THE OLYMPIC GAMES

Li Xiaoshuang
Atlanta, 1996

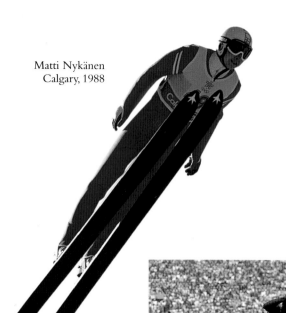

Matti Nykänen
Calgary, 1988

Florence Griffith-Joyner
Seoul, 1988

Ed Moses
Los Angeles, 1984

Jayne Torvill and
Christopher Dean
Sarajevo, 1984

Linford Christie
Barcelona, 1992

Alberto Tomba
Albertville, 1992

Vitali Sherbo
Barcelona, 1992

THE OLYMPIC GAMES

Bobsleigh
Nagano, 1998

Carl Lewis
Los Angeles, 1984

Maurice Greene
Sydney, 2000

Haile Gebrselassie
Atlanta, 1996

LONDON, NEW YORK, MUNICH, MELBOURNE, DELHI

Copyright © Chronik Verlag, im Bertelsmann Lexikon Verlag GmbH
Gütersloh/München 1995

This edition © 2004 Dorling Kindersley Limited, London

This book is an updated version of Chronicle of the Olympics,
first published in 1996 by Dorling Kindersley Limited,
80 Strand, London WC2R 0RL

A Penguin Company

Updated for Dorling Kindersley by
Amber Books Ltd
Bradley's Close
74–77 White Lion Street
London N1 9PF
www.amberbooks.co.uk

2 4 6 8 10 9 7 5 3 1

A CIP catalog record for this book is available from the British Library,
and a Cataloging-in-Publication record from the Library of Congress.

UK ISBN: 1 4053 0322 0
US ISBN: 0-7566-0400-1

Printed and bound by L. Rex Printing Company Limited, China

See our complete catalog at
www.dk.com

Contents

Carl Lewis
Barcelona, 1992

Kitty McKane
Antwerp, 1920

THE OLYMPIC GAMES
page 8

ATHENS 1896 TO BEIJING 2008
page 14

Katarina Witt
Calgary, 1988

ATHENS 1896
page 16

PARIS 1900
page 20

ST. LOUIS 1904
page 24

LONDON 1908
page 28

STOCKHOLM 1912
page 32

ANTWERP 1920
page 36

CHAMONIX 1924
page 40

PARIS 1924
page 44

ST. MORITZ 1928
page 48

AMSTERDAM 1928
page 52

LAKE PLACID 1932
page 56

LOS ANGELES 1932
page 60

GARMISCH 1936
page 64

BERLIN 1936
page 68

ST. MORITZ 1948
page 72

LONDON 1948
page 76

OSLO 1952
page 80

HELSINKI 1952
page 84

CORTINA 1956
page 88

MELBOURNE 1956
page 92

Olga Korbut
Munich, 1972

Muhammad Ali
Rome, 1960.
Gold medal re-presented,
Atlanta, 1996

NAGANO 1998
page 216

SYDNEY 2000
page 222

SQUAW VALLEY 1960
page 96

LAKE PLACID 1980
page 148

SALT LAKE CITY 2002
page 232

ROME 1960
page 100

MOSCOW 1980
page 152

ATHENS 2004
page 238

INNSBRUCK 1964
page 106

SARAJEVO 1984
page 158

TORINO 2006
page 248

TOKYO 1964
page 110

LOS ANGELES 1984
page 162

BEIJING 2008
page 250

GRENOBLE 1968
page 116

CALGARY 1988
page 170

ABBREVIATIONS • *page 252*

MEXICO CITY 1968
page 120

SEOUL 1988
page 174

STATISTICS • *page 253*

SAPPORO 1972
page 126

ALBERTVILLE 1992
page 184

INDEX • *page 368*

MUNICH 1972
page 130

BARCELONA 1992
page 190

INNSBRUCK 1976
page 138

LILLEHAMMER 1994
page 200

MONTREAL 1976
page 142

ATLANTA 1996
page 206

Cathy Freeman
Sydney, 2000

The Olympic Games: *From ancient times to the 21st century*

Since their renaissance in 1896, the Olympic Games have become the greatest sports event in the world. No matter how many world or continental championship titles an athlete wins, to compete in the Olympic Games often remains his or her supreme ambition.

SINCE THEIR BEGINNING THE modern Olympic Games have faced many political crises and their demise has been often predicted. However, the Olympic movement has survived two world wars as well as periods of upheaval, coups d'état, and revolutions – although in most cases there have been changed external circumstances and political considerations to be taken into account.

The origin of the Olympic Games lies in the ancient world where they were treated as a ritual festival. The idea of winning was of far more significance in those games than in the Olympic philosophy established by Pierre de Coubertin more than 2,500 years later. In fact, victory was of paramount importance, with defeat bringing disgrace for the whole *polis* (city-state). Because no measurements or times were recorded, few performances have been handed down through the ages. However, it is known that the victors were awarded an olive wreath.

Although we have details of the winners only from 776 B.C. onwards, archaeologists have demonstrated that the Olympics can be traced far back into the second millennium before Christ. The five-day-long games included running, wrestling, the pentathlon, horse riding, and chariot races, as well as competitions to determine the best trumpeters and heralds. The ceremonies to honor the victors were all held on the last day of the Olympic Games. A temporary end to the Olympic movement came in A.D. 391, when a decree issued by the Roman emperor Theodosius I prohibited all pagan worship, which included the Olympic Games.

During the Middle Ages, athletic activities had little significance and did not have any importance afterward.

"The Discus Thrower"
This is a copy of the bronze original by the sculptor Myron (c. 450 B.C.). Greek discuses were made of various materials (lead, bronze, or iron) and were between 3½ and 11¼ pounds (1.5 and 5kg) in weight and between 6 and 12 inches (17 and 32cm) in diameter. A competition was decided on the best of five attempts.

The Wrestlers
The decoration on this ancient vase depicts a wrestling bout. In these times, there were not any weight categories and there was also not a time limit inside which a fight had to be finished. Wrestling first became an "Olympic" sport in 708 B.C.

By the 19th century, though, new sports had evolved, including boxing, golf, and cricket. Soccer, tennis, and gymnastics increased in importance from the late 1800s onward. More and more people gathered to play and exercise together and founded sports clubs and associations. Scientists discussed the role of sport in society in general, and for adolescent people in particular. The Greek ideal of developing one's body and mind in harmony, one with the other, was rediscovered. At this time, the new sports were played predominantly by the upper classes and the aristocracy.

In the 1880s, Pierre de Coubertin (born on January 1, 1863 in Paris), who belonged to a long-established French family of noble descent, made a study of the impact of sport on society. In his youth, he had been greatly taken with the ancient Olympic Games and was very interested in archaeological excavations in Greece. Even though it was as early as in 1766 that the British scientist Richard Chandler discovered the location of the ancient Olympia, it took more

than 100 years before the mud-covered remains were laid open in 1875-81 by Ernst Curtius, a German archaeologist from Berlin.

In his studies of physical exercise, de Coubertin was influenced by the ancient concept of the human being on the one hand and by the views held by the British educationalist Thomas Arnold on the other. He became convinced that exercise had to be the basis of sensible education. The fact that France had had great difficulty in getting over its defeat by Germany in the War of 1870/71, plus the desire of his homeland to regain national pride and strength, formed the background to de Coubertin's theories. However, the new French social order was not to be based on the development of new animosities. Rather, it was to be expressed by means of fair competition between nations. De Coubertin was convinced that equal opportunity for all participants was a prerequisite for these competitions. As well as physical education, as practiced in Britain, it was again the ancient Greek concept that served as de Coubertin's ideal, since in those days all athletes had trained together for competition. The amateur ideal was to be the indispensable prerequisite for de Coubertin to underline the "noble and chivalrous character" of physical exercise. Rewards were expected to come from the sporting activities themselves. Material gifts, desire for profit, and business interest were not allowed in sport because it was believed they would prejudice the coming together of athletes.

To start with, the impact of these theories was limited to the aristocracy, who could afford to pursue sporting activities in this way. Difficulties soon arose, however, as the lower social classes refused to be excluded. Eventually, in the late 1920s, after many years of negotiations, the IOC gave its permission for loss-of-income compensation to be paid to athletes.

Despite his initial difficulties in recruiting followers for his "religion of sport," de Coubertin continued to look for a way of spreading his ideas of an Olympic renaissance. He first mentioned the idea of reviving the Olympic Games during a lecture in 1892, when it was met with little comprehension. Undeterred, he invited interested persons from all over the world to participate in a sports congress in Paris in June 1894. The congress, which was held at the Sorbonne, part of Paris University, closed with unanimous support for a resolution to revive the Olympic Games in 1896. The plan was that after the first celebration in Athens, the competitions would be hosted in turns by all capitals at four-year intervals.

The new Olympic movement was to be coordinated and led by a panel entitled the International Olympic Committee (IOC). Besides de Coubertin himself, its members included Lord Arthur O. Ampthill (Great Britain), Viktor Balck

1 Attic chalice: This chalice dates from 510-500 B.C. Prior to the ancient Olympic Games, the athletes were made ready for competition with massage and oil. However, the actual period of preparation started weeks earlier. All athletes gathered at a special training camp for at least the last 30 days before the beginning of the Games. At the training sessions they were all fed the same diet and lived in the same kind of accommodation. Besides being coached in their sports, the athletes were given lectures about the importance of participating in the Olympic Games. Additionally, the athletes were briefed on how they were expected

to comport themselves during the competitions.

2 Inside of a drinking bowl (c. 500 B.C.): In classical times, competitors in the jumping events were required to carry extra weights in their hands. The ancient Olympic pentathlon consisted of long jump, discus, javelin, running, and wrestling events. According to Greek mythology, the hero Jason was responsible for creating the pentathlon.

3 Renaissance of the Olympic Games accomplished: The delegates to the International Congress of Paris, which was held at the

Sorbonne (part of the University of Paris) in 1894, gave their approval to Pierre de Coubertin's proposal to revive the Olympic Games. At the conclusion of the congress, an international committee was set up to implement this resolution. Here International Olympic Committee (IOC) members pose for the camera on the occasion of the first modern Olympic Games in Athens. They are (from left to right): Willibald Gebhardt (Germany), Pierre de Coubertin (France), Jiri Guth (Bohemia), Dimitrios Vikelas (Greece, president), Ferenc Kemeny (Hungary), Aleksei Butovsky (Russia), and Viktor Balck (Sweden).

(Sweden), Dimitrios Vikelas (Greece), Aleksei Butovsky (Russia), Ernest Callot (France), Leonard A. Cuff (New Zealand), Jiri Guth (Bohemia), Charles Herbert (Great Britain), Ferenc Kemeny (Hungary), Ferdinando Lucchesi-Palli (Italy), William M. Sloane (USA), and José B. Zubiaur (Argentina). Pierre de Coubertin, who initially acted as the committee's secretary general, went on to hold the IOC's presidency from 1896 until 1925.

After a promising start with the Athens Games of 1896, the Olympic movement stuttered a little, with the Games of 1900 and 1904 being something of a disappointment. Held as part of world fairs of those years, they were hardly noticed. Matters took a turn for the better with the 1906 'Intermediate' celebration. Although they rescued a foundering Olympic movement and helped establish the Olympic Games as a sporting event, the 1906

Games were not originally considered an official Olympic celebration in the eyes of the IOC.

Political developments began to affect events in the stadium from an early stage. World War I resulted in the cancellation of the VI Olympic Games, which had been scheduled to take place in Berlin in 1916. Nevertheless, the Olympic movement was still in existence when hostilities came to an end, and the first postwar celebration was awarded to Antwerp, in Belgium, a country that had been ravaged by the conflict. Even though the Berlin Games had not taken place, their designation as the VI Olympiad was not carried over and the Antwerp Games became the VII Olympics. The Belgians excelled themselves in organizing the Games at such short notice and in such circumstances. Twenty-nine nations were represented. Among those missing were Germany, Austria, Hungary, and Bulgaria, excluded from the IOC as a result of the war.

Except for the inclusion of figure skating in the program for the London Games of 1908 and of ice hockey and figure skating in the schedule for Antwerp, winter sports, in general, remained outside the scope of the Olympic movement. Winter sports lovers had long been campaigning for their introduction, and by the early 1920s this lobby had gained so much recognition that in 1924, despite initial resistance, the IOC allowed an "International Winter Sports Week" to be staged at Chamonix in France. It was highly successful, and a year later the IOC agreed to stage the Winter Olympic Games. They were to be held in the same year as the Summer Games but would be organized as separate celebrations. The Scandinavian nations, which had believed that winter sports competitions already established in their countries would be in danger if Winter Olympics took place, dropped their objections. In 1925, the Belgian Henri de Baillet-Latour took over from Pierre de Coubertin as IOC president. He continued the work started by the Frenchman until 1942.

Like his predecessor, de Baillet-Latour attempted to prevent the increasing participation of women in the Olympics, but momentum was gathering. In the ancient Olympic Games, women were strictly forbidden to take part (in fact, they were allegedly put to death if they were so much as watching), and in the early years of the modern Olympics, the IOC also frowned on the idea of women competing in the Games. Although there were female competitors as early as 1900, the IOC did not regard their presence as official until 1912, when women's swimming events were sanctioned. The number of women participants grew steadily with each Games, but it was not until 1928 that the IOC finally

Dimitrios Vikelas
(Born February 15, 1835, Syros; died July 20, 1908 Athens). Dimitrios Vikelas was one of the original founder members of the International Olympic Committee and acted as its first president from 1894–96.

Pierre de Coubertin
(Born January 1, 1863, Paris; died September 2, 1937, Geneva). De Coubertin was IOC secretary general and then president from 1896–1925. His dream was of the "youth of the world" meeting in peaceful competition.

Henri de Baillet-Latour
(Born March 1, 1876, Brussels; died January 6, 1942, Brussels). The Belgian was IOC president from 1925–42. He gained much experience as head of the organizing committee of the 1920 Antwerp Games.

Johannes Sigfrid Edström
(Born November 21, 1870, Gothenburg; died March 18, 1964, Stockholm) He was vice president of the IOC from 1937–42, acting president from 1942, and elected president from 1946 to 1952.

Avery Brundage
(Born September 26, 1887, Detroit; died May 8, 1975, Garmisch-Partenkirchen). He was a US Olympic athlete in 1912. As IOC president (1952–72), he was considered a supporter of the idea of amateurism.

Michael Morris Killanin
(Born July 30, 1914, London; died April 25, 1999, Dublin). An Irishman, Killanin was IOC president from 1972–80. After his retirement, the committee appointed the journalist, writer, and film producer its honorary chairman for life.

Hand over:
Juan Antonio Samaranch (left; born July 17, 1920, IOC president 1980–2001) hands over the presidency of the IOC to Jacques Rogge (born May 2, 1942) on 16 July 2001. Samaranch's presidency saw the rise of the Olympics in international stature and success, while Rogge is looking toward reducing the Games in terms of their cost. Rogge hopes to take the Olympics eventually to Africa and South America.

allowed women to take part in track-and-field competitions. Nevertheless, after the 1928 Games, which were held in Amsterdam, the IOC barred women from running distances of more than 200 meters – a decision that lasted until 1960.

The last Games before World War II took place in 1936 in Berlin, and the Nazis turned them into a unique propaganda event, with the public being presented with a picture of a peace-loving German Reich. War then intervened. In 1938, the XII Summer Games, scheduled to take place in Japan in 1940, were transferred to Helsinki, Finland, due to the outbreak of the Sino-Japanese War in 1937. The Winter Games, also awarded originally to Japan, were moved first to St. Moritz and then to Garmisch-Partenkirchen. However, the Soviet invasion of Finland in 1939 and the outbreak of World War II the same year prevented either Games from taking place. The 1944 Games, scheduled for Cortina d'Ampezzo and London, were likewise cancelled, and few IOC members were able to attend the ceremony marking the 50th anniversary of the renaissance of the Olympic ideal, which was held in Lausanne in 1944.

In 1948, in the presence of the Swede Sigfrid Edström, elected IOC president in 1946, the Olympic Games resumed, with London as the venue. However, as the postwar era progressed, first-class sporting performances could not disguise the fact that these peaceful meetings of the "youth of the world" were developing into a struggle for prestige. The Cold War between the East and the West extended into the stadiums, while the idea of international under-standing was abandoned as a result of ideological incompatibilities and the prohib-ition of contact between athletes. With the suppression of the uprising in Hungary, the British-French inter-vention in the Suez crisis, the practice of apartheid in South Africa and Rhodesia (now Zimbabwe) as well as the Soviet invasion of Afghanistan, boycotts and exclusions overshad-owed the Olympic Games from 1956 onward.

In 1952, the IOC had appointed the American Avery Brundage its new president, and he served until 1972. He was regarded as a vigorous supporter of amateurism and penalized any breaches by immediately banning the offender, as in the case of the Austrian alpine skier Karl Schranz in 1972. The last days of Brundage's term were overshadowed by the devastating attack on Israel's team in the Munich Olympic village in 1972. This confirmed Brundage's fear that the bigger and more important the Olympic Games became, the more they would suffer from eco-nomic, political, and, from that point on, criminal pressure as well.

In the boycotts of 1980 and 1984, the political pressures reached a temporary peak. The Games in Moscow were boycotted by the USA and several other allied countries, because of the Soviet invasion of Afghanistan. Four years later the USSR and allies reacted with a counter-boycott of the Los Angeles Games. The USSR and their allies cited worries over local security arrangements as the reason.

The Summer Games of 1984 revealed for the first time that the Olympic Games were no longer affordable without marketing, sponsor-ship, and revenue from television rights. Televi-sion companies had to pay hundreds of millions of dollars to obtain these rights. The fact that the most popular disciplines were scheduled for times with the highest advertising appeal consti-tuted a sacrifice to increasing commercialism.

The pressure on athletes intensified too, as the public were only interested in champions. Furthermore, the business world would only take on champions to advertise their products.

Spain's Juan Antonio Samaranch, who took over the IOC presidency in 1980, recognized these facts. He pushed ahead with the commercialization of the Olympics, overseeing a huge increase in the Games' profitability. Some criticized his tenure, pointing to what many felt was the over-commercialization of the 1996 Atlanta Games. However, Samaranch did much to raise the international profile and sporting standards of the Games. In 1981 he helped bring to an end the controversial clause 26 – a regulation regarding the exclusive admission of amateur athletes. He also championed the cause of female athletes in the Olympics and was a vigorous opponent of any form of sporting apartheid. The magnificent Sydney 2000 Games were a fitting testament to Samaranch's presidency.

Samaranch's baton was passed to the Belgian Jacques Rogge in July 2001. Rogge, as with Samaranch, faces some great challenges during his presidency, particularly regarding illegal drug use in Olympic sport. With the 2002 Winter Olympics in Salt Lake City marred by several prominent incidents of drug taking, the world is looking to Athens 2004, Torino 2006 and Beijing 2008 to see how Rogge has tackled this problem.

1 Symbolic emblem: The Olympic flag, which was designed and presented to the IOC by Pierre de Coubertin, has flown above Olympic Games since the 1920 celebration at Antwerp. The five colored rings intertwined symbolize the five continents whose athletes meet for fair competition. When the symbol was devised, the flags of all the nations of the world could be made up from the five colors and white background.

2 Olympic flame: Since 1928, the lighting of the Olympic flame has been traditional. Since 1936, torchbearers have been carrying the flame from Greece to the host venue in commemoration of the ancient games.

3 Farewell for four years: At the closing ceremony of each Olympic Games, the host of the next Games is ceremonially presented with the Olympic flag.

4 The joy of victory: The Chinese government invested $24 million into securing the Olympics for Beijing, with the full backing of an enthusiastic city population.

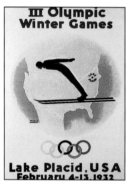

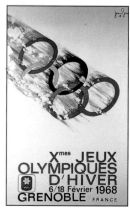

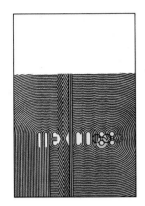

Athens 1896
to
Athens 2004

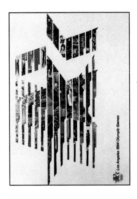

Athens

On April 6, 1896, in Athens, King George I of Greece opened the I Olympic Games of modern times. An audience of over 60,000 had gathered in the city's newly refurbished stadium to witness the event.

INITIALLY, PIERRE DE COUBERTIN had intended to stage the first Games in Paris in 1900 in association with the World's Fair. However, it was eventually decided that the first Olympiad should take place in 1896, with the Greek capital Athens as host city. Consequently, Dimitrios Vikelas, Greek delegate to the 1894 International Congress of Paris, which had revived the Games, was appointed president of the newly formed International Olympic Committee – the IOC.

Greece ran into financial difficulties as it prepared for the Games, and Budapest repeatedly offered itself as an alternative site, since Hungary was getting ready for its millennium celebrations. In the end, however, thanks to the efforts of Crown Prince Constantine of Greece, who set up and presided over an organizing committee, donations started to roll in. One gift of more than 900,000 gold drachmas by Greek businessman Georgios Averoff went toward the rebuilding of the city's stadium. In addition, the first sports postage stamps were issued and a lottery organized to raise additional funds. The Olympic Games were able to go ahead in Athens as planned.

The opening ceremony coincided with the 75th anniversary of the start of the Greek independence movement. At the beginning of the Games, therefore, the hosts' national enthusiasm was at a peak. Approximately 200 men from 14 countries competed in nine events. The majority of the participants were Greeks.

Many of the other competitors had made their way to Athens under their own steam. The Irishman John Pius Boland, for example, who competed for Britain, spent four weeks in Athens ahead of the Games to prepare himself. It paid off; Boland went on to win the individual tennis event and also the doubles competition, in which he was partnered by Fritz Traun, a German who also took part in the 800 meters.

Local Hero
On the last day of the Games, the Greek athlete Spyridon Louis (in traditional dress) is honored for his win in the marathon.

Classical Theme
The cover of the report on the 1896 Games evoked the Olympics' classical ancestry. At Athens, as in early times, only men took part.

In addition to tennis and track and field, fencing, weightlifting, cycling, wrestling, shooting, swimming, and gymnastics also featured. Rowing and sailing competitions were also due to be contested, but were canceled because of poor weather. The cricket and soccer tournaments were also called off – in their case because of a lack of participating teams.

Event winners were presented with an olive branch, a certificate, and a silver medal. The runners-up received a laurel sprig and a copper medal. The first man to win an Olympic competition was the American James Brendan Connolly, who took the triple jump, clearing 44' 11$\frac{3}{4}$" (13.71 meters).

The hosts had to wait until the final event to record their first Olympic win. A French archaeologist had suggested a race from Marathon to Athens be included in the schedule in commemoration of the legendary run by a herald after the battle of Marathon in 490 BC. The organizers concurred, and the 26-mile race was commandingly won by the Greek runner Spyridon Louis, who was immediately hailed as a national hero.

Long-Jump King
The American Ellery Clark won the long jump with a leap of 20' 10" (6.35 meters).

US All-Rounder
James B. Connolly (USA) was victorious in the triple jump, and came away from Athens with one second and one third place as well.

Double Victor
Robert Garrett (USA) outperformed Connolly: he was a double champion, as well as picking up two second places.

German Wins Four
Having already lifted three gymnastics titles, Carl Schuhmann of Germany added a fourth win, taking the wrestling championship.

1 **Olympic enthusiasm:** The Greek spectators followed the 1896 Athens Games with great interest. On the first day, thousands packed the stadium, hearing a speech by the president of the organizing committee, Crown Prince Constantine, before the Games were declared open by King George I. The picture shows the Athens stadium during the 1906 Games, held to celebrate the tenth anniversary of the inaugural competition.

2 **US athletes dominate:** The Americans were by far the most successful team at Athens. Herbert Jamison (second from left) took second place in the 400-meters behind Thomas Burke, with third place being taken by the German Fritz Hofmann. Robert Garrett (second from right) became discus champion ahead of the Greeks Panagiotis Paraskevopoulo and Sotirios Versis. Garrett secured his second title in the shot event, once again consigning Greek competitors, this time Miltiades Gouskos and Georgios Papasideris, to second and third places. In the long jump, Garrett had to settle for second place behind his teammate Ellery Clark. Third place went to another American, James B. Connolly. In the high jump, meanwhile, Garrett came equal second with Connolly, behind Clark. Albert Tyler (right) was second in the pole vault, won by his teammate William Hoyt who cleared 10' 10" (3.3 meters). Francis Lane (left) had to be content with fourth place in the 100-meter final.

3 **Souvenir photographs:** Athletes and officials had numerous group pictures taken of themselves in the Greek capital. Souvenir photographs like this were so popular, it seems, because many participants, notably those from the United States, wanted to be able to prove on their return home that they had taken part in an historic event – the first Olympic Games of modern times.

4 **Starting in style:** Using various techniques, the athletes take their marks for the start of the second heat of the 100-meters. While Thomas Curtis (USA, second from left) prefers to start from a crouching position, the Dane Eugen Schmidt (middle) leans on two short sticks. The remaining competitors opt for the traditional starting position. The eventual champion was Thomas Burke (USA), who won the final in 12.0 seconds.

5 **Six cycling events:** The Frenchman Paul Masson was the most successful cyclist of the Games: he won the one-lap race ahead of the Greek Stamatios Nikolopoulos and the Austrian Adolf Schmal. In the 2,000-meter sprint, Masson once again

defeated Nikolopoulos, with Frenchman Léon Flameng coming home third. Masson secured his third title by winning the 10,000-meter track race ahead of Flameng and Schmal. It was Flameng, though, who took the 100-kilometer track title, while Schmal also scored a success in the 12-hour race. In the meanwhile, the cycling marathon was won by Aristidis Konstantinidis, ahead of German August Goedrich.

6 British strongman: In 1896, the Olympic weightlifting competition was not divided into categories as it is today, but consisted of a one-armed lifting event and a two-armed event. Britain's Launceston Elliott came first in the one-armed, lifting 156¼ pounds (71 kilograms). He was followed by Viggo Jensen of Denmark and Alexandros Nikolopoulos of Greece. In the two-armed event, both Elliott and Jensen lifted 245¼ pounds (111.5 kilograms), but the Dane was named the winner because Elliott had moved one of his feet. Third place went to the Greek lifter Sotirios Versis.

7 Unbeatable Greeks and French: The fencing was dominated by athletes from two nations. In the individual foil event, Eugène-Henri Gravellote (FRA) won ahead of his compatriot Henri Callot and Greek swordsman Perikles Pierrakos-Mavromichalis. The foil for masters event was claimed by Leon Pyrgos (GRE), and the saber competition by Ioannis Georgiadis (GRE) ahead of team mate Telemachos Karakalos.

8 Greeks on high: The home crowd saw the Greek athletes Nicolaos Andriakopoulos and Thomas Xenakis come first and second in the rope climbing. Fritz Hofmann (GER) was third.

9 Royal congratulations: Athletes and officials assemble for a medal ceremony in the Olympic Stadium. King George I was keen on conducting the ceremonies himself. At the Athens Olympics, there were not any gold medals, because a silver medal was the winner's prize.

10 Team gymnastics in the open air: In front of the judges and audience in the middle of the Olympic Stadium, gymnasts put themselves through their paces in the team events. Having won the parallel bars ahead of both Greek teams, the German team moved on to claim the Olympic title in the horizontal bar competition.

11 Versatility: The German Carl Schuhmann added the Olympic wrestling title to his successes in gymnastics, beating the Greeks Georgios Tsitas and Stephanos Christopoulos. The picture shows a wrestling match from the Athens Games of 1906.

Paris

The sporting events that accompanied the world's fair were regarded by the IOC and international media as the II Olympic Games. However, public interest in these Games was relatively subdued.

THERE HAD BEEN SOME controversy before these Games, because Greece had laid claim to the right to stage all future Olympiads. However, the Cretan Revolt and the subsequent Greek-Turkish war effectively put Greece out of the running for 1900. Consequently, the Olympic committee fell back on its resolution of 1894 to bring the Olympic Games to Paris. However, because of a lack of organization and information, the public took hardly any notice of the Games. Another reason for people's indifference was that the competitions took place throughout the complete five-month duration of the world's fair. And the Games could hardly be called a meeting of athletes when the track-and-field competitions were held in July in the Bois de Boulogne, while the swimming events took place during August in a pool on the Seine River. Also, athletes' complaints about the sometimes miserable state of facilities went unheeded. Competitions in the Bois de Vincennes, for example, were reputedly disrupted by odors drifting across from the agricultural show nearby.

Sailing was among the sports featured for the first time. Also, women took part in the Olympic Games for the first time, though they competed in only a limited number of events, among them golf and tennis. America's Margaret Abbott won the golf tournament, while Great Britain's Charlotte Cooper was victorious in the tennis, taking both the singles and mixed doubles titles. She was partnered in the latter by fellow Briton Reggie Doherty, who won the men's doubles with his brother Laurie, the men's singles champion.

The long-jump final ended in bizarre fashion by today's standards. Because in 1900 the results from the qualifying rounds were taken into account in the final result, America's Myer Prinstein finished second in the competition without having made a single jump in

Rendezvous in Paris
The Games lasted from May to October. A range of trophies were awarded, because the modern medal system was not yet in place.

the final. Prinstein was absent from the final because it took place on Sunday, and his Methodist college would not allow him to compete on that day.

By winning three titles (high jump, standing long jump, and standing triple jump), the great American track-and-field athlete Ray Ewry embarked upon a glittering Olympic career. He competed until 1908 and won no less than ten titles, making him, in terms of first places, the most successful Olympic competitor of all time. The most successful competitor of the 1900 Games, however, was Alvin Kraenzlein. The son of German emigrants to America, he won the 60-meters, both the 110-meter and 200-meter hurdles, as well as the long jump.

The hosts dominated the fencing, taking five of the seven titles contested. With one win each, only the Cuban Ramón Fonst and the Italian Antonio Conte were able to break the French monopoly. In rowing, the Netherlands celebrated their first Olympic title win, François Brandt and Roelof Klein triumphing in the coxed pairs final.

Paris 1900
The Eiffel Tower, erected for the world's fair in 1889, and a huge globe were the symbols of the 1900 fair.

Ace Alvin
Alvin Kraenzlein (USA) won four track-and-field titles to become the Games' most successful competitor.

Australia Advances
The Australian swimmer Frederick Lane won two events at Paris.

Mighty Magyar
Rudolf Bauer of Hungary out-threw all rivals to become discus champion.

Frenchman Foils All
The Frenchman Albert Ayat won two fencing events – the épée for masters and the épée for amateurs and masters.

1 **Little Olympic interest:** The Olympic Games formed part of the world's fair in Paris, and it was often, rather by chance, that passersby came across the sporting events that were taking place at various places across the city. Even the athletes themselves seem to have had little chance to savor the Olympic spirit that should have pervaded the meeting of the "youth of the world." The majority of participants went straight home to their respective countries once the events had been decided.

2 **Discontinued events:** The American Charles Sands (pictured here) won the golf tournament ahead of the Britons Walter Rutherford and David Robertson. In the women's event, Margaret Abbott was victorious, leaving second and third places to her fellow Americans Pauline Whittier and Daria Pratt. By the 1908 Games, however, golf had ceased to be an Olympic sport. A number of other sports have fallen by the wayside over the years, including cricket. The only Olympic cricket tournament took place in 1900, and the winner was Great Britain. Rugby is another discontinued Olympic sport that was first contested in 1900, when France ran out winners. But they had to settle for second-place behind the USA when rugby made its final Olympic appearance in 1924.

3 **Bows and arrows:** The French and Belgians dominated in archery. Among the Olympic champions of 1900 were the Frenchmen Henri Herouin (in the *Au cordon doré* 50-meter event), Eugène Mougin (*Au chapelet* 50-meter), Emmanuel Foulon (*Sur la perche à la herse*) and Emile Grumiaux (*Sur la perche à la pyramide*). In the *Au cordon doré* 33-meter and *Au chapelet* 33-meter events, the Belgian Hubert van Innis was the victor. Archery continued as an Olympic competition until 1908. It reappeared in 1920 before vanishing once again. In 1972, it was reinstated for the Munich Games and has been an Olympic sport ever since, though the number of events is much reduced compared with the early days.

4 **Professional touch:** As well as the amateur sportsmen who flocked to Paris in 1900, professional athletes were invited to the World's Fair to take part in a number of events, some of which were seen as world championships. The professional high jump was won by the much-fancied world-record holder Michael Sweeney from the USA, whereas the amateur event was taken by the American Irving Baxter, ahead of the Irishman Patrick Leahy, who was competing in the British team. Third place went to the Hungarian Lajos Gönczy. In the amateur standing high jump, Ray Ewry (USA) out-jumped fellow countrymen Irving Baxter and Lewis P. Sheldon. Ewry added two other Olympic titles to his collection by winning the standing long jump, once again ahead of Baxter, with Emile Torcheboeuf of France in third place, and the standing triple jump, defeating Baxter yet again, along with Robert Garrett, a double champion at Athens. The triple jump was won by America's Myer Prinstein, while his rival Alvin Kraenzlein took the long jump. Kraenzlein had a great time, winning the 60-meter sprint, and the 110-meter and 200-meter hurdles titles as well.

5 **Different high jumping techniques:** In the high jump events, the athletes used a wide variety of techniques to get themselves over the bar. Here the American Alvin Schoenfield "rolls" himself over. A professional athlete, Schoenfield was taking part in the world championships being held at the 1900 World's Fair at the same time as the Olympic Games.

6 **Authority on the move:** IOC president Pierre de Coubertin was eager to attend as many sporting events as possible and pedaled all over the city on his tricycle to and from the various venues. It was not long before the father of the modern Olympic Games came to realize that it did not make much sense to link the Olympic Games to a world's fair. De Coubertin regretted the fact that under these circumstances the intrinsic value of the Olympic Games could not really be appreciated. However, besides the 1906 "Intermediate Games," it was a further eight years before the Games gained the status of an independent event.

7 Consolation for Norway in athletics: In the pole vault, the Norwegian Carl-Albert Andersen (pictured here) came third with a jump of 10' 5¾" (3.20 meters). This was just two inches (5 cm) short of American Meredith Colket's second-placed effort. Colket, in turn, was only two inches (5 cm) behind his compatriot Irving Baxter. The Scandinavian countries had a disappointing time in the track-and-field competitions. Indeed, apart from Andersen, the Scandinavians managed only three top-three track-and-field finishes – Ernst Schulz (DEN), third in the 400-meters, Ernst Fast (SWE), third in the marathon, and the joint Swedish and Danish team, which won the tug-of-war event.

8 Long wait for his win: With a jump of 10' 9¾" (3.30 meters) America's Irving Baxter was a worthy victor in the pole vault. However, he had to wait for his title win to be confirmed. Originally, the pole vault had been scheduled to take place on a Sunday. It was then rescheduled and then put back once again to Sunday. Many competitors, in particular a number of Americans, failed to turn up because their colleges were religious institutions. Following a protest, a second competition was organized for another day. Even though some athletes managed to clear heights that would have won them the title, Daniel Horton (USA), for example, jumped more than 11 feet, their efforts were little more than statistics.

9 First and second for the USA: With a throw of 42' 1¾" (12.85 meters), the American shot putter Josiah McCracken (shown here) secured second place behind his compatriot Richard Sheldon. Both Sheldon, who added a third place in the discus to his shot title, and McCracken no doubt benefited from the absence of world-record holder Dennis Horgan.

10 Unsuccessful defense: Robert Garrett, who had won the shot (and the discus) at the Athens Olympic Games, had to settle for third place in Paris. The American also finished third in the standing triple jump.

11 First champion in new event: The Irish-born American John Flanagan became the first Olympic champion in the hammer. Second and third places were taken by Flanagan's fellow Americans Truxton Hare and Josiah McCracken.

12 Swimming marked by great variety: In 1900, the swimming competition was held in the Seine River. Among the events contested were two that have long since vanished from the Olympic program – the 200-meter obstacle race and the underwater swimming event. In the former, the competitors had to climb over a bar and a chain of boats, as well as dive under another chain of boats. In the end, it was the Australian Frederick Lane who took the title. He added another win in the 200-meter freestyle, ahead of the Hungarian Zoltàn Halmay and the Austrian Karl Ruberl. Britain's John Jarvis also secured two title wins. In the 1,000-meter freestyle, he beat the Austrian Otto Wahle and Halmay, and in the 4,000-meter freestyle, he defeated Halmay once again and France's Louis Martin in fine style. In the 200-meter backstroke, it was Germany's turn to triumph with Ernst Hoppenberg coming in ahead of Austria's Ruberl and Johannes Drost of Holland. Charles de Vendeville of France won the underwater swimming event ahead of his compatriot P. Alexandre Six and the Dane Peder Lykkeberg. The Germans won the 5 x 200-meter team event convincingly, leaving two French teams trailing in their wake, while in the water polo tournament, Great Britain ran out winners ahead of Belgium and France.

13 Scandinavians pull out the stops: Since Sweden and Denmark were unable to come up with the required six athletes each for the tug-of-war, the two countries joined forces to form a combined team, which won the competition ahead of the USA and France. Some authorities believe, however, that the Americans' participation may have been limited to an exhibition pull. Tug-of-war featured in every Olympic Games from 1900 until 1920. It was then dropped as an Olympic sport and has never reappeared. Great Britain was the most successful tug-of-war country, with two first places, two second places, and a third.

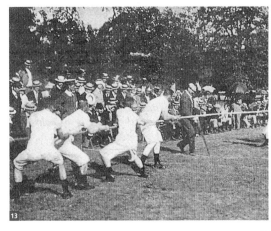

St. Louis

In St. Louis, as in Paris, the Olympics took place as part of the world's fair. As a result, the inscription on the winners' medals read "Universal Exhibition" on the front and "Olympiad" on the reverse.

Ewry Again
Ray Ewry (USA) successfully defended his Olympic titles in the standing high jump, long jump, and triple jump.

Help for Hicks
As he approached the finish in the marathon, Thomas Hicks (USA) was grateful for every kind of support.

ONCE AGAIN THE SPORTS EVENTS failed to stand out from the rest of the 1904 World's Fair schedule. And once again, the public took hardly any notice of the Games as an independent entity. The general lack of interest was further increased by the long duration of the Games, as had also been the case in Paris, and the high number of competitions. The organizers wanted to avoid an overlap, and from July until November nearly 400 competitions were held. However, not all of them could call themselves "Olympic events," since some were for professionals or students. As far as the Olympics were concerned, the organizers announced competitions in 16 sports with 104 titles to be won. For the first time, boxing was included in the Olympic program.

IOC president Pierre de Coubertin could not attend the Games and was disappointed that the Olympic spirit had not been sufficiently stressed. He also criticized the so-called Anthropological Days, on which contests such as stone-throwing and steeplechase running were organized for ethnic minorities by the world's fair ethnological department. De Coubertin considered these "competitions" discriminatory.

The enormous cost of travel resulted in the number of athletes decreasing by almost half compared with 1900. Six hundred-twenty-five competitors took part, with more than 500 of them coming from the USA and 50 from Canada. American domination in track and field was broken by the Irishman Thomas Kiely, who won the combined events (later to become the decathlon). The program for this was punishing: all ten events – 100- and 1,500-meters, 110-meter hurdles, walking, high jump, long jump, pole vault, shot, hammer, and weight throwing – had to be completed in a day.

The American marathon runner Fred Lorz triggered a scandal when it was

Meet Me in St. Louis
The program of the St. Louis World's Fair, during which the 1904 Olympic Games took place.

discovered that he allowed an escort to give him a lift and drop him off a short distance away from the finish. Lorz received a lifetime ban, but it was lifted a short time later.

In 1906, a second celebration of the Olympic Games was held in Athens. Against de Coubertin's will, the IOC had decided in 1901 to stage Olympiads at two-year intervals, with Athens and other international cities taking turns as host.

In the event, the 1906 Games turned out to be decisive for the Olympic movement. After the difficulties encountered in Paris and St. Louis, these Games were just as successful as those held in the Greek capital a decade earlier. For the first time, the teams paraded for the opening ceremony, while gold, silver, and bronze medals were awarded in most events. Despite providing a much needed boost to the ailing Olympic movement, the 1906 Games were later downgraded, becoming known as the Intermediate, or Intercalated, Games.

Ireland's Finest
Thomas Kiely of Ireland (left) won the combined events, the forerunner of the decathlon. With Kiely is his fellow Irishman J.J. Holloway.

Rausch Wins Twice
The German swimmer Emil Rausch won two titles in St. Louis and added a third place in the 200-meter freestyle.

All-Purpose Daniels
In the swimming, Charles Daniels (USA) secured three title wins, one second place, and a third.

Flanagan's Reprise
John Flanagan (USA) repeated his Olympic title win of 1900 by taking the hammer event. In the weight throwing, he could manage only second.

1 On his way to victory: The American sprinter Archie Hahn scorched home in the 60-meters, defeating his fellow Americans William Hogenson and Fay Moulton. Hahn also triumphed in the finals of the 100- and 200-meters. In both races he left Nathaniel Cartmell and Hogenson to fight it out for second and third.

2 Tough fight: Out of 32 entrants in the marathon, only 14 made it to the finish line. America's Thomas Hicks came first, Albert Coray of France second, and Arthur Newton (USA) third.

3 Favorite in the jump events remains unbeaten: The great Ray Ewry (USA) entered three events and was a three-time winner, thus repeating his performance in Paris in 1900. In the standing high jump, he cleared 5' 3" (1.6 meters), putting six inches (15 cm) between himself and Joseph Stadler and Lawson Robertson, both also representing the USA. In the standing triple jump, Ewry took the title with a leap of 34' 7¼" (10.54 meters), some 15¼ inches (38 cm) ahead of Charles King (USA), with Stadler in third place. Ewry's third title win was in the standing long jump. He became champion with a world record jump of 11' 4⅞" (3.476 meters). Charles King (USA) was once again runner-up, and John Biller, another American athlete, came third.

4 Dramatic decider settles discus title: At the end of the competition, Martin Sheridan (pictured here) and Ralph Rose (both USA) jointly led the discus event with 128' 10½" (39.28 meters). In the subsequent "throw-off" Sheridan out-distanced Rose by just under five feet (1.52 meters). Rose, who won the shot competition and came third in the hammer, had to settle for second ahead of the Greek Nicolaos Georgantas.

5 Triple victory: James Lightbody (USA) is rewarded for one of his many victories at the 1904 Olympics. Over 800 meters, Lightbody beat his compatriots Howard Valentine and Emil Breitkreuz to the tape, while in the 1,500-meters he pushed W. Frank Verner and Lacey Hearn (both also USA) into second and third spots. Lightbody's third win came in the steeplechase, ahead of the Irishman John Daly, who was competing for the British team. Third place in the steeplechase was taken by Arthur Newton of the USA. Lightbody added a second place in the four-mile team event.

6 Strychnine sulfate to enhance performance: By the day after the marathon, the winner Thomas Hicks (USA, shown here) had recovered from his physical exhaustion and was able to pose for photographers in front of his trophies. His coach explained how Hicks had managed to finish the race. He stated that he had noticed that Hicks was in distress some ten miles from the finishing line. To rally his man, the coach had felt compelled to give him a small amount of strychnine sulfate dissolved in egg white. After this ministration, Hicks was able to continue, but the last mile was an ordeal. The athlete was barely able to lift his feet and, although conscious, was suffering from hallucinations. Eventually, completely drained, Thomas Hicks staggered to the finishing line, supported by stewards.

7 Gold in the pole vault: The American Charles Dvorak cleared a height of 11' 6" (3.505 meters), which was enough to secure him the Olympic title ahead of fellow countrymen LeRoy Samse and Louis Wilkins.

8 Starting from the landing stage: The 440-yard freestyle was won by Charles Daniels (USA), who also secured victory in the 220 yards. He added a third victory to his collection as a member of the winning 4 x 50-yard relay team.

9 German gymnasts: A photograph of the gymnasts that represented Germany at St. Louis. Team captain F. Hofmann is seated front with his team behind (from right): A. Weber, E. Mohr, O. Wiegand, W. Lemke, H. Peitsch, C. Busch, W. Weber, and A. Spinnler (a member of the Swiss team).

10 Little interest in the sporting competitions: James E. Sullivan (second from right), chairman of the organizing committee, could do nothing to prevent the Games being simply a part of the World's Fair.

The IV Olympiad in London opened a new chapter in Olympic history. As at Athens in 1906, the Games were not merely a part of a world exhibition, but were staged as an event in their own right.

THESE GAMES WERE ORIGINALLY to be held in Rome, but the Italians withdrew their capital's candidacy after the 1906 eruption of Mount Vesuvius – the money that would have been spent on the Olympics was now badly needed elsewhere. In the event, Britain declared itself willing, at short notice, to organize and hold the 1908 Games in London.

The London Games were held in the White City Stadium in the Shepherd's Bush district of west London. Constructed for the Franco-British exhibition earlier in the year, the stadium was equipped with a running track and a velodrome, as well as having a large swimming pool, which featured an adjustable diving board, in front of the stands. A crowd of almost 100,000 watched the proceedings. For the first time, stands supported by simple steel tubes were erected, helping to reduce costs.

As they had done at the opening ceremony of the second Athens Games in 1906, the participating athletes paraded behind their respective national flags on their entry into the stadium. However, they were not dressed in uniform.

The first medals had been awarded even before the opening ceremony took place. The indoor tennis and real tennis (*Jeu de paume*) tournaments had been held in the spring. The actual Games got underway in July, with the track-and-field events, including tug-of-war and the first Olympic 1,600-meter relay, which consisted of two 200-meter legs together with one of 400 meters, and one of 800 meters. Motorboating, polo, wrestling, and rowing were also part of the program. In the fall, figure skating became the first winter sport to be included. There were also soccer, field hockey, and lacrosse tournaments. Again, women took part in a limited number of sports: archery, figure skating, yachting, and tennis.

Tragic Hero
Officials rush to help race leader Dorando Pietri to the finish of the marathon. Sadly, the Italian was disqualified, but was rewarded with the crowd's sympathy.

Welcome to London
The official program featured a high jumper in action at the White City.

Controversy arose between the American delegation and the British. The US team management accused the host nation's judges of partiality. As a result, the IOC announced its intention to use judges from various nations on future occasions.

The most successful competitors at the London Games, with three gold medals each, were the British swimmer Henry Taylor (400-meter and 1,500-meter freestyle and 4 x 200-meter freestyle relay) and the American athlete Melvin Sheppard (800-meters, 1,500-meters, and medley relay).

In the 110-meter hurdles, the 27-year-old US athlete Forrest Smithson showed his class. In the final, he took the gold medal with a time of 15.0 seconds, ahead of fellow Americans John Garrels and Arthur Shaw. Meanwhile, the great Ray Ewry, in his last Olympics before retirement, successfully defended his Olympic titles in the standing high jump and long jump. These successes raised his first-place tally to ten, when his wins in 1906 are taken into account.

Marathon Success
After the disqualification of Italy's Dorando Pietri, the 22-year-old American John Joseph Hayes was declared Olympic marathon champion.

Triple Winner
With three gold medals, the middle distance runner Melvin Sheppard (USA) shared the honor of being the most successful competitor of the Games with British swimmer Henry Taylor.

Determined Douglas
Britain's Johnny Douglas won the middleweight boxing title. An all-round sportsman, he won an England amateur football cap and captained Essex and his country at cricket.

Discus Double
America's Martin Sheridan claimed two discus golds, winning both the Greek-style and modern-style competitions.

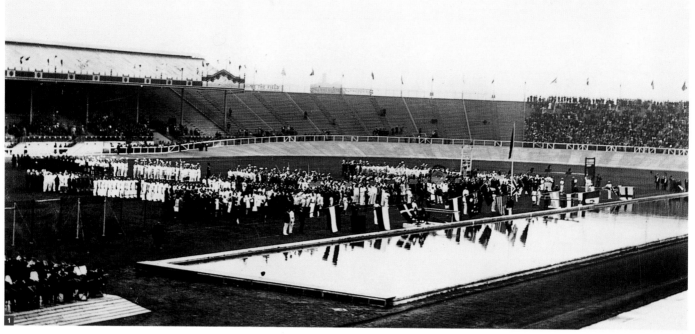

1 **Olympic Games open at the White City:** After the teams had paraded into the brand new White City stadium, the national flags were lowered to greet the Royal Family. In the foreground is the 100-meter open-air pool where the swimming events were held.

2 **Successful title defense:** The American Ralph Rose repeated his shot put success of the 1904 Games.

3 **Three silver winners:** Harry Porter (USA, pictured here) won the high jump, clearing 6' 3" (1.905 meters). Three competitors jumped 6' 2" (1.88 meters) to share the silver: Georges André (FRA), Con Leahy (GBR/ IRL), and István Somody (HUN).

4 **Swan song for a great champion:** With a gold medal in the standing high jump, the legendary American athlete Ray Ewry continued his winning run in the Olympics, uninterrupted since 1900. The silver medal was jointly won by Greece's Konstantin Tsiklitiras and the American John Biller. In the standing long jump, Ewry was victorious for the fourth time in a row, with the silver medal going to Tsiklitiras ahead of Martin Sheridan (USA). No one has yet beaten Ewry's incredible haul of ten first places from 1900 to 1908,

which included two at Athens in 1906. After the London Games, 34-year-old Ewry retired from competitive sports.

5 **Hat trick for Sheridan:** Following his victories in St. Louis in 1904 and Athens in 1906, discus maestro Martin Sheridan (USA) triumphed once again. He won the modern-style event with a throw of 134' 2" (40.89 meters), ahead of his compatriots Merritt Giffin and Marquis Horr. He also won the Greek-style event. At the London Games, discus Greek-style had the athletes ascend a small podium and hurl the discus from it. However, it seems that this was an incorrect interpretation of the ancient technique.

6 **Exciting finish:** Canadian Robert Kerr (second from left) becomes Olympic champion over

200 meters. Robert Cloughen (USA, left) takes the silver ahead of Nathaniel Cartmell (USA, second from right). George Hawkins (GBR, right) is fourth.

7 **Wyndham's walkover:** Britain's Wyndham Halswelle on his way to qualifying for the 400-meter final, which he won on a walkover.

8 **One and two for US hurdlers:** Charles Bacon (right) won the 400-meter hurdles final ahead of Harry Hillman. Britain's Leonard Tremeer picked up the bronze medal.

9 **Smithson protests:** The US hurdles star Forrest Smithson appears to be in action clutching a Bible. In fact, Smithson posed for this shot in protest at having to compete on a Sunday.

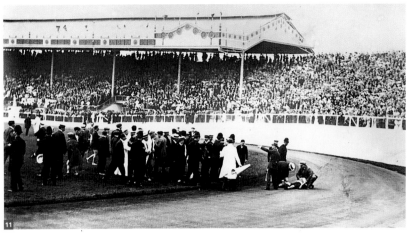

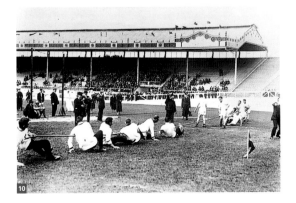

10 **Britain pulls ahead:** In the tug-of-war event, the gold, silver, and bronze medals all went to British teams.

11 **13** **Marathon drama:** (Picture 11) Inside the stadium and on his last lap, the marathon race leader, Dorando Pietri of Italy, collapsed four times from exhaustion. Each time, he struggled back to his feet and staggered on toward the line. For the final few yards to the finish, the nearly unconscious Italian was supported by, among others, the stadium announcer (picture 12, second from left) and a second official, thought by some to be Arthur Conan Doyle (right). The spectators celebrated what they believed to be Pietri's Olympic title win. However, the Italian was disqualified for having "used external support." The gold medal was awarded to John Joseph Hayes (USA), who finished in a time of 2:55:18.4, ahead of South Africa's Charles Hefferon and USA's Joseph Forshaw (USA). Pietri later vigorously denied having asked for help. However, things took a turn for the better when on the following day he received a golden trophy from Queen Alexandra, donated by herself in acknowledgement of his heroic performance (picture 13).

The Swedish hosts ensured that the V Olympic Games ran smoothly. For the first time, there were athletes representing all the continents of the world.

THE ORGANIZATION AND SPORTS facilities in Stockholm were both impeccable, making the V Games a model for future Olympiads. The diplomatic controversies of the time were almost forgotten in the general atmosphere of harmony. That said, the opening parade, in which teams marched behind signs bearing the name of their country, threatened to lead to serious disturbances. The Austrians criticized the participation in the Games of a separate team representing Bohemia, since it was part of the Austro-Hungarian Empire, and Russia objected to a team being fielded by the Grand Duchy of Finland, which then belonged to the Russian Empire. In the end, for the parade, the Bohemians and Finns were asked to march directly behind the Austrian and Russian teams respectively, to use smaller print on the signs bearing their country names, and to enter the stadium without their national flags. However, during medal ceremonies small pennants bearing the countries' national colors were hoisted together with the flags of the respective empires.

In total, 2,547 athletes from 28 countries took part in the Games. The Japanese made their Olympic debut, and women increased the range of sports in which they took part by participating in the swimming events.

Trailblazing technological innovations at the Stockholm Games included the photo-finish for track-and-field events and the electronic timer to back up the conventional stopwatch.

For the second time, equestrianism featured in the Olympic program and has been included ever since. Equestrian events were first contested at the Paris Games, but were discontinued. They had been scheduled for London in 1908, but the organizers had been unable to cope with the vast number of entries.

The Swedish "sports philosophy," which demanded that people exercise

It's Official
Elements of athletics, art, and several national flags intermingle to form the first official Olympic Games poster.

their bodies in a balanced fashion, had a major impact upon the timetable. The shot, javelin, and discus events each had two competitions scheduled. In the one, the athletes threw using their strong arm; in the other, they were to use both arms alternately, and the result was an aggregate of both throws. A further addition to the Olympic program was the modern pentathlon. Designed by de Coubertin, it consisted of horse riding, fencing, swimming, shooting, and cross-country running.

The American athlete Jim Thorpe was outstanding in Stockholm. He won the track-and-field pentathlon and the decathlon. The following year, however, it was revealed that, in his youth, Thorpe had received payment for playing baseball. As a result of rigid interpretation of the IOC's rules on amateurism, he became the first athlete to be disqualified as a "professional." He was stripped of his medals. Only in 1982 was Jim Thorpe rehabilitated and his medals restored. They were presented in 1983 to his family, since, sadly, the great man himself had died in 1953.

The Greatest?
Jim Thorpe, a Native American, was perhaps the greatest athlete of all time. After winning two Olympic golds, he went on to play major league baseball and NFL football.

Double Act
The Finn Armas Taipale took the gold medals in the one-handed and two-handed discus events.

Rose Returns
Ralph Rose (USA) picked up the gold medal in the two-handed shot and silver in the one-handed event.

Dazzling Duke
Duke Paoa Kahanamoku (USA), of Hawaiian royal descent, won the 100-meter freestyle and was a silver medalist in the 4 x 200-meter freestyle relay.

First Flying Finn
Finland's Hannes Kolehmainen (right) was victorious in the 5,000-meters, the 10,000-meters, and the individual cross-country event, and won a silver in the team cross-country event.

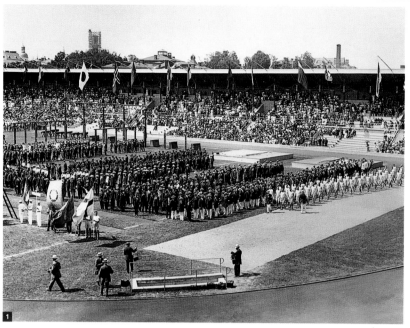

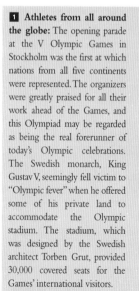

1 **Athletes from all around the globe:** The opening parade at the V Olympic Games in Stockholm was the first at which nations from all five continents were represented. The organizers were greatly praised for all their work ahead of the Games, and this Olympiad may be regarded as being the real forerunner of today's Olympic celebrations. The Swedish monarch, King Gustav V, seemingly fell victim to "Olympic fever" when he offered some of his private land to accommodate the Olympic stadium. The stadium, which was designed by the Swedish architect Torben Grut, provided 30,000 covered seats for the Games' international visitors.

2 **Wrestlers fight to the point of exhaustion:** The Greco-Roman wrestling bout between Russia's Martin Klein (left) and the Finn Alfred Asikainen lasted for more than 11 hours before Klein clinched victory. Completely exhausted by their exertions, both wrestlers had to pull out of their scheduled fights against Claes Johansson of Sweden. Thus, the Swede was declared Greco-Roman middleweight champion, with Klein second and Asikainen third. At light-heavyweight, the fight between the Swede Anders Ahlgren and the Finn Ivar Böhling was abandoned after nine hours. Both wrestlers received a silver medal, without a gold medal being awarded. The bronze medal was taken by the Hungarian Béla Varga.

3 **Women make their debut at swimming:** Setting a world record time of 5:52.8, the Great Britain team, comprising Bella Moore, Jennie Fletcher, Annie Speirs, and Irene Steer, shown here with their chaperone Clara Jarvis, won the 4 x 100-meter freestyle relay ahead of the German four of Margarete Rosenberg, Wally Dressel, Louise Otto, and Hermine Stindt. In third place came the Austrian quartet, made up of Margarete Adler, Klara Milch, Josefine Sticker, and Berta Zahourek. In the women's individual 100-meter freestyle, the Australian Fanny Durack became Olympic champion in a time of 1:22.2, ahead of her fellow Australian Wilhelmina Wylie and Great Britain's Jennie Fletcher. In the women's highboard diving event "Greta" Johansson of Sweden defeated her teammate Lisa Regnell and Isabelle White (GBR).

4 **Enormous variety in gymnastics:** The team event in the so-called "Swedish system" was won by the hosts, ahead of Denmark and Norway, while the gold medal in the "free system" team event went to Norway, ahead of Finland and Denmark. These two gymnastic events were introduced in 1912, contested once more in 1920, and then discontinued. In the individual combined exercises, Italy's Alberto Braglia took the gold. Silver went to the Frenchman Louis Ségura, ahead of Adolfo Tunesi of Italy. In the team event, Italy finished above Hungary and Great Britain.

5 **Gold medal in the high jump:** Alma Richards (USA) clears at 6' 4" (1.93 meters) to win the high-jump gold medal, ahead of the German Hans Liesche and George Horine (USA). The remaining jump events were mainly dominated by the Americans and the Swedes. The long jump was taken by Albert Gutterson (USA) ahead of Calvin Bricker (CAN) and Georg Aberg (SWE). The hosts completed a clean sweep in the triple jump, while America's Harry Babcock won the pole vault with 12' 11½" (3.95 meters). Joint second were Frank Nelson and Marcus Wright (both USA).

6 **A premature celebration:** Anchorman Richard Rau (left) is jubilant about what he believes is a German 4 x 100-meter win. The German team, though, was disqualified for an incorrect changeover, a ruling that was hotly disputed. As a result, Britain (anchorman William Applegarth, pictured right) took the gold.

7 **Results in horse riding:** In the team three-day event, the Germans (pictured here) picked up the silver medal, behind the Swedish hosts, with the bronze being taken by the USA In the individual three-day event, Axel Nordlander of Sweden became champion, ahead of Friedrich von Rochow (GER) and Jean Cariou (FRA). In the dressage competition, Sweden won all three medals, with the gold going to Carl Bonde, ahead of Gustav-Adolf Boltenstern and Hans von Blixen-Finecke. The hosts added another gold medal in the team show jumping, which they won ahead of France and Germany. The individual show jumping event was won by France's Jean Cariou, ahead of Rabod Wilhelm von Kröcher of Germany and Emanuel de Blommaert de Soye of Belgium.

8 **New technology:** The Stockholm Olympics were the first at which the photo finish was available to verify judges' decisions. In the 1,500-meters, a photo managed to separate silver medalist Abel Kiviat (USA) from bronze medalist Norman Taber (also USA).

9 **Wins in rowing:** In the coxed fours event, the German team of Albert Arnheiter, Otto Fickeisen, Rudolf Fickeisen, Hermann Wilker, and coxswain Otto Maier (middle) took the gold medal ahead of Great Britain, with Denmark and Norway sharing bronze-medal position. In the coxed eights event, Great Britain took first and second places, ahead of Germany, while in the single sculls, there was success for Britain again as William Kinnear

secured gold ahead of Polydore Veirman of Belgium, with Everard Butler of Canada and Russia's Michail Kusik coming joint third.

10 **The Americans fete their winners:** On their return from the Stockholm Olympics, the US winners were welcomed with a festive parade. Here mayor of New York William J. Gaynor (left) congratulates Jim Thorpe, champion in the pentathlon and decathlon. There is a wonderful story concerning this remarkable athlete from Prague, Oklahoma, and King Gustav V of Sweden. It is said that when Thorpe was presented to the king to receive his medals, the Swedish monarch told him, "Sir, you are the greatest athlete in the world". Thorpe is reputed to have replied simply – "Thanks, King."

Antwerp

There had been no more "intermediate" celebrations after Athens, and war stopped the 1916 Games from taking place. It was 1920 before the Olympics were staged again – in the Belgian city of Antwerp.

IN THE PRELIMINARY TO THE EVENT, the public passionately debated whether or not athletes should be admitted from those countries that were held responsible for the outbreak of the Great War. For its part, the IOC excluded the delegates from the Central Powers (Austria, Bulgaria, Germany, Hungary, and Turkey). In so doing, it prevented those countries from being invited to the Games, since it was customary to invite only nations represented on the IOC.

Whereas during the previous Games there had been hardly any ceremonial or symbolic acts, at Antwerp, doves of peace were released at the opening ceremony, a repeat of events at Athens in 1896. The Belgian fencer and water polo player Victor Boin took the first Olympic oath, which is still taken today on behalf of all competitors by a representative of the host nation, who pledges that the athletes will take part in the Games "in the true spirit of sportsmanship."

Throughout the Games, the Olympic flag flew above and inside all sports facilities. Bearing five colored rings interwoven to symbolize the unity of the five continents, the flag had been presented to the Olympic movement on its 20th anniversary by Pierre de Coubertin. Now, for the first time, it became the official symbol of the Games.

Spectators at Antwerp witnessed the last Olympic tug-of-war contest. Tug-of-war had first appeared in 1900, when the event was won by a joint Swedish and Danish team. This time, on an especially designed strip in the stadium, the British team outclassed all comers. A number of other events were also discontinued after 1920. Weight throwing vanished, as did the 3,000-meter walk, the 400-meter breaststroke, and several sailing events. Ice hockey, on the other hand, made its debut – a sure indication of the increasing importance of winter sports.

America First
Charles Paddock (USA, right) secures the 100-meter title. He added a second gold medal in the 4 x 100-meter relay, but had to be content with silver in the 200-meters.

Assembly at Antwerp
The official poster for the first Games after World War I showed a classical discus thrower alongside flags of the participating nations.

In the track-and-field events, only a handful of countries were represented. The number of actual participants was less than expected as a number of athletes had been killed in the war. Of the four track-and-field world records set, two were in the hurdles: Earl Thompson (CAN) ran 14.8 seconds in the 110-meters, while Frank Loomis (USA) recorded 54.0 seconds in the 400-meters.

The throwing events were dominated by the Finns, who took first and second in both shot and discus and picked up all three medals in the javelin. The 1920 Games were also significant for the emergence of another major Finnish distance running talent: Paavo Nurmi.

However, the most important conclusion to be drawn from the Antwerp Games was that the Olympic movement had survived the turmoil of the Great War. That this was the case can be attributed to Pierre de Coubertin and to the chairman of the Belgian organizing committee, Henri de Baillet-Latour.

Stylish Suzanne
In tennis, France's Suzanne Lenglen won two gold medals and a bronze.

Nurmi Arrives
Finland's Paavo Nurmi attracted a lot of attention at Antwerp with his three gold medals and one silver.

Youngest Champ
American Aileen Riggin became the youngest Olympic champion up to that time when she won the springboard diving gold medal at 14 years old.

Gold for Sweden
The long jump was won by Sweden's William Petersson.

1 **The Olympic flag:** At Antwerp, the flag bearing five interwoven rings fluttered over an Olympic celebration for the first time. The colored rings symbolize the five continents.

2 **General air of jubilation:** Following his win at 10,000 meters, the Finn Paavo Nurmi (right) is the center of attention. However, the Italian Augusto Maccario (left), fourth in the race behind Joseph Guillemot (FRA) and James Wilson (GBR), is also paraded by his fans. Nurmi added two more gold medals to his collection by winning the individual cross-country event and being in the winning Finnish cross-country team. In the 5,000-meters, Nurmi had to settle for second place behind Guillemot.

3 **Commanding victory:** Percy Hodge (GBR, left) gets within reach of the Olympic 3,000-meter steeplechase title. The American Patrick Flynn (second left) was second, ahead of Ernesto Ambrosini of Italy.

4 **Collecting tennis medals:** Suzanne Lenglen (FRA) secured her first gold medal by defeating Dorothy Holman (GBR) in the singles final. In the mixed doubles, she and her compatriot Max Décugis beat the British pairing of Kitty McKane and Max Woosnam. Together with French partner Elisabeth d'Ayen, Lenglen also won a bronze medal in the women's doubles.

5 **Figure skating brought forward:** In April, before the official Games got underway, the Finnish couple Ludovika and Walter Jakobsson won the pairs figure skating event. They are shown here on the left of the picture, next to fellow Finn Sakari Ilmanen, fifth in the men's event. Gillis Grafström and Magda Julin (both SWE) won the individual competitions.

6 **Triple victory for the USA:** The springboard diving event from the one-meter and three-meter boards was won by the American Aileen Riggin ahead of her US teammates Helen Wainwright and Thelma Payne. In the highboard diving event, she took fifth place. The medalists were Stefani Clausen of Denmark, Eileen Armstrong (GBR), and Eva Olliwier (SWE).

7 **Medals for Kitty:** Kitty McKane (later Godfree) won gold in the women's doubles (with Winifred McNair), silver in the mixed, and a singles bronze. She later won Wimbledon twice.

8 **Royal congratulations:** Albert I of Belgium presenting medals. Here he is congratulating Warren Paoa Kealoha (USA) on his victory in the 100-meter backstroke. Kealoha won the final in 1:15.2, ahead of Raymond Kegeris (USA) and the Belgian Gérard Blitz.

9 **Further congratulations:** The youngest Olympic gold-medal winner so far (in 1920), 14-year-old diver Aileen Riggin (USA), stands atop the winners' podium to receive her prize.

10 **Prize for success:** Triple Olympic champion Ethelda Bleibtrey (USA), winner of the 100-meter freestyle, the 300-meter freestyle, and in the 4 x 100-meter freestyle relay, is delighted to accept this trophy from the Belgian king.

11 **Unusual finish:** In the 100-meter final, Olympic champion Charles Paddock's leap across the finish line caused a sensation. Clocking the same time, Morris M. Kirksey (also USA, right) was left with the silver medal, ahead of Harry Edward (GBR, left).

Chamonix

Because the IOC did not sanction Winter Games until 1925, the Chamonix meet was staged as International Winter Sports Week. Nevertheless, it is now recognized as the first Winter Olympics.

Repeat Performance
Sweden's Gillis Grafström won the men's figure skating competition, as he had at the 1920 Antwerp Olympics.

WITH FIGURE SKATING HAVING been included as part of the Olympic program for the London Games of 1908, the Italian Eugène Brunetta d'Usseaux suggested, in 1911, that separate Winter Games be held. His idea met with resistance from the Scandinavian countries, who believed that such a move might jeopardize the Nordic games, which had been regularly staged in Sweden since 1901. Despite these protests, medals were awarded for figure skating and ice hockey at the Antwerp Games of 1920.

Then, in 1922, a meeting of the French Olympic Committee decided to organize an International Winter Sports Week in Chamonix in 1924. Sixteen nations were represented by a total of some 294 athletes, including 13 women. The preparations included the construction of a new ice stadium, which covered an area of 27,000 square meters and was equipped with two adjacent ice-hockey rinks and a 400-meter-long ice track. Sadly, the well-organized competitions were beset by poor weather conditions, which brought Chamonix both drops in temperature and thaws.

The Scandinavians demonstrated their dominance in all five disciplines – bobsled, ice hockey, figure skating, speed skating, and Nordic competitions. Norway topped the medals table with four gold medals, seven silver medals, and six bronze medals. Finland came next with four gold medals, three silver medals, and three bronze medals.

Finland boasted the outstanding athlete of the week, too – speed skater Clas Thunberg. Thunberg won three gold medals, one silver medal, and one bronze medal to earn himself the nickname "Nurmi on ice" – a reference to the great Finnish distance runner and multiple-medalist Paavo Nurmi. Meanwhile, Norway's Thorleif Haug was being celebrated as the "king on skis" after his

Celebration in Chamonix
The official poster for International Winter Sports Week does not identify the event as a separate Winter Olympic Games, but does make a connection with the VIII Olympic Games being held in Paris later that year.

victories in the 18- and 50-kilometer cross-country skiing, and the Nordic combined event, consisting of cross-country skiing and ski jumping. Gillis Grafström of Sweden won the figure skating title, adding to his success at Antwerp in 1920.

Britain picked up a handful of medals at this first winter celebration. There was a silver in the four-man bob, and bronze medals for the British ice hockey team and for figure skater Ethel Muckelt. At the closing ceremony, Pierre de Coubertin awarded a prize for "Merit for Alpinism" to Charles Granville Bruce. Bruce, a British general, had been leader of the 1922 expedition that attempted to climb Mount Everest.

Spurred on by the huge success of International Winter Sports Week, the IOC resolved the following year to begin staging Winter Games at four-year intervals. These Games were to be separate from the summer competitions.

1 International Winter Sports Week: The Nordic combined event, consisting of an 18-kilometer cross-country ski race and a ski jump competition, was won by the Norwegian Thorleif Haug, ahead of his compatriots Thoralf Strömstad and Johan Gröttumsbraaten. The Olympic rings at the top of the hill indicate IOC patronage for the meeting, held in early 1924, even though it was only granted the title of I Winter Olympic Games retrospectively. Among the demonstration sports (as opposed to official medal sports) on view at Chamonix were military patrol and curling. Curling has appeared on a number of occasions since and became a full medal sport at Nagano, Japan, in 1998.

2 Eight teams contest ice hockey: Members of the Belgian ice hockey squad pose for the camera on their arrival at Chamonix. Following defeats by the USA (0-19), Great Britain (3-19), and France (5-7), the Belgians finished second from bottom. Canada won the eight-team tournament easily ahead of the USA and Great Britain. During the tournament, the Canadians scored 110 goals and conceded only three. Having also won the ice hockey at Antwerp, Canada dominated Olympic ice hockey for many years, winning in 1924, 1928, and 1932, before taking the silver behind Great Britain in 1936.

3 Speedster on ice: Charles Jewtraw won the 500-meter speed skating gold medal, finishing in a time of 44.0 seconds, registering the United States' only gold of the Games. The remaining speed skating events were won by Finns, with Clas Thunberg taking the 1,500, 5,000, and the all-round event. The 10,000-meters was won by Julius Skutnabb, with Thunberg second. Thunberg also picked up a bronze in the 500-meters.

4 The finishing line: The finish for the cross-country skiing events was right next to the ice rink. Cheered on by the spectators, the triple Olympic champion Thorleif Haug of Norway comes in ahead of his teammates Thoralf Strömstad and Johan Gröttumsbraaten in the 50-kilometer event. On the ice rink, the Swede Gillis Grafström took the figure-skating title, ahead of Austrian Willy Böckl and Georges Gautschi of Switzerland. The women's event was won by world champion Herma Planck-Szabo (AUT). The silver medal was claimed by the American Beatrix Loughran, and the bronze medal went to Britain's Ethel Muckelt. However, the favorite with the crowd was 11-year-old Norwegian Sonja Henie, who won hearts even though she finished without a medal. Little could the spectators have known that the girl who came last would go on to become the finest woman figure skater of all time. Her Olympic reign was still four years away.

5 Germany still barred: German ski jumpers pictured at the national championships in

the Harz Mountains. In the while, the top international performers competed in Chamonix. The first Olympic ski jump event was won by the Norwegian Jacob Tullin Thams ahead of his compatriot Narve Bonna and the Norwegian-born American jumper Anders Haugen. Olympic ski jumping took place only on a small hill until 1964.

6 Risky discipline: This picture shows a bobsled competition from the early 1920s. At that time, runs had few safety features, making the sport exceptionally perilous. At Chamonix, Switzerland II won ahead of Great Britain II and Belgium I. The two-man event was introduced in 1932.

7 Participation is all: The Italians took 23 competitors to Chamonix, including the ski jumping team shown here. In the end, there were not any Italian medalists, but it is taking part, rather than winning, that lies at the heart of the Olympic idea.

Paris

For the second time in the young history of the modern Olympic Games, athletes from all over the world – more than 3,000 competitors from 44 countries – met to do battle in Paris.

AFTER THE ORGANIZATIONAL blunders made during the competitions in 1900, the 1924 Paris Games saw the French work particularly hard to ensure that the event ran smoothly. For the first time since 1906, a so-called Olympic Village was erected to accommodate the athletes, and a new track-and-field stadium near Colombes, equipped with a 500-meter track, was finished just in time for the beginning of the Games. It was also the first time in the history of the Olympic Games that events could be followed through live radio transmissions. Another innovation was at the newly built, 10,000-seat swimming arena at Tourelles; competitors' lanes were separated by ropes supported by cork floats.

Technical problems had prevented construction of a regatta course for the rowing competitions. Even though the bend in the Seine River near Argenteuil seemed an ideal location for the rowing tournaments, medal chances were considerably affected by the drawing of lanes; certain areas of the bend put crews at a disadvantage, and strong currents offered further handicaps.

Despite the efforts of IOC president Pierre de Coubertin to have the Germans reinstated, they were banned from these Games as they had been four years previously. The crowds celebrated Paavo Nurmi as their star of the Games. The Finnish runner won five gold medals, two of which were secured in the space of one hour.

Other athletics competitions ended rather bizarrely. One example was in the men's 400-meters, where the world record was improved three times. Having set a new world record of 48.0 seconds in the preliminary heat, the Swiss competitor Joseph Imbach fell in the final. In the intermediate heat, this record

French Pride
The 1924 Olympic poster was dominated by a picture of athletes and the French tricolor.

time was improved on again by the silver medal winner Horatio Fitch (USA, 47.8 seconds). The gold medal was eventually taken by Britain's Eric Liddell, who clocked a further record-breaking time of 47.6 seconds. However, the long track meant that competitors in the 400-meters had to run around only one bend, and this meant Liddell's performance was not officially recognized as a world record time until 1936.

The 1924 Paris Games was the last time tennis was seen as a full medal sport until it was reintroduced more than 60 years later in Seoul. The reasoning behind this was that the IOC had doubts about the top players' amateur status, amateurism being a prerequisite of Olympic participation. Three competitors, all of whom were American, won two golds each in Paris: Vincent Richards in the men's singles and doubles, Helen Wills in the women's singles and doubles, and Hazel Wightman in the women's doubles and the mixed doubles.

Go Johnny Go
The American swimmer Johnny Weissmuller remained unbeaten in the 100-meter and 400-meter freestyle events as well as in the 4 x 200-meter freestyle relay. He also collected a bronze medal with the water polo team.

Flying Scotsman
Britain's Eric Liddell, a Scottish rugby union international, won the 400-meters and picked up a bronze in the 200-meters.

Chariot of Fire
The Briton Harold Abrahams won the gold medal over 100-meters and took a silver medal in the 4 x 100-meter relay.

Double Gold
Harold Osborn (USA) was a double Olympic champion, winning the high jump and the decathlon.

1 Olympic oath: Surrounded by the standard-bearers of the participating nations, the French athlete Georges André takes the Olympic oath during the opening ceremony and sets the VIII Olympic Games in motion.

2 Abrahams strikes: Britain's Harold Abrahams (No. 419) dips to win the 100-meters in 10.6 seconds ahead of America's Jackson Scholz (no. 274, 10.7)

3 Experienced champion: Albin Stenroos (FIN) won the marathon by a margin of almost six minutes, beating the Italian Romeo Bertini and the American Clarence DeMar.

4 British success: In the 800-meter event, Britain's Douglas Lowe beat the Swiss Paul Martin

by a fifth of a second to secure one of the three British track victories. Bronze went to the American Schuyler Enck.

5 "Rolling" toward gold: The high jump competition is taken by Harold Osborn (USA). His successful attempt at 6' 6" (1.98 meters), using the rolling technique with crossed legs, secured his win over fellow American Leroy Brown and the Frenchman Pierre Lewden.

6 Scandinavian domination: The 5,000-meter field is led by the Swede Edvin Wide (right). The eventual winner was the Finn Paavo Nurmi (left), who set an Olympic record only an hour after his triumph in the 1,500-meters. The 27-year-old athlete defeated his compatriot Ville

Ritola (middle), with Wide taking bronze. In the cross-country event, Ritola and Earl Johnson (USA) did not stand a chance against Nurmi. The cross-country team event was taken by Finland, as was the 3,000-meter team race. These provided Nurmi's fourth and fifth golds and confirmed his status as a quite exceptional athlete.

7 Champion in the shadow: Although Fred Tootell (USA) won the hammer, his compatriot Matthew McGrath became the hero of this event, winning the silver at the age of 45. McGrath had already collected a silver medal during the Games in London in 1908 and a gold medal in Stockholm in 1912. In Antwerp in 1920, he had finished in fifth position. Third in the

hammer in Paris was Britain's Malcolm Nokes.

8 Three gold medals: Johnny Weissmuller (USA) was the first Olympic swimmer to record a sub-one-minute (59.0 seconds) time in the 100-meter freestyle event. In the 400-meter freestyle, he defeated the Swede Arne Borg. He collected another gold medal when the United States won the 4 x 200-meter freestyle relay event; Australia and Sweden took second and third places.

9 World record bronze: With a distance of 25' 4" (7.76 meters), the American Robert LeGendre improved the long jump world record by almost 3 inches (7 centimeters). However, this achievement did not secure him a gold medal because the

jump was part of the pentathlon competition. In the final standings of that event, he took third place, behind the Finn Eero Lehtonen (who successfully defended the title he won in Antwerp) and the Hungarian Elemé Somfay. In the long jump event, 24' 5" (7.445 meters) secured William DeHart Hubbard his gold medal.

10 Triumphs for the USA: In the springboard diving event, Elizabeth Becker relegated the Olympic champion of 1920, Aileen Riggin, to second place. The bronze medal was taken by Caroline Fletcher. In the high-board diving, Caroline Smith picked up the gold medal, ahead of Becker. The competitor who prevented a clean sweep by the Americans was the Swede Hjördis Töpel, who finished third.

St. Moritz

The IOC awarded the II Winter Olympic Games to Switzerland. Even though early February usually brings snow to the Engadin region, unseasonably mild weather conditions disrupted many events.

Ice Success
The Norwegian speed skater Ivar Ballangrud won a gold medal over 5,000 meters in impressive style, and added a bronze over 1,500 meters.

AT ST. MORITZ, THE ORGANIZERS were fortunate enough to be able to exploit existing sports facilities at what was already a well-established ski resort. Athletes from 25 nations were full of praise for the organization and proposed timetable of events for these Winter Olympics and, for the first time since World War I, German athletes were admitted to Olympic competition.

However, weather conditions caused some concern: a thaw resulted in the 10,000-meter speed skating competition being canceled, and only two of the usual four bobsled runs went ahead. Nordic skiing was affected, too, as the outcome of the 50-kilometer cross-country skiing event very much depended on the right choice of ski wax. This was because the athletes began the competition in the morning with temperatures around freezing and finished at midday with temperatures above 66°F (20°C).

Skeleton sledding made its debut as an Olympic discipline and proved popular with spectators. With athletes lying head first on a heavy sled and hurtling down St. Moritz's famous Cresta Run, this exhilarating, yet dangerous, competition was won by the American brothers Jennison Heaton, with his brother John coming second. However, the event was only ever held when the Olympics were in St. Moritz, in 1928 and 1948. As in 1924, bobsled teams were left the choice of whether to compete with four or five athletes; all teams decided to enter the competitions with five-man crews.

Even though the International Ski Federation (*Fédération Internationale de Ski* – FIS) had been founded in 1924, Alpine skiing did not form part of the St. Moritz Games. The first international competitions featuring these events took place in March 1928; until 1936, the Winter Olympics remained the exclusive domain of the Nordic disciplines.

Young Winner
The figure skating gold medal won by Norway's Sonja Henie was the first of her many Olympic accomplishments.

Swiss Hospitality
The peaks of the Engadin mountains dominate an Olympic poster that also featured the Swiss and IOC flags.

As happened four years before in Chamonix, Norway were the most successful team, winning six gold medals. Second place went to the USA, with two gold, two silver, and two bronze medals, ahead of Sweden and Finland. The two most successful competitors each claimed two titles. The Norwegian Johan Gröttumsbraaten won the Nordic combined and the 18-kilometer cross-country skiing, while Clas Thunberg of Finland was victorious in the 500-meter and 1,500-meter speed skating events. As expected, the title holders Canada won the ice hockey. With no US team in the tournament, there was no stopping the Canadians, who stormed to victory, scoring 38 goals and conceding none.

Norway's Sonja Henie was the star of the Games. At 15 years of age, she became the youngest person to win the figure skating title, with the first of three consecutive Olympic golds in the event.

Third Gold
The Swede Gillis Grafström skated superbly to secure his third Olympic figure skating title at the age of 30.

Norway's Hero
Cross-country skier Johan Gröttumsbraaten from Norway became a double Olympic champion.

Personal Best
The Swede Per Erik Hedlund won the 50-kilometer cross-country skiing event, with fellow countrymen taking the other two medal places.

1 Swiss hosts: The opening ceremony of the II Winter Olympic Games in St. Moritz takes place in the midst of a snow-covered landscape that will soon melt. Surrounded by standard-bearers of all the teams, the skier Hans Eidenbenz (center of picture with Swiss flag) takes the Olympic oath.

2 Triumph for Norway: The Scandinavians celebrated three medals in the 18-kilometer cross-country skiing event. Here Johan Gröttumsbraaten is on his way to his first gold medal, ahead of fellow Norwegians Ole Hegge and Reidar Ödegaard.

3 Group photograph: Female athletes from eight nations took part in the women's figure skating event and pose for the cameras before the start of the competition. World and European champion Sonja Henie won convincingly, ahead of the Austrian Fritzi Burger and the American Beatrix Loughran.

4 Royal observer: Numerous guests of honor traveled to St. Moritz to attend the opening ceremony and the competitions that followed. A seat in the Royal Box was occupied by Prince Henry (front left), husband of Queen Wilhelmina of the Netherlands. With Amsterdam due to host the IX Summer Olympics later that year, his presence was not surprising.

5 The crowds' favorite: The Olympic figure skating champion Sonja Henie (NOR) is pictured acting as a "judge" for her colleagues. Even though this was only her second Olympics, the 15-year-old was already a popular star with the crowd and competitors alike.

6 Gold for France: Andrée Joly and Pierre Brunet won the pairs figure skating competition. Initially, the event had to be postponed because of a thaw. Behind the French couple, who were bronze medalists at

Chamonix in 1924, Lilly Scholz and Otto Kaiser (AUT) secured the silver medal, ahead of their compatriots Melitta Brunner and Ludwig Wrede. The victors would retain their title four years later at Lake Placid.

7 Best American skater: Beatrix Loughran (USA) delivers an expressive performance on the ice rink. She was the best-placed non-European figure skater, finishing the competition in bronze medal position. The figure skating competition consisted of two sections: a compulsory section containing 13 mandatory elements and a four-minute-long free program.

8 Three Swedish medals: The start and finish line of the 50-kilometer cross-country skiing competition, an event that was affected by a daily temperature swing of over 66°F (20°C). The Swedish skiers coped best with the difficult conditions, with Per Erik Hedlund winning gold,

ahead of his teammates Gustav Jonsson and Volger Andersson. His winning margin of over 13 minutes is unmatched in Olympic history.

9 Repeat victory: The Finnish speed skater Clas Thunberg became joint Olympic champion in the 500-meter event. Four years earlier he had finished joint third, but now he shared joint first place with Norwegian Bernt Evensen. Both finished in the Olympic record time of 43.4 seconds. Roald Larsen (NOR), John Farrell (USA), and Jaakko Friman (FIN) took joint third place, all recording 43.6 seconds. In the 1,500-meters, which he won in 1924, Thunberg struck gold again. The silver medal in this event went to Evensen ahead of Ivar Ballangrud (NOR). The 5,000-meters went to Ballangrud ahead of Julius Skutnabb (FIN) and Evensen. A continuing thaw forced the 10,000-meter competition to be abandoned.

10 Comprehensive coverage: The German media followed the Games closely, primarily because this was the first time a German team had been allowed to participate in the winter meeting of the "youth of the world." Newspapers and magazines – including *Die Woche*, printed in Berlin – regularly reported training sessions, results, and other happenings at the Winter Olympic Games at St. Moritz.

11 Five in the four-man bob: The participating nations utilized the opportunity to compete using five men in the bobsleds, even though the heavy thaw that affected the Games meant that only two (not the usual four) runs were possible. Germany II, with pilot Hanns Kilian, Valentin Krempl, Hans Hess, Sebastian Huber, and Hans Nägle (from front), secured the bronze medal, behind the two American teams. It was Germany's only medal at these Winter Olympics.

TRAINING ZUR WINTER-OLYMPIADE

Amsterdam

The Olympic Stadium in Amsterdam was the outstanding arena of the IX Summer Olympic Games. Its Dutch architect, Jan Wils, won a gold medal for the stadium's design at the Olympic arts competition.

Titled Hurdler
The British athlete Lord David Burghley became Olympic champion in the 400-meter hurdles.

THERE WAS A CONTROVERSIAL start to the IX Summer Olympics when the organizers decided to grant exclusive photographic rights to one company and prohibited all private photography in the stadiums. To prevent spectators from smuggling cameras into the stadiums, checks were carried out at the entrances, resulting in long delays and numerous protests. These measures were eventually abandoned, and the attempt at imposing a photographic monopoly failed.

Win Again
Johnny Weissmuller (USA) repeated his Paris feats with wins in the 100-meter freestyle and the 4 x 200-meter freestyle relay.

Three thousand fourteen athletes (including 290 women) from 46 nations competed in these "universal" Games. The German team, readmitted to the Summer Olympics after 16 years of Olympic exile, had a victorious return. Their ten golds secured them the runners-up position in the medals table, although still some way behind the USA's 22 victories. The swimmer Johnny Weissmuller (USA) and the Finnish runner Paavo Nurmi, who at his third Games picked up his tenth, eleventh, and twelfth Olympic medals, were the most successful athletes.

The spectators in the Olympic Stadium greeted Henri de Baillet-Latour as the new IOC president as he had succeeded Pierre de Coubertin in September 1925. Illness prevented the 65-year-old de Coubertin from attending the Games, the first that he had missed since 1908. However, the creator of the modern Olympic movement listened to news of the events through radio broadcast.

The Amsterdam Olympics saw new procedures introduced that are still in use today. For the first time, a flame was ignited on the marathon tower in front of the newly built Olympic Stadium, thereby introducing the Olympic flame to the Olympic Games. Greece, founders of the original Olympic competition, led the parade of the nations' teams. The admission of women to track-and-field events at Amsterdam was a new

Amsterdam Hosts
A runner dominates the official poster of the Summer Games in Amsterdam. The Olympic flag is in the background.

Good Sign
The javelin competition was won by Erik Lundkvist, a sign painter from Sweden. He set a new world record two weeks later.

development that was to have far-reaching consequences. De Coubertin had always spoken out against women's participation and, until 1928, women had been ineligible for Olympic track-and-field athletics. However, a world women's organization, which had organized its own games for women, forced the IOC to compromise. Excellent performances by female competitors in Amsterdam only served to justify their right to compete in Olympic competition.

The German Lina Radke-Batschauer accomplished what had previously been achieved only by the tug-of-war team back in 1906: a German gold medal in a track-and-field event. In the 800-meter competition, she crossed the finish line in a world record time of 2:16.8. Behind her, many women runners completed the race in an "exhausted" state, a fact that influenced the IOC's decision not to allow women to compete in middle distance running events again until the 1960 Rome Games.

Breaststroke Win
Hilde Schrader (GER) won the 200-meter breaststroke event, equaling the world record set in her semifinal.

Momentous Gold
Lina Radke-Batschauer's victory over 800 meters was Germany's first individual track-and-field gold medal.

1 Big interest: A view of the award-winning stadium in Amsterdam, full to capacity for the opening ceremony of the Summer Games.

2 Gold for Japan: Mikio Oda wins the triple jump, ahead of Levi Casey (USA) and Vilho Tuulos (FIN).

3 Narrow victory: In the 100-meters, Percy Williams (CAN, second from left) beats Jack London (GBR, left) and Georg Lammers (GER, second from right). Williams also won the 200-meters.

4 The favorites beaten: Britain's David Burghley (second from right) defeats the favored American runners Frank Cuhel and Morgan Taylor in the 400-meter hurdles.

5 Golden quartet: Florence Bell, Myrtle Cook, Fanny Rosenfeld, and Ethel Smith of Canada won the 4 x 100-meter relay in the world-record time of 48.4 seconds.

6 Scandinavian victories: In the 10,000-meters, Paavo Nurmi (FIN, centre) won ahead of Ville Ritola (FIN, left) and Edvin Wide (SWE, right). In the 5,000-meters and 3,000-meter steeplechase, Nurmi collected silver medals.

7 World record victory: A throw of 52' 0¾" (15.87 meters)

meant victory for the American John Kuck in the shot put.

8 Strongest athlete: Weightlifter Josef Strassberger (GER) won the gold medal in the heavyweight category

9 Victory for the USA: Pete Desjardins became Olympic highboard diving champion. He won the springboard diving event as well, having come second in Paris.

10 Favorites ahead: In the eights rowing event, the US crew (nearer camera) won, ahead of Great Britain and Canada.

11 German medals: In the 200-meter breaststroke, Hilde Schrader (GER, lane 6) won, with Mietje Baron (HOL, lane 2) coming second and Lotte Mühe (GER, lane 5) third.

12 Extra time decision: The German water polo team beat Hungary 5-2 in the final, netting three goals in extra time. The score was 2-2 after normal time.

13 Hockey winners: A strong Indian team (nearest the camera) won the tournament, ahead of the Netherlands (left) and Germany (dark bands on shirts).

14 Fencing medal: Queen Wilhelmina of the Netherlands presents the gold medal to Helene Mayer (GER) for her win in the individual foil.

Lake Placid

Despite the worldwide Depression, the III Winter Olympic Games went ahead. Unfortunately, they turned out to be a financial disaster for the organizers, who faced a huge loss.

HARDLY ANY COUNTRY IN THE world had sufficient financial means to be able to send a well-prepared and well-equipped team to these Olympic Games. As a result, only 306 athletes from 17 nations competed for medals in the Adirondack Mountains in the state of New York. The credibility of the competitions was further undermined by the fact that over half of these athletes were from the U.S.A. or from Canada.

For all this, the hosts had not spared any expense in creating a setting worthy of exciting competition. The Olympic Stadium had been newly built, as was the bobsled run on Mount Hoevenberg – notorious for being one of the fastest and most dangerous runs in the world. Only the weather foiled the organizers' plans: warm weather continually turned ice and snow into slush. As a result, competitions had to be rescheduled and postponed, and the Games actually finished two days late, with the four-man bobsled event being the final competition to take place.

In Lake Placid, three disciplines were presented for demonstration purposes only: the women's speed skating (officially admitted as an Olympic discipline in 1960), dog sled racing, and curling. This last discipline, which was also included as an official Olympic sport at the 1998 Winter Olympics at Nagano, Japan, was dominated by the Canadians. Their teams from Manitoba, Ontario, and Quebec took the first three places. Medals in the Nordic skiing events were monopolized by the Scandinavians, among them the Norwegians Johan Gröttumsbraaten (Nordic combined) and Birger Ruud (ski jumping). The cross-country com-petitions were also beset by adverse weather conditions, and an added organizational oversight hampered participants in the 50-kilometer event: the course wound through a solitary stretch of woods where there were no stewards to show

Retains Gold
The Norwegian skier Johan Gröttumsbraaten became Olympic champion in the Nordic combined and successfully defended the title he won at St. Moritz in 1928.

III Olympic Winter Games

Lake Placid, USA
February 4-13, 1932

The American Games
A ski jumper as well as a map of the USA showing Lake Placid are featured on the poster advertising the Olympic Games.

competitors the way nor any spectators to cheer them on.

The remaining competitions were dominated by the Americans and Canadians. Two of Lake Placid's celebrated stars were the American speed skaters John Shea (gold medal winner over 500 and 1,500 meters) and Irving Jaffee (gold medalist over 5,000 and 10,000 meters).

After three Olympic wins in 1920, 1924, and 1928, the Swedish figure skater Gillis Gräfström could manage only second place and retired from international competition. Here he had to yield the ice to the Austrian Karl Schäfer, who had swum for his country in the Amsterdam Summer Games four years before. Sonja Henie from Norway repeated her victory of 1928 in the figure skating competition. Still only 19 years old, she won standing ovations from the crowds for the sensational interpretations of popular shows that she included in her free program.

Repeat Victory
In Lake Placid, the ever popular Norwegian figure skater Sonja Henie repeated her Olympic title win of 1928.

King of the Ice
In front of his home crowd, the American Irving Jaffee won two long distance speed skating gold medals and was part of a clean sweep for the Americans in the speed skating events.

Figure Skating Win
By winning the gold medal, the Austrian Karl Schäfer ended the remarkable winning run of the triple Olympic champion Gillis Gräfström (SWE), who had to settle for second place.

Sven's Gold
Sweden's Sven Utterström took the 18-kilometer cross-country skiing gold medal with two minutes to spare over fellow Swede Axel Wikström.

1 Standard-bearers: At the opening ceremony, the US ice sprinter John Shea – who went on to win two golds – takes the Olympic oath, which is received by Admiral Byrd, the aviator who flew to the South Pole.

2 The crowds' favourite: Sonja Henie (NOR) secured her second Olympic win. The Norwegian figure skater's free program included extracts from popular stage shows and enthralled the judges just as much as it did the audience. The Austrian Fritzi Burger and Maribel Vinson from the United States took silver and bronze medals respectively.

3 Most successful winner: Winning two gold medals each, John Shea (USA, front) and his teammate Irving Jaffee were the most successful competitors of the Winter Games in Lake Placid. In the 500-meter speed skating event, John Shea beat the Norwegian Bernt Evensen and the Canadian Alexander Hurd. In the 1,500-meter event, Shea stopped an overwhelming triumph by the Canadians who took places two to four; the silver medal was won by Hurd ahead of William Logan and Frank Stack.

4 Lack of snow: The shortage of snow that disrupted the Games can be best seen from the ski jump hill. As four years before, the Nordic combined, consisting of an 18-kilometer cross-country race and a ski jump competition, was won by the Norwegian competitor Johan Gröttumsbraaten ahead of his compatriots Ole Stenen and Hans Vinjarengen. The ski jump competition finished with another three medals for the Norwegians: Birger Ruud won the gold medal ahead of Hans Beck and Kaare Wahlberg. Ruud went on to successfully defend his title four years later at Garmisch-Partenkirchen.

5 Preliminary decision: The start to one of the two qualifying heats in the 10,000-meter speed skating event. The first four in each of the two heats reached the final. The final was won by the American Irving Jaffee ahead of world record holder Ivar Ballangrud of Norway and the Canadian Frank Stack. Jaffee also became

Olympic champion over 5,000 meters, with the silver medal won by his team mate Edward Murphy and the bronze going to the Canadian William Logan.

6 A limited competition: The four teams in the ice hockey competition played each other twice. The title was decided by the first of two matches between Canada (white jerseys) and the host nation, USA. A 2-1 win by the Canadians in the first leg, followed by a 2-2 draw in the second leg, were enough to win them the gold medal. Germany took the bronze medal, with Poland clearly defeated back in fourth place.

7 The strongest survive: American rules dictated that instead of the usual procedure whereby skaters went out in pairs, the speed skating events had to have mass starts, and this was highly controversial among the European skaters. Pushing and pulling often resulted in the judges having to remind competitors to compete fairly. The unpopular starting method was reason enough for the multiple world record holder and combined world champion Clas Thunberg (NOR) not to enter the competition.

8 Dangerous course: Bobsled USA I, with pilot William Fiske, Edward Eagan, Clifford Gray, and Jay O'Brien, won the four-man bobsled competition on the natural ice channel at Mount Hoevenberg. Not only was the course notorious for its bends, it was also considerably longer than a normal Olympic course. The silver medal was won by USA II ahead of Germany I. This was Edward Eagan's second gold. He had won his first as a light-heavyweight boxer at the 1920 Summer Games in Antwerp. He remains the only Olympian to have won gold medals at both Winter and Summer Games.

9 New two-man bob: The two-man bobsled competition was held here for the first time and consisted of four runs. The American brothers, Hubert and Curtis Stevens (USA I), won the gold medal ahead of Reto Capadrutt/Oscar Geier (SUI II) and John Heaton/Robert Minton (USA II).

Los Angeles

Around 3,500 musicians created a festive atmosphere at the opening of the X Olympic Games. In the midst of the Great Depression, the American "dream factory" captivated spectators and athletes alike.

A CROWD MORE THAN 100,000 strong gathered in the Coliseum to watch the opening ceremony. As a result of the worldwide depression, only 1,408 athletes from 37 nations were able to travel to the USA. Male competitors lived in an especially built Olympic Village, as they had at the 1906 Olympic Games in Athens and again in Paris in 1924. However, female participants stayed in hotels. Once again, the number of athletes each nation could enter in each competition was limited, with a maximum of three entries per country per event permitted.

Even before the Games commenced, they were rocked by controversy: the IOC banned Paavo Nurmi for violation of amateur regulations. On a number of occasions, the Finnish runner had claimed travel expenses to fund his journeys to meets. Thus, the 35-year-old Nurmi was denied the chance to compete for the marathon gold medal, with which he had hoped to mark the end of his career. It had been a glittering career, during which this athletics legend set 22 official world records and won nine Olympic gold medals, plus three silvers. At home in Finland, Nurmi was not banned and continued to race for a couple of years. In fact, his portrait featured on the official poster for the Helsinki Games of 1952. It then irritated the IOC when Nurmi, a "professional" athlete banned for life from Olympic competition, was given the honor of carrying the torch into the Helsinki stadium.

Scandal aside, the Los Angeles Games had many other points of interest. Innovations included the use of a three-level podium for the medal ceremonies and automatic timing for track events. For the first and only time since 1900, soccer was missing as a sport. In show jumping, meanwhile, medals were not awarded in the team event, because no team could get the required three riders

Tolan Triumphs
At 5' 5" (1.65 meters) tall, Eddie Tolan (right, with Ralph Metcalfe) was thought too short to be a sprinter. He proved his doubters wrong by winning both the 100- and 200-meters.

Come to LA
The official poster calls on the "youth of the world" to come together at Los Angeles for the Olympic Games.

around the difficult circuit successfully.

There were bizarre happenings in the 3,000-meter steeplechase. A mistake by the lap counter caused the athletes to run an extra lap. While this was not of any consequence for the Finn Volmari Iso-Hollo, who was well in the lead, the American Joseph McCluskey was overtaken during this unscheduled lap. Nevertheless, he did not lodge a protest and settled for bronze, behind Britain's Thomas Evenson.

The 1932 Games were a showcase for Mildred "Babe" Didrikson, who turned in a fine all-round performance. A superb sportswoman, she turned to golf on giving up track and field, becoming perhaps the greatest woman player to date.

Once again a gold medal was awarded in the Merit for Alpinism category. The Germans Toni and Franz Schmid were honored for making the first ascent of the North Face of the Matterhorn.

Olympic Record
Japanese swimmer Yasuji Miyazaki shaved 0.8 seconds off Johnny Weissmuller's 100-meter freestyle record in the semifinal, touching in 58.0 seconds. In the final, a time of 58.2 was enough for victory.

Hampson for Britain
Britain's Thomas Hampson comes home to win the 800-meter gold medal, ahead of Alexander Wilson of Canada. Wilson's fellow Canadian Phil Edwards was third.

Polish Express
The Pole Stanislawa Walasiewicz won the women's 100-meters. She had been living in the USA since 1913 and in 1947 became a US citizen.

Rowing Repeat
After a dramatic race against William Miller (USA), the Australian rower Henry Pearce retained the Olympic single sculls title he had won in 1928.

1 Solemn oath: After the Games have been opened by US vice president Charles Curtis, the American fencer George Calnan, épée bronze medalist in 1928, takes the Olympic oath on behalf of all participants. Because of the global economic crisis, the turn-out at Los Angeles was only half that of the 1928 Games.

2 India's superiority: Only three teams competed in the field hockey tournament. The Indians (pictured here during their match against Japan) were unbeaten, scoring 35 goals and conceding two. Japan took the silver medal, and the USA, beaten 24-1 by the victorious Indians, were third. India had also won in 1928, and remained invincible until 1960.

3 Photo finish: Only the camera could decide who had won the final of the men's 100-meters at the Los Angeles Games. Although the electronic timer showed the same time (a world record 10.38 seconds) for first and second, Eddie Tolan (USA, right) was declared the winner, ahead of Ralph Metcalfe (also USA, second from right). The bronze medal went to the German sprinter Arthur Jonath (third from right), who recorded 10.40 seconds.

4 New procedure for medal ceremonies: Since 1932, medal ceremonies have taken place on a special three-step podium. This picture shows the winner of the women's 100-meter freestyle, Helene Madison (USA, middle), flanked by Holland's Willemijntje den Ouden (left) and the USA's Eleanor Garatti-Saville.

5 Green walks to victory: Britain's Thomas Green (No. 98) on his way to winning the 50-kilometer road walk, a new Olympic event at Los Angeles, in 4:50:10. Second was the Latvian athlete Janis Dalinsh in 4:57:20, and the bronze was won by Italy's Ugo Frigerio, who finished in 4:59:06.

6 A record performance: With a throw of 133' 1½" (40.58 meters) American discus thrower Lillian Copeland set a new Olympic record and picked up the gold, medal ahead of her team mate Ruth Osborn and the Polish world record holder Jadwiga Wajsowna.

7 Results of the water polo: This match between eventual silver medalists Germany and the USA, who finished in third place, ended in a 4-4 draw. The gold medal was taken by the Hungarian team, who dominated the event, handing out heavy defeats to Germany (6-2), Japan (17-0), and the USA (7-0). Hungary went on to repeat their success at the 1936 Berlin Games.

8 **The versatile "Babe":** By winning gold medals in the 80-meter hurdles and the javelin, and a silver medal in the high jump, America's Mildred Didrikson (right) became the most successful track-and-field athlete of the Games.

9 **Successful gymnast:** In addition to two gold medals in the floor and pommel horse competitions, István Pelle (HUN) won silver medals in the combined exercises and parallel bars.

The Winter Games at the Bavarian resort of Garmisch-Partenkirchen were the first of two Olympic celebrations on German soil in 1936. They were officially opened by Adolf Hitler.

WORRIED ABOUT NEWS OF discrimination against Jews in Germany, the IOC repeatedly demanded that Olympic rules be respected: Jewish athletes could not be specifically excluded from the German team. However, an attempt by German emigrants living in the USA to prompt a boycott of the Games by all democratic countries failed. The Nazi regime, for its part, used the Games as an opportunity to present itself as peace loving in front of more than half-a-million spectators from around the world. The newly built sports facilities, such as the Olympic ski jump hill, the ice rink, and the bobsled run near the Riessersee, were opened amid a great deal of pomp and ceremony.

From the start, negative press coverage of the Games was suppressed. Only German photographers were admitted to the venues, and only after extensive censorship by the propaganda ministry were "suitable" pictures released for publication in international newspapers and magazines.

As for the Games themselves, 28 nations attended, among which Australia, Bulgaria, Greece, Liechtenstein, Spain, and Turkey were being represented for the first time at an Olympic winter competition. The increasing popularity of Alpine skiing was reflected in the IOC's introduction of an Alpine combined competition, consisting of downhill and slalom events. However, by classing Austrian and Swiss hotel skiing instructors as professionals and banning them from taking part, the IOC sparked a controversy. The men's gold medal in the new event was taken by German skier Franz Pfnür, with fellow countryman "Guzzi" Lantschner second, and France's Emile Allais third. Germany also struck gold and silver in the women's Alpine combined, with Christl Cranz winning ahead of Käthe Grasegger.

German Winter Games
The poster for the 1936 Winter Games suggests an athlete giving the Nazi salute.

Another newly introduced discipline was the Nordic 4 x 10-kilometer relay event, which was won by the Finnish team. Meanwhile, the British ice hockey team registered the upset of the Games. They defeated the much-favored Canadian side and went on to win the gold medal. It then emerged that eight of the players in the British team lived and played their ice hockey in Canada. Nevertheless, they were eligible to represent Britain by virtue of having been born there.

The most successful individual at Garmisch was 31-year-old Norwegian speed skater Ivar Ballangrud. Taking part in his third Olympics, he added three gold medals and a silver medal to his collection, and then retired from competitive sport. His teammate, Sonja Henie, said goodbye to amateur sports and turned professional, after winning her third consecutive Olympic figure skating title. Britain's Cecilia Colledge took silver.

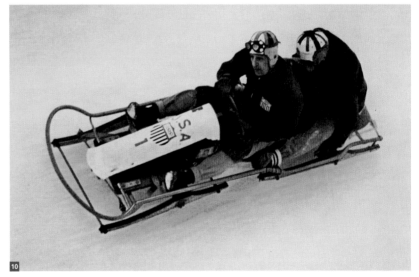

1 **The Games draw to a close:** The closing ceremony at Garmisch featured a fireworks display by torchlight.

2 **Hat trick:** With her third title in a row, Sonja Henie of Norway became (and still is) the most successful individual woman figure skater in Olympic history. The silver medal at Garmisch was won by Britain's Cecilia Colledge.

3 **Successful start:** A good performance in the compulsory section set world champion Karl Schäfer (AUT, right) on the way to the men's Olympic figure skating title, ahead of Ernst Baier (GER) and Felix Kaspar (AUT).

4 **Finnish relay:** First skier Sulo Nurmela (FIN, left) hands over to Klaes Karppinen during the 4 x 10-kilometer cross-country, which Finland won ahead of Norway and Sweden. The 4 x 10-kilometers was a new event at Garmisch.

5 **Swedish expertise:** The first four places in the 50-kilometer skiing competition were taken by Swedes. The gold was won by Elis Wiklund, ahead of (from left) Axel Wikström, Nils-Joel Englund, and Hjalmar Bergström.

6 **Curling demonstration:** Curling featured at Garmisch as a demonstration sport, as it had at Chamonix and at Lake Placid. Austria won the team event, and Georg Edenhauser (AUT) came out on top in the individual competition.

7 **Italy on patrol:** The military patrol event, another demonstration sport, was won by the Italian team.

8 **Bobsled win:** Switzerland II, with (from right to left) pilot Pierre Musy, Arnold Gartmann, Charles Bouvier, and Joseph Beerli, won the four-man bob, ahead of Switzerland I and Great Britain I.

9 **Change of fortune:** Having led after the downhill, Laila Schou Nielsen (NOR) could not find the same form in the slalom and finished third overall in the Alpine combined.

10 **Medals for the USA:** Ivan Brown (left), partnered by Alan Washbond in USA I took the gold medal in the two-man bob. Switzerland II was second and USA II third.

11 **Scandinavians fly to victory:** The ski jump was won by Birger Ruud ahead of the Swede Sven Eriksson. Third was Ruud's fellow Norwegian, Reidar Andersen.

12 **Norway again:** In the Nordic combined competition, Norway's Oddbjörn Hagen claimed the gold.

67

The first Summer Olympic Games to be held in Germany were used by the Nazi party as a gigantic propaganda exercise. Because of World War II, these were the last Olympics until 1948.

DESPITE IOC CONCERNS ABOUT the Nazis' rise to power in Germany, the committee was unable to move the 1936 Games away from Berlin. The German IOC members and the German Reich repeatedly gave assurances that they would abide by the rules of Olympic competition. Before the event, the chairman of the US National Olympic Committee and future IOC president, Avery Brundage, had rejected calls by Jewish emigrants for a boycott, and warned that politics should not interfere with sports. In addition, the world had seen how smoothly the Germans had run the Winter Games at Garmisch-Partenkirchen earlier that year, and there is no doubt that helped to dispel much of the skepticism that had prevailed before the Games.

A suggestion by Carl Diem, the head of the German organizing committee, was adopted, and this was the first time the Olympic flame was ignited by the sun in Olympia, Greece. It was then relayed to the impressive new 100,000-seat stadium in the German capital by no less than 3,075 torchbearers, each running slightly more than half a mile of the journey.

By employing the Third Reich's efficient propaganda machine, Adolf Hitler was able to use these Olympics as a platform from which to promote the host nation to a worldwide audience. This was typified by *Olympische Spiele*, Leni Riefenstahl's epic documentary on the Berlin Games, which although undoubtedly propaganda is also a respected cinematic work.

To deflect criticism of Germany's race legislation, the German team manager selected two "half Jews" for the national team. Furthermore, ice hockey player Rudi Ball and the 1928 Olympic fencing champion Helene Mayer were included without having to go through the usual qualification process. However, one of

Jesse's Games
Winning four gold medals (100-meters, 200-meters, long jump, 4 x 100-meter relay), the American athlete Jesse Owens was the Games' undisputed star.

Berlin in the Limelight
An over-sized athlete and the quadriga of the Brandenburg Gate dominate the official poster of the Berlin Games.

the world's most accomplished high jumpers, Jewish athlete Gretel Bergmann, was not chosen.

The ruling powers had supported the German athletes' preparations in every conceivable way because the athletes were expected to prove the superiority of the "Aryan race" over athletes from other parts of the world. This was much undermined by the success of American black athletes. Nevertheless, Germany's 33 golds meant that the national team finished as overall medal winners in the competition, ahead of the United States' 24 golds and Hungary's ten.

Outdoor 11-a-side handball was introduced to the tournament for the first and last time, with Germany beating Austria in the final. Other new disciplines were canoeing and basketball. The Americans triumphed in the latter, embarking on a winning run which was interrupted only by the USSR in 1972.

1 **Big interest:** Tens of thousands of spectators followed the competitions each day: this is a view of the swimming stadium and the Olympic Stadium, both seemingly filled to capacity.

2 **The oath is taken:** Following the parade of nations, German weightlifter Rudolf Ismayr (who was Olympic champion in Los Angeles in 1932) takes the Olympic oath. He was not, however, able to retain his title in Berlin.

3 **Italian in front:** Trebisonda Valla (third from left) won the 80-meter hurdles, ahead of the German Anni Steuer and the Canadian Elizabeth Taylor. It took a photo-finish to finally decide the positions of the first four athletes.

4 **"King of the athletes":** The US decathletes turned out to be invincible. Glenn Morris (middle) picked up the gold medal, ahead of Robert Clark (left) and Jack Parker (right).

5 **Third victory for India:** The seemingly invincible Indian hockey team became Olympic champions for the third time in a row. In the final, they beat the Germans 8-1. The Netherlands secured the bronze medal.

6 **German riding success:** The three-day event was won by Ludwig Stubbendorff (pictured here) on Nurmi, ahead of the American Earl Thomson and Hans Mathiesen-Lunding of Denmark. Stubbendorff picked up his second gold medal in the team event with Rudolf Lippert and Konrad von Wangenheim, outclassing Poland and Great Britain. The German riders emphasized their superiority by winning gold (Heinz Pollay) and silver (Friedrich Gerhard) medals in the individual dressage event, a gold medal in the team dressage event, and through victories in the individual (Kurt Hasse) and team show jumping events. Hazardous conditions caused three horses to be killed.

7 **German foil:** The Jewish fencer Helene Mayer (right) was included in the German team to dispel growing international concern about Germany's blatantly racist and anti-Semitic laws. At the medal ceremony for the foil competition (shown here), she received the silver, behind the Hungarian Ilona Elek (middle) and ahead of bronze medalist, Ellen Preis of Austria.

8 **US pool win:** The 400-meter freestyle swimming event

was decided when America's Jack Medica (lane 2) beat his Japanese rivals Shumpei Uto (nearer the camera) and Shozo Makino. The men's swimming medals were generally contested by just two nations. Apart from the gold in the 100-meter freestyle event (won by Ferenc Csik of Hungary) and the silver in the 200-meter breaststroke (Erwin Sietas of Germany), all the individual men's medals went to swimmers from either Japan or the United States.

9 **Three gymnastics golds:** Konrad Frey (GER) won gold medals in the pommel horse and parallel bars competitions, a silver in the horizontal bar event, and bronze medals in the floor and combined exercises. Frey secured his third gold in the team event, thus becoming Germany's most successful competitor in Berlin.

10 **Japanese record:** Japan won the final of the 4 x 200-meter freestyle relay in a new world record time of 8:51.5. The

USA finished more than ten seconds behind in second position, with Hungary securing the bronze medal.

11 **British rowing gold:** In the double sculls, Jack Beresford (rear) and Leslie Southwood are ahead of Germany and Poland. They went on to take the title. The German crew had beaten the British in the heats.

12 **Canoeing debut:** Gregor Hradetzky (AUT) won the

1000-meter single-seat kayak event. He also took the 10,000-meter folding kayak event.

13 **Estonian strength:** Wrestler Kristjan Palusalu (top, against the German Kurt Hornfischer) took the freestyle wrestling match. He also won the Greco-Roman heavyweight wrestling event.

14 **Diving medals:** The American Marshall Wayne won the highboard diving competition, ahead of his

compatriot Elbert Root and Hermann Stork of Germany. Wayne also won the silver medal in the springboard diving event. American success was completed by Richard Degener's gold medal and Albert Greene's bronze medal.

15 **Tandem gold:** The German duo Ernst Ihbe (left) and Carl Lorenz won the 2,000-meter tandem competition, ahead of teams from the Netherlands and France.

St. Moritz

For the first time since Garmisch-Partenkirchen in 1936, athletes from all over the world met for Winter Olympic competition. The Olympic spirit had once again survived the horrors of a world war.

WHEN THE 1940 SUMMER Olympic Games were due to be staged in Tokyo, the Japanese organizers proposed Sapporo as the venue for the Winter Games. However, as a result of the outbreak of war between Japan and China, Japan withdrew, and it was suggested that the Winter Games be held in St. Moritz instead. Organizational disagreements ensued and the event was eventually handed to Garmisch-Partenkirchen. The outbreak of World War II, however, saw the whole planning process grind to a halt.

During the war years, the IOC had a change of leadership. After Henri de Baillet-Latour's death in 1942, vice president Sigfrid Edström duly took over as acting president, becoming elected president in 1946. Also in 1946, a newly expanded IOC decided to award the next Winter Games to Switzerland, which had remained neutral during the war; St. Moritz was again selected as the venue. The town had gained Olympic experience as hosts of the 1928 Winter Games, and its facilities, which had remained undamaged during the war, had only to be modernized, not rebuilt.

However, these first postwar Games were still very much in the shadow of World War II. For a start, most athletes had only improvised equipment. In addition, a shortage of hard currency, combined with restrictions on foreign travel for citizens in countries such as Great Britain, meant that many visitors stayed away. Local hotel owners suffered as a consequence.

At St. Moritz, slalom and downhill skiing events for men and women were included for the first time as Olympic disciplines. This raised Alpine skiing to the same level as Nordic skiing. The surprise Alpine skiing sensation turned out to be the 28-year-old American skier Gretchen Fraser, who started the competition as a complete outsider, and went on to take the gold medal in the women's slalom event.

Nils Wins
At the first post-war Winter Olympics, the four-time winner of the Wasa cross-country event, Nils Karlsson of Sweden, became Olympic champion in the 50-kilometer Nordic competition.

JEUX OLYMPIQUES D'HIVER
1948 St MORITZ SUISSE

New Entries
Out of the 28 nations competing at St. Moritz, Chile, Denmark, Iceland, Korea, and Lebanon were present for the first time.

Contrary to the IOC's emphatic plea for it not to go ahead, the military patrol competition was held, but still for demonstration purposes only. The winter pentathlon – consisting of cross-country skiing, shooting, downhill skiing, fencing, and horse riding – was also a demonstration event, but it did not turn out to be very successful.

The newspaper headlines were dominated by the controversy concerning the ice hockey competition. The United States had sent two teams to Switzerland, each claiming to represent their country; one was nominated by the US National Olympic Committee, and another nominated by the Amateur Hockey Association of the United States (AHAUS). The International Olympic Committee vice president Avery Brundage accused the AHAUS team of violating amateur rules. Yet, he was not able to prevent them from participating. The AHAUS team went on to finish fourth. A year later, though, they were retroactively disqualified.

Final Victory
The United States took their first Olympic skiing medal when Gretchen Fraser won the women's slalom event. She retired after the Games.

Alpine King
The Frenchman Henri Oreiller won gold in the downhill and combined skiing events. With bronze in the slalom, he became the most successful athlete at St. Moritz.

Best Yet to Come
Britain's Jeannette Altwegg took the figure skating bronze behind Canada's Barbara Ann Scott and Austria's Eva Pawlik. Four years later, though, Altwegg was to be Olympic champion.

Crammond Third
Britain's John Crammond picked up the bronze medal in the skeleton sled toboganing event. The event, now discontinued, was won by the Italian Nino Bibbia, with John Heaton of the United States in second place.

1 Alpine first: With the introduction of the downhill and slalom events as Olympic disciplines, Alpine competitions finally won full recognition after the combined event had been included at the 1936 Winter Olympics in Garmisch-Partenkirchen. At St. Moritz, the downhill was won by the Frenchman Henri Oreiller, ahead of the Austrian Franz Gabl. Oreiller picked up his second gold medal in the combined event, with Karl Molitor (SUI) second and James Couttet (FRA) third. Oreiller also took a bronze medal in the slalom event, behind Edy Reinalter (SUI) and Couttet.

2 Momentous gold: Richard "Dick" Button was the first American to become Olympic figure skating champion. His athletic presentation secured him the gold medal, ahead of Hans Gerschwiler of Switzerland and the Austrian Edi Rada. The pairs event was taken by the much-favored world and European champions from Belgium, Micheline Lannoy and Pierre Baugniet.

3 Favorite's victory: The women's figure skating competition was won by the Canadian Barbara Ann Scott. The Austrian skater Eva Pawlik took the silver medal, ahead of Jeanette Altwegg of Great Britain.

4 Joint silver: IOC president Sigfrid Edström (second from left) presents medals to the winners in the 500-meter speed skating. The Norwegian Finn Helgesen (fourth from left) took the gold. His compatriot Thomas Byberg (third from left) shared silver with Americans Robert Fitzgerald (second from right) and Kenneth Bartholomew (right).

5 Speed skating results: The Swede Ake Seyffarth won the 10,000-meter event. The Norwegians took all remaining speed skating golds. Seyffarth added to his gold medal by winning the silver medal, behind Sverre Farstad of Norway in the 1,500-meter event.

6 **Surprise winner:** With an advantage of half a second, American Gretchen Fraser relegates the Swiss skier Antoinette Meyer and Austria's Erika Mahringer to second and third positions in the women's slalom. Fraser added a silver medal to her tally when she secured second place in the Alpine combined competition.

7 **Double Swiss victory:** Felix Endrich (in cockpit) and Friedrich Waller won the two-man bobsled gold medal, ahead of Fritz Feierabend and Paul Eberhard in the other Swiss bobsled. Feierabend's innovative bobsled design, in which the runners were individually suspended under a new aerodynamic cover, attracted a lot of attention during the competition.

8 **Medals for Austria:** Trude Beiser of Austria won the Alpine combined event, which consisted of a downhill competition and a slalom. Another Austrian, Erika Mahringer, came third behind America's Gretchen Fraser. The silver medal in the women's downhill event was taken by Beiser behind the surprise winner, the Swiss skier Hedy Schlunegger. Beiser's fellow Austrian Resi Hammerer secured the bronze medal.

9 **Finns in front:** The Finn Heikki Hasu took the gold medal in the Nordic combined event, ahead of his compatriot Martti Huhtala and the Swede Sven Israelsson. The Nordic combined is made up of an 18-kilometer cross-country skiing section and three attempts from the Olympic ski jump hill, of which the best two jumps are then taken into account.

10 **Ruud end:** With his Olympic title in the ski jumping competition, Petter Hugsted (NOR) took over from his compatriot and mentor Birger Ruud, who had collected gold in both 1932 and 1936. Ruud had to be content with the silver, ahead of another Norwegian, Thorleif Schjeldrup.

London

After a break of 12 years, the Summer Olympic Games were to be staged once again. For the second time since 1908, the IOC selected London – originally earmarked for the 1944 Games – as the venue.

LONDON WAS A LIKELY OPTION FOR the first postwar Summer Olympics because its existing facilities had remained largely intact through the war. In front of King George VI, the Swedish IOC president, Sigfrid Edström, and more than 80,000 spectators, the XIV Summer Olympic Games were opened at the Empire Stadium of Wembley, in northwest London. Despite some concerns, the IOC continued the tradition of relaying the Olympic torch from Athens, but decided to re-route the runners. On their way from Olympia to London, the torchbearers were diverted via Pierre de Coubertin's tomb in Lausanne, thereby avoiding having to run through Germany.

Not surprisingly, the Games took place without teams from Germany and Japan. Both countries were the alleged aggressors of World War II, and as a result were excluded from participating. Athletes from the Soviet Union did not take part either, because the USSR was not affiliated to the IOC. Before the Games, the organizers dropped the idea of building an Olympic village because of anticipated high costs; Britain was, after all, almost bankrupt in the years following World War II. Instead, the athletes stayed in military barracks and colleges around the capital; rationing meant that many teams had to bring their own food along with them.

Polo and outdoor handball were no longer included in the competitions, while the Olympic arts competitions were held for the last time, thus ending Pierre de Coubertin's original idea of combining art with sports.

The women's competitions were expanded by the addition of the 200-meter, long jump, and shot events. Fanny Blankers-Koen of the Netherlands became the star of the Games, making history as the "flying housewife." A mother of two children, she won gold medals over 100 meters, 200 meters, in

OLYMPIC GAMES

29 JULY 1948 14 AUGUST
LONDON

London Statistics
Fifty-nine countries sent a total of 4,099 athletes to the 1948 Summer Olympic Games.

the 4 x 100-meter relay, and in the 80-meter hurdles, where a photo finish confirmed her win over Britain's Maureen Gardner. Even though the 30-year-old Blankers-Koen was already past her expected athletic prime, a more favorable timetable might have seen her win even more medals.

However, with three gold medals (combined, team, and pommel horse events), one silver (parallel bars), and a bronze (horizontal bar), the Finnish gymnast Veikko Huhtanen managed to surpass the Dutch athlete's medal tally. The Hungarian fencer Ilona Elek won a much-celebrated gold medal and retained her 1936 Olympic title. Her compatriot Aladár Gerevich won two golds in London. He competed in Olympic Games from 1932 right up until 1960, winning seven gold, one silver, and two bronze medals in various fencing events. In winning 38 events, the USA became the most successful team of the Games, ahead of Sweden with 16 golds and France with ten Olympic titles.

Dutch Joy
With four gold medals, the Dutch athlete Fanny Blankers-Koen was the most successful female competitor of the Games.

Swedish Double

The Swede John Mikaelsson won the 10-kilometer walking event, with compatriot John Ljunggren taking the 50-kilometer title.

Good Start

A gold medal over 10,000 meters and a silver medal over 5,000 meters were the first medals of a highly successful Olympic career for the Czechoslovakian Emil Zátopek.

Javelin Gold

With his win in the javelin event, Tapio Rautavaara continued traditional Finnish success in this discipline.

Olga's First

The Hungarian Olga Gyarmati won the first Olympic women's long jump competition. The world record holder was Fanny Blankers-Koen.

1 **Flame burns once more:** Spectators watch events at Wembley Stadium, built for the 1924 British Empire Exhibition.

2 **Swedish victory:** Henry Eriksson is surrounded by well-wishers after his victory in the 1,500-meters.

3 **800-meter injury:** The Dane Hans Christensen has to retire with a fractured leg.

4 **US triple:** William Porter (middle) won the 110-meter hurdles, ahead of Clyde Scott (left) and Craig Dixon (right).

5 **Narrow decision:** In the 5,000-meters, Emil Zátopek (TCH, left) is defeated by the Belgian Gaston Reiff (right).

6 **Star of the Games:** Fanny Blankers-Koen (HOL, middle) wins the 100-meters, ahead of Dorothy Manley (GBR) and Shirley Strickland (AUS).

7 **Sprint final:** Harrison Dillard (USA, left) wins the 100-meters, ahead of "Barney" Ewell (USA, second right) and Lloyd La Beach (PAN, third right).

8 **French golds:** Micheline Ostermeyer won gold medals in the discus and shot competitions. She also secured a bronze in the high jump.

9 **Australian win:** John Winter won the high jump with a jump of 6' 6" (1.98 meters).

10 **Golden discus:** Adolfo Consolini (ITA) defeated his compatriot Giuseppe Tosi and Fortune Gordien (USA).

11 **Two wins:** Hungarian fencer Aládar Gerevich (right) won golds in the individual and team saber events.

12 **Pool drama:** The 100-meter freestyle winner, Greta Andersen (DEN), has to be rescued after fainting during the 400-meter freestyle.

13 **Swedish success:** The pentathlon was won by William Grut (right), while Gösta Gärdin (left) took the bronze.

14 **Swedish canoeing gold:** Hans Berglund and Lennart Klingström won the 1,000-meter kayak pairs event.

15 **Double diving winners:** Double gold medal winner Victoria Draves (USA) congratulates Samuel Lee (USA) on his gold in the highboard and bronze in the springboard.

Oslo

For the first time, the Winter Olympics were held in a Scandinavian country. The event was received with great enthusiasm by the Norwegians, and a record number of spectators attended the Games.

BEFORE THESE GAMES BEGAN, THE organizers were concerned about Oslo's ability to stage the event; the city did not really have sports facilities that met Olympic standards. However, this was remedied by refurbishing existing facilities and building new ones, which were ready well before the opening ceremony. In the end, the worries proved unfounded, because the facilities, as well as the courses for the newly introduced men's and women's giant slalom and women's 10-kilometer cross-country skiing, met the high expectations of athletes and officials alike.

Ahead of the Games, the Norwegians had picked up Carl Diem's idea and decided to relay the Olympic torch to the Winter Games in the same way as it was to the Summer Games. There had been plans for a "torch relay of friendship" from the venue of the first Winter Games (Chamonix) to Garmisch-Partenkirchen in 1940, but World War II scuttled the Games. The Norwegians started their relay run in the southern Norwegian town of Morgedal, situated in the province of Telemark. Morgedal was the birthplace of the peasant Sondre Nordheim who, in 1868, had invented the first operational ski binding, making him one of the founders of modern skiing. As an added historical touch, the anchor runner carrying the torch into the Bislett Stadium was 19-year-old Egil Nansen, grandson of the polar explorer Fridtjof Nansen, also regarded as an early skiing pioneer.

For the first time since the end of World War II, German and Japanese teams were allowed to compete at the Olympic Games. The organizing committee had made certificates of de-nazification mandatory for entry into Norway, but any fears that the Norwegians might have been hostile to athletes of the former occupying power turned out to be unsubstantiated. The atmosphere was, instead, marked by the enthusiasm and impartiality of the spectators.

Attracting 150,000 spectators, the ski jump event at Mount Holmenkollen set a record in terms of crowd numbers that remains unbeaten. On the cross-country skiing slopes, it was difficult to distinguish between spectators and athletes because the majority of spectators had made their way there on skis. The American figure skater Richard "Dick" Button dominated the headlines when, during the successful defense of his 1948 figure skating title, he became the first skater to perform a triple jump and a toe-loop, and a double axle.

Victory by the 31-year-old Finn Lydia Wideman, turned out to be one of the highlights of the Games. Despite being the oldest competitor, she won the 10-kilometer cross-country skiing event, and became the first athlete to win a women's Olympic Nordic skiing event. Finnish athletes also took the silver and bronze medal positions.

Home Win
Hjalmar "Hjallis" Andersen (right) after his race against the Japanese Sugawara. Winning three gold medals (over 1,500 meters, 5,000 meters, and 10,000 meters), the Norwegian skater was the most successful athlete in Oslo.

Norwegian Hosts
Tied to ski poles, the national flag of host nation Norway and the Olympic flag wave side by side on the official poster of the VI Olympic Winter Games.

Ice Victor
The American Richard "Dick" Button proudly displays his figure skating gold medal. His triple loop was the first by a figure skater.

Slalom Queen
Andrea Mead Lawrence (USA) won two gold medals in the slalom and giant slalom Alpine skiing events. She was the first American to secure two golds in a Winter Olympics.

Norway's Star
The Norwegian skier Stein Eriksen put on an impressive display in front of his home crowd by becoming Olympic champion in the giant slalom and taking the silver medal in the slalom.

German Gold
Andreas Ostler led the German four-man bobsled team to victory by a margin of more than two seconds over the four runs.

1 **Expressive Briton:** The 21-year-old British athlete Jeanette Altwegg, born in India and daughter of a Swiss father, won the figure skating gold medal, ahead of the American Tenley Albright and Jacqueline du Bief of France.

2 **Olympic title retained:** Following his win at the 1948 Winter Games in St. Moritz, Richard "Dick" Button again took the figure skating gold medal, well ahead of the Austrian Helmut Seibt and James Grogan of the United States. After his retirement from an outstanding career as a competitive figure

skater, Button went on to achieve more success as a television sports commentator.

3 **Norway celebrates:** In front of more than 30,000 spectators, the VI Winter Olympic Games were officially opened in the Norwegian capital, Oslo. The readmitted German team members, led by standard-bearer Hermann Böck, found themselves warmly welcomed. Thirty countries participated, a record for a Winter Olympics.

4 **US speed skating success:** Olympic champion Kenneth

Henry (right), silver medalist Donald McDermott (left), and their coach (centre) celebrate a US 1–2 in the 500-meter speed skating event. The bronze medal position was taken by two athletes: the Norwegian Arne Johansen and Gordon Audley of Canada, both clocked the same time. Henry had finished fifth in this event in the Games at St. Moritz in 1948.

5 **Harmony on ice:** Reigning world and European figure skating champions, of the time, Ria and Paul Falk (GER) continued their winning run in the Oslo Olympics. The married

couple took the gold medal, ahead of the American brother and sister Karol and Michael Kennedy. The bronze medal was secured by Marianna and László Nagy of Hungary. Following their Olympic win, the Germans successfully defended their world championship title and moved on to pursue professional careers.

6 **Experienced winner:** The men's downhill was won by the Italian woodcutter Zeno Coló. The icy slope made great demands on the athletes' technical skills. Coló, who was also world champion, relegated the Austrians Othmar Schneider

and Christian Pravda to positions two and three respectively. The Italian almost collected another two medals but instead had to be content with fourth place in both the slalom and giant slalom.

7 **Austrian's silver and gold:** After coming a disappointing second in the men's downhill competition, the Austrian Othmar Schneider took the slalom gold. He defeated the Norwegians Stein Eriksen and Guttorm Berge in the process.

8 **Fastest time:** Andreas "Anderl" Ostler, Friedrich Kuhn,

Lorenz Nieberl, and Franz Kemser (GER) took the gold medal in the four-man bobsled competition. The line-up was put together from the two existing German teams before the event, after the other nations' bobsleds, manned by considerably heavier athletes, had achieved much faster times in training. During the competition, the four German athletes, weighing a combined total of more than 1,000 pounds, turned in the fastest time four runs in a row and finished well ahead of the USA I and Switzerland I teams. It was Germany's first gold medal in

this event. German success continued in the two-man bobsled, which was won by Ostler and Nieberl, ahead of USA I and Switzerland I. Ostler became the first pilot to win both bobsled competitions at the same Olympics. After the Games, the International Bobsled Association imposed overall weight limits.

9 Hosts celebrate victories:
By pushing the Austrians Christian Pravda and Toni Spiss into second and third places, the Norwegian Stein Eriksen (pictured) secured the men's giant slalom gold medal. He

won the silver medal in the slalom event. In the downhill, Eriksen had to settle for sixth position. His gold and silver were the only Olympic medals he ever won.

10 The favorite in front: The 1950 world champion Trude Jochum-Beiser (middle, gold) of Austria, the German Annemarie "Mirl" Buchner (left, silver, also a double bronze medal winner in the slalom and giant slalom), and the Italian Giuliana Minuzzo (bronze) show their delight during the medal ceremony for the women's downhill.

Helsinki

There was a wonderful atmosphere at the XV Olympics, which were held in the Finnish capital, Helsinki. To the delight of the crowd, the final torchbearers were their heroes, the great distance runners Paavo Nurmi and Hannes Kolehmainen.

FOR THE FIRST TIME SINCE 1912, athletes from Russia took part in an Olympic Games. In 1912, they had participated representing the Tsarist empire; now they were representing a communist Soviet Union. However, problems arose before the Games when the Soviet team refused to be accommodated alongside athletes from capitalist countries in the Olympic village at Kapyla. Following a declaration of solidarity from the other Eastern Bloc countries attending the Games, teams and officials were put up in alternative accommodation in students' quarters.

Having participated as part of a "united" Korea in 1948, South Korea now made its Olympic debut as a country in its own right. It had been the focal point of the Cold War that had developed between the United States and the Soviet Union, both of whom were involved in the conflict between North and South Korea. Unfortunately, the Helsinki Games were overshadowed by the polarization of the two systems; team officials considered every win achieved by "their" athletes as proof of the superiority of their own social system.

This was also the first time since World War II that a German team participated in a Summer Olympic Games. However, a united German team could not be assembled. Before the event, the Federal Republic of Germany and the German Democratic Republic could not agree on the selection criteria, resulting in the East German athletes remaining at home. One interesting addition was Saarland; as an independent German region with its own National Olympic Committee, it was allowed to send its own team to the Games.

The finest sporting achievements were those of Emil Zátopek. The army officer they called the "Czech Express"

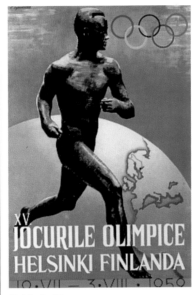

Pride in Paavo
As well as featuring a globe that highlighted the venue of the Summer Games, the official poster also illustrated the legendary Finnish long-distance runner, Paavo Nurmi.

secured victories over 5,000 meters, 10,000 meters, and in the marathon, enthralling spectators all the way. An additional milestone was set by the American Bob Mathias, who became the first decathlete to successfully defend an Olympic title. However, the greatest personal success was achieved by the Danish rider Lis Hartel on her dressage horse, Jubilee. She won a silver medal in the event and thereby triumphed over the poliomyelitis (inflammation of the spinal cord) which required that she be lifted on and off her horse at the Games.

The Dutch athlete Fanny Blankers-Koen, the undisputed star of the previous Games in London in 1948, had a disappointing end to her international career in Helsinki. In the 80-meter hurdles final – won by the Australian Shirley Strickland – the 34-year-old struck a hurdle and fell; she left the arena in tears never to compete again.

Czech This
Emil Zátopek on his way to victory in the marathon. He also took the 5,000- and 10,000-meter events.

Sprint Queen
The Australian track-and-field athlete Marjorie Jackson was victorious in the 100- and 200-meter finals. Her time of 11.5 seconds in the 100-meters was a world record.

Soviet Strength
In Helsinki, the Soviet gymnast Viktor Chukarin took four gold and two silver medals. In 1956, he went on to add another three golds, one silver, and one bronze to his medal collection.

Hungary to Win
The Hungarian swimmer Váleria Gyenge was victorious in the 400-meter freestyle event in what was a successful Olympics in the pool for the Hungarians.

Bob's Back
Bob Mathias (USA) repeated his 1948 Olympic decathlon win, securing victory by the largest margin in Olympic history. It was also a world record.

1 Legend lights the flame: Inside the stadium, Paavo Nurmi handed the torch to fellow Finnish running legend Hannes Kolehmainen, who ignited the Olympic flame.

2 Gold medal for Brazil: Adhemar Ferreira da Silva took the triple jump gold medal, ahead of Leonid Shcherbakov (URS) and Arnoldo Devonish (VEN).

3 On her way to gold: The South African Esther Brand won the high jump, ahead of Britain's Sheila Lerwill and Alexandra Chudina (URS).

4 US quartet in front: The Americans won the men's 4 x 100-meter relay, ahead of the Soviet Union and Hungary.

5 Star performer: In a final sprint, Emil Zátopek (TCH, right) won the 5,000-meters. Alain Mimoun (FRA, second right) took silver, ahead of Herbert Schade (GER, second left). Britain's Chris Chataway (left) falls, before finishing fifth.

6 Flush of victory: In the 4 x 400-meter event, Jamaica's relay team beat the Americans (left) by only a tenth of a second, and set a world record. Germany (right) took the bronze.

7 Running in the family: Like her husband Emil Zátopek, Dana Zátopková (TCH) was victorious. On the same day as Emil's 5,000-meter win, she won gold in the javelin, ahead of

Alexandra Chudina and Yelena Gorchakova of the USSR.

8 Photo-finish: Lindy Remigino (USA, third right) wins the 100-meters in front of Herb McKenley (JAM, second right) and Emmanuel McDonald Bailey (GBR, second left).

9 Swimming gold: In the 100-meter freestyle, Katalin Szöke (HUN) defeated Johanna Termeulen (HOL) and her fellow Hungarian Judit Temes.

10 Surprise winner: In the 400-meter freestyle final, the Frenchman Jean Boiteux beat

Ford Konno (USA) and Per-Olof Östrand (SWE).

11 Fastest walker: The Swede John Mikaelsson (right) won the 10-kilometer walking event in just over 45 minutes.

12 Multiple champion:

Viktor Chukarin (URS) won gold in the combined exercises, the pommel horse, the horse vault, and the team event, and also secured silver in the rings and parallel bars.

13 Swiss Gold: The parallel bars final was won by Hans

Eugster, thus denying Viktor Chukarin a fifth gold medal.

14 US clean sweep: The American David Browning won the springboard with compatriots, Miller Anderson and Robert Clotworthy, second and third respectively.

Cortina d'Ampezzo

Cortina d'Ampezzo in the Italian Dolomites had bid three times to host the Winter Olympics, but it was not until 1956 that this resort had the opportunity to welcome the world's best athletes.

THE NORTHERN ITALIAN TOWN OF Cortina d'Ampezzo had been earmarked for the 1944 Winter Games but World War II forced this plan to be abandoned. Eight years later and more disappointment: Oslo was given preference over Cortina's renewed attempt to stage a Winter Olympic Games. In 1956, however, all the persistence paid off.

To finance the necessary construction projects, the organizers were able to rely on the support of Italian industrial groups, and the event itself was also supported by a number of Italian companies. Even so, compared with the levels of sponsorship offered to later Olympic organizers, the amount of financial backing involved was very small indeed: Fiat and Olivetti provided a couple of cars and typewriters respectively.

Before the Games began, a lack of snow cast a shadow over the competition timetable. Adverse weather conditions meant that athletes had insufficient opportunity to train and this resulted in numerous complaints. Such was the concern that a few days before the start, snow had to be transported down to the valley from higher snow fields. Ironically, heavy snow fell on the day of the opening ceremony and much of the imported snow had to be removed.

These Games saw the Olympic debut of a pan-German team of 75 athletes. As recently as 1955, the East German National Olympic Committee had provisionally been recognized by the IOC. Winning 16 medals and becoming the most successful nation, the Soviet team also made their debut at a Winter Olympics. Entries of 818 athletes from 32 countries set a record for participation in a Winter Olympic Games. Giuliana Chenal-Minuzzi, who was third in the downhill in Oslo in 1952, was the first woman athlete to take the Olympic oath at the opening ceremony.

In 1954, the Italian television station

Cortina's Finest Hour
The VII Winter Olympic Games in Cortina d'Ampezzo were as colorful as the poster that advertised them.

RAI had launched regular programs and now offered live coverage from Cortina – a first in the history of the Winter Games. Thanks to "Eurovision," television audiences in Central Europe also followed the competitions.

They witnessed the triumphs of the Austrian Anton "Toni" Sailer. The 20-year-old outclassed his rivals in all three Alpine skiing events. These wins also counted as world championship titles, and secured him an additional world championship classification in the new combined event. Sailer was the most successful athlete in Cortina, ahead of the Soviet speed skater Yevgeni Grischin who won gold over 500 and 1,500 meters.

The ice hockey tournament saw an end to Canada's dominance in this event. Apart from Great Britain's gold medal in 1936, the Canadians had taken all Olympic ice hockey titles since 1920. The victorious Soviet team that beat them included Vsevolod Bobrov, who had been a member of his country's soccer team during the 1952 Summer Olympics in Helsinki.

King Toni
In a reference to his home town, Kitzbühel, the triple gold medal winner Toni Sailer (AUT) was known to his fans as the "Blitz from Kitz."

Tenley Wins
The American Tenley Albright, world figure skating champion in 1953 and 1955, added an Olympic gold to the silver she collected in 1952.

Medals Galore
Veikko Hakulinen (FIN) was gold medalist in the 30-kilometer Nordic skiing competition, and collected silver in the 50-kilometers and 4 x 10-kilometer relay cross-country events.

Swiss Success
Renée Colliard, from Switzerland, secured the gold medal in the women's slalom. The women's downhill was won by her teammate Madeleine Berthod.

Soviet Tie
The Soviet speed skater Yevgeni Grischin was Olympic champion over 500 meters and, in a dead heat with compatriot Yuri Mikhailov, became joint 1,500-meter title holder.

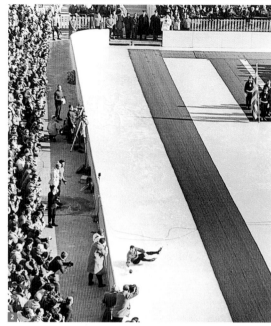

1 **Natural ice rink:** The 400-meter-long ice rink on Lake Misurina accommodated 8,500 spectators.

2 **Opening ceremony:** Moments before the Olympic flame is lit, the speed skater Guido Caroli stumbles over a cable on the ice rink. The torch had originally been lit on the Capitoline Hill in Rome.

3 **Soviet debut:** Winning all seven games in the ice hockey tournament, the Soviet Union (dark shirts) concluded their Olympic debut in impressive style. In the final (pictured here), the Soviet team beat the eventual bronze medal winners

Canada, 2-0. The silver medal went to the United States. The USSR won a total of seven gold, three silver, and six bronze medals, to become the most successful nation at the Winter Games in Cortina d'Ampezzo.

4 **Figure skating pairs:** The Austrian pair Elisabeth Schwarz and Kurt Oppelt defeated the Canadian world champions Frances Dafoe and Norris Bowden by a tiny margin, with Marianne and László Nagy from Hungary in third.

5 **Triple US triumph:** The men's figure skating competition was won by an American for the

third consecutive time, as Hayes Alan Jenkins beat teammate Ronald Robertson and his own younger brother, David.

6 **Figure skating win:** Despite a badly injured foot, the American Tenley Albright took the figure skating event, ahead of her compatriot Carol Heiss and the Austrian Ingrid Wendl. Later in the year, Heiss beat Albright in the world championships.

7 **Swiss gold medal:** Renée Colliard was a surprise winner in the women's slalom. The silver medal was taken by the Austrian Regina Schöpf, ahead of Yevgeniya Sidorova of the Soviet Union.

8 **Successful bobsleds:** Pilot Franz Kapus with Gottfried Diener, Robert Alt, and Heinrich Angst took the gold medal for Switzerland I. The silver went to Italy II, ahead of USA I. In the two-man bob, it was Italy first and second with the Swiss team third.

9 **Happy winner:** The slalom silver medalist at Oslo in 1952, Ossi Reichert (FRG), and her coach are jubilant about her win in the giant slalom. The silver and bronze medals were taken by the Austrians Josefine Frandl and Dorothea Hochleitner.

10 **Wonderful present:** On her 25th birthday, the Swiss Madeleine Berthod became Olympic downhill champion. The silver medal was won by her teammate Frieda Dänzer, while the bronze went to Lucile Wheeler of Canada.

11 **Nordic skiing victories:** At his third Olympic Games, the Finn Veikko Hakulinen won the newly introduced 30-kilometer cross-country event, ahead of the Swede Sixten Jernberg and Pavel Kolschin of the USSR. Hakulinen added another two silver medals to his collection in the 50-kilometer event (he won the gold in 1952) and the 4 x 10-kilometer relay. He secured seven medals in his Olympic career.

Melbourne

The XVI Olympic Games were opened in Melbourne by the Duke of Edinburgh in late November 1956. As the northern hemisphere moved into winter, Australia was just getting ready for summer.

Fraser First
Australian swimming phenomenon Dawn Fraser (left) is congratulated after winning her heat of the 100-meter freestyle. Fraser went on to win the gold in a new world record time.

T HE FIRST OLYMPIC GAMES to be held south of the equator posed a particular set of problems for athletes from Europe and America. For a start, many athletes did not have sufficient funds to spend a period of time acclimatizing before the Games. In addition, the late timing of the competition within the athletics season meant that athletes had to retain their peak fitness over a longer period than usual. Contrary to the regulations laid down in the Olympic Charter, one discipline had to be separated from the rest of the program. As the Australian government were unwilling to shorten the usual six-month quarantine period for horses entering the country, the horse riding events were forced to take place in June in Stockholm.

Because of the high cost of traveling to Australia, fewer athletes participated in these Games than, for example, in Berlin 20 years previously. The already relatively low number of competitors decreased even more when China pulled out (because of Taiwan's participation), and Egypt and Lebanon decided not to attend (because of the Suez crisis). Liechtenstein, the Netherlands, Spain, and Switzerland also withdrew, in protest at the Soviet invasion of Hungary. In the end, 3,342 athletes attended.

The competitions themselves also suffered from the effects of political crises. One water polo match in the final round between Hungary and the USSR was abandoned because of the misconduct of some of the players. However, by beating Yugoslavia in the final, Hungary successfully defended their 1952 title.

Outstanding athletes in Melbourne included the Soviet gymnast Larissa Latynina, who won four gold medals (in the team, the combined exercises, the horse vault, and the floor competitions), a silver medal (in the asymmetrical bars event), and a bronze medal (in the portable apparatus). Betty Cuthbert

Australian Hosts
The Australian host city's coat of arms is featured on the Olympic poster for the XVI Olympic Games, held in Melbourne.

turned on the style in front of her home crowd with three track-and-field wins: the 100- and 200-meters and the 4 x 100-meter relay. In the 5,000- and 10,000-meter events, the Soviet Vladimir Kuts took the titles held by Emil Zátopek; the Czechoslovakian retired from international competition after finishing sixth in the marathon. After winning two gold medals over the 80-meter hurdles and in the 4 x 100-meter relay, the Australian athlete Shirley de la Hunty (née Strickland) also retired. Between 1948 and 1956, she had collected a total of three gold, one silver, and three bronze medals.

The Australian swimmer Dawn Fraser marked the beginning of her Olympic career by taking two gold medals (100-meter and 4 x 100-meter freestyle) and one silver (400-meter freestyle). Her compatriot Murray Rose became the first male swimmer to win two individual freestyle events (400-meters and 1,500-meters) since Johnny Weissmuller's achievements of 1924.

Soviet Star
With four golds, one silver, and one bronze, the Soviet gymnast Larissa Latynina was a favorite with the crowds; she was the Games' most successful competitor.

Home to Glory
British boxing gold medalist Dick McTaggart is held aloft by ecstatic fans as he returns home to Dundee with not only the lightweight gold medal but also the Val Barker Cup for the Games' most stylish boxer.

Long Distance Hero
Vladimir Kuts (URS) became double Olympic champion over 5,000-meters and 10,000-meters, achieving a new Olympic record in the latter event.

More Boxing Gold
British flyweight Terry Spinks brought home gold from Melbourne. He later turned professional and became British champion in 1960.

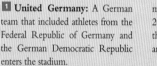

1 United Germany: A German team that included athletes from the Federal Republic of Germany and the German Democratic Republic enters the stadium.

2 Three home golds: The 18-year-old Australian Betty Cuthbert (No. 468) takes her first gold medal in the women's 100-meter sprint. Two days later, she secured her second gold in the 200-meters and went on to win her third with the 4 x 100-meter relay team.

3 Duel decided: Vladimir Kuts of the Soviet Union (left) won this duel against Britain's Gordon Pirie (right) in the 5,000-meter event. In the 10,000-meters, he crossed the finishing line ahead of the Hungarian Jozsef Kovács. Allan Lawrence gained a notable bronze for the host nation.

4 Bravo Brasher!: Christopher Brasher (GBR) heads for victory in the 3,000-meter steeplechase. Brasher had been a pacemaker in Roger Bannister's four-minute mile and founded the London marathon.

5 Exciting final: Bobby Joe Morrow (USA, right) wins the 100-meters. He secured victory in the 200-meters three days later and with the 4 x 100-meter relay team added another gold to his medal collection.

6 Efforts rewarded: Alain Mimoun of France is the first athlete to enter the Olympic stadium in the marathon competition.

7 Favorites win rowing gold: The American eight secured a narrow victory over the Canadian and Australian crews.

8 Diving accolades: America's Pat McCormick won the springboard and highboard diving competitions in convincing style. She had also won both titles at Helsinki in 1952.

9 Hat-trick in the boxing: At his third Olympics, and at the age of 30, the Hungarian boxer László Papp (right) became the first boxer to win three Olympic titles.

10 Swimming gold and record: European champion Ursula Happe (GER) after the medal ceremony for her victory in the 200-meter breaststroke, where she set a new Olympic record of 2:53.1.

11 A win despite injury: Having sustained an injury in the first round, the German show jumper Hans Günter Winkler was in severe pain, but still managed to guide his horse, Halla, over the course without any mistakes. He won gold medals in the individual and team events. In an Olympic career that lasted until 1976, Winkler won five gold medals.

12 Six medals: The Hungarian gymnast Agnes Keleti won golds in the floor, the beam, the asymmetrical bars, and the team portable apparatus event, and silvers in the combined exercises and the team event.

13 Soviet wins: Boris Shakhlin became the Olympic pommel horse champion. The Soviet team's success was wrapped up by Viktor Chukarin, with wins in the parallel bars and combined exercises, a silver in the floor event, and a bronze in the pommel horse. Valentin Muratov also won two golds in the floor and horse vault competitions and a silver in the rings. Other Soviet medals were Albert Azaryan's gold in the rings event, and Yuri Titov's silver in the horizontal bar and bronze in the combined exercises and the vault.

Squaw Valley

The organizers were unable to fully allay the skepticism that greeted the award of the VIII Winter Games to Squaw Valley in the Sierra Nevada. Nevertheless, the celebration passed off smoothly.

Home Win
America's Carol Heiss, who had taken the Olympic oath during the opening ceremony, won the women's figure skating gold medal.

WHEN THE DECISION WAS MADE in 1955 on the venue for the 1960 Games, the area around Lake Tahoe was completely undeveloped as a winter sports center. However, within four years, Squaw Valley, 6,000 feet (1,829 meters) above sea level, was ready, with sports facilities and accommodation for participants, as well as infrastructure for more than two million visitors. This came about thanks to the organizing committee and financial backing from the states of California and Nevada, together with subsidies from the federal government.

Nevertheless, preparing the slopes for the Alpine skiing competitions was fiercely expensive, because they had to have man-made obstacles incorporated to meet the high standard required for the Olympic Games. And despite the subsidies, the organizers delayed construction of a bobsled run for too long, with the result that the IOC had to call off both bob competitions. (As usual two-man and four-man events had been scheduled.)

For these VIII Winter Olympic Games, the flame had once again been lit in the Norwegian town of Morgedal. During the opening ceremony, which was stage-managed by Walt Disney, a pan-German team paraded into the stadium beneath a flag bearing the national colors of Germany (black, red, and yellow) and the five Olympic rings. This compromise had been worked out by officials after the East German delegation had initially insisted on marching behind the East German flag. South Africa was represented for the first time at a Winter Games, but because of the country's policy of apartheid, this first appearance was also its last until 1994.

Spectators at Squaw Valley were the first to watch the biathlon as an Olympic discipline. A combined event, consisting of cross-country skiing and shooting, the biathlon had been a recognized sport in

Monopoly Broken
Georg Thoma (GER) became the first non-Scandinavian to win a Nordic skiing event, taking the Nordic combined title.

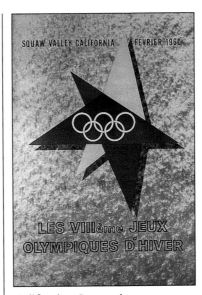

Californian Connection
The five rings take pride of place on the official poster of the 1960 Winter Olympic Games, held in Squaw Valley, California.

the Scandinavian countries for many years. It is perhaps unsurprising, then, that the first Olympic champion was a Swede – Klas Lestander.

Another newcomer to the Winter Olympic program was women's speed skating. There were four events – the 500-meters, in which the gold medal was won by the German Helga Haase; the 1,000-meters, won by Klara Guseva (URS); and the 1,500- and 3,000-meters, both of which were won by Lidia Skoblikova of the Soviet Union.

The figure skating turned out to be an all-American "family affair." The men's event was won by David Jenkins, the brother of Hayes Alan Jenkins, the Olympic champion of 1956. The women's title was won by David Jenkins' future sister-in-law, Carol Heiss.

The Germans Georg Thoma and Helmut Recknagel made headlines when they became the first non-Scandinavians to win the Nordic combined competition (Thoma) and the ski jump (Recknagel).

Ski and Shoot
The first Olympic biathlon competition was held over a 20-kilometer course, and was won by Sweden's Klas Lestander.

Teenage Triumph
The 19-year-old Heidi Biebl (GER) became the Olympic women's downhill champion.

Flying Flag-Bearer
Helmut Recknagel (GER), the pan-German team's standard-bearer at the opening ceremony, secured the gold medal in the ski jump.

1 **Lighting the Olympic flame:** During the opening ceremony, the Olympic flame is lit by the 1952 500-meter speed skating champion, the American Kenneth Henry.

2 **Hockey gold for the hosts:** In the semi-final of the ice hockey tournament, the eventual champions, USA (dark shirts) caused an upset by defeating the USSR 3-2. The Soviet team were the favored side. They had taken the gold at Cortina, and had not been beaten in international competition since 1956. The US. team had qualified for the semi-finals by beating Czechoslovakia 7-5 and Australia 12-1 during their group matches. In the second qualifying group, Canada, six-times Olympic champions (1920 to 1932 and 1948 to 1952), had initially lived up to expectations by beating Sweden 5-2 and Japan 19-1. However, in the end they had to settle for second place, with the Soviet side taking the bronze medal.

3 **Tight finish:** With only 0.8 seconds in it, Veikko Hakulinen (right), anchorman of the Finnish 4 x 10-kilometer relay team, secured his country the Olympic gold medal. Haakon Brusveen (left) is on the Finn's shoulder to earn Norway the silver medal. The bronze was picked up by the Soviet team.

4 **Skiing "marathon":** In the 50-kilometer cross-country skiing race, Kalevi Hämäläinen (FIN) beat his fellow countryman Veikko Hakulinen and the Swede Rolf Rämgard. Previously, the 30-kilometer event had been won by Sixten Jernberg (SWE), ahead of Rämgard and Nikolai Anikin (URS). The 15-kilometer event was won by Haakon Brusveen (NOR) from Jernberg and Hakulinen.

5 **Two titles:** The speed skater Yevgeni Grischin (URS) made headlines by becoming a double Olympic champion. Over 500-meters, he defeated the Americans William Disney and Rafael Gratsch, while in the 1,500-meters, he shared the title with Norwegian Roald Aas, the bronze medal going to Boris Stenin from the USSR. The Soviets took another speed skating gold with Viktor Kositschkin winning the 5,000-meters ahead of the Norwegian Knut Johannesen and Holland's Jan Pesman. In the 10,000-meters Johannesen took his revenge on Kositschkin, beating him into second place, with Kjell Bäckman of Sweden coming in third.

6 **Women make their debut:** Helga Haase (GER) became the first woman to win an Olympic speed skating event. In the 500-meters, she clocked 45.9 seconds, 0.1 seconds better than Natalia Dontschenko (URS). America's Jeanne Ashworth was third. In the 1,000-meters, Haase picked up a silver medal, being beaten to the gold by Klara Guseva (URS). The bronze medal in this event went to Tamara Rylova (also URS). In the two remaining women's speed skating competitions, Lidia Skoblikova of the USSR displayed the talent that was to make her a major force in the discipline for many years to come. Skoblikova had just missed out on a medal in the 1,000-meters, but she won the 1,500-meters, pushing the Poles Elvira Seroczynska and Helena Pilejczyk into second and third spots. Over 3,000 meters, Skoblikova picked up another gold medal ahead of her teammate Valentina Stenina and Eevi Huttunen of Finland.

7 **Gold and bronze medals for France:** Jean Vuarnet won the downhill skiing by 0.5 seconds ahead of Hans-Peter Lanig (GER). Vuarnet's fellow Frenchman Guy Perillat took the bronze.

8 **Medal ceremony:** The Canadians Barbara Wagner and Robert Paul (middle) clutch their figure skating gold medals, which they secured ahead of Marika Kilius and Hans-Jürgen Bäumler (GER, left) and Nancy and Ronald Ludington (USA, right).

9 **Gold medal for Switzerland:** In the giant slalom, Swiss Alpine skier Roger Staub commandingly beat his Austrian rivals, Josef Stiegler and Ernst Hinterseer. However, Hinterseer collected a gold medal in the slalom event, ahead of his compatriot Matthias Leitner and Charles Bozon of France.

10 **Concentrating on victory:** The women's downhill competition is won by Germany's Heidi Biebl. The American Penny Pitou, a second adrift of the Olympic champion, picked up the silver medal, while Traudl Hecher of Austria took third place.

11 **Favorite wins:** In the figure skating, Carol Heiss (USA) won, with Sjoukje Dijkstra (HOL) and Barbara Roles (USA) coming second and third. In this Olympic year, Heiss also won the world title for the fifth consecutive time.

Rome

Pierre de Coubertin had wanted to stage the 1908 Olympics in Rome, but the eruption of Vesuvius in southern Italy had intervened. In 1960, 52 years later, the Games finally arrived in the Italian capital.

A COMBINATION OF NEW SPORTS facilities and historic buildings provided the backdrop to the XVII Olympics in Rome. The organizers successfully mixed traditional values with the demands of modern sport. For example, the gymnastics events were held in the Baths of Caracalla, while the wrestlers fought in the Basilica of Maxentius. The start and finish of the marathon were, untypically, sited outside the Olympic Stadium. The runners started on their 26-mile journey on the Capitoline Hill and finished at the Arch of Constantine. The indoor arena, the *Palazzetto dello Sport*, designed by Pier Luigi Nervi, fitted perfectly into its surroundings and was considered an outstanding example of modern architecture. Nevertheless, Nervi was accused of having taken his inspiration for the building from the Fascists' *Foro Italico*.

The opening ceremony, featuring the now-traditional parade by the participating nations, took place in front of more than 100,000 spectators in the Olympic Stadium. All but the Soviet athletes had received the blessing by Pope John XXIII in St. Peter's Square.

The Rome Games were broadcast by television to all European countries and were watched by millions. Sadly, the competitions themselves were overshadowed by the rivalry between the USA and the USSR. In the final medal table, the Soviet Union, with a total of 43 gold medals, finished ahead of the USA who had 34.

The American sprinter Wilma Rudolph captured the public's imagination. As a child, the 20-year-old had suffered from polio. In Rome, she was a triple gold medalist, winning the 100-meters, 200-meters, and running in the winning 4 x 100-meter relay team.

In the men's 100-meters, the German Armin Hary's victory broke the monopoly the USA had always had in the event, ever since the Games in Los Angeles in 1932.

Black Gazelle
America's Wilma Rudolph won two individual sprint gold medals and a relay gold in Rome.

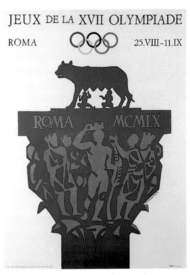

JEUX DE LA XVII OLYMPIADE

ROMA   25.VIII-11.IX

ROMA MCMLX

In the City of Romulus and Remus
The official Olympic poster featured the Roman legend of the twins Romulus and Remus, who were suckled by a she-wolf.

Another sensation in Rome was the Ethiopian runner Abebe Bikila, who won the marathon barefoot. His performance suggested that the sports equipment industry might be wrong in its claims that success depended completely on continual improvements in equipment.

In addition to the medals won, there were remarkable personal milestones reached at the Rome Games. At the age of 50, the Hungarian saber maestro Aladár Gerevich rounded off his extraordinary career by winning his seventh gold medal to add to a silver and two bronzes. Gerevich had competed in no less than six Games (1932 to 1960). Another veteran fencer also called it a day. With a record tally for fencing of 13 medals (six golds, five silvers, and two bronzes), including a last victory in the team épée event, the Italian Edoardo Mangiarotti retired after having taken part in five Olympic Games (1936 to 1960).

Meanwhile, in gymnastics, Larissa Latynina was still in the middle of a career that would eventually yield 18 medals. In Rome, she added three golds (including the team combined), two silvers, and a bronze to her collection.

Breaking the Run
The German sprinter Armin Hary won the men's 100-meters, breaking America's domination. He won a second gold medal as a member of the victorious German 4 x 100-meter relay team.

Veteran Bows Out
The Hungarian fencer Aladár Gerevich crowned a career spanning six Games with victory in the team saber.

Number One
With three gold medals, two silvers, and one bronze, Soviet gymnast Larissa Latynina was the most successful female competitor of the Games.

First Ethiopian
In winning the marathon, Abebe Bikila became the first Ethiopian athlete to win a gold medal.

1 Let the Games begin: The "youth of the world" gather once more under the Olympic flag. At the opening ceremony, athletes from 83 nations paraded, and doves of peace were released. Adolfo Consolini, the 1948 discus champion, took the oath.

2 Thompson marches on: Don Thompson of Britain strides out on his way to triumph in the 50-kilometer walk. Thompson set a new Olympic record for the event of 4:25:30. Second was John Ljunggren of Sweden with Italy's Abdon Pamich third.

3 Favorite first: A leap of 26' 7½" (8.12 meters) was enough to secure Ralph Boston, the world record holder, the Olympic long jump title in Rome. Boston beat his fellow American Irvin Robertson (26'7¼"/8.11 meters) and the Soviet athlete Igor Ter-Ovanesian (26'4½"/8.04 meters).

4 All three for the USA: Al Oerter successfully defends his discus title, with a winning throw of 194' 1½" (59.18 meters). Silver and bronze were picked up by Richard Babka and Richard Cochran (both also USA).

5 Sensational final: The world 100-meter record holder, Armin Hary (GER, second from right), defeats the American David Sime (right) and Britain's Peter Radford (second from left). Hary was the first male German athlete to win an Olympic gold medal in a running event.

6 Three gold medals for track-and-field star: American women athletes in high spirits. Wilma Rudolph (standing, right) had plenty to be cheerful about. In the 100-meter final, she beat Britain's Dorothy Hyman and the Italian Giuseppina Leone. Over 200 meters, she again showed her superiority, this time beating Jutta Heine (GER), and Dorothy Hyman. Rudolph added a third gold medal in the US 4 x 100-meter relay team that won ahead of Germany and Poland.

7 Romanian win: Iolanda Balas (ROM) won the women's high jump, going clear at 6' 0¾" (1.85 meters). Silver was shared by Jaroslawa Jozwiakowska of Poland and Britain's Dorothy Shirley.

8 Results in the diving: In the diving competitions, Ingrid Krämer of Germany reigned supreme. In the springboard event, she won the gold, ahead of Paula Myers-Pope from the USA and Britain's Elizabeth Ferris. In the highboard event, Krämer again showed her class to defeat Myers-Pope and the Soviet diver Ninelia Krutova.

9 US victories in the pool: The American swimmer Lynn Burke won the 100-meter backstroke. Second and third places went to Britain's Natalie Steward and Satoko Tanaka of Japan respectively. Burke was also a member of America's 4 x 100-meter medley team that won from Australia and Germany.

10 Swim win for Britain: Britain's Anita Lonsbrough (middle) wears the gold medal for the 200-meter breaststroke, having set a world record time of 2:49.5 in the final. Wiltrud Urselmann (GER, right) and Barbara Göbel (GER, left) were second and third.

11 Narrow decision: Otis Davis of the United States became the Olympic champion over 400 meters, clocking a world record of 44.9 seconds. However, it needed a photograph to separate him from Carl Kaufmann of Germany, who had to settle for the silver medal, although he recorded the same time. The bronze medal was taken by the South African Malcolm Spence (45.5 seconds).

12 Joy and anguish for the US relay teams: The American 4 x 100-meter relay team was disqualified as a result of an illegal changeover involving Ray Norton (left) and Frank Budd, which took place outside the zone. The gold medal was won by the German team (Bernd Cullmann, Armin Hary, Martin Lauer, and Walter Mahlendorf), ahead of the USSR and Great Britain. The Americans were more successful in the 4 x 400-meter, winning the gold medal in 3:02.2, ahead of Germany and the Antilles and cutting 1.7 seconds off the world record held by Jamaica.

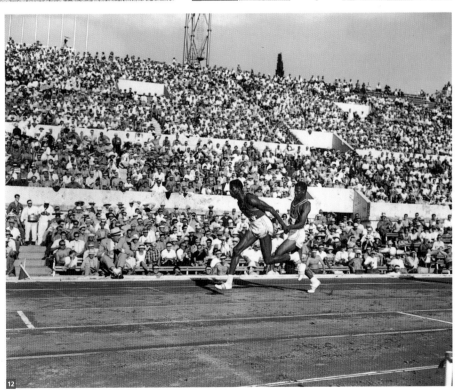

1 **Double win for Italy:** Brothers Raimondo (right) and Piero D'Inzeo (left) won gold and silver respectively in the show jumping. Britain's David Broome took the bronze. In the team event, the Italians finished third, behind the Germans and the USA. The D'Inzeos both appeared at eight Games, winning six medals each.

2 **Success of the Games:** By winning four gold medals, two silver medals, and one bronze medal, the Soviet gymnast Boris Shakhlin became the Games' most successful competitor. He won the combined exercises from Takashi Ono (JPN) and Yuri Titov (URS), and picked up his second gold in the parallel bars, ahead of Giovanni Carminucci (ITA) and Ono once again. In the horse vault, he shared the title with Ono, and he also split the pommel horse title, this time with Eugen Ekman of Finland. He won a silver medal as a member of the Soviet team that finished second behind Japan, a second silver in the rings behind teammate Albert Azaryan, and a bronze in the horizontal bar. Shakhlin's career tally was 13 medals, including seven golds. Ten medals were individual; the rest for team events.

3 **USA dominates basketball:** The picture shows the highly talented US basketball team beating Italy 112–81 on their way to winning the gold medal. The Americans, possibly the best ever amateur Olympic team, met the USSR in the final, winning 81–57. Brazil collected the bronze medal.

4 **Successful heavyweight:** Wilfried Dietrich of Germany (right), shown here in his fight against the Swede Stan Svenson, won the heavyweight (unlimited weight) freestyle wrestling title, ahead of Turkey's Hamit Kaplan and Savkus Dzarasov of the Soviet Union. Dietrich also won a silver medal at heavyweight (unlimited weight) in the Greco-Roman style, as he had at Melbourne four years earlier. In Rome, he was defeated by Ivan Bogdan of the Soviet Union, while the bronze was won by the Czechoslovak Bohumil Kubát.

5 **Gold medal for US boat:** Arthur Ayrault, Ted Nash, John

Sayre, and Richard Wailes are tired but elated when they receive their gold medals for the coxless fours. Italy and the USSR were second and third. The USA also picked up a bronze in the coxed pairs through Richard Draeger, Conn Findlay, and H. Kent Mitchell (cox). The event was won by Germany with the Soviet Union second.

6 **Celebration for shooting star:** Peter Kohnke (GER) is delighted at winning gold in the small-bore rifle (prone position). He is held aloft by Georg von Opel, president of the German shooting association. James Hill (USA) and Forcella Pelliccioni (VEN) were second and third.

7 **"The Greatest" wins:** An Olympic title win in Rome in the light-heavyweight category proved a stepping stone to greater things for America's 18-year-old Cassius Clay (right).

8 **Rowing success:** The Germans won the gold in the coxed eights, ahead of Canada and Czechoslovakia.

Innsbruck

With the IX Winter Games due to start, the Innsbruck area found itself with a shortage of snow. However, the Austrian army came to the rescue, shipping in thousands of tons of snow from elsewhere.

ALTHOUGH THE ORGANIZERS OF the IX Winter Olympic Games had made all the preparations they could for the competitions, the weather turned out to be beyond their sphere of influence. Innsbruck's mildest February for 58 years meant that Austrian troops had to transport more than 25,000 tons of snow from higher snow fields to the River Inn valley so the slopes would be ready for the Alpine skiing competitions. The cross-country skiers, meanwhile, competing in the town of Seefeld, farther up the Inn valley, found conditions to be ideal.

For the first time at a Winter Olympics, the number of competitors exceeded the 1,000 mark, with around 900 male and 200 female athletes participating at Innsbruck. The schedule comprised a record 34 events, and luge tobogganing made its Olympic debut. In lugeing, competitors descend an ice run lying face upwards on the toboggan. (In 1928 and 1948, there had been skeleton sledding competitions, in which the athletes lay face down.) At Innsbruck there were three luge events – the singles and two-man for male competitors and the singles for women.

The bobsled competitions returned after their enforced break in Squaw Valley (1960) when the organizers had failed to build a bobsled run. Meanwhile in the ski jump competition new rules were implemented, replacing those that had been in effect since 1930. Two separate events were now held: one on the small hill and one on the big hill. The athletes were granted three attempts, of which the shortest jump was ruled out by the judges. The winner on the small hill at Innsbruck was Veikko Kankkonen of Finland, while the large hill victor was Toralf Engan of Norway. However, the complicated judging procedure made the ski jump competitions

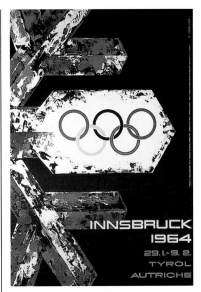

Crystal Promise
Only the official Olympic poster of the Winter Games in Innsbruck was dominated by snow crystals; the Games themselves are were disrupted by a serious lack of snow.

rather confusing, and as a result, the rules were simplified for the 1968 Games in Grenoble.

The figure skating event held a surprise. After losing nine times in the European and world championships at the hands of their old rivals Marika Kilius and Hans-Jürgen Bäumler, the Soviet couple Ludmilla Belousova and Oleg Protopopov took the Olympic title. Their adversaries finished second, but were disqualified for having taken part in a professional ice show before the Games, though they were later reinstated.

Soviet speed skater Lidia Skoblikova was the most successful competitor of the Winter Games, winning all four speed skating competitions. The Swede Sixten Jernberg crowned his career by taking the 50-kilometer cross-country skiing gold. At three Winter Games, Jernberg collected four gold, three silver, and two bronze medals, giving him a long-standing record in the Nordic disciplines.

1 **Opening ceremony:** Josef Rieder lights the Olympic flame in the Bergisel Stadium. For the first time the Winter torch had been lit in Olympia, Greece, and was relayed across Europe to Innsbruck.

2 **Jubilant sisters:** In the slalom event, the French skier Marielle Goitschel (pictured) was defeated by her older sister, Christine. Positions were reversed in the giant slalom, where Marielle took gold.

3 **Female figure skaters:** World champion Sjoukje Dijkstra (HOL) took the gold medal, ahead of Regine Heitzer (AUT) and Petra Burka (CAN).

4 **Successful season:** Manfred Schnelldorfer (GER) won the figure skating event, ahead of Alain Calmat (FRA) and Scott Allen (USA). A few weeks later, he also claimed the world championship title.

5 **Norwegian treble:** Knut Johannesen (NOR) won the 5,000-meter speed skating event, ahead of his teammates Per Ivar Moe and Fred Anton Maier. Over 10,000 meters, Johannesen was defeated by the Swede Jonny Nilsson and by Maier, but still collected his fifth medal.

6 **Speed skating star:** Over 500 meters, Lidia Skoblikova (URS) beat her compatriots Irina Yegorova and Tatyana Sidorova. She was again victorious in the 1,000-meter event, defeating Yegorova and the Finn Kaija Mustonen. Her third gold medal was won over the 1,500-meter distance, ahead of Mustonen and Berta Kolokoltseva (URS). She completed her amazing gold medal collection by winning over 3,000 meters.

7 **Two medals:** The ski jump event from the small hill was won by Veikko Kankonnen (FIN), ahead of the Norwegians Toralf Engan and Torgeir Brandtzæg. On the big hill, he added another silver medal when beaten by Engan.

8 **Ice hockey jubilation:** The Soviet team celebrate their second Olympic title since 1956. The silver was taken by Sweden, ahead of Czechoslovakia.

9 **French family wins:** In the giant slalom, Marielle (pictured, gold medal) and Christine Goitschel (silver) swapped their first and second places from the earlier slalom event. Christine shared the silver medal with Jean Saubert (USA).

10 **Gold medal for Austria:** In the slalom, Pepi Stiegler defeated the Americans William Kidd and James Heuga. In the giant slalom, he took bronze, behind French Olympic champion François Bonlieu and Karl Schranz of Austria.

11 **Female luge champion:** Ortrun Enderlein of Germany won the first women's single-seater luge event. She defeated her German teammate Ilse Geisler and Helene Thurrier of Austria.

12 **British bobsled win:** Tony Nash (pilot) and Robin Dixon in Great Britain I hurtle to victory in the two-man bob to become Britain's first gold medalists at a Winter Olympics for 12 years. In second place were Italy II, with Italy I taking bronze.

13 **Three skiing golds:** Klaudia Boyarskikh (URS) won golds in the 5-kilometer Nordic skiing event ahead of Mirja Lehtonen (FIN) and Alevtina Koltschina (URS), the 10-kilometer competition, ahead of her teammates Yevdokia Mekshilo and Maria Gusakova, and with the Soviet 3 x 5-kilometer relay team.

14 **Finn's Nordic win:** Eero Mäntyranta won the 15- and 30-kilometer distances. He added another silver medal with the 4 x 10-kilometer relay team.

15 **"King" of Nordic skiing:** Sixten Jernberg (SWE) won golds in the 50-kilometer event and with the relay team. He had to settle for bronze over 15 kilometers, however, behind Eero Mäntyranta (FIN) and Harald Grönningen (NOR).

Tokyo

For the first time, the Olympic Games went to Asia. Tokyo's appointment as host city of the XVIII Olympiad confirmed Japan's readmission to the international community after World War II.

TOKYO HAD BEEN PENCILED IN to host the 1940 Olympic Games, but the outbreak of the Sino-Japanese war in 1937 saw its bid fall through. Twenty-six years later, the Japanese organizing committee set new standards in preparing for the Games. The hosts invested heavily in the most modern sports facilities, as well as in improving the infrastructure of a city containing ten million inhabitants. The extraordinary architectural design of the swimming stadium led Avery Brundage to call it a "cathedral of sports." Other outstanding new buildings included the judo hall, which was modeled on the style of traditional Japanese temples.

The opening ceremony offered a convincing combination of established and contemporary elements. The first record was broken right away when, watched by the Imperial Japanese family, teams from 93 nations (ten more than in Rome in 1960) paraded into the Meiji Stadium. It was to be the last time until 1992 that a combined German team would participate at an Olympic Games. With 377 competitors, the united German squad represented the largest team at the Tokyo Games.

Two events were newly introduced as Olympic disciplines: volleyball (wins for the Soviet men's team and for the Japanese women's team), and the traditional Japanese discipline of judo, where the hosts intended to demonstrate their superiority. However, they had to concede defeat in the most prestigious of the judo events (the open category) to the Dutchman Antonius Geesink.

In the swimming pool, the American Don Schollander won four gold medals, and was celebrated as Tokyo's most successful participant. The Soviet gymnast Larissa Latynina crowned her final appearance before retiring with two

Land of the Rising Sun
The symbol of Japan's national flag dominated the poster of the Olympic Games in Tokyo.

gold, two silver, and two bronze medals. At three Olympic Games (1956 to 1964), she was on the podium no less than 18 times. In Tokyo, the Czechoslovakian Vera Cáslavská (three gold medals) became Latynina's successor.

The crowds reacted with great enthusiasm as many new world records were set. The Ethiopian distance runner Abebe Bikila, for example, received a hero's welcome when he successfully defended, in world record time, the Olympic marathon title he had won in Rome four years before. However, the high standards set by athletes at the Tokyo Games led some critics to warn about exaggerated expectations for the future development of all the Olympic disciplines.

The Soviet rower Vyacheslav Ivanov won his third consecutive Olympic gold in the single sculls event; a similar feat was achieved by the Australian swimmer Dawn Fraser in the 100-meter freestyle, in which she set a new Olympic record.

Tired Victor
German athlete Willi Holdorf has to be supported by fellow athletes after the final decathlon event, the 1,500 meters. He was rewarded with the gold medal, ahead of Rein Aun (URS) and Hans-Joachim Walde (GER).

King Don
The American swimmer Don Schollander picked up gold medals in two individual and two relay events, the first swimmer to achieve this feat.

Double Victor
Soviet track-and-field athlete Tamara Press successfully defended her Olympic shot put title, and added the discus gold for good measure.

Lynn's Leap
Britain's Lynn Davies won the long jump gold, ahead of reigning champion Ralph Boston. His winning leap was 26' 5½" (8.07 meters), just one-and-a-half inches (4 cm) longer than Boston's best.

Dutch Upset
The Dutch judo star Antonius Geesink was lauded after his Olympic title win in the open category, which was expected to be won by one of the Japanese competitors.

1 **Symbol of peace:** Yoshinoi Sakai lights the Olympic flame. The student was born near Hiroshima on August 6, 1945, the day when the Japanese city was razed by an American atomic bomb.

2 **Freestyle specialist:** Over the 100-meter distance, Don Schollander of the United States beat Britain's Bobby McGregor and Hans-Joachim Klein from Germany. In the 400-meter event, he showed his superiority over Frank Wiegand (GER) and Allan Wood (AUS). He added two more gold medals as a member of the 4 x 100-meter and 4 x 200-meter relay teams.

3 **Solemn ceremony:** During the opening ceremony, hundreds of doves of peace are released in the National Stadium.

4 **Australian pool gold:** In the 100-meter freestyle event, Dawn Fraser (middle) beat Sharon Stouder (USA, left) and Kathleen Ellis (USA, right). As part of the 4 x 100-meter freestyle relay, Fraser won a silver medal.

5 **Clear victory:** Irina Press (URS, seen here during the 80-meter hurdles event) took the pentathlon with a new world record score of 5,246 points, ahead of Mary Rand (GBR, 5,035 points) and Galina Bystrova (URS, 4,956 points)

6 **Winner's joy:** Following her victory in the women's 800-meter event, Britain's Ann Packer is congratulated by her boyfriend, Robbie Brightwell, himself a silver medalist with Britain's 4 x 400-meter relay team.

7 **Fourth gold medal:** A triple gold medalist in the Melbourne Games back in 1956, Australia's Betty Cuthbert defeated Britain's Ann Packer and fellow Australian Judith Amoore in the first women's 400-meter event.

8 **Pole vault "marathon":** After seven hours of competition, the pole vault tournament ended with a victory for Fred Hansen (USA). Silver and bronze medals went to Germans Wolfgang Reinhardt and Klaus Lehnertz.

9 **Successful title defense:** Peter Snell (NZL, right) successfully defended his Olympic 800-meter title, ahead of Bill Crothers (CAN, second from left) and the Kenyan Wilson Kiprugut (third from left).

10 **Versatile athlete:** Britain's Mary Rand took the long jump with a new world record performance of 22' 2¼" (6.76 meters). She took the silver medal in the pentathlon, and was a bronze medalist with the British 4 x 100-meter relay team, behind Poland and the United States.

1 **The way to the top:** Joe Frazier (USA) shows off his gold medal after winning the heavyweight boxing competition at Tokyo. He defeated West Germany's Hans Huber in the final. Frazier went on to fight as a professional in an era that boasted Muhammad Ali (who as Cassius Clay won the 1960 light-heavyweight gold) and George Foreman, who was Olympic heavyweight boxing champion at Mexico City in 1968. Nevertheless "Smokin' Joe" Frazier stood out as a great boxer even in this company and had a stint as undisputed world heavyweight champion from 1970, when he beat Jimmy Ellis, to 1973, when he was defeated by George Foreman. Frazier fought three epic duels with Muhammad Ali, including the "Thriller in Manila" in September 1975, which Ali won to retain his title. Several Olympic champions have gone on to win world titles, including Floyd Patterson (USA, middleweight gold, 1952), Sugar Ray Leonard (USA, light-welterweight gold, 1976), Michael Spinks (USA, middleweight gold, 1976), Leon Spinks (USA, light-heavyweight gold, 1976), and Lennox Lewis (CAN, super-heavyweight gold, 1988).

2 **Repeating his Olympic title win:** Twelve years after his victory in Helsinki, the Frenchman Pierre Jonquères d'Oriola took the show jumping title again. On this occasion, it was the turn of Hermann Schridde (GER) and Britain's Peter Robeson to be defeated by the Frenchman. The team event was won by the Germans ahead of France and Italy.

3 **Successful German dressage:** Harry Boldt, Reiner Klimke, and Josef Neckermann (GER, middle) won the dressage gold medal, ahead of Switzerland (left) and the Soviet Union (right). The individual event was won by the Swiss rider Henri Chammartin, ahead of Boldt and Sergei Filatov of the Soviet Union. The Italian Mauro Checcoli won the three-day event, with Carlos Alberto Moratorio (ARG) taking silver and Fritz Ligges (GER) taking the bronze. The Italians had additional success in the team event, where they took the gold medal, ahead of the US and German teams.

4 **Olympic judo debut:** The first Olympic judo competition saw world champion Antonius Geesink (HOL, left) take the open category by beating his world championship final opponent, Akio Kaminaga of Japan. The bronze medal was jointly secured by the Australian Theodore Boronovskis and German Klaus Glahn.

5 **Cáslavská takes over:**
With three gold medals and one silver, the Czechoslovakian Vera Cáslavská was seen as the successor to gymnastics star Larissa Latynina (URS). Cáslavská won the combined exercises, ahead of Latynina and Polina Astakhova (URS). In the horse vault, she took the gold, ahead of Latynina and Birgit Rodochla (GER), who shared silver with identical points. Cáslavská secured her third gold medal in the balance beam event, defeating Soviet teammates Tamara Manina and Latynina. A silver medal was added in the team competition, behind the Soviets and ahead of the Japanese. After her four golds in 1968, she controversially spoke out against the events surrounding the quelling of the Prague uprising. In 1990, she became chairwoman of the Czech NOC and in 1995 became an IOC member.

6 **Last Olympic Games:** At her third Olympic Games, Larissa Latynina (URS, middle) won her third successive gold medal in the floor event, shrugging off opposition from the silver and bronze medalists Polina Astakhova (URS) and Anikó Ducza (HUN). In addition to her second gold medal in the team competition, Latynina also added two silvers in the combined exercises individual and in the horse vault, as well as two bronze medals in the balance beam and asymmetrical bars events. With a tally of 18 Olympic medals (nine golds), Latynina is the most successful Olympic athlete ever.

7 **Triumph for the hosts:**
In front of his home crowd, the Japanese Yukio Endo was the most successful male gymnast in Tokyo. In the individual combined exercises, he won, ahead of the joint silver medalists Shuji Tsurumi (JPN), Boris Shakhlin (URS), and Viktor Lisitsky (URS). In the parallel bars event, Endo was again victorious, this time beating his compatriot Tsurumi and Franco Menichelli of Italy. Endo secured his third gold medal with the Japanese team who won ahead of the USSR and Germany in the team event. In the floor event, Endo shared the silver medal with Lisitsky, behind Menichelli.

Grenoble

Hosting the X Winter Olympics provided Grenoble with an economic boost. However, the long distances between the different venues created problems for athletes and spectators alike.

Killy's Games
The Grenoble Olympics were dominated by the three gold medals won by the legendary French Alpine skier Jean-Claude Killy.

BEFORE THE INDUSTRIAL CITY OF Grenoble was able to become a suitable venue for the X Winter Games, large amounts of money needed to be invested in the construction of new sports facilities and an improved infrastructure. Even though this money was spent, Grenoble itself did not have sufficient sports facilities, so competitions took place in the whole of the surrounding region, and athletes were accommodated in seven Olympic Villages. Although some critics complained this meant the Games could not be considered as a true meeting of the "youth of the world," and that many spectators had to travel a long way for particular competitions, the Games were a triumph for the French.

The opening ceremony, conducted by the French president Charles de Gaulle, was held in a stadium whose improvised stands stood on steel girders. This was the first time at a Winter Games that two separate German teams paraded into the stadium. They were united only by their black, red, and yellow flag bearing the five Olympic rings, and a joint anthem (Beethoven's "Song of Joy"). During the competition, relationships between the two teams were decidedly frosty.

For the first time, the IOC ordered drug tests to be carried out after each competition. In addition, gender testing was introduced.

Twelve years after the triple win in all three Alpine skiing competitions by the Austrian Toni Sailer, the Frenchman Jean-Claude Killy equaled this achievement. These Games were often referred to as the "Killympics," and France had a new national hero. However, the 24-year-old earned his slalom win only through the disqualification, for missing gates, of the Austrian Karl Schranz and the Norwegian Haakon Mjoen who had

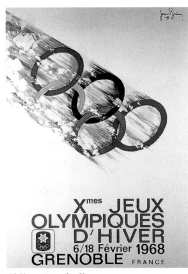

Skiing Symbolism
The five Olympic rings featured on the official poster of the X Winter Games in Grenoble were shown as though in a fast downhill skiing competition.

been ahead of him. After the Games, Killy retired and made a profitable living out of his successful sporting career. His contribution to the organization of the 1992 Winter Games in Albertville earned him the highest Olympic distinction, and in 1995, he became a member of the International Olympic Committee.

In the luge competition, the female East German competitors, reigning champion Ortrun Enderlein, Angela Knösel, and Anna-Maria Müller, were disqualified for warming up the runners on their sleds before the race to achieve faster times on the ice.

The speed skating was once more dominated by the Dutch: Cornelis Verkerk won a gold medal over 1,500 meters and a silver medal over 5,000 meters; Carolina Geijssen took gold over 1,000 meters and a silver medal over 1,500 meters; and Johanna Schut secured her win in the 3,000-meter event. In the bobsled, Italy's Eugenio Monti won two gold medals at the age of 40.

1 Italian gold: Eugenio Monti and Luciano de Paolis secured their gold medal in the two-man bob, ahead of West Germany I and Romania I. Having clocked an identical overall time to that of the West Germans after the four runs, the fastest time set by the Italians in the last run secured their win. Five days later, Monti and de Paolis claimed their second title, this time together with Mario Armano and Roberto Zandonella in the four-man bob, ahead of Austria I and Switzerland I. After his silver medal win in the two-man in Cortina d'Ampezzo in 1956 and his two bronze medals in Innsbruck in 1964, these two Olympic titles constituted the crowning achievement of 40-year-old Monti's Olympic bobsled career.

2 Favorite takes gold: The world record holder Erhard Keller (FRG) won the 500-meter speed skating sprint in 40.3 seconds. Magne Thomassen of Norway and Richard McDermott (USA) shared the silver, finishing 0.2 seconds behind Keller.

3 Two medals for Canada: In the giant slalom, Nancy Greene of Canada defeated the French skier Annie Famose and the Swiss Fernande Bochatay. The defending champion, Marielle Goitschel of France, could manage only seventh place. Two days earlier, Greene had won the slalom silver

behind Goitschel and ahead of Famose. In the downhill, Famose missed out on a medal when she finished fifth, behind Olga Pall of Austria, Isabelle Mir (FRA), Christl Haas, and Brigitte Seiwald (both AUT).

4 Successful title defense: Despite this 4-5 defeat at the hands of the eventual silver medalists, Czechoslovakia, the Soviet ice hockey team went on to successfully defend their Olympic title. The Czech team missed out on a possible gold medal win when they were held to a 2-2 draw by Sweden and then beaten 2-3 by the bronze medal winners, Canada. The Soviet team, for their part completely outclassed the Canadians, handing out a 5-0 thrashing.

5 Flying to gold: The gold medal winner in the ski jump from the small hill was Jiri Raska (TCH). Silver and bronze medals were taken by the Austrians Reinhold Bachler and Baldur Preiml respectively. Raska added a silver medal in the big hill event.

6 Surprise winner: Experts were taken by surprise and expectations totally upset when Vladimir Belusov (pictured) won the ski jump from the big hill in front of 58,000 spectators. He defeated the Czech Jiri Raska and Lars Grini of Norway. This title win in Grenoble was to remain the

1

2

3

4

5

6

7

8

9

Soviet ski jumper's sole international success.

7 Swiss athlete defeated: The Nordic combined athlete Alois Kälin of Switzerland had to settle for a silver medal, behind his West German rival Franz Keller. His clear win in the 15-kilometer event proved to be too little too late to catch up with the German, who had established a commanding lead after the ski jump event. In the end, Keller had a 1.05 point lead over his rival.

8 Scandinavians broken: The Italian Francesco Nones won the 30-kilometer cross-country skiing title ahead of Odd Martinsen of Norway and the Finn Eero Mäntyranta. Nones was the first athlete not from Scandinavia or the USSR to win a gold medal in a cross-country skiing event.

9 German Nordic win: Franz Keller (FRG) became Olympic champion in the Nordic combined competition. With a narrow lead, he left second and third places to Alois Kälin of Switzerland and Andreas Kunz of East Germany respectively.

10 Killy cleans up: Jean-Claude Killy (middle) was the first Alpine skier to repeat the Austrian Toni Sailer's 1956 feat of winning all three Alpine skiing events. The Frenchman took the downhill title, ahead of his compatriot Guy Périllat and the Swiss skier Jean-Daniel Dätwyler. He had failed to

finish in the same event at Innsbruck four years earlier. In a slalom event shrouded by dense fog, he defeated the two Austrians Herbert Huber and Alfred Matt. Killy was happy to secure a third gold in the giant slalom competition, which he won ahead of Willy Favre of Switzerland (left) and Heinrich Messner of Austria (right).

11 Twilight gold medals: Following their 1964 title win, the gold medalists in the pairs figure skating event were once again the Soviet married couple, Ludmilla Belousova and Oleg Protopopov. Their teammates Tatyana Shuk and Alexander Gorelik took the silver medal, ahead of the West German couple Margot Glockshuber and Wolfgang Danne. During 1968, the Soviet Olympic champions also took their fourth European and world championship titles in a row. Belousova and Protopopov defected to Switzerland and turned professional. The pair's comeback attempt in 1971 was unsuccessful.

12 Austrian success: Following his Olympic figure skating title, Wolfgang Schwarz was another skater who moved on to pursue a professional career in a figure skating show. The silver medal was taken by the American Timothy Wood, ahead of Patrick Péra of France. The women's event was won by the American Peggy Fleming, ahead of the East German skater Gaby Seyfert and Hana Maskova of Czechoslovakia.

10

11

12

Mexico City

Mexico City's high altitude made life difficult for distance runners, but in the "explosive" events, the XIX Olympiad was a festival of record breaking, with 34 world and 38 Olympic records set.

THE INCREASING INFLUENCE OF politics on society, which had been evident in many countries during the late 1960s, played its part in the run-up to the 1968 Summer Olympic Games. Before the opening of the Games, complaints by ordinary Mexicans that the exorbitant amounts of money being invested in facilities could not be justified when placed alongside Mexico's own social problems culminated in violent riots. Police and army units were forced to quell protests led by Mexican students.

Arguments also resulted from the question of South Africa's participation at these Games; the majority of black African countries threatened a boycott if South Africa was allowed to compete. The IOC eventually gave in to the pressure and withdrew its invitation to South Africa's athletes. As a result of resolutions made by the IOC, two separate German teams paraded into the stadium under one flag for the first time at a Summer Olympics. And the Mexican hurdler Norma Enriqueta Basilio de Sotela became the first woman to light the Olympic flame.

Controversy would also continue once the competitions had begun. The medal ceremony for the winners of the men's 200-meters, for example, turned into a political demonstration. During the playing of the American national anthem, the US sprinters Tommie Smith and John Carlos raised their black-gloved fists, a symbol of the radical black power movement, which had been fighting for the equal rights of black citizens in the United States. The team's management banned the two athletes from the national team and sent them home.

The avalanche of first-class performances during the Games was mainly a result of Mexico City's high altitude (almost 7,350 feet/2,240 meters). The altitude issue had dominated much of the pre-Games discussion, the

Innovative Design
The especially commissioned poster for the XIX Summer Games in Mexico City.

consensus being that athletes from lowland countries would be at a disadvantage in Mexico City. However, several weeks of high altitude training for many of these athletes led to an increased oxygen supply to the muscles and enhanced performances.

In the sprint events, American athletes were dominant. Olympic champion Jim Hines set a new world record of 9.9 seconds for the 100-meters. This was later officially recognized as an inaugural electronic timing record of 9.95 seconds. In the running events from 1,500-meters up to the marathon, African athletes established themselves as world champions. However, the most outstanding track-and-field performance was achieved by American Bob Beamon. He improved the world long jump record by a staggering 21¾" (55 cm) to 29' 2½" (8.90 meters). It was not until 23 years later that Mike Powell (USA) managed to improve on Beamon's "leap into the 21st century".

It was not American high jumper "Dick" Fosbury's winning jump of 7' 4¼" (2.24 meters) itself that caused a sensation, but his technique. The so-called "Fosbury Flop" – with the high jumper attempting to clear the bar shoulders first – revolutionized high jumping, and replaced the conventional straddle technique.

Legendary Leap
With a jump of 29' 2½" (8.90 meters), American long jumper Bob Beamon set an historic world record, which remained unbeaten until 1991.

Record Success
Al Oerter of the United States won his fourth Olympic discus title, and became the first Olympic athlete to win four consecutive titles in the same event.

Prolific Medalist
The Czech gymnast Vera Cáslavská won four gold and two silver medals and became the "queen" of the Games. She added these to the three gold medals and one silver secured in Tokyo four years earlier.

Triple Champion
In the pool, 16-year-old American Debbie Meyer secured three gold medals in the freestyle events, and became the first swimmer to take three golds in individual events.

Sprint Nation
Jim Hines (USA) won the 100-meter final and picked up a second gold medal with the 4 x 100-meter relay team to reinforce American dominance in the sprints.

1 **Colorful opening:** At the opening ceremony, thousands of balloons are released into the sky.

2 **Hemery victorious:** Britain's David Hemery comes home to win the 400-meter hurdles gold in a new world record time of 48.12 seconds. Fellow Briton John Sherwood was third.

3 **Black demonstration:** During the medal ceremony for the 200-meters, Olympic champion Tommie Smith (middle) and the third-

placed John Carlos (right, both USA) raise their black-gloved fists. The US team management did not tolerate this demonstration for black rights and sent both sprinters home. On the left is the silver medalist Peter Norman (AUS).

4 Africans win: The field of 5,000-meter athletes is led by Ron Clarke (AUS), who eventually finished in fifth place. In the closing stages, the Tunisian Mohamed Gammoudi (second right) sprinted past the Kenyan Kipchoge Keino (fifth from right) to take the gold medal.

5 Lillian Board: The hugely talented Lillian Board (left) won 400-meter silver, behind Colette Besson (FRA, middle). Tragically, the "golden girl" of British athletics died of cancer in 1970.

6 Smiling winner: The gold medalist over 1,500 meters, Kipchoge Keino (KEN, right), and the runner-up Jim Ryun (USA) at the medal ceremony. The bronze medal went to Bodo Tümmler (FRG).

7 Pentathlon excitement: Ingrid Becker (FRG, seen here in the shot event) secured her

pentathlon gold medal only in the final 200-meter event when she pushed the leading Austrian Liese Prokop and Annamária Tóth of Hungary into second and third positions respectively.

8 Winning flop technique: Richard "Dick" Fosbury (USA) invented the "Fosbury Flop" and used it to become Olympic high jump champion. The silver medal was taken by Edward Caruthers (USA), ahead of Valentin Gavrilov (URS).

9 Two East German golds: The start of the 100-meter

backstroke final, which was eventually won by Roland Matthes, ahead of the Americans Charles Hickcox and Ron Mills. Matthes secured his second gold medal in the 200-meter backstroke. He completed his medal collection with another silver in the 4 x 100-meter medley relay.

10 USA victorious: In the 4 x 200-meter freestyle relay, the USA proved to be invincible. The silver medal went to Australia, ahead of the Soviet quartet.

11 Double champion: Michael Wenden (AUS, bottom)

wins the 100-meter freestyle. Wenden took a second gold medal when he won the 200-meter freestyle.

12 Freestyle specialist: Debbie Meyer (USA) won three gold medals in the 200-, 400-, and 800-meter freestyle events.

13 Highboard diving medals: Klaus Dibiasi (ITA, second left) picks up the gold medal, ahead of Alvaro Gaxiola (MEX, left) and Edwin Young (USA, second right). In the three-meter springboard event, the Italian took silver, behind Bernie Wrightson (USA).

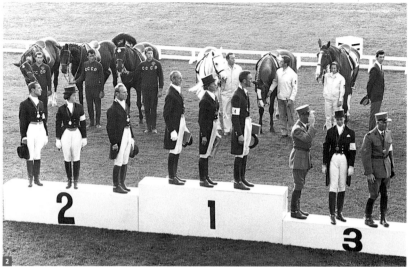

1 Finnegan's gold: Chris Finnegan, Britain's Olympic middleweight champion sports his gold medal as he arrives at Heathrow airport. He later turned professional and won the British and European titles.

2 German riding success: Josef Neckermann, Liselotte Linsenhoff, and Reiner Klimke (FRG, middle) seen during the medal ceremony for the dressage team event, after beating the Soviet Union (left) and Switzerland (right). Neckermann and Klimke added additional individual medals for West Germany.

3 Last win as an amateur: Following this victory over Jonas Chepulis (URS) in the heavyweight division, George Foreman pursued a successful career as a professional boxer.

4 Gold medal disallowed: The gold medals are pesented to the victorious Danish cycling pursuit team. West Germany's initial win in the 4,000-meter team pursuit was disallowed, and the team was subsequently demoted to the silver medal position. Third place was taken by the Italian team.

5 Strong-men: In the freestyle wrestling, heavyweight Alexander Medved (URS, middle) took gold, ahead of Osman Duraliev (BUL, left) and Wilfried Dietrich (FRG, right).

6 Four gymnastics golds: Vera Cáslavská (TCH) won the gold medal in the horse vault, with Erika Zuchold (GDR) second and Zinaida Voronina (URS) third. In the asymmetrical bars event, she beat Karin Janz (GDR) and Voronina. In the floor event, Cáslavská shared her title with Larissa Petrik (URS). Her fourth gold came in the combined exercises, defeating Voronina and Natalya Kuchinskaya (URS).

7 Soccer champions: Hungary (red shirts) took the gold by beating Bulgaria 4–1.

8 Japanese triumph: In the rings event, Mikhail Voronin (URS) and the Japanese Sawao Kato had to surrender to Akinori Nakayama's (JPN, pictured) superiority; he also took gold in the parallel bars, the horizontal bar, and the team events. He added a silver medal in the floor event and a bronze in the combined exercises.

9 Dutch winner: Olympic single sculls champion Henri Jan Wienese (right) is congratulated by the runner-up, Jochen Meissner (FRG, left).

10 Jubilation in Mexico: The 17-year-old Mexican Felipe Muñoz secured a popular win in front of his home crowd in the 200-meter breaststroke final, ahead of Vladimir Kosinsky (URS) and Brian Job (USA). It was the hosts' first gold medal.

11 German eight-man win: The West German rowing eight picked up the gold medal, ahead of Australia and the USSR.

Sapporo

The award of the XI Winter Games meant success at the third time of asking for Sapporo. The city had previously bid for the 1940 Games, which did not take place, and for the 1968 celebration.

Gustavo's Gold
Gustavo Thöni picked up Italy's first gold medal in Alpine skiing for 20 years by winning the giant slalom. He also collected a silver medal in the slalom.

Ard Luck
With three gold medals over 1,500 meters, 5,000 meters, and 10,000 meters under his belt, Dutch speed skater Ard Schenk became the most successful male athlete of the Winter Games in Sapporo.

THE JAPANESE GOVERNMENT regarded the XI Winter Games in Sapporo as a prestige event and invested enormous sums of money in the construction of new sports facilities. As a result, these Games turned out to be the most extravagant and expensive so far, but this was offset by selling the rights for television coverage; this constituted the main source of income for the organizers. While $2.6 million had been sufficient for purchasing the television transmission rights at the last Winter Games in Grenoble, this amount went up by more than 300 percent to $8.47 million. Two-thirds of this money was netted by the organizers.

The day before the opening ceremony at Sapporo, the "Schranz case" hit the headlines. The Austrian Alpine skier Karl Schranz had to leave the Olympic Village for breaching amateur regulations. At a time when many top skiers were making money from the sport – such as through sponsorships – Schranz was singled out for punishment. His ban was meant to be a warning against the increasing commercialism of sports, as outlined by the IOC president Avery Brundage in the year when his term was coming to an end. His demand to ban some 40 other alleged "professional" athletes from competing was rejected by a majority of IOC members.

The issue of amateur status also cast a shadow over the ice hockey tournament. The Canadians intended to include several players in their team who were employed in the North American professional league, as East European countries were also sending so-called state-sponsored amateurs to the Games, and the Canadians regarded them as *de facto* professionals. After the International Ice Hockey Federation and the IOC had vigorously turned down Canada's request, the Canadian team decided to pull out of the event.

Island Games
The official poster of the XI Winter Olympic Games, from February 3 to 13 in Sapporo, the capital of the Japanese island of Hokkaido. The resort was renowned for its winter sports facilities.

The Games offered some sporting surprises. For the first time in the history of the Winter Games, all three medal positions in one discipline were taken by athletes from a non-European country: Yukio Kasaya, Akitsugu Konno, and Seiji Aochi won the small hill ski jump for Japan. Poland earned its first gold medal, with Wojciech Fortuna winning the ski jump from the big hill, as did Spain, through Francisco Fernandez Ochoa's victory in the slalom.

Winning three gold medals each, the Soviet cross-country skier Galina Kulakova and the Dutch speed skater Ard Schenk were the Games' most successful competitors. Schenk missed out on a fourth gold when he fell at the start of the 500-meter event.

For the last time, figure skaters with a good compulsory program benefited from the 50-50 judging system. Thus, the Austrian Beatrix Schuba won the gold medal even though she had been in ninth position after the free program.

Swiss Double
Marie-Theres Nadig (SUI) was a jubilant gold medal winner in the giant slalom event; she had already won the downhill event three days earlier.

X-Country Golds
Winning three gold medals in the 5-kilometer, 10-kilometer, and 3 x 5-kilometer cross-country skiing events, Galina Kulakova (URS) was the most successful female athlete in Sapporo.

Keller Again
Erhard Keller of West Germany successfully defended his 1968 Olympic 500-meter speed skating title and set a new Olympic record for good measure.

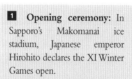

1 Opening ceremony: In Sapporo's Makomanai ice stadium, Japanese emperor Hirohito declares the XI Winter Games open.

2 Closing ceremony: The Olympic flag is folded together, symbolizing the end of the Games. It was due to be handed over to Denver, scheduled host city of the 1976 Games; however, it was kept in Sapporo for another four years until just before the next Olympiad.

3 Favorite wins: Ondrej Nepela (TCH) became figure skating champion, ahead of Sergei Chetverukhin (URS) and the Frenchman Patrick Péra. During the Olympic year, Nepela added to his world (1971–73) and European (1969–73) championship titles.

4 Austrian skating gold: The European and world champion, Beatrix Schuba, took the women's figure skating title ahead of the Canadian Karen Magnussen. The bronze medal was won by Janet Lynn (USA).

5 Champions victorious: The figure skating pair of Irina Rodnina and Alexei Ulanov (URS), who were undefeated in all world and European championships from 1969, beat compatriots Ludmilla Smirnova and Andrei Suraikin, with Manuela Gross and Uwe Kagelmann (GDR) third.

6 New record and gold: The speed skater Monika Pflug (FRG) set a new Olympic record over 1,000 meters with a time of 1:31.40. She won by 0.21 seconds from Atje Keulen-Deelstra (HOL). The American Anne Elizabeth Henning was third, just 0.01 seconds slower. Monika Pflug was a competitor in five Olympic Games and finished her Olympic career in Calgary in 1988, where she took seventh place in the 500-meter event.

7 Fastest speed skater: Ahead of the Olympic Games, the speed skater Erhard Keller (FRG) had lost his world record over 500 meters (38.3 seconds) to the Finn Leo Linkovesi (38.0 seconds). However, in Sapporo, the West German regained the initiative and successfully defended his 1968 Olympic title by defeating the Swede Hasse Börjes and Valeri Muratov of the Soviet Union. Linkovesi was able to finish in only sixth position.

8 First gold for Spain: The first gold medal for Spain at a Winter Olympic Games was won by Francisco Fernandez Ochoa in the slalom competition. He defeated the Italian cousins Gustavo (silver medal) and Rolando Thöni (bronze medal). This was also the first time since 1948 that Austria did not take a medal in the slalom. The women's slalom was taken by the American Barbara Ann Cochran.

9 Successful Alpine skier: The Italian Gustavo Thöni on his way to victory in the giant slalom, beating the Swiss skiers Edmund Bruggmann and Werner Mattle. Thöni also won the silver medal in the slalom and was to return to the limelight 16 years later as coach of the double Olympic champion, the great Alberto Tomba (ITA).

10 Swiss gold and silver: Bernhard Russi clocked the best time in the downhill to become the first Swiss skier to win this event. His compatriot Roland Collombin took the silver medal.

11 Third Soviet gold medal: The Soviet ice hockey team receive their medals after winning the Olympic title for the third time in a row. The silver medal went to the Americans, with the Czechs, whose 14-1 victory over Poland was the most emphatic win of the tournament, taking bronze.

12 Double victory: The two-man bobsled event was taken by the West German duo Wolfgang Zimmerer and Peter Utzschneider, ahead of their compatriots Horst Floth and Pepi Bader. The bronze medal was taken by Switzerland I, driven by Jean Wicki and Edy Hubacher. In the four-man event, West Germany I, comprising team members Stefan Gaisreiter, Walter Steinbauer, Utzschneider, and pilot Zimmerer, took the bronze medal after being beaten by Switzerland I and Italy I.

13 X-Country skiing wins: Galina Kulakova (URS) outclassed her rivals in the 5-kilometer and 10-kilometer events. Together with her Soviet teammates Lyubov Mukhatshova and Alevtina Olyunina, she also secured a commanding relay win ahead of Finland and Norway.

Munich

The XX Summer Olympic Games set out to be full of hope and expectation. Instead, a terrorist attack by Palestinian guerrillas on Israel's team in the Olympic Village brought shock and outrage.

ELEVEN ATHLETES, FIVE TERRORISTS, and one policeman were killed during the kidnapping of Israeli athletes at Munich and the subsequent attempt to rescue them. Even though numerous competitors and officials had advocated abandoning the Games after the tragedy, the IOC decided to continue the competitions, thus conforming to the wishes of the Israeli government and team which refused to give in to any Palestinian pressure. Avery Brundage demanded: "The Games must go on." The IOC president, who was due to retire after these Games and hand over the presidency to Lord Killanin, would not allow the peaceful spirit of the Olympic movement to be ruined by "a handful of terrorists." Despite his appeals, however, several athletes left Munich, concerned about inadequate security. The day after the memorial service, competitions were continued, with the Olympic flag at half-mast. All supporting events were called off.

But controversy did not stop there. Following the banning of South Africa and a threat of boycott by 27 African nations, the IOC were now forced to expel Rhodesia – admitted into the Olympic fold a year earlier and having already sent a team of 30 athletes to Munich – for its apartheid politics.

In Munich, indoor handball had its debut and became one of 195 Olympic disciplines. After its 1964 premiere, judo also established itself as a permanent sport. Having enjoyed a short Olympic spell between 1900 and 1908 and a reappearance in 1920, archery was another discipline that returned to the Olympic schedule.

With 20 gold medals, the East Germans confirmed their claim to be the third sports nation in the world behind the USSR (50 gold medals) and the USA (33 wins). In subsequent years, East

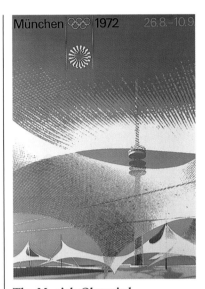

The Munich Olympiad
The sensational tent construction covering the Olympic park and the Olympic tower in Munich are the themes illustrated on the official poster for the XX Olympic Games.

Germany would continue to improve its world standing even more. West Germany won 40 medals (13 gold, 11 silver, and 16 bronze), and finished in fourth position in the medals table.

The sporting highlight of the Games was the performance of the American swimmer Mark Spitz. He won four gold medals in world record times in the 100- and 200-meter freestyle and in the 100- and 200-meter butterfly. He also took golds in the 4 x 100- and 4 x 200-meter freestyle relays, and in the 4 x 100-meter medley relay, thus becoming the most successful swimmer of all time. The female swimming star was the Australian Shane Gould, who picked up three gold medals, as well as one silver and a bronze.

The Soviet gymnast Olga Korbut became the crowds' favorite. The elfin Korbut thrilled audiences with victories in the floor and balance beam events, and took a silver medal in the asymmetrical bars event. She added a third gold in the combined exercises team event.

Star Spitz
The winner of seven gold medals in the swimming pool, Mark Spitz (USA) is hoisted aloft by his teammates.

Star Performer

The 17-year-old Soviet gymnast Olga Korbut hit the headlines by winning three gold medals and establishing Soviet dominance in the female gymnastics events.

Gould's Golds

By securing three gold medals, one silver and a bronze, Australia's Shane Gould became the most successful female swimmer at the Munich Games.

European Judo Wins

Wilhelm Ruska of Holland won two judo victories at Munich – in the heavyweight and open categories.

Track Success

Anchor runner Heide Rosendahl (right) and her teammate Ingrid Mickler are elated about the gold medal won by West Germany in the 4 x 100-meter relay event.

1 Stunning arenas: The Olympic Stadium and the adjacent park, with general sports and swimming halls, set new architectural standards for Olympic arenas.

2 In Nurmi's footsteps: The Finnish policeman Lasse Viren (front) won the 5,000-meters (in a new Olympic record time) and the 10,000-meters (in a world record time). In doing so, he followed in the footsteps of his compatriot Paavo Nurmi, who won nine gold medals between 1920 and 1928.

3 Narrow victory: The new Olympic champion in the javelin was Klaus Wolfermann (FRG). With a distance of 296' 10" (90.48 meters), he took first place, ahead of Janis Lusis from the USSR and Bill Schmidt of the USA.

4 Marathon win: Frank Shorter (USA) wins the marathon. Clocking a time of 2:12:19.8, he won by more than two minutes ahead of Belgian

Karel Lismont (2:14:31.8). Third place went to Mamo Wolde of Ethiopia.

5 Fastest walker: Bernd Kannenberg of West Germany was the winner in the 50-kilometer walk. He defeated the Soviet athlete Venyamin Soldatenko and the American Larry Young.

6 Winning 16-year-old: Experts regarded the Olympic high jump title win by the German Ulrike Meyfarth, ahead of the Bulgarian Yordanka Blagoyeva and the Austrian Ilona Gusenbauer, as a sensation. At the time, Meyfarth was the youngest gold medalist in an individual track-and-field event, and her winning height of 6' 3½" (1.92 meters) equaled Gusenbauer's world record.

7 Kenya first and second: Kipchoge Keino won the 3,000-meter steeplechase in an Olympic record time, ahead of his compatriot Benjamin Jipcho and Tapio Kantanen (FIN).

8 Three medals: Heide Rosendahl proved her versatility by winning golds in the long jump and with the West German 4 x 100-meter relay team. She also took a silver medal in the pentathlon, behind Mary Peters (GBR).

9 Favorite wins: The European champion Valeri Borzov (URS) secured gold in the 100-meters, ahead of Robert Taylor (USA) and Lennox Miller (JAM). Borzov also won the 200-meters, with Larry Black (USA) and Pietro Mennea (ITA) second and third.

10 Two gold medals: By beating Raelene Boyle (AUS) and Silvia Chivas (CUB), Renate Stecher (GDR) proved invincible over 100 meters. Five days later, she added a second gold medal in the 200-meters, ahead of Boyle and the Olympic champion of 1968, Irena Szewinska (POL). She also took a silver medal with the East German 4 x 100-meter relay team, behind West Germany.

1 Mary rises to occasion: Mary Peters in high jump action on her way to becoming Britain's first pentathlon winner. Heide Rosendahl (FRG) and Burglinde Pollak (GDR) were second and third.

2 First round secures gold: In his first attempt in the shot put, the Pole Wladyslaw Komar achieved a distance of 69' 6" (21.18 meters), enough to win him the gold medal ahead of the American George Woods and Hartmut Briesenick (GDR).

3 Hero of the Games: Winning seven gold medals, Mark Spitz was the most successful competitor of the Games. In the 100-meter freestyle, he beat his compatriot Jerry Heidenreich and Vladimir Bure of the Soviet Union. In the 200-meter freestyle final, he reduced to second and third place Steven Genter (USA) and Werner Lampe (FRG). His third gold medal in an individual event followed in the 100-meter butterfly, where he beat Bruce Robertson (CAN) and Heidenreich. Over the longer distance of 200 meters in the butterfly, he won again by defeating teammates Gary Hall and Robin Backhaus. His collection of four individual gold medals was complemented by three golds in relay events, secured as a member of what was an all-conquering American squad: the 4 x 100-meter freestyle, the 4 x 200-meter freestyle, and the 4 x 100-meter medley relay.

4 Australian star: With a new world record time of 2:03.56, the Australian Shane Gould won the 200-meter freestyle, ahead of the Americans Shirley Babashoff (2:04.33) and Keena Rothhammer (2:04.92). In the 400-meter freestyle, she could not be contained by the second-placed Italian Novella Calligaris or by the bronze medalist Gudrun Wegner (GDR). Gould picked up her third gold medal in the 200-meter medley, where she defeated the favorites Kornelia Ender (GDR) and Lynn Vidali (USA). She also took silver in the 800-meter freestyle and bronze in the 100-meter freestyle, behind Sandra Neilson and Babashoff (both USA).

5 Canoeing first: For the first and last time until 1992, slalom canoeing competitions (also known as whitewater canoeing) took place. Siegbert Horn from East Germany won the K1 by beating the Austrian Norbert Sattler and his fellow East German teammate Harald Gimpel. The women's event produced more East German success when Angelika Bahmann took the gold medal, ahead of Gisela Grothaus and Magdalena Wunderlich from West Germany.

6 Kato's three golds: Sawao Kato (JPN) won the parallel bars event for the first time. In the combined exercise individual and team events, he successfully defended the titles he won in 1968. His medal collection was completed by two silvers in the pommel horse event (gold went to Viktor Klimenko, URS) and in the horizontal bar event, where he had to yield to his compatriot Mitsuo Tsukahara.

7 Five gymnastics medals: Karin Janz (GDR) took two gold medals in the asymmetrical bars and horse vault. Two silver medals followed in the combined exercises individual and team events. In the balance beam event, she had to settle for bronze when she was defeated by Olga Korbut and Tamara Lazakovitch (both URS).

8 Fight for gold medal: In the light flyweight (Greco-Roman style) final, the Romanian wrestler Gheorghe Berceanu (blue jersey) defeated the Iranian Rahim Aliabadi.

9 Darling Olga: Olga Korbut of the Soviet Union won two gold medals in the floor event and in the balance beam event. In the latter, she beat compatriot Tamara Lazakovitch and Karin Janz (GDR). She picked up her third gold in the combined exercises team. In the asymmetrical bars event, Korbut shared second place with Erika Zuchold (GDR), behind gold medalist Janz.

10 Dutch victory: Judo star Wilhelm Ruska (HOL) was the only athlete to win two judo gold medals, which he took in the heavyweight and open categories.

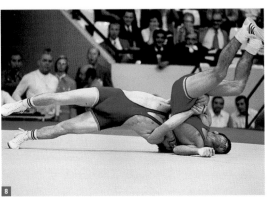

1 **Wins for British riders:** Richard Meade (middle on Laurieston) won the gold medal in the individual three-day event, ahead of Italy's Alessandro Argenton (left, on Woodland) and Sweden's Jan Jönsson (right, on Sarajevo). Great Britain also won the three-day team event, ahead of the USA and West Germany. The British team consisted of Richard Meade (on Laurieston), Mary Gordon-Watson (on Cornishman), and Bridget Parker (on Cornish Gold).

2 **Narrow decision:** The water polo final between the USSR (white caps) and the eventual silver medalists Hungary ended in a 3-3 draw. In the final placings, the Soviet

Union were established as Olympic champions on the grounds of their better goal difference. The bronze medal was taken by the United States.

3 **First hockey gold:** For the first time in the history of the Olympic Games, West Germany (white shirts) won the hockey tournament. In the final, they dethroned title holders Pakistan by beating them 1-0.

4 **Favorites beaten:** The soccer tournament ended with the Polish team (red shirts) taking the gold medal when they beat the three-time Olympic champions (1952, 1964, and 1968) Hungary 2-1 in the final. The bronze medal was shared by the Soviet Union and East Germany after they tied

their third place play-off.

5 **Gold medal for quartet:** The West German quartet of (from left) Jürgen Colombo, Günter Haritz, Udo Hempel, and Günther Schumacher won the 4,000-meter team pursuit, ahead of teams from East Germany and Great Britain.

6 **USSR victorious:** In the volleyball final, the women's team from Japan (blue shirts) suffered a 2-3 defeat at the hands of the Soviets. The bronze medal was taken by North Korea. The Japanese men's team were more successful when they beat East Germany 3-1 in the final. Third place was taken by the Soviets.

7 **Games are continued:** After the memorial service for

the victims of the attack on the Israeli team, the Olympic and national flags flew at half-mast until the end of the tournament. Although criticized in some quarters for the insensitivity of some of his remarks, IOC president Avery Brundage was successful in advocating that the Games should continue. In addition, the German president Gustav Heinemann appealed to all nations of the world "to overcome hatred" and "to pave the way for reconciliation."

8 **Athletes taken hostage:** An armed policeman readies his weapon in the Olympic Village where Arab terrorists went into hiding with their Israeli hostages. Germany's interior minister Hans-Dietrich Genscher twice negotiated an extension of the time limit set by the terrorists for the fulfilment of their conditions. The terrorists demanded that the Israeli government release 200 Arabs held in Israeli prisons. The kidnappers also demanded a flight for themselves and their hostages from Munich to Egypt. Under the watchful eye of special police units, the kidnappers and their hostages left the Olympic Village and boarded two helicopters that were provided for them on the evening of September 5, 1972.

9 **Violent end:** The rescue operation carried out by the German police ended in a bloodbath. The helicopters had brought the terrorists and their hostages to Munich's military air base at Fürstenfeldbruck, where the group intended to board an aircraft. After a shoot-out with police marksmen, three of the guerrillas were killed; the remaining terrorists blew up the helicopters and shot the athletes. The terrorist attack claimed the lives of 11 Israeli athletes, one policeman, and five of the eight terrorists.

10 **Munich's mourning:** Athletes and officials of the Israeli delegation are overcome with grief during the memorial service at the Olympic Stadium in honor of their dead compatriots. In his address to the watching world, the Israeli ambassador to Bonn, Eliashiv Ben-Horin, made a plea for people to oppose the politics of killing, kidnapping, and terror. They were troubled times indeed.

Innsbruck

For the second time in 12 years, Innsbruck hosted the Winter Olympic Games. Two Olympic flames were lit in the Bergisel Stadium – one to symbolize the present Games, the other to commemorate 1964.

DENVER WAS THE INITIAL CHOICE to host the XII Winter Olympic Games because the 100th anniversary of the state of Colorado coincided with celebrations for the 200th anniversary of the birth of the United States. However, a 300 percent increase in costs, as well as the anticipated environmental damage of winter tourism and the construction of new sports facilities, led to a referendum in which the majority of people voted against the event being hosted in Denver.

It was instead Innsbruck that had the privilege of staging its second Winter Games only 12 years after hosting its first successful games in 1964. The organizers were able to use existing sports facilities, with only minor refurbishments and modernization work needed to upgrade the resort. Projects such as the construction of a motorway through the River Inn valley and the building of publicly funded residential blocks (accommodation for more than 1,250 athletes) were brought forward. Funding was partially raised through donations, and Austrian army troops helped out with the construction work.

One idea that was not very well received was that of conducting the medal ceremonies in the ice rink each evening after the day's competitions. The spectators would have preferred to see the medal ceremonies held on the spot.

The first competition of the Games, the blue riband downhill skiing event, was won by the Austrian Franz Klammer. While the hosts had to wait until the last day for another gold medalist (ski jumper Karl Schnabl), German fans were gripped by "Rosi fever." Twenty-five-year-old Rosi Mittermaier, who during her ten-year career had never been able to win a World Cup downhill race, won the downhill and slalom events and took a silver medal in the giant slalom.

In 1975, the International Figure Skating Federation had introduced a

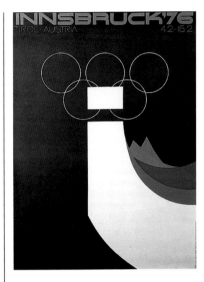

Hosts Once More
The official Olympic poster shows a ski jump hill in front of Tyrolean mountains.

reorganized competition, consisting of a short compulsory program and a long freestyle program. Thus, the share of the obligatory section in the overall mark, which was unpopular with most athletes, fell from 50 percent to 30 percent. Ice dancing also made its debut as an Olympic discipline; its first gold medal went to the Soviet pair, Ludmilla Pakhomova and Alexander Gorshkov.

The Dutch continued their long-standing success in the speed skating events. In the men's competitions over distances in excess of 1,000 meters, Piet Kleine (gold medal over 10,000 meters and silver medal over 5,000 meters) and Hans van Helden (bronze medals over 1,500, 5,000, and 10,000 meters) took five of the nine medals that were on offer.

The ice hockey tournament had begun before the official opening with a series of preliminary qualifying matches. The Soviet Union, the title holders, benefited when the Czechoslovakian team (who went on to win silver) were deducted one point after their captain, Frantisek Pospisil, was found guilty of taking a banned substance.

Rosi's Gold
The West German Rosi Mittermaier on the way to her downhill gold medal. With two gold medals and one silver medal each, she and the Nordic skier Raisa Smetanina from the Soviet Union were the most successful competitors at Innsbruck.

Flying Franz
The favorite Franz Klammer withstood intense mental pressure to win the downhill event in front of an expectant home crowd.

Record Breaker
Clocking a new Olympic record time of 14:50.59 minutes over 10,000 meters (ten seconds better than the previous record), the Dutch speed skater Piet Kleine secured gold in style.

Debut Winner
At her first Olympic Games, Raisa Smetanina (URS) won two gold medals in the 10-kilometers and 4 x 5-kilometers cross-country skiing events. She added a silver medal in the 5-kilometer event.

British Victor
Third at the world championships in 1975 and European champion in 1976, the British skater John Curry crowned his amateur career with a gold medal in the men's figure skating competition.

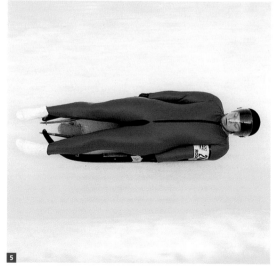

6

7

8

9

1 Double symbolism: During these Winter Games, two flames were visible above the Bergisel Stadium; one for the current Olympics, the other for Innsbruck's first Games back in 1964.

2 New skating rules: In 1976, the US figure skater Dorothy Hamill won the Olympic title to add to her world championship title, becoming the first Olympic champion under the new figure skating scoring system, which allotted only 30 percent of marks to the compulsory program. She was

coached by Carlo Fassi, who also helped Britain's John Curry to Olympic gold in Innsbruck.

3 Skating without jumps: Athletes competed in the ice dance event for the first time in Innsbruck. The discipline had staged its own world championships since 1952. Here the title was won by the Soviet favorites, Ludmilla Pakhomova and Alexander Gorshkov. The Soviet pair remained unbeaten at the European and world championships later that year.

4 Career change: Speed skater Sheila Young (USA) won a gold medal over 500 meters, a silver medal over 1,500 meters, and a bronze over 1,000 meters. She retired from speed skating after the Games, but continued to be in the sporting limelight by pursuing a career as a sprint cyclist.

5 East Germans clean up: The luge titles were all taken by athletes from East Germany and competitors from other nations had to be content with silver or bronze medals. The singles were

won by Margit Schumann (pictured) and Detlef Günther; the two-man title went to Hans Rinn and Norbert Hahn.

6 Lucky number 1: In the women's giant slalom, the Canadian Kathy Kreiner clocked a time of 1:29.13 minutes, which meant that she took the title by just 0.12 seconds.

7 Nordic "marathon" win: The Norwegian Ivar Formo dominated the 50-kilometers cross-country skiing and won from

Gert-Dietmar Klause (GDR). However, this gold medal was to be his only international success.

8 Home ski jump victory: On the closing day of the Games, Karl Schnabl thrilled the home crowd when he won a gold medal in the ski jump from the big hill.

9 Austria's great start: On the opening day of the Games, the Austrian downhiller Franz Klammer won the most demanding and prestigious of all alpine disciplines.

Montreal

After being beset by numerous problems, including a major boycott, ahead of the event, the XXI Olympic Games, held in the Canadian city of Montreal, were characterized by perfect organization and strict security.

BUILDING CRANES DOMINATED the skyline during the opening ceremony for the XXI Olympiad, with speeches held in both languages of the host nation, English and French. Industrial disputes, an unusually long winter, and a severe lack of funds had made it impossible to finish work on the Olympic facilities in time. As a result, the opening ceremony took place under improvised conditions. To this day the city of Montreal is still repaying debts accrued during these Olympics.

With memories of the terrorist attack in Munich still very fresh in people's minds, the Montreal Olympics were marked by rigid security measures. Commemorating their murdered team mates of four years before, each member of the Israeli delegation paraded into the stadium at the opening ceremony wearing a black armband.

Once again, politics played a major role in these Olympic Games, with 24 of the 116 registered teams boycotting the competition. The explanation given (by the 22 black African countries who refused to take part and Guyana) was that they objected to New Zealand's participation on the grounds that New Zealand's rugby team had played in apartheid South Africa. The Taiwanese team withdrew after a disagreement with the Canadians. Also, as in 1971, the IOC reiterated its banning of Rhodesia from the Games, due to its system of apartheid. Overall, this meant that the number of athletes participating in Montreal was 6,085 – 1,071 fewer than had competed at the Munich Games in 1972.

Because the media were mainly interested in the winners of each event, many surprising results were given scant coverage; the silver medals won by the Belgian Ivo van Damme over 800 meters and 1,500 meters were just one example.

A New Star
The 14-year-old Romanian gymnast Nadia Comaneci was the crowds' favorite in Montreal. She won three gold medals, a silver, and a bronze.

Summer in Canada
The official poster of the Montreal Summer Games featured a design based on the five intertwined Olympic rings.

The fifth place in the marathon taken by the Finn Lasse Viren was another momentous run, considering he had already successfully defended his 5,000- and 10,000-meter titles. In doing so, he had earned himself a place in the history books. Although numerous experts expressed their doubts about the value of the running competitions in the absence of the strong African nations, new world and Olympic records on the track showed that standards remained high.

In the swimming competitions, the United States, with 13 gold medals, and East Germany, with 11 wins, dominated. Britain's David Wilkie and the Soviet Marina Koshevaia (both winning their respective 200-meter breaststroke finals) were the only swimmers to upset the US-German monopoly, both swimmers setting new world records for good measure. Women's rowing was admitted for the first time, with East Germany taking four of the six gold medals. Basketball and handball were also new disciplines for women.

Ed's Record
The American Edwin Moses won the Olympic title in the 400-meter hurdles with a new world record time of 47.64 seconds. It was the third consecutive time at an Olympics that this record had been broken.

Wilkie Wins
British swimming ace David Wilkie powers to victory in the final of the 200-meter breaststroke. Wilkie's time of 2:15.11 was a new world record.

Second Gold
At her fourth Olympic Games, Irena Szewinska (POL) crowned her career with an Olympic title and world record in the 400-meters. She had won the 200-meter event in Mexico eight years before and another gold in the 1964 4 x 100 meter relay.

Viren Again
Lasse Viren (FIN) became the first athlete to successfully defend his Olympic 5,000- and 10,000-meter titles. He finished the 5,000-meters more than 30 yards in front of his nearest rival.

1 Second Olympic flame: As had been customary since 1936, the Olympic flame was lit at all Olympic venues, including Kingston on Lake Ontario, where the yachting events took place. These included the Finn class (gold for Jochen Schümann of East Germany), the Soling (Denmark), the Tornado (Great Britain), and the Flying Dutchman (West Germany).

2 Triple Soviet medals: In the hammer, Yuri Sedykh won with a distance of 254' 4" (77.52 meters), beating compatriots Alexei Spiridonov (249' 7"/76.08 meters) and Anatoli Bondarchuk (247' 8"/75.48 meters).

3 World record win: The American Bruce Jenner won the decathlon. The silver medal was picked up by Guido Kratschmer (FRG), ahead of the 1972 gold medal winner, Nikolai Avilov

(URS). In eight of the events, Jenner improved on his own personal best performances. Until the penultimate event, the three leading competitors were separated by only 76 points. Jenner subsequently increased his lead and improved his own world record by 80 points to 8,618 points.

4 Favorite wins: The Olympic high jump champion was world record holder Rosemarie Ackermann (GDR), clearing a height of 6' 4" (1.93 meters). Second and third places were taken by Sara Simeoni (ITA) and Yordanka Blagoyeva (BUL).

5 Years of success: By winning the 400-meter title in 49.29 seconds, the Polish track-and-field athlete Irena Szewinska (No. 277) set a new world record. The East Germans Christina Brehmer (50.51

seconds) and Ellen Streidt (50.55 seconds) had to settle for silver and bronze respectively. During an Olympic career that spanned 16 years (1964–80), Szewinska (formerly known as Kirszenstein) amassed a collection of three gold, two silver, and two bronze medals.

6 First-time double: The Cuban Alberto Juantorena (No. 217) celebrates his Olympic 800-meter win. He had only run four 800-meter races before the Games, and all of those were in 1976. Improving the three-year-old world record held by the Italian Marcello Fiasconaro by 0.2 seconds to 1:43.50, he defeated Ivo van Damme (BEL) and Richard Wohlhuter (USA). Juantorena completed an outstanding double by winning the 400-meters, beating the Americans Fred Newhouse and Herman Frazier.

144

8

9

10

11

7 **Sprint record:** The finish line of the 100-meters is crossed by Annegret Richter (FRG, lane 7), ahead of the East German title holder Renate Stecher (lane 4) and Richter's teammate, Inge Helten (lane 1). Richter had set a new world record time of 11.01 seconds in an earlier heat. Over 200 meters, she added a silver medal when defeated by Bärbel Eckert (GDR); Stecher picked up bronze. Richter's third medal came in the 4 x 100-meter relay event, where the West German team took the silver medal behind the East German runners and ahead of the Soviet quartet.

8 **Favorite beaten:** The Finnish rower Pertti Karppinen (left) was the surprise Olympic winner in the single sculls. Over the last couple of yards, he overtook the world and European champion Peter-

Michael Kolbe (FRG, nearest the camera). The bronze medal was taken by Joachim Dreifke (GDR). Winning the coxed and coxless pairs, the quadruple sculls, the coxless fours, as well as the eights, East Germany were by far the most successful nation in the men's rowing events. The East German women also achieved success, in the single sculls (Christine Scheiblich), the quadruple sculls, the coxed fours, and the eights.

9 **Swimming success:** The American John Naber was the first backstroke swimmer to clock a sub-two-minute time over 200 meters when he won in 1:59.19 and beat his compatriots Peter Rocca and Dan Harrigan. He took an additional backstroke gold over 100 meters, with Rocca second and Roland Matthes of East Germany third. Two more gold

medals followed when the USA 4 x 200-meter freestyle relay team beat the USSR and Great Britain, and the 4 x 100-meter medley relay team beat Canada and West Germany. His medal collection was completed by a silver medal in the 200-meter freestyle event, losing out to compatriot Bruce Furniss.

10 **Queen of the pool:** Kornelia Ender (GDR, top) is overjoyed about her victory in the 100-meter freestyle final, beating Petra Priemer (GDR) and Enith Brigitha (HOL). Ender finished the Games with four gold medals plus a silver medal, picked up with the East German freestyle relay team.

11 **Kim's golds:** Nelli Kim (URS) won golds in the floor, horse vault, and combined exercise team events, and a silver in the individual combined.

145

7

8

1 Fencing victories: Alexander Pusch (FRG, right) took the gold medal in the individual épée event. Second and third places were taken by Pusch's teammate Jürgen Hehn (left) and the Hungarian Győző Kulcsár. In the team épée event, the West German team were not able to contain the Swedes, who took the gold medal.

2 Team cycling gold: In the 4,000-meter team pursuit, the West Germans (from left) Peter Vonhof, Hans Lutz, Günter Schumacher, and Gregor Braun beat the USSR and Great Britain. Braun picked up a second gold medal in the 4,000-meter individual pursuit event, with the Dutchman Herman Ponsteen second and Thomas Huschke (GDR) third.

3 Yachting medals: Jörg and Eckart Diesch (FRG) celebrate their gold medal in the Flying Dutchman category, ahead of Rodney Pattisson and Julian

Brooke Houghton (GBR, left). The Brazilians Reinaldo Conrad and Peter Eicker took third place.

4 Surprise win: Harro Bode and Frank Hübner (FRG) took an unexpected gold in the 470 yachting category.

5 Basketball's debut: In the first women's Olympic basketball tournament, the Soviet team (white shirts, seen during their 112-77 win over silver medalists, USA) took the gold medal. The bronze medal was claimed by Bulgaria.

6 Equestrian medals: Alwin Schockemöhle (FRG) won the individual show jumping event, ahead of Michel Vaillancourt (CAN) and François Mathy (BEL). The successful West Germans also took a silver medal in the show jumping team event, silver and bronze medals for Harry Boldt and Reiner Klimke respectively in the individual dressage, a bronze

medal for Karl Schultz in the individual three-day event, a gold medal in the dressage team event, and a silver medal in the team three-day event.

7 USSR victorious: The men's handball final was won by the Soviet team (red shirts), who defeated Romania 19-15. The Polish team finished in third place. The Soviet women's team also took gold.

8 Polish delight: In the men's volleyball final, Poland (white shirts) beat the USSR 3-2; Cuba took the bronze. The women's tournament was won by the Japanese, who defeated the Soviets 3-0, with South Korea taking the bronze medal.

9 Weightlifting supremo: Vasili Alexeyev (URS) successfully defended his 1972 super-heavyweight Olympic title. Silver and bronze medals went to the East Germans Gerd Bonk and Helmut Losch.

9

Lake Placid

In 1980, the Winter Olympic Games came to the New York resort of Lake Placid for the second time. Insufficient natural snow forced the organizers to use artificial snow, which made its Olympic debut.

IN 1974, THE IOC AWARDED THE XIII Winter Games to Lake Placid, a resort in New York State's Adirondack Mountains. Lake Placid's first encounter with the Winter Olympic Games had been in 1932, and in 1980, as had happened 48 years before, the organizers had to cope with a snow shortage and with moving enormous crowds to and from a small town of 3,000 inhabitants. Tens of thousands of people were sometimes forced to wait hours for the shuttle buses that served the venues. And many journalists were critical of the one-hour walk to the press center. Many athletes also considered the Olympic village too confined; after the Games it would actually be used as a prison for young offenders. The sports facilities themselves, on the other hand, received high praise, even though they were some distance apart from each other.

At Lake Placid, artificial snow was used for the first time in Olympic competition, at a cost of $5 million. However, the fake snow was extremely demanding on the athletes, especially when mixed with newly fallen snow – the two types formed a cocktail that produced somewhat unpredictable characteristics. Nevertheless, the snow shortage problem had been resolved.

Despite international political unrest, most spectators were impartial when it came to acknowledging sporting performance and achievement. Although the reception for the Soviet delegation was rather subdued during the opening ceremony, the display turned on by the figure skater Irina Rodnina, with her partner Alexander Zaitsev, earned standing ovations. One year after having given birth to a son, she won her third successive Olympic title. In a glorious career, Rodnina also took ten world championship titles, making her the most successful female figure skater of all time.

The battle for prestige between the two superpowers was evident in the ice

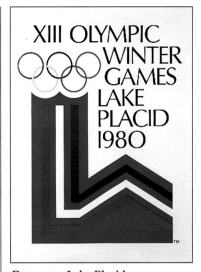

Return to Lake Placid
The official poster of the XIII Winter Olympic Games shows a ski jump hill beneath the five Olympic rings.

hockey tournament. The Soviets had been gold medalists in the sport at each Winter Olympics since their shocking defeat at the hands of the Americans at Squaw Valley in 1960. They were hot favorites to continue the run, especially since they had thrashed the American team 10–3 only a week before the start of the Games. Once again, however, playing in front of a home crowd seemed to bring out the best in the Americans. They met the Soviets in the semi-finals and beat them 4–3, before going on to defeat Finland in the final. Carried away by this success, the media rather ignored the achievements of the American speed skater Eric Heiden, who won five gold medals, set a world record over 10,000 meters, and four other Olympic records.

For 12 days, sporting events dominated. However, late in 1979, the Soviet Union had invaded Afghanistan, and before the start of the Lake Placid celebration, President Jimmy Carter had threatened a US boycott of the Summer Olympics due to be held in Moscow later that year. The specter of international politics lurked close by.

King Eric
American speed skater Eric Heiden, who had taken the Olympic oath at the opening ceremony, won five gold medals, for 500, 1,000, 1,500, 5,000, and 10,000 meters.

Downhill Gold
The Austrian Annemarie Pröll crowned her career by winning the women's downhill, ahead of Liechtenstein's Hanni Wenzel and the Swiss skier Marie-Theres Nadig.

Final Glory
Ulrich Wehling (GDR) was the first winter sports athlete to win three successive gold medals in the Nordic combined event. Following his win in Lake Placid, he retired from competitive sports.

Third Gold
Irina Rodnina (URS) ended her career after winning her third consecutive Olympic pairs figure skating title. In 1972 she had won with Alexei Ulanov, and in 1976 and 1980 with Alexander Zaitsev.

Successful Recovery
The Swede Ingemar Stenmark took two gold medals – in the slalom and giant slalom events – and confirmed a return to form after a bad fall had put him out of action five months before the Games.

1 Opening of the Games: The nations parade as the Olympic flame is carried into the stadium.

2 Hockey sensation: The USA won the ice hockey tournament, with the Soviets, who had won gold at every Games since 1964, taking silver.

3 Three medals: Hanni Wenzel, born in Bavaria but skiing for Liechtenstein, took gold in the slalom and giant slalom, and a downhill silver.

4 East German luge win: Hans Rinn and Norbert Hahn defeated Peter Gschnitzer and Karl Brunner (ITA) and Georg Fluckinger and Karl Schrott (AUT) in the two-man event.

5 Surprise winner: The men's downhill was won by the outsider Leonhard Stock (AUT).

6 Double gold: Ingemar Stenmark (SWE) won the giant slalom ahead of Andreas Wenzel (LIE) and Hans Enn (AUT). He also won the slalom.

7 Final skating gold: Anett Pötzsch (GDR) retired after taking gold in Lake Placid.

8 Springboard to success: After the Games, figure skating champion Robin Cousins (GBR) turned professional.

9 In a spin: Figure skater Denise Biellmann (SUI) had to settle for fourth place in the women's event. However, the audience was spellbound by her freestyle program.

10 Figure skating win: Irina Rodnina and Alexander Zaitsev (URS) won the pairs title, ahead of compatriots Marina Cherkassova and Sergei Shakhray.

11 X-country victory: Over 10 kilometers, Barbara Petzold (GDR) beat the Finns into second and third.

12 Nikolai's title: In the 50-kilometers Nordic skiing event, Nikolai Simyatov (URS) outclassed Juha Mieto (FIN) and Alexander Savyalov (URS).

13 Consecutive wins: Ulrich Wehling (GDR) took his third Nordic combined title.

Moscow

The XXII Olympiad was the first to be staged in a country with a communist regime. However, it was overshadowed by a large-scale boycott in protest at the 1979 Soviet invasion of Afghanistan.

Home Victor
During the Summer Games in Moscow, Soviet swimmer Vladimir Salnikov won three gold medals in front of his home crowd.

ONLY 80 COUNTRIES WERE represented at the Moscow Games, a third less than had participated in Munich eight years before. Notable absentees included Japan, West Germany, and the large team from the United States. After the terrible events at Munich and the African boycott in Montreal, the Moscow controversy was the last thing the Olympic movement needed. A question mark hung over the future of the Olympic idea, and it was impossible to predict whether the nations of the world would ever again assemble for sporting competition. Three days before the 1980 Games opened, Juan Antonio Samaranch was elected IOC president to succeed Lord Killanin. He inherited a very difficult task.

The Games were opened on July 19 by the Soviet president, Leonid Brezhnev. The opening ceremony was perfectly staged, with groups dressed in colorful traditional costumes from all the Soviet republics. Gestures of protest, such as the entry of some delegations under the Olympic flag, rather than their national flags, were largely ignored by television cameras.

Western countries have frequently referred to the Moscow Games as being of a low standard, and time and time again raised doubts about the sporting value of the results and medals. Experts seem in little doubt that Ed Moses would have won the 400-meter hurdles, as he had in Montreal in 1976 and went on to do once again in Los Angeles in 1984. Some other results might also have been different if certain athletes had not been absent. Nevertheless, although not of the highest caliber, the Moscow Games were hardly substandard; 36 world records, 39 European records, and 73 Olympic records were testimony to the high level of talent and competition on display. Vladimir Salnikov (URS), for example, became the first swimmer to break the magic 15-minute barrier in the 1,500-meter freestyle when he clocked a time of 14:58.27. In the women's pentathlon, the Soviet Nadia Tkachenko scored 5,083 points to become the first athlete to exceed 5,000 points in the event during Olympic competition. In the long-distance events, the Ethiopian Miruts Yifter enthused the crowds with his blistering sprint finishes. At Moscow, "Yifter the Shifter," as he was dubbed, became only the sixth runner to do the long distance double of 5,000- and 10,000-meters. He won the latter with a scorching final lap of 54.0 seconds.

Perhaps the most eagerly awaited contest was between the two British running stars Steve Ovett and Sebastian Coe in the 800- and 1,500-meters. At the end of 1979, Coe held the world records for both events (as well as for the mile), but in the run-up to the Games, Ovett equaled Coe's 1,500-meter record and bettered his time over the mile. The stage was set for a showdown in Moscow. In an interesting final twist, Ovett won at Coe's preferred distance of 800 meters, while Coe triumphed in the 1,500-meters.

Poor Turnout
The official poster of the 1980 Moscow Olympics, from which teams from the USA and other Western countries were absent.

Multimedalist
The Soviet gymnast Alexander Ditiatin picked up three gold medals, four silvers, and a bronze. He became the first gymnast to score a perfect 10 in the horse vault event.

Champion Jumper
The new Olympic champion in the women's high jump was the Italian world record holder, Sara Simeoni. She had secured a silver medal in the event four years earlier.

Triple Gold
Rica Reinisch (GDR) won three swimming gold medals, in the 100- and 200-meter backstroke, and with the 4 x 100-meter medley relay team.

King Daley
In winning the decathlon, Britain's Daley Thompson became "king of the athletes," and disappointed the home crowd by pushing the Soviet athlete Yuri Kutsenko into second position.

1 Colorful opening: During the opening ceremony, a section of the 102,000 crowd transformed the stands of the Lenin Stadium into alternating pictures by using colorful scarves. This type of visual display was customary during mass rallies in countries with communist regimes.

2 Italian win: Italy's Pietro Mennea (third from left), who had secured a bronze medal in this event at the Munich Games eight years before, wins the men's 200-meters in a time of 20.19 seconds. Britain's Allan Wells (fourth from left) took the silver medal, ahead of Don Quarrie of Jamaica (second from right). By taking bronze, Quarrie added another Olympic 200-meter medal to the gold that he won in Montreal four years before.

3 Gold at 100 meters: Britain's Allan Wells leads Don Quarrie of Jamaica, the Montreal silver medalist, in the first heat of the 100-meters. Wells went on to win the final in 10.25 seconds in a photo-finish ahead of Silvio Leonard (CUB) to become the first Briton to win the 100-meters since Harold Abrahams did so in Paris in 1924. Petr Petrov of Bulgaria took the bronze medal.

4 Soviet superiority: In the women's 1,500-meters final, Tatyana Kazankina (URS, right) won gold as she had in Montreal. Christiane Wartenberg (GDR) and Nadyezhda Olizarenko of the Soviet Union came second and third respectively. Olizarenko made no mistake in the 800-meter event, where she underlined her Olympic title

win by setting a new world record of 1:53.43 minutes.

5 British battle: Sebastian Coe (GBR, right) becomes the new Olympic champion over 1,500-meters. He beat second-placed Jürgen Straub (GDR, centre) and Steve Ovett (GBR, left), joint world record holder (with Coe) over this distance.

6 Ovett overtakes: Though beaten in the 1,500-meters, Steve Ovett (GBR, third right) made no mistake over the 800-meters, taking the gold. Fellow Briton Sebastian Coe, world record holder over 800-meters and clear favorite for this event, took the silver medal, ahead of Nikolai Kirov (URS).

7 High jump gold: In Moscow, the silver medalist in

Montreal four years previously, the Italian Sara Simeoni, took the gold medal ahead of Urszula Kielan of Poland and Jutta Kirst of East Germany.

8 World record gold: The Pole Wladyslaw Kosakiewicz took the gold medal in the pole vault event and set a new world record (for the first time during Olympic competition since 1920) of 18' 11½" (5.78 meters). His compatriot Tadeusz Slusarski and Konstantin Volkov (URS) shared the silver medal after they both cleared 18' 6½" (5.65 meters).

9 Long distance star: The Ethiopian Miruts Yifter (left) defeated Suleiman Nyambui of Tanzania (right) and the Finn Kaarlo Maaninka in the men's 5,000-meters. Yifter won his second gold medal in the

10,000-meter event when he beat Maaninka and his Ethiopian compatriot Mohammed Kedir. Yifter's unconventional running style, where a steady pace was interrupted with numerous unexpected sprinting bursts, kept his rivals guessing.

10 Duncan does it: Duncan Goodhew won a swimming gold for Britain by taking the 100-meters breaststroke in 1:03.34 minutes ahead of Arsen Miskarov (URS) and Australia's Peter Evans. He could manage only sixth in the 200-meters, which was won by Robertas Zhulpa (URS), with second and third going to Alban Vermes (HUN) and Miskarov of the Soviet Union. Goodhew was, however, part of the British medley relay team that came third behind Australia and the Soviet Union.

1 East Germans dominate: Bernd and Jörg Landvoigt celebrate their win in the coxless pairs event.

2 Soviet winners: Vladimir Parfenovich and Sergei Chukhrai (front) take gold in the 1,000-meter K2.

3 Fencing medals: France won the final of the épée team competition when it beat Poland 8-4 (photograph shows the contest between Andrzej Lis and Hubert Gardas). France was also victorious in both the men's and women's foil team events. In addition, Pascale Trinquet secured another gold medal for France by winning the individual foil tournament.

4 Home gold: In the individual cycling road race, Sergei Sukhoruchenkov (URS) defeated Czeslaw Lang (POL) by a huge margin of nearly three minutes. Yuri Barinov (URS) took bronze. The Soviets also won the 100-kilometer team time trial.

5 Winner's joy: Players and officials celebrate the Soviet water polo team's victory.

6 Narrow decision: The East German handball team (white shirts) won the tournament by defeating the USSR 23-22 in the final. The women's tournament was won by the Soviet Union.

7 Swiss judo win: In the middleweight division, Jörg Röthlisberger beat the Cuban Isaac Azcuy Oliva (standing) to secure a momentous victory.

8 Most successful athlete: Alexander Ditiatin (URS) took three gold medals, in the individual and team combined exercise competitions and in the rings event. He added four silvers to his medal collection and completed his tally with a bronze medal in the floor event.

9 Strongest lifter: With an overall lift of 970 pounds (440 kilograms) in the combined competition, the 30-year-old Soviet weight lifter Sultan Rakhmanov took gold in the super-heavyweight category, ahead of Jürgen Heuser (GDR).

10 Wrestling medals: The freestyle super-heavyweight champion was Soslan Andiev (URS, blue shirt). Silver went to József Balla (HUN), with Adam Sandurski (POL, red shirt) taking bronze.

11 Shooting for gold: In the prone small-bore rifle event, Karoly Varga (HUN) won the gold medal, ahead of Hellfried Heilfort (GDR) and Petr Zaprianov (BUL).

12 Two home golds: The modern pentathlon title was taken by Anatoli Starostin (URS), who picked up a second gold medal as part of the USSR's team event victory.

Sarajevo

When Sarajevo was selected ahead of Sapporo or Gothenburg, even the host's organizing committee was surprised. Nevertheless, 1984 saw the Winter Games held in the Balkans for the first time.

WHEN THESE GAMES WERE awarded to Sarajevo in 1978, the organizers knew they had six years to prepare. Funding was raised from the sale of television rights, sponsorships, and advertising contracts, as well as through the efforts of the people of Sarajevo themselves.

The organizers demonstrated their improvisational skills on a number of occasions. For example, they equipped the downhill slope with an elevated starting area to comply with regulations that insisted on a start-finish altitude difference of 800 meters. The Yugoslavs also coped well with the numerous schedule changes resulting from the adverse weather conditions. For the first time, the IOC agreed to pay the expenses of one male and one female member of each team. The number of participating nations was up from the 37 at Lake Placid to 49, although Egypt, the Virgin Islands, Mexico, Monaco, Puerto Rico, and Senegal were represented by only one competitor each.

The most successful teams in Sarajevo were the East Germans, with nine golds, the USSR, with six golds, and the USA, Finland, and Sweden with four golds. The most successful participant was the Finnish cross-country skier Marja-Liisa Hämäläinen, who won the 5-, 10-, and 20-kilometer individual events, and claimed a bronze medal as a member of the Finnish 4 x 5-kilometer relay team.

The Americans had considerable success on the ski slopes, with Bill Johnson winning the men's downhill, Phil Mahre winning the slalom, and Debbie Armstrong taking the gold medal in the women's giant slalom event. In the individual figure skating events, America's Scott Hamilton took the men's gold, while the women's event was won by East Germany's Katarina Witt.

Balkan Glory
A snowflake is the main image on the official poster of the XIV Winter Olympic Games held in the Bosnian capital, Sarajevo.

However, the stars of the Sarajevo Games were the British ice dance pair Jayne Torvill and Christopher Dean, whose performances marked the dawn of a new era in this discipline. Their interpretation of Ravel's "Bolero" was one of the truly great moments in sport, for which they achieved a perfect score for artistic presentation – all nine judges awarded them the maximum six points. In the competition overall, they gained 12 out of a possible 18 sixes.

Tragically, Sarajevo and its sports facilities were reduced to rubble in the fighting that later engulfed the former Yugoslavia. During the Lillehammer Winter Olympics of 1994, IOC president Juan Antonio Samaranch flew to the Bosnian capital and appealed to the warring sides to impose a temporary cease-fire for the duration of the Games.

Dream Team
The British ice dancers Jayne Torvill and Christopher Dean were the undisputed stars in Sarajevo. They crowned their amateur career with an Olympic title win and their fourth world championship title in 1984.

X-Country Queen
Winning three gold medals and one bronze, Marja-Liisa Hämäläinen of Finland was the most successful athlete at the Winter Games in Sarajevo.

Twins Peak
The twin brothers Phil (right) and Steve Mahre of the United States took first and second positions respectively in the men's slalom. It was the first gold for the USA in this discipline.

Katarina's Grace
East Germany's Katarina Witt won her first Olympic figure skating gold medal; she would successfully defend her title four years later in Calgary.

German Success
East Germany I, with the legendary Wolfgang Höppe in the team, won the four-man bobsled competition, ahead of East Germany II. Höppe also took gold with Dietmar Schauerhammer in the winning East German two-man bob.

1 The Olympic flame is lit: After the Olympic torch had been carried through Yugoslavia by 1,600 relay runners, the Olympic flame was lit by the figure skater Sandra Dubravcic in Sarajevo's Olympic Stadium. The site was badly damaged in the Balkan conflict a few years later.

2 Facelift for Olympic city: A view of Sarajevo, where sports facilities and the city's infrastructure were modernized with the help of investment of tens of millions of dollars. During the 13 days of competition, posters bearing the Olympic symbol made Sarajevo's streets beautifully colorful.

3 Successful flight: The Finn Matti Nykänen jumps from the big (90-meter) hill. He finished the competition as Olympic champion, beating Jens Weissflog (GDR) with an Olympic record 389½-foot (116-meter) jump. Weissflog had beaten Nykänen in the small (70-meter) hill contest a few days before.

4 Double medals for USA: After the two runs in the women's giant slalom, the American Debbie Armstrong became the new Olympic champion, ahead of her compatriot Christin Cooper and Perrine Pelen of France.

5 Swedish "king of skiing": In the 50-kilometer cross-country skiing competition, Thomas Wassberg was invincible. He secured a second gold medal as part of the Swedish 4 x 10-kilometer relay team.

6 Biathlete's three medals: The West German biathlete Peter Angerer recorded his greatest personal success by winning a gold medal over 20 kilometers, a silver over 10 kilometers, and a bronze with the 4 x 7.5-kilometer relay team.

7 Giant gold: Clocking a time of 2:41.18, Max Julen (SUI) won the giant slalom, ahead of Juriy Franko (YUG) and Andreas Wenzel (LIE). There was further success for Switzerland when Peter Müller took second position in the blue riband men's downhill event.

8 Favorite wins: After his Olympic figure skating win, Scott Hamilton (USA), who was world champion from 1981 to 1984, turned professional.

9 USSR too strong: The ice hockey world champions from the Soviet Union commandingly took the Olympic title, with the Czechoslovakian and Swedish teams taking silver and bronze. The Soviets conceded only five goals in their seven games. Here at the medal ceremony, goalkeeper Vladislav Tretyak (middle) cannot hide his elation – this was his third gold medal in four Olympic Games. In 1980, he had to be content with a silver medal.

10 Fastest speed skater: Karin Enke (GDR) won two gold medals over 1,000 and 1,500 meters, as well as two silver medals over 500 and 3,000 meters. The stunning success of the East German women speed skaters was completed by Christa Rothenburger's gold medal over 500 meters, Andrea Schöne's gold over 3,000 and silver in both the 1,000- and 1,500-meters, and finally Gabi Schönbrunn's bronze over 3,000 meters.

11 East German bobs win: Wolfgang Höppe was successful in the two-man and four-man bobsled events. In the two-man bob, he was victorious with Dietmar Schauerhammer, ahead of his compatriots Bernhard Lehmann, and Bogdan Musiol. In the four-man bob, he and his teammates Schauerhammer, Andreas Kirchner, and Roland Wetzig clinched the title, ahead of East Germany II, represented by Lehmann, Musiol, Ingo Voge, and Eberhard Weise, and Switzerland I (Rico Freiermuth, Silvio Giobellina, Urs Salzmann, and Heinz Stettler).

Los Angeles

In 1984, Olympic athletes met in Los Angeles for the second time, having first gathered there in 1932. The Games were remarkable for being the first privately funded tournament in Olympic history.

THE DRIVING FORCE BEHIND Los Angeles' successful bid was the city's mayor, Tom Bradley, while entrepreneur Peter Ueberroth dedicated his time to bringing the project to fruition once the Games had been awarded. Ueberroth was able to attract more than 30 sponsors, who between them contributed more than $500 million. Other companies funded the building of new sports facilities, in a deal that allowed them to advertise on the admission tickets. The ABC television network paid $225 million for the exclusive television transmission rights, thereby ensuring that most events started in the evenings during prime television time. With these vast amounts of money involved, many critics held the view that what had once been a festival of amateur sport had been converted into a purely commercial spectacle.

The Games were overshadowed by a boycott imposed by the Soviet Union and many of its allies, who explained their absence by alleging that they were not satisfied with security arrangements. However, their nonparticipation was generally seen as retaliation for the US-instigated boycott of the Moscow Olympics four years before.

The star of the Los Angeles Games was undoubtedly Carl Lewis, the American track-and-field athlete, who followed in Jesse Owens's footsteps by taking four Olympic titles. Forty-eight years after Owens's triumphs in Berlin, Lewis emulated his achievements exactly, taking golds in the 100- and 200 meters, the 4 x 100-meter relay, and the long jump. Only the 17-year-old Romanian gymnast Ecaterina Szabó won more medals, claiming four golds and a silver.

Britain's Daley Thompson successfully defended his decathlon title, becoming only the second man (after Bob Mathias) to do so. Meanwhile, teammate Sebastian Coe recovered from serious illness to successfully defend the Olympic 1,500-

Star Games
The official Olympic poster shows different facets of life in the USA.

meter title, the first man ever to achieve this feat. As in Moscow, Coe also picked up a silver medal in the 800- meters, this time losing out to Brazil's Joaquim Cruz; the Brazilian set a new Olympic record in the process.

In the women's 400-meter hurdles, Nawal El Moutawakel, competing in her first Games, became the first Moroccan sportswoman to win an Olympic gold medal. Other surprise winners included Holland's Ria Stalman, who won the discus, West Germany's Ulrike Meyfarth, who repeated her 1972 high jump success, and the little-known Australian Glynis Nunn, who took gold in the first Olympic heptathlon. However, it seems likely that some of the medal winners at Los Angeles might have struggled to reach the finals had the East European teams been participating.

Among the new disciplines at Los Angeles were women's synchronized swimming, in which the solo event was won by Tracie Ruiz from the USA, and windsurfing, won by Holland's Stephan van den Berg. During the Olympic Congress of 1981, the term "Olympic amateur" had been removed from the Olympic Charter. This gave individual sports associations the power to decide on an athlete's eligibility for the Olympics. As a result, professional soccer players were eligible for the Olympics, though European and South American countries considered only players that had not appeared in the World Cup.

King Carl
With four Olympic titles, Carl Lewis (USA) was the star of the 1984 Los Angeles Summer Games.

Daley Retains
Briton Daley Thompson celebrates a successful attempt in the discus, which put him on the road to victory in the decathlon. His winning points tally equalled the world record.

Double Diving Gold
The American diver Greg Louganis remained unbeaten from the three-meter springboard as well as from the ten-meter highboard, and wowed the crowd with his precision.

Pool Giant
Michael Gross (FRG), whose nickname was "Albatross" because of the span of his outstretched arms, set a new world record when winning the 200-meter freestyle event.

Gymnast's Accolades
Winning four gold medals and a silver, the Romanian gymnast Ecaterina Szabó was the most successful competitor in Los Angeles. The judges awarded her a perfect 10 in one round of the floor exercises event.

1 **Spectacular opening:** During the parade of nations, the home spectators gave the American team an enthusiastic reception. One of the many attractions at the opening ceremony in the Coliseum was a jet-propelled "rocket man," who flew through the air then landed in the stadium. A crowd of more than 90,000 in the stadium, as well as a worldwide television audience in the hundreds of millions, followed the four-and-a-half-hour spectacle, executed by more than 10,000 performers. The Olympics had come to the United States.

2 **New 100-meter record:** In the absence of her East German rivals, the American Evelyn Ashford (right) set a new Olympic record of 10.97 seconds in the womens 100-meter sprint. The silver medal

was picked up by Alice Brown (USA, 11.13 seconds), ahead of the Jamaican Merlene Ottey (11.16 seconds). Ashford secured a second gold medal as part of the US 4 x 100-meter relay team win (along with Brown, Jeanette Bolden, and Chandra Cheeseborough). Canada were second and Great Britain third.

3 **Olympic debut:** Los Angeles witnessed the debut of the womens 400-meter hurdles competition, with Nawal El Moutawakel becoming the first Moroccan sportswoman to win a gold medal in Olympic competition. Clocking a time of 54.61 seconds, she defeated the American Judi Brown and Cristina Cojocaru of Romania. After her surprise victory, the winner was proud to wave her country's national flag and soak up the applause from the crowd.

4 **Second gold medal:** The American 400-meter hurdles world record holder, Edwin Moses, took the Olympic oath on behalf of all athletes during the opening ceremony. Following his victory in 1976, the world champion of 1983 and 1987 secured his second Olympic title. Silver and bronze medals went to compatriot Danny Harris and the European champion Harald Schmid (FRG) respectively.

5 **Battling with the heat:** At their debut Olympic marathon, the women athletes were caught by the midday heat, which led to many athletes suffering from exhaustion. Unlike the women, the men were allowed to start their event late in the afternoon. In addition, the rules were changed at short notice to allow athletes to be provided with

water at an increased number of refreshment stands. This put the 37-year-old Portuguese Carlos Lopes in a position to set a new Olympic record of 2:09:21. Second and third places were taken by the Irishman John Treacy (2:09:56) and Britain's Charlie Spedding (2:09:58) respectively. The women's event was won by the American Joan Benoit in 2:24:52. The exhausted Swiss athlete Gaby Andersen-Schiess caused some concern when she was seen to visibly waver over the track during the final lap in the stadium, but she finished the race.

6 Glory for Tessa: Britain's Tessa Sanderson shows off her Olympic javelin gold medal. She threw 228' 2" (69.56 meters) to beat Tiina Lillak (226' 4"/69.00 meters) into second place. Sanderson's British rival Fatima

Whitbread (220'/67.14 meters), who was to be world champion in 1987, took the bronze. Tessa Sanderson is the only British athlete to have taken part in five Olympic Games (1976 to 1992).

7 Star of the Games: After the medal ceremony for the victorious American 4 x 100-meter relay team, Carl Lewis is carried around by his teammates on a lap of honor. On the final day of the Games, Ron Brown, Sam Graddy, Lewis, and Calvin Smith set a new world record in the event of 37.83 seconds, defeating Jamaica (38.62 seconds) and Canada, (38.70 seconds). It was Lewis's fourth gold medal of the Games after his 100-meter win over Graddy and Ben Johnson (CAN) and his success in the 200-meter final, in which he beat his compatriots Kirk Baptiste and Thomas Jefferson in

a time of 19.80 seconds. Lewis also won the long jump, with a winning leap of 28' 0¼" (8.54 meters), pushing the Australian Gary Honey and the Italian Giovanni Evangelisti (both just over 27 feet) into second and third places.

8 "King" once again: Britain's Daley Thompson (seen during the decisive pole vault event) successfully defended the Olympic decathlon title he won in Moscow four years before. Setting a new Olympic record of 8,798 points, equaling Jürgen Hingsen's (FRG) world record, Thompson relegated Hingsen (8,673 points) to the silver medal position. The West German team was still able to be proud of its achievements, however, as Siegfried Wentz (8,412 points) and Guido Kratschmer (8,326 points) took positions three and

four respectively. At the European championships in Stuttgart two years later, Thompson again beat Hingsen to take the title. However, after a disappointing ninth place at the world championships in Rome in 1987, the then 30-year-old Thompson came back once more to Olympic competition in Seoul. Despite carrying an injury, he came a respectable fourth and ended a marvelous career with dignity.

9 Surprise winner: Not even experts had expected the West German discus thrower Rolf Danneberg to be a serious medal contender. At his fourth attempt, the 6' 6" (2 meters) tall athlete threw 218' 6" (66.60 meters). Second place went to the American Mac Wilkins (217' 6"/66.30 meters), who had been champion at Montreal, ahead of

John Powell (also USA, 214' 9"/65.46 meters).

10 First heptathlon gold: The Olympic debut of the heptathlon (which replaced the pentathlon) at Los Angeles saw the relatively unknown Australian athlete, Glynis Nunn (middle, here at the medal ceremony), win the event. The two-day-long competition consisted of 100-meter hurdles, high jump, shot, 200-meter sprint, long jump, javelin, and 800-meter run. The Australian (6,390 points) finished only a whisker ahead of the favored American Jackie Joyner (6,385 points) and the West German Sabine Everts (6,363 points). This was one event where the absence of Soviet athletes may have lowered standards; Soviet athletes had taken all the medals in the pentathlon at the Moscow Games four years before.

1 **Double diving victory:**
The American diver Greg Louganis won the highboard event with 710.91 points, ahead of his compatriot Bruce Kimball and the Chinese diver, Li Kongzheng. Never before had a diver achieved more than 700 points in this event. Four days earlier, he had secured the springboard title with the largest ever margin of victory, ahead of Tan Liangde (CHN) and Ronald Merriott (USA). This double Olympic diving victory had previously been accomplished

only twice – by the Americans Albert White (in Paris in 1924) and Ulise Joseph Desjardins (in Amsterdam in 1928).

2 **Favorite takes first title:**
In Los Angeles, world champion Tracie Ruiz (USA, front) became the first Olympic synchronized swimming champion. The silver medal went to the Canadian Carolyn Waldo, with Miwako Motoyoshi of Japan third. In the duet, Ruiz and her partner, Candy Costie, were again in a class of their own when they beat

Sharon Hambrook and Kelly Kryczka (CAN) and Motoyoshi and Saeko Simura (JPN).

3 **Double victory for Gross:**
In the 100-meter butterfly, Michael Gross (FRG) set a new world record time of 53.08 seconds, which secured him the gold medal, ahead of Pablo Morales (USA) and Glenn Buchanan (AUS). In the 200-meter freestyle event, he set another world record (1:47.44) and demonstrated his superiority over Michael Heath (USA) and

his fellow West German Thomas Fahrner. He finished second in the 200-meter butterfly, beaten by Jon Sieben (AUS). The 20-year-old German picked up another silver as part of the 4 x 200-meter freestyle relay team, with the USA winning, and Britain third.

4 **Pool world records:** The Canadian Alex Baumann won the 200-meter medley in a new world record time of 2:01.42. He secured another victory and another world record in the 400-

meter medley, with a time of 4:17.41.

5 **Three gold medals:** Mary T. Meagher (USA) won three gold medals, in the 100- and 200-meter butterfly events, and with the American 4 x 100-meter medley relay team.

6 **Gymnast's five medals:**
The crowd's favorite, Mary Lou Retton (USA, seen during her floor performance which won her a bronze medal), won the individual combined exercises

competition, picked up two silvers in the horse vault and the team event, and took a bronze in the asymmetrical bars event.

7 **Prolific winner:** The Romanian gymnast Ecaterina Szabó won the floor, balance beam (jointly), and horse vault events, and contributed to her country's gold medal in the team combined exercise competition. In the individual combined exercises, she had to settle for a silver medal, behind Mary Lou Retton (USA).

8 **Olympic wins for China:** The gymnast Li Ning won three gold medals in the floor, rings, and pommel horse (picture) events, two silvers in the horse vault and in the team combined exercises competition, as well as a bronze in the individual combined exercises. Chinese success was completed by Lou Yun, who took gold in the horse vault and silver in the floor event.

9 **Fencing success:** The West German fencers celebrate the

gold medals won in the women's team foil event, ahead of Romania and France. Cornelia Hanisch (second left) added a silver medal in the individual foil competition.

10 **Italian swordsmen:** The Italian Mauro Numa (left) took the gold medal in the men's individual foil ahead of West Germany's Matthias Behr (right). Numa secured a second gold as part of the Italian foil team. West Germany and France were second and third.

1 Chinese win: In the women's volleyball tournament the American team (left) were no match for the gold medalists China, at whose hands they suffered a straight sets defeat. The USA had to settle for silver ahead of the Japanese team. The men's tournament was won by the USA after they managed a 3-0 victory over silver medalists Brazil. The Italians finished in bronze medal position.

2 Yugoslavia win: The final of the men's handball tournament between Yugoslavia (blue shirts) and West Germany was decided by the narrow margin of 18-17, in favor of the team from the Balkans. The Romanian team won the bronze medal, thanks to a 23-19 victory over Denmark. The women's handball tournament also saw the Yugoslavs (who were the silver medalists in Moscow) take the gold, in this case ahead of Korea and China.

3 Dutch hockey gold: The Dutch women field hockey players celebrate their Olympic title. This second Olympic field hockey tournament for women saw only six teams taking part. West Germany picked up the silver medal, with the USA taking bronze. The men's tournament was won by Pakistan for the third time (having also been gold medalists in 1960 and 1968). The West Germans took second place, this time ahead of bronze medalists Great Britain.

4 Invincible USA: In the basketball competition, none of the teams were able to prevent the favorites, the hosts, from taking their ninth Olympic title. In the final, the USA comprehensively beat Spain 96-65. The picture shows Pat Ewing (right) and Spain's Fernando Romay. Yugoslavia finished in bronze medal position.

5 US basketball gold: Six teams competed in the women's basketball tournament. In the final round, the US team, which remained undefeated in the competiton, beat South Korea 85-55. The picture shows Cheryl Miller targeting the basket, with the Korean Moon Kyung-Ya (left) too late to take any defensive action. The bronze was picked up by China, beating Canada 63-57.

6 Greco-Roman Wrestling success: In the bantamweight division (up to 125¾ lb/57kg body weight), the West German

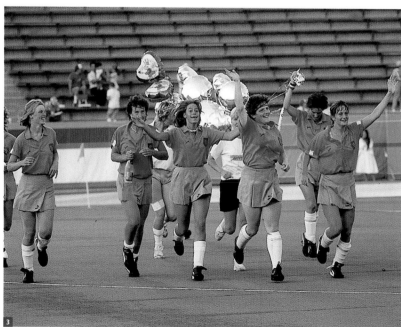

wrestler Pasquale Passarelli (blue top) took the gold medal thanks to a win over Japan's Masaki Eto (red top). Greek wrestler Haralambos Holidis finished in bronze medal position. The West Germans won another silver medal when the light-flyweight (up to 105¾ lb/48kg) Markus Scherer lost out to the impressive Olympic champion, Vincenzo Maenza of Italy, in the final.

7 Strong men: Rolf Milser (FRG, pictured) dominated the first heavyweight weightlifting category. Silver went to the Romanian Vasile Gropa and bronze to the Finn Pekka Niemi. Previously, Karl-Heinz Radschinsky had won the gold medal in the middleweight category ahead of Jacques Demer (CAN) and Dragomir Cioroslan (ROM). West German success was completed by the bronze secured in the super-heavyweight category by Manfred Nerlinger, who had to concede to the superiority of champion Dean Lukin (AUS) and Mario Martinez (USA).

8 Rowing hat-trick: The Finnish rower Pertti Karppinen won his third consecutive Olympic title in the single sculls

event by a margin under two seconds from his greatest rival, and world champion, Peter-Michael Kolbe (FRG). He had to settle for a silver medal, with Canadian Robert Mills taking bronze. Canada took gold in the eights competition.

9 US cycling double: Americans Connie Carpenter (gold, middle) and Rebecca Twigg (silver, left) showed their delight at the medal ceremony for the women's individual road race over 49¾ miles (79.2 kilometers). Bronze went to Sandra Schumacher (FRG, right).

10 Financial expert: Los Angeles mayor Tom Bradley (left) had suggested that Peter Ueberroth (right) be chairman of the organizing committee for the first privately funded Games. Following the success of the event, Ueberroth was praised for his achievements.

11 Favorite wins: World champion Reiner Klimke (FRG) rode Ahlerich to a commanding win in the dressage competition. The West German trio of Herbert Krug, Uwe Sauer, and Klimke also won the gold medal in the dressage team event.

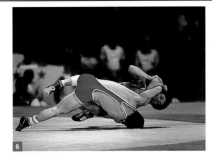

Calgary

In 1981, 24 years after it first formed its bidding committee, the Canadian city of Calgary, at the foot of the Rocky Mountains, was finally awarded the Winter Olympic Games by the IOC.

FUNDS FOR THE CALGARY GAMES originated from three sources. Half of the budget was put up by the Canadian government; sponsors, official suppliers, and licensees contributed another $90 million; and the US television network ABC paid $309 million for the broadcasting rights. ABC benefited from a decision made by the IOC in 1984 to extend the Games from 12 to 16 days. The consequence for the competitors was that start times for many events were chosen not for sporting reasons, but to meet the demands of television advertisers in the United States.

The Olympic program was again extended to include new disciplines. In Nordic skiing, team competitions in the combined and in the ski jump events made their Olympic debut. Further developments in Nordic skiing came as a result of the "skating technique" used by the Finnish skier Siitonen in Sarajevo in 1984. Modified regulations for the cross-country events were introduced: while the shorter distances – the men's 15- and 30-kilometers, and the women's 5- and 10-kilometers – were to be covered using the classic style, the freestyle (skating technique) could now be used in the men's 50- and the women's 20-kilometer competitions and also in the relay events. In Alpine skiing, meanwhile, the super giant slalom ("Super G") made its first appearance, and for the first time since 1948, there was an Alpine combined competition. Another first was that the speed skating events were held indoors, and the 5,000-meter event was added to the women's speed skating program.

Although the spectators enjoyed the Calgary Games, many saw them more as a well-rehearsed show than a series of competitive sporting competitions. Among the winners they cheered on were the Finnish ski jumper Matti Nykänen and the Dutch speed skater Yvonne van Gennip, who each won

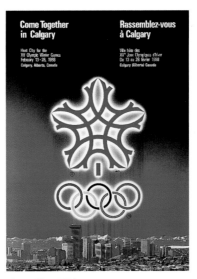

Canadian Welcome
The official poster of these Winter Olympic Games features a bilingual appeal for the youth of the world to come together.

three gold medals. The real favorites, though, were the Italian Alberto Tomba, who managed to attract considerable attention both through his gold medals in the slalom and giant slalom, and his well-publicized laid-back lifestyle, and Katarina Witt, who was dubbed "Carmen on ice." The East German became the first female figure skater since Sonja Henie (1928 to 1936) to successfully defend her individual Olympic title.

For the first time since 1968, the Winter Games included demonstration sports. At Calgary, curling, short track speed skating, and freestyle skiing were all exhibited, with an encouraging response from the watching crowds. As a mark of the IOC's recognition of their sporting achievements, disabled athletes were given their own timetable of competitions. This had actually been introduced four years before at the Sarajevo Games, but was now a more comprehensive program. However, officials turned down suggestions to integrate the competitions for disabled athletes into the official program.

Italian Hero
The Italian Alberto Tomba won two gold medals in the slalom and giant slalom to become the most successful Alpine competitor of the Games.

Close Result
America's Brian Boitano took the men's figure skating gold, just ahead of Canada's Brian Orser.

Triple Jump Wins
With Olympic titles in the small hill, big hill, and team ski jumping events, the 24-year-old Finn Matti Nykänen was the most successful male competitor at these Winter Games.

Gennip's Golds
The Dutch speed skater Yvonne van Gennip demonstrated her superiority in this discipline by winning over the 1,500-, 3,000-, and 5,000-meter distances.

Ski Champ
In Calgary, the 1985 world combined and downhill champion, and the 1987 Super G world champion, Pirmin Zurbriggen (SUI), took a gold medal in the downhill and a bronze medal in the giant slalom.

1 Cheerful mascots: The official mascots for the Calgary Games, two polar bears called Hidy and Howdy, were conceived by the Canadian designer Sheila Scott. Marketed in many different ways, they were a prominent sight at the venues and on television screens.

2 Successful Alpine skier: The Frenchman Franck Piccard won the first Olympic super giant slalom event, ahead of the Austrian Helmut Mayer and Lars-Böerje Eriksson of Sweden. Piccard picked up a bronze medal in the downhill, behind the two Swiss skiers, Pirmin Zurbriggen and Peter Müller (who also came second in this event in 1984).

3 West Germans win: Adverse weather conditions forced the women's downhill race to be postponed by one day.

Marina Kiehl coped best with the demanding course and exceptionally strong winds to take gold. The West German skier defeated Brigitte Oertli of Switzerland and the Canadian Karen Percy, and was the only German Alpine skiing gold medalist.

4 First giant slalom wins: In the women's Super G, Sigrid Wolf (middle) clocked a time of 1:19.03, which secured her the gold medal, ahead of the Swiss skier Michela Figini (left, 1:20.03) and the Canadian, Karen Percy (right, 1:20.29), who was also bronze medalist in the downhill.

5 Vreni's double: Switzerland's Vreni Schneider lived up to expectations when she took two gold medals in the skiing competitions. In the slalom, she beat the Yugoslav Mateja Svet and the West German

Christa Kinshofer-Güthlein. In the giant slalom event, the 23-year-old Schneider defeated Kinshofer-Güthlein and Maria Walliser of Switzerland, 1984 silver medalist in the downhill.

6 Title and award to Witt: In the summer of 1988, the East German figure skater Katarina Witt (seen here during her interpretation of "Carmen" in the freestyle program) received an Olympic award from IOC president Juan Antonio Samaranch. She was the first female figure skater since Sonja Henie (1928 to 36) to defend her Olympic title.

7 Unbeaten favorites: In the ice dancing competition, the Soviet pair of Natalya Bestemianova and Andrei Bukin lived up to their billing to win the gold medal, ahead of their compatriots Marina

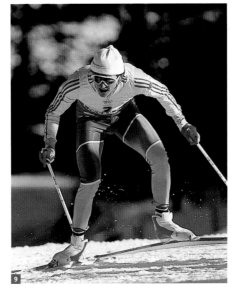

Klimova and Sergei Ponomarenko. The Canadians Tracy Wilson and Robert McCall took the bronze medal. The champions were invincible throughout the Olympic year, in which they won their fourth successive world championship title.

8 **Racing to gold:** Tomas Gustafson (SWE) won the gold medal in the 5,000-meter speed skating event (and successfully defended his 1984 Olympic title) when he defeated Leo Visser and Gerard Kemkers (both HOL). Four days later, he took the 10,000-meter event, and improved the world record held by the Norwegian Geir Karlstad by 0.31 seconds to 13:48.20. Second and third places in the 10,000-meters were taken by the Austrian Michael Hadschieff and Visser respectively.

9 **Medals for Switzerland:** Hippolyt Kempf (SUI) (seen here during the cross-country skiing) had been a world-class Nordic combined athlete for a year by the time he competed at Calgary. He was part of the successful Swiss team that took silver in the team event, beaten by West Germany.

10 **Double victory:** At his second Olympic Games, Frank-Peter Roetsch (GDR), the silver medalist over 20 kilometers in Sarajevo, picked up two gold medals in the 10-kilometer and 20-kilometer biathlon events at Calgary.

11 **Swiss on a roll:** In the four-man bobsled event, the Switzerland I team of Ekkehard Fasser, Marcel Fässler, Kurt Meier, and Werner Stocker took the gold medal ahead of East Germany I and USSR II.

Seoul

Happily, the large-scale boycotts of Moscow and Los Angeles did not recur at Seoul. For the first time in 12 years, all leading Olympic nations, except Cuba and Ethiopia, took part in the Olympic Games.

TWENTY-FOUR YEARS AFTER THE Tokyo Games of 1964, the Summer Olympics returned to Asia. However, the warm welcome given by the hosts could not cover up the tense political relations between the pro-Western South Korean government and the communist rulers of North Korea, who decided not to send a team. During the 16 days of the Games, athletes from 159 nations participated, and 27 new world records were set.

Sadly, though, the results on the track were overshadowed by the most spectacular drugs case in Olympic history. Three days after Ben Johnson had won the men's 100-meter gold in a new world record of 9.79 seconds, official drug testers announced that the 26-year-old Canadian had tested positive for performance-enhancing drugs. Johnson was stripped of both his world record and gold medal, and banned from ever representing Canada again. The ban was later reduced to two years.

Once again, the Soviet Union (55 gold medals) and East Germany (37) demonstrated their superiority over the Western nations by finishing first and second in the medals table. The East German swimmer Kristin Otto won six golds, coming close to equaling the phenomenal performance of America's Mark Spitz, who won seven gold medals in 1972. The US swimmer Matt Biondi won five gold medals, as well as a silver and a bronze. In the 100-meter butterfly, however, he lost to Anthony Nesty, the only swimmer representing Surinam. In the women's sprints, American Florence Griffith-Joyner was outstanding. Having been a respected but not brilliant sprinter on the international circuit for some time, "Flo-Jo" suddenly blossomed in 1988, winning golds in the 100-meters, 200-meters, and 4 x 100-meter relay, and taking a silver as a member of the 4 x 400-meter team that finished second

Seoul Man
The dramatic official poster for the Games shows a torch bearer carrying the Olympic flame to Seoul beneath the five intertwined Olympic rings.

behind the USSR. She set a new world record of 21.34 seconds in the 200-meter final and also ran the fastest Olympic time ever over 100 meters (10.54 seconds). Unfortunately, that run was considered wind-assisted and did not count as a record.

The men's middle distance events were both won by Kenyans, with Paul Ereng taking the 800-meters and Peter Rono the 1,500-meters. A Kenyan, John Ngugi, also won the 5,000-meters, while the 10,000-meter gold went to Brahim Boutaib of Morocco. The Africans had to settle for silver and bronze in the marathon, though, when Italy's Gelindo Bordin picked up the gold.

After 64 years, tennis regained its status as a full Olympic sport. The singles competitions were won by West Germany's Steffi Graf and Miloslav Mecir of Czechoslovakia The newly introduced sport of table tennis was almost completely dominated by the Chinese and Korean competitors.

Colorful Flo
The sprinter Florence Griffith-Joyner (USA) won three gold medals and a silver. She captured the public's attention not only through her athletic performances, but also by her outgoing personality.

Cooper Collects
Britain's Malcolm Cooper retained his Olympic title in the small-bore (three positions) event. Alister Allan (also GBR) took the silver medal, having taken bronze at Los Angeles in 1984.

Multimedalist
The Romanian Daniela Silivas picked up gold medals in the floor, balance beam, and asymmetrical bars events, and added two silver medals in the individual and team combined exercises events. She also took the bronze medal in the horse vault.

Six Golds
The East German swimmer Kristin Otto won six gold medals and helped to set a number of new Olympic records to become the most successful competitor in Seoul.

Legendary Bubka
Sergei Bubka (URS) won the pole vault with his one and only valid attempt. He set a new Olympic record in an event where the Russians secured the first three places.

1 **Colorful spectacle:** During the athletes' parade at the opening ceremony of the Games in Seoul, some of the participating athletes appeared dressed in their national costumes.

2 **Short-lived victory:** Three days after what Ben Johnson (CAN, right) believed to be his personal triumph in the 100-meters came sobering news. He was disqualified for drug taking, and Carl Lewis (USA, left) was declared Olympic champion.

3 **Heptathlon result:** Scoring 7,291 points, Jackie Joyner-Kersee (USA, right) improved her own world record by 79 points. She defeated Sabine John and Auke Behmer (both GDR). In the women's long jump, Joyner-Kersee leapt 24' 3½" (7.40 meters) to become the first American to win this event. Heike Drechsler (GDR) and Galina Chistyakova (URS) took second and third positions respectively.

4 **African victories:** Once again, Kenyans demonstrated their talent for middle-distance running. Paul Ereng (left) won the 800-meters ahead of Joaquim Cruz of Brazil (right) and Said Aouita (MAR, centre). In the 1,500-meters, Ereng's compatriot, Peter Rono, became the first Kenyan since the legendary Kip Keino (in Mexico City, 1968) to win this event. Britain's Peter Elliott was second.

6

7

5 **More African success:**
Over 5,000 meters, John Ngugi (KEN) ran a very controlled race. His finishing sprint secured him an advantage of 3.82 seconds over second place Dieter Baumann (FRG), with third place going to Hansjörg Kunze (GDR). In the 10,000-meters, gold went to Brahim Boutaib (MAR), ahead of Salvatore Antibo (ITA).

6 **Led from the start:**
The women's marathon was dominated by Rosa Mota (POR). Silver went to Lisa Martin (AUS), and bronze to Katrin Dörre (GDR).

7 **East German double:**
Christian Schenk was the first East German to win the decathlon, ahead of his compatriot Torsten Voss.

8 **Fashion-conscious:** The US triple Olympic champion Florence Griffith-Joyner in one of the 100-meters heats.

9 **One vault victory:** On his third attempt at 19' 4½" (5.90 meters), Sergei Bubka (URS) kept his composure to win the pole vault over team-mates Rodion Gataullin (19' 2¼"/5.85 meters) and Grigori Yegorov (19' 04"/5.8 meters).

10 **Win over arch rival:**
With a distance of 245' (74.68 meters), Petra Felke (GDR) won the javelin competition, ahead of her arch rival, the British world and European champion, Fatima Whitbread. The bronze medal went to Beate Koch (GDR).

8

9

10

1 **Six wins in six starts:**
Winning six gold medals,
Kristin Otto (GDR) was
without doubt the outstanding
athlete of the Summer Games
in Seoul. She won the first
Olympic 50-meter freestyle
event for women. In the 100-
meter freestyle, she beat
Zhuang Yong (CHN) and
Cathérine Plewinski (FRA). In
the 100-meter backstroke, 23-
year-old Otto defeated the
Hungarian Krisztina Egerszegi
and fellow East German
Cornelia Sirch. She proved her
versatility by winning the 100-
meter butterfly final, beating
Birte Weigang (GDR) and the
Chinese swimmer Qian Hong.
Her gold medal collection was
completed by her two relay
wins with the 4 x 100-meter
freestyle and 4 x 100-meter
medley teams.

2 **Wins for Matt Biondi:**
The star of the men's
swimming was the American
Matt Biondi (nearest the
camera). He took five gold
medals, one silver, and a
bronze. He won the first
50-meter freestyle event for
men since 1904, ahead of
his teammate Thomas Jager and
Gennadi Prigoda of the
USSR. In the 100-meter
freestyle, he outclassed his
compatriot Christopher Jacobs
and the Frenchman Stephan
Caron to set a new Olympic
record. He took silver in
the 100-meter butterfly, and
finished third behind Duncan
Armstrong (AUS) and Anders
Holmertz (SWE) in the 200-
meter freestyle. He won
further gold medals as a
member of the winning US
4 x 100-meter and 4 x 200-
meter freestyle teams and
the 4 x 100-meter medley
team.

3 **Maestro Moorhouse:**
Britain's Adrian Moorhouse
(right) clinched the 100-meter
breaststroke gold in a time of
1:02.04, ahead of Károly
Guttler (HUN, 1:02.05) and
Dmitri Volkov (URS, 1:02.20).
Moorhouse won European
titles at 100 meters in 1985,
1987, and 1989 (the last in a
world record time of 1:01.49),
and in the 200-meters
breaststroke in 1983.

4 **Victorious eights:**
Twenty years after their win in

Mexico City, West Germany
reclaimed the Olympic
eights title. In the final, cox
Manfred Klein, Thomas
Möllenkamp, Matthias
Mellinghaus, Ansgar Wessling,
Eckhardt Schultz, Armin
Eichholz, Thomas Domian,
Wolfgang Maennig, and
Bahne Rabe (from right to
left) beat the crews from the
USSR and USA by just one
length. Further successes for
the West German rowers came
courtesy of Peter-Michael
Kolbe, who won the silver
medal behind Thomas Lange
(GDR) in the single sculls, and
the coxless fours, who took the
bronze medal, behind teams
from East Germany and the
USA. The most successful
rowing nation was East
Germany, with five gold medals
in the women's competitions
and three golds in the men's
events.

5 **Favorite wins:** The
American Greg Louganis
remained unbeaten in Seoul.
The world champion in the three-
meter springboard dominated
the competition and successfully defended his Olympic title.
In the ten-meter highboard
diving, Louganis repeated his
winning performance to leave
second and third places to
Xiong Ni (CHN) and Jesus
Mena (MEX). In the women's
competitions, the Chinese
divers Gao Min (three-meter)
and Xu Yanmei (ten-meter)
were in a class of their own.

6 **Dutch rowing gold:**
The double sculls event
produced a surprise win
for the Dutchmen Roland
Florijn (left) and Nicolas
Rienks. They defeated
Switzerland by 1.46 seconds.
The Soviet Union took the
bronze. Florijn and Rienks
were Holland's only medal
providers in the rowing
competitions at Seoul.

7 **Italian boat wins:** In the
coxed pairs, the Italians Carmine
(left) and Giuseppe (middle)
Abbagnale successfully defended
their 1984 Olympic title. On the
right is cox Giuseppe di Capua.
The silver medal was taken by the
East Germans, with the bronze
going to the British team.
Carmine and Giuseppe's brother
Agusto was in the winning
Italian quadruple sculls team.

1 Perfect presentation: In the rhythmic gymnastics event, Marina Lobach (URS) gave an immaculate display. In the all-round competition, she won the gold medal, ahead of Adriana Dunavska (BUL) and her compatriot Alexandra Timoshenko.

2 Soviet superiority: With five medals under his belt, Vladimir Artemov was the Games' most successful gymnast. He won golds in the parallel bars and horizontal bar, and the individual and team combined exercises events; and a silver in the floor event.

3 Dressage win: Nicole Uphoff (FRG) picked up the gold medal, ahead of Margitt Otto-Crepin (FRA) and Christine Stückelberger (SUI). Uphoff won a gold in the team event.

4 On his way to gold: The New Zealander Mark Todd, on Charisma, coped best with the demanding circuit to successfully defend his 1984 three-day-event Olympic title, beating the Britons Ian Stark and Virginia Leng.

5 Chinese triumph: All medals in the women's table tennis singles went to China: Chen Jing (pictured) took gold, Li Huifeng the silver, and Jiao Zhimin the bronze.

6 Korean 1-2: The men's table tennis singles title went to Yoo Nam Kyu ahead of team-mate Kim Ki Taik.

7 Men's saber final: This was won by Jean-François

Lamour (FRA, right) over Janusz Olech (POL, left).

8 **Flood of medals:** Svetlana Boginskaya (URS) won the horse vault and was in the winning Soviet combined exercises team. She also won a silver and a bronze.

9 **The favorite wins:** Daniela Silivas (ROM) became a triple champion at Seoul. In the balance beam event, she won ahead of Elena Shushunova (URS).

10 **Doubling up:** Christa Luding-Rothenburger (GDR, right,) the Olympic 1,000-meter speed skating champion at the Calgary Winter Games, won a silver medal in the sprint cycling event, having been defeated by Erika Salumäe (URS, left).

11 **Dutch gold medal:** Eventual winner Monique Knol (HOL, No. 32) leads the pack in the women's road race.

12 **Tennis back:** The first Olympic men's full-medal tournament for 64 years was won by Miloslav Mecir (TCH).

13 **Steffi's gold:** The West German tennis ace Steffi Graf won the women's singles, beating Gabriela Sabatini (ARG).

14 **West German success:** Sabine Bau (left, silver), Anja Fichtel (middle, gold), and Zita Funkenhauser (right, bronze) celebrate their medals in the individual foil event – and gold in the team event.

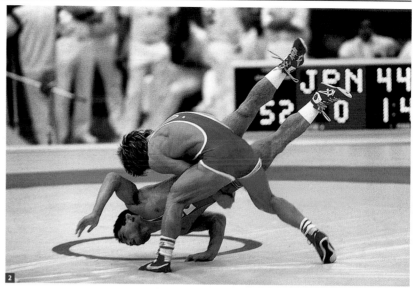

1 **USSR leading nation:** In the super-heavyweight wrestling category, Alexander Karelin (URS) took the gold medal, ahead of Rangel Guerovski (BUL) and Tomas Johansson (SWE). The USSR clinched four gold medals, one silver medal, and a bronze in the Greco-Roman competitions, as well as four golds, three silvers, and two bronze medals in the freestyle events, thus becoming the most successful nation in the wrestling competitions.

2 **Norwegian win:** Jon Rönningen (blue top) won the flyweight wrestling (Greco-Roman style) final against Atsuji Miyahara of Japan.

3 **Maske is champion:** Henry Maske (GDR, right) beat Egerton Marcus (CAN, left) to win the middleweight boxing gold. Following German reunification, he pursued a professional career and became world light-heavyweight champion in 1993.

4 **Turkish delight:** With a lift of 755lb (342.5kg), the weightlifter Nahim Süleymanoglu (TUR) secured gold in the featherweight contest, ahead of Stefan Topourov (BUL, 688¾lb/ 312.5kg) and Ye Huanming (CHN, 633¾lb/287.5kg).

5 **Lewis leads:** Lennox Lewis won the super-heavyweight boxing gold for Canada, to which he emigrated as a child. Lewis later became the first British-born world heavyweight champion this century.

6 **First win for 68 years:** For the first time since 1920, Great Britain took the gold medal in the men's hockey tournament, beating West Germany 3-1 in the final. Holland took the bronze medal. The women's tournament was won by Australia.

7 **Soviet champions:** In the final of the soccer tournament (pictured here) a winning goal in extra time gave the USSR victory over Brazil. This was the Soviets' first football gold medal since 1956. In the third-place play off for the bronze medal, the West German team defeated Italy 3-1.

8 **Scintillating volleyball:** The USSR lost the final in four sets (15-13, 10-15, 4-15, and 8-15) to the United States. In the women's tournament, the Soviet team eventually beat Peru to win 10-15, 12-15, 15-13, 15-7, 17-15.

9 **Medal ceremony:** The Olympic small-bore rifle (prone) champion at Seoul was Miroslav Varga (TCH, middle). The Korean Cha Yuong Chul (right) took silver and Attila Zahonyi (HUN) secured bronze.

10 **Shooting star:** Silvia Sperber (FRG) defeated Vessela Lecheva (BUL) and Valentina Cherkassova (URS) in the small-bore rifle (three positions). She also took a silver medal behind Irina Chilova (URS) in the air rifle competition.

Albertville

With the award of the XVI Winter Games, France joined the USA in the exclusive club of three-time hosts: in 1924, it had been Chamonix; in 1968, Grenoble; in 1992, it was to be Albertville.

ALBERTVILLE'S SUCCESSFUL BID TO stage the Winter Olympics had been inspired by the French triple Olympic skiing champion of 1968, Jean-Claude Killy. He was chairman of the organizing committee, which also included the politician Michele Barnier. With support from the French government, Killy wanted to stimulate the economic development of the Savoy region, an area whose winter sports and tourism potential had been largely untapped. The "Olympic venture" was paid for through sponsoring contracts, the sale of exclusive television broadcasting rights to a US television network, as well as through license agreements that declared certain companies to be "official suppliers."

During the preparatory stage, there was increasing criticism about the decision to spread the competitions over 12 different venues. Additionally, extra construction work led to protests from environmentalists. As a result, the IOC president announced the Committee's future intention to allow certain competitions within a Games to take place in different regions or countries if it meant that such a move would decrease the chances of damage to the environment.

The main venue at Albertville saw all the athletes from the 64 participating nations convene only for the opening and closing ceremonies. The results of the political changes in Central and Eastern Europe were clearly noticeable during the nations' parade at the opening ceremony. Lithuania competed under its own flag for the first time since 1928; likewise, Estonia and Latvia for the first time since 1936. In addition, competitors from other parts of the former Soviet Union formed a team that went under the name of the Unified Team (EUN). For the first time in 28 years, athletes

A French Celebration
The official logo of the XVI Winter Olympics held in Albertville features the colors of the French national flag beneath the stylized Olympic flame.

from all over Germany were reunited in one team for the Winter Olympics.

For Albertville, the Winter Olympic program was augmented by short track speed skating and freestyle skiing on the moguls slope. With her three gold and two silver medals, the Nordic skier Lyubov Yegorova (EUN) was the most successful female athlete of the Games. Her team-mate Raisa Smetanina crowned her career with a gold medal as part of the relay team. The 39-year-old had picked up ten medals in a total of five Olympic Games.

After having won the bronze medal in 1984 and the silver medal in 1988, the Russian ice dancing pair of Marina Klimova and Sergey Ponomarenko clinched their first Olympic title with a dazzling display on the ice. With Bart Veldkamp's success over 10,000 meters, the Netherlands celebrated their first men's Olympic speed-skating title since Piet Kleine's Olympic-record-breaking triumph at Innsbruck in 1976.

Björn Again and Again
The Nordic skiing specialist, Björn Daehlie of Norway, took gold medals in the new combined styles event (10 kilometers in the classical style and 15 kilometers freestyle), in the 50-kilometer cross-country freestyle, and with the 4 x 10-kilometer relay team. He also took a silver medal in the 30-kilometer classical.

Norwegian Triple
The Norwegian Vegard Ulvang won three gold medals in Nordic skiing events over 10 kilometers (classical), 30 kilometers (classical), and with the Norwegian 4 x 10-kilometer relay team.

Success on the Piste
There was double success for Petra Kronberger. The Austrian won both the slalom and the Alpine combined, the latter ahead of her compatriot Anita Wachter (seen left).

Finn Wins
Ski jumper Toni Nieminen of Finland won two gold medals in the big hill (90-meter) and team events. He added a bronze medal in the small hill (70-meter) event.

Full Marks
Double Olympic biathlon champion Mark Kirchner (GER) won the 10-kilometers and added a second gold medal as part of the German 4 x 7.5-kilometer relay team. Over 20 kilometers, he took second place behind Yevgeni Redkin (EUN).

1 Opening ceremony: 2,500 performers present a stunning "festival of the senses."

2 Next Games in 1994: During the closing ceremony, Viking ships prepare for Lillehammer 1994.

3 16-year-old wins: Using the V-style technique, Toni Nieminen (FIN) won the big hill event, ahead of Martin Höllwarth and Heinz Kuttin (both AUT).

4 Double win for Austria: On the small hill, Ernst Vettori beat his Austrian compatriot Martin Höllwarth.

5 Norwegian success: Vegard Ulvang on his way to gold in the 30-kilometer cross-country event.

6 French domination: In the Nordic combined discipline, Fabrice Guy (FRA, left) picked up the gold medal.

7 Gold medal for Italy: Stefania Belmondo (ITA) won the 30-kilometer event, ahead of Lyubov Yegorova and Yelena Wälbe (both EUN).

8 Japanese favorites: Japan's victory over Norway and Austria in the Nordic combined team event came as no surprise to the experts. The picture shows Japanese anchorman Kenji Ogiwara.

9 Alpine surprise: Having never won a world cup event before, the Austrian Patrick Ortlieb picked up a surprise gold in the downhill at Albertville.

10 Most successful biathlete: Mark Kirchner of Germany won two gold medals and a silver to become the most successful biathlete at Albertville.

11 Tomba's triumph: Alberto Tomba successfully defended his Olympic title in the giant slalom.

12 Austria celebrates: With two gold medals under her belt, the Austrian Petra Kronberger was the most successful Alpine skier at the Games. She took the slalom and combined events.

13 Outsider wins: Christian Jagge (NOR) won a surprise gold medal in the men's slalom.

14 Norway's medals: Kjetil Andre Aamodt demonstrated his strength by taking the gold medal in the Super G and the bronze medal in the giant slalom.

15 Winning trio: Katja Seizinger (GER, left) celebrated after taking the bronze medal in the Super G, behind Deborah Compagnoni (ITA, middle) and Carole Merle (FRA, right).

1 Ice dance win: After their bronze medal in Sarajevo in 1984 and silver medal in Calgary in 1988, it was third time lucky for the favorites Marina Klimova and Sergei Ponomarenko of St. Petersburg. They took the ice dance gold medal in Albertville, and left Isabelle and Paul Duchesnay (FRA) trailing in second place.

2 Germans on ice: Gunda Niemann, Germany's most successful speed skater, won two gold medals (3,000- and 5,000-meters) and a silver (1,500-meters). Further German successes were Jacqueline Börner's gold over 1,500 meters, Heike Warnicke's silvers over 3,000 and 5,000 meters, and the bronzes won by Christa Luding, Monique Garbrecht, and Claudia Pechstein's over 500, 1,000, and 5,000 meters respectively.

3 Favorite clinches title: The women's world figure skating champion Kristi Yamaguchi (USA) beat Midori Ito (JPN) and Nancy Kerrigan (USA) to win the gold. The

European champion, Surya Bonaly (FRA) had to settle for fifth position.

4 Win on old sled: On the luge track, the men had to cope with a 0.78-mile (1,250-meter) run with a gradient of 8.8 percent and a difference in altitude of 360 feet (110 meters). After having difficulties with a new type of sled during preliminary training sessions, the German Georg Hackl started the luge competition with an old sled. His ability shone through as he won the competition and pushed the Austrian duo of Markus Prock and Markus Schmidt into silver and bronze medal positions. In the women's event, sisters Doris (gold) and Angelika Neuner (silver) secured a double win for Austria. Susi Erdmann (GER) finished in third position.

5 Defeated favorites: Stefan Krausse and Jan Behrendt (GER) on their way to the gold medal in the two-seater luge. Favorites Hansjörg Raffl and Norbert Huber (ITA) had to settle for a bronze medal, behind

silver medalists Yves Mankel and Thomas Rudolph (GER).

6 Swiss duo's success: The Olympic champions in the two-man bob were Gustav Weder and Donat Acklin. They picked up a bronze with Lorenz Schindelholz and Curdin Morell in the four-man bob, beaten by the Austrian and German teams.

7 Ice hockey enthusiasm: Despite the collapse of the Soviet Union, coach Viktor Tikhonov ensured that the new-look EUN team were a gold-medal-winning side. In the final, they beat Canada 3-1 and gave a Russian-based team their sixth ice hockey gold out of the last seven Olympics. Next came the Canadian team, who clinched their first Olympic ice hockey medal since 1968. The Czechs took the bronze medal.

8 Exciting jumps: The exhibition sport of freestyle skiing (moguls) was introduced for the first time, and enthralled the spectators. Curling was once again a demonstration sport.

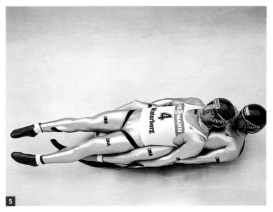

Barcelona

A crowd of 100,000 spectators in Barcelona's stadium, plus a television audience of two billion, watched one of the most spectacular Olympic opening ceremonies of all time.

Dream Team
In basketball no team stood a chance against the United States. Earvin "Magic" Johnson was the star player at Barcelona.

THESE TURNED OUT TO BE THE Olympic Games of the Spanish IOC president, Juan Antonio Samaranch, who had managed to bring the 1992 Games to his home region of Catalonia. Being an advocate of the commercialization of sport, he expressed his gratitude to the Games' sponsors at the end of the Barcelona celebration. The IOC registered millions of dollars in revenue from these Olympics, partly through the sale of television broadcasting rights. However, the IOC president's stance was not greeted with universal approval. Many athletes complained that the start times of several events were arranged to suit the TV and advertising industries.

Christie Wins for Britain
After taking silver in Seoul in 1988, British sprinter Linford Christie achieved his greatest triumph in winning the 100-meter final. In 1986 and again in 1990 he had been European champion over this distance.

Besides the splendid cultural activities that accompanied the Games, the modernization and construction work carried out on sports facilities and in other key areas of the city attracted praise. The neoclassical Olympic Stadium on Montjuic and the velodrome were refurbished, while the 1,700-seat Sant Jordi Sports Palace (named for the Catalonian patron saint) was built from scratch.

The 1992 Olympic Games were significant in that they marked the emergence, or re-emergence, of a number of teams onto the world sporting stage, following the recent waves of political change in Europe and elsewhere. The first appearance since 1964 of a pan-German team was greeted with pleasure. A similarly warm reception was extended to South Africa, which was welcomed back to the Olympic Games having last competed in 1960, in response to the government's reform program. Despite the far-reaching upheaval in the former Soviet Union, a Unified Team (EUN) was again fielded by the Commonwealth of Independent States. In the Balkans, meanwhile, the bloody fight for Tito's legacy dragged on, and Yugoslavia, Bosnia-Herzegovina, Slovenia, and

Spanish Summer
The official poster of the XXV Summer Olympics echoes the style of the Spanish painter Joán Miro.

Croatia each sent its own team to Barcelona.

As for the sports, there were major upsets in some of the individual events. In the women's 100-meter hurdles, for example, Paraskevi Patoulidou became the first Greek sportswoman to claim an Olympic gold, and in the 800-meters, Holland's Ellen van Langen could hardly believe that she had won. There were also triumphs over adversity. Gail Devers (USA) overcame serious illness to win the 100-meters. Only a year earlier she had been suffering from Graves' disease, and there had been fears that she might have to have a leg amputated.

The single most successful individual participant at the Barcelona Olympics was the gymnast Vitali Sherbo (EUN), with six gold medals. He was followed in the medal list by swimmers Yevgeni Sadovi (EUN) and Krisztina Egerszegi (HUN), with three golds each. The subject of drugs was again on the agenda, and both China and Cuba were criticized for having refused to take part in international drugs testing prior to the Games.

Sherbo's Song
During the five individual medal ceremonies for Vitali Sherbo, even though he was a member of the Unified Team, the flag of Belorussia was raised and the national anthem of the republic played for the first time ever at the Olympic Games.

Drechsler Delighted
Heike Drechsler of Germany, one of the most successful track-and-field athletes of the early 1990s, emerged as the winner in the long jump.

Triple Gold
Krisztina Egerszegi of Hungary, world champion and world record holder in the 100- and 200-meter backstroke, and reigning European champion for the 400-meter freestyle, confirmed her status as a favorite in Barcelona with three gold medals.

1 **Mystical narratives:** Among the extravagant tableaux that characterized the Barcelona Games' opening ceremony was the battle between humans and an ocean full of monsters (shown here). Other highlights were performances by Spanish opera stars Teresa Berganza, Montserrat Caballe, Jose Carreras, and Placido Domingo. A further treat for the audience was the appearance of the queen of Flamenco, Christina Hoyos, on horseback.

2 **Linford is the fastest:** Britain's Linford Christie won the men's 100-meter final, ahead of Namibia's Frankie Fredericks (who also picked up the silver medal in the 200-meters) and the American Dennis Mitchell. The oldest man by four years to win this sprint title, Christie added the

world championship to his collection the following year.

3 **Gail's force:** Gail Devers (USA, right) wins the women's 100-meters, beating Jamaica's Juliet Cuthbert (second from the right) and Irina Privalova (EUN, left) by one-hundredth of a second. Gwen Torrence (USA) and Jamaica's Merlene Ottey (second and third from the left) are left empty-handed. Devers's hopes of a second title were dashed when she fell in the 100-meter hurdles, leaving Paraskevi Patoulidou to claim the first gold medal ever for a Greek woman athlete.

4 **Golden Sally:** In a time of 53.23 seconds, Britain's Sally Gunnell (right) wins the 400-meter hurdles. In 1993, Gunnell won the 400-meter hurdles world title, and in 1994 she took the European and Commonwealth titles as well.

5 **Long-distance scandal:** In an extraordinary finish to the 10,000-meters, the Kenyan athlete Richard Chelimo (left) was obstructed by Morocco's Hammou Boutaib, who had already been lapped. Khalid Skah (also Morocco, right), who was lying in second place, went on to cross the finishing line first. Skah was initially disqualified, but later declared Olympic champion. The silver went to Chelimo, who was, however, celebrated as the moral victor.

6 **New record in hurdles:** American Kevin Young won the 400-meter hurdles in 46.78 seconds, breaking the nine-year-old world record set by Ed Moses, and becoming the first athlete to break 47 seconds for the event. Young was followed in by Winthrop Graham of Jamaica and Britain's Kriss Akabusi.

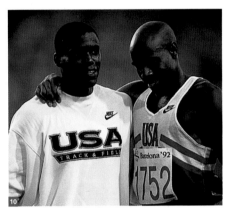

7 **Queen of track and field:** America's Jackie Joyner-Kersee was unbeatable in the heptathlon. With 7,044 points, the 30-year-old decisively relegated Irina Belova (EUN, 6,845 points) and Germany's Sabine Braun (6,649 points) to second and third place. Jackie is the sister of the 1984 triple-jump champion, Al Joyner.

8 **Czech cashes in:** Czech athlete Robert Zmelik secured the decathlon gold medal at the end of two days of battle in the heat, amassing 8,611 points. US champion Dave Johnson was involved in an incident during this event. Although he overstepped the base line when putting the shot, Johnson was not disqualified but was given a fourth attempt. He went on to win bronze with 8,309 points. In the meantime, Spain's Antonio Penalver gave the home crowd

plenty to cheer about, taking the silver with 8,412 points.

9 **Lithuania's first gold:** Lithuania had not been represented at the Summer Olympics since 1928 and had never won a medal. Discus thrower Romas Ubartas – who had won the 1986 European title and the 1988 Olympic silver medal on behalf of the USSR – changed all that, bringing home gold from Barcelona.

10 **First jump wins:** No other athlete could match the 28' 5¼" (8.67 meters) that Carl Lewis (USA, left) achieved in his first jump during the long jump finals. Thus Lewis got his own back for his defeat by fellow American Mike Powell (right) at the 1991 world championships in Tokyo. In that competition, Powell had beaten Bob Beamon's 1968 world record of 29' 2½" (8.90

meters) by two inches (5 cm). In Barcelona, Powell jumped into second place, with Joe Greene coming third to ensure a US clean sweep. Gold in the long jump was at least some consolation for the legendary Lewis, who had failed to gain an individual sprint place with the US Olympic team.

11 **High jump nail-biter:** Heike Henkel (GER) was faced with an early departure from the high jump after twice failing to clear 6' 5½" (1.97 meters). But unlike her great rival, the Bulgarian Stefka Kostadinova (who set the world record in 1987 and won the 1988 Olympic silver medal), Henkel succeeded in her final attempt. She went on to jump 6' 7¼" (2.02 meters) to win the event. Second was Romania's Galina Astafei, while the Cuban Joanet Quintero took the bronze medal home.

1 Team spirit: The EUN swimming team won the 4 x 200-meter freestyle relay ahead of Sweden and the USA.

2 Star swimmer: With three golds in the 100- and 200-meter backstroke and the 400-meter individual medley, Krisztina Egerszegi was the Games' most successful female swimmer.

3 Three gold medals: Yevgeni Sadovyi (EUN) won the 200- and 400-meter freestyle, and picked up a third gold in the 4 x 200-meter freestyle relay.

4 Medley specialist: Tamas Darnyi (HUN) retained his Olympic titles in the 200- and 400-meter medley events.

5 Surprise win: Dagmar Hase was the only German swimmer to win a gold medal. In the 400-meter freestyle, she defeated the title holder Janet Evans (USA). She added two silver medals – in the 200-meter backstroke and the 4 x 100-meter medley relay.

6 Winning twins: The synchronized swimming duet event was won by Karen and Sarah Josephson (USA). Penny and Vicky Vilagos (CAN) were second, and Fumiko Kuno and Aki Takayama (JPN) third.

7 Scintillating final: The Italian water polo team proudly present their gold medals. The longest final in the history of the Olympics, against the host nation Spain, was decided by a goal shortly before the end of the sixth period of extra time that gave Italy a 9-8 victory.

8 Wildwater renaissance: For the first time since its Olympic debut in Munich, slalom canoeing was in the Olympic program. In the Canadian pairs, the Americans Scott Strausbaugh (pictured front) and Joe Jacobi won, ahead of Miroslav Simek and Jiri Rohan (TCH) and the French pair of Franck Adisson and Wilfrid Forgues.

9 Title for Great Britain: The British rowers Steven Redgrave (left) and Matthew Pinsent are exhausted but happy, having won the Olympic coxless pairs title.

10 And another British rowing victory: Cox Garry Herbert (right) and oarsmen Jonathan and Greg Searle celebrate their victory in the coxed pairs.

11 Chinese domination: After Gao Min and Fu Mingxia had captured the women's springboard and highboard titles respectively, Sun Shuwei (pictured here) claimed a third gold for China with his win in the men's highboard event. In the men's springboard, Tan Liangde had to settle for silver.

12 French sailing gold: Yves Loday and Nicolas Henard demonstrated their invincibility in the Tornado class. Randy Smyth and Keith Notary (USA) and Mitch Booth and John Forbes (AUS) took second and third places respectively.

13 Fastest surfer: Windsurfing was enjoying its third Olympic appearance at the Barcelona Games. In the Lechner A-390 class, Franck David of France (pictured here) defeated the American Mike Gebhardt and Lars Kleppich of Australia.

1 Perfect program: The Chinese gymnast Li Lu won the asymmetrical bars with a mark of 10, and was also second in the balance beam event.

2 Reward for perfection: Alexandra Timoshenko of the Unified Team presented a demanding program in the rhythmic gymnastics to earn herself the gold medal.

3 Sole medal: Trent Dimas's win in the horizontal bars, ahead of Grigori Misyutin (EUN) and Andreas Wecker (GER) gave the US men's gymnastics team its only medal.

4 Celebrated gymnast: Vitali Sherbo (EUN) underlined his superiority by winning gold medals in the rings, pommel horse, horse vault, and parallel bars, as well as in the individual and team combined exercises.

5 More Unified success: Tatyana Lyssenko picked up gold medals in the balance beam and team events, plus a bronze in the horse vault.

6 Floor triumph: Lavinia Milosovici (ROM) was the deserved gold medal winner in the floor exercises event.

7 Gold medal for Estonia: In the 1,000-meter sprint, Erika Salumäe (EST) defeated Annett Neumann (GER) and Ingrid Haringa (HOL).

8 Boardman first: Britain's Chris Boardman won the 4,000-meter individual pursuit, ahead of Jens Lehmann (GER) and Gary Anderson (NZL).

9 Home win: José Moreno Perinan (ESP) won the 1,000-meter time trial with Shane Kelly (AUS) and Erin Hartwell (USA) coming second and third respectively.

10 Fencing win: France's Philippe Omnes celebrates his individual foil gold medal win.

11 Italian title: The world champion in the foil, Giovanna Trillini, also clinched the Olympic title. She won a second gold as part of the victorious Italian foil team.

12 Shooting star: Michael Jakosits (GER) claimed the gold medal in the running game target event, ahead of Anatoli Asrabayev (EUN) and Lubos Racansky (TCH).

13 Chinese accuracy: In the skeet shooting competition, Shan Zhang (CHN) defeated all comers. The second-placed Juan Jorge Giha Yarur (PER, left) and the bronze medalist Bruno Rossetti of Italy (right) congratulate her.

14 French win: The archery title was won by Sebastien Flute (FRA) from Chung Jae-Hun (KOR). Britain's Simon Terry took the bronze medal.

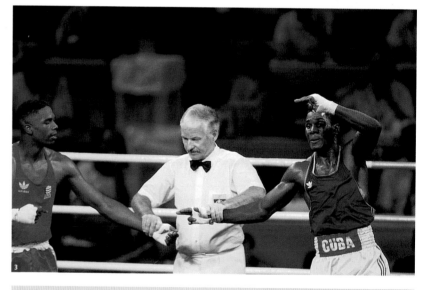

1 Strongest athlete: In the super-heavyweight weightlifting category (for lifters of over 242½lb/110kg bodyweight), Alexander Kurlovich (EUN) won the gold medal ahead of his teammate Leonid Taranenko and the German Manfred Nerlinger.

2 Jubilation in front of home crowd: Spain's Miriam Blasco could hardly believe that she was the new Olympic judo champion in the lightweight category.

3 Cubans dominate: Cuban boxers clinched Olympic titles in seven out of twelve weight categories. At middleweight, Ariel Hernandez (right) won the gold, with America's Chris Byrd (left) taking silver.

4 Featherweight gold: In the final, Andreas Tews (GER, right) was too good for Faustino Reyes (ESP, left).

5 Favorite wins: Hakki Busar (TUR, red shirt) could not prevent the 1989-91 world champion, Maik Bullmann (GER, blue shirt), from claiming the Olympic title in the light-heavyweight category (Greco-Roman style).

6 Light-heavyweight judo: Antal Kovacs (HUN, left) beat Britain's Raymond Stevens (right) to win the gold medal.

7 Wasted home advantage: In the women's doubles final, Arantxa Sanchez-Vicario and Conchita Martinez (ESP) were defeated by the Americans Gigi (left) and Mary Jo (right) Fernandez , 7-5, 2-6, 6-2.

8 Tennis pros at Olympics: The Germans Michael Stich (right) and Boris Becker (left) made early departures from the singles. In the doubles, however, they won the gold, beating

Wayne Ferreira and Piet Norval (RSA), 7-6, 4-6, 7-6, 6-3.

9 **USA defeated:** America's most popular sport, baseball, was introduced to the 1992 Olympic schedule as a gesture toward Atlanta in 1996. However, the USA was represented by a second-choice team and finished fourth behind Cuba, Chinese Taipei, and Japan.

10 **Basketball dream:** No other team stood a chance against the USA's "Dream Team" of National Basketball Association all-stars. In the final, the Croatians were

defeated 117-85.

11 **Badminton's debut:** Indonesian players won both singles titles in the inaugural badminton tournament. Alan Kusuma (pictured here) won the men's, and Susi Susanti took the women's gold medal.

12 **Dressage gold medal for Germany:** The German team of (from left) Klaus Balkenhol, Nicole Uphoff, Monica Theodorescu, and Isabelle Werth claimed the gold medal in dressage. Second and third places went to the Netherlands and the USA respectively.

Lillehammer

Following Oslo's 1952 example, the Norwegian town of Lillehammer tried to organize a Winter Olympics "for everyone." The 16-day celebration took place in a festive atmosphere.

IN 1986, THE OLYMPIC CHARTER, which stipulated that Winter and Summer Games be held in the same year, was changed by the IOC. The Winter and Summer Olympics would now be held alternately every two years. In introducing the two-year interval, officials had envisaged better marketing prospects, partly because television companies had reached their limit under the previous arrangement. They could not attract the amount of advertising they needed in order to pay for Olympic television broadcasting rights twice a year – an outlay of millions of dollars. However, from now on, the Winter Games would fall in the same year as soccer's World Cup finals.

Before its appointment as the site of the XVII Winter Games, Lillehammer was a town of 21,000 inhabitants, hardly known outside Norway. Within four years, however, the organizers had turned it into a first-rate Olympic site. They modernized existing sports facilities, built new ones from scratch where necessary, and generated the infrastructure required to stage a modern Olympic Games. The Norwegians were particularly concerned about environmental aspects. Future usage was a major consideration in the siting of buildings and in their architecture. Excessive tree-felling was avoided.

The political changes in South Africa and its readmission to the IOC allowed South African competitors to participate in a Winter Olympics for the first time in 34 years. Meanwhile, the Unified Team that had taken part at Albertville and Barcelona no longer existed. Instead, teams from Georgia, Russia, Ukraine, and other newly independent former Soviet republics arrived in Norway to compete. Among the 67 teams taking part at Lillehammer was a small one from Bosnia-Herzegovina, whose homeland was in the grip of a bloody civil war.

Logo for Lillehammer
The logo for the XVII Winter Games held in Lillehammer, Norway, was designed by the artist Sarah Rosenbaum.

New competitions included additional short track skating events and the free-style skiing aerials. The women's figure skating attracted most of the media's attention. Before the Games, favorite Nancy Kerrigan, of the USA, had been assaulted by persons believed to be connected with her rival, Tonya Harding. Harding, the 1994 US champion, was nevertheless allowed to take part at Lillehammer, though she did not place. Ukraine's Oksana Bayul eventually won, with Kerrigan finishing second.

The 1,000-meter short track skating event finished in unique fashion. After numerous falls and disqualifications, only the gold (Kim Ki-Hoon, KOR) and silver medals (Chae Ji-Hoon, KOR) were awarded in the usual manner. The bronze went to the winner of the "B" final, Marc Gagnon (CAN), who had, in fact, clocked a faster time than the two Koreans. Italian skier Alberto Tomba augmented his medal collection by winning another slalom silver, bringing his overall tally to five.

Medals Galore
With a total of six gold and three silver medals from her two Olympics, Russian Lyubov Yegorova became one of the most successful female Winter Olympics competitors of all time.

Winning Streak
At her second Olympic Games, the Russian Lyubov Yegorova won three gold medals (5-kilometers, combined pursuit event, and 4 x 5-kilometer relay) and one silver medal (15-kilometers).

High Point
Having won the giant slalom world title in 1985, Markus Wasmeier (GER) crowned his career in Lillehammer with gold medals in the giant slalom and the Super G.

Koss Cruises to Gold
In front of his home crowd, the speed skater Johann Olav Koss won three gold medals – over 1,500, 5,000, and 10,000 meters. In each event, Koss improved on the world record.

Nordic Master
With two gold and two silver medals, Norway's Björn Daehlie emphasized his standing as one of the finest cross-country skiers in the world.

1 **Festival of winter sports:** The opening ceremony of the Lillehammer Games was conducted by King Harald V of Norway. The pageant included local people in national costume driving traditional sleighs, pulled by reindeer.

2 **Joy of victory:** Markus Wasmeier (GER) celebrates his win in the giant slalom, ahead of Urs Kälin (SUI) and Christian Mayer (AUT). The German picked up his second gold medal in the Super G.

3 **"Grande dame" of skiing:** With her slalom win, the Swiss skier Vreni Schneider became the only female Alpine skier to claim three Olympic gold medals, having won the slalom and giant slalom in Calgary. At Lillehammer, she added a silver medal in the combined event and a bronze medal in the giant slalom to her collection.

4 **Comeback to gold:** Having suffered from countless injuries, Diann Roffe (USA) staged a brilliant comeback. She took the super giant slalom (Super G), ahead of the Russian, Svetlana Gladysheva, and Isolde Kostner of Italy.

5 **Three medals for Kazakhstan:** Vladimir Smirnov of the former Soviet republic of Kazakhstan won the gold medal in the 50-kilometer cross-country skiing (classical), and silver medals in the 10-kilometers (classical) and the combined pursuit event.

6 **Most successful male competitor:** By increasing his tally of gold medals to five, the Norwegian skier Björn Daehlie became the most successful male competitor in the history of the Winter Olympics in terms of gold medals. He has also won three silvers.

7 **Alaskan picks up gold medal:** The American Tommy Moe, who lives near Anchorage, Alaska, won the men's downhill, ahead of Kjetil Andre Aamodt of Norway and Canada's Edward Podvinsky.

8 **Five celebrations:** The Italian skier Manuela Di Centa (left, with teammate Stefania Belmondo) secured the gold medal in the 30-kilometers. She also won the gold in the 15-kilometers, silver medals in the 5-kilometers and the combined pursuit, and a bronze in the 4 x 5- kilometer relay.

9 **Double victory for Norway:** Espen Bredesen on his way to the gold medal in the small hill ski jump. The silver medal was clinched by teammate Lasse Ottesen, ahead of Dieter Thoma (GER).

10 **Bédard dominates the biathlon:** In the 7.5-kilometer event, Canada's Myriam Bédard defeated Svetlana Paramygina (BLR) and Valentina Zerba (UKR). Bédard also won the 15-kilometer biathlon, ahead of Anne Briand Bouthiaux (FRA) and Uschi Disl (GER).

11 **Happy biathletes:** The German 4 x 7.5-kilometer biathlon relay team of Ricco Gro, Frank Luck, Mark Kirchner, and Sven Fischer celebrate their Olympic victory over Russia and France.

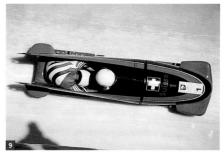

1 Favorite wins: Russia's Alexei Urmanov claimed the Olympic figure skating title, ahead of Elvis Stojko (CAN) and Philippe Candeloro (FRA).

2 Gold medal for Ukraine: Oksana Bayul secured the Olympic women's figure skating title. America's Nancy Kerrigan and the Chinese skater Lu Chen were placed second and third respectively.

3 Russians take ice dance gold: Oksana Grichuk and Yevgeni Platov (RUS, middle) were the ice dance gold medalists. Jayne Torville and Christopher Dean (right) took the bronze medal, behind the second-placed Russian pair, the world title holders, Maya Usova and Alexander Shulin (left). The British pair, who had won the Olympic title in Sarajevo in 1984, staged a marvelous comeback after ten years away from competition to become European champions earlier in the year. The favorites with the crowd, they were disappointed not to have come first at Lillehammer.

4 Most successful female US athlete: At her fourth Olympics, the speed skater Bonnie Blair won the 500-meters and 1,000-meters to take her gold medal tally to five, and make her the most successful female US Winter Olympic athlete. In the 500-meter sprint, she defeated Susan Auch (CAN) and Franziska Schenk (GER), while Anke Baier (GER) and the Chinese Ye Quiaobo had to concede Blair's superiority over 1,000-meters.

5 Gold medal for Sweden: The Swedish ice hockey team were clearly elated about winning the Olympic tournament. In the final, the Swedes defeated the Canadians 3-2, to record their first Olympic ice hockey title win. Finland took the bronze.

6 Spectacular performer: The Canadian trick skier Jean-Luc Brassard became the new Olympic moguls champion, ahead of the Russian Sergei Shupletsov and Edgar Grospiron of France.

7 Italian double victory: Kurt Brugger and Wilfried Huber (ITA) claimed the gold medal in the two-man luge. The event took place on the Hunderfossen ice track, which has an average gradient of 8.5 percent. Their fellow Italians, Hansjörg Raffl and Norbert Huber, won the silver medal, ahead of the German team of Stefan Krausse and Jan Behrendt.

8 Commanding win: The Italian luge tobogganist Gerda Weissensteiner turned out to be unbeatable. Her 3:15.517 put her clear of Germany's Susi Erdmann (3:16.276) and Andrea Tagwerker of Austria (3:16.652).

9 Swiss bob team win: The Switzerland I team, of Gustav Weder (right) and Donat Acklin, (left) on their way to the two-man bobsled gold medal. The silver was picked up by Switzerland II (Reto Götschi/ Guido Acklin), ahead of Italy I (Günther Huber/Stefano Ticci).

10 Medals in short track: Britain's Nicholas Gooch (leading) won a bronze medal in the 500-meter short track speed skating behind Chae Ji-Hoon of Korea and Mirko Vuillermin of Italy. The Koreans dominated the short track, winning gold in four of the six events. In addition to Chae Ji-Hoon's success, Kim Ki-Hoon won the men's 1,000-meters, Chun Lee-Kyung the women's 1,000-meters and the Koreans also won the women's 3,000-meter relay. Korea also picked up a silver and a bronze.

Atlanta

The Games to celebrate the centenary of the renaissance of the Olympic ideal took place not in Athens, venue of the first Olympic Games of modern times, but in the United States at Atlanta, Georgia.

The World's Greatest Athlete
America's Michael Johnson became the first man ever to win both the 200-meters and the 400-meters at the same Games after the track program was altered to allow him to run in both events.

PERHAPS THE FACT THAT THE terrorist bomb that exploded in Centennial Park, the festive heart of the Atlanta Olympics, is not the abiding memory of the Games is the greatest testimony of all to the spectacle that was the Centennial Olympics. These 1996 Games will be remembered as the Olympics at which sport conquered all, even the efforts of a terrorist to spoil the world's party. Centennial Olympic Park, 21 acres of corporate tents and sponsored soundstages, was the people's village, a place where sports fans from around the world went to have a great time. Three days after the bombing, as soon as the park was reopened, the people came back and it was as if they had never been away.

But the Olympics are about nothing if not athletic endeavor, and once again in many events the competitors went faster, higher, and proved they were stronger than ever before, as the Olympic motto *Citius, Altius, Fortius* enjoins them to do.

Initially, there were murmurs of discontent when the IOC decided to alter the sequence of events on the track so that America's Michael Johnson could attempt a 200-meter and 400-meter double, something no man had ever done successfully before. But no one was complaining after Johnson not only completed the double but did so in the manner less of an athlete and more of a god. His world record in the 200-meters, 19.32 seconds, was a time that most experts thought would not be run until well into the next century.

Surely only Superman could upstage that. And he did, in the shape of King Carl. Carl Lewis, that is, who won his ninth Olympic gold medal in four Games by taking the long jump title.

But that was not all. There was drama in the weightlifting, in which Russia's Andrei Chemerkin's world record lift caused the man who finished in second

Atlantan Adventure
The Atlanta logo featured a stylized flame emitting stars. The number 100 referred to the centenary of the modern Olympics.

place – the German Ronny Weller – to faint with shock. There was the opening ceremony, at which one of the greatest Olympians ever, Muhammad Ali, movingly lit the flame, hampered by the shaking hands inflicted on him by Parkinson's syndrome.

And there was the gymnastics. When America's Kerri Strug stepped up to take her vault in the team event, everyone in the hall thought the United States needed at least 9.6 to win gold. In her initial effort, Strug landed badly, twisting her ankle and leaving her leg numb. But despite her injury, the 4 ft 9 in (1.44 m) 18-year-old bravely took a second vault, for which she scored 9.712. Later it was revealed that the Americans would have won without her score. But the hearts of sports fans throughout the world had been won over. Her coach had to pick Strug up and carry her to the medal podium. That is the abiding memory of the 1996 Atlanta Olympic Games.

American Gold Rush
United States swimmer Amy van Dyken won four swimming gold medals – two in individual races and two in relay events.

Spanish Success
After failing to win his sixth Tour de France title only weeks earlier, cyclist Miguel Indurain (ESP) made up for his disappointment by winning gold in the inaugural Olympic road time trial.

Ireland's Golden Girl
Irish swimmer Michelle Smith won three gold medals and one bronze to become the most successful individual swimmer of the Games.

Four for Redgrave
Coxless pairs rower Steve Redgrave's fourth gold medal in successive Games led to many hailing him as Britain's greatest ever Olympian.

1 Magic moment: In a moving opening ceremony, former world heavyweight boxing champion Muhammad Ali, here with former US swimming gold medalist Janet Evans, lit the Olympic flame.

2 The time, the race: America's Michael Johnson won the 200-meters in a world record time of 19.32. Most experts thought nobody would run that fast until at least 2050.

3 US relay gold: Atlantan Gwen Torrence anchors the US women's 4 x 100-meter team to victory in her home town.

4 Russian surprise: Russia's Svetlana Masterkova was the surprise winner of both the 800-meters and 1500-meters.

5 World's fastest man: Donovan Bailey (CAN) wins the 100-meters in a world record 9.84 after defending champion Linford Christie was disqualified after two false starts.

6 French double: José-Marie Perec (FRA) won the women's 200-meters and the 400-meters.

7 Distance king: Ethiopia's Haile Gebrselassie won 10,000-meter gold after a classic race in which Kenya's Paul Tergat, who was second, tried all he could to wear him down.

8 All-round best: Dan O'Brien of the United States won the decathlon to ease the disappointment of not making the US team four years earlier.

9 Close call: American sprinter Gail Devers retained her 100-meter title by 0.005 seconds over her archrival, Jamaica's Merlene Ottey.

10 German win: Astrid Kumbernuss won the women's shot. She beat China's Sun Xinmei (left) and Russia's Irina Khudorozhkina into second and third places respectively.

11 Nine and out: American legend Carl Lewis laid claim to being the greatest Olympian ever by winning the long jump to take his tally of golds to nine.

12 Successful favorite: Jan Zelezny of the Czech Republic won the javelin by almost two and a half feet.

1 Four for Ireland: Michelle Smith surprised the world by winning three gold medals and a bronze in individual swimming events. It meant she individually won more gold medals in one Games than any Irish team in the history of the Olympics.

2 Relay gold: The United States won the women's 4 x 100-meter relay ahead of Russia in second and China in third.

3 Peerless Popov: Alexander Popov (RUS) proved he was still the world's greatest sprint swimmer by retaining the 50-meter and 100-meter freestyle swimming titles. Popov also picked up two silvers as a member of Russian relay teams.

4 US rules the pool: The United States were the leading force in the women's swimming,

winning seven of the sixteen titles on offer and grabbing five second places. Amy van Dyken (pictured) was the most successful US woman swimmer, with individual golds in the 50-meter freestyle and the 100-meter butterfly and two wins with relay teams.

5 Synchronized success: Not only did the United States have the speed, they also had the grace. A great performance by the United States synchronized swimming team saw them lift the gold medal ahead of Canada and Japan.

6 America's most vaunted: Gary Hall Jr.'s two team gold medals and two individual silver medals made him the most successful United States man in the pool and put him in the top five medal winners at Atlanta.

7 Flying high: Russia's Denis Pankratov did the double in the men's butterfly by winning gold in both the 100-meter and 200-meter races.

8 Diving to defense: China's 18-year-old Fu Mingxia won the women's springboard and highboard diving events by huge margins to successfully defend the titles she first won as a 13-year-old in Barcelona.

9 Thank You, Lord: The captain of the victorious Spanish water polo team offers up a prayer after his team had beaten Croatia in the final. Italy, gold medalists at Barcelona, took the bronze medal.

10 Gold for Oliver: Oliver Fix (GER) on his way to winning the canoe slalom K1 event ahead of Andraz Vehovar of Slovenia.

Fix's compatriot Thomas Becker came third.

11 The joy and the pain: British rowers Matthew Pinsent (left) and Steve Redgrave were both overjoyed and exhausted after winning the coxless pairs. For the British pair, it was a second gold, after Barcelona, and for Redgrave a fourth successive win.

12 Nikolas is top sailboarder: Greece's Nikolas Kaklamanakis came up trumps in the Mistral sailboard competition. The Hong Kong sailboarder Lee Lai-Shan won the women's competition.

13 Dangerous Dane: In the Europe women's yachting event, Denmark's Kristine Roug took gold, with Margit Matthijsse of the Netherlands coming second, and America's Courtney Becker-Dey finishing third.

1 Perfect balance: America's Shannon Miller in action on the balance beam. Her gold medal in this event was one of the most popular among the partisan crowd in the gymnastics hall.

2 America's darling: Brave Kerri Strug is carried to the medal podium by her coach. Despite sustaining serious injury in her first vault in the team gymnastics event, Strug carried on in a bid to see America through to gold. The United States duly triumphed.

3 All-round excellence: China's Li Xiaoshuang was the surprise winner of the men's individual combined exercises gold medal.

4 Boxing clever: Cuba's Felix Savon (right) retained his heavyweight boxing title. Cuban fighters featured in seven of the twelve boxing finals, winning four gold medals.

5 More Cuban joy: Driulis Gonzalez (CUB) beat Korea's Jun Sun-Jong (with head on the ground) to win a bruising encounter in the women's lightweight judo final.

6 Turkish delight: The man known as Pocket Hercules – Turkey's Naim Süleymanoglu – lifted 413 lbs/187kg, more than three times his own bodyweight, to retain the featherweight weightlifting crown.

7 Strongest man in the world: A brilliant competition saw Andrei Chemerkin (RUS) hoist the greatest poundage in history, 573 lbs/260 kg, to beat the already celebrating German Ronny Weller into second place.

8 Red, white, and blue arrows: The United States had a clean sweep in men's archery, winning both the team event and the individual, in which Justin Huish (pictured) took gold.

9 Italy first: Paola Pezzo of Italy won the inaugural women's cross-country cycling event ahead of Alison Sydor (CAN) and America's Susan DiMattei.

10 Point to prove: In fencing, the women's individual épée was contested for the first time. The inaugural winner was France's Laura Flessel (right).

11 Horses for courses: Germany's Ulrich Kirchhoff (left) won gold in both the individual and team jumping competitions.

12 Time traveler: Master cyclist Miguel Indurain of Spain triumphed in the first ever Olympic road time trial.

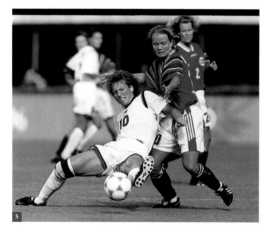

1 **Déja vu:** As at Barcelona, the United States "Dream Team" were victorious in the men's basketball final. In Atlanta, their victims were Yugoslavia, who went down 95-69 after giving the Americans a tough first 30 minutes. Lithuania were third. The American women beat Brazil 111-87 to complete a US basketball double.

2 **US tennis triumph:** America's Andre Agassi, whose father boxed for Iran at the 1948 and 1952 Games, won the men's singles gold medal, beating Spain's Sergi Bruguera 6-2, 6-3, 6-1 in the final. India's Leander Paes took the bronze to bring India its first medal of any kind since 1980 and its first individual medal since the 1952 Games in Helsinki.

3 **Lindsay's turn:** Lindsay Davenport conquered Arantxa Sanchez Vicario of Spain 7-6, 6-2 in the women's singles final. Jana Novotna (CZE) was third. Like Agassi, Davenport comes from a family of Olympians. Her father played volleyball for the United States in Mexico City in 1968. The United States also won the women's doubles through Mary Jo and Gigi Fernandez.

4 **African soccer gold:** Nigeria became the first African team to win a major soccer tournament when they beat Argentina 3-2 in the Olympic final with goals from Celestine Babayaro, Daniel Amokachi, and Emmanuel Amunike. Their battle for gold was hard fought: in the semi-final they faced the favorites, Brazil.

5 **US women's soccer win:** The Atlanta Games witnessed the debut of women's soccer as an Olympic sport. The United States (in white here against bronze medalists Norway) beat China 2-1 in the final thanks to goals from Tiffeny Milbrett and Shannon MacMillan.

6 **Strike two:** For the second successive Olympic Games, Cuba won the baseball gold medal, with Japan in second place, and the United States a surprising third.

7 **Brazil's beach:** Beach volleyball was another sport making its first appearance at the Olympics. In the women's pairs event, the Brazilians proved unbeatable, except by one another. The Brazilian first and second teams contested the final and walked off with gold and silver. Australia were third. The US men put up a better showing, taking gold and silver. Canada took the men's bronze.

8 **Croatian handball kings:** Croatia won the men's handball gold medal, beating Sweden 27-26 in the final. Spain finished in third place.

9 **Terror in the park:** A video camera catches the flash from the Centennial Park explosion on July 27. Two people were killed and 111 injured in the bombing.

10 **Citizens to the rescue:** Almost as soon as the bomb went off, people began to help the injured.

11 **Flag is down:** The Olympic flag flies at half-staff as a mark of respect to the dead and injured.

12 **The show goes on:** If the bomb was meant to disrupt the program, it failed. No event was postponed or cancelled. Three days afterward, people flocked back into the reopened park.

Nagano

The Japanese city of Nagano, 90 minutes by train from Tokyo, was host to the final Winter Olympics of the twentieth century, with 67 events in seven winter sports being held over a period of 16 days.

IN JUNE 1991, IN BIRMINGHAM, England, the International Olympic Committee announced that the 1998 Winter Olympics would be held in Nagano, Japan, from Saturday, February 7 to Sunday, February 22. The announcement prompted Eishiro Saito, president of the organizing committee for the Games, to say that it was "the fulfilment of a dream held for half a century, and earned the city the honor of writing a new chapter in the illustrious history of the Olympic Games".

One criticism of some past Winter Games was that the competition sites were too far from the central areas. The Nagano organizers ensured this was not the case in 1998. The competition sites were divided into specified areas: Nagano City, Hakuba, Shiga Kogen, Izuna Kogen, Karuizawa, and Nozawa Onsen. All of them are within a 25-mile radius of Nagano City.

Situated about 125 miles west of Tokyo, Nagano is the most southerly city ever to host a Winter Olympics. Notwithstanding its location, Nagano turned on some hostile weather for the events: heavy snow forced officials to postpone some races, including the men's downhill and combined slalom events.

Curling and snowboarding made their debut at the Nagano Games, along with women's ice hockey. The gold in curling went to Denmark, and it was their first Winter medal ever – an impressive achievement for a nation that does not have a functioning curling rink. Canada's Ross Rebagliati took the first ever Olympic Snowboard Giant Slalom gold medal, turning on a captivating display, but then stayed in the headlines when a drugs test detected traces of marijuana. Rebagliati was stripped of his gold medal, but this was reinstated following an appeal. It was an emotional moment when the US women's ice hockey team

defeated four-time world champions, Canada, to take gold: the intense rivalry of the two teams made the historic victory doubly sweet.

As host nation, Japan rode on the wave of enthusiasm from faithful fans to win more golds in the 16 days of the Nagano Games than it has won in 70 years of Winter Games. It was a fitting reward for the warm welcome with which they greeted the rest of the world and the perfectionism they brought to the eighteenth Winter Olympic Games.

The Nagano Games were the biggest yet, with representatives of 72 countries participating, five more than at Lillehammer in 1994. The debut events brought the total number being contested up to 68 in all. Germany topped the medal table with 12 golds, 9 silver, and 8 bronze, followed by Norway with 10 gold, 10 silver, and 5 bronze, and Russia with 9 gold, 6 silver, and 3 bronze.

Record Breaker

Wayne Gretzky is generally regarded as the greatest ice hockey star ever to skate. He has set and surpassed almost every conceivable scoring record in his long career in North America's National Hockey League. The Nagano Games was the first in which professionals like Gretzky played, but for all his skills he was unable to help Canada progress beyond the semifinals.

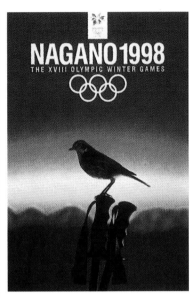

In Harmony with Nature
One of five official posters for Nagano shows a bird atop a ski pole. The work of Masuteru Aoba, the poster emphasizes the quest for harmony between the Olympics and nature.

Japanese Joy
Japan's Hiroyasu Shimuzu tearfully acknowledges the applause of the home crowd as he is presented with the gold medal for his win in the 500 meters speed skating event.

Three More Gold
The great cross-country skier Björn Dæhlie came to the Nagano games with five Olympic golds (joint top of the all-time list) and three silvers already in his trophy cabinet. At Nagano he took his tally to an amazing eight golds and four silvers.

Furious Scramble
Big scramble during the Sweden v USA men's ice hockey match. This encounter during the group stages went Sweden's way by four goals to two. Both teams qualified for the later knock-out stages but both were eliminated in the quarter-finals.

Masked Man
Goalkeeper Andrei Mezin of Belorussia wore an elaborate and colorful face mask but it did not bring success to his team in the ice hockey competition. Mezin conceded 21 goals in all and Belorussia were eliminated in the group stages of the tournament.

1 Björn Dæhlie (45), who has just won gold in the 10-kilometers classical cross-country ski race, has time for a word with the only African in the event, Kenya's Philip Boit.

2 Ross Rebagliati of Canada was the controversial winner of the men's snowboard giant slalom. His celebrations were cut short by the news that he had tested positive for marijuana. His gold medal was initially taken away, but was reinstated after an appeal.

3 Hans-Petter Buraas of Norway celebrates by waving his national flag after he took the gold medal in the slalom skiing competition. He won despite breaking the tip of his ski during the first of his two runs.

4 Hermann Maier of Austria demonstrates the spectacular and daring style that brought him two skiing golds. Maier came to the games with the reputation of being the fastest man on skis but fell heavily in the downhill event. Despite his crashing fall, he recovered to win both the giant slalom and super-G within a week.

5 King of the Moguls: Jonny Moseley, who was – unusually for a skier perhaps – born in Puerto Rico and now lives in California, screams for joy following his successful dance down the mogul piste.

His performance proved good enough to take the freestyle moguls gold medal.

6 In keeping with tradition, the carrying of the Olympic torch and the lighting of the Olympic flame were high points in the preparation for the Games and in the opening ceremony.

7 Katrin Apel took part in the biathlon events at Nagano. She was a member of the German team that won the women's relay event and took the bronze position herself in the individual 7.5-kilometers sprint.

8 Anita Moen-Guidon of Norway gets a time check on the other competitors from an official during the women's 5-kilometers classical cross-country skiing event. Moen-Guidon gained an individual bronze medal in the 15-kilometers classical event.

9 Norway's Halvard Hanevold made a supreme last-minute effort to take the gold medal in the men's 20-kilometers biathlon.

10 Mario Reiter of Austria had been having a poor season right up to the time of the Olympic Games. If neither his spirits nor his expectations were high, his compensation eventually came in the shape of a gold in the combined downhill/slalom competition.

1 Russian pair Pasha Grishuk and Yevgeni Platov, winners of the ice dance competition, performing the tango in the compulsory dance phase of the event.

2 Rintje Risma of the Netherlands took the silver in the 5000 meters race.

3 Germany's Claudia Pechstein came to the Games as the women's world record holder in the 3000 meters speed skating event. She had to settle, however, for silver

behind her compatriot Gunda Niemann-Stirnemann.

4 Hiroyasu Shimizu of Japan (centre) took gold in the 500 meters speed skating event. Canada's Jeremy Wotherspoon (left) and Kevin Overland (right) took silver and bronze respectively .

5 Action in the short track speed skating is fast and furious. Skaters rarely recover from even the slightest mistake.

6 Germany's Rene Lohse lies back in the arms of his partner Kati Winklers during the pairs figure skating event.

7 Austria's Angelika Neuner finished third in the luge event, half a second behind the Germans Silke Kraushaar (gold) and Barbara Niedernhuber (silver).

8 The Czech Republic men's ice hockey team beat Russia 1-0 to secure the first ever Czech ice hockey gold.

9 Germany II, driven by Christopher Langen, fought off stiff competition to win the four-man bob competition.

10 Barbara Niedernhuber of Germany finished in the silver medal position in the women's luge competition, one of the most closely contested series ever.

11 Curling made its debut at Nagano as a full Olympic sport with competitions for both men and women.

Sydney

The Sydney 2000 Games were one of the greatest success stories in Olympic history. Over 10,000 athletes from 200 countries delivered the ultimate sporting event in a superb venue.

AT THE CLOSING CEREMONY of the Sydney 2000 Games, outgoing president of the International Olympic Committee (IOC) Juan Antonio Samaranch declared to the host nation, "I am proud and happy to proclaim that you have presented to the world the best Olympic Games ever." Quite a plaudit, but one few would argue with. Everything seemed perfect – the organization, the athletic performance, the setting, the climate. Sydney elevated the popularity of the Olympics, and the events were watched by an international television audience of more than 3.5 billion.

The host nation also excelled in their sporting achievements. Australia began its climb up the medal rankings in Atlanta in 1996, when it secured 41 medals, including nine gold, to place them fifth on the medals table behind the United States, Germany, Russia and China. In the Sydney Olympics, Australia finished in fourth place with 58 medals, including 16 gold, raising them above Germany in the rankings. Possibly the crowning moment for the host country came when Cathy Freeman, who also lit the Olympic torch, became the first Aboriginal athlete to win an athletics gold in the 400 meters.

The United States held onto its top position at the medals table, winning a total of 97 medals – 40 gold, 24 silver, and 33 bronze. US sprinter Marion Jones won five medals, including three golds. Maurice Greene took the 100 meters gold in 9.87 seconds. Michael Johnson ran to 400 meters gold in 43.84 seconds. Outside of athletics, the US women's softball and basketball teams won golds in hard-fought battles against Australia and Japan respectively.

Australia's Shapes and Colors
This logo creates the figure of a running athlete from boomerang shapes.

The UK also had one of its best Olympics, taking home 28 medals, including 11 golds. Denise Lewis won gold in the heptathlon, and Britain's veteran triple-jumper Jonathan Edwards claimed the gold he had missed in Atlanta. Another veteran, the rower Steve Redgrave, helped the British coxless fours win gold, bringing Redgrave his fifth straight gold in five Olympics. In boxing, Audley Harrison beat Mukhtarkhan Dildabekov for the gold, the first for UK boxers at the Olympics since 1968.

Brazil won six silvers and six bronzes, but no golds, despite being favorites in beach volleyball and equestrian. Canada fell to 18th ranking with only three golds.

The only blot on the Sydney Games was the rash of athletes removed after failing drugs tests – a record total of 35. However, it is undeniable that the Sydney Games were the high watermark of the modern Olympics, and something that future Olympic hosts will have to live up to.

1 **Home win:** Australia's Louise Sauvage won the 800 meters wheelchair race with a time of 1:56.07.

2 **Ethiopian dominance:** Maintaining Ethiopia's dominance of the long-distance running events, Gezahegne Abera won the men's marathon event in 2:10:11. Silver was taken by Kenya's Eric Wainaina, while another Ethiopian, Tesfaye Tola, secured bronze.

3 **Crowning glory:** British triple-jumper Jonathan Edwards capped an amazing career with a 17.71 meter jump. The jump was just short of his world record, but it still brought him the gold.

4 **Beating the baton:** The USA 4 x 100 meters relay team had previously been dogged by poor baton changes, but in the Sydney games they won gold with a time of 37.61.

5 **Veteran medal winner:** Michael Johnson (USA) won the men's 400 meters race in 43.84 seconds. Sydney 2000 was Johnson's last performance in an Olympic event, topping a career which had brought in five Olympic gold medals.

6 **Best jump:** Yelena Yelesina (RUS) took gold in the women's high jump, with Hestrie Cloete of South Africa in silver position. Cloete added 2 cm to her previous best height, but a miss at 1.96 meters placed her behind Yelesina.

7 **Cuban gold:** Ivan Pedroso of Cuba beat Australia's Jai Taurima to the gold in the men's long jump with a final leap of 8.55 meters. Taurima had initially led with a fifth-round jump of 8.49 meters, setting a new Australian record and sending the home crowd wild. Taurima's final jump, however, was only 8.29 meters.

8 **Impressive time:** The 100 meters world record holder, Maurice Greene (USA), won the Sydney 100 meters gold in 9.87 seconds. Greene's fastest ever time was 9.79 seconds, achieved in Athens on June 16, 1999.

9 **Struggling for bronze:** The US women's 4 x 100 meters relay team missed gold and silver placings through poor handovers. Despite having the formidable Marion Jones on the team, the Americans lost out to the Bahamas, who took gold with 41.95 seconds.

10 **Golden throw:** Szymon Ziolkowski (POL) threw 80.02 meters in the men's hammer-throw event. Ziolkowski threw in conditions of driving rain, and several competitors purposely disqualified themselves in protest at the wet throwing circle. Nicola Vizzoni of Italy was in silver position with a throw of 79.64 meters.

11 **Algerian win in 1500 meters:** Algeria's Nouria Merah-Benida won the women's 1500 meters event at Sydney with 4:05.10. Suzy Favor-Hamilton (USA) fell and was injured during the race.

12 **Narrow gold:** Nick Hysong (USA) won gold in the pole vault by the tightest of margins. Hysong and three other competitors all ended on 5.90 meters, but Hysong was awarded gold because he had failed fewer heights in earlier jumps.

13 **Breaking records:** Trine Hattestad (NOR) set a world women's javelin record in Rome in June 2000 with 68.22 meters. In Sydney she went on to achieve a distance of 68.91 meters in her first throw and take gold. Mirella Maniani-Tzelili (GRE) took the silver with 67.51 meters, while Cuba's Osleidys Menendez threw 66.18 meters to win the bronze.

1 World record swim: Dutchman Pieter van den Hoogenband set a world record of 47.84 in the men's 100 meters freestyle semi-final. He went on to win the 100 meters and 200 meters freestyle, only the third man to win the double.

2 Team effort: Australian swimming teams won the 4 x 100 meters and 4 x 200 meters freestyle relays, setting new world records with times of 3:13.67 and 7:07.05 respectively.

3 Triple gold for UK: The British sailing team put in an outstanding performance to win three gold and two silver medals. The golds came in the Finn, Laser and women's Europe classes. They formed a major part of the UK's final tally of 11 gold medals.

4 Hyman beats champion: In a shock upset for the home crowd, Misty Hyman (USA) took gold from Australia's defending champion Susie O'Neill in the women's 200 meters butterfly. Her time – 2:05.08 – was only seven one-hundredths of a second slower than O'Neill's world record.

5 Redgrave's fifth gold: Steve Redgrave helped power the British rowing coxless four team to gold at Sydney. Redgrave battled diabetes to become the first Olympian to win five consecutive gold medals in an endurance event.

6 Hungary water polo win: Hungary won the gold in the water polo, beating Russia 13–6. Hungary has traditionally been dominant in Olympic water polo, the Sydney result being their seventh gold in the event.

7 Kayak final: Germany's Birgit Fischer and Katrin Wagner won gold in the women's K2 500 meters kayaking. The win made Fischer only the second woman to take Olympic medals 20 years apart.

8 Backstroke world beater: Lenny Krayzelburg (USA) confirmed his excellence in the 200 meters backstroke event. He won gold with 1:56.76, putting fellow American Aaron Peirsol in silver position with 1:57.35.

9 French rowing medal: Jean Cristophe Rolland (left) and Michel Andrieux won gold in the men's coxless pairs rowing final. Ted Murphy and Sebastien Bea (USA) won silver, while Matthew Long and James Tomkins (AUS) took bronze.

10 China dominates diving: Hu Jia and Tian Liang wear the silver medals won in the men's synchronized 10 meters platform diving. They battled against one another in the individual platform event, Tian taking gold and Hu silver.

11 Synchronized success: The Russian synchronized swimming team won gold in the free routine final with a score of 64.566. They added to gold already secured by Olga Brusnikina and Maria Kisseleva in the duet competition.

1 **Russian shock victory:** Russian Viacheslav Ekimov beat some of cycling's biggest names – including the twice winner of the Tour de France, Lance Armstrong (USA) – to take gold in the individual road trials. He covered 46.8 km in 57:40.

2 **Chinese gold on beam:** Xuan Liu won gold in the women's beam event. She scored 9.825, beating the traditional leaders of the event – Russia and Romania – back into silver to fourth place rankings.

3 **Pezzo mountainbike gold:** Paolo Pezzo of Italy took gold in the cross-country mountainbike event after an enthralling race which saw her collide with top Spanish cyclist Margarite Fullana, who finished in bronze position.

4 **Uneven bars win:** The Russian gymnast Svetlana Khorkina won gold in the uneven bars, scoring 9.862. She had not lost a major competition in uneven bars since 1994.

5 **Russian excellence:** Russia took gold and silver positions in the women's artistic floor exercise. Here the gold medal winner Elena Zamolodtichikova performs the routine which brought a score of 9.850.

6 **Urzica takes gold:** Marius Urzica of Hungary won gold in the men's individual apparatus pommel horse, scoring 9.862. Many in the crowd booed the decision, believing Alexi Nemov deserved the gold rather than his bronze medal (score: 9.800). France's Eric Poujade took silver place with 9.825.

7 **Spanish vault gold:** Spanish gymnast Gervasio Deferr clearly won gold in the men's vault with a leading score of 9.712. The silver medalist Aleksei Bondarenko (RUS) scored 9.587.

8 **Riding High:** David O'Connor (USA) rode the Irish thoroughbred gelding Custom Made to win the three-day equestrian event, also producing the best eventing dressage score in Olympic history. He later received the USA Equestrian of the Year Award.

9 **Artistic rings win:** Szilveszter Csollany of Hungary took gold in the men's artistic rings final after a performance that earned him a score of 9.850. Dimosthenis Tampakos of Greece took silver with 9.762, and Iordan Iovtchev (BUL) took bronze, scoring 9.737.

10 **Sad ending:** Gymnast Andreea Raducan (ROM) was stripped of her Olympic all-round champion gold after testing positive for a banned drug. The IOC, however, recognized she had taken the drug innocently, as it was contained in a cold remedy prescribed by the team doctor.

11 **Slip to bronze:** During her hoop routine Alina Kabaeva (RUS), favourite to win the individual women's rhythmic gymnastics, dropped the hoop – a mistake that relegated her to bronze place.

12 **Bonfire's last ride:** Anky van Grunsven of the Netherlands rode Bonfire to gold in the Grand Prix Dressage freestyle with a world record score of 86.05. The event was Bonfire's last international competition.

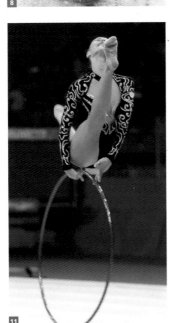

1 Australian archery gold: Australia's own Simon Fairweather won the Olympic archery gold after a 12-arrow victory over Victor Wunderle. His final score was 113, Wunderle's 106.

2 Massive lift: Hossein Rezazadeh (IRI) won gold in the super-heavyweight weightlifting event with two awesome lifts which totaled 472.5 kgs. The first lift was of 212.5 kg, the second 260 kg.

3 Third Cuban gold: The Cuban women's volleyball team beat Russia 3–2 in the Sydney final and won their third straight Olympic gold.

4 Italy triumphant: Italian fencer Valentina Vezzali won gold in the women's individual foil event and the women's team event, beating Poland 45–36. Vezzali was previously a silver medalist in Atlanta in 1996.

5 Chinese battle: Wang Nan beat Li Ju in a five-set battle to take the women's singles table tennis gold. Together the Chinese women had taken gold in the doubles.

6 Controversial win: David Douillet (FRA) beat Shinichi Shinohara (JPN) for the Judo heavyweight gold. The result caused uproar in Japan, however. Many felt that New Zealand referee Craig Monaghan had awarded a yuko (scoring point) to Douillet but ignored a counter-throw technique from Shinohara that would have clinched a Japanese gold.

7 Taekwondo master: South Korean martial artist Kim Kyong Hun used his height and reach advantage to good effect in the final of his Taekwondo event. He beat Australia's Daniel Trenton 7–2, despite incurring a knee injury during the bout.

8 Ukrainian sharpshooter: Mykola Milchev won the men's Olympic skeet shooting event with 150 hits. In silver position was Petr Malek of the Czech Republic with 148 while James Graves (USA) took the bronze with 147.

9 US giants: As expected, the United States won the gold in the men's basketball, but only against valiant French opposition. France pulled back in the second half to produce a final score of 85–75 to the Americans.

10 Power play: Venus Williams produced an awesome display of tennis to blast the Russian, Elena Dementieva, off court in the women's tennis final.

11 Wrestling gold: Alireza Dabir of Iran won the gold medal 58kg freestyle wrestling event. It took him five and a half minutes to beat his Ukrainian adversary, Yevgeni Buslyovych.

Controversy and sporting excellence sat side by side in the 2002 Winter Olympics. However, among drug scandals and corruption emerged some of the Games' best winter performances.

THE 2002 WINTER OLYMPICS, hosted by Salt Lake City, Utah, from 8–24 February, were marked by shocks and upsets. Worst of all were a rash of disqualifications for drug offences. On the last day of the Games alone, three cross-country skiers – including Johann Muehlegg (ESP) – were disqualified after testing positive for Darbepoetin. It was a particularly sad end to the Olympics for Muehlegg, who had already won two golds for the 10 km and 30 km events, but was stripped of his gold medal for the 50 km classic. British skier Alain Baxter also lost a bronze medal after failing a drugs test, although the Court of Arbitration for Sport ruled that he was in no way a cheat.

There was also controversy in the skating. In the finals of the pairs figure skating, Russia was awarded the gold despite an apparently superior performance from the Canadians. An investigation revealed that the French judge had been put under pressure to vote for Russia. In response, the medals were reissued and both Canada and Russia took golds, standing together on the same podium.

"Skategate", as it became known, and the drug scandals unfortunately took the attention of the media, but they should not overshadow the sporting achievements. Both the UK and USA had their best games in decades. The US team won 34 medals – 10 gold, 13 silver and 11 bronze. Many different athletes helped them this new standard, including 16-year-old figure-skater Sarah Hughes and Vonetta Flowers, whose win in the bobsleigh with Jill Bakken made her the first African-American to take gold in a Winter Olympics.

It was the UK's best Winter Games for over 60 years. Alex Coomber won

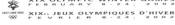

SALT LAKE 2002
XIX OLYMPIC WINTER GAMES
FEBRUARY 8-24, 2002
XIXᵉˢ JEUX OLYMPIQUES D'HIVER
FÉVRIER 8-24, 2002

Salt Lake Snowflake
The emblem on the flag is a stylized snow crystal in yellow, orange, and blue – the colors found in the Utah landscape.

bronze in the men's skeleton, while the British curling team took gold, and instantly became national heroes.

In two North American upsets, Canada beat the USA in both the men's and women's finals. Another surprise came when Australia won its first ever Winter Olympics gold; short-track speed skater Steven Bradbury survived a mass tumble in the 1000 meters event to cross the finishing line alone.

Many of the highest performers of the Games came from the usual European winter sports giants, including Germany, Norway, and Russia. In the women's events, the undoubted star was Janica Kostelic of Croatia. She won gold medals in the slalom, giant slalom and combined event, and a silver from the super-G. The exceptional ability of such sportsmen and women ensured that the Salt Lake City Games would not be remembered entirely for their controversies.

Lost Bronze
British skier Alain Baxter lost his bronze medal from the men's slalom after failing a drugs test. Although he was cleared of any wrongdoing – the trace of non-performance-enhancing drug came from a nasal cold remedy – strict Olympic rules meant the loss of the medal.

Downhill Victory
The men's downhill gold went to the Austrian Fritz Strobl at the testing Snowbasin course. He ran the course in 1:39.13, while the Norwegian Lasse Kjus took silver with 1:39.35.

Slalom Win
Stephan Eberharter of Austria finally clinched an Olympic gold medal by winning the men's giant slalom with a combined time of 2:23.28 seconds for two runs. At 32 years old he was one of the oldest Olympic medalists and the slalom was not his natural race.

Emotional Gold
Jack Shea (USA) won the men's skeleton in 1:49.96. His 91-year-old grandfather, also called Jack Shea, was a former Olympic gold medalist speed skater. He had died shortly before the Games following a car accident.

1 Gold-winning jump: Simon Ammann of Switzerland jumped to gold in the individual small and large hills jumping. He was only the second athlete in the history of the Olympics to win both events.

2 Retirement race: Picabo Street (USA), a veteran skier and former (1998) Olympic Super-G champion, finished 16th in the women's downhill race. She subsequently announced her retirement from professional skiing.

3 Clear win: Samppa Lajunen of Finland took his third gold of the 2002 Winter Olympics by winning the Nordic combined event. He won the final 7.5 km sprint in 16:40.1, nine seconds faster than Ronny Ackermann (GER) who took silver.

4 Shock win: The Italian skier Daniela Ceccarelli, who had never before won a major race, beat off some of the world's best to take gold in the women's Super-G event in 1:13.59.

5 Move to gold: Ales Valenta of Czechoslovakia won the men's aerials gold by clinching the title with a quintuple-twisting triple flip to score 257.02pts. Valenta had been in fifth place until the final.

6 Women's downhill: Carole Montillet of France won the gold in the women's downhill skiing in 1:39.56. Isolde Kostner of Italy and Renate Goetschl of Austria took silver and bronze medals respectively.

7 Stripped of medal: Johann Muelegg (ESP) was stripped of his 50 km cross-country gold medal after testing positive for the banned blood agent Darbepoetin. He kept two other gold medals from pre-test events (10 and 30 km).

8 Triple golds: Janica Kostelic (CRO) became one of only three alpine skiers to win three golds in a single Olympic Games when she took gold in the giant slalom. She had already won golds in the slalom and the combined event.

9 Slalom slip: In alpine skiing Bode Miller (USA) won silver in the combined event and the giant slalom. In the slalom, however, a combination of slips and lost rhythms resulted in a plunge to 24th place, although he persisted in finishing the race. Bode Millar's medals were the only ones won by the US team in the alpine events.

1 Gold record: Ole Einar Bjoerndalen (NOR) won gold in the persuit biathlon and the 10 km, 20 km and relay events. He became the first biathlete to win four gold medals in a single Olympic Games.

2 US bobsleigh win: Jill Bakken and Vonetta Flowers of the USA fought off two German teams to win the women's bobsleigh. Bakken and Flowers actually comprised the USA's No. 2 team in bobsleigh. The USA 1 finished fifth.

3 Royal crash: Prince Albert of Monaco's four-man bobsleigh team crashed out of the Olympics after the bobsleigh overturned on a bend. The Prince slid across the finishing line.

4 Australian first: Speed skater Steven Bradbury won Australia's first ever Winter Olympics gold in the men's 1000 meters. Bradbury survived a mass fall caused when Chinese skater Li Jiajun fell on the last turn.

5 Scottish heroines: The sport of curling was thrust into the limelight in the UK when the Scottish team, comprised of Rhona Martin, Margaret Morton, Fiona MacDonald, Debbie Knox, and Janice Rankin, took gold. The medal was the UK's first Winter Olympics gold for 18 years.

6 Surprise gold: Sarah Hughes, a 16-year-old American, shocked the skating world by winning gold in the women's figure skating. She beat favorites Michelle Kwan (USA) and Irina Slutskaya (RUS) with a performance that included seven triple jumps.

7 50-year gap: Fifty years since they last won the Olympic men's ice hockey, Canada once again took gold. The Canadian team beat the USA 5-2. Russia was in bronze position.

8 Skating controversy: Jamie Sale and David Pelletier (CAN) shared the gold-medal platform with Elena Berezhnaya and Anton Sikharulidze (RUS) for the ice dancing routine. The Canadian's silver from the pairs skating final was upgraded to a second gold after an investigation concluded that French judge Marie Reine Le Gougne had been pressured to vote for the Russians.

9 Flawless Performance: Alexei Yagudin (RUS) defeated reigning world champion Evgeny Plushenko to take gold in the men's figure skating. His performance neared total perfection, and won him four 6.0s from the judges.

10 US Hat-trick: Ross Powers (USA) won gold in the men's snowboard half-pipe with a best score of 46.1. The USA dominated the event; Danny Cass and Jarret Thomas took silver and bronze.

6

7

8

9

10

Athens

In the year 2004, the Olympics will return to their spiritual birthplace, Greece. The Greek capital, Athens, will host a Games featuring more than 10,200 athletes from 200 countries.

Athens Celebrates
Adults, children and all the members of the Athens Olympic Committee celebrated in Athens in September 1997 when it was announced that Athens would hold the XXVIII Olympic Games in 2004.

THE XXVIII OLYMPIAD IN Athens will hark back to the origins of international competitive sport. Greece was hosting probably the world's earliest major multi-state athletic competition, the Olympics, by the second millennium B.C., with formal records of winners listed from around 776 B.C. Athens itself hosted the very first modern Olympic games in 1896. With the 2004 Games returning to Athens, Greek people feel that sporting history has come full circle.

Interest in the hosting the 2004 Games reached unprecedented levels when the bids were opened in the mid-1990s. The countries that had submitted bid proposals to the International Olympic Commission (IOC) by the submission deadline of January 10, 1996 were: Russian Federation, Sweden, France, Argentina, Brazil, Italy, Puerto Rico, South Africa, Turkey), Spain, and Greece.

On March 6, 1997, Olympic committees from each of the bidding nations presented their cases to the IOC Selection College. The original list was then whittled down to five contenders: Stockholm, Rome, Buenos Aires, Cape Town, and Athens. After the disappointment of missing out on hosting the 1996 Centenary Games, the Athens team was determined to make their case.

Part of the Athens bid involved plans to slash city air pollution levels by 35 percent through traffic-reduction measures, use solar and wind energy to provide electricity for the Olympic Village, and initiate many other biodiversity, recycling, and green-space programs. Adding commitments to build state-of-the-art sporting facilities, Athens swung the IOC behind it. On September 5, 1997 Athens was

Laurel Wreath
The Athens 2004 logo, shown here on a postage stamp, features the Olympic rings set beneath a laurel wreath – the headdress worn by athletic victors in ancient times.

announced as the host of the 2004 Olympic Games.

Since then, Athens has been on a roller-coaster ride in its preparations. The scale of transformation in the city has been immense. Using a $13bn (£9 billion) budget, the redevelopment of the city has involved the building of 28 new hotels and the construction of a new international airport, plus the development of the numerous sporting facilities demanded by the Games. The enormity of the project has given cause for concern – at one point then IOC president felt that Athens was in danger of losing the Games because so many essential projects were behind schedule. However, under the presidency of Rogge the IOC has exuded more confidence.

Troubles aside, the 2004 Games promise to be as exciting as ever. Expectations are high that the birthplace of the modern Olympics can provide a memorable Games over 100 years after its conception.

Angelopoulos Rejoices
Gianna Angelopoulos-Daskalaki was a Greek conservative politician and the driving force behind Athens' successful Olympic bid. In 1990, Athens had lost the bid to hold the Centennial Games of 1996, which went to Atlanta instead.

Profitable Games
Hosting the Olympics in a vastly expansive undertaking. Merchandizing is a central way of recouping some of the costs, as is the selling the television broadcasting rights to the Games.

The Final Candidates
President of the IOC, Juan Antonio Samaranch, congratulates Gianna Angelopoulos on winning the bid to host the 2004 Olympics on March 7, 1997. The final group was Rome, Buenos Aires, Cape Town, Stockholm, and Athens.

New Medals
For the first time since 1928, the imagery on the Olympic medals has been changed to incorporate specifically Greek elements. The new medal was designed by Greek artist Elena Votsi.

Greece and the Games

Despite its vaunted position in Olympic history, Greece remains one of the smallest competitors in the Games. As such, it has generally come low in the medal rankings in each Olympic Games. However, this has not stopped the country from producing athletes of individual excellence who have been high achievers in their own right.

On April 6–15, 1896, Athens was host to the first modern Olympic Games. It was a glorious first Games for the host nation. In track and field, while the United States was unquestionably laying its foundations for supremacy, Greece's own Spyridon (Spyros) Louis won the marathon event (then 40 km) in 2:58:50. Louis was the epitome of Greek identity (he wore nothing but traditional Greek costume). Born in 1872, he showed ability as a runner during military service and became a national hero with his marathon victory. He did not compete in another Olympic Games, although he made an appearance at the 1936 Olympics in Berlin as

an official representative of Greece, and remains a legend in Greek sporting history.

He was not the only Greek athlete to triumph in the 1896 Games. Inspired by their home surroundings, Greek sportsmen also attained medals in shooting, fencing, wrestling, cycling, gymnastics, and swimming, and came second in the medals table after the USA. Yet in the 1900 Games in Paris, Greek fortunes in the Games dipped significantly. They plummeted downward in the medals tables as the number of participating countries jumped from 14 to 26 and the quality of athletes rose. In 1904 in St Louis, Perikles Kalkousis' weightlifting gold and Nicolaos Georgantas' bronze in the discus were the only medals for Greece.

Since 1904 the Games have presented sporadic moments of glory for Greece. In the 1912 Games in Stockholm, Konstantinos Tsiklitiras won gold in the standing long jump. In the 1956 Games in Melbourne, Georgios Roubanis won a bronze in the pole vault, while in Los Angeles in 1984

Haralambos Holidis took bronze in the Greco-Roman wrestling. Though golds have been sparse for Greek Olympic athletes since 1896, there have been signs of a modern revival of fortunes. In the Barcelona Games in 1992 Pyrros Dimas hoisted a two-lift combined weight of 390 kg in the men's –82.5 kg weightlifting to take gold. A silver followed in the 1996 Atlanta games when Niki Bakogianni came a close second to the world record holder Stefka Kostadinova (BUL) in the women's high jump.

Golds returned to Greece more substantially in Sydney 2000, most memorably in Konstantinos Kenteris' gold-medal winning run in the men's 200 meters. Three other golds were also won by Greece, two in weightlifting and one in taekwondo, as well as six silver and four bronze medals. With such an excellent performance preceding the Athens 2004 Games, many eyes will be watching to see whether Greece can attain something of the athletic position it attained in the original modern Olympics.

1 Greek legend: A statue of the Greek marathon runner, Spyros Louis. Construction for the 2004 Olympics can be seen taking place in the background. Louis won the marathon in the first modern Olympic Games in 1896 in 2:58:50, but he never ran again in the Olympics.

2 Lifting gold: Perikles Kaklousis (GRE) won gold for the two-handed lift in the 1904 Olympics in St Louis. In silver position was Oscar Osthoff of the USA, with fellow American Frank Kungler taking bronze.

3 Sprint finish: Greece had an unexpected triumph in the athletics at Sydney 2000. Konstantinos Kenteris (GRE) beat the UK's Darren Campbell to take gold in the 200 meters final.

4 Greek hurdling gold: Paraskevi Patoulidou (GRE) won a surprise gold

in the women's 100 meters hurdles in Barcelona in 1992, the first major track-and-field win for Greece since 1956.

5 Close call: Niki Bakogianni (GRE) came close to the gold when she jumped 2.03 meters in the high jump at Atlanta, 1996. She was, however, beaten to gold by Stefka Kostadinova (BUL), who jumped 2.05 meters.

6 Precious gold: After a long period of little major Olympic success, Greece finally took a gold when Pyrros Dimas won the light-heavyweight weightlifting in Barcelona, 1992. He retained the title at the next two Games.

7 Wrestling bronze: Greek freestyle wrestler Admiran Karntanov won a bronze medal in the 54 kg class after defeating German Kontoev (BLR) 5–4. He took the winning point in the final two seconds.

Athens' Olympic Venues

Athens has had its infrastructure revitalized for the 2004 Games, particularly in terms of transport. Officials expect thousands of visitors to make around one million cross-city journeys during the competition. A new international airport has been built in Attica (the region in which Athens resides), and is connected to the city by a new six-lane motorway. In addition, a new Metro network has been commissioned and car traffic can take advantage of a new ring road. To enhance the appearance of the city, more than one million trees have been planted.

The Olympic venues themselves are spread fairly broadly throughout Attica, although all will be easily accessible via public transport. At the heart of the venues, set in the northern suburbs of the city, is the Athens Olympic Sports Complex (OCO). Containing five different sports venues, the complex will host the opening and closing ceremonies (Olympic Stadium), athletics, gymnastics, trampoline, basketball, tennis, swimming, water polo, diving, and track cycling.

South-east of the OCO is the Goudi Olympic Complex (modern pentathlon and badminton), the Helinko Olympic Complex (baseball, softball, hockey, handball, canoeing/kayaking), the Markopoulo Olympic Shooting Center, and the Markopoulo Olympic Equestrian Center. There is also the Panathinaiko Stadium, the stadium where the original 1896 games were held. This will be used for archery events and, fitting with tradition, as the finishing point for the marathon. The marathon starting point is in Marathon itself, and will be identical to the 1896 route.

On the western Attic coast is the Vouliagmeni Olympic Center for the triathlon and Agios Kosmas Olympic Sailing Center.

Moving to the immediate south-west of the OCO is the Galatsi Olympic Hall, the destination for rhythmic gymnastics and table tennis. Extending further out toward the coast is the Peristeri Olympic Boxing Hall, the Athens City Center Cycling Road Race Course, the Nikaia Olympic Weightlifting Hall and, next to Athens' Piraeus harbor, the Faliro Coastal Zone Olympic Complex, where the taekwondo and handball preliminaries and volleyball/beach volleyball will be held.

Now we extend farther north toward Greece's mountainous interior. North-west of the OCO is the Ano Liossia Olympic Hall, a 9300-seat venue for wrestling and judo, while

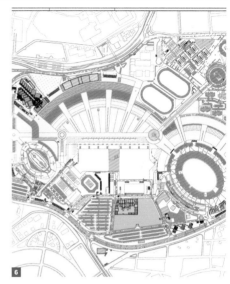

still farther north is the Parnitha Olympic Mountain Bike Venue. Just east of this is the Olympic Village, a state-of-the-art home for 16,000 athletes and officials. The Olympic Village features bio-climate building design, over 30,000 m² of sports facilities and even its own fire brigade and schools. On the adjacent north-eastern Attica coast is the Shinias Olympic Rowing and Canoeing Center, featuring a 2000-meter course for the rowing and kayaking events.

The many venues of the 2004 Olympics are integrated by public transport. The only sport demanding travel outside Athens is football, which is spread over four stadia ranging from Heraklio on the island of Crete in the far south to Volos in the north, although the Karaiskaki Stadium in Athens is the scene for the men's and women's finals.

1 City construction: In preparation for the 2004 Olympic Games, the Greeks have undertaken a major construction effort. Competitions for the Games will be contested in newly-built arenas as well as existing complexes that have been modified and upgraded.

2 Olympic Stadium: The Olympic Stadium is situated at Marousi, northern Athens. Part of the Olympic Sports Complex, it will hold 75,000 spectators and will be the major focus for track and field events.

3 Olympic Aquatic Center: The Aquatic Center features three pools: two outdoor and one indoor. The 11,000-seat Main Pool (outdoor) will host the race swimming and water polo, and the Indoor Pool (6500 seats) will host the diving.

4 Olympic Rowing and Canoeing Center: 4,000 spectators will be able to watch the 26 different rowing and canoeing events from the Schinias center, located in the northeast part of the Attica region.

5 Volleyball Center: The 10,000-seat Olympic Beach Volleyball Center is at Faliro, southern Athens. In addition to the competition area, the center has six training courts and two warm-up courts.

6 Aerial view: The Athens Olympic Sports Complex will be the centerpiece of the Games. The complex will be the venue for six of the twenty-eight sports as well as Opening and Closing Ceremonies.

7 Equestrian Center: The Markopoulo Equestrian Center is situated 23 miles (37 km) south east of the Olympic Village. It covers an area of 21,000m², and features stabling for 300 horses. There will be 20,000 seats for jumping events, 8000 for dressage, and 40,000 for cross-country.

8 Sailing Center: The Agios Kosmas Olympic Sailing Center, located in southern Attica, is where the all the sailing competition will take place from August 14 to 28, 2004.

1 Long-jump contenders: The UK has seen a recent rise in the quality of its long jumpers. In August 2003, Chris Tomlinson was became the first Briton to reach the final of the long jump in the World Athletics Championships.

2 African race: Kenya and Ethiopia have been traditional rivals in distance-running categories. The great Haile Gebrselassie (ETH), world record holder in 5000 and 10,000 meters events; has recently been beaten his countryman, Kenenisa Bekele, twice world cross-country champion.

3 Record breaker: 17-year-old Elizabeth Tweddle has already achieved more than any female gymnast in British history. Elizabeth won the nation's first European Championships medal – a bronze on the uneven bars – in 2002, and took bronze for the same event at the 2003 World Championships.

4 US distance hopeful: Deena Drosin is one of the USA's key contenders for distance running events such as the 10,000 meters or marathon. In April 2003 she broke an 18-year record for the US women's marathon.

5 Track glory: In recent Olympics, US athletes have been powerful in sprint races while African athletes have dominated 5000 meters+ races. Here Stephanie Graf (AUT) competes in the heats of the women's 800 meters at the World Athletics Championships in France, August 2003.

6 Lithuanian powerhouse: The Lithuanian Virgilijus Alekna won the gold for discus in the Sydney Olympics, and also took gold in the 2003 World Athletics Championships with a throw of 69.69 meters.

7 Javelin strength: Northern and Eastern European countries are strong in the javelin event, Czechoslovakia taking men's gold for the last two Olympics. The Russian, Sergey Makarov (RUS), however, recently beat Czechoslovakia's Jan Zelezny in the 2003 World Championships.

The Competition

The Athens 2004 Olympics will run from August 11–29, 2004. It will feature 28 Olympic sports, within which there are a total of over 300 individual disciplines ranging from the 100 meters sprint to the 10 meters air-pistol shooting. In total there will be around 10,500 athletes competing from 200 different countries, with 3,000 team officials accompanying them. Sporting events will actually begin two days before the opening ceremony on August 13 with two days of football preliminaries.

The main bulk of the events, however, begins on August 14 with highlights including the men's cycling road race final. Thereafter there is a packed schedule every day. Other highlights include: August 15 – women's fencing individual epee final; August 16 – men's artistic gymnastics team final; August 17– the women's artistic gymnastics team final and the men's 4 x 200 meters swimming freestyle relay; August 18 – men's 100 meters swimming freestyle final; August 19 – women's individual artistic gymnastics final and women's 100 meters freestyle swimming final; August 20– men's athletics 10,000 meters final and men's 50 meters swimming

freestyle final; August 21– women's swimming 50 meters freestyle final, women's athletics 100 meters final, finals in the men's and women's pairs rowing; August 22 – men's athletics 100 meters final, men's triple-jump and high jump finals, women's marathon; August 23 – women's triple-jump final and individual dressage Grand Prix in the equestrian; August 24 – women's athletics 100 meters hurdles and 400 meters finals; August 25 – women's 200 meters final; August 26 – men's athletics 200 meters final and the modern pentathlon, plus finals of the men's triathlon; August 27 – men's 110 meters hurdles final, women's 4 x 100 meters relay final; August 28 – men's football final, women's high jump final, men's 4 x 100 meters final, canoeing and kayaking flatwater racing finals; August 29 – men's marathon and boxing finals.

Changes to the list of events compared with Sydney have been fairly minor. A women's sabre event, for example, has been added to the fencing program. Yet the Games promise to be as exciting as ever. Naturally, many will expect the United States to be the dominant nation at the medals table, a position largely derived from their excellence

in athletics, gymnastics, basketball, and swimming. However, their supremacy will not be uncontested. In the Sydney 2000 games, Russia won a total of 88 medals compared with the United States' 97, including 32 golds as against 40 for the USA. Russian excellence in gymnastics, wrestling, weightlifting, diving, and fencing will no doubt make leadership of the medals table a hotly contested privilege.

Yet other nations will also make the rankings unpredictable. China took a total of 59 medals, including 28 golds, and will be looking to continue its excellent record in diving, synchronized swimming, table tennis, and gymnastics. A question mark hangs over Australia. Will it be able to improve on its fourth position achieved in Sydney 2000, relying on its massive strength in swimming and other talents in rowing and cycling? The UK is also fielding a strong team, with good opportunities for gold medals in athletics, boxing, cycling, rowing, sailing, and shooting.

As we know from experience, correctly predicting the results of the Olympics is incredibly difficult. Competing in such a historic venue should bring out the best in all the world's athletes, and make for an enthralling event.

1 US dominance: Basketball events are dominated by the USA. In 1989 Olympic basketball was opened to NBA players. They are clear favorites to win in Athens.

2 High kicking: Taekwondo is one of the newest Olympic disciplines, having become an official Olympic sport at Sydney 2000. Korea, China, Australia, and the USA have emerged as the front-runners, although Michalis Mouroutsis (GRE) won gold in the under 58 kg category at Sydney.

3 Shooting true: There are a total of 10 different shooting events for men, and seven for women, in the Olympics. Luna Tao, who entered the Chinese national shooting team in 1998, is one of the world's finest pistol and rifle shots. In Sydney she won the 10 meters air pistol and took silver in the 25 meters pistol.

4 Fencing tradition: Fencing was part of the original Olympic games in 1896. In Sydney 2000, Germany, Russia, Hungary, and Italy continued their medal-winning runs. Here is Alessandro Puccini (ITA) having won gold in the individual foil at Atlanta, 1996.

5 Punching for gold: Up to the 2000 Games, an Olympic bout was three three-minute rounds, but this has been changed to four two-minute rounds.

6 US vaulter: Annia Hatch is a major US contender for medals in the 2004 gymnastics events. Annia hails from Cuba, and won Cuba's first World Championships medal for the vault in 1996. She became a US citizen in December 2001.

7 Chinese golds: China has a huge lead in world table tennis. During the Sydney Olympics, out of 12 medals available in four table tennis events (singles and doubles, men and women), eight were won by China, including a men's singles gold for Kong Linghui, seen here.

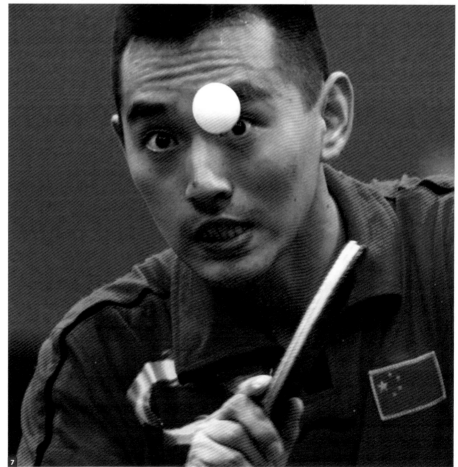

Torino

The world's best winter sportsmen and women are already looking ahead to the 2006 Winter Olympics in Torino, Italy. Eighty medals will be up for grabs in 15 different sports.

ITALY'S SUCCESS IN ITS BID TO HOST the 2006 XX Winter Olympics was announced at the 109th session of the International Olympic Committee (IOC) in Seoul. The IOC had initially evaluated six bids from Sion (Switzerland), Zakopane (Poland), Poprad-Tatry (Slovakia), a joint bid from Helsinki (Finland) and Lillehammer (Norway), Klagenfurt (Austria), and finally Torino itself. The IOC reduced the candidate list to Sion and Torino, and Torino won the final vote 53–36 on June 19, 1999.

Torino is already a major venue for winter sports enthusiasts and athletes, and has, or is developing, first-class facilities for the forthcoming games. It is set in the region of Piedmont in the north-west of Italy, and has an aristocratic lineage evident in the beautiful and imposing architecture. During the Games, Torino city will use its two stadia – Comunale and Delle Alpi – to host ice hockey, figure skating, short track and speed skating. The Olympic Village will also be located in the village

Torino city, however, is just one of six major competition sites set deep in the Italian Alps. These are, with their associated sports: Bardonecchia (snowboarding), Pinerolo (curling), Pragelato (Nordic combined, ski jumping, cross country), Sestriere (alpine skiing), Sauze d'Oulx (freestyle), and Cesana San Sicario (biathlon, women's alpine time trials, downhill, combined downhill, super-G, plus bobsleigh, luge and skeleton at Pariol-Greniere). In addition, there are training facilities at Claviere and Torre Pelice.

The Games will be 17 days in duration, from 10 to 26 February, and will feature over 2500 athletes competing in 15 traditional events: alpine skiing, biathlon, bobsleigh, nordic combined, cross-country skiing, curling, figure skating, ice hockey, luge, freestyle, speed skating, short-track, skeleton, ski jumping, and snowboard. The Italians themselves have high hopes for the Games. During the 2002 Winter Olympics in the USA they came a respectable seventh position in the medals tables with four gold, four silver, and four bronze medals. Italian women were particularly strong, with Daniela Ceccarelli taking gold in the women's super-G, Stefania Belmondo winning the 15 km cross-country, and Gabriella Paruzzi taking the 30 km classical, with Belmondo in silver position. Competing on home soil, the Italians stand a good chance of pushing themselves higher up the rankings.

The 2002 Winter Olympics saw the US team in second place, and in 2006 no doubt they will be going all out to dislodge Germany from the No. 1 position they have held since Nagano in 1998. US strengths are concentrated in snowboarding, speed skating, bobsleigh and skeleton, and figure skating. The 2002 Games were a bitter disappointment for the USA in the alpine skiing events, Bode Miller being the only medal winner with two silvers. Yet the US team fields some especially strong skiers, and the team will be hoping that Torino rectifies past mistakes and poor times. In the skating events, Russia will hope to maintain its traditional presence against fierce competition from the USA as well as countries such as Canada, France, Japan, and China. For the UK, there will be hopes that the curling gold can be kept and that British skiers manage a medal placing after the disappointing disqualification of Alain Baxter in Salt Lake City.

Training For Gold
The US bobsleigh team in training during the 2002 Olympics. The USA took 10 gold medals during the 2002 Games, and will be hoping to achieve first place in the medals table at Torino.

Major Venue
The events in the 2006 Winter Olympics in Torino will be held in nine main locations. These are broken down into seven venue locations: Bardonecchia, Pinerolo, Pragelato, Cesana, Sauze d'Oulx, Sestriere, Torino, and two training locations: Claviere and Torre Pellice.

Torino City
The city of Torino itself will host figure skating, speed skating, short track, and ice hockey, plus the Olympic ceremonies. It will also be home to the Olympic village for the athletes.

Pragelato
Pragelato is the venue for ski-jumping, Nordic combined, and cross-country events. It features a total of 50km of ski runs snaking through the Chisone Valley in the Val Troncea National Park.

Bobsleigh Run
The bobsleigh track in Torino will cost in its first phase of construction alone around 15 million euros, and is built within a frame of local soil to minimize its environmental impact.

Beijing

The selection of Beijing to host the 2008 Olympics was a controversial decision, but the Chinese are now 100 percent committed to producing a first-class modern Games.

Winning Celebrations

Tens of thousands of people took to the streets of Shanghai to celebrate winning the 2008 Olympics bid. Chinese President Jiang Zemin declared, "I welcome our friends around the world to visit Beijing in 2008."

THE CITY OF BEIJING, CHINA, was elected the Host City for the Games of the XXIX Olympiad in 2008 on Friday July 13, 2001. The vote followed a statement from the International Olympic Committee (IOC) Evaluation Commission: "a Beijing Games would leave a unique legacy to China and to sports". Prior to the decision by the IOC, two other cities had been in the running, Paris and Toronto, both presenting extremely strong bids. Two other cities – Istanbul in Turkey and Osaka in Japan – had already fallen by the wayside.

Despite the strong competition, Beijing was the favorite to win. It had been a runner-up in the 1993 IOC vote which awarded the 2000 Games to Sydney (China lost by two votes), and many in the IOC felt it was time to give China the opportunity to host the Games. The clear leaning towards China was evident when the final votes came in – Beijing had captured 56 votes, against 22 for Toronto and 18 for Paris. Many politicians, human rights organizations, and atheletes were angered by the decision; there remains a widespread feeling that China's poor human rights record should have precluded it from the bid process entirely. Yet the IOC argued that giving the 2008 Games to Beijing was a way of leading China into the global community, and would actually assist the reform of its human rights agenda.

Beijing's preparations for 2008 have now begun in earnest. It plans to invest a total of $20 billion on stadia and city improvements, with an extended subway system helping transport the anticipated millions of visitors. Thirty-five stadia are proposed, 30 within Beijing itself, and 15 of these are new buildings. They will be located in four zones, the largest being the Olympic Central Area containing 12 stadia, including the National Stadium and National Swimming Center. The University Zone – so called because of its location within Beijing's university establishments – will feature four stadiums for table tennis, badminton, wrestling and judo. The Western Community will have six stadia, including the basketball stadium, while the Northern Tourism Community will have facilities for equestrian and aquatic sports.

A major issue is Beijing's chronic pollution problem, something the city officials are hoping to solve with a major clean-air initiative and a water-treatment system costing $12 billion. Government officials have stated that by mid-2006 the bulk of the physical redevelopment work, including the stadia, will be completed and the time left before the Games will be spent on testing the facilities.

With such intense preparations underway, what can we predict about the Games themselves, which will be held from August 8 to August 24, 2008? Being some years away, the only thing we can say with certainty is that China will go all out to dominate the medals tables. The USA will continue to reign in many events, particularly athletics, so the Chinese may well focus on their key strengths of gymnastics, diving, table tennis, and other sports requiring unusual dexterity and precision. Already a new generation of Chinese athletes are being prepared for the event, with athletically talented school-children undergoing particularly rigorous training regimes. In 2008 the hopes and aspirations of a few of them may well be realized.

Olympic Unveiling
Chinese officials applaud the unveiling of the 2008 Beijing Olympics emblem. The unveiling took place at the Temple of Heaven, Beijing, on August 3, 2003.

Committee Celebrates
The team that campaigned for China to host the 2008 Olympics celebrates on hearing the news that their campaign has been successful.

Beijing Stadium
The main stadium in Beijing will be a state-of-the-art facility, funded by a consortium of commercial and government bodies to a total cost of 3.5 billion yuan (USD$423 million).

Rising Giant
Beijing is rapidly becoming one of the most modern and dynamic cities in Asia. The city was established in 1045 B.C. and currently has a population of over 11 million.

Country Abbreviations

AFG	Afghanistan		ITA	Italy
AHO	Netherlands Antilles		JAM	Jamaica
ALB	Albania		JOR	Jordan
ALG	Algeria		JPN	Japan
ANG	Angola		KAZ	Kazakhstan
ANT	Antigua and Barbuda		KEN	Kenya
ARG	Argentina		KOR	South Korea
ARM	Armenia		LAT	Latvia (to 1939; from 1992)
AUS	Australia		LIB	Lebanon
AUT	Austria		LIE	Liechtenstein
AZE	Azerbaijan		LIT	Lithuania (to 1939; from 1992)
BAH	Bahamas		LUX	Luxemburg
BEL	Belgium		MAR	Morocco
BLR	Belarus/Belorussia		MAS	Malaysia
BOH	Bohemia (to 1918)		MDA	Moldova
BOL	Bolivia		MDV	Maldives
BRA	Brazil		MEX	Mexico
BSH	Bosnia-Herzegovina		MGL	Mongolia
BUL	Bulgaria		MON	Monaco
BUR	Burkina Faso		MOZ	Mozambique
CAN	Canada		NAM	Namibia
CHI	Chile		NED	Netherlands (formerly HOL)
CHN	China		NGR	Nigeria
CIV	Ivory Coast		NIG	Niger
CMR	Cameroon		NOR	Norway
COL	Colombia		NZL	New Zealand
CRC	Costa Rica		PAK	Pakistan
CRO	Croatia		PER	Peru
CUB	Cuba		PHI	Philippines
CZE	Czech Republic (from 1994)		POL	Poland
DEN	Denmark		POR	Portugal
DJI	Djibouti		PRK	North Korea
DOM	Dominican Republic		PUR	Puerto Rico
ECU	Ecuador		ROM	Romania
EGY	Egypt		RSA	South Africa (formerly SAF)
ESP	Spain		RUS	Russia (to 1919; from 1994)
EST	Estonia (to 1939; from 1992)		SAF	South Africa (now RSA)
ETH	Ethiopia		SEN	Senegal·
EUN	Unified Team (Commonwealth of Independent States, 1992)		SER	Serbia (from 1992)
FIN	Finland		SLO	Slovenia (from 1992)
FRA	France		SUI	Switzerland
FRG	West Germany (1949-1990; then GER)		SUR	Surinam
GBR	Great Britain		SVK	Slovakia (from 1994)
GDR	East Germany (1949-1990; then GER)		SWE	Sweden
GEO	Georgia		SYR	Syria
GER	Germany (to 1949; from 1990)		TCH	Czechoslovakia (to 1993)
GER★	pan-German team 1956–1964		TGA	Tonga
GHA	Ghana		THA	Thailand
GRE	Greece		TPE	Taiwan
HAI	Haiti		TRI	Trinidad and Tobago
HKG	Hong Kong		TUN	Tunisia
HOL	Netherlands (now NED)		TUR	Turkey
HUN	Hungary		UAE	United Arab Emirates
INA	Indonesia		UGA	Uganda
IND	India		UKR	Ukraine
IOP	Independent Olympic Participant		URS	Soviet Union (to 1992)
IRI	Iran (formerly IRN)		URU	Uruguay
IRL	Ireland		USA	United States of America
IRN	Iran (now IRI)		UZB	Uzbekistan
IRQ	Iraq		VEN	Venezuela
ISL	Iceland		YUG	Yugoslavia
ISR	Israel		ZAM	Zambia
ISV	Virgin Islands			

Athens 1896

April 6 – April 15

Participants: ca. 200 / Men: 200, Women: 0, Countries: 14,
Sports: 9, Events: 43

Medals Table

PLACE	COUNTRY	GOLD	SILVER	BRONZE
1	USA	11	6	2
2	Greece	10	19	18
3	Germany	7	5	3
4	France	5	4	2
5	Great Britain	3	3	1

Outstanding Athletes

PLACE	NAME (NATIONALITY)	DISCIPLINE	G	S	B
1	Carl Schuhmann (GER)	Gym/Wrestling	4	–	–
2	Hermann Weingärtner (GER)	Gymnastics	3	2	1
3	Alfred Flatow (GER)	Gymnastics	3	1	–
4	Paul Masson (FRA)	Cycling	3	–	–
5	Fritz Hofmann (GER)	Athletics/Gym	2	1	2

EVENT	GOLD		SILVER		BRONZE	
Athletics						
100 m	Thomas Burke (USA)	12.0	Fritz Hofmann (GER)	12.2	Alajos Szokolyi (HUN)	12.6
400 m	Thomas Burke (USA)	54.2	Herbert Jamison (USA)	55.2	Fritz Hofmann (GER)	55.6
800 m	Edwin Flack (AUS)	2:11.0	Nandor Dani (HUN)	2:11.8	Dimitrios Golemis (GRE)	2:28.0
1500 m	Edwin Flack (AUS)	4:33.2	Arthur Blake (USA)	4:34.0	Albin Lermusiaux (FRA)	4:36.0
Marathon (25 miles 28 yds)	Spyridon Louis (GRE)	2:58:50	Charilaos Vasilakos (GRE)	3:06:03	Gyula Kellner (HUN)	3:09:35
110 m Hurdles	Thomas Curtis (USA)	17.6	Grantley Goulding (GBR)	18.0		
High Jump	Ellery Clark (USA)	5'11¼"	James B. Connolly (USA)	5'5"		
			Robert Garrett (USA)	5'5"		
Long Jump	Ellery Clark (USA)	20'10"	Robert Garrett (USA)	20'3¼"	James B. Connolly (USA)	20'0½"
Pole Vault	William Hoyt (USA)	10'10"	Albert Tyler (USA)	10'6"	Evangelos Damaskos (GRE)	8'6¼"
Triple Jump	James B. Connolly (USA)	44'11¾"	Alexandre Tuffère (FRA)	41'8"	Ioannis Persakis (GRE)	41'0¾"
Shot	Robert Garrett (USA)	36'9¾"	Miltiades Gouskos (GRE)	36'9"	Georgios Papasideris (GRE)	34'0"
Discus	Robert Garrett (USA)	95'7½"	Panagiotis Paraskevopoulo (GRE)	95'0"	Sotirios Versis (GRE)	91'1¾"
Weight Lifting						
One-arm Lifts	Launceston Elliott (GBR)	156¼lb	Viggo Jensen (DEN)	125¾lb	Alexandros Nikolopoulos (GRE)	125¾lb
Two-arm Lifts	Viggo Jensen (DEN)	245¼lb	Launceston Elliott (GBR)	245¼lb	Sotirios Versis (GRE)	220lb
Wrestling						
	Carl Schuhmann (GER)		Georgios Tsitas (GRE)		Stephanos Christopoulos (GRE)	
Fencing						
Individual Foil	Eugène-Henri Gravelotte (FRA)	4	Henri Callot (FRA)	3	Perikles Pierrakos-Mavromichalis (GRE)	2
Foil for Fencing Masters	Leon Pyrgos (GRE)	1	M. Perronet (FRA)	0		
Individual Saber	Ioannis Georgiadis (GRE)	4	Telemachos Karakalos (GRE)	3	Holger Nielsen (DEN)	2
Shooting						
Free Rifle (200 m)	Pantelis Karasevdas (GRE)	2320	P. Pavlidis (GRE)	1978	Nicolaos Trikupis (GRE)	1718
Free Rifle (300 m)	Georgios Orphanidis (GRE)	1583	Jean Phrangoudis (GRE)	1312	Viggo Jensen (DEN)	1305
Rapid-Fire Pistol (25 m)	Jean Phrangoudis (GRE)	344	Georgios Orphanidis (GRE)	249	Holger Nielsen (DEN)	
Military Revolver (25 m)	John Paine (USA)	442	Sumner Paine (USA)	380	N. Morakis (GRE)	205
Free Pistol (50 m)	Sumner Paine (USA)	442	Viggo Jensen (DEN)	285	Holger Nielsen (DEN)	
Cycling						
One-lap race	Paul Masson (FRA)	24.0	Stamatios Nikolopoulos (GRE)	25.4	Adolf Schmal (AUT)	26.6
2000 m	Paul Masson (FRA)	4:56.0	Stamatios Nikolopoulos (GRE)	5:00.2	Léon Flameng (FRA)	
10,000 m	Paul Masson (FRA)	17:54.2	Léon Flameng (FRA)	17:54.2	Adolf Schmal (AUT)	
100 km	Léon Flameng (FRA)	3:08:19.2	G. Kolettis (GRE)			
12 Hours Track	Adolf Schmal (AUT)	314.997	F. Keeping (GBR)	314.664	Georgios Paraskevopoulos (GRE)	313.330
Marathon (87 km)	Aristidis Konstantinidis (GRE)	3:22:31	August Goedrich (GER)	3:42:18	F. Battel (GBR)	
Gymnastics						
Parallel Bars – Individual	Alfred Flatow (GER)		Jules Zutter (SUI)		Hermann Weingärtner (GER)	
Parallel Bars – Team	Germany		Greece		Greece	
Horse Vault	Carl Schuhmann (GER)		Jules Zutter (SUI)			
Horizontal Bar – Individual	Hermann Weingärtner (GER)		Alfred Flatow (GER)		Pet Messas (GRE)	
Horizontal Bar – Team	Germany					
Rings	Ioannis Mitropoulos (GRE)		Hermann Weingärtner (GER)		Petros Persakis (GRE)	
Pommel Horse	Jules Zutter (SUI)		Hermann Weingärtner (GER)		Gyula Kakas (HUN)	
Rope Climbing	Nicolaos Andriakopoulos (GRE)		Thomas Xenakis (GRE)		Fritz Hofmann (GER)	

EVENT	GOLD		SILVER		BRONZE
Swimming					
100 m Freestyle	Alfred Hajós (HUN)	1:22.2	Efstathios Chorophas (GRE)	1:23.0	Otto Herschmann (AUT)
500 m Freestyle	Paul Neumann (AUT)	8:12.6	Antonios Pepanos (GRE)		Efstathios Chorophas (GRE)
1200 m Freestyle	Alfred Hajós (HUN)	18:22.2	Jean Andreou (GRE)	21:03.4	Efstathios Chorophas (GRE)
100 m Freestyle (Sailors)	Ioannis Malokinis (GRE)	2:20.4	S. Chasapis (GRE)		Dimitrios Drivas (GRE)
Tennis					
Singles	John Pius Boland (GBR)		Dennis Kasdaglis (GRE)		
Doubles	John Pius Boland (GBR)/ Fritz Traun (GER)		Demis Kasdaglis (GRE)/ Demetrios Petrokokkinos (GRE)		

Paris 1900

May 14 – October 28

Participants: 1225 / Men: 1206, Women: 19, Countries: 26, Sports: 24, Events: 166

Medals Table

PLACE	COUNTRY	GOLD	SILVER	BRONZE
1	**France**	29	41	32
2	**USA**	20	14	9
3	**Great Britain**	17	8	10
4	**Belgium**	8	7	5
5	**Switzerland**	6	2	1

Outstanding Athletes

PLACE	NAME (NATIONALITY)	DISCIPLINE	G	S	B
1	**Alvin Kraenzlein (USA)**	**Athletics**	4	–	–
2	**Konrad Stäheli (SUI)**	**Shooting**	3	–	1
3	**Ray Ewry (USA)**	**Athletics**	3	–	–
4	**Irving Baxter (USA)**	**Athletics**	2	3	–
5	**Walter Tewksbury (USA)**	**Athletics**	2	2	1

EVENT	GOLD		SILVER		BRONZE	
Athletics						
60 m	Alvin Kraenzlein (USA)	7.0	Walter Tewksbury (USA)	7.1	Stanley Rowley (AUS)	7.2
100 m	Francis Jarvis (USA)	11.0	Walter Tewksbury (USA)	11.1	Stanley Rowley (AUS)	11.2
200 m	Walter Tewksbury (USA)	22.2	Norman Pritchard (IND)	22.8	Stanley Rowley (AUS)	22.9
400 m	Maxwell Long (USA)	49.4	William Holland (USA)	49.6	Ernst Schultz (DEN)	
800 m	Alfred Tysoe (GBR)	2:01.2	John Cregan (USA)	2:03.0	David Hall (USA)	
1500 m	Charles Bennett (GBR)	4:06.2	Henri Deloge (FRA)	4:06.6	John Bray (USA)	4:07.2
5000 m Team Event	Great Britain	26	France	29		
Marathon (25 miles 28 yds)	Michel Theato (FRA)	2:59:45	Emile Champion (FRA)	3:04:17	Ernst Fast (SWE)	3:37:14
110 m Hurdles	Alvin Kraenzlein (USA)	15.4	John McLean (USA)	15.5	Fred Moloney (USA)	15.6
200 m Hurdles	Alvin Kraenzlein (USA)	25.4	Norman Pritchard (IND)	26.6	Walter Tewksbury (USA)	
400 m Hurdles	Walter Tewksbury (USA)	57.6	Henri Tauzin (FRA)	58.3	George Orton (CAN)	
2500 m Steeplechase	George Orton (CAN)	7:34.4	Sidney Robinson (GBR)	7:38.0	Jacques Chastanié (FRA)	
4000 m Steeplechase	John Rimmer (GBR)	12:58.4	Charles Bennett (GBR)	12:58.6	Sidney Robinson (GBR)	12:58.8
High jump	Irving Baxter (USA)	6'2¾"	Patrick Leahy (GBR/IRL)	5'10"	Lajos Gönczy (HUN)	5'8¾"
Standing High Jump	Ray Ewry (USA)	5'5"	Irving Baxter (USA)	5'0"	Lewis Sheldon (USA)	4'11"
Pole Vault	Irving Baxter (USA)	10'9¾"	Meredith Colket (USA)	10'7¾"	Carl-Albert Andersen (NOR)	10'5¾"
Long Jump	Alvin Kraenzlein (USA)	23'6¾"	Myer Prinstein (USA)	23'6¼"	Patrick Leahy (GBR/IRL)	22'9½"
Standing Long Jump	Ray Ewry (USA)	10'6½"	Irving Baxter (USA)	10'3¼"	Emile Torcheboeuf (FRA)	9'11½"
Triple Jump	Myer Prinstein (USA)	47'5½"	James Connolly (USA)	45'10"	Lewis Sheldon (USA)	44'9"
Standing Triple Jump	Ray Ewry (USA)	34'8½"	Irving Baxter (USA)	32'8"	Robert Garrett (USA)	31'2"
Shot	Richard Sheldon (USA)	46'3"	Josiah McCracken (USA)	42'1¾"	Robert Garrett (USA)	40'7"
Discus	Rudolf Bauer (HUN)	118'2½"	Frantisek Janda-Suk (BOH)	115'7½"	Richard Sheldon (USA)	113'6"
Hammer	John Flanagan (USA)	163'1½"	Truxton Hare (USA)	161'2"	Josiah McCracken (USA)	139'3½"
Tug-of-War	Sweden/Denmark		USA		France	
Swimming						
200 m Freestyle	Frederick Lane (AUS)	2:25.2	Zoltán Halmay (HUN)	2:31.4	Karl Ruberl (AUT)	2:32.0
1000 m Freestyle	John Jarvis (GBR)	13:40.2	Otto Wahle (AUT)	14:53.6	Zoltán Halmay (HUN)	15:16.4
4000 m Freestyle	John Jarvis (GBR)	58:24.0	Zoltán Halmay (HUN)	1:08:55.4	Louis Martin (FRA)	1:13:08.4
200 m Backstroke	Ernst Hoppenberg (GER)	2:47.0	Karl Ruberl (AUT)	2:56.0	Johannes Drost (HOL)	3:01.0
200 m Team Swimming	Germany	32	France	51	France	61
200 m Obstacle Event	Frederick Lane (AUS)	2:38.4	Otto Wahle (AUT)	2:40.0	Peter Kemp (GBR)	2:47.4
Underwater Swimming	Charles de Vendeville (FRA)	516'7¼"	P. Alexandre Six (FRA)	508'4¾"	Peder Lykkeberg (DEN)	403'1¼"
Water Polo	Great Britain		Belgium		France	

EVENT	GOLD		SILVER		BRONZE	
Fencing						
Individual Foil	Emile Coste (FRA)		Henri Masson (FRA)		Jacques Boulenger (FRA)	
Foil for Fencing Masters	Lucien Mérignac (FRA)		Alphonse Kirchhoffer (FRA)		Jean-Baptiste Mimiague (FRA)	
Individual Épée	Ramón Fonst (CUB)		Louis Perrée (FRA)		Léon Sée (FRA)	
Épée for Fencing Masters	Albert Ayat (FRA)		Emile Bougnol (FRA)		Henri Laurent (FRA)	
Épée for Amateurs and Fencing Masters	Albert Ayat (FRA)		Ramón Fonst (CUB)		Léon Sée (FRA)	
Individual Saber	Georges de la Falaise (FRA)		Léon Thiébaut (FRA)		Siegfried Flesch (AUT)	
Sabre for Fencing Masters	Antonio Conte (ITA)		Italo Santelli (ITA)		Milan Neralic (AUT)	
Rowing						
Single Sculls	Henri Barrelet (FRA)	7:35.6	André Gaudin (FRA)	7:41.6	St. George Ashe (GBR)	8:15.6
Coxed Pairs	Netherlands	7:34.2	France I	7:34.4	France II	7:57.2
Coxless Fours	Belgium	7:16.8	France I	7:23.8	France II	7:47.2
Coxed Fours	France	7:11.0	France I	7:18.0	Germany	7:18.2
2nd Final★	Germany	5:59.0	Netherlands	6:33.0	Germany	6:35.0
Coxed Eights	USA	6:09.8	Belgium	6:13.8	Netherlands	6:23.0
Yachting						
Open Class	Great Britain		Germany		France	
0.5 Ton Class	France		France		France	
0 5-1.0 Ton Class	Great Britain		France		France	
1-2 Ton Class	Germany		Switzerland		France	
2-3 Ton Class	Great Britain		France		France	
3-10 Ton Class	France		Netherlands		France/Great Britain	
10-20 Ton Class	France		France		Great Britain	
Cycling						
2000 m Sprint	Georges Taillandier (FRA)		Fernand Sanz (FRA)		John Lake (USA)	
Equestrianism						
Grand Prix (Jumping)	Aimé Haegeman (BEL)	2:16.0	Georges van de Poele (BEL)	2:17.6	Pierre de Champsavin (FRA)	2:26.0
Equestrian High Jump	Dominique M. Gardères (FRA)	1.85	Giangiorgio Trissino (ITA)†	1.85	André Moreau (FRA)	1.70
Equestrian Long Jump	C. van Langhendonck (BEL)	6.10	Giangiorgio Trissino (ITA)	5.70	Henri de Prunelle (FRA)	5.30
†Equal first.						
Shooting						
Rapid-Fire Pistol	Maurice Larrouy (FRA)	58	Léon Moreaux (FRA)	57	Eugène Balme (FRA)	57
Free Pistol (50 m)	Karl Röderer (SUI)	503	Achille Paroche (FRA)	466	Konrad Stäheli (SUI)	453
Olympic Trap Shooting	Roger de Barbarin (FRA)	17	René Guyot (FRA)	17	Justinien de Clary (FRA)	17
Running Game Target	Louis Debray (FRA)	20	Pierre Nivet (FRA)	20	Comte de Lambert (FRA)	19
Live Pigeon Shooting	Léon de Lunden (BEL)	21	Maurice Faure (FRA)	20	Donald Macintosh (AUS)	18
					Crittenden Robinson (GBR)	18
Military Rifle	Emil Kellenberger (SUI)	930	Anders Nielsen (DEN)	921	Ole Östmo (NOR)	917
					Paul van Asbroeck (BEL)	917
Military Rifle – Three Positions						
Standing	Lars Madsen (DEN)	305	Ole Östmo (NOR)	299	Charles du Verger (BEL)	298
Kneeling	Konrad Stäheli (SUI)	324	Emil Kellenberger (SUI)	314		
			Anders Nielsen (DEN)	314		
Prone	Achille Paroche (FRA)	332	Anders Nielsen (DEN)	330	Ole Östmo (NOR)	329
Military Rifle (Team)	Switzerland	4399	Norwegen	4290	France	4278
Team Events	Switzerland	2271	France	2203	Netherlands	1876
Archery						
Au cordon doré (50 m)	Henri Herouin (FRA)	31	Hubert van Innis (BEL)	29	Emile Fisseux (FRA)	28
Au chapelet (50 m)	Eugène Mougin (FRA)		Henri Helle (FRA)		Emile Mercier (FRA)	
Au cordon doré (33 m)	Hubert van Innis (BEL)		Victor Thibaud (FRA)		Charles Petit (FRA)	
Au chapelet (33 m)	Hubert van Innis (BEL)		VictorThibaud (FRA)		Charles Petit (FRA)	
Sur la perche à la herse	Emmanuel Foulon (FRA)		Pierre Serrurier (FRA)		Emile Druart (BEL)	
Sur la perche à la pyramide	Emile Grumiaux (FRA)		Louis Glineux (BEL)			
Gymnastics						
Individual Combined Exercises	Gustave Sandras (FRA)	302	Noël Bas (FRA)	295	Lucien Démanet (FRA)	293
Soccer						
	Great Britain		France		Belgium	
Cricket						
	Great Britain		France			
Golf						
Men's Singles	Charles Sands (USA)	167	Walter Rutherford (GBR)	168	David Robertson (GBR)	175
Women's Singles	Margaret Abbott (USA)	47	Polly Whittier (SUI)	49	Daria Pratt (USA)	55

EVENT	GOLD	SILVER	BRONZE
Polo	Great Britain	Great Britain	France
Rugby	France	Germany	Great Britain
Tennis			
Men's Singles	Hugh Doherty (GBR)	Harold Mahony (GBR/IRL)	Reginald Doherty (GBR) A. B. J. Norris (GBR)
Men's Doubles	Reginald Doherty (GBR)/ Hugh Doherty (GBR)	Spalding de Garmendia (USA)/ Max Decugis (FRA)	André Prévost (FRA)/ Gerard de la Chapelle (FRA)/ Harold Mahony (GBR/IRL)/ A. B. J. Norris (GBR)
Women's Singles	Charlotte Cooper (GBR)	Hélène Prévost (FRA)	Marion Jones (USA) Hedwiga Rosenbaumová (BOH)
Mixed	Charlotte Cooper (GBR) Reginald Doherty (GBR)	Hélène Prévost (FRA) | Harold Mahony (GBR/IRL)	Hedwiga Rosenbaumová (BOH)/ Anthony Warden (GBR) Marion Jones (USA)/ Hugh Doherty (GBR)

★Various protests and delayed starts during the heats led to there being two finals; the winners' medals were awarded to the crews of the second final.

St. Louis 1904

July 1 – November 23

Participants: 687 / Men: 681, Women: 6, Countries: 13,
Sports: 6, Events: 104

Medals Table

PLACE	COUNTRY	GOLD	SILVER	BRONZE
1	USA	80	86	72
2	Germany	5	4	6
3	Cuba	5	3	3
4	Canada	4	1	1
5	Hungary	2	1	1

Outstanding Athletes

PLACE	NAME (NATIONALITY)	DISCIPLINE	G	S	B
1	Anton Heida (USA)	Gymnastics	5	1	
2	Marcus Hurley (USA)	Cycling	4		
3	George Eyser (USA)	Gymnastics	3	2	1
4	James Lightbody (USA)	Athletics	3	1	
	Charles Daniels (USA)	Swimming	3	1	

EVENT	GOLD		SILVER		BRONZE	
Athletics						
60 m	Archie Hahn (USA)	7.0	William Hogenson (USA)	7.2	Fay Moulton (USA)	7.2
100 m	Archie Hahn (USA)	11.0	Nathaniel Cartmell (USA)	11.2	William Hogenson (USA)	11.2
200 m	Archie Hahn (USA)	21.6	Nathaniel Cartmell (USA)	21.9	William Hogenson (USA)	
400 m	Harry Hillman (USA)	49.2	Frank Waller (USA)	49.9	Herman Groman (USA)	50.0
800 m	James Lightbody (USA)	1:56.0	Howard Valentine (USA)	1:56.3	Emil Breitkreuz (USA)	1:56.4
1500 m	James Lightbody (USA)	4:05.4	W. Frank Verner (USA)	4:06.8	Lacey Hearn (USA)	
Marathon (24 miles 1503 yds)	Thomas Hicks (USA)	3:28:35	Albert Coray (FRA)	3:34:52	Arthur Newton (USA)	3:47:33
110 m Hurdles	Frederick Schule (USA)	16.0	Thaddeus Shideler (USA)	16.3	Lesley Ashburner (USA)	16.4
200 m Hurdles	Harry Hillman (USA)	24.6	Frank Castleman (USA)	24.9	George Poage (USA)	
400 m Hurdles	Harry Hillman (USA)	53.0	Frank Waller (USA)	53.2	George Poage (USA)	
Steeplechase	James Lightbody (USA)	7:39.6	John Daly (GBR/IRL)	7:40.6	Arthur Newton (USA)	
Team Cross-Country	USA	21:17.8	USA		France	
High jump	Samuel Jones (USA)	5'11"	Garret Serviss (USA)	5'10"	Paul Weinstein (GER)	5'10"
Standing High Jump	Ray Ewry (USA)	5'3"	Joseph Stadler (USA)	4'9"	Lawson Robertson (USA)	4'9"
Pole Vault	Charles Dvorak (USA)	11'6"	LeRoy Samse (USA)	11'3"	Louis Wilkins (USA)	11'3"
Long Jump	Myer Prinstein (USA)	24'1"	Daniel Frank (USA)	22'7¼"	Robert Stangland (USA)	22'7"
Standing Long Jump	Ray Ewry (USA)	11'4⅞"	Charles King (USA)	10'9"	John Biller (USA)	10'8½"
Triple Jump	Myer Prinstein (USA)	47'1"	Frederick Englehardt (USA)	45'7¼"	Robert Stangland (USA)	43'10¼"
Standing Triple Jump	Ray Ewry (USA)	34'7¼"	Charles King (USA)	33'4"	James Stadler (USA)	31'3½"
Shot	Ralph Rose (USA)	48'7"	William W. Coe (USA)	47'3"	Leon Feuerbach (USA)	43'10½"
Discus	Martin Sheridan (USA)	128'10½"	Ralph Rose (USA)	128'10½"	Nicolaos Georgantas (GRE)	123'7½"
Hammer	John Flanagan (USA)	168'0½"	John DeWitt (USA)	164'10½"	Ralph Rose (USA)	150'0"
56 lb Weight Throw	Etienne Desmarteau (CAN)	28'8¼"	John Flanagan (USA)	27'10¼"	James Mitchell (USA)	27'9½"
Tug-of-War	USA		USA		USA	
Combined events	Thomas Kiely (GBR/IRL)	6036	Adam Gunn (USA)	5907	Truxton Hare (USA)	5813

EVENT	GOLD		SILVER		BRONZE	
Swimming						
50 yards Freestyle	Zoltán Halmay (HUN)	28.0	Scott Leary (USA)	28.6	Charles Daniels (USA)	
100 yards Freestyle	Zoltán Halmay (HUN)	1:02.8	Charles Daniels (USA)		Scott Leary (USA)	
220 yards Freestyle	Charles Daniels (USA)	2:44.2	Francis Gailey (USA)	2:46.0	Emil Rausch (GER)	2:56.0
440 yards Freestyle	Charles Daniels (USA)	6:16.2	Francis Gailey (USA)	6:22.0	Otto Wahle (AUT)	6:39.0
880 yards Freestyle	Emil Rausch (GER)	13:11.4	Francis Gailey (USA)	13:23.4	Géza Kiss (HUN)	
1 mile Freestyle	Emil Rausch (GER)	27:18.2	Géza Kiss (HUN)	28:28.2	Francis Gailey (USA)	28:54.0
100 yards Backstroke	Walter Brack (GER)	1:16.8	Georg Hoffmann (GER)	1:18.0	Georg Zacharias (GER)	1:19.6
440 yards Breaststroke	George Zacharias (GER)	7:23.6	Walter Brack (GER)	7:33.0	Jamison Handy (USA)	
4 x 50 yards Relay	USA	2:04.6	USA		USA	
Highboard Diving	George Sheldon (USA)	12.66	Georg Hoffmann (GER)	11.66	Frank Nehoe (USA)	11.33
					Alfred Braunschweiger (GER)	11.33
Plunge for Distance	W. E. Dickey (USA)	62'6¼"	Edgar Adams (USA)	57'6¼"	Leo Goodwin (USA)	57'0½"
Water Polo	USA		USA		USA	
Boxing						
Flyweight (-105 lb)	George Finnegan (USA)		Miles Burke (USA)			
Bantamweight (-115 lb)	Oliver Kirk (USA)		George Finnegan (USA)			
Featherweight (-125 lb)	Oliver Kirk (USA)		Frank Haller (USA)		Fred Gilmore (USA)	
Lightweight (-135 lb)	Harry Spanger (USA)		James Eagan (USA)		Russell van Horn (USA)	
Welterweight (-143¾ lb)	Albert Young (USA)		Harry Spanger (USA)		Joseph Lydon (USA)	
Middleweight (-158 lb)	Charles Mayer (USA)		Benjamin Spradley (USA)			
Heavyweight (+158 lb)	Samuel Berger (USA)		Charles Mayer (USA)		William Michaels (USA)	
Weightlifting						
One-arm Lifts (10 Lifts)	Oscar Paul Osthoff (USA)	48pts	Frederik Winters (USA)	45pts	Frank Kungler (USA)	10pts
Two-arm Lifts	Perikles Kakousis (GRE)	246 lb	Oscar Paul Osthoff (USA)	186 lb	Frank Kungler (USA)	176 lb
Freestyle Wrestling						
Light Flyweight (-105¾ lb)	Robert Curry (USA)		John Heim (USA)		Gustav Thiefenthaler (USA)	
Flyweight (-115 lb)	George Mehnert (USA)		Gustave Bauer (USA)		William Nelson (USA)	
Bantamweight (-125 lb)	Isaac Niflot (USA)		August Wester (USA)		Z. B. Strebler (USA)	
Featherweight (-135 lb)	Benjamin Bradshaw (USA)		Theodore McLear (USA)		Charles Clapper (USA)	
Lightweight (-145 lb)	Otto Roehm (USA)		Rudolph Tesing (USA)		Albert Zirkel (USA)	
Welterweight (-158 lb)	Charles Erickson (USA)		William Beckmann (USA)		Jerry Winholtz (USA)	
Heavyweight (+158 lb)	Bernhuff Hansen (USA)		Frank Kungler (USA)		Fred Warmbold (USA)	
Fencing						
Foil (Individual)	Ramón Fonst (CUB)		Albertson Van Zo Post (CUB)		Charles Tatham (CUB)	
Foil (Team)	Cuba		USA		Cuba	
Épée (Individual)	Ramón Fonst (CUB)		Charles Tatham (CUB)		Albertson Van Zo Post (CUB)	
Saber (Individual)	Manuel Diaz (CUB)		William Grebe (USA)		Albertson Van Zo Post (CUB)	
Single Sticks	Albertson Van Zo Post (CUB)		William Grebe (USA)		William Scott O'Connor (USA)	
Rowing						
Single Sculls	Frank Greer (USA)	10:08.5	James Juvenal (USA)		Constance Titus (USA)	
Double Sculls	USA	10:03.2	USA		USA	
Coxless Fours	USA	9:53.8	USA			
Coxed Eights	USA	7:50.0	Canada			
Archery						
Men						
York Round	Phillip Bryant (USA)	820	Robert Williams (USA)	819	William Thompson (USA)	816
American Round	Phillip Bryant (USA)	1048	Robert Williams (USA)	991	William Thompson (USA)	949
Team Round	USA	1344	USA	1341	USA	1268
Women						
National Round	Lida Howell (USA)	620	Jessie Pollock (USA)	419	Emma Cooke (USA)	419
Columbia Round	Lida Howell (USA)	867	Emma Cooke (USA)	630	Jessie Pollock (USA)	630
Team Round	USA	506	USA			
Gymnastics						
Individual Combined Exercises	Julius Lenhart (AUT)	69.80	Wilhelm Weber (GER)	69.10	Adolf Spinnler (SUI)	67.99
Team	USA	374.43	USA	356.37	USA	349.69
Parallel Bars	George Eyser (USA)	44	Anton Heida (USA)	43	John Duha (USA)	40
Horse Vault	Anton Heida (USA)/	36			William Merz (USA)	31
	George Eyser (USA)	36				

EVENT	GOLD		SILVER		BRONZE	
Pommel Horse	Anton Heida (USA)	42	George Eyser (USA)	33	William Merz (USA)	29
Horizontal Bar	Anton Heida (USA)	40			George Eyser (USA)	39
	Edward Hennig (USA)	40				
Rings	Hermann Glass (USA)	45	William Merz (USA)	35	Emil Voigt (USA)	32
Rope Climbing	George Eyser (USA)	7.0	Charles Krause (USA)	7.8	Emil Voigt (USA)	9.8
Club Swinging	Edward Hennig (USA)	13.0	Emil Voigt (USA)	9.0	Ralph Wilson (USA)	5.0
Four Event Competition	Anton Heida (USA)	161	George Eyser (USA)	152	William Merz (USA)	135
Nine Event Competition	Adolf Spinnler (SUI)	43.49	Julius Lenhart (AUT)	43.00	Wilhelm Weber (GER)	41.60
Triathlon	Max Emmerich (USA)	35.70	John Grieb (USA)	34.00	William Merz (USA)	33.90
Tennis						
Men's Singles	Beals Wright (USA)		Robert LeRoy (USA)			
Men's Doubles	Edgar Leonard/		Alonzo Bell/			
	Beals Wright (USA)		Robert LeRoy (USA)			
Lacrosse						
	Canada		USA			
Roque						
	Charles Jacobus (USA)		S. O. Streeter (USA)		Charles Brown (USA)	
Basketball						
	USA		USA		USA	
Soccer						
	Canada		USA		USA	

London 1908

Participants: 2035 / Men: 1999, Women: 36, Countries: 22,
Sports: 21, Events: 110

April 27 – October 31
(Official Opening Ceremony on July 13)

Medals Table

PLACE	COUNTRY	GOLD	SILVER	BRONZE
1	Great Britain	56	50	39
2	USA	23	12	12
3	Sweden	7	5	10
4	France	5	5	9
5	Germany	3	5	5

Outstanding Athletes

PLACE	NAME (NATIONALITY)	DISCIPLINE	G	S	B
1	Melvin Sheppard (USA)	Athletics	3	–	–
	Henry Taylor (GBR)	Swimming	3	–	–
3	Benjamin Jones (GBR)	Cycling	2	1	–
4	Martin Sheridan (USA)	Athletics	2	–	1
	Oscar Swahn (SWE)	Shooting	2	–	1

EVENT	GOLD		SILVER		BRONZE	
Athletics						
100 m	Reginald Walker (SAF)	10.8	James Rector (USA)	10.9	Robert Kerr (CAN)	11.0
200 m	Robert Kerr (CAN)	22.6	Robert Cloughen (USA)	22.6	Nathaniel Cartmell (USA)	22.7
400 m	Wyndham Halswelle (GBR)	50.0				
800 m	Melvin Sheppard (USA)	1:52.8	Emilio Lunghi (ITA)	1:54.2	Hanns Braun (GER)	1:55.2
1500 m	Melvin Sheppard (USA)	4:03.4	Harold Wilson (GBR)	4:03.6	Norman Hallows (GBR)	4:04.0
5 Miles (8046.57 m)	Emil Voigt (GBR)	25:11.2	Edward Owen (GBR)	25:24.0	John Svanberg (SWE)	25:37.2
3 Miles Team Race	Great Britain	6	USA	19	France	32
Marathon	John Joseph Hayes (USA)	2:55:18.4	Charles Hefferon (SAF)	2:56:06.0	Joseph Forshaw (USA)	2:57:10.4
110 m Hurdles	Forrest Smithson (USA)	15.0	John Garrels (USA)	15.7	Arthur Shaw (USA)	
400 m Hurdles	Charles Bacon (USA)	55.0	Harry Hillman (USA)	55.3	Leonard Tremeer (GBR)	57.0
3200 m Steeplechase	Arthur Russel (GBR)	10:47.8	Archie Robertson (GBR)	10:48.4	John Lincoln Eisele (USA)	
Medley Relay	USA	3:29.4	Germany	3:32.4	Hungary	3:32.5
3500 m Walk	George Larner (GBR)	14:55.0	Ernest Webb (GBR)	15:07.4	Harry Kerr (NZL)	15:43.4
10 Miles Walk (16 093.4 m)	George Larner (GBR)	1:15:57.4	Ernest Webb (GBR)	1:17:31.0	Edward Spencer (GBR)	1:21:20.2
High Jump	Harry Porter (USA)	6'3"	Con Leahy (GBR/IRL)	6'2"		
			István Somody (HUN)	6'2"		
			Georges André (FRA)	6'2"		

EVENT	GOLD		SILVER		BRONZE	
Standing High Jump	Ray Ewry (USA)	5'2¼"	Konstantin Tsiklitiras (GRE)	5'7½"		
			John Biller (USA)	5'7½"		
Pole Vault	Edward Cooke (USA)	12'2"	Ed Archibald (CAN)	11'9"		
	Alfred Gilbert (USA)	12'2"	Charles Jacobs (USA)	11'9"		
			Bruno Söderström (SWE)	11'9"		
Long Jump	Francis Irons (USA)	24'6½"	Daniel Kelly (USA)	23'3¾"	Calvin Bricker (CAN)	23'3"
Standing Long Jump	Ray Ewry (USA)	10'11½"	Konstantin Tsiklitiras (GRE)	10'7¼"	Martin Sheridan (USA)	10'7"
Triple Jump	Timothy Ahearne (GBR/IRL)	48'11¼"	J. Garfield McDonald (CAN)	48'5¼"	Edvard Larsen (NOR)	47'2¾"
Shot	Ralph Rose (USA)	46'7½"	Dennis Horgan (GBR)	44'8¼"	John Garrels (USA)	43'3"
Discus	Martin Sheridan (USA)	134'2"	Merritt Giffin (USA)	133'6½"	Marquis Horr (USA)	129'5"
Greek Style	Martin Sheridan (USA)	124'9"	Marquis Horr (USA)	122'6¾"	Werner Järvinen (FIN)	119'9¼"
Hammer	John Flanagan (USA)	170'4"	Matthew McGrath (USA)	167'11"	Cornelius Walsh (USA)	159'1½"
Javelin	Erik Lemming (SWE)	179'10½"	Arne Halse (NOR)	165'11"	Otto Nilsson (SWE)	154'6"
Freestyle	Erik Lemming (SWE)	178'9"	Michel Dorizas (GRE)	168'7"	Arne Halse (NOR)	163'3"
Tug-of-War	Great Britain		Great Britain		Great Britain	
Swimming						
100 m Freestyle	Charles Daniels (USA)	1:05.6	Zoltán Halmay (HUN)	1:06.2	Harald Julin (SWE)	1:08.0
400 m Freestyle	Henry Taylor (GBR)	5:36.8	Frank Beaurepaire (AUS)	5:44.2	Otto Scheff (AUT)	5:46.0
1500 m Freestyle	Henry Taylor (GBR)	22:48.4	Sydney Battersby (GBR)	22:51.2	Frank Beaurepaire (AUS)	22:56.2
100 m Backstroke	Arno Bieberstein (GER)	1:24.6	Ludwig Dam (DEN)	1:26.6	Herbert Haresnape (GBR)	1:27.0
200 m Breaststroke	Frederick Holman (GBR)	3:09.2	William Robinson (GBR)	3:12.8	Pontus Hansson (SWE)	3:14.6
4 x 200 m Freestyle Relay	Great Britain	10:55.6	Hungary	10:59.0	USA	11:02.8
Springboard Diving	Albert Zürner (GER)	85.5	Kurt Behrens (GER)	85.3	George Gaidzik (USA)	80.8
					Gottlob Walz (GER)	80.8
Highboard Diving	Hjalmar Johansson (SWE)	83.75	Karl Malmström (SWE)	78.73	Arvid Spångberg (SWE)	74.00
Water Polo	Great Britain		Belgium		Sweden	
Boxing						
Bantamweight (-116 lb)	A. Henry Thomas (GBR)		John Condon (GBR)		W. Webb (GBR)	
Featherweight (-126 lb)	Richard Gunn (GBR)		C. W. Morris (GBR)		Hugh Roddin (GBR)	
Lightweight (-140 lb)	Frederick Grace (GBR)		Frederick Spiller (GBR)		H. H. Johnson (GBR)	
Middleweight (-158 lb)	John Douglas (GBR)		Reginald Baker (AUS)		W. Philo (GBR)	
Heavyweight (+158 lb)	A. L. Oldham (GBR)		S. C. H. Evans (GBR)		Frederick Parks (GBR)	
Greco-Roman Wrestling						
Lightweight (-146¾ lb)	Enrico Porro (ITA)		Nikolai Orlov (RUS)		Arvid Linden (FIN)	
Middleweight (-161 lb)	Frithiof Märtensson (SWE)		Mauritz Andersson (SWE)		Anders Andersen (DEN)	
Light-Heavyweight (-205 lb)	Verner Weckman (FIN)		Yrjö Saarela (FIN)		Carl Jensen (DEN)	
Heavyweight (+205 lb)	Richard Weisz (HUN)		Alexander Petrov (RUS)		Sören Marius Jensen (DEN)	
Freestyle Wrestling						
Bantamweight (-125 lb)	George Mehnert (USA)		William Press (GBR)		Aubert Côté (CAN)	
Featherweight (-13 lb)	George Dole (USA)		James Slim (GBR)		William McKie (GBR)	
Lightweight (-146¾ lb)	George de Relwyskow (GBR)		William Wood (GBR)		Albert Gingell (GBR)	
Middleweight (-161 lb)	Stanley Bacon (GBR)		George de Relwyskow (GBR)		Frederick Beck (GBR)	
Heavyweight (+161 lb)	George Con O'Kelly (GBR /IRL)		Jacob Gundersen (NOR)		Edmond Barrett (GBR/IRL)	
Fencing						
Épée (Individual)	Gaston Alibert (FRA)	5	Alexandre Lippmann (FRA)	4+2	Eugène Olivier (FRA)	4+1
Épée (Team)	France		Great Britain		Belgium	
Saber (Individual)	Jenö Fuchs (HUN)	6+1	Béla Zulavsky (HUN)	6	Vilém Goppold von Lobsdorf (BOH)	4
Saber (Team)	Hungary		Italy		Bohemia	
Rowing						
Single Sculls	Harry Blackstaffe (GBR)	9:26.0	Alexander McCulloch (GBR)		Bernhard von Gaza (GER)	
					Károly Levitzky (HUN)	
Coxless Pairs	Great Britain	9:41.0	Great Britain		Canada	
Coxless Fours	Great Britain	8:34.0	Great Britain		Netherlands	
Coxed Eights	Great Britain	7:52.0	Belgium		Great Britain II	
Yachting						
6 m	Great Britain		Belgium		France	
7 m	Great Britain					
8 m	Great Britain		Sweden		Great Britain	
12 m	Great Britain		Great Britain			

London 1908

EVENT	GOLD		SILVER		BRONZE	
Motorboating						
Open Class	E. B. Thubron (FRA)	2:26.53				
60 Foot	Thomas Thornycroft/					
	Bernard Redwood (GBR)	2:28:58				
8 m	Thomas Thornycroft/					
	Bernard Redwood (GBR)	2:28:36				
Cycling						
660 yards Track	Victor Johnson (GBR)		Emile Demangel (FRA)		Karl Neumer (GER)	
100 km Track	Charles Bartlett (GBR)	2:41:48.6	Charles Denny (GBR)		Octave Lapize (FRA)	
1000 m Sprint	Declared void; riders exceeded the time limit.					
20 km Track	Charles Kingsbury (GBR)	34:13.6	Benjamin Jones (GBR)		Joseph Werbrouck (BEL)	
2000 m Tandem	France	3:07.6	Great Britain		Great Britain	
5000 m	Benjamin Jones (GBR)	8:36.2	Maurice Schilles (FRA)		André Auffray (FRA)	
4000 m Team Pursuit	Great Britain	2:18.6	Germany	2:28.6	Canada	2:29.6
Shooting						
Free Rifle (3 positions)	Albert Helgerud (NOR)	909	Harry Simon (USA)	887	Ole Saether (NOR)	883
Free Rifle (Team)	Norway	5055	Sweden	4711	France	4652
Free Rifle	Jerry Millner (GBR)	98	Kellogg Casey (USA)	93	Maurice Blood (GBR)	92
Military Rifle	Louis Richardet (SUI)	238	Jean Reich (SUI)	234	Raoul de Boigne (FRA)	232
Military Rifle (Team)	USA	2531	Great Britain	2497	Canada	2439
Small-Bore Rifle (Prone)	A. A. Carnell (GBR)	387	Harry Humby (GBR)	386	George Barnes (GBR)	385
Small-Bore Rifle (Moving Target)	A. F. Fleming (GBR)	24	M.K. Matthews (GBR)	24	W. B. Marsden (GBR)	24
Small Bore Rifle (Disappearing Target)	William Styles (GBR)	45	H. J. Hawkins (GBR)	45	E. J. Amoore (GBR)	45
Small-Bore Rifle (Team)	Great Britain	771	Sweden	737	France	710
Rapid-Fire Pistol	Paul van Asbroeck (BEL)	490	Reginald Storms (BEL)	487	James Edward Gorman (GBR)	485
Rapid-Fire (Team)	USA	1914	Belgium	1863	Great Britain	1817
Olympic Trap Shooting	Walter Henry Ewing (CAN)	72	Georg Beattie (CAN)	60	Alexander Maunder (GBR)	57
Clay Pigeons (Team)	Great Britain	407	Canada	405	Great Britain	372
Running Deer Shooting	Oscar Swahn (SWE)	25	Ted Ranken (GBR)	24	Alexander Rodgers (GBR)	24
Running Deer Shooting (Team)	Sweden	86	Great Britain	85		
Running Deer Shooting (Double Shot)	Walter Winans (USA)	46	Ted Ranken (GBR)	46	Oscar Swahn (SWE)	38
Archery						
Men						
York Round	William Dod (GBR)	815	R. B. Brooks-King (GBR)	768	Henry B. Richardson (USA)	760
Continental Round	E. G. Grisot (FRA)	263	Louis Vernet (FRA)	256	Gustave Cabaret (FRA)	255
Women						
National Round	Q. F. Newall (GBR)	688	Lottie Dod (GBR)	642	Hill-Lowe (GBR)	618
Gymnastics						
Individual Combined Exercises	Alberto Braglia (ITA)	317.0	S. W. Tysal (GBR)	312.0	Louis Ségura (FRA)	297.0
Team	Sweden	438	Norway	425	Finland	405
Soccer						
	Great Britain		Denmark		Netherlands	
Hockey						
	Great Britain		Great Britain/Ireland		Great Britain/Scotland	
					Great Britain/Wales	
Jeu de Paume						
	Jay Gould (USA)		Eustace Miles (GBR)		Neville Lytton (GBR)	
Lacrosse						
	Canada		Great Britain			
Polo						
	Great Britain		Great Britain II		Great Britain III	
Rugby						
	Australia		Great Britain			
Tennis						
Men's Singles	Josiah Ritchie (GBR)		Otto Froitzheim (GER)		Wilberforce Eaves (GBR)	
Men's Singles (Indoor)	Wentworth Gore (GBR)		George Caridia (GBR)		Josiah Ritchie (GBR)	

EVENT	GOLD	SILVER	BRONZE
Men's Doubles	George W. Hillyard/Reginald Doherty (GBR)	Josiah Ritchie/James Cecil Parke (GBR)	Charles Cazalet/Charles Dixon(GBR)
Men's Doubles (Indoor)	Arthur W. Gore/Herbert Ropel-Barrett (GBR)	George Simond/George Caridia (GBR)	Gunnar Setterwall/Wollmar Boström (SWE)
Women's Singles	Dorothea Chambers (GBR)	Dorothy Boothby (GBR)	Joan Winch (GBR)
Women's Singles (Indoor)	Gwendoline Eastlake-Smith (GBR)	Angela Greene (GBR)	Martha Adlerstrâhle (SWE)
Rackets	Evan B. Noel (GBR)	Henry Leaf (GBR)	John Astor (GBR)
Doubles	Vane Pennel/John Astor (GBR)	Edward Bury/Cecil Browning (GBR)	Evan Noel/Henry Leaf (GBR)
Figure Skating			
Women	Florence Syers (GBR)	Elsa Rendschmidt (GER)	Dorothy Greenhough-Smith (GBR)
Men	Ulrich Salchow (SWE)	Richard Johansson (SWE)	Per Thorén (SWE)
Pairs	Annie Kübler/Heinrich Burger (GER)	Phyllis Johnson/James Johnson (GBR)	Florence Syers/Edgar Syers (GBR)

Stockholm 1912

Participants: 2547 / Men: 2490, Women: 57, Countries: 28,
Sports: 13, Events: 102

May 5 – July 22
(Official Opening Ceremony on July 6)

Medals Table

PLACE	COUNTRY	GOLD	SILVER	BRONZE
1	Sweden	24	24	17
2	USA	23	19	1
3	Great Britain	10	15	16
4	Finland	9	8	9
5	France	7	4	3

Outstanding Athletes

PLACE	NAME (NATIONALITY)	DISCIPLINE	G	S	B
1	Hannes Kolehmainen (FIN)	Athletics	3	1	–
	Wilhelm Carlberg (SWE)	Shooting	3	1	–
	Alfred Lane (USA)	Shooting	3	1	–
4	Johan von Holst (SWE)	Shooting	2	1	1
5	Eric Carlberg (SWE)	Shooting	2	1	–

EVENT	GOLD		SILVER		BRONZE	
Athletics						
100 m	Ralph Cook Craig (USA)	10.8	Alvah Meyer (USA)	10.9	Donald Lippincott (USA)	10.9
200 m	Ralph Cook Craig (USA)	21.7	Donald Lippincott (USA)	21.8	William Applegarth (GBR)	22.0
400 m	Charles Reidpath (USA)	48.2	Hanns Braun (GER)	48.3	Edward Lindberg (USA)	48.4
800 m	James Meredith (USA)	1:51.9	Melvin Sheppard (USA)	1:52.0	Ira Davenport (USA)	1:52.0
1500 m	Arnold Jackson (GBR)	3:56.8	Abel Kiviat (USA)	3:56.9	Norman Taber (USA)	3:56.9
3000 m Team Race	USA	9	Sweden	13	Great Britain	23
5000 m	Hannes Kolehmainen (FIN)	14:36.6	Jean Bouin (FRA)	14:36.7	George Hutson (GBR)	15:07.6
10,000 m	Hannes Kolehmainen (FIN)	31:20.8	Louis Tewanima (USA)	32:06.6	Albin Stenroos (FIN)	32:21.8
Marathon (24 miles 1723 yds)	Kenneth McArthur (SAF)	2:36:54.8	Christian Gitsham (SAF)	2:37:52.0	Gaston Strobino (USA)	2:38:42.4
110 m Hurdles	Frederick Kelly (USA)	15.1	James Wendell (USA)	15.2	Martin Hawkins (USA)	15.3
Individual Cross-Country	Hannes Kolehmainen (FIN)	45:11.6	Hjalmar Andersson (SWE)	45:44.8	John Eke (SWE)	46:37.6
Team Cross-Country	Sweden	10	Finland	11	Great Britain	49
4 x 100 m	Great Britain	42.4	Sweden	42.6		
4 x 400 m	USA	3:16.6	France	3:20.7	Great Britain	3:23.2
10 km Walk	George Goulding (CAN)	46:28.4	Ernest Webb (GBR)	46:50.4	Fernando Altimani (ITA)	47:37.6
High Jump	Alma Richards (USA)	6'4"	Hans Liesche (GER)	6'3¼"	George Horine (USA)	6'2½"
Standing High Jump	Platt Adams (USA)	5'4¼"	Benjamin Adams (USA)	5'3"	Konstantin Tsiklitiras (GRE)	5'1¼"
Pole Vault	Harry Babcock (USA)	12'11½"	Marcus Wright (USA)	12'7½"		
			Frank Nelson (USA)	12'7½"		
Long Jump	Albert Gutterson (USA)	24'11"	Calvin Bricker (CAN)	23'7¾"	Georg Aberg (SWE)	23'6½"
Standing Long Jump	Konstantin Tsiklitiras (GRE)	11'0¾"	Platt Adams (USA)	11'0½"	Benjamin Adams (USA)	10'9¼"
Triple Jump	Gustaf Lindblom (SWE)	48'5"	Georg Aberg (SWE)	47'7¼"	Erik Almlöf (SWE)	89'8¼"
Shot	Patrick McDonald (USA)	50'4"	Ralph Rose (USA)	50'0¼"	Lawrence Whitney (USA)	46'5"
(Both Hands)	Ralph Rose (USA)	90'11"	Patrick McDonald (USA)	90'4½"	Elmer Niklander (FIN)	89'8¼"
Discus	Armas Taipale (FIN)	148'3½"	Richard Byrd (USA)	138'10"	James Duncan (USA)	138'8½"
(Both Hands)	Armas Taipale (FIN)	272'0¾"	Elmer Niklander (FIN)	255'11½"	Emil Magnusson (SWE)	254'0½"
Hammer	Matthew McGrath (USA)	179'7"	Duncan Gillis (CAN)	158'9"	Clarence Childs (USA)	158'0"
Javelin	Erik Lemming (SWE)	198'11"	Juho Saaristo (FIN)	192'5"	Mór Kóczán (HUN)	182'1"
(Both Hands)	Julio Saaristo (FIN)	359'3"	Väinö Siikaniemi (FIN)	332'0½"	Urho Peltonen (FIN)	329'8½"
*Pentathlon	Ferdinand Bie (NOR)	16	James Donahue (USA)	24	Frank Lukemann (CAN)	24

EVENT	GOLD		SILVER		BRONZE	
*Decathlon	Hugo Wieslander (SWE)	7724.495	Charles Lomberg (SWE)	7413.510	Gösta Holmér (SWE)	7347.855
Tug-of-War	Sweden		Great Britain			
*In 1982 Jim Thorpe (USA) the original gold medal winner in the Pentathlon and Decathlon was reinstated.						
Swimming						
Men						
100 m Freestyle	Duke Kahanamoku (USA)	1:03.4	Cecil Healey (AUS)	1:04.6	Kenneth Huszagh (USA)	1:05.6
400 m Freestyle	George Hodgson (CAN)	5:24.4	John Hatfield (GBR)	5:28.8	Harold Hardwick (AUS)	5:31.2
1500 m Freestyle	George Hodgson (CAN)	22:00.0	John Hatfield (GBR)	22:39.0	Harold Hardwick (AUS)	23:15.4
100 m Backstroke	Harry Hebner (USA)	1:21.2	Otto Fahr (GER)	1:22.4	Paul Kellner (GER)	1:24.0
200 m Breaststroke	Walter Bathe (GER)	3:01.8	Wilhelm Lützow (GER)	3:05.0	Kurt Malisch (GER)	3:08.0
400 m Breaststroke	Walter Bathe (GER)	6:29.6	Thor Henning (SWE)	6:35.6	Percy Courtman (GBR)	6:36.4
4 x 200 m Freestyle	Australia	10:11.6	USA	10:20.2	Great Britain	10:28.2
Springboard Diving	Paul Günther (GER)	79.23	Hans Luber (GER)	76.78	Kurt Behrens (GER)	73.73
Highboard Diving	Erik Adlerz (SWE)	73.94	Albert Zürner (GER)	72.60	Gustaf Blomgren (SWE)	69.56
Plain High Diving	Erik Adlerz (SWE)	40.0	Hjalmar Johansson (SWE)	39.3	John Jansson (SWE)	39.1
Water Polo	Great Britain		Sweden		Belgium	
Women						
100 m Freestyle	Fanny Durack (AUS)	1:22.2	Wilhelmina Wylie (AUS)	1:25.4	Jennie Fletcher (GBR)	1:27.0
4 x 100 m Freestyle	Great Britain	5:52.8	Germany	6:04.6	Austria	6:17.0
Highboard Diving	Greta Johansson (SWE)	39.9	Lisa Regnell (SWE)	36.0	Isabelle White (GBR)	34.0
Greco-Roman Wrestling						
Featherweight (-132¼ lb)	Kaarlo Koskelo (FIN)		Georg Gerstacker (GER)		Otto Lasanen (FIN)	
Lightweight (-148¾ lb)	Eemel Väre (FIN)		Gustaf Malmström (SWE)		Edvin Matiasson (SWE)	
Middleweight (-165¼ lb)	Claes Johansson (SWE)		Martin Klein (RUS)		Alfred Asikainen (FIN)	
Light-Heavyweight (-181¾ lb)			Anders Ahlgren (SWE)		Béla Varga (HUN)	
			Ivar Böhling (FIN)			
Heavyweight (+181¾ lb)	Yrjö Saarela (FIN)		Johan Olin (FIN)		Sören Jensen (DEN)	
Fencing						
Individual Foil	Nedo Nadi (ITA)	7	Pietro Speciale (ITA)	5	Richard Verderber (AUT)	4
Individual Épée	Paul Anspach (BEL)	6	Ivan Osiier (DEN)	5	Philippe Le Hardy de Beaulieu (BEL)	4
Team Épée	Belgium		Great Britain		Netherlands	
Individual Saber	Jenö Fuchs (HUN)	6	Béla Békéssy (HUN)	5/5	Ervin Mészáros (HUN)	5/6
Team Saber	Hungary		Austria		Netherlands	
Modern Pentathlon						
	Gustaf Lilliehöök (SWE)	27	Gösta Asbrink (SWE)	28	Georg de Laval (SWE)	30
Rowing						
Single Sculls	William Kinnear (GBR)	7:47.6	Polydore Veirman (BEL)	7:56.0	Everard Butler (CAN)	
					Mikhail Kusik (RUS)	
Coxed Fours	Germany	6:59.4	Great Britain		Denmark/Norway†	
Coxed Fours (Inriggers)	Denmark	7:47.0	Sweden	7:56.2	Norway	
Coxed Eights	Great Britain	6:15.0	Great Britain	6:19.0	Germany	
†Denmark and Norway were joint bronze medalists.						
Yachting						
6 m	France		Denmark		Sweden	
8 m	Norway		Sweden		Finland	
10 m	Sweden		Finnland		Russia	
12 m	Norway		Sweden		Finland	
Cycling						
Individual Road Race (200 miles)	Rudolph Lewis (SAF)	10:42:39.0	Frederick Grubb (GBR)	10:51:24.2	Carl Schutte (USA)	10:52:38.8
Team Road Race	Sweden	44:35:33.6	Great Britain	44:44:39.2	USA	44:47:55.5
Equestrianism						
Three-Day Event	Axel Nordlander (SWE)	46.59	Friedrich v. Rochow (GER)	46.42	Jean Cariou (FRA)	46.32
Three-Day Event Team	Sweden	139.06	Germany	138.48	USA	137.33
Grand Prix (Dressage)	Carl Bonde (SWE)	15	Gustav Adolf Boltenstern (SWE)	21	Hans v. Blixen-Finecke (SWE)	32
Grand Prix (Jumping)	Jean Cariou (FRA)	186	Rabod Wilhelm v. Kröcher (GER)	186	Emanuel de Blommaert de Soye (BEL)	185
Grand Prix (Jumping) Team	Sweden	545	France	538	Germany	530
Shooting						
Free Rifle (3 Positions)	Paul Colas (FRA)	987	Lars Jörgen Madsen (DEN)	981	Niels Larsen (DEN)	962
Free Rifle (Team)	Sweden	5655	Norway	5605	Denmark	5529
Military Rifle	Paul Colas (FRA)	94	Carl Osburn (USA)	94	Joseph Jackson (USA)	93

EVENT	GOLD		SILVER		BRONZE	
Military Rifle (Team)	USA	1687	Great Britain	1602	Sweden	1570
Small-Bore Rifle (Prone)	Frederick Hird (USA)	194	William Milne (GBR)	193	Harry Burt (GBR)	192
Small-Bore Rifle (Team)	Sweden	925	Great Britain	917	USA	881
Small-Bore Rifle (Disappearing Target)	Wilhelm Carlberg (SWE)	242	Johan von Holst (SWE)	233	Gustaf Ericsson (SWE)	231
Rapid-Fire Pistol	Alfred Lane (USA)	499	Paul Palen (SWE)	286	Johan von Holst (SWE)	283
Free Pistol (50 m)	Alfred Lane (USA)	96	Peter Dolfen (USA)	474	Charles Stewart (GBR)	470
Team Event	USA	1916	Sweden	1849	Great Britain	1804
Olympic Trap Shooting	James Graham (USA)	96	Alfred Goldel (GER)	94	Harry Blau (RUS)	91
Clay Pigeons (Team)	USA	532	Great Britain	511	Germany	510
Running Deer Shooting	Alfred Swahn (SWE)	41	Ake Lundberg (SWE)	41	Nestori Toivonen (FIN)	41
Running Deer Shooting (Team)	Sweden	151	USA	132	Finland	123
Running Deer Shooting (Double Shot)	Ake Lundberg (SWE)	79	Edward Benedicks (SWE)	74	Oscar Swahn (SWE)	72

Gymnastics

Individual Combined Exercises	Alberto Braglia (ITA)	135.0	Louis Ségura (FRA)	132.5	Adolfo Tunesi (ITA)	131.5
Team	Italy	265.75	Hungary	227.25	Great Britain	184.50
Swedish System (Men's Teams)	Sweden	937.46	Denmark	898.84	Norway	857.21
Free System (Men's Teams)	Norway	114.25	Finland	109.25	Denmark	106.25

Tennis

Men's Singles	Charles Winslow (SAF)		Harold Kitson (SAF)	Oscar Kreuzer (GER)
Men's Singles (Indoor)	André Gobert (FRA) 8:6. 6:4. 6:4		Charles Dixon (GBR)	Anthony Wilding (AUS)
Men's Doubles	Charles Winslow / Harold Kitson (SAF)		Felix Pipes / Arthur Zborzil (AUT)	Albert Canet / Marc de Marangue (FRA)
Men's Doubles (Indoor)	André Gobert / Maurice Gernot (FRA)		Gunnar Setterwall / Carl Kempe (SWE)	Charles Dixon / Alfred Beamish (GBR)
Women's Singles	Marguerite Broquedis (FRA)		Dora Köring (GER)	Molla Bjurstedt (NOR)
Women's Singles (Indoor)	Edith Hannan (GBR)		Thora Castenschiold (DEN)	Mabel Parton (GBR)
Mixed Doubles	Dora Köring / Heinrich Schomburgk (GER)		Sigrid Fick / Gunnar Setterwall (SWE)	Marguerite Broquedis / Albert Canet (FRA)
Mixed Doubles (Indoor)	Edith Hannan / Charles Dixon (GBR)		Helen Aitchison / Herbert Roper-Barre (GBR)	Sigrid Fick / Gunnar Setterwall (SWE)

Soccer

	Great Britain	Denmark	Netherlands

Antwerp 1920

July 7 – September 12
(Figure Skating and Ice Hockey April 23–29)
(Official Opening Ceremony August 14)

Participants: 2668 / Men: 2591, Women: 77, Countries: 29,
Sports: 21, Events: 154

Medals Table

PLACE	COUNTRY	GOLD	SILVER	BRONZE
1	USA	41	26	27
2	Sweden	17	19	26
3	Great Britain	15	15	13
4	Belgium	14	11	10
5	Finland	14	10	8

Outstanding Athletes

PLACE	NAME (NATIONALITY)	DISCIPLINE	G	S	B
1	Willis Lee (USA)	Shooting	5	1	1
2	Nedo Nadi (ITA)	Fencing	5	–	–
3	Hubert van Innis (BEL)	Archery	4	2	–
4	Lloyd Spooner (USA)	Shooting	4	1	2
5	Carl Osburn (USA)	Shooting	4	1	1

EVENT	GOLD		SILVER		BRONZE	
Athletics						
100 m	Charles Paddock (USA)	10.8	Morris Kirksey (USA)	10.8	Harry Edward (GBR)	11.0
200 m	Allen Woodring (USA)	22.0	Charles. Paddock (USA)	22.1	Harry Edward (GBR)	22.2
400 m	Bevil Rudd (SAF)	49.6	Guy Butler (GBR)	49.9	Nils Engdahl (SWE)	50.0
800 m	Albert Hill (GBR)	1:53.4	Earl Eby (USA)	1:53.6	Bevil Rudd (SAF)	1:54.0
1500 m	Albert Hill (GBR)	4:01.8	Philip Noel-Baker (GBR)	4:02.4	Lawrence Shields (USA)	4:03.1
3000 m Team Race	USA	10	Great Britain	20	Sweden	24
5000 m	Joseph Guillemot (FRA)	14:55.6	Paavo Nurmi (FIN)	15:00:0	Erik Backman (SWE)	15:13.0
10,000 m	Paavo Nurmi (FIN)	31:45.8	Joseph Guillemot (FRA)	31:47.2	James Wilson (GBR)	31:50.8

EVENT	GOLD		SILVER		BRONZE	
Marathon (26 miles 991 yds)	Hannes Kolehmainen (FIN)	2:32:35.8	Juri Lossman (EST)	2:32:48.6	Valerio Arri (ITA)	2:36:32.8
110 m Hurdles	Earl Thomson (CAN)	14.8	Harold Barron (USA)	15.1	Frederick Murray (USA)	15.2
400 m Hurdles	Frank Loomis (USA)	54.0	John Norton (USA)	54.3	August Desch (USA)	54.5
3000 m Steeplechase	Percy Hodge (GBR)	10:00.4	Patrick Flynn (USA)		Ernesto Ambrosini (ITA)	
Individual Cross-Country	Paavo Nurmi (FIN)	27:15.0	Erik Backman (SWE)	27:15.6	Heikki Liimatainen (FIN)	27:37.4
Team Cross-Country	Finland	10	Great Britain	21	Sweden	23
4 x 100 m	USA	42.2	France	42.6	Sweden	42.9
4 x 400 m	Great Britain	3:22.2	South Africa	3:24.2	France	3:24.8
3 km Walk	Ugo Frigerio (ITA)	13:14.2	George Parker (AUS)		Richard F. Remer (USA)	
10 km Walk	Ugo Frigerio (ITA)	48:06.2	Joseph Pearman (USA)		Charles Gunn (GBR)	
High jump	Richmond Landon (USA)	6'4¼"	Harold Muller (USA)	6'2¾"	Bo Ekelund (SWE)	6'2¾"
Pole Vault	Frank Foss (USA)	13'5"	Henry Petersen (DAN)	12'1½"	Edwin Myers (USA)	11'9½"
Long Jump	William Petersson (SWE)	23'5¼"	Carl Johnson (USA)	23'3¼"	Erik Abrahamsson (SWE)	23'2½"
Triple Jump	Vilho Tuulos (FIN)	47'7"	Folke Jansson (SWE)	47'6"	Erik Almlöf (SWE)	49'9¾"
Shot	Ville Pörhölä (FIN)	48'7"	Elmer Niklander (FIN)	46'5¼"	Harry Liversedge (USA)	46'5"
Discus	Elmer Niklander (FIN)	146'7"	Armas Taipale (FIN)	144'11½"	Augustus Pope (USA)	138'2½"
Hammer	Patrick Ryan (USA)	173'5½"	Carl Johan Lind (SWE)	158'10½"	Basil Bennet (USA)	158'3½"
Javelin	Jonni Myyrä (FIN)	215'9½"	Urho Peltonen (FIN)	208'4"	Paavo Jaale-Johansson (FIN)	207'0"
56lb Weight Throw	Patrick McDonald (USA)	36'11½"	Patrick Ryan (USA)	36'0"	Carl Johan Lind (SWE)	33'7¾"
Pentathlon	Eero Lehtonen (FIN)	14	Everett Bradley (USA)	24	Hugo Lahtinen (FIN)	26
Decathlon	Helge Lövland (NOR)	6804.355	Brutus Hamilton (USA)	6771.085	Bertil Ohlson (SWE)	6580.030
Tug-of-War	Great Britain		Netherlands		Belgium	
Swimming						
Men						
100 m Freestyle	Duke Kahanamoku (USA)	1:01.4	Pua Kealoha (USA)	1 :02.2	William Harris (USA)	1:03.0
400 m Freestyle	Norman Ross (USA)	5 :26.8	Ludy Langer (USA)	5 :29.0	George Vernot (CAN)	5:29.8
1500 m Freestyle	Norman Ross (USA)	22:23.2	George Vernot (CAN)	22 :36.4	Frank Beaurepaire (AUS)	23:04.0
100 m Backstroke	Warren Kealoha (USA)	1:15.2	Raymond Kegeris (USA)	1:16.2	Gérard Blitz (BEL)	1:19.0
200 m Breaststroke	Hakan Malmroth (SWE)	3:04.4	Thor Henning (SWE)	3:09.2	Arvo Aaltonen (FIN)	3:12.2
400 m Breaststroke	Hakan Malmroth (SWE)	6:31.8	Thor Henning (SWE)	6:45.2	Arvo Aaltonen (FIN)	6:48.0
4 x 200 m Freestyle Relay	USA	10:04.4	Australia	10:25.4	Great Britain	10:37.2
Springboard Diving	Louis Kuehn (USA)	05.11.1901	Clarence Pinkston (USA)	655.3	Louis Balbach (USA)	649.5
Highboard Diving	Clarence Pinkston (USA)	100.67	Erik Adlerz (SWE)	99.08	Harry Prieste (USA)	93.73
Plain High Diving	Arvid Wallmann (SWE)	183.5	Nils Skoglund (SWE)	183.0	John Jansson (SWE)	175.0
Water Polo	Great Britain		Belgium		Sweden	
Women						
100 m Freestyle	Ethelda Bleibtrey (USA)	1:13.6	Irene Guest (USA)	1:17.0	Frances Schroth (USA)	1:17.2
300 m Freestyle	Ethelda Bleibtrey (USA)	4:34.0	Margaret Woodbridge (USA)	4:42.8	Frances Schroth (USA)	4:52.0
4 x 100 m Freestyle Relay	USA	5:11.6	Great Britain	5:40.8	Sweden	5:43.6
Springboard Diving	Aileen Riggin (USA)	539.9	Helen Wainwright (USA)	534.8	Thelma Payne (USA)	534.1
Highboard Diving	Stefani Fryland-Clausen (DEN)	34.6	Eileen Armstrong (GBR)	33.3	Eva Olliwier (SWE)	33.3
Boxing						
Flyweight (-112 lb)	Frank di Genaro (USA)		Anders Petersen (DEN)		William Cuthbertson (GBR)	
Bantamweight (-118 lb)	Clarence Walker (SAF)		Christopher Graham (CAN)		James McKenzie (GBR)	
Featherweight (-126 lb)	Paul Fritsch (FRA)		Jean Gachet (FRA)		Edoardo Garzena (ITA)	
Lightweight (-135 lb)	Samuel Mosberg (USA)		Gotfred Johansen (DEN)		Chris Newton (CAN)	
Welterweight (-147 lb)	Albert Schneider (CAN)		Alexander Ireland (GBR)		Frederick Colberg (USA)	
Middleweight (-160 lb)	Harry Mallin (GBR)		Georges Prud'Homme (CAN)		Montgomery Herscovitch (CAN)	
Light-Heavyweight (- 175 lb)	Edward Eagan (USA)		Sverre Sörsdal (NOR)		Harry Franks (GBR)	
Heavyweight (+175 lb)	Ronald Rawson (GBR)		Sören Petersen (DEN)		Xavier Eluère (FRA)	
Weightlifting						
Featherweight (-132¼ lb)	Frans de Haes (BEL)	220.0	Alfred Schmidt (EST)	212.5	Eugène Ryther (SUI)	210.0
Lightweight (-148¾ lb)	Alfred Neuland (EST)	257.5	Louis Williquet (BEL)	240.0	Florimond Rooms (BEL)	230.0
Middleweight (-165½ lb)	Henri Gance (FRA)	245.0	Pietro Bianchi (ITA)	237.5	Albert Pettersson (SWE)	237.5
Light-Heavyweight (-182 lb)	Ernest Cadine (FRA)	290.0	Fritz Hünenberger (SUI)	275.0	Erik Pettersson (SWE)	272.5
Heavyweight (+182 lb)	Filippo Bottino (ITA)	270.0	Joseph Alzin (LUX)	255.0	Louis Bernot (FRA)	250.0
Greco-Roman Wrestling						
Featherweight (-132¼ lb)	Oskari Friman (FIN)		Heikki Kähkönen (FIN)		Fridtjof Svensson (SWE)	
Lightweight (-148¾ lb)	Eemeli Väre (FIN)		Taavi Tamminen (FIN)		Fridtjof Andersen (NOR)	
Middleweight (-165¼ lb)	Carl Westergren (SWE)		Artur Lindfors (FIN)		Matti Perttilä (FIN)	
Light-Heavyweight (-181¾ lb)	Claes Johansson (SWE)		Edil Rosenqvist (FIN)		Johannes Eriksen (DEN)	
Heavyweight (+181¾ lb)	Adolf Lindfors (FIN)		Poul Hansen (DEN)		Martti Nieminen (FIN)	

EVENT	GOLD		SILVER		BRONZE	
Freestyle Wrestling						
Featherweight (-132¼ lb)	Charles Ackerly (USA)		Samuel Gerson (USA)		Peter W. Bernard (GBR)	
Lightweight (-148¾ lb)	Kalle Antilla (FIN)		Gottfried Svensson (SWE)		Peter Wright (GBR)	
Middleweight (-165¼ lb)	Eino Leino (FIN)		Väinö Penttala (FIN)		Charles Johnson (USA)	
Light-Heavyweight (-181¾ lb)	Anders Larsson (SWE)		Charles Courant (SUI)		Walter Maurer (USA)	
Heavyweight (+181¾ lb)	Robert Roth (SUI)		Nathan Pendleton (USA)		Ernst Nilsson (SWE)	
					Frederick Meyer (USA)	
Fencing						
Individual Foil	Nedo Nadi (ITA)	10	Philippe Cattiau (FRA)	9/14	Roger Ducret (FRA)	9/19
Team Foil	Italy		France		USA	
Individual Épée	Armand Massard (FRA)	9	Alexandre Lippmann (FRA)	7	Gustave Buchard (FRA)	6
Team Épée	Italy		Belgium		France	
Individual Saber	Nedo Nadi (ITA)	11	Aldo Nadi (ITA)	9	Adrianus E. W. de Jong (HOL)	7
Team Saber	Italy		France		Netherlands	
Modern Pentathlon						
	Gustav Dyrssen (SWE)	18	Erik de Laval (SWE)	23	Gösta Runö (SWE)	27
Rowing						
Single Sculls	John Kelly sen. (USA)	7:35.0	Jack Beresford jun. (GBR)	7:36.0	Clarence Hadfield d'Arcy (NZL)	
						7:48.0
Double Sculls	USA	7:09.0	Italy	7:19.0	France	7:21.0
Coxed Pairs	Italy	7:56.0	France	7:57.0	Switzerland	
Coxed Fours	Switzerland	6:54.0	USA	6:58.0	Norway	7:02.0
Coxed Eights	USA	6:02.6	Great Britain	6:05.0	Norway	6:36.0
Yachting						
12 Foot Dinghy	Netherlands		Netherlands			
18 Foot Dinghy	Great Britain					
6 m	Norway		Belgium			
6 m (1907 Rating)	Belgium		Norway		Norway	
6.5 m (1919 Rating)	Netherlands		France			
7 m	Great Britain					
8 m	Norway		Norway		Belgium	
8 m (1907 Rating)	Norway		Norway			
10 m	Norway					
10 m (1907 Rating)	Norway					
12 m (1903 Rating)	Norway					
12 m	Norway					
Sharpie 30 m2	Sweden					
Sharpie 40 m2	Sweden		Sweden			
Cycling						
Individual Road Race (109 miles)	Harry Stenqvist (SWE)	4:40:01.8	Henry Kaltenbrunn (SAF)	4:41:26.6	Fernand Canteloube (FRA)	4:42:54.4
Team Road Race	France	19:16:43.2	Sweden	19:23:10.0	Belgium	19:28:44.4
50 km Track	Henry George (BEL)	1:16:43.2	Cyril Alden (GBR)		Piet Ikelaar (HOL)	
1000 m Sprint	Maurice Peeters (HOL)	1 :38.3	Thomas Johnson (GBR)		Harry Ryan (GBR)	
2000 m Tandem	Great Britain	2:49.4	South Africa		Netherlands	
4000 m Team Pursuit	Italy	5:20.0	Great Britain		South Africa	
Equestrianism						
Three-Day Event	Helmer Mörner (SWE)	1775.00	Åge Lundström (SWE)	1738.75	Ettore Caffaratti (ITA)	1733.75
Three-Day Event (Team)	Sweden	5057.50	Italy	4735.00	Belgium	4560.00
Grand Prix (Dressage)	Janne Lundblad (SWE)	27.937	Bertil Sandström (SWE)	26.312	Hans von Rosen (SWE)	25.125
Grand Prix (Jumping)	Tommaso Lequio (ITA)	-2	Alessandro Valerio (ITA)	-3	Gustaf Lewenhaupt (SWE)	-4
Grand Prix (Jumping) Team	Sweden	-14	Belgium	-16.25	Italy	-18.75
Figure Riding	Bouckaert (BEL)	30.5	Fiel (FRA)	29.5	Finet (BEL)	29.0
Figure Riding (Team)	Belgium		France		Sweden	
Shooting						
Free Rifle (Three Positions)	Morris Fisher (USA)	997	Niels Larsen (DEN)	985	Östen Östensen (NOR)	980
Free Rifle (Team)	USA	4876	Norway	4741	Switzerland	4698
Military Rifle (Prone) 300 m	Otto Olsen (NOR)	60	Léon Johnson (FRA)	59	Fritz Kuchen (SUI)	59
Military Rifle (Team)	USA	289	France	283	Finland	281
Military Rifle (Standing) 300 m	Carl Osburn (USA)	56	Lars Madsen (DEN)	55	Lawrence Adam Nuesslein (USA)	54
Military Rifle (Team)	Denmark	266	USA	255	Sweden	255
Military Rifle (Prone) 600 m	Hugo Johansson (SWE)	58	Mauritz Eriksson (SWE)	56	Lloyd Spooner (USA)	56

EVENT	GOLD		SILVER		BRONZE	
Military Rifle (Team) 600 m	USA	287	South Africa	287	Sweden	287
Military Rifle (Prone) 600 +300 m	USA	573	Norway	565	Switzerland	563
Small-Bore Rifle (Standing)	Lawrence A.Nuesslein (USA)	391	Arthur Rothrock (USA)	386	Dennis Fenton (USA)	385
Small-Bore Rifle (Team)	USA	1899	Sweden	1873	Norway	1866
Rapid-Fire Pistol	Guilherme Paraense (BRA)	274	Raymond Bracken (USA)	272	Fritz Zulauf (SUI)	269
Free Pistol (50 m)	Carl Frederick (USA)	496	Afranio da Costa (BRA)	489	Alfred Lane (USA)	481
Olympic Trap Shooting	Mark Arie (USA)	95	Frank Troeh (USA)	93	Frank Wright (USA)	87
Clay Pigeons (Team)	USA	547	Belgium	503	Sweden	500
Running Deer Shooting	Otto Olsen (NOR)	43	Alfred Swahn (SWE)	41	Harald Natvig (NOR)	41
Running Deer (Team)	Norway	178	Finland	159	USA	158
Running Deer (Double Shot)	Ole Lilloe-Olsen (NOR)	82	Fredrik Landelius (SWE)	77	Einar Liberg (NOR)	71
Running Deer (Double Shot) (Team)	Norway	343	Sweden	336	Finland	284
Military Revolver (Team) 50 m	USA	2372	Sweden	2289	Brazil	2264
Military Revolver (Team) 30 m	USA	1310	Greece	1285	Switzerland	1270
Archery						
Fixed Bird Target – Small Birds – Individual	Edmond van Moer (BEL)	11	Louis van de Perck (BEL)	8	Joseph Hermans (BEL)	6
Fixed Bird Target – Large Birds – Individual	Edouard Cloetens (BEL)	13	Louis van de Perck (BEL)	11	Firmin Flamand (BEL)	7
Fixed Bird Target – Sm and Lrg Birds – Team	Belgium					
Moving Bird Target – 28 m – Individual	Hubert van Innis (BEL)	144	Léonce Quentin (FRA)	115		
Moving Bird Target – 28 m – Team	Netherlands	3087	Belgium	2924	France	2317
Moving Bird Target – 33 m – Individual	Hubert van Innis (BEL)	139	Julien Brulé (FRA)	94		
Moving Bird Target – 33 m – Team	Belgium	2958	France	2586		
Moving Bird Target – 50 m – Individual	Julien Brulé (FRA)	134	Hubert van Innis (BEL)	106		
Moving Bird Target – 50 m – Team	Belgium	2701	France	2493		
Gymnastics						
Individual Combined Exercises	Giorgio Zampori (ITA)	88.35	Marco Torrès (FRA)	87.62	Jean Gounot (FRA)	87.45
Team	Italy	359.855	Belgium	346.785	France	340.100
Swedish System (Men's Teams)	Sweden	1364	Denmark	1325	Belgium	1094
Free System (Men's Teams)	Denmark		Norway			
Tennis						
Men's Singles	Louis Raymond (SAF)		Ichiya Kumagae (JPN)		Charles Winslow (SAF)	
Men's Doubles	O. G. Noel Turnbull / Max Woosnam (GBR)		Ichiya Kumagae/ Seiichiro Kashio (JPN)		Max Décugis/ Pierre Albarran (FRA)	
Women's Singles	Suzanne Lenglen (FRA)		Dorothy Holman (GBR)		Kitty McKane (GBR)	
Women's Doubles	Winifred Margaret McNair/ Kitty McKane (GBR)		Geraldine Beamish/ Dorothy Holman (GBR)		Suzanne Lenglen/Elisabeth d'Ayen (FRA)	
Mixed	Suzanne Lenglen/ Max Décugis (FRA)		Kitty McKane/ Max Woosnam (GBR)		Milada Skrbková/Ladislav Zmela (TCH)	
Football						
	Belgium		Spain		Netherlands	
Hockey						
	Great Britain		Denmark		Belgium	
Polo						
	Great Britain		Spain		USA	
Rugby						
	USA		France			
Figure Skating						
Women	Magda Julin (SWE)	12	Svea Noren (SWE)	12.5	Theresa Weld (SWE)	15.5
Men	Gillis Gräfström (SWE)	7	Andreas Krogh (NOR)	18	Martin Stixrud (NOR)	24.5
Pairs	Ludovika Jakobsson/ Walter Jakobsson (FIN)	7	Alexia Bryn/Yngvar Bryn (NOR)	15.5	Phyllis Johnson / Basil Williams (GBR)	25
Ice Hockey						
	Canada		USA		Czechoslovakia	

Chamonix 1924

January 24 – February 5

Participants: 258 / Men: 245, Women: 13, Countries: 16,
Sports: 5, Events: 14

Medals Table

PLACE	COUNTRY	GOLD	SILVER	BRONZE
1	Norway	4	7	6
2	Finland	4	3	3
3	Austria	2	1	–
4	USA	1	2	1
5	Switzerland	1	–	1

Outstanding Athletes

PLACE	NAME (NATIONALITY)	DISCIPLINE	G	S	B
1	Clas Thunberg (FIN)	Speed Skating	3	1	1
2	Thorleif Haug (NOR)	Nordic Skiing	3	–	–
3	Julius Skutnabb (FIN)	Speed Skating	1	1	1

EVENT	GOLD		SILVER		BRONZE	
Nordic Skiing						
18 km Cross-Country Skiing	Thorleif Haug (NOR)	1:14:31.0	Johan Gröttumsbraaten (NOR)	1:15:51.0	Tapani Niku (FIN)	1:26:26.0
50 km Cross-Country Skiing	Thorleif Haug (NOR)	3:44:32.0	Thoralf Strömstad (NOR)	3:46:23.0	Johan Gröttumsbraaten (NOR)	3:47:46.0
Ski Jumping	Jacob Tullin Thams (NOR)	18.960	Narve Bonna (NOR)	18.689	Thorleif Haug (NOR)	18.000*
					Anders Haugen (USA)	17.916*
Nordic Combined	Thorleif Haug (NOR)	18.906	Thoralf Strömstad (NOR)	18.219	Johan Gröttumsbraaten (NOR)	17.854
Figure Skating						
Women	Herma Planck-Szabo (AUT)		Beatrix Loughran (USA)		Ethel Muckelt (GBR)	
Men	Gillis Gräfström (SWE)		Willy Böckl (AUT)		Georges Gautschi (SUI)	
Pairs	Helene Engelmann/Alfred Berger (AUT)		Ludovika Jakobsson/Walter Jakobsson (FIN)		Andée Joly/Pierre Brunet (FRA)	
Speed Skating						
500 m	Charles Jewtraw (USA)	44.0	Oskar Olsen (NOR)	44.2	Roald Larsen (NOR)	44.8
					Clas Thunberg (FIN)	44.8
1500 m	Clas Thunberg (FIN)	2:20.8	Roald Larsen (NOR)	2:22.0	Sigurd Moen (NOR)	2:25.6
5000 m	Clas Thunberg (FIN)	8:39.0	Julius Skutnabb (FIN)	8:48.4	Roald Larsen (NOR)	8:50.2
10,000 m	Julius Skutnabb (FIN)	18:04.8	Clas Thunberg (FIN)	18:07.8	Roald Larsen (NOR)	18:12.2
All-Round Championship	Clas Thunberg (FIN)	5.5	Roald Larsen (NOR)	9.5	Julius Skutnabb (FIN)	11
Bobsledding						
4-Man Bob	Switzerland I	5:45.54	Great Britain II	5:48.83	Belgium I	6:02.29
Ice hockey						
	Canada		USA		Great Britain	

*Owing to incorrect calculations which were first discovered and corrected in 1974 Haug was awarded the bronze medal although his actual score was 17.821. Haugen was awarded his bronze medal at a later date.

Paris 1924

May 4 – July 27
(Official Opening Ceremony July 5)

Participants: 3092 / Men: 2956, Women: 136, Countries: 44,
Sports: 17, Events: 126

Medals Table

PLACE	COUNTRY	GOLD	SILVER	BRONZE
1	USA	45	27	27
2	Finland	14	13	10
3	France	13	15	10
4	Great Britain	9	13	12
5	Italy	8	3	5

Outstanding Athletes

PLACE	NAME (NATIONALITY)	DISCIPLINE	G	S	B
1	Paavo Nurmi (FIN)	Athletics	5	–	–
2	Ville Ritola (FIN)	Athletics	4	2	–
3	Roger Ducret (FRA)	Fencing	3	1	–
4	Johnny Weissmuller (USA)	Swimming	3	–	1
5	Vincent Richards (USA)	Tennis	2	1	–

EVENT	GOLD		SILVER		BRONZE	
Athletics						
100 m	Harold Abrahams (GBR)	10.6	Jackson Scholz (USA)	10.7	Arthur Porritt (NZL)	10.8
200 m	Jackson Scholz (USA)	21.6	Charles Paddock (USA)	21.7	Eric Liddell (GBR)	21.9
400 m	Eric Liddell (GBR)	47.6	Horatio Fitch (USA)	48.4	Guy Butler (GBR)	48.6
800 m	Douglas Lowe (GBR)	1:52.4	Paul Martin (SUI)	1:52.6	Schuyler Enck (USA)	1:53.0
1500 m	Paavo Nurmi (FIN)	3:53.6	Willy Schärer (SUI)	3:55.0	Henry Stallard (GBR)	3:55.6
3000 m Team Race	Finland	8	Great Britain	14	USA	25
5000 m	Paavo Nurmi (FIN)	14:31.2	Ville Ritola (FIN)	14:31.4	Edvin Wide (SWE)	15:01.8
10,000 m	Ville Ritola (FIN)	30:23.2	Edvin Wide (SWE)	30:55.2	Eero Berg (FIN)	31:43.0
Marathon (26 miles 385 yds)	Albin Stenroos (FIN)	2:41:22.6	Romeo Bertini (ITA)	2:47:19.6	Clarence DeMar (USA)	2:48:14.0
110 m Hurdles	Daniel Kinsey (USA)	15.0	Sidney Atkinson (SAF)	15.0	Sten Pettersson (SWE)	15.4
400 m Hurdles	F. Morgan Taylor (USA)	52.6	Erik Vilén (FIN)	53.8	Ivan Riley (USA)	54.2
3000 m Steeplechase	Ville Ritola (FIN)	9:33.6	Elias Katz (FIN)	9:44.0	Paul Bontemps (FRA)	9:45.2
Individual Cross-Country	Paavo Nurmi (FIN)	32:54.8	Ville Ritola (FIN)	34:19.4	Earl Johnson (USA)	35:21.0
Team Cross-Country	Finland	11	USA	14	France	20
4 x 100 m Relay	USA	41.0	Great Britain	41.2	Netherlands	41.8
4 x 400 m Relay	USA	3:16.0	Sweden	3:17.0	Great Britain	3:17.4
10 km Walk	Ugo Frigerio (ITA)	47:49.0	Gordon Goodwin (GBR)		Cecil McMaster (SAF)	
High Jump	Harold Osborn (USA)	6'6"	Leroy Brown (USA)	6'4¾"	Pierre Lewden (FRA)	6'3¼"
Pole Vault	Lee Barnes (USA)	12'11½"	Glen Graham (USA)	12'11½"	James Brooker (USA)	12'9½"
Long Jump	William DeHart Hubbard (USA)	24'5"	Edward Gourdin (USA)	23'10¼"	Sverre Hansen (NOR)	23'9¾"
Triple Jump	Anthony Winter (AUS)	50'11¼"	Luis Bruneto (ARG)	50'7¼"	Vilho Tuulos (FIN)	50'5"
Shot	Clarence Houser (USA)	49'2"	Glenn Hartranft (USA)	49'1¾"	Ralph Hills (USA)	48'0¼"
Discus	Clarence Houser (USA)	151'5"	Vilho Niittymaa (FIN)	147'5½"	Thomas Lieb (USA)	147'0½"
Hammer	Frederick Tootell (USA)	174'10"	Matthew McGrath (USA)	166'9½"	Malcolm Nokes (GBR)	158'3½"
Javelin	Jonni Myyrä (FIN)	206'6½"	Gunnar Lindström (SWE)	199'10"	Eugene Oberst (USA)	191'5"
Pentathlon	Eero Lehtonen (FIN)	14	Elemér Somfay (HUN)	16	Robert LeGendre (USA)	18
Decathlon	Harold Osborn (USA)	7710.775	Emerson Norton (USA)	7350.895	Alexander Klumberg (EST)	7329.360
Swimming						
Men						
100 m Freestyle	Johnny Weissmuller (USA)	59.0	Duke Kahanamoku (USA)	1:01.4	Sam Kahanamoku (USA)	1:01.8
400 m Freestyle	Johnny Weissmuller (USA)	5:04.2	Arne Borg (SWE)	5:05.6	Andrew Charlton (AUS)	5:06.6
1500 m Freestyle	Andrew Charlton (AUS)	20:06.6	Arne Borg (SWE)	20:41.4	Frank Beaurepaire (AUS)	21:48.4
100 m Backstroke	Warren Paoa Kealoha (USA)	1:13.2	Paul Wyatt (USA)	1:15.4	Károly Bartha (HUN)	1:17.8
200 Breaststroke	Robert Skelton (USA)	2:56.6	Joseph de Combe (BEL)	2:59.2	William Kirschbaum (USA)	3:01.0
4 x 200 m Freestyle Relay	USA	9:53.4	Australia	10:02.2	Sweden	10:06.8
Springboard Diving	Albert White (USA)	696.4	Peter Desjardins (USA)	693.3	Clarence Pinkston (USA)	653.0
Highboard Diving	Albert White (USA)	97.46	David Fall (USA)	97.30	Clarence Pinkston (USA)	94.60
Plain High Diving	Richmond Eve (AUS)	160.0	John Jansson (SWE)	157.0 *	Harold Clarke (GBR)	158.0 *
Water Polo	France		Belgium		USA	
*Handicap: Jansson 14.5 - Clarke 15.5						
Women						
100 m Freestyle	Ethel Lackie (USA)	1:12.4	Mariechen Wehselau (USA)	1:12.8	Gertrude Ederle (USA)	1:14.2
400 m Freestyle	Martha Norelius (USA)	6:02.2	Helen Wainwright (USA)	6:03.8	Gertrude Ederle (USA)	6:04.8
100 m Backstroke	Sybil Bauer (USA)	1:23.2	Phyllis Harding (GBR)	1:27.4	Aileen Riggin (USA)	1:28.2
200 m Breaststroke	Lucy Morton (GBR)	3:33.2	Agnes Geraghty (USA)	3:34.0	Gladys Carson (GBR)	3:35.4
4 x 100 m Freestyle Relay	USA	4:58.8	Great Britain	5:17.0	Sweden	5:35.6
Springboard Diving	Elizabeth Becker (USA)	474.5	Aileen Riggin (USA)	460.4	Caroline Fletcher (USA)	436.4
Highboard Diving	Caroline Smith (USA)	33.2 *	Elizabeth Becker (USA)	33.4 *	Hjördis Töpel (SWE)	32.8
*Handicap: Smith 10.5 - Becker 11.0						
Boxing						
Flyweight (-112 lb)	Fidel LaBarba (USA)		James McKenzie (GBR)		Raymond Fee (USA)	
Bantamweight (-118 lb)	William Smith (SAF)		Salvatore Tripoli (USA)		Jean Ces (FRA)	
Featherweight (-126 lb)	John Fields (USA)		Joseph Salas (USA)		Pedro Quartucci (ARG)	
Lightweight (-135 lb)	Hans Nielsen (DEN)		Alfredo Copello (ARG)		Frederick Boylstein (USA)	
Welterweight (-147 lb)	Jean Delarge (BEL)		Héctor Mendez (ARG)		Douglas Lewis (CAN)	
Middleweight (-160 lb)	Harry Mallin (GBR)		John Elliott (GBR)		Joseph Beecken (BEL)	
Light-Heavyweight (-175 lb)	Harry Mitchell (GBR)		Thyge Petersen (DEN)		Sverre Sörsdal (NOR)	
Heavyweight (+175 lb)	Otto von Porrat (NOR)		Sören Petersen (DEN)		Alfredo Porzio (ARG)	
Weightlifting						
Featherweight (-132¼ lb)	Pierino Gabetti (ITA)	402.5	Andreas Stadler (AUT)	385.0	Arthur Reinmann (SUI)	382.5
Lightweight (-148¾ lbg)	Edmond Decottignies (FRA)	440.0	Anton Zwerina (AUT)	427.5	Bohumil Durdis (TCH)	425.0
Middleweight (- 165½ lb)	Carlo Galimberti (ITA)	492.5	Alfred Neuland (EST)	455.0	Johannes Kikas (EST)	450.0

EVENT	GOLD		SILVER		BRONZE	
Light-Heavyweight (–182 lb)	Charles Rigoulot (FRA)	502.5	Fritz Hünenberger (SUI)	490.0 ★	Leopold Friedrich (AUT)	490.0 ★
Heavyweight (+182 lb)	Guiseppe Tonani (ITA)	517.5	Franz Aigner (AUT)	515.0	Harald Tammer (EST)	497.5

★Body Weight: Hünenberger 81.9 kg. Friedrich 82.0 kg

Greco-Roman Wrestling

Bantamweight (–127¾ lb)	Eduard Pütsep (EST)		Anselm Ahlfors (FIN)		Väinö Ikonen (FIN)	
Featherweight (–136½ lb)	Kalle Antilla (FIN)		Aleksanteri Toivola (FIN)		Erik Malmberg (SWE)	
Lightweight (– 148¾ lb)	Oskari Friman (FIN)		Lajos Keresztes (HUN)		Kalle Westerlund (FIN)	
Middleweight (–165¼ lb)	Edvard Westerlund (FIN)		Artur Lindfors (FIN)		Roman Steinberg (EST)	
Light-Heavyweight (–181¾ lb)	Carl Westergren (SWE)		Rudolf Svensson (SWE)		Onni Pellinen (FIN)	
Heavyweight (+181¾ lb)	Henri Deglane (FRA)		Edil Rosenqvist (FIN)		Raymund Badó (HUN)	

Freestyle Wrestling

Bantamweight (–123½ lb)	Kustaa Pihlajamäki (FIN)		Kaarlo Mäkinen (FIN)		Bryant Hines (USA)	
Featherweight (–134½ lb)	Robin Reed (USA)		Chester Newton (USA)		Katsutoshi Naito (JPN)	
Lightweight (–145½ lb)	Russell Vis (USA)		Volmari Vikström (FIN)		Arvo Haavisto (FIN)	
Welterweight (–158½ lb)	Hermann Gehri (SUI)		Eino Leino (FIN)		Otto Müller (SUI)	
Middleweight (–174 lb)	Fritz Hagemann (SUI)		Pierre Olivier (BEL)		Vilho Pekkala (FIN)	
Light-Heavyweight (–1913/4 lb)	John Spellman (USA)		Rudolf Svensson (SWE)		Charles Courant (SUI)	
Heavyweight (+191¾ lb)	Harry Steele (USA)		Henri Wernli (SUI)		Andrew McDonald (GBR)	

Fencing

Individual Foil - Men	Roger Ducret (FRA)	6	Philippe Cattiau (FRA)	5	Maurice van Damme (BEL)	4
Team Foil - Men	France		Belgium		Hungary	
Individual Épée	Charles Delporte (BEL)	8	Roger Ducret (FRA)	7	Nils Hellsten (SWE)	7
Team Épée	France		Belgium		Italy	
Individual Saber	Sándor Posta (HUN)	5	Roger Ducret (FRA)	5	János Garay (HUN)	5
Team Saber	Italy		Hungary		Netherlands	
Individual Foil - Women	Ellen Osiier (DEN)	5	Gladys Muriel Davis (GBR)	4	Grete Heckscher (DEN)	3

Modern Pentathlon

Individual	Bo Lindman (SWE)	18	Gustaf Dyrssen (SWE)	39.5	Bertil Uggla (SWE)	45

Rowing

Single Sculls	Jack Beresford jun. (GBR)	7:49.2	William Garrett Gilmore (USA)	7:54.0	Josef Schneider (SUI)	8:01.1
Double Sculls	USA	6:34.0	France	6:38.0	Switzerland	
Coxless Pairs	Netherlands	8:19.4	France	8:21.6		
Coxed Pairs	Switzerland	8:39.0	Italy	8:39.1	USA	
Coxless Fours	Great Britain	7:08.6	Canada	7:18.0	Switzerland	
Coxed Fours	Switzerland	7:18.4	France	7:21.6	USA	
Coxed Eights	USA	6:33.4	Canada	6:49.0	Italy	

Yachting

Olympic Monotype	Léon Huybrechts (BEL)	2	Henrik Robert (NOR)	7	Hans Dittmar (FIN)	8
6 m	Norway	2	Denmark	5	Niederlande	5
8 m	Norway	2	Great Britain	5	France	5

Cycling

Individual Road Race (116¾ miles)	Armand Blanchonnet (FRA)	6:20:48.0	Henri Hoevenaers (BEL)	6:30:27.0	René Hamel (FRA)	6:40:51.6
Team Road Race	France	19:30:13.4	Belgium	19:46:55.4	Sweden	19:59:41.4
50 km Track	Jacobus Willems (HOL)	1:18:24.0	Cyril Alden (GBR)		Frederick Wyld (GBR)	
1000 m Sprint	Lucien Michard (FRA)		Jakob Meijer (HOL)		Jean Cugnot (FRA)	
2000 m Tandem	France		Denmark		Netherlands	
4000 m Team Pursuit	Italy	5:15.0	Polen		Belgium	

Equestrianism

Three-Day Event	Adolph v. d. Voort v. Zijp (HOL)	1976.0	Frode Kirkebjerg (DEN)	1853.5	Sloan Doak (USA)	1845.5
Three-Day Event Team	Netherlands	5297.5	Sweden	4743.5	Italy	4512.5
Grand Prix (Dressage)	Ernst Linder (SWE)	276.4	Bertil Sandström (SWE)	275.8	Xavier Lesage (FRA)	265.8
Grand Prix (Jumping)	Alphonse Gemuseus (SUI)	-6	Tommaso Lequio (ITA)	-8.75	Adam Królikiewicz (POL)	-10
Grand Prix (Jumping) Team	Sweden	-42.25	Switzerland	-50.0	Portugal	-53.0

Shooting

Free Rifle (3 Positions)	Morris Fisher (USA)	95	Carl Osburn (USA)	95	Niels Larsen (DEN)	93
Free Rifle (Team)	USA	676	France	646	Haiti	646
Small-Bore Rifle (Prone)	Pierre Coquelin de Lisle (FRA)	398	Marcus Dinwiddle (USA)	396	Josias Hartmann (SUI)	394
Rapid-Fire Pistol	H. M. Bailey (USA)	18	Vilhelm Carlberg (SWE)	18	Lennart Hannelius (FIN)	18
Olympic Trap Shooting	Gyula Halasy (HUN)	98	Konrad Huber (FIN)	98	Frank Hughes (USA)	97

EVENT	GOLD		SILVER		BRONZE	
Clay Pigeons (Team)	USA	363	Canada	360	Finland	360
Running Deer Shooting (Single Shot)	John Boles (USA)	40	Cyril Mackworth-Praed (GBR)	39	Otto Olsen (NOR)	39
Running Deer Shooting (Team)	Norway	160	Sweden	154	USA	148
Running Deer Shooting (Double Shot)	Ole Lilloe-Olsen (NOR)	76	Cyril Mackworth-Praed (GBR)	72	Alfred Swahn (SWE)	72
Running Deer Shooting (Team)	Great Britain	263	Norway	262	Sweden	250
Gymnastics						
Individual Combined Exercises	Leon Stukelji (YUG)	110.340	Robert Prazak (TCH)	110.323	Bedrich Supcik (TCH)	106.930
Team	Italy	839.058	France	820.528	Switzerland	816.661
Parallel Bars	August Güttinger (SUI)	21.63	Robert Prazak (TCH)	21.61	Giorgio Zampori (ITA)	21.45
Horse Vault	Frank Kriz (USA)	9.98	Jan Koutny (TCH)	9.97	Bohumil Morkovsky (TCH)	9.93
Horizontal Bar	Leon Stukelji (YUG)	19.730	Jean Gutweniger (SUI)	19.236	André Higelin (FRA)	19.163
Rings	Franco Martino (ITA)	21.553	Robert Prazak (TCH)	21.483	Ladislav Vácha (TCH)	21.430
Pommel Horse	Josef Wilhelm (SUI)	21.23	Jean Gutweniger (SUI)	21.13	Antoine Rebetez (SUI)	20.73
Sidehorse Vault	Albert Ségiun (FRA)	10.00	Jean Gounot (FRA)	9.93		
			François Gangloff (FRA)	9.93		
Rope Climbing	Bedrich Supck (TCH)	7.2	Albert Séguin (FRA)	7.4	August Güttinger (SUI)	7.8
					Ladislav Vácha	7.8
Tennis						
Men's Singles	Vincent Richards (USA)		Henri Cochet (FRA)		Umberto De Morpurgo (ITA)	
Men's Doubles	Vincent Richards/Frank Hunter (USA)		Jacques Brugnon/ Henri Cochet (FRA)		Jean Borotra/ René Lacoste (FRA)	
Women's Singles	Helen Wills (USA)		Julie Vlasto (FRA)		Kitty McKane (GBR)	
Women's Doubles	Hazel Wightman/ Helen Wills (USA)		Edith Covell/ Kitty McKane (GBR)		Dorothy C. Shepherd-Barron/ Evelyn L. Colyer (GBR)	
Mixed	Hazel Wightman/ R. Norris Williams (USA)		Marion Jessup/ Vincent Richards (USA)		Cornelia Bouman/ Hendrik Timmer (HOL)	
Soccer						
	Uruguay		Switzerland		Sweden	
Polo						
	Argentina		USA		Great Britain	
Rugby						
	USA		France		Romania	

St. Moritz 1928

February 11 – February 19

Participants: 464 / Men: 438, Women: 26, Countries: 25,
Sports: 6, Events: 14

Medals Table

PLACE	COUNTRY	GOLD	SILVER	BRONZE
1	Norway	6	4	5
2	USA	2	2	2
3	Sweden	2	2	1
4	Finland	2	1	1
5	France	1	–	–

Outstanding Athletes

PLACE	NAME (NATIONALITY)	DISCIPLINE	G	S	B
1	Johan Gröttumsbraaten (NOR)	Nordic Skiing	2	–	–
	Clas Thunberg (FIN)	Speed Skating	2	–	–
3	Bernt Evenson (NOR)	Speed Skating	1	1	1
4	Ivar Ballangrud (NOR)	Speed Skating	1	–	1

EVENT	GOLD		SILVER		BRONZE	
Nordic Skiing						
18 km Cross-Country Skiing	Johan Gröttumsbraaten (NOR)	1:37:01.0	Ole Hegge (NOR)	1:39:01.0	Reidar Ödegaard (NOR)	1:40:11.0
50 km Cross-Country Skiing	Per Erik Hedlund (SWE)	4:52:03.0	Gustaf Jonsson (SWE)	5:05:30.0	Volger Andersson (SWE)	5:05:46.0
Ski Jumping	Alf Andersen (NOR)	19.208	Sigmund Ruud (NOR)	18.542	Rudolf Burkert (TCH)	17.937
Nordic Combined	Johan Gröttumsbraaten (NOR)	17.833	Hans Vinjarengen (NOR)	15.303	John Snersrud (NOR)	15.021

EVENT	GOLD		SILVER		BRONZE	
Figure Skating						
Women	Sonja Henie (NOR)		Fritzi Burger (AUT)		Beatrix Loughran (USA)	
Men	Gillis Grafström (SWE)		Willy Böckl (AUT)		Robert van Zeebroeck (BEL)	
Pairs	Andrée Joly/ Pierre Brunet (FRA)		Lilly Scholz/ Otto Kaiser (AUT)		Melitta Brunner/ Ludwig Wrede (AUT)	
Speed Skating						
500 m	Clas Thunberg (FIN)	43.4			John Farrell (USA)	43.6
	Bernt Evensen (NOR)	43.4			Roald Larsen (NOR)	43.6
					Jaakko Friman (FIN)	43.6
1500 m	Clas Thunberg (FIN)	2:21.1	Bernt Evensen (NOR)	2:21.9	Ivar Ballangrud (NOR)	2:22.6
5000 m	Ivar Ballangrud (NOR)	8:50.5	Julius Skutnabb (FIN)	8:59.1	Bernt Evensen (NOR)	9:01.1
10,000 m	Event abandoned in the 5th heat owing to thawing conditions					
Bobsledding						
4-Man Bob	USA II	3:20.5	USA I	3:21.0	Germany II	3:21.9
Skeleton Sled	Jennison Heaton (USA)	181.8	John R. Heaton (USA)	182.8	David Earl of Northesk (GBR)	185.1
Ice Hockey						
	Canada		Sweden		Switzerland	

Amsterdam 1928

May 17 – August 12
(Official Opening Ceremony July 28)

Participants: 3014 / Men: 2724, Women: 290, Countries: 46,
Sports: 14, Events: 109

Medals Table

PLACE	COUNTRY	GOLD	SILVER	BRONZE
1	**USA**	**22**	**18**	**16**
2	**Germany**	**10**	**7**	**14**
3	**Finland**	**8**	**8**	**9**
4	**Sweden**	**7**	**6**	**12**
5	**Italy**	**7**	**5**	**7**

Outstanding Athletes

PLACE	NAME (NATIONALITY)	DISCIPLINE	G	S	B
1	**Georges Miez (SUI)**	**Gymnastics**	3	1	–
2	**Lucien Gaudin (FRA)**	**Fencing**	2	2	–
3	**Hermann Hänggi (SUI)**	**Gymnastics**	2	1	1
4	**Eugen Mack (SUI)**	**Gymnastics**	2	–	1

EVENT	GOLD		SILVER		BRONZE	
Athletics						
Men						
100 m	Percy Williams (CAN)	10.8	Jack London (GBR)	10.9	Georg Lammers (GER)	10.9
200 m	Percy Williams (CAN)	21.8	Walter Placeeley (GBR)	21.9	Helmut Körnig (GER)	21.9
400 m	Raymond Barbuti (USA)	47.8	James Ball (CAN)	48.0	Joachim Büchner (GER)	48.2
800 m	Douglas Lowe (GBR)	1:51.8	Erik Byléhn (SWE)	1:52.8	Hermann Engelhard (GER)	1:53.2
1500 m	Harry Larva (FIN)	3:53.2	Jules Ladoumégue (FRA)	3:53.8	Eino Purje (FIN)	3:56.4
5000 m	Ville Ritola (FIN)	14:38.0	Paavo Nurmi (FIN)	14:40.0	Edvin Wide (SWE)	14:41.2
10,000 m	Paavo Nurmi (FIN)	30:18.8	Ville Ritola (FIN)	30:19.4	Edvin Wide (SWE)	31:00.8
Marathon	Mohammed El Quafi (FRA)	2:32:57	Miguel Plaza (CHI)	2:33:23	Martti Marttelin (FIN)	2:35:02
110 m Hurdles	Sidney Atkinson (SAF)	14.8	Stephen Anderson (USA)	14.8	John Collier (USA)	14.9
400 m Hurdles	David Burghley (GBR)	53.4	Frank Cuhel (USA)	53.6	F. Morgan Taylor (USA)	53.6
3000 m Steeplechase	Toivo Loukola (FIN)	9:21.8	Paavo Nurmi (FIN)	9:31.6	Ove Andersen (FIN)	9:35.6
4 x 100 m	USA	41.0	Germany	41.2	Great Britain	41.8
4 x 400 m	USA	3:14.2	Germany	3:14.8	Canada	3:15.4
High Jump	Robert King (USA)	6'4¼"	Benjamin Hedges (USA)	6'3¼"	Claude Ménard (FRA)	6'3¼"
Pole Vault	Sabin William Carr (USA)	13'9¼"	William Droegemueller (USA)	13'5¼"	Charles McGinnis (USA)	12'11½"
Long Jump	Edward Hamm (USA)	25'4¼"	Silvio Cator (HAI)	24'10¼"	Alfred Bates (USA)	24'3¼"
Triple Jump	Mikio Oda (JPN)	49'10¾"	Levi Casey (USA)	49'9"	Vilho Tuulos (FIN)	49'6¾"
Shot	John Kuck (USA)	52'0¾"	Herman Brix (USA)	51'8"	Emil Hirschfeld (GER)	51'6¾"
Discus	Clarence Houser (USA)	155'2½"	Antero Kivi (FIN)	154'11"	James Corson (USA)	154'6"
Hammer	Patrick O'Callaghan (IRL)	168'7"	Ossian Skiöld (SWE)	168'3"	Edmund Black (USA)	160'10"
Javelin	Erik Lundkvist (SWE)	218'6"	Béla Szepes (HUN)	214'1"	Olav Sunde (NOR)	209'10½"
Decathlon	Paavo Yrjölä (FIN)	8053	Akilles Järvinen (FIN)	7931	John Kenneth Doherty (USA)	7706

EVENT	GOLD		SILVER		BRONZE	
Women						
100 m	Elizabeth Robinson (USA)	12.2	Fanny Rosenfeld (CAN)	12.3	Ethel Smith (CAN)	12.3
800 m	Lina Radke-Batschauer (GER)	2:16.8	Kinue Hitomi (JPN)	2:17.6	Inga Gentzel (SWE)	2:17.8
4 x 100 m	Canada	48.4	USA	48.8	Germany	49.2
High Jump	Ethel Catherwood (CAN)	5'2½"	Carolina Gisolf (HOL)	5'1¼"	Mildred Wiley (USA)	5'1¼"
Discus	Halina Konopacka (POL)	129'11½"	Lillian Copeland (USA)	121'7½"	Ruth Svedberg (SWE)	117'10"
Swimming						
Men						
100 m Freestyle	Johnny Weissmuller (USA)	58.6	István Bárány (HUN)	59.8	Katsuo Takaishi (JPN)	1:00.0
400 m Freestyle	Alberto Zorilla (ARG)	5:01.6	Andrew Charlton (AUS)	5:03.6	Arne Borg (SWE)	5:04.6
1500 m Freestyle	Arne Borg (SWE)	19:51.8	Andrew Charlton (AUS)	20:02.6	Clarence Crabbe (USA)	20:28.8
100 m Backstroke	George Kojac (USA)	1:08.2	Walter Laufer (USA)	1:10.0	Paul Wyatt (USA)	1:12.0
200 m Breaststroke	Yoshiyuki Tsuruta (JPN)	2:48.8	Erich Rademacher (GER)	2:50.6	Teofilo Yldefonzo (PHI)	2:56.4
4 x 200 m Freestyle Relay	USA	9:36.2	Japan	9:41.4	Canada	9:47.8
Springboard Diving	Ulise Joseph Desjardins (USA)	185.04	Michael Galitzen (USA)	174.06	Farid Simaika (EGY)	172.46
Highboard Diving	Ulise Joseph Desjardins (USA)	98.74	Farid Simaika (EGY)	99.58	Michael Galitzen (USA)	92.34
Water Polo	Germany		Hungary		France	
Women						
100 m Freestyle	Albina Osipowich (USA)	1:11.0	Eleonor Garatti (USA)	1:11.4	Joyce Cooper (GBR)	1:13.6
400 m Freestyle	Martha Norelius (USA)	5:42.8	Maria-Johanna Braun (HOL)	5:57.8	Josephine McKim (USA)	6:00.2
100 m Backstroke	Maria-Johanna Braun (HOL)	1:22.0	Ellen King (GBR)	1:22.2	Joyce Cooper (GBR)	1:22.8
200 m Breaststroke	Hilde Schrader (GER)	3:12.6	Mietje Baron (HOL)	3:15.2	Lotte Mühe (GER)	3:17.6
4 x 100 m Freestyle Relay	USA	4:47.6	Great Britain	5:02.8	South Africa	5:13.4
Springboard Diving	Helen Meany (USA)	78.62	Dorothy Poynton (USA)	75.62	Georgia Coleman (USA)	73.38
Highboard Diving	Elizabeth Pinkston-Becker (USA)	31.60	Georgia Coleman (USA)	30.60	Lala Sjöqvist (SWE)	29.20
Boxing						
Flyweight (-112 lb)	Antal Kocsis (HUN)		Armand Appel (FRA)		Carlo Cavagnoli (ITA)	
Bantamweight (-118 lb)	Vittorio Tamagnini (ITA)		John Daley (USA)		Harry Isaacs (SAF)	
Featherweight (-126 lb)	Bep van Klaveren (HOL)		Victor Peralta (ARG)		Harold Devine (USA)	
Lightweight (-135 lb)	Carlo Orlandi (ITA)		Stephen Halaiko (USA)		Gunnar Berggren (SWE)	
Welterweight (- 147 lb)	Edward Morgan (SWE)		Raúl Landini (ARG)		Raymond Smillie (CAN)	
Middleweight (-160 lb)	Piero Toscani (ITA)		Jan Hermánek (TCH)		Léonard Steyaert (BEL)	
Light-Heavyweight (-175 lb)	Victor Avendano (ARG)		Ernst Pistulla (GER)		Karl Leendert Miljon (HOL)	
Heavyweight (+175 lb)	Arturo Rodrigues Jurado (ARG)		Nils Ramm (SWE)		Jacob Michaelsen (DEN)	
Weightlifting						
Featherweight (-132¼ lb)	Franz Andrysek (AUT)	287.5	Pierino Gabetti (ITA)	282.5	Hans Wölpert (GER)	282.5
Lightweight (-148¾ lb)	Kurt Helbig (GER)	322.5			Fernand Arnout (FRA)	302.5
	Hans Haas (AUT)	322.5				
Middleweight (-165½ lb)	Roger Francois (FRA)	335.0	Carlo Galimberti (ITA)	332.5	August Scheffer (HOL)	327.5
Light-Heavyweight (-182 lb)	Sayed Nosseir (EGY)	355.0	Louis Hostin (FRA)	352.5	Johannes Verheijen (HOL)	337.5
Heavyweight (+182 lb)	Josef Strassberger (GER)	372.5	Arnold Luhäär (EST)	360.0	Jaroslav Skobla (TCH)	357.5
Greco-Roman Wrestling						
Bantamweight (- 127¾ lb)	Kurt Leucht (GER)		Jindrich Maudr (TCH)		Giovanni Gozzi (ITA)	
Featherweight (-136½ lb)	Voldemar Väli (EST)		Erik Malmberg (SWE)		Gerolamo Quaglia (ITA)	
Lightweight (-148¾ lb)	Lajos Keresztes (HUN)		Eduard Sperling (GER)		Edvard Westerlund (FIN)	
Middleweight (-165¼ lb)	Väino Kokkinen (FIN)		László Papp (HUN)		Albert Kusnets (EST)	
Light-Heavyweight (-181¾ lb)	Ibrahim Moustafa (EGY)		Adolf Rieger (GER)		Onni Pellinen (FIN)	
Heavyweight (+181¾ lb)	Rudolf Svensson (SWE)		Hjalmar E. Nyström (FIN)		Georg Gehring (GER)	
Freestyle Wrestling						
Bantamweight (-123½ lb)	Kaarlo Mäkinen (FIN)		Edmond Spapen (BEL)		James Trifunov (CAN)	
Featherweight (-134½ lb)	Allie Morrison (USA)		Kustaa Pihlajamäki (FIN)		Hans Minder (SUI)	
Lightweight (- 145½ lb)	Osvald Käpp (EST)		Charles Pacôme (FRA)		Eino Leino (FIN)	
Welterweight (-158½ lb)	Arvo Haavisto (FIN)		Lloyd Appleton (USA)		Maurice Letchford (CAN)	
Middleweight (-174 lb)	Ernst Kyburz (SUI)		Donald P. Stockton (CAN)		Samuel Rabin (GBR)	
Light-Heavyweight (-191¾ lb)	Thure Sjöstedt (SWE)		Arnold Bögli (SUI)		Henri Lefébre (FRA)	
Heavyweight (+191¾ lb)	Johan Richthoff (SWE)		Aukusti Sihvola (FIN)		Edmond Dame (FRA)	
Fencing						
Individual Foil - Men	Lucien Gaudin (FRA)	9+2	Erwin Casmir (GER)	9+1	Giulio Gaudini (ITA)	9
Team Foil - Men	Italy		France		Argentina	
Individual Épée	Lucien Gaudin (FRA)	8	Georges Buchard (FRA)	7	George Calnan (USA)	6
Team Épée	Italy		France		Portugal	

EVENT	GOLD		SILVER		BRONZE	
Individual Saber	Ödön Tersztyánsky (HUN)	9+1	Attila Petschauer (HUN)	9	Bino Bini (ITA)	8
Team Saber	Hungary		Italy		Poland	
Individual Foil - Women	Helene Mayer (GER)	7	Muriel Freeman (GBR)	6	Olga Oelkers (GER)	4
Modern Pentathlon						
Individual	Sven Thofelt (SWE)	47	Bo Lindman (SWE)	50	Helmuth Kahl (GER)	52
Rowing						
Single Sculls	Henry Pearce (AUS)	7:11.0	Kenneth Myers (USA)	7:20.8	David Collet (GBR)	7:29.8
Double Sculls	USA	6:41.4	Canada	6:51.0	Austria	6:58.8
Coxless Pairs	Germany	7:06.4	Great Britain	7:08.8	USA	7:20.4
Coxed Pairs	Switzerland	7:42.6	France	7:48.4	Belgium	7:59.4
Coxless Fours	Great Britain	6:36.0	USA	6:37.0	Italy	
Coxed Fours	Italy	6:47.8	Switzerland	7:03.4	Poland	7:12.8
Coxed Eights	USA	6:03.2	Great Britain	6:05.6	Canada	
Yachting						
Olympic Monotype	Sven Thorell (SWE)		Henrik Robert (NOR)		Bertil Broman (FIN)	
6 m	Norway		Denmark		Estonia	
8 m	France		Netherlands		Sweden	
Cycling						
Individual Road Race (104½ miles)	Henry Hansen (DEN)	4:47:18	Frank Southall (GBR)	4:55:06	Gösta Carlsson (SWE)	5:00:17
Team Road Race	Denmark	15:09:14	Great Britain	15:14:49	Sweden	15:27:49
1000 m Time Trial	Willy Falck-Hansen (DEN)	1:14.4	Gerard Bosch (HOL)	1:15.2	Edgar Gray (AUS)	1:15.6
1000 m Sprint	René Beaufrand (FRA)		Antoine Mazairac (HOL)		Willy Falck-Hansen (DEN)	
2000 m Tandem	Netherlands		Great Britain		Germany	
4000 m Team Pursuit	Italy	5:01.8	Netherlands	5:06.2	Great Britain	5:02.4
Equestrianism						
Three-Day Event	Charles Pahud de Mortanges (HOL)	1969.92	Gerard Pieter de Kruyff (HOL)	1967.26	Bruno Neumann (GER)	1944.42
Three-Day Event - Team	Netherlands		Norway		Poland	
Grand Prix (Dressage)	Carl von Langen (GER)	237.42	Charles Marion (FRA)	231.0	Ragnar Olson (SWE)	229.78
Dressage - Team	Germany		Sweden		Netherlands	
Grand Prix (Jumping)	Franticek Ventura (TCH)	0/0/0	Pierre Bertran de Balanda (FRA)	0/0/2	Charley Kuhn (SUI)	0/0/4
Grand Prix (Jumping) Team	Spain	-4	Poland	-8	Sweden	-10
Gymnastics						
Men						
Individual Combined Exercises	Georges Miez (SUI)	247.500	Hermann Hänggi (SUI)	246.625	Leon Stukelji (YUG)	244.875
Team	Switzerland	1718.625	Czechoslovakia	1712.250	Yugoslavia	1648.750
Parallel Bars	Ladislav Vácha (TCH)	18.83	Josip Primozic (YUG)	18.50	Hermann Hänggi (SUI)	18.08
Horse Vault	Eugen Mack (SUI)	9.58	Emanuel Löffler (TCH)	9.50	Stane Derganc (YUG)	9.46
Horizontal Bar	Georges Miez (SUI)	19.17	Romeo Neri (ITA)	19.00	Eugen Mack (SUI)	18.92
Rings	Leon Stukelji (YUG)	19.25	Ladislav Vácha (TCH)	19.17	Emanuel Löffler (TCH)	18.83
Pommel Horse	Hermann Hänggi (SUI)	19.75	Georges Miez (SUI)	19.25	Heikki Savolainen (FIN)	18.83
Women						
Team	Netherlands	316.75	Italy	289.00	Great Britain	258.25
Soccer						
	Uruguay		Argentina		Italy	
Hockey						
	India		Netherlands		Germany	

Lake Placid 1932

February 4 – February 15

Participants: 252 / Men: 231, Women: 21, Countries: 17,
Sports: 5, Events: 14

Medals Table

PLACE	COUNTRY	GOLD	SILVER	BRONZE
1	USA	6	4	2
2	Norway	3	4	3
3	Sweden	1	2	–
4	Canada	1	1	5
5	Finland	1	1	1

Outstanding Athletes

PLACE	NAME (NATIONALITY)	DISCIPLINE	G	S	B
1	John Shea (USA)	Speed Skating	2	–	–
	Irving Jaffee (USA)	Speed Skating	2	–	–
3	Veli Saarinen (FIN)	Nordic Skiing	1	–	1

EVENT	GOLD		SILVER		BRONZE	
Nordic Skiing						
18 km Cross-Country Skiing	Sven Utterström (SWE)	1:23:07	Axel T. Wikström (SWE)	1:25:07	Veli Saarinen (FIN)	1:25:24
50 km Cross-Country Skiing	Veli Saarinen(FIN)	4:28:00	Väinö Liikkanen (FIN)	4:28:20	Arne Rustadstuen (NOR)	4:31:53
Ski Jumping	Birger Ruud (NOR)	228.1	Hans Beck (NOR)	227.0	Kaare Wahlberg (NOR)	219.5
Nordic Combined	Johan Gröttumsbraaten (NOR)	446.00	Ole Stenen (NOR)	436.05	Hans Vinjarengen (NOR)	434.60
Figure Skating						
Women	Sonja Henie (NOR)		Fritzi Burger (AUT)		Maribel Vinson (USA)	
Men	Karl Schäfer (AUT)		Gillis Gräfström (SWE)		Montgomery Wilson (CAN)	
Pairs	Andrée Brunet/Pierre Brunet (FRA)		Beatrix Loughran/Sherwin Badger (USA)		Emilia Rotter/László Szollás (HUN)	
Speed Skating						
500 m	John Shea (USA)	43.4	Bernt Evensen (NOR)		Alexander Hurd (CAN)	
1500 m	John Shea (USA)	2:57.5	Alexander Hurd (CAN)		William Logan (CAN)	
5000 m	Irving Jaffee (USA)	9:40.8	Edward Murphy (USA)		William Logan (CAN)	
10,000 m	Irving Jaffee (USA)	19:13.6	Ivar Ballangrud (NOR)		Frank Stack (CAN)	
Bobsledding						
2-Man Bob	USA I	8:14.14	Switzerland II	8:16.28	USA II	8:29.15
4-Man Bob	USA I	7:53.68	USA II	7:55.70	Germany I	8:00.04
Ice Hockey						
	Canada		USA		Germany	

Los Angeles 1932

July 30 – August 14

Participants: 1408 / Men: 1281, Women: 127, Countries: 37,
Sports: 14, Events: 117

Medals Table

PLACE	COUNTRY	GOLD	SILVER	BRONZE
1	USA	41	32	30
2	Italy	12	12	12
3	France	10	5	4
4	Sweden	9	5	9
5	Japan	7	7	4

Outstanding Athletes

PLACE	NAME (NATIONALITY)	DISCIPLINE	G	S	B
1	Helen Madison (USA)	Swimming	3	–	–
	Romeo Neri (ITA)	Gymnastics	3	–	–
3	István Pelle (HUN)	Gymnastics	2	2	–
4	Mildred Didrikson (USA)	Athletics	2	1	–

EVENT	GOLD		SILVER		BRONZE	
Athletics						
Men						
100 m	Eddie Tolan (USA)	10.38	Ralph Metcalfe (USA)	10.38	Arthur Jonath (GER)	10.40
200 m	Eddie Tolan (USA)	21.2	George Simpson (USA)	21.4	Ralph Metcalfe (USA)	21.5
400 m	William Carr (USA)	46.2	Benjamin Eastman (USA)	46.4	Alexander Wilson (CAN)	47.4

EVENT	GOLD		SILVER		BRONZE	
800 m	Thomas Hampson (GBR)	1:49.7	Alexander Wilson (CAN)	1:49.9	Philip Edwards (CAN)	1:51.5
1500 m	Luigi Beccali (ITA)	3:51.2	John Cornes (GBR)	3:52.6	Philip Edwards (CAN)	3:52.8
5000 m	Lauri Lehtinen (FIN)	14:30.0	Ralph Hill (USA)	14:30.0	Lauri Virtanen (FIN)	14:44.0
10,000 m	Janusz Kusocinski (POL)	30:11.4	Volmari Iso-Hollo (FIN)	30:12.6	Lauri Virtanen (FIN)	30:35.0
Marathon	Juan Carlos Zabala (ARG)	2:31:36.0	Samuel Ferris (GBR)	2:31:55.0	Armas Toivonen (FIN)	2:32:12.0
110 m Hurdles	George Saling (USA)	14.6	Percy Beard (USA)	14.7	Donald Finlay (GBR)	14.8
400 m Hurdles	Robert Tisdall (IRL)	51.7	Glenn Hardin (USA)	51.9	Morgan Taylor (USA)	52.0
3000 m Steeplechase	Volmari Iso-Hollo (FIN)	10:33.4	Thomas Evenson (GBR)	10:46.0	Joseph McCluskey (USA)	10:46.2
4 x 100 m	USA	40.0	Germany	40.9	Italy	41.2
4 x 400 m	USA	3:08.2	Great Britain	3:11.2	Canada	3:12.8
50 km Walk	Thomas Green (GBR)	4:50.10	Janis Dalinsh (LAT)	4:57:20	Ugo Frigerio (ITA)	4:59:06
High Jump	Duncan McNaughton (CAN)	6'5½"	Robert Van Osdel (USA)	6'5½"	Simeon Toribio (PHI)	6'5½"
Pole Vault	William Miller (USA)	14'1¾"	Shuhei Nishida (JPN)	14'0"	George Jefferson (USA)	13'9"
Long Jump	Edward Gordon (USA)	25'0¾"	Charles L. Redd (USA)	24'11¼"	Chuhei Nambu (JPN)	24'5¼"
Triple Jump	Chuhei Nambu (JPN)	51'7"	Erik Svensson (SWE)	50'3¼"	Kenkichi Oshima (JPN)	49'7¼"
Shot	Leo Sexton (USA)	52'5¾"	Harlow Rothert (USA)	51'5"	Frantisek Douda (TCH)	51'2½"
Discus	John Anderson (USA)	162'4½"	Henri J. Laborde (USA)	159'0½"	Paul Winter (FRA)	157'0"
Hammer	Patrick O'Callaghan (IRL)	176'11"	Ville Pörhölä (FIN)	171'6"	Peter Zaremba (USA)	165'1½"
Javelin	Matti Järvinen (FIN)	238'6½"	Matti Sippala (FIN)	229'0"	Eino Penttilä (FIN)	225'4½"
Decathlon	James Bausch (USA)		Akilles Järvinen (FIN)		Wolrad Eberle (GER)	
Women						
100 m	Stanislawa Walasiewicz (POL)	11.9	Hilda Strike (CAN)	11.9	Wilhelmina v. Bremen (USA)	12.0
80 m Hurdles	Mildred Didrikson (USA)	11.7	Evelyne Hall (USA)	11.7	Marjorie Clark (SAF)	11.8
4 x 100 m	USA	47.0	Canada	47.0	Great Britain	47.6
High Jump	Jean Shiley (USA)	5'5"	Mildred Didrikson (USA)	5'5"	Eva Dawes (CAN)	5'3"
Discus	Lillian Copeland (USA)	133'1½"	Ruth Osburn (USA)	131'7½"	Jadwiga Wajsowna (POL)	128'1"
Javelin	Mildred Didrikson (USA)	143'4"	Ellen Braumüller (GER)	142'8½"	Tilly Fleischer (GER)	142'1¼"
Swimming						
Men						
100 m Freestyle	Yasuji Miyazaki (JPN)	58.2	Tatsugo Kawaishi (JPN)	58.6	Albert Schwartz (USA)	58.8
400 m Freestyle	Clarence Crabbe (USA)	4:48.4	Jean Taris (FRA)	4:48.5	Tsutomu Oyokota (JPN)	4:52.3
1500 m Freestyle	Kusuo Kitamura (JPN)	19:12.4	Shozo Makino (JPN)	19:14.1	James Cristy (USA)	19:39.5
200 m Breaststroke	Yoshiyuki Tsuruta (JPN)	2:45.4	Reizo Koike (JPN)	2:46.4	Teofilo Yldefonzo (PHI)	2:47.1
100 m Back Stroke	Masaji Kiyokawa (JPN)	1:08.6	Toshio Irie (JPN)	1:09.8	Kentaro Kawatsu (JPN)	1:10.0
4 x 200 m Freestyle Relay	Japan	8:58.4	USA	9:10.5	Hungary	9:31.4
Springboard Diving	Michael Galitzen (USA)	161.38	Harold Smith (USA)	158.54	Richard Degener (USA)	151.82
Highboard Diving	Harold Smith (USA)	124.80	Michael Galitzen (USA)	124.28	Frank Kurtz (USA)	121.98
Water Polo	Hungary	8	Germany	5	USA	5
Women						
100 m Freestyle	Helene Madison (USA)	1:06.8	Willie den Ouden (HOL)	1:07.8	Eleonor Garatti (USA)	1:08.2
400 m Freestyle	Helene Madison (USA)	5:28.5	Lenore Kight (USA)	5:28.6	Jennie Makaal (SAF)	5:47.3
200 m Breaststroke	Claire Dennis (AUS)	3:06.3	Hideko Maehata (JPN)	3:06.4	Else Jacobsen (DEN)	3:07.1
100 m Backstroke	Eleanor Holm (USA)	1:19.4	Philomena Mealing (AUS)	1:21.3	Elizabeth Davies (GBR)	1:22.5
4 x 100 m Freestyle Relay	USA	4:38.0	Netherlands	4:47.5	Great Britain	4:52.4
Springboard Diving	Georgia Coleman (USA)	87.52	Katherine Rawls (USA)	82.56	Jane Fauntz (USA)	82.12
Highboard Diving	Dorothy Poynton (USA)	40.26	Georgia Coleman (USA)	35.56	Marion Roper (USA)	35.22
Boxing						
Flyweight (-112 lb)	István Enekes (HUN)		Francisco Cabanas (MEX)		Louis Salica (USA)	
Bantamweight (-118 lb)	Horace Gwynne (CAN)		Hans Ziglarski (GER)		José Villanueva (PHI)	
Featherweight (-126 lb)	Carmelo Robledo (ARG)		Josef Schleinkofer (GER)		Carl Carlsson (SWE)	
Lightweight (-135 lb)	Lawrence Stevens (SAF)		Thure Ahlqvist (SWE)		Nathan Bor (USA)	
Welterweight (-147 lb)	Edward Flynn (USA)		Erich Campe (GER)		Bruno Ahlberg (FIN)	
Middleweight (-160 lb)	Carmen Barth (USA)		Amado Azar (ARG)		Ernest Pierce (SAF)	
Light-Heavyweight (-175 lb)	David Carstens (SAF)		Gino Rossi (ITA)		Peter Jörgensen (DEN)	
Heavyweight (+175 lb)	Santiago Lovell (ARG)		Luigi Rovati (ITA)		Frederik Feary (USA)	
Weightlifting						
Featherweight (-132¼ lb)	Raymond Suvigny (FRA)	287.5	Hans Wölpert (GER)	282.5	Anthony Terlazzo (USA)	280.0
Lightweight (-148¾lb)	Réne Duverger (FRA)	325.0	Hans Haas (AUT)	307.5	Gastone Pierini (ITA)	302.5
Middleweight (-165¼ lb)	Rudolf Ismayr (GER)	345.0	Carlo Galimberti (ITA)	340.0	Karl Hipfinger (AUT)	337.5
Light-Heavyweight (-182 lb)	Louis Hostin (FRA)	365.0	Svend Olsen (DEN)	360.0	Henry Duey (USA)	330.0
Heavyweight (+182 lb)	Jaroslav Skobla (TCH)	380.0	Vaclav Psenicka (TCH)	377.5	Josef Strassberger (GER)	377.5

EVENT	GOLD		SILVER		BRONZE	
Greco-Roman Wrestling						
Bantamweight (-123¼ lb)	Jakob Brendel (GER)		Marcello Nizzola (ITA)		Louis François (FRA)	
Featherweight (-134¼ lb)	Giovanni Gozzi (ITA)		Wolfgang Ehrl (GER)		Lauri Koskela (FIN)	
Lightweight (-145½ lb)	Erik Malmberg (SWE)		Abraham Kurland (DEN)		Eduard Sperling (GER)	
Welterweight (-158½ lb)	Ivar Johansson (SWE)		Väinö Kajander (FIN)		Ercole Gallegati (ITA)	
Middleweight (-174 lb)	Väinö Kokkinen (FIN)		Jean Földeák (GER)		Axel Cadier (SWE)	
Light-Heavyweight (-191¾ lb)	Rudolf Svensson (SWE)		Onni Pellinen (FIN)		Mario Gruppioni (ITA)	
Heavyweight (+191¾ lb)	Carl Westergren (SWE)		Josef Urban (TCH)		Nikolaus Hirschl (AUT)	
Freestyle Wrestling						
Bantamweight (-123¼ lb)	Robert Pearce (USA)		Ödön Zombori (HUN)		Aatos Jaskari (FIN)	
Featherweight (-134¼ lb)	Hermanni Pihlajamäki (FIN)		Edgar Nemir (USA)		Einar Karlsson (SWE)	
Lightweight (-145½ lb)	Charles Pacôme (FRA)		Károly Kárpáti (HUN)		Gustaf Klarén (SWE)	
Welterweight (-158½ lb)	Jack van Bebber (USA)		Daniel MacDonald (CAN)		Eino Leino (FIN)	
Middleweight (-174 lb)	Ivar Johansson (SWE)		Kyösti Luukko (FIN)		Jósef Tunyogi (HUN)	
Light-Heavyweight (-191¾ lb)	Peter Mehringer (USA)		Thure Sjöstedt (SWE)		Eddie Scarf (AUS)	
Heavyweight (+191¾ lb)	Johan Richthoff (SWE)		John Riley (USA)		Nikolaus Hirschl (AUT)	
Fencing						
Individual Foil - Men	Gustavo Marzi (ITA)	9	Joseph Levis (USA)	6	Giulio Gaudini (USA)	5
Team Foil - Men	France		Italy		USA	
Individual Épée	Giancarlo Cornaggia-Medici (ITA)	8/18	Georges Buchard (FRA)	7	Carlo Agostoni (ITA)	7
Team Épée	France		Italy		USA	
Individual Saber	György Piller (HUN)	8	Giulio Gaudini (ITA)	7	Endre Kabos (HUN)	5
Team Saber	Hungary		Italy		Poland	
Individual Foil - Women	Ellen Preis (AUT)	8/1	Heather Guinness (GBR)	8	Erna Bogen (HUN)	7
Modern Pentathlon						
Individual	Johan Oxenstierna (SWE)	32	Bo Lindmann (SWE)	35.5	Richard Mayo (USA)	38.5
Rowing						
Single Sculls	Henry Pearce (AUS)	7:44.4	William Miller (USA)	7:45.2	Guillermo Douglas (URU)	8:13.6
Double Sculls	USA	7:17.4	Germany	7:22.8	Canada	7:27.6
Coxless Pairs	Great Britain	8:00.0	New Zealand	8:02.4	Poland	8:08.2
Coxed Pairs	USA	8:25.8	Poland	8:31.2	France	8:41.2
Coxless Fours	Great Britain	6:58.2	Germany	7:03.0	Italy	7:04.0
Coxed Fours	Germany	7:19.0	Italy	7:19.2	Poland	7:26.8
Coxed Eights	USA	6:37.6	Italy	6:37.8	Canada	6:40.4
Yachting						
Olympic Monotype	Jacques Lebrun (FRA)	87	Adriaan L. J. Maas (HOL)	85	Santiago A. Cansino (ESP)	76
International Star	USA	46	Great Britain	35	Sweden	28
6 m	Sweden	18	USA	12	Canada	4
8 m	USA	8	Canada	4		
Cycling						
Individual Road Race (62 miles)	Attilio Pavesi (ITA)	2:28:05.6	Guglielmo Segato (ITA)	2:29:21.4	Bernhard Britz (SWE)	2:29:45.2
Team Road Race	Italy	7:27:15.2	Denmark	7:38:50.2	Sweden	7:39:12.6
1000 m Time Trial	Edgar Gray (AUS)	1:13.0	Jacobus v. Egmond (HOL)	1:13.3	Charles Rampelberg (FRA)	1:13.4
1000 m Sprint	Jacobus v. Egmond (HOL)	12.6	Louis Chaillot (FRA)		Bruno Pellizzari (ITA)	
2000 m Tandem	France	12.0	Great Britain		Denmark	
4000 m Team Pursuit	Italy	4:53.0	France	4:55.7	Great Britain	4:56.0
Equestrianism						
Three-Day Event	Charles F. P. de Mortanges (HOL)	1813.833	Earl Thomson (USA)	1811.000	Clarence von Rosen jun. (SWE)	1809.416
Three-Day Event - Team	USA		Netherlands			
Grand Prix (Dressage)	Xavier Lesage (FRA)	343.75	Charles Marion (FRA)	305.42	Hiram Tuttle (USA)	300.50
Grand Prix (Jumping)	France		Sweden		USA	
Grand Prix (Jumping) - Team	Takeichi Nishi (JPN)	-8	Harry Chamberlain (USA)	-12	Clarence von Rosen jun. (SWE)	-16
Shooting						
Small-Bore Rifle (Prone)	Bertil Rönmark (SWE)	294	Gustavo Huet (MEX)	294	Zoltan Hradetzky-Soós (HUN)	293
Rapid-Fire Pistol	Renzo Morigi (ITA)	36	Heinz Hax (GER)	36	Domenico Matteucci (ITA)	36

EVENT	GOLD		SILVER		BRONZE	
Gymnastics						
Individual Combined Exercises	Romeo Neri (ITA)	140.625	István Pelle (HUN)	134.925	Heikki Savolainen (FIN)	134.575
Team	Italy	541.850	USA	522.275	Finland	509.995
Parallel Bars	Romeo Neri (ITA)	18.97	István Pelle (HUN)	18.60	Heikki Savolainen (FIN)	18.27
Floor	István Pelle (HUN)	9.60	Georges Miez (SUI)	9.47	Mario Lertora (ITA)	9.23
Horse Vault	Savio Guglielmetti (ITA)	18.03	Alfred Jochim (USA)	17.72	Edward Carmichael (USA)	17.53
Horizontal Bar	Dallas Bixler (USA)	18.33	Heikki Savolainen (FIN)	18.07	Einari Teräsvirta (FIN)	18.07
Rings	George Gulack (USA)	18.97	William Denton (USA)	18.60	Giovanni Lattuada (ITA)	18.50
Pommel Horse	István Pelle (HUN)	19.07	Omero Bonoli (ITA)	18.87	Frank Haubold (USA)	18.57
Rope Climbing	Raymond Bass (USA)	6.7	William Galbraith (USA)	6.8	Thomas Connelly (USA)	7.0
Tumbling	Rowland Wolfe (USA)	18.90	Edward Gross (USA)	18.67	William Hermann (USA)	18.37
Club Swinging	George Roth (USA)		Philip Erenberg (USA)		William Kutrmeier (USA)	
Hockey						
	India		Japan		USA	

Garmisch–Partenkirchen 1936

February 6 – February 16

Participants: 668 / Men: 588, Women: 80, Countries: 28,
Sports: 6, Events: 17

Medals Table

PLACE	COUNTRY	GOLD	SILVER	BRONZE
1	Norway	7	5	3
2	Germany	3	3	–
3	Sweden	2	2	3
4	Finland	1	2	3
5	Switzerland	1	2	–

Outstanding Athletes

PLACE	NAME (NATIONALITY)	DISCIPLINE	G	S	B
1	Ivar Ballangrud (NOR)	Speed Skating	3	1	–
2	Oddbjörn Hagen (NOR)	Nordic Skiing	1	2	–
3	Ernst Baier (GER)	Figure Skating	1	1	–
4	Erik-August Larsson (SWE)	Nordic Skiing	1	–	1

EVENT	GOLD		SILVER		BRONZE	
Alpine Skiing						
Alpine Combined						
Men	Franz Pfnür (GER)	08.04.1900	Adolf Lantschner (GER)	96.26	Emile Allais (FRA)	94.69
Women	Christl Cranz (GER)	06.04.1900	Käthe Grasegger (GER)	95.26	Laila Schou Nilsen (NOR)	93.48
Nordic Skiing						
18 km Cross-Country Skiing	Erik-August Larsson (SWE)	1:14:38	Oddbjörn Hagen (NOR)	1:15:33	Pekka Niemi (FIN)	1:16:59
50 km Cross-Country Skiing	Elis Wiklund (SWE)	3:30:11	Axel Wikström (SWE)	3:33:20	Nils-Joel Englund (SWE)	3:34:10
4 x 10 km Relay	Finland	2:41:33	Norway	2:41:39	Sweden	2:43:03
Ski Jumping	Birger Ruud (NOR)	232.0	Sven Ivan Eriksson (SWE)	230.5	Reidar Andersen (NOR)	228.9
Nordic Combined	Oddbjörn Hagen (NOR)	430.3	Olaf Hoffsbakken (NOR)	419.8	Sverre Brodahl (NOR)	408.1
Figure Skating						
Women	Sonja Henie (NOR)		Cecilia Colledge (GBR)		Vivi-Anne Hultén (SWE)	
Men	Karl Schäfer (AUT)		Ernst Baier (GER)		Felix Kaspar (AUT)	
Pairs	Maxi Herber/Ernst Baier (GER)		Ilse Pausin/Erik Pausin (AUT)		Emilia Rotter/László Szollás (HUN)	
Speed Skating						
500 m	Ivar Ballangrud (NOR)	11.02.1900	Georg Krog (NOR)	43.5	Leo Freisinger (USA)	44.0
1500 m	Charles Mathisen (NOR)	2:19.2	Ivar Ballangrud (NOR)	2:20.2	Birger Vasenius (FIN)	2:20.9
5000 m	Ivar Ballangrud (NOR)	8:19.6	Birger Vasenius (FIN)	8:23.3	Antero Ojala (FIN)	8:30.1
10000 m	Ivar Ballangrud (NOR)	17:24.3	Birger Vasenius (FIN)	17:28.2	Max Stiepl (AUT)	17:30.0
Bobsledding						
2-Man Bob	USA I	5:29.29	Switzerland II	5:30.64	USA II	5:33.96
4-Man Bob	Switzerland II	5:19.85	Switzerland I	5:22.73	Great Britain I	5:23.41
Ice Hockey						
	Great Britain		Canada		USA	

Berlin 1936

August 1 – August 16

Participants: 4066 / Men: 3738, Women: 328, Countries: 49,
Sports: 19, Events: 129
Final Torchbearer: Fritz Schilgen

Medals Table

PLACE	COUNTRY	GOLD	SILVER	BRONZE
1	Germany	33	26	30
2	USA	24	20	12
3	Hungary	10	1	5
4	Italy	8	9	5
5	Finland	7	6	6

Outstanding Athletes

PLACE	NAME (NATIONALITY)	DISCIPLINE	G	S	B
1	Jesse Owens (USA)	Athletics	4	–	–
2	Konrad Frey (GER)	Gymnastics	3	1	2
3	Hendrika Mastenbroek (HOL)	Swimming	3	1	–
4	Alfred Schwarzmann (GER)	Gymnastics	3	–	2
5	Robert Charpentier (FRA)	Cycling	3	–	–

EVENT	GOLD		SILVER		BRONZE	
Athletics						
Men						
100 m	Jesse Owens (USA)	10.3	Ralph Metcalfe (USA)	10.4	Martinus Osendarp (HOL)	10.5
200 m	Jesse Owens (USA)	20.7	Matthew Robinson (USA)	21.1	Martinus Osendarp (HOL)	21.3
400 m	Archie Williams (USA)	46.5	Godfrey Brown (GBR)	46.7	James LuValle (USA)	46.8
800 m	John Woodruff (USA)	1:52.9	Mario Lanzi (ITA)	1:53.3	Philip Edwards (CAN)	1:53.6
1500 m	John Lovelock (NZL)	3:47.8	Glenn Cunningham (USA)	3:48.4	Luigi Beccali (ITA)	3:49.2
5000 m	Gunnar Hoeckert (FIN)	14:22.2	Lauri Lehtinen (FIN)	14:25.8	Henry Jonsson (SWE)	14:29.0
10,000 m	Ilmari Salminen (FIN)	30:15.4	Arvo Askola (FIN)	30:15.6	Volmari Iso-Hollo (FIN)	30:20.2
Marathon	Kitei Son (JPN)	2:29:19.2	Ernest Harper (GBR)	2:31:23.2	Shoryu Nan (JPN)	2:31:42.0
110 m Hurdles	Forrest Towns (USA)	14.2	Donald Finlay (GBR)	14.4	Frederick Pollard (USA)	14.4
400 m Hurdles	Glenn Hardin (USA)	52.4	John Loaring (CAN)	52.7	Miguel White (PHI)	52.8
3000 m Steeplechase	Volmari Iso-Hollo (FIN)	9:03.8	Kaarlo Tuominen (FIN)	9:06.8	Alfred Dompert (GER)	9:07.2
4 x 100 m	USA	39.8	Italy	41.1	Germany	41.2
4 x 400 m	Great Britain	3:09.0	USA	3:11.0	Germany	3:11.8
50 km Walk	Harold Whitlock (GBR)	4:30:41.1	Arthur Schwab (SUI)	4:32:09.2	Adalbert Bubenko (LAT)	4:32:42.2
High Jump	Cornelius Johnson (USA)	6'7¾"	David Albritton (USA)	6'6¾"	Delos Thurber (USA)	6'6¾"
Pole Vault	Earle Meadows (USA)	14'3¼"	Shuhei Nishida (JPN)	14'0"	Sueo Oe (JPN)	13'11¼"
Long Jump	Jesse Owens (USA)	26'5¼"	Luz Long (GER)	25'9¾"	Naoto Tajima (JPN)	25'4½"
Triple Jump	Naoto Tajima (JPN)	52'5¾"	Masao Harada (JPN)	51'4½"	John P. Metcalfe (AUS)	50'10"
Shot	Hans Woellke (GER)	53'1¾"	Sulo Bärlund (FIN)	52'10½"	Gerhard Stöck (GER)	51'4½"
Discus	Kenneth Carpenter (USA)	165'7"	Gordon Dunn (USA)	161'11"	Giorgio Oberweger (ITA)	161'6"
Hammer	Karl Hein (GER)	185'4"	Erwin Blask (GER)	180'6½"	Fred Warngard (SWE)	179'10½"
Javelin	Gerhard Stöck (GER)	235'8"	Yrjö Nikkanen (FIN)	232'2"	Kalervo Toivonen (FIN)	232'0"
Decathlon	Glenn Morris (USA)	7900	Robert Clark (USA)	7601	Jack Parker (USA)	7275
Women						
100 m	Helen Stephens (USA)	11.5	Stanislawa Walasiewicz (POL)	11.7	Käthe Krauß (GER)	11.9
80 m Hurdles	Trebisonda Valla (ITA)	11.7	Ann Steuer (GER)	11.7	Elizabeth Taylor (CAN)	11.7
4 x 100 m	USA	46.9	Great Britain	47.6	Canada	47.8
High Jump	Ibolya Csák (HUN)	5'3"	Dorothy Odam (GBR)	5'3"	Elfriede Kaun (GER)	5'3"
Discus	Gisela Mauermayer (GER)	156'3"	Jadwiga Wajsowna (POL)	151'7½"	Paula Mollenhauer (GER)	130'6½"
Javelin	Tilly Fleischer (GER)	148'2½"	Luise Krüger (GER)	142'0"	Maria Kwasniewska (POL)	137'1½"
Swimming						
Men						
100 m Freestyle	Ferenc Csik (HUN)	57.6	Masanori Yusa (JPN)	57.9	Shiego Arai (JPN)	58.0
400 m Freestyle	Jack Medica (USA)	4:44.5	Shumpei Uto (JPN)	4:45.6	Shozo Makino (JPN)	4:48.1
1500 m Freestyle	Noboru Terada (JPN)	19:13.7	Jack Medica (USA)	19:34.0	Shumpei Uto (JPN)	19:34.5
100 m Backstroke	Adolf Kiefer (USA)	1:05.9	Albert van de Weghe (USA)	1:07.7	Masaji Kiyokawa (JPN)	1:08.4
200 m Breaststroke	Tetsuo Hamuro (JPN)	2:42.5	Erwin Sietas (GER)	2:42.9	Reizo Koike (JPN)	2:44.2
4 x 200 m Freestyle	Japan	8:51.5	USA	9:03.0	Hungary	9:12.3
Springboard Diving	Richard Degener (USA)	163.57	Marshall Wayne (USA)	159.56	Albert Greene (USA)	146.29
Highboard Diving	Marshall Wayne (USA)	113.58	Elbert Root (USA)	110.60	Hermann Stork (GER)	110.31
Water Polo	Hungary		Germany		Belgium	
Women						
100 m Freestyle	Hendrika Mastenbroek (HOL)	1:05.9	Jeanette Campbell (ARG)	1:06.4	Gisela Arendt (GER)	1:06.6
400 m Freestyle	Hendrika Mastenbroek (HOL)	5:26.4	Ragnhild Hveger (DEN)	5:27.5	Lenore Wingard-Kight (USA)	5:29.0
200 m Breaststroke	Hideko Maehata (JPN)	3:03.6	Martha Genenger (GER)	3:04.2	Inge Sörensen (DEN)	3:07.8
100 m Backstroke	Dina W. Senff (HOL)	1:18.9	Hendrika Mastenbroek (HOL)	1:19.2	Alice Bridges (USA)	1:19.4

EVENT	GOLD		SILVER		BRONZE	
4 x 100 m Freestyle	Netherlands	4:36.0	Germany	4:36.8	USA	4:40.2
Springboard Diving	Marjorie Gestring (USA)	89.27	Katherine Rawls (USA)	88.35	Dorothy Poynton-Hill (USA)	82.36
Highboard Diving	Dorothy Poynton-Hill (USA)	33.93	Velma Dunn (USA)	33.63	Käthe Köhler (GER)	33.43
Boxing						
Flyweight (-112 lb)	Willy Kaiser (GER)		Gavino Matta (ITA)		Louis D. Laurie (USA)	
Bantamweight (- 118 lb)	Ulderico Sergo (ITA)		Jack Wilson (USA)		Fidel Ortiz (MEX)	
Featherweight (-126 lb)	Oscar Casanovas (ARG)		Charles Catterall (SAF)		Josef Miner (GER)	
Lightweight (-135 lb)	Imre Harangi (HUN)		Nikolai Stepulov (EST)		Erik Agren (SWE)	
Welterweight (-147 lb)	Sten Suvio (FIN)		Michael Murach (GER)		Gerhard Petersen (DEN)	
Middleweight (-160 lb)	Jean Despeaux (FRA)		Henry Tiller (NOR)		Raul Villareal (ARG)	
Light-Heavyweight (-175 lb)	Roger Michelot (FRA)		Richard Vogt (GER)		Francisco Risiglione (ARG)	
Heavyweight (+175 lb)	Herbert Runge (GER)		Guillermo Lovell (ARG)		Erling Nilsen (NOR)	
Weightlifting						
Featherweight (-132¼ lb)	Anthony Terlazzo (USA)	312.5	Saleh Mohammed Soliman (EGY)	305.0	Ibrahim Shams (EGY)	300.0
Lightweight (-148¾ lb)	Anwar Mesbah (EGY)	342.5			Karl Jansen (GER)	327.5
	Robert Fein (AUT)	342.5				
Middleweight (-165½ lb)	Khadr Sayed El Touni (EGY)	387.5	Rudolf Ismayr (GER)	352.5	Adolf Wagner (GER)	352.5
Light-Heavyweight (-182 lb)	Louis Hostin (FRA)	372.5	Eugen Deutsch (GER)	365.0	Ibrahim Wasif (EGY)	360.0
Heavyweight (+182 lb)	Josef Manger (GER)	410.0	Václav Psenicka (TCH))	402.5	Arnold Luhaäär (EST)	400.0
Greco-Roman Wrestling						
Bantamweight (-123¼ lb)	Márton Lörincz (HUN)		Egon Svensson (SWE)		Jakob Brendel (GER)	
Featherweight (-134¼ lb)	Yasar Erkan (TUR)		Aarne Reini (FIN)		Einar Karlsson (SWE)	
Lightweight (-145½ lb)	Lauri Koskela (FIN)		Josef Herda (TCH)		Voldemar Väli (EST)	
Welterweight (-158½ lb)	Rudolf Svedberg (SWE)		Fritz Schäfer (GER)		Eino Virtanen (FIN)	
Middleweight (-174 lb)	Ivar Johansson (SWE)		Ludwig Schweickert (GER)		Jósef Palotás (HUN)	
Light-Heavyweight (-191¾ lb)	Axel Cadier (SWE)		Edwin Bietags (LAT)		August Neo (EST)	
Heavyweight (+191¾ lb)	Kristjan Palusalu (EST)		John Nyman (SWE)		Kurt Hornfischer (GER)	
Freestyle Wrestling						
Bantamweight (-123¼ lb)	Ödön Zombori (HUN)		Ross Flood (USA)		Johannes Herbert (GER)	
Featherweight (-134¼ lb)	Kustaa Pihlajamäki (FIN)		Francis Millard (USA)		Gösta Jönsson (SWE)	
Lightweight (-145½ lb)	Károly Kárpáty (HUN)		Wolfgang Ehrl (GER)		Hermanni Pihlajamäki (FIN)	
Welterweight (-158½ lb)	Frank Lewis (USA)		Ture Andersson (SWE)		Joseph Schleimer (CAN)	
Middleweight (-174 lb)	Emile Poilvé (FRA)		Richard Voliva (USA)		Ahmet Kirecci (TUR)	
Light-Heavyweight (-191¾ lb)	Knut Fridell (SWE)		August Neo (EST)		Erich Siebert (GER)	
Heavyweight (+191¾ lb)	Kristjan Palusalu (EST)		Josef Klapuch (TCH)		Hjalmar Nyström (FIN)	
Fencing						
Individual Foil - Men	Giulio Gaudini (ITA)	7	Edward Gardière (FRA)	6	Giorgio Bocchino (ITA)	4
Team Foil	Italy		France		Germany	
Individual Épée	Franco Riccardi (ITA)	5	Saverio Ragno (ITA)	6	Giancarlo Cornaggia-Medici (ITA)	6
Team Épée	Italy		Sweden		France	
Individual Saber	Endre Kabos (HUN)	7	Gustavo Marzi (ITA)	6	Aladár Gerevich (HUN)	6
Team Saber	Hungary		Italy		Germany	
Individual Foil - Women	Ilona Elek (HUN)	6	Helene Mayer (GER)	5	Ellen Preis (AUT)	5
Modern Pentathlon						
Individual	Gotthard Handrick (GER)	31.5	Charles Leonard (USA)	39.5	Silvano Abba (ITA)	45.5
Canoeing						
1000 m Kayak Singles K1	Gregor Hradetzky (AUT)	4:22.9	Helmut Cämmerer (GER)	4:25.6	Jacob Kraaier (HOL)	4:35.1
10,000 m Kayak Singles K1	Ernst Krebs (GER)	46:01.6	Fritz Landertinger (AUT)	46:14.7	Ernest Riedel (USA)	47:23.9
1000 m Kayak Pairs K2	Austria	4:03.8	Germany	4:08.9	Netherlands	4:12.2
10,000 m Kayak PairsK2	Germany	41:45.0	Austria	42:05.4	Sweden	43:06.1
1000 m Canadian Singles C1	Francis Amyot (CAN)	5:32.1	Bohuslav Karlik (TCH)	5:36.9	Erich Koschik (GER)	5:39.0
1000 m Canadian Pairs C2	Czechoslovakia	4:50.1	Austria	4:53.8	Canada	4:56.7
10,000 m Canadian PairsC2	Czechoslovakia	50:33.5	Canada	51:15.8	Austria	51:28.0
10,000 m Folding Kayak Singles F1	Gregor Hradetzky (AUT)	50:01.2	Henri Eberhardt (FRA)	50:04.2	Xaver Hörmann (GER)	50:06.5
10,000 m Folding Kayak Pairs F2	Sweden	45:48.9	Germany	45:49.2	Netherlands	46:12.4
Rowing						
Single Sculls	Gustav Schäfer (GER)	8:21.5	Josef Hasenöhrl (AUT)	8:25.8	Daniel Barrow (USA)	8:28.0
Double Sculls	Great Britain	7:20.8	Germany	7:26.2	Poland	7:36.2
Coxless Pairs	Germany	8:16.1	Denmark	8:19.2	Argentina	8:23.0
Coxed Pairs	Germany	8:36.9	Italy	8:49.7	France	8:54.0

EVENT	GOLD		SILVER		BRONZE	
Coxless Fours	Germany	7:01.8	Great Britain	7:06.5	Switzerland	7:10.6
Coxed Fours	Germany	7:16.2	Switzerland	7:24.3	France	7:33.3
Coxed Eights	USA	6:25.4	Italy	6:26.0	Germany	6:26.4
Yachting						
Olympic Monotype	Daniel Kagchelland (HOL)	163	Werner Krogmann (GER)	150	Peter Scott (GBR)	131
International Star	Germany	80	Sweden	64	Netherlands	63
6 m	Great Britain	67	Norway	66	Sweden	62
8 m	Italy	55	Norway	53	Germany	53
Cycling						
Individual Road Race (62 miles)	Robert Charpentier (FRA)	2:33:05.0	Guy Lapébie (FRA)	2:33:05.2	Ernst Nievergelt (SUI)	2:33:05.8
Team Road Race	France	7:39:16.2	Switzerland	7:39:20.4	Belgium	7:39:21.0
1000-m-Time Trial	Arie van Vliet (HOL)	1:12.0	Pierre Georget (FRA)	1:12.8	Rudolf Karsch (GER)	1:13.2
1000-m-Sprint	Toni Merkens (GER)	11.8	Arie van Vliet (HOL)		Louis Chaillot (FRA)	
2000-m-Tandem	Germany	11.8	Netherlands		France	
4000-m-Team Pursuit	France	4:45.0	Italy	4:51.0	Great Britain	4:52.6
Equestrianism						
Three-Day Event	Ludwig Stubbendorff (GER)	-37.70	Earl Thomson (USA)	-99.90	Hans Mathiesen-Lunding(DEN)	-102.20
Three-Day Event - Team	Germany	-676.65	Poland	-991.70	Great Britain	-9195.50
Grand Prix (Dressage)	Heinz Pollay (GER)	1760.0	Friedrich Gerhard (GER)	1745.5	Alois Podhajsky (AUT)	1721.5
Grand Prix (Dressage) - Team	Germany	5074.0	France	4846.0	Sweden	4660.5
Grand Prix (Jumping)	Kurt Hasse (GER)	4	Henri Rang (ROM)	4	József von Platthy (HUN)	8
Grand Prix (Jumping) - Team	Germany	-44.00	Netherlands	-51.50	Portugal	-56.00
Shooting						
Small-Bore Rifle (Prone)	Willy Rögeberg (NOR)	300	Ralf Berzseny (HUN)	296	Wladyslaw Karas (POL)	296
Rapid-Fire Pistol	Cornelius van Oyen (GER)	36	Heinz Hax (GER)	35	Torsten Ullman (SWE)	34
Free Pistol (50 m)	Torsten Ullmann (SWE)	559	Erich Krempel (GER)	544	Charles des Jammonières (FRA)	540
Gymnastics						
Men						
Individual Combined Exercises	Alfred Schwarzmann (GER)	113.100	Eugen Mack (SUI)	112.334	Konrad Frey (GER)	111.532
Team	Germany	657.430	Switzerland	654.802	Finland	638.468
Parallel Bars	Konrad Frey (GER)	19.067	Michael Reusch (SUI)	19.034	Alfred Schwarzmann (GER)	18.967
Floor	Georges Miez (SUI)	18.666	Josef Walter (SUI)	18.500	Eugen Mack (SUI)	18.466
					Konrad Frey (GER)	18.466
Horse Vault	Alfred Schwarzmann (GER)	19.200	Eugen Mack (SUI)	18.967	Matthias Volz (GER)	18.467
Horizontal Bar	Aleksanteri Saarvala (FIN)	19.367	Konrad Frey (GER)	19.267	Alfred Schwarzmann (GER)	19.233
Rings	Alois Hudec (TCH)	19.433	Leon Stukelji (YUG)	18.867	Matthias Volz (GER)	18.667
Pommel Horse	Konrad Frey (GER)	19.333	Eugen Mack (SUI)	19.167	Albert Bachmann (SUI)	19.067
Women						
Team	Germany	506.50	Czechoslovakia	503.60	Hungary	499.00
Basketball						
	USA		Canada		Mexico	
Soccer						
	Italy		Austria		Norway	
Handball						
	Germany		Austria		Switzerland	
Hockey						
	India		Germany		Netherlands	
Polo						
	Argentina		Great Britain		Mexico	

St. Moritz 1948

January 30 – February 8

Participants 669 / Men: 529, Women: 77, Countries: 28,
Sports: 7, Events: 22
Final Torchbearer: Richard Torriani

Medals Table

PLACE	COUNTRY	GOLD	SILVER	BRONZE
1	Norway	4	3	3
	Sweden	4	3	3
3	Switzerland	3	4	3
4	USA	3	4	2
5	France	2	1	2

Outstanding Athletes

PLACE	NAME (NATIONALITY)	DISCIPLINE	G	S	B
1	Henri Oreiller (FRA)	Alpine Skiing	2	–	1
2	Martin Lundström (SWE)	Nordic Skiing	2	–	–
3	Trude Beiser (AUT)	Alpine Skiing	1	1	–
	Gretchen Fraser (USA)	Alpine Skiing	1	1	–
	Nils Östensson (SWE)	Nordic Skiing	1	1	–

EVENT	GOLD		SILVER		BRONZE	
Alpine Skiing						
Men						
Downhill	Henri Oreiller (FRA)	2:55.0	Franz Gabl (AUT)	2:59.1	Karl Molitor (SUI)	3:00.3
					Rolf Olinger (SUI)	3:00.3
Slalom	Edy Reinalter (SUI)	130.3	James Couttet (FRA)	130.8	Henri Oreiller (FRA)	132.8
Alpine Combined	Henri Oreiller (FRA)	3.27	Karl Molitor (SUI)	6.44	James Couttet (FRA)	6.95
Women						
Downhill	Hedy Schlunegger (SUI)	2:28.3	Trude Beiser (AUT)	2:29.1	Resi Hammerer (AUT)	2:30.2
Slalom	Gretchen Fraser (USA)	117.2	Antoinette Meyer (SUI)	117.7	Erika Mahringer (AUT)	118.0
Alpine Combined	Trude Beiser (AUT)	6.58	Gretchen Fraser (USA)	6.95	Erika Mahringer (AUT)	7.04
Nordic Skiing						
18 km Cross-Country Skiing	Martin Lundström (SWE)	1:13:50	Nils Östensson (SWE)	1:14:22	Gunnar Eriksson (SWE)	1:16:06
50 km Cross-Country Skiing	Nils Karlsson (SWE)	3:47:48	Harald Eriksson (SWE)	3:52:20	Benjamin Vanninen (FIN)	3:57:28
4 x 10 km	Sweden	2:32:08	Finland	2:41:06	Norway	2:44:33
Ski Jumping	Petter Hugsted (NOR)	228.1	Birger Ruud (NOR)	226.6	Thorleif Schjeldrup (NOR)	225.1
Nordic Combined	Heikki Hasu (FIN)	448.80	Martti Huhtala (FIN)	433.65	Sven Israelsson (SWE)	433.40
Figure Skating						
Women	Barbara Ann Scott (CAN)		Eva Pawlik (AUT)		Jeanette Altwegg (GBR)	
Men	Richard Button (USA)		Hans Gerschwiler (SUI)		Edi Rada (AUT)	
Pairs	Micheline Lannoy/ Pierre Baugniet (BEL)		Andrea Kékessy/ Ede Király (HUN)		Suzanne Morrow/ Wallace Diestelmeyer (CAN)	
Speed Skating						
500 m	Finn Helgesen (NOR)	43.1	Kenneth Bartholomew (USA)	43.2		
			Thomas Byberg (NOR)	43.2		
			Robert Fitzgerald (USA)	43.2		
1500 m	Sverre Farstadt (NOR)	2:17.6	Ake Seyffarth (SWE)	2:18.1	Odd Lundberg (NOR)	2:18.9
5000 m	Reidar Liaklev (NOR)	8:29.4	Odd Lundberg (NOR)	8:32.7	Göte Hedlund (SWE)	8:34.8
10,000 m	Ake Seyffarth (SWE)	17:26.3	Lauri Parkkinen (FIN)	17:36.0	Pentti Lammio (FIN)	17:42.7
Bobsledding						
2-Man Bob	Switzerland II	5:29.2	Switzerland I	5:30.4	USA II	5:35.3
4-Man Bob	USA II	5:20.1	Belgium	5:21.3	USA I	5:21.5
Skeleton Sled						
	Nino Bibbia (ITA)	323.2	John R. Heaton (USA)	324.6	John Crammond (GBR)	325.1
Ice Hockey						
	Canada		Czechoslovakia		Switzerland	

London 1948

July 29 – August 14

Participants: 4099 / Men:3714, Women: 385, Countries: 59,
Sports: 17, Events: 136
Final Torchbearer: John Mark

Medals Table

PLACE	COUNTRY	GOLD	SILVER	BRONZE
1	USA	38	27	19
2	Sweden	16	11	17
3	France	10	6	13
4	Hungary	10	5	12
5	Italy	8	12	9

Outstanding Athletes

PLACE	NAME (NATIONALITY)	DISCIPLINE	G	S	B
1	Fanny Blankers-Koen (HOL)	Athletics	4	–	–
2	Veikko Huhtanen (FIN)	Gymnastics	3	1	1
3	Paavo Aaltonen (FIN)	Gymnastics	3	–	1
4	James McLane (USA)	Swimming	2	1	–
	Anne Curtis (USA)	Swimming	2	1	–

EVENT	GOLD		SILVER		BRONZE	
Athletics						
Men						
100 m	Harrison Dillard (USA)	10.3	Norwood Ewell (USA)	10.4	Lloyd LaBeach (PAN)	10.4
200 m	Melvin Patton (USA)	21.1	Norwood Ewell (USA)	21.1	Lloyd LaBeach (PAN)	21.2
400 m	Arthur Wint (JAM)	46.2	Herbert McKenley (JAM)	46.4	Malvin Whitfield (USA)	46.9
800 m	Malvin Whitfield (USA)	1:49.2	Arthur Wint (JAM)	1:49.5	Marcel Hansenne (FRA)	1:49.8
1500 m	Henry Eriksson (SWE)	3:49.8	Lennart Strand (SWE)	3:50.4	Willem Slijkhuis (HOL)	3:50.4
5000 m	Gaston Reiff (BEL)	14:17.6	Emil Zátopek (TCH)	14:17.8	Willem Slijkhuis (HOL)	14:26.8
10,000 m	Emil Zátopek (TCH)	29:59.6	Alain Mimoun (FRA)	30:47.4	Bertil Albertsson (SWE)	30:53.6
Marathon	Delfo Cabrera (ARG)	2:34:51.6	Thomas Richards (GBR)	2:35:07.6	Etienne Gailly (BEL)	2:35:33.6
110 m Hurdles	William Porter (USA)	13.9	Clyde Scott (USA)	14.1	Craig Dixon (USA)	14.1
400 m Hurdles	Leroy Cochran (USA)	51.1	Duncan White (CEY)	51.8	Rune Larsson (SWE)	52.2
3000 m Steeplechase	Thore Sjöstrand (SWE)	9:04.6	Erik Elmsäter (SWE)	9:08.2	Gösta Hagström (SWE)	9:11.8
4 x 100 m	USA	40.6	Great Britain	41.3	Italy	41.5
4 x 400 m	USA	3:10.4	France	3:14.8	Sweden	3:16.0
10 km Walk	John Mikaelsson (SWE)	45:13.2	Ingemar Johansson (SWE)	45:43.8	Fritz Schwab (SUI)	46:00.2
50 km Walk	John Ljunggren (SWE)	4:41:52	Gaston Godel (SUI)	4:48:17	Tebbs Lloyd-Johnson (GBR)	4:48:31
High Jump	John Winter (AUS)	6'6"	Björn Paulson (NOR)	6'4¾"	George Stanich (USA)	6'4¾"
Pole Vault	Guinn Smith (USA)	14'1¼"	Erkki Kataja (FIN)	13'9¼"	Robert Richards (USA)	13'9¼-
Long Jump	Willie Steele (USA)	25'7¾"	Thomas Bruce (AUS)	24'9"	Herbert Douglas (USA)	24'8¾"
Triple Jump	Arne Ahman (SWE)	50'6¼"	George Avery (AUS)	50'4¾"	Ruhi Sarialp (TUR)	49'3½"
Shot	Wilbur Thomson (USA)	56'2"	Francis Delaney (USA)	54'8½"	James Fuchs (USA)	53'10¼"
Discus	Adolfo Consolini (ITA)	173'1½"	Giuseppe Tosi (ITA)	169'10½"	Fortune Gordien (USA)	166'6½"
Hammer	Imre Németh (HUN)	183'11"	Ivan Gubijan (YUG)	178'0½"	Robert Bennett (USA)	176'3"
Javelin	Tapio Rautavaara (FIN)	228'10½"	Steve Seymour (USA)	221'7½"	József Várszegi (HUN)	219'10½"
Decathlon	Robert Mathias (USA)	7139	Ignace Heinrich (FRA)	6974	Floyd Simmons (USA)	6950
Women						
100 m	Fanny Blankers-Koen (HOL)	11.9	Dorothy Manley (GBR)	12.2	Shirley Strickland (AUS)	12.2
200 m	Fanny Blankers-Koen (HOL)	24.4	Audrey Williamson (GBR)	25.1	Audrey Patterson (USA)	25.2
80 m Hurdles	Fanny Blankers-Koen (HOL)	11.2	Maureen Gardner (GBR)	11.2	Shirley Strickland (AUS)	11.4
4 x 100 m	Netherlands	47.5	Australia	47.6	Canada	47.8
High Jump	Alice Coachman (USA)	5'6"	Dorothy Tyler-Odam (GBR)	5'6"	Micheline Ostermeyer (FRA)	5'3¼"
Long Jump	Olga Gyarmati (HUN)	18'8"	Noëmi Simonetto De Portela (ARG)	18'4¼"	Ann-Britt Leyman (SWE)	18'3¼"
Shot	Micheline Ostermeyer (FRA)	45'1¼"	Amelia Piccinini (ITA)	42'11½"	Ine Schäffer (AUT)	42'10¾"
Discus	Micheline Ostermeyer (FRA)	137'6"	Edera Gentile-Cordiale (ITA)	35'0½"	Jacqueline Mazeas (FRA)	132'9"
Javelin	Herma Bauma (AUT)	149'6"	Kaisa Parviainen (FIN)	143'8"	Lily Carlstedt (DEN)	140'6½"
Swimming						
Men						
100 m Freestyle	Walter Ris (USA)	57.3	Alan Ford (USA)	57.8	Géza Kádas (HUN)	58.1
400 m Freestyle	William Smith (USA)	4:41.0	James McLane (USA)	4:43.4	John Marshall (AUS)	4:47.7
1500 m Freestyle	James McLane (USA)	19:18.5	John Marshall (AUS)	19:31.3	György Mitró (HUN)	19:43.2
100 m Backstroke	Allen Stack (USA)	1:06.4	Robert Cowell (USA)	1:06.5	Georges Vallerey (FRA)	1:07.8
200 m Breaststroke	Joseph Verdeur (USA)	2:39.3	Keith Carter (USA)	2:40.2	Robert Sohl (USA)	2:43.9
4 x 200 m Freestyle	USA	8:46.0	Hungary	8:48.4	France	9:08.0
Springboard Diving	Bruce Harlan (USA)	163.64	Miller Anderson (USA)	157.29	Samuel Lee (USA)	145.52
Highboard Diving	Samuel Lee (USA)	130.05	Bruce Harlan (USA)	122.30	Joaquin Caprilla Pérez (MEX)	113.52
Water Polo	Italy		Hungary		Netherlands	

EVENT	GOLD		SILVER		BRONZE	
Women						
100 m Freestyle	Greta Andersen (DEN)	1:06.3	Ann Curtis (USA)	1:06.5	Marie-Louise Vaessen (HOL)	1:07.6
400 m Freestyle	Ann Curtis (USA)	5:17.8	Karen-Margrete Harup (DEN)	5:21.2	Catherine Gibson (GBR)	5:22.5
100 m Backstroke	Karen-Margrete Harup (DEN)	1:14.4	Suzanne Zimmermann (USA)	1:16.0	Judy Davies (AUS)	1:16.7
200 m Breaststroke	Petronella van Vliet (HOL)	2:57.2	Beatrice Lyons (AUS)	2:57.7	Evá Novák (HUN)	3:00.2
4 x 100 m Freestyle	USA	4:29.2	Denmark	4:29.6	Netherlands	4:31.6
Springboard Diving	Victoria Draves (USA)	108.74	Zoe Ann Olsen (USA)	108.23	Patricia Elsener (USA)	101.30
Highboard Diving	Victoria Draves (USA)	68.87	Patricia Elsner (USA)	66.28	Birte Christofferson (DEN)	66.04
Boxing						
Flyweight (-112½ lb)	Pascual Perez (ARG)		Spartaco Bandinelli (ITA)		Han Soo-Ann (KOR)	
Bantamweight (-119 lb)	Tibor Csik (HUN)		Giovanni Battista Zuddas (ITA)		Juan Venegas (PUR)	
Featherweight (-127¾ lb)	Ernesto Formenti (ITA)		Dennis Shepherd (SAF)		Aleksy Antkiewicz (POL)	
Lightweight (-136½ lb)	Gerald Dreyer (SAF)		Joseph Vissers (BEL)		Sven Wad (DEN)	
Welterweight (-148 lb)	Julius Torma (TCH)		Horace Herring (USA)		Alessandro D'Ottavio (ITA)	
Middleweight (-161 lb)	László Papp (HUN)		John Wright (GBR)		Ivano Fontana (ITA)	
Light-Heavyweight (-176¼ lb)	George Hunter (SAF)		Donald Scott (GBR)		Maurio Cia (ARG)	
Heavyweight (+176¼ lb)	Rafael Iglesias (ARG)		Gunnar Nilsson (SWE)		John Arthur (SAF)	
Weightlifting						
Bantamweight (-123½ lb)	Joseph Di Pietro (USA)	307.5	Julian Creus (GBR)	297.5	Richard Tom (USA)	295.0
Featherweight (-132¼ lb)	Mahmoud Fayad (EGY)	332.5	Rodney Wilkes (TRI)	317.5	Jaffar Salmassi (IRN)	312.5
Lightweight (-148¾ lb)	Ibrahim Shams (EGY)	360.0	Attia Hamouda (EGY)	360.0	James Halliday (GBR)	340.0
Middleweight (-165½ lb)	Frank Spellman (USA)	390.0	Peter George (USA)	382.5	Kim Sung-Jip (KOR)	380.0
Light-Heavyweight (-182 lb)	Stanley Stanczyk (USA)	417.5	Harold Sakata (USA)	380.0	Gösta Magnusson (SWE)	375.0
Heavyweight (+182 lb)	John Davis (USA)	452.5	Norbert Schemansky (USA)	425.0	Abraham Charité (HOL)	412.5
Greco-Roman Wrestling						
Flyweight (- 114½ lb)	Pietro Lombardi (ITA)		Kenan Olcay (TUR)		Reino Kangasmäki (FIN)	
Bantamweight (-125¾ lb)	Kurt Pettersen (SWE)		Ali Mahmoud Hassan (EGY)		Halil Kaya (TUR)	
Featherweight (-136½ lb)	Mehmet Oktav (TUR)		Olle Anderberg (SWE)		Ferenc Tóth (HUN)	
Lightweight (-147½ lb)	Gustav Freij (SWE)		Aage Eriksen (NOR)		Károly Ferencz (HUN)	
Welterweight (-160¾ lb)	Gösta Andersson (SWE)		Miklós Szilvási (HUN)		Henrik Hansen (DEN)	
Middleweight (-174 lb)	Axel Grönberg (SWE)		Muhlis Tayfur (TUR)		Ercole Gallegati (ITA)	
Light-Heavyweight (-191¾ lb)	Karl-Erik Nilsson (SWE)		Kaelpo Gröndahl (FIN)		Ibrahim Orabi (EGY)	
Heavyweight (+191¾ lb)	Ahmet Kirecci (TUR)		Tor Nilsson (SWE)		Guido Fantoni (ITA)	
Freestyle Wrestling						
Flyweight (-114½ lb)	Lennart Viitala (FIN)		Halat Balamir (TUR)		Thure Johansson (SWE)	
Bantamweight (-125¾ lb)	Nasuh Akar (TUR)		Gerald Leeman (USA)		Charles Kouyos (FRA)	
Featherweight (-136½ lb)	Gazanfer Bilge (TUR)		Ivar Sjölin (SWE)		Adolf Müller (SUI)	
Lightweight (-147½ lb)	Celal Atik (TUR)		Gösta Frändfors (SWE)		Hermann Baumann (SUI)	
Welterweight (-160¾ lb)	Yasar Dogu (TUR)		Richard Garrard (AUS)		Leland Merrill (USA)	
Middleweight (-174 lb)	Glen Brand (USA)		Adil Candemir (TUR)		Erik Linden (SWE)	
Light-Heavyweight (-191¾ lb)	Henry Wittenberg (USA)		Fritz Stöckli (SUI)		Bengt Fahlkvist (SWE)	
Heavyweight (+191¾ lb)	Gyula Bóbis (HUN)		Bertil Antonsson (SWE)		Joseph Armstrong (AUS)	
Fencing						
Individual Foil - Men	Jehan Buhan (FRA)	7	Christian d'Oriola (FRA)	5	Lajos Maszlay (HUN)	4
Team Foil - Men	France		Italy		Belgium	
Individual Épée	Luigi Cantone (ITA)	7	Oswald Zappelli (SUI)	5	Edoardo Mangiarotti (ITA)	5
Team Épée	France		Italy		Sweden	
Individual Saber	Aladár Gerevich (HUN)	7	Vicenzo Pinton (ITA)	5	Pál Kovacs (HUN)	5
Team Saber	Hungary		Italy		USA	
Individual Foil - Women	Ilona Elek (HUN)	6	Karen Lachmann (DEN)	5	Ellen Müller-Preis (AUT)	5
Modern Pentathlon						
Individual	Wiliam Grut (SWE)	16	George Moore (USA)	47	Gösta Gärdin (SWE)	49
Canoeing						
Men						
1000 m Kayak Singles K1	Gert Fredriksson (SWE)	4:33.2	Johan Kobberup (DEN)	4:39.9	Henri Eberhardt	4:41.4
10,000 m Kayak Singles K1	Gert Fredriksson (SWE)	50:47.7	Kurt Wires (FIN)	51:18.2	Ejvind Skabo (NOR)	51:35.4
1000 m Kayak Pairs K2	Sweden	4:07.3	Denmark	4:07.5	Finland	4:08.7
10,000 m Kayak Pairs K2	Sweden	46:09.4	Norway	46:44.8	Finland	46:48.2
1000 m Canadian Singles C1	Josef Holecek (TCH)	5:42.0	Douglas Bennett (CAN)	5:53.3	Robert Boutigny (FRA)	5:55.9
10,000 m Canadian SinglesC1	Frantisek Capek (TCH)	1:02.05	Frank Havens (USA)	1:02.40	Norman Lane (CAN)	1:04.35

EVENT	GOLD		SILVER		BRONZE	
1000 m Canadian Pairs C2	Czechoslovakia	5:07.1	USA	5:08.2	France	5:15.2
10,000 m Canadian Pairs C2	USA	55:55.4	Czechoslovakia	57:38.5	France	58:00.8
Women						
500 m Kayak Singles K1	Karen Hoff (DEN)	2:31.9	Alide van der Anker-Doedans (HOL)	2:32.8	Fritzi Schwingl (AUT)	2:32.9
Rowing						
Single Sculls	Mervyn Wood (AUS)	7:24.4	Eduardo Risso (URU)	7:38.2	Romolo Catasta (ITA)	7:51.4
Double Sculls	Great Britain	6:51.3	Denmark	6:55.3	Uruguay	7:12.4
Coxless Pairs	Great Britain	7:21.1	Switzerland	7:23.9	Italy	7:31.5
Coxed Pairs	Denmark	8:00.5	Italy	8:12.2	Hungary	8:25.2
Coxless Fours	Italy	6:39.0	Denmark	6:43.5	USA	6:47.7
Coxed Fours	USA	6:50.3	Switzerland	6:53.3	Denmark	6:58.6
Coxed Eights	USA	5:56.7	Great Britain	6:06.9	Norway	6:10.3
Yachting						
Olympic Monotype	Paul Elvström (DEN)	5543	Ralph Evans jun. (USA)	5408	Jacobus de Jong (HOL)	5204
International Star	USA	5828	Cuba	4949	Netherlands	4731
Swallow	Great Britain	5625	Portugal	5579	USA	4352
Dragon	Norway	4746	Sweden	4621	Denmark	4223
6 m	USA	5472	Argentina	5120	Sweden	4033
Cycling						
Individual Road Race (121 miles)	José Beyaert (FRA)	5:18:12.6	Gerardus Voorting (HOL)	5:18:16.2	Lode Wouters (BEL)	5:18:16.2
Team Road Race	Belgium	15:58:17.4	Great Britain	16:03:31.6	France	16:08:19.4
1000 m Time-Trial	Jacques Dupont (FRA)	1:13.5	Pierre Nihant (BEL)	1:14.5	Thomas Godwin (GBR)	1:15.0
1000 m Sprint	Mario Ghella (ITA)		Reginald Harris (GBR)		Axel Schandorff (DEN)	
2000 m Tandem	Italy		Great Britain		France	
4000 m Team Pursuit	France	4:57.8	Italy	5:36.7	Great Britain	4:55.8
Equestrianism						
Three-Day Event	Bernard Chevallier (FRA)	+4	Frank Henry (USA)	-21	Robert Selfelt (SWE)	-25
Three-Day Event (Team)	USA	-161.50	Sweden	-165.00	Mexico	-305.25
Grand Prix (Dressage)	Hans Moser (SUI)	492.5	André Jousseaume (FRA)	480.0	Gustav-Adolf Boltenstern jun. (SWE)	477.5
Grand Prix (Dressage) Team	France	1269.0	USA	1256.0	Portugal	1182.0
Grand Prix (Jumping)	Humberto Marileo Cortés (MEX)	6.25	Rubén Uriza (MEX)	8	Jean François d'Orgeix (FRA)	8
Grand Prix (Jumping) Team	Mexico	-34.25	Spain	-56.50	Great Britain	-67.00
Shooting						
Free Rifle (3 Positions)	Emil Grünig (SUI)	1120	Pauli Janhonen (FIN)	1114	Willy Rögeberg (NOR)	1112
Small-Bore Rifle (Prone)	Arthur Cook (USA)	599	Walter Tomsen (USA)	599	Jonas Jonsson (SWE)	597
Rapid-Fire Pistol	Károly Takács (HUN)	580	Carlos E. Diaz Sáenz Valiente (ARG)	571	Sven Lundqvist (SWE)	569
Free Pistol (5 0m)	Edwin Vasquez Cam (PER)	545	Rudolf Schnyder (SUI)	539	Torsten Ullman (SWE)	539
Gymnastics						
Men						
Individual Combined Exercises	Veikko Huhtanen (FIN)	229.70	Walter Lehmann (SUI)	229.00	Paavo Aaltonen (FIN)	228.80
Team	Finland	1358.30	Switzerland	1356.70	Hungary	1330.85
Parallel Bars	Michael Reusch (SUI)	39.50	Veikko Huhtanen (FIN)	39.30	Christian Kipfer (SUI)	39.10
					Josef Stalder (SUI)	39.10
Floor	Ferenc Pataki (HUN)	38.70	János Mogyorósi-Klencs (HUN)	38.40	Zdenek Ruzicka (TCH)	38.10
Horse Vault	Paavo Aaltonen (FIN)	39.10	Olavi Rove (FIN)	39.00	János Mogyorósi-Klencs (HUN)	38.50
					Ferenc Pataki (HUN)	38.50
					Leo Sotornik (TCH)	38.50
Horizontal Bar	Josef Stalder (SUI)	39.70	Walter Lehmann (SUI)	39.40	Veikko Huhtanen (FIN)	39.20
Rings	Karl Frei (SUI)	39.60	Michael Reusch (SUI)	39.10	Zdenek Ruzicka (TCH)	38.50
Pommel Horse	Veikko Huhtanen (FIN)	38.70	Luigi Zanetti (ITA)	38.30	Guido Figone (ITA)	38.20
	Paavo Aaltonen (FIN)	38.70				
	Heikki Savolaien (FIN)	38.70				
Women						
Team	Czechoslovakia	445.45	Hungary	440.55	USA	422.63
Basketball	USA		France		Brazil	
Soccer	Sweden		Yugoslavia		Denmark	
Hockey	India		Great Britain		Netherlands	

Oslo 1952

Participants: 694 / Men: 585, Women: 109, Countries: 30,
Sports: 6, Events: 22
Final Torchbearer: Eigil Nansen

Medals Table

PLACE	COUNTRY	GOLD	SILVER	BRONZE
1	Norway	7	3	6
2	USA	4	6	1
3	Finland	3	4	2
4	Germany	3	2	2
5	Austria	2	4	2

Outstanding Athletes

PLACE	NAME (NATIONALITY)	DISCIPLINE	G	S	B
1	Hjalmar Andersen (NOR)	Speed Skating	3	–	–
2	Andrea Mead Lawrence (USA)	Alpine Skiing	2	–	–
	Andreas Ostler (GER)	Bobsledding	2	–	–
	Lorenz Nieberl (GER)	Bobsledding	2	–	–

EVENT	GOLD		SILVER		BRONZE	
Alpine Skiing						
Men						
Downhill	Zeno Colò (ITA)	2:30.8	Othmar Schneider (AUT)	2:32.0	Christian Pravda (AUT)	2:32.4
Slalom	Othmar Schneider (AUT)	2:00.0	Stein Eriksen (NOR)	2:01.2	Guttorm Berge (NOR)	2:01.7
Giant Slalom	Stein Eriksen (NOR)	2:25.0	Christian Pravda (AUT)	2:26.9	Toni Spiss (AUT)	2:28.8
Women						
Downhill	Trude Jochum-Beiser (AUT)	1:47.1	Annnemarie Buchner (GER)	1:48.0	Giuliana Minuzzo (ITA)	1:49.0
Slalom	Andrea Mead Lawrence (USA)	2:10.6	Ossi Reichert (GER)	2:11.4	Annemarie Buchner (GER)	2:13.3
Giant Slalom	Andrea Mead Lawrence (USA)	2:06.8	Dagmar Rom (AUT)	2:09.0	Annemarie Buchner (GER)	2:10.0
Nordic Skiing						
Men						
18 km Cross-Country Skiing	Hallgeir Brenden (NOR)	1:01:34.0	Tapio Mäkelä (FIN)	1:02:09.0	Paavo Lonkila (FIN)	1:02:20.0
50 km Cross-Country Skiing	Veikko Hakulinen (FIN)	3:33.33.0	Eero Kolehmainen (FIN)	3:38:11.0	Magnar Estensad (NOR)	3:38:28.0
4 x 10 km	Finland	2:20:16.0	Norway	2:23:13.0	Sweden	2:24:13.0
Ski Jumping	Arnfinn Bergmann (NOR)	226.0	Torbjörn Falkanger (NOR)	221.5	Karl Holmstöm (SWE)	219.5
Nordic Combined	Simon Slåttvik (NOR)	451.621	Heikki Hasu (FIN)	447.500	Sverre Stenersen (NOR)	436.335
Women						
10 km Cross-Country Skiing	Lydia Widemann (FIN)	41:40.0	Mirja Hietamies (FIN)	42:39.0	Siiri Rantanen (FIN)	42:50.0
Figure Skating						
Women	Jeanette Altwegg (GBR)		Tenley Albright (USA)		Jacqueline du Bief (FRA)	
Men	Richard Button (USA)		Helmut Seibt (AUT)		James Grogan (USA)	
Pairs	Ria Falk/ Paul Falk (GER)		Karol Estelle Kennedy/ Michael Kennedy (USA)		Marianne Nagy/ László Nagy (HUN)	
Speed Skating						
500 m	Kenneth Henry (USA)	43.2	Donald McDermott (USA)	43.9	Arne Johansen (NOR)	44.0
					Gordon Audley (CAN)	44.0
1500 m	Hjalmar Andersen (NOR)	2:20.4	Willem van der Voort (HOL)	2.20.6	Roald Aas (NOR)	2:21.6
5000 m	Hjalmar Andersen (NOR)	8:10.6	Cornelis Broekman (HOL)	8:21.6	Sverre Haugli (NOR)	8:22.4
10,000 m	Hjalmar Andersen (NOR)	16:45.8	Cornelis Broekman (HOL)	17:10.6	Carl-Erik Asplund (SWE)	17:16.6
Bobsledding						
2-Man Bob	Germany	5:24.54	USA I	5:26.89	Switzerland I	5:27.71
4-Man Bob	Germany	5:07.84	USA I	5:10.48	Switzerland I	5:11.70
Ice Hockey						
	Canada		USA		Sweden	

Helsinki 1952

July 19 – August 3

Participants: 4925 / Men: 4407, Women: 518, Countries: 69,
Sports: 17, Events: 149
Final Torchbearer: Paavo Nurmi

Medals Table

PLACE	COUNTRY	GOLD	SILVER	BRONZE
1	USA	40	19	17
2	USSR	22	30	19
3	Hungary	16	10	16
4	Sweden	12	12	10
5	Italy	8	9	4

Outstanding Athletes

PLACE	NAME (NATIONALITY)	DISCIPLINE	G	S	B
1	Viktor Chukarin (URS)	Gymnastics	4	2	–
2	Emil Zátopek (TCH)	Athletics	3	–	–
3	Maria Gorochovskaya (URS)	Gymnastics	2	5	–
4	Edoardo Mangiarotti (ITA)	Fencing	2	2	–
	Grant Shaginyan (URS)	Gymnastics	2	2	–
	Nina Bocharova (URS)	Gymnastics	2	2	–

EVENT	GOLD		SILVER		BRONZE	
Athletics						
Men						
100 m	Lindy Remigino (USA)	10.4	Herbert McKenley (JAM)	10.4	Emmanuel McDonald-Bailey (GBR)	10.4
200 m	Andrew Stanfield (USA)	20.7	Thane Baker (USA)	20.8	James Gathers (USA)	20.8
400 m	George Rhoden (JAM)	45.9	Herbert McKenley (JAM)	45.9	Ollie Matson (USA)	46.8
800 m	Malvin Whitfield (USA)	1:49.2	Arthur Wint (JAM)	1:49.4	Heinz Ulzheimer (GER)	1:49.7
1500 m	Josy Barthel (LUX)	3:45.1	Bob McMillen (USA)	3:45.2	Werner Lueg (GER)	3:45.4
5000 m	Emil Zátopek (TCH)	14:06.6	Alain Mimoun (FRA)	14:07.4	Herbert Schade (GER)	14:08.6
10,000 m	Emil Zátopek (TCH)	29:17.0	Alain Mimoun (FRA)	29:32.8	Alexander Anufriyev (URS)	29:48.2
Marathon	Emil Zátopek (TCH)	2:23:03.2	Reinaldo Gorno (ARG)	2:25:35.0	Gustaf Jansson (SWE)	2:26:07.0
110 m Hurdles	Harrison Dillard (USA)	13.7	Jack Davis (USA)	13.7	Arthur Barnard (USA)	14.1
400 m Hurdles	Charles Moore (USA)	50.8	Yuri Lituyev (URS)	51.3	John Holland (NZL)	52.2
3000 m Steeplechase	Horace Ashenfelter (USA)	8:45.4	Vladimir Kazantsev (URS)	8:51.6	John Disley (GBR)	8:51.8
4 x 100 m	USA	40.1	USSR	40.3	Hungary	40.5
4 x 400 m	Jamaica	3:03.9	USA	3:04.0	Germany	3:06.6
10 km Walk	John Mikaelsson (SWE)	45:02.8	Fritz Schwab (SUI)	45:41.0	Bruno Yunk (URS)	45:41.0
50 km Walk	Giuseppe Dordoni (ITA)	4:28:07.8	Josef Dolezal (TCH)	4:30:17.8	Antal Róka (HUN)	4:31:27.2
High Jump	Walter Davis (USA)	6'8¼"	Ken Wiesner (USA)	6'7"	J. Telles da Conceiceião (BRA)	6'6"
Pole Vault	Bob Richards (USA)	14'11"	Donald Laz (USA)	14'9"	Ragnar Lundberg (SWE)	14'5"
Long Jump	Jerome Biffle (USA)	24'10"	Meredith Gourdine (USA)	24'8¼"	Ödön Földessy (HUN)	23'11¼"
Triple Jump	Adhemar Ferreira da Silva (BRA)	53'2½"	Leonid Shcherbakov (URS)	52'5"	Arnoldo Devonish (VEN)	50'11"
Shot	Parry O'Brien (USA)	57'1¼"	Darrow Hooper (USA)	57'0½"	Jim Fuchs (USA)	55'11½"
Discus	Sim Iness (USA)	180'6½"	Adolfo Consolini (ITA)	176'5"	James Dillion (USA)	174'9½"
Hammer	József Csermák (HUN)	197'11½"	Karl Storch (GER)	193'1"	Imre Németh (HUN)	189'5"
Javelin	Cyrus Young (USA)	242'0½"	William Miller (USA)	237'8½"	Toivo Hyytiäinen (FIN)	235'10"
Decathlon	Robert Mathias (USA)	7887	Milton Campbell (USA)	6975	Floyd Simmons (USA)	6788
Women						
100 m	Marjorie Jackson (AUS)	11.5	Daphne Hasenjager-Robb (SAF)	11.8	Shirley de la Hunty-Strickland (AUS)	11.9
200 m	Marjorie Jackson (AUS)	23.7	Bertha Brouwer (HOL)	24.2	Nadyezhda Khnykhina (URS)	24.2
80 m Hurdles	Shirley de la Hunty-Strickland (AUS)	10.9	Maria Golubnichaya (URS)	11.1	Maria Sander (GER)	11.1
4 x 100 m Relay	USA	45.9	Germany	45.9	Great Britain	46.2
High Jump	Esther Brand (SAF)	5'5½"	Sheila Lerwill (GBR)	5'5"	Alexandra Chudina (URS)	5'4"
Long Jump	Yvette Williams (NZL)	20'5½"	Alexandra Chudina (URS)	20'1½"	Shirley Cawley (GBR)	19'5"
Shot	Galina Zybina (URS)	50'1½"	Marianne Werner (GER)	47'9½"	Klavdiya Tochenova (URS)	47'6¾"
Discus	Nina Romashrova (URS)	168'8"	Elizaveta Bagriantseva (URS)	154'5½"	Nina Dumbadze (URS)	170'8"
Javelin	Dana Zátopková (TCH)	165'7"	Alexandra Chudina (URS)	164'0½"	Yelena Gorchakova (URS)	163'3"
Swimming						
Men						
100 m Freestyle	Clarke Scholes (USA)	57.4	Hiroshi Suzuki (JPN)	57.4	Göran Larsson (SWE)	58.2
400 m Freestyle	Jean Boiteux (FRA)	4:30.7	Ford Konno (USA)	4:31.3	Per-Olof Östrand (SWE)	4:35.2
1500 m Freestyle	Ford Konno (USA)	18:30.3	Shiro Hashizune (JPN)	18:41.4	Tetsuo Okamoto (BRA)	18:51.3
100 m Backstroke	Yoshinobu Oyakawa (JPN)	1:05.4	Gilbert Bozon (FRA)	1:06.2	Jack Taylor (USA)	1:06.5
200 m Breaststroke	John Davies (AUS)	2:34.4	Bowen Stassforth (USA)	2:34.7	Herbert Klein (GER)	2:35.9
4 x 200 m Freestyle	USA	8:31.1	Japan	8:33.5	France	8:45.9
Springboard Diving	David Browning (USA)	205.29	Miller Anderson (USA)	199.84	Robert Clotworthy (USA)	184.92
Highboard Diving	Samuel Lee (USA)	156.28	Joaquin Capilla Pérez	145.21	Günther Haase (GER)	141.31
Water Polo	Hungary		Yugoslavia		Italy	

EVENT	GOLD		SILVER		BRONZE	
Women						
100 m Freestyle	Katalin Szöke (HUN)	1:06.8	Johanna Termeulen (HOL)	1:07.0	Judit Temes (HUN)	1:07.1
400 m Freestyle	Váleria Gyenge (HUN)	5:12.1	Eva Novák (HUN)	5:13.7	Evelyn Kawamoto (USA)	5:14.6
100 m Backstroke	Joan Harrison (SAF)	1:14.3	Geertje Wielema (HOL)	1:14.5	Jean Stewart (NZL)	1:15.8
200 m Breaststroke	Eva Székely (HUN)	2:51.7	Eva Novák (HUN)	2:54.4	Helen Gordon (GBR)	2:57.6
4 x 100 m Freestyle Relay	Hungary	4:24.4	Netherlands	4:29.0	USA	4:30.1
Springboard Diving	Patricia McCormick (USA)	147.30	Mady Moreau (FRA)	139.34	Zoe Ann Jensen-Olsen (USA)	127.57
Highboard Diving	Patricia McCormlck (USA)	79.37	Paula Jean Myers (USA)	71.63	Juno Irwin-Stover (USA)	70.49

Boxing

EVENT	GOLD	SILVER	BRONZE
Flyweight (-112½ lb)	Nathan Brooks (USA)	Edgar Basel (GER)	Anatoli Bulakov (URS)
			Bill Toweel (SAF)
Bantamweight (-119 lb)	Pentti Hämäläinen (FIN)	John McNally (IRL)	Gennadi Garbusov (URS)
			Kang Joon-Ho (KOR)
Featherweight (-126 lb)	Jan Zachara (TCH)	Sergio Caprari (ITA)	Joseph Ventaja (FRA)
			Leonard Leisching (SAF)
Lightweight (-132 lb)	Aureliano Bolognesi (ITA)	Aleksy Antkiewicz (POL)	Erkki Pakkanen (FIN)
			Gheorge Fiat (ROM)
Light-Welterweight (-140 lb)	Charles Adkins (USA)	Viktor Mednov (URS)	Erkki Mallenius (FIN)
			Bruno Visintin (ITA)
Welterweight (-148 lb)	Zygmunt Chychla (POL)	Sergei Shcherbakov (URS)	Victor Jörgensen (DEN)
			Günther Heidemann (GER)
Light-Middleweight (-157 lb)	László Papp (HUN)	Theunis van Schalkwyk (SAF)	Boris Tishin (URS)
			Eladio Herrera (ARG)
Middleweight (-165 lb)	Floyd Patterson (USA)	Vasile Tita (ROM)	Stig Sjölin (SWE)
			Boris Nikolov (BUL)
Light-Heavyweight (-178½ lb)	Norvel Lee (USA)	Antonio Pacenza (ARG)	Anatoli Perov (URS)
			Harri Siljander (FIN)
Heavyweight (+178½lb)	Hayes Edward Sanders (USA)	Ingemar Johansson (SWE)*	Andries Nieman (SAF)
			Jekka Koski (FIN)

*Disqualified; reinstated as silver medallist in 1982.

Weightlifting

EVENT	GOLD		SILVER		BRONZE	
Bantamweight (-123½ lb)	Ivan Udodov (URS)	315.0	Mahmoud Namdjou (IRN)	307.5	Ali Mirzai (IRN)	300.0
Featherweight (-132¼ lb)	Rafael Chimishkyan (URS)	337.5	Nikolai Saksonov (URS)	332.5	Rodney Wilkes (TRI)	322.5
Lightweight (-148¾ lb)	Thomas Kono (USA)	362.5	Yevgeni Lopatin (URS)	350.0	Verne Barberis (AUS)	350.0
Middleweight (-165½ lb)	Peter George (USA)	400.0	Gerard Gratton (CAN)	390.0	Kim Sung-Jip (KOR)	382.5
Light-Heavyweight (-182 lb)	Trofin Lomakin (URS)	417.5	Stanley Stanczyk (USA)	415.0	Arkadi Vorobiev (URS)	407.5
Middle-Heavyweight (-198½ lb)	Norbert Schemansky (USA)	445.0	Grigori Novak (URS)	410.0	Lennox Kilgour (TRI)	402.5
Heavyweight (+198½ lb)	John Davis (USA)	460.0	James Bradford (USA)	437.5	Humberto Selvetti (ARG)	432.5

Greco-Roman Wrestling

EVENT	GOLD	SILVER	BRONZE
Flyweight (- 114½ lb)	Boris Gurevich (URS)	Ignazio Fabra (ITA)	Leo Honkala (FIN)
Bantamweight (- 125¾ lb)	Imre Hódos (HUN)	Zakaria Chihab (LIB)	Artem Teryan (URS)
Featherweight (-136½ lb)	Yakov Punkin (URS)	Imre Polyak (HUN)	Abdel Rashed (EGY)
Lightweight (-147½lb)	Shazam Safin (URS)	Gustaf Freij (SWE)	Mikulás Athanasov (TCH)
Welterweight (-160¾ lb)	Miklós Szilvási (HUN)	Gösta Andersson (SWE)	Khalil Taha (LIB)
Middleweight (-174 lb)	Axel Grönberg (SWE)	Kalervo Ranhala (FIN)	Nikolai Belov (URS)
Light-Heavyweight (-191¾ lb)	Kaelpo Gröndahl (FIN)	Shalva Shikhladze (URS)	Karl-Erik Nilsson (SWE)
Heavyweight (+191¾ lb)	Johannes Kotkas (URS)	Josef Ruzicka (TCH)	Tauno Kovanen (FIN)

Freestyle Wrestling

EVENT	GOLD	SILVER	BRONZE
Flyweight (-114½ lb)	Hasan Gemici (TUR)	Yushu Kitano (JPN)	Mahmoud Mollaghassemi (IRN)
Bantamweight (-125¾ lb)	Shohachi Ishii (JPN)	Rashid Mamedbekov (URS)	Kha-Shaba Jadav (IND)
Featherweight (-136½ lb)	Bayram Sit (TUR)	Nasser Guivehtchi (IRN)	Josiah Henson (USA)
Lightweight (-147½ lb)	Olle Anderberg (SWE)	Thomas Evans (USA)	Djahanbakte Tovfighe (IRN)
Welterweight (- 160¾ lb)	William Smith (USA)	Per Berlin (SWE)	Abdullah Modjtabavi (IRN)
Middleweight (-174 lb)	David Tsimakuridze (URS)	Gholam Reza Takhti (IRN)	György Gurics (HUN)
Light-Heavyweight (-191¾ lb)	Wiking Palm (SWE)	Henry Wittenberg (USA)	Adil Atan (TUR)
Heavyweight (+191¾ lb)	Arsen Mekokishvili (URS)	Bertil Antonsson (SWE)	Kenneth Richmond (GBR)

Fencing

EVENT	GOLD		SILVER		BRONZE	
Individual Foil - Men	Christian d'Oriola (FRA)	8	Edoardo Mangiarotti (ITA)	6	Manlio Di Rosa (ITA)	5
Team Foil - Men	France		Italy		Hungary	
Individual Épée	Edoardo Mangiarotti (ITA)	7	Dario Mangiarotti (ITA)	6	Oswald Zappelli (SUI)	6
Team Épée	Italy		Sweden		Switzerland	

EVENT	GOLD		SILVER		BRONZE	
Individual Saber	Pál Kovács (HUN)	8	Aladár Gerevich (HUN)	7	Tibor Berczelly (HUN)	5
Team Saber	Hungary		Italy		France	
Individual Foil – Women	Irene Camber (ITA)	5+1	Ilona Elek (HUN)	5	Karen Lachmann (DEN)	4
Modern Pentathlon						
Individual	Lars Hall (SWE)	32	Gábor Benedek (HUN)	39	István Szondy (HUN)	41
Team	Hungary	166	Sweden	182	Finland	213
Canoeing						
Men						
1000 m Kayak Singles K1	Gert Fredriksson (SWE)	4:07.9	Thorvald Strömberg (FIN)	4:09.7	Luis Gantois (FRA)	4:20.1
10 000 m Kayak Singles K1	Thorvald Strömberg (FIN)	47:22.8	Gert Fredriksson (SWE)	47:34.1	Michael Scheuer (GER)	47:54.5
1000 m Kayak Pairs K2	Finland	3:51.1	Sweden	3:51.1	Austria	3:51.4
10,000 m Kayak Pairs K2	Finland	44:21.3	Sweden	44:21.7	Hungary	44:26.6
1000 m Canadian Singles C1	Josef Holecek (TCH)	4:56.3	János Parti (HUN)	5:03.3	Olavi Ojanpara (FIN)	5:08.5
10,000 m Canadian Singles C1	Frank Havens (USA)	57:41.1	Gábor Novák (HUN)	57:49.2	Alfred Jindra (TCH)	57:53.1
1000 m Canadian Pairs C2	Denmark	4:38.3	Czechoslovakia	4:42.9	Germany	4:48.3
10,000 m Canadian Pairs C2	France	54:08.3	Canada	54:09.9	Germany	54:28.1
Women						
500 m Kayak Singles K1	Sylvi Saimo (FIN)	2:18.4	Gertrude Liebhart (AUT)	2:18.8	Nina Savina (URS)	2:21.6
Rowing						
Single Sculls	Yuri Tyukalov (URS)	8:12.8	Mervyn Wood (AUS)	8:14.5	Teodor Kocerka (POL)	8:19.4
Double Sculls	Argentina	7:32.2	USSR	7:38.3	Uruguay	7:43.7
Coxless Pairs	USA	8:20.7	Belgium	8:23.5	Switzerland	8:32.7
Coxed Pairs	France	8:28.6	Germany	8:32.1	Denmark	8:34.9
Coxless Fours	Yugoslavia	7:16.0	France	7:18.9	Finland	7:23.3
Coxed Fours	Czechoslovakia	7:33.4	Switzerland	7:36.5	USA	7:37.0
Coxed Eights	USA	6:25.9	USSR	6:31.2	Australia	6:33.1
Sailing						
Finn Class	Paul Elvström (DEN)	8209	Charles Currey (GBR)	5449	Rickard Sarby (SWE)	5051
International Star	Italy	7635	USA	7216	Portugal	4903
Dragon	Norway	6130	Sweden	5556	Germany	5352
5.5 m	USA	5751	Norway	5325	Sweden	4554
6 m	USA	4870	Norway	4648	Finland	3944
Cycling						
Individual Road Race (118¼ miles)	André Noyelle (BEL)	5:06:03.6	Robert Grondelaers (BEL)	5:06:51.2	Edi Ziegler (GER)	5:07:47.5
Team Road Race	Belgium	15:20:46.6	Italy	15:33:27.3	France	15:38:58.1
1000 m Time Trial	Russel Mockridge (AUS)	1:11.1	Marino Morettini (ITA)	1:12.7	Raymond Robinson (SAF)	1:13.0
1000 m Sprint	Enzo Sacchi (ITA)		Lionel Cox (AUS)		Werner Potzernheim (GER)	
2000 m Tandem	Australia		South Africa		Italy	
4000 m Team Pursuit	Italy	4:46.1	South Africa	4:53.6	Great Britain	4:51.5
Equestrianism						
Three-Day Event	Hans v. Blixen-Finecke (SWE)	-28.33	Guy Lefrant (FRA)	-54.50	Wilhelm Büsing (GER)	-55.50
Three-Day Event (Team)	Sweden	-221.49	Germany	-235.49	USA	-587.16
Grand Prix (Dressage)	Henri Saint Cyr (SWE)	561.0	Lis Hartel (DEN)	541.5	André Jousseaume (FRA)	541.0
Grand Prix (Dressage) Team	Sweden	1597.5	Switzerland	1579.0	Germany	1501.0
Grand Prix (Jumping)	Pierre Jonquères d'Oriola (FRA)	-8/0	Oscar Cristi (CHI)	-8/4	Fritz Thiedemann (GER)	-8/8
Grand Prix (Jumping) Team	Great Britain	-40.75	Chile	-45.75	USA	-52.25
Shooting						
Free Rifle (3 Positions)	Anatoli Bogdanov (URS)	1123	Robert Bürchler (SUI)	1120	Lev Weinstein (URS)	1109
Small-Bore Rifle (Prone)	Josif Sarbu (ROM)	400/33	Boris Andreyev (URS)	400/28	Arthur Jackson (USA)	399
Small-Bore Rifles (3 Positions)	Erling Konshaug (NOR)	1164/53	Vilho Ylönen (FIN)	1164/49	Boris Andreyev (URS)	1163
Rapid-Fire Pistol	Károly Takács (HUN)	579	Szilárd Kun (HUN)	578	Gheorghe Lichiardopol (ROM)	578
Free Pistol (50 m)	Huelet Benner (USA)	553	Angel L. de Gozalo (ESP)	550	Ambrus Balogh (HUN)	549
Olympic Trap Shooting	George P. Généreux (CAN)	192	Knut Holmqvist (SWE)	191	Hans Liljedahl (SWE)	190
Running Deer Shooting	John Larsen (NOR)	413	Per Olof Sköldberg (SWE)	409	Tauno Mäki (FIN)	407
Gymnastics						
Men						
Individual Combined Exercises	Viktor Chukarin (URS)	115.70	Grant Shaginyan (URS)	114.95	Josef Stalder (SUI)	114.75
Team	USSR	575.4	Switzerland	567.50	Finland	564.20
Parallel Bars	Hans Eugster (SUI)	19.65	Viktor Chukarin (URS)	19.60	Josef Stalder (SUI)	19.50

EVENT	GOLD		SILVER		BRONZE	
Floor	Karl William Thoresson (SWE)	19.25	Tadao Uesako (JPN)	19.15		
			Jerzy Jokiel (POL)	19.15		
Horse Vault	Viktor Chukarin (URS)	19.20	Masao Takemoto (JPN)	19.15	Takashi Ono (JPN)	19.10
					Tadao Uesako (JPN)	19.10
Horizontal Bar	Jack Günthard (SUI)	19.55	Josef Stalder (SUI)	19.50		
			Alfred Schwarzmann (GER)	19.50		
Rings	Grant Shaginyan (URS)	19.75	Viktor Chukarin (URS)	19.55	Hans Eugster (SUI)	19.40
					Dmitri Leonkin (URS)	19.40
Pommel Horse	Viktor Chukarin (URS)	19.50	Yevgeni Korolkov (URS)	19.40		
			Grant Shaginyan (URS)	19.40		
Women						
Individual Combined Exercises	Maria Gorochovskaya (URS)	76.78	Nina Bocharova (URS)	75.94	Margit Korondi (HUN)	75.82
Team	USSR	527.03	Hungary	520.96	Czechoslovakia	503.32
Floor	Agnes Keleti (HUN)	19.36	Maria Gorochovskaya (URS)	19.20	Margit Korondi (HUN)	19.00
Horse Vault	Yekaterina Kalinchuk (URS)	19.20	Maria Gorochovskaya (URS)	19.19	Galina Minaitscheva (URS)	19.16
Beam	Nina Bocharova (URS)	19.22	Maria Gorochovskaya (URS)	19.13	Margit Korondi (HUN)	19.02
Asymmetrical Bars	Margit Korondi (HUN)	19.40	Maria Gorochovskaya (URS)	19.26	Agnes Keleti (HUN)	19.16
Portable Apparatus (Women's Teams)	Sweden	74.20	USSR	73.00	Hungary	71.60
Basketball						
	USA		USSR		Uruguay	
Soccer						
	Hungary		Yugoslavia		Sweden	
Hockey						
	India		Netherlands		Great Britain	

Cortina d'Ampezzo 1956

January 26 – February 5

Participants: 820 / Men: 688, Women: 132, Countries: 32,
Sports: 6, Events: 24
Final Torchbearer: Guido Caroli

Medals Table

PLACE	COUNTRY	GOLD	SILVER	BRONZE
1	USSR	7	3	6
2	Austria	4	3	4
3	Finland	3	3	1
4	Switzerland	3	2	1
5	Sweden	2	4	4

Outstanding Athletes

PLACE	NAME (NATIONALITY)	DISCIPLINE	G	S	B
1	Toni Sailer (AUT)	Alpine Skiing	3	–	–
2	Yevgeni Grischin (URS)	Speed Skating	2	–	–
3	Sixten Jernberg (SWE)	Nordic Skiing	1	2	1
4	Veikko Hakulinen (FIN)	Nordic Skiing	1	2	–
5	Lyubov Kosyryeva (URS)	Nordic Skiing	1	1	–
	Sigvard Ericsson (SWE)	Speed Skating	1	1	–

EVENT	GOLD		SILVER		BRONZE	
Alpine Skiing						
Men						
Downhill	Toni Sailer (AUT)	2:52.2	Raymond Fellay (SUI)	2:55.7	Andreas Molterer (AUT)	2:56.2
Slalom	Toni Sailer (AUT)	3:14.7	Chiharu Igaya (JPN)	3:18.7	Stig Sollander (SWE)	3:20.2
Giant Slalom	Toni Sailer (AUT)	3:00.1	Andreas Molterer (AUT)	3:06.3	Walter Schuster (AUT)	3:07.2
Women						
Downhill	Madeleine Berthod (SUI)	1:40.7	Frieda Dänzer (SUI)	1:45.4	Lucile Wheeler (CAN)	1:45.9
Slalom	Renée Colliard (SUI)	1:52.3	Regina Schöpf (AUT)	1:55.4	Yevgeniya Sidorova (URS)	1:56.7
Giant Slalom	Ossi Reichert (GER)*	1:56.5	Josefine Frandl (AUT)	1:57.8	Dorothea Hochleitner (AUT)	1:58.2
Nordic Skiing						
Men						
15 km Cross-Country Skiing	Hallgeir Brenden (NOR)	49:39.0	Sixten Jernberg (SWE)	50:14.0	Pavel Kolschin (URS)	50:17.0
30 km Cross-Country Skiing	Veikko Hakulinen (FIN)	1:44:06.0	Sixten Jernberg (SWE)	1:44:30.0	Pavel Kolschin (URS)	1:45:45.0

EVENT	GOLD		SILVER		BRONZE	
50 km Cross-Country Skiing	Sixten Jernberg (SWE)	2:50:27.0	Veikko Hakulinen (FIN)	2:51:45.0	Fedor Terentyev (URS)	2:53:32.0
4 x 10 km	USSR	2:15:30.0	Finland	2:16:31.0	Sweden	2:17:42.0
Ski Jumping	Antti Hyvärinen (FIN)	227.0	Aulis Kallakorpi (FIN)	225.0	Harry Glass (GER)★	224.5
Nordic Combined	Sverre Stenersen (NOR)	455.000	Bengt Eriksson (SWE)	437.000	Franciszek Gron-Gasienica (POL)	436.800
Women						
10 km Cross-Country Skiing	Lyubov Kosyryeva (URS)	38:11.0	Radya Yeroschina (URS)	38:16.0	Sonja Edström (SWE)	38:23.0
3 x 5 km	Finland	1:09:01.0	USSR	1:09:28.0	Sweden	1:09:48.0
Figure Skating						
Women	Tenley Albright (USA)		Carol Heiss (USA)		Ingrid Wendl (AUT)	
Men	Hayes Alan Jenkins (USA)		Ronald Robertson (USA)		David Jenkins (USA)	
Pairs	Elisabeth Schwarz/Kurt Oppelt (AUT)		Frances Dafoe/Norris Bowden (CAN)		Marianne Nagy/László Nagy (HUN)	
Speed Skating						
500 m	Yevgeni Grischin (URS)	40.2	Rafael Gratsch (URS)	40.8	Alv Gjestvang (NOR)	41.0
1500 m	Yevgeni Grischin (URS)	2:08.6			Toivo Salonen (FIN)	2:09.4
	Yuri Mikhailov (URS)	2:08.6				
5000 m	Boris Schilkov (URS)	7:48.7	Sigvard Ericsson (SWE)	7:56.7	Oleg Gontscharenko (URS)	7:57.5
10,000 m	Sigvard Ericsson (SWE)	16:35.9	Knut Johannesen (NOR)	16:36.9	Oleg Gontscharenko (URS)	16:42.3
Bobsledding						
2-Man Bob	Italy I	5:30.14	Italy II	5:31.45	Switzerland I	5:37.46
4-Man Bob	Switzerland I	5:10.44	Italy II	5:12.10	USA I	5:12.39
Ice Hockey						
	USSR		USA		Canada	

★Representing a combined German team.

Melbourne 1956

Participants: 3184 / Men: 2813, Women: 371, Countries: 67,
Sports: 17, Events: 151
Final Torchbearer: Ron Clarke (Melbourne)
Hans Wikne/Karin Lindberg/Henri Eriksson (Stockholm)

November 22 – December 8
(Equestrian Games in Stockholm June 10–17)
Participants: 158 / Men: 145, Women: 145,
Countries 29

Medals Table

PLACE	COUNTRY	GOLD	SILVER	BRONZE
1	USSR	37	29	32
2	USA	32	25	17
3	Australia	13	8	14
4	Hungary	9	10	7
5	Italy	8	8	9

Outstanding Athletes

PLACE	NAME (NATIONALITY)	DISCIPLINE	G	S	B
1	Larissa Latynina (URS)	Gymnastics	4	1	–
2	Agnes Keleti (HUN)	Gymnastics	3	2	–
3	Viktor Chukarin (URS)	Gymnastics	3	1	1
4	Valentin Muratov (URS)	Gymnastics	3	1	–
5	Betty Cuthbert (AUS)	Athletics	3	–	–
	Robert Morrow (USA)	Athletics	3	–	–
	Murray Rose (AUS)	Swimming	3	–	–

EVENT	GOLD		SILVER		BRONZE	
Athletics						
Men						
100 m	Robert Morrow (USA)	10.5	Thane Baker (USA)	10.5	Hector Hogan (AUS)	10.6
200 m	Robert Morrow (USA)	20.6	Andrew Stanfield (USA)	20.7	Thane Baker (USA)	20.9
400 m	Charles Jenkins (USA)	46.7	Karl-Friedrich Haas (GER)★	46.8	Voitto Hellsten (FIN)	47.0
					Ardalion Ignatiev	47.0
800 m	Tom Courtney (USA)	1:47.7	Derek Johnson (GBR)	1:47.8	Andun Boysen (NOR)	1:48.1
1500 m	Ronald Delany (IRL)	3:41.2	Klaus Richtzenhain (GER)★	3:42.0	John Landy (AUS)	3:42.0
5000 m	Vladimir Kuts (URS)	13:39.6	Gordon Pirie (GBR)	13:50.6	Derek Ibbotson (GBR)	13:54.4
10,000 m	Vladimir Kuts (URS)	28:45.6	József Kovács (HUN)	28:52.4	Allan Lawrence (AUS)	28:53.6
Marathon	Alain Mimoun (FRA)	2:25:00.0	Franjo Mihalic (YUG)	2:26:32.0	Veikko Karvonen (FIN)	2:27:47.0
110 m Hurdles	Lee Calhoun (USA)	13.5	Jack Davis (USA)	13.5	Joel Shankle (USA)	14.1
400 m Hurdles	Glenn Davis (USA)	50.1	Eddie Southern (USA)	50.8	Joshua Culbreath (USA)	51.6
3000 m Steeplechase	Chris Brasher (GBR)	8:41.2	Sándor Rozsnyói (HUN)	8:43.6	Ernst Larsen (NOR)	8:44.0

EVENT	GOLD		SILVER		BRONZE	
4 x 100 m	USA	39.5	USSR	39.8	Germany★	40.3
4 x 400 m	USA	3:04.8	Australia	3:06.2	Great Britain	3:07.2
20 km Walk	Leonid Spirin (URS)	1:31:27.4	Antonas Mikenas (URS)	1:32:03.0	Bruno Yunk (URS)	1:32:12.0
50 km Walk	Norman Read (NZL)	4:30:42.8	Yevgeni Maskinskov (URS)	4:32:57.0	John Lundgren (SWE)	4:35:02.0
High Jump	Charles Dumas (USA)	6'11½"	Charles Porter (AUS)	6'10½"	Igor Kashkarov (URS)	2.08
Pole Vault	Bob Richards (USA)	14'11½"	Bob Gutowski (USA)	14'10¼"	Georgios Roubanis (GRE)	4.50
Long Jump	Greg Bell (USA)	25'8¼"	John Bennett (USA)	25'2¼"	Jorma Valkama (FIN)	7.48
Triple Jump	Adhemar Ferreira da Silva (BRA)	53'7½"	Vilhjálmur Einarsson (ISL)	53'4"	Vitold Kreyer (URS)	16.02
Shot	Parry O'Brien (USA)	60'11"	Bill Nieder (USA)	59'7½"	Jiri Skobla (TCH)	17.65
Discus	Al Oerter (USA)	184'10½"	Fortune Gordien (USA)	179'9½"	Desmond Koch (USA)	54.40
Hammer	Harold Connolly (USA)	207'3½"	Mikhail Krivonosov (URS)	206'9"	Anatoli Samotsvetov (URS)	62.56
Javelin	Egil Danielsen (NOR)	281'2"	Janusz Sidlo (POL)	262'4"	Viktor Tsibulenko (URS)	79.50
Decathlon	Milton Campbell (USA)	7937	Rafer Johnson (USA)	7587	Vasili Kusnetsov (URS)	7465
Women						
100 m	Betty Cuthbert (AUS)	11.5	Christa Stubnick (GER)★	11.7	Marlene Matthews (AUS)	11.7
200 m	Betty Cuthbert (AUS)	23.4	Christa Stubnick (GER)★	23.7	Marlene Matthews (AUS)	23.8
80 m Hurdles	S. de la Hunty-Strickland (AUS)	10.7	Gisela Köhler (GER)★	10.9	Norma Thrower (AUS)	11.0
4 x 100 m	Australia	44.5	Great Britain	44.7	USA	44.9
High Jump	Mildred McDaniel (USA)	5'9¼"	Maria Pisaryeva (URS)	5'5½"	Thelma Hopkins (GBR)	5'5½"
Long Jump	Elzbieta Krzesinska (POL)	20'10"	Willye White (USA)	19'11¾"	Nadyezhda Dvalishvili (URS)	19'10¾"
Shot	Tamara Tyshkevich (URS)	54'5"	Galina Zybina (URS)	54'2¾"	Marianne Werner (GER)★	51'2½"
Discus	Olga Fikotová (TCH)	176'1½"	Irina Beglyakova (URS)	172'4½"	Nina Ponomaryeva (URS)	170'8"
Javelin	Inese Jaunzeme (URS)	176'8"	Marlene Ahrens (CHI)	165'3"	Nadyezhda Konyayeva (URS)	164'11½
Swimming						
Men						
100 m Freestyle	Jon Henricks (AUS)	55.4	John Devitt (AUS)	55.8	Gary Chapman (AUS)	56.7
400 m Freestyle	Murray Rose (AUS)	4:27.3	Tsuyoshi Yamanaka (JPN)	4:30.4	George Breen (USA)	4:32.5
1500 m Freestyle	Murray Rose (AUS)	17:58.9	Tsuyoshi Yamanaka (JPN)	18:00.3	George Breen (USA)	18:08.2
100 m Backstroke	David Theile (AUS)	1:02.2	John Monckton (AUS)	1:03.2	Frank McKinney (USA)	1:04.5
200 m Breaststroke	Masaru Furukawa (JPN)	2:34.7	Masahiro Yoshimura (JPN)	2:36.7	Charis Yunitschev (URS)	2:36.8
200 m Butterfly	William Yorzik (USA)	2:19.3	Takashi Ishimoto (JPN)	2:23.8	György Tumpek (HUN)	2:23.9
4 x 200 m Freestyle Relay	Australia	8:23.6	USA	8:31.5	USSR	8:34.7
Springboard Diving	Robert Clotworthy (USA)	159.56	Donald Harper (USA)	156.23	Joaquin Capilla Pérez (MEX)	150.69
Highboard Diving	Joaquin Capilla Pérez (MEX)	152.44	Gary Tobian (USA)	152.41	Richard Connor (USA)	149.79
Water Polo	Hungary		Yugoslavia		USSR	
Women						
100 m Freestyle	Dawn Fraser (AUS)	1:02.0	Lorraine Crapp (AUS)	1:02.3	Faith Leech (AUS)	1:05.1
400 m Freestyle	Lorraine Crapp (AUS)	4:54.6	Dawn Fraser (AUS)	5:02.5	Sylvia Ruuska (USA)	5:07.1
100 m Backstroke	Judith Grinham (GBR)	1:12.9	Carin Cone (USA)	1:12.9	Margaret Edwards (GBR)	1:13.1
200 m Breaststroke	Ursula Happe (GER)★	2:53.1	Eva Ezékely (HUN)	2:54.8	Eva-Maria ten Elsen (GER)★	2:55.1
100 m Butterfly	Shelley Mann (USA)	1:11.0	Nancy Ramey (USA)	1:11.9	Mary Sears (USA)	1:14.4
4 x 100 m Freestyle Relay	Australia	4:17.1	USA	4:19.2	South Africa	4:25.7
Springboard Diving	Patricia McCormick (USA)	142.36	Jeanne Stunyo (USA)	125.89	Irene MacDonald (CAN)	121.40
Highboard Diving	Patricia McCormick (USA)	84.85	Juno Irwin (USA)	81.64	Paula Jean Myers (USA)	81.58
Boxing						
Flyweight (-112½ lb)	Terence Spinks (GBR)		Mircea Dobrescu (ROM)		John Caldwell (IRL) René Libeer (FRA)	
Bantamweight (-119 lb)	Wolfgang Behrendt (GER)★		Song Soon-Chung (KOR)		Frederick Gilroy (IRL) Claudio Barrientos (CHI)	
Featherweight (-126 lb)	Vladimir Safronov (URS)		Thomas Nicholls (GBR)		Hendryk Niedzwiedzki (POL) Pentti Hämäläinen (FIN)	
Lightweight (- 132 lb)	Richard McTaggart (GBR)		Harry Kurschat (GER)★		Anthony Byrne (IRL) Anatoli Lagetko (URS)	
Light-Welterweight (-140 lb)	Vladimir Yengibaryan (URS)		Franco Nenci (ITA)		Henry Loubscher (SAF) Constantin Dumitrescu (ROM)	
Welterweight (-148 lb)	Nicolae Lince (ROM)		Frederick Tiedt (IRL)		Kevin John Hogarth (AUS) Nicholas Gargano (GBR)	
Light-Middleweight (-157 lb)	László Papp (HUN)		José Torres (USA)		John McCormack (GBR) Zbigniew Pietrzykowski (POL)	
Middleweight (-165 lb)	Gennadi Schatkov (URS)		Ramon Tapia (CHI)		Gilbert Chapron (FRA) Victor Zalazar (ARG)	
Light-Heavyweight (-178½ lb)	James Felton Boyd (USA)		Gheorghe Negrea (ROM)		Romualdas Murauskas (URS) Carlos Lucas (CHI)	
Heavyweight (+178½ lb)	Peter Rademacher (USA)		Lev Mukhin (URS)		Daniel Bekker (SAF) Giacomo Bozzano (ITA)	

EVENT	GOLD		SILVER		BRONZE	
Weightlifting						
Bantamweight (-123½ lb))	Charles Vinci (USA)	342.5	Vladimir Stogov (URS)	337.5	Mahmoud Namdjou (IRN)	332.5
Featherweight (-132¼ lb)	Isaac Berger (USA)	352.5	Yevgeni Minayev (URS)	342.5	Marian Zielinski (POL)	335.0
Lightweight (-148¾ lb)	Igor Rybak (URS)	380.0	Ravil Khabutdinov (URS)	372.5	Kim Chang-Hee (KOR)	370.0
Middleweight (-154½ lb)	Fyodor Bogdanovski (URS)	420.0	Peter George (USA)	412.5	Ermanno Pignatti (ITA)	382.5
Light-Heavyweight (-182 lb)	Thomas Kono (USA)	447.5	Vasili Stepanov (URS)	427.5	James George (USA)	417.5
Middle-Heavyweight (-198½ lb)	Arkadi Vorobyev (URS)	462.5	David Sheppard (USA)	442.5	Jean Debuf (FRA)	425.0
Heavyweight (+198½ lb)	Paul Anderson (USA)	500.0	Humberto Selvetti (ARG)	500.0	Alberto Pigaiani (ITA)	452.5
Greco-Roman Wrestling						
Flyweight (-114½ lb)	Nikolai Solovyov (URS)		Ignazio Fabra (ITA)		Durum Ali Egribas (TUR)	
Bantamweight (-125¾ lbg)	Konstantin Vyrupayev (URS)		Edvin Vesterby (SWE)		Francisco Horvat (ROM)	
Featherweight (-136½ lb)	Rauno Mäkinen (FIN)		Imre Polyák (HUN)		Roman Dzneladze (URS)	
Lightweight (-147½ lb)	Kyösti Lehtonen (FIN)		Riza Dogan (TUR)		Gyula Tóth (HUN)	
Welterweight (-160¾ lb)	Mithat Bayrak (TUR)		Vladimir Maneyev (URS)		Per Berlin (SWE)	
Middleweight (-174 lb)	Givy Kartoziya (URS)		Dimiter Dobrev (BUL)		Rune Jansson (SWE)	
Light-Heavyweight (-191¾ lb)	Valentin Nikolayev (URS)		Petko Sirakov (BUL)		Karl-Erik Nilsson (SWE)	
Heavyweight (+191¾ lb)	Anatoli Parfenov (URS)		Wilfried Dietrich (GER)*		Adelmo Bulgarelli (ITA)	
Freestyle Wrestling						
Flyweight (- 114½ lb)	Mirian Tsalkalamanidze (URS)		Mohamed Ali Khojastehpour (IRN)		Hüseyin Akbas (TUR)	
Bantamweight (-125¾ lb)	Mustafa Dagistanli (TUR)		Mohamad Yaghoubi (IRN)		Mikhail Chachov (URS)	
Featherweight (-136½ lb)	Shozo Sasahara (JPN)		Joseph Mewis (BEL)		Erkki Penttilä (FIN)	
Lightweight (-147½ lb)	Emamali Habibi (IRN)		Shigeru Kasahara (JPN)		Alimberg Bestayev (URS)	
Welterweight (-160¾ lb)	Mitsuo Ikeda (JPN)		Ibrahim Zengin (TUR)		Vakhtang Balavadze (URS)	
Middleweight (-174 lb)	Nikola Stantschev (BUL)		Daniel Hodge (USA)		Georgi Skhirtladze (URS)	
Light-Heavyweight (- 191¾ lb)	Gholam-Reza Takhti (IRN)		Boris Kulayev (URS)		Peter Steele Blair (USA)	
Heavyweight (+191¾ lb)	Hamit Kaplan (TUR)		Hussein Mehmedov (BUL)		Taisto Kangasniemi (FIN)	
Fencing						
Individual Foil - Men	Christian d'Oriola (FRA)	6	Giancarlo Bergamini (ITA)	5	Antonio Spallino (ITA)	5
Team Foil - Men	Italy		France		Hungary	
Individual Épée	Carlo Pavesi (ITA)	5/1/2	Guiseppe Delfino (ITA)	5/1/1	Edoardo Mangiarotti (ITA)	5/1/10
Team Épée	Italy		Hungary		France	
Individual Saber	Rudolf Kárpáti (HUN)	6	Jerzy Pawlowski (POL)	5	Lev Kuznetsov (URS)	4
Team Saber	Hungary		Poland		USSR	
Individual Foil - Women	Gillian Sheen (GBR)	6+1	Olga Orban (ROM)	6	Renée Garilhe (FRA)	5
Modern Pentathlon						
Individual	Lars Hall (SWE)	4833	Olavi Nannonen (FIN)	4774.5	Väinö Korhonen (FIN)	4750
Team	USSR	13 690.5	USA	13 482	Finland	13 185.5
Canoeing						
Men						
1000 m Kayak Singles K1	Gert Fredriksson (SWE)	4:12.8	Igor Pissaryev (URS)	4:15.3	Lajos Kiss (HUN)	4:16.2
10,000 m Kayak Singles K1	Gert Fredriksson (SWE)	47:43.4	Ferenc Halaczky (HUN)	47:53.3	Michael Scheuer (GER)*	48:00.3
1000 m Kayak Pairs K2	Germany*	3:49.6	USSR	3:51.4	Austria	3:55.8
10,000 m Kayak Pairs K2	Hungary	43:37.0	Germany*	43:40.6	Australia	43:43.2
1000 m Canadian Singles C1	Leon Rotman (ROM)	5:05.3	István Hernek (HUN)	5:06.2	Gennadi Bukharin (URS)	5:12.7
10,000 m Canadian Singles C1	Leon Rotman (ROM)	56:41.0	János Parti (HUN)	57:11.0	Gennadi Bukharin (URS)	57:14.5
1000 m Canadian Pairs C2	Romania	4:47.4	USSR	4:48.6	Hungary	4:54.3
10,000 m Canadian Pairs C2	USSR	54:02.4	France	54:48.3	Hungary	55:15.6
Women						
500 m Kayak Singles K1	Elisaveta Dementyeva (URS)	2:18.9	Therese Zenz (GER)*	2:19.6	Tove Söby (DEN)	2:22.3
Rowing						
Single Sculls	Vyacheslav Ivanov (URS)	8:02.5	Stuart Mackenzie (AUS)	8:07.7	John Kelly jun. (USA)	8:11.8
Doubles Sculls	USSR	7:24.0	USA	7:32.2	Australia	7:37.4
Coxless Pairs	USA	7:55.4	USSR	8:03.9	Austria	8:11.8
Coxed Pairs	USA	8:26.1	Germany*	8:29.2	USSR	8:31.0
Coxless Fours	Canada	7:08.8	USA	7:18.4	France	7:20.9
Coxled Fours	Italy	7:19.4	Sweden	7:22.4	Finland	7:30.9
Coxed Eights	USA	6:35.2	Canada	6:37.1	Australia	6:39.2
Yachting						
Finn Class	Paul Elvström (DEN)	7509	André Nelis (BEL)	6254	John Marvin (USA)	5953
International Star	USA	5876	Italy	5649	Bahamas	5223

EVENT	GOLD		SILVER		BRONZE	
Sharpie	New Zealand	6086	Australia	6068	Great Britain	4859
Dragon	Sweden	5723	Denmark	5723	Great Britain	4547
5.5 m	Sweden	5527	Great Britain	4050	Australia	4022
Cycling						
Individual Road Race (116¾ miles)	Ercole Baldini (ITA)	5:21:17.0	Arnaud Geyre (FRA)	5:23:16.0	Alan Jackson (GBR)	5:23:16.0
Team Road Race	France	22	Great Britain	23	Germany★	27
1000 m Time Trial	Leandro Faggin (ITA)	1:09.8	Ladislav Foucek (TCH)	1:11.4	Alfred Swift (SAF)	1:11.6
1000 m Sprint	Michel Rousseau (FRA)		Guglielmo Pesenti (ITA)		Richard Ploog (AUS)	
2000 m Tandem	Australia		Czechoslovakia		Italy	
4000 m Team Pursuit	Italy	4:37.4	France	4:39.4	Great Britain	4:42.2
Equestrianism						
Three-Day Event	Petrus Kastennmann (SWE)	-66.53	August Lütke-Westhues (GER)★	-84.87	Frank Weldon (GBR)	-85.48
Three-Day Event (Team)	Great Britain	-355.48	Germany★	-475.91	Canada	-572.72
Grand Prix (Dressage)	Henri Saint Cyr (SWE)	860.0	Lis Hartel (DEN)	850.0	Liselott Linsenhoff (GER)★	832.0
Grand Prix (Dressage) Team	Sweden	2475	Germany★	2346	Switzerland	2346
Grand Prix (Jumping)	Hans Günter Winkler (GER)★	-4	Raimondo D'Inzeo (ITA)	-8	Piero D'Inzeo (ITA)	-11
Grand Prix (Jumping) Teams	Germany★	-40.00	Italy	-66.00	Great Britain	-69.00
Shooting						
Free Rifle (3 Positions)	Vasili Borissov (URS)	1138	Allan Erdman (URS)	1137	Vilho Ylönen (FIN)	1128
Small-Bore Rifle (Prone)	Gerald R. Ouelette (CAN)	600	Vasili Borissov (URS)	599	Gilmour St. Boa (CAN)	598
Small-Bore Rifle (3 Positions)	Anatoli Bogdanov (URS)	1172	Otakar Horinek (TCH)	1172	Nils Johan Sundberg (SWE)	1167
Rapid-Fire Pistol	Stefan Petrescu (ROM)	587	Yevgeni Schcherkasov (URS)	585	Gheorghe Lichiardopol (ROM)	581
Free Pistol (50 m)	Pentti Linnosvuo (FIN)	556 126	Makhmud Umarov (URS)	556 124	Offutt Pinion (USA)	551
Olympic Trap Shooting	Galliano Rossini (ITA)	195	Adam Smelczynski (POL)	190	Alessandro Ciceri (ITA)	188
Running Deer Shooting	Vitali Romanenko (URS)	441	Per Olof Sköldberg (SWE)	432	Vladimir Sevrugin (URS)	429
Gymnastics						
Men						
Individual Combined Exercises	Viktor Chukarin (URS)	114.25	Takashi Ono (JPN)	114.20	Yuri Titov (URS)	113.80
Team	USSR	568.25	Japan	566.40	Finland	555.95
Parallel Bars	Viktor Chukarin (URS)	19.20	Masami Kubota (JPN)	19.15	Takashi Ono (JPN)	19.10
					Masao Takemoto (JPN)	19.10
Floor	Valentin Muratov (URS)	19.20	Nobuyuki Aihara (JPN)	19.10		
			William Thoresson (SWE)	19.10		
			Viktor Chukarin (URS)	19.10		
Horse Vault	Helmut Bantz (GER)★	18.85			Yuri Titov (URS)	18.75
	Valentin Muratov (URS)	18.85				
Horizontal Bar	Takashi Ono (JPN)	19.60	Juri Titov (URS)	19.40	Masao Takemoto (JPN)	19.30
Rings	Albert Azaryan (URS)	19.35	Valentin Muratov (URS)	19.15	Masao Takemoto (JPN)	19.10
Pommel Horse	Boris Shakhlin (URS)	19.25	Takashi Ono (JPN)	19.20	Viktor Chukarin (URS)	19.10
Women						
Individual Combined Exercises	Larissa Latynina (URS)	74.933	Agnes Keleti (HUN)	74.633	Sofia Muratova (URS)	74.466
Team	USSR	444.80	Hungary	443.50	Romania	438.20
Floor	Agnes Keleti (HUN)	18.733	Elena Leustean (ROM)	18.700		
	Larissa Latynina (URS)	18.733				
Horse Vault	Larissa Latynina (URS)	18.833	Tamara Manina (URS)	18.800	Ann-Sofi Colling (SWE)	18.733
Beam	Agnes Keleti (HUN)	18.800	Tamara Manina (URS)	18.633		
	Eva Besáková (TCH)	18.633				
Asymmetrical Bars	Agnes Keleti (HUN)	18.966	Larissa Latynina (URS)	18.833	Sofia Muratova (URS)	18.800
Portable Apparatus (Women's Teams)	Hungary	75.20	Sweden	74.20	Poland	74.00
Basketball						
	USA		USSR		Uruguay	
Soccer						
	USSR		Yugoslavia		Bulgaria	
Hockey						
	India		Pakistan		Germany★	

★ representing a combined German team

Squaw Valley 1960   February 18 – February 28

Participants: 665 / Men: 522, Women: 143, Countries: 30,
Sports: 6, Events: 27
Final Torchbearer: Kenneth Henry

Medals Table

PLACE	COUNTRY	GOLD	SILVER	BRONZE
1	USSR	7	5	9
2	Germany★	4	3	1
3	USA	3	4	3
4	Norway	3	3	–
5	Sweden	3	2	2

Outstanding Athletes

PLACE	NAME (NATIONALITY)	DISCIPLINE	G	S	B
1	Lidia Skoblikova (URS)	Speed Skating	2	–	–
	Yevgeni Grischin (URS)	Speed Skating	2	–	–
3	Veikko Hakulinen (FIN)	Nordic Skiing	1	1	1
4	Maria Gusakova (URS)	Nordic Skiing	1	1	–
	Helga Haase (GER)★	Speed Skating	1	1	–
	Sixten Jernberg (SWE)	Nordic Skiing	1	1	–
	Knut Johannesen (NOR)	Speed Skating	1	1	–
	Viktor Kositschkin (URS)	Speed Skating	1	1	–

EVENT	GOLD		SILVER		BRONZE	
Alpine Skiing						
Men						
Downhill	Jean Vuarnet (FRA)	2:06.0	Hans-Peter Lanig (GER)★	2:06.5	Guy Perillat (FRA)	2:06.9
Slalom	Ernst Hinterseer (AUT)	2:08.9	Matthias Leitner (AUT)	2:10.3	Charles Bozon (FRA)	2:10.4
Giant Slalom	Roger Staub (SUI)	1:48.3	Josef Stiegler (AUT)	1:48.7	Ernst Hinterseer (AUT)	1:49.1
Women						
Downhill	Heidi Biebl (GER)★	1:37.6	Penny Pitou (USA)	1:38.6	Traudl Hecher (AUT)	1:38.9
Slalom	Anne Heggtveit (CAN)	1:49.6	Betsy Snite (USA)	1:52.9	Barbara Henneberger (GER)★	1:56.6
Giant Slalom	Yvonne Rüegg (SUI)	1:39.9	Penny Pitou (USA)	1:40.0	Giuliana Chenal-Minuzzo (ITA)	1:40.2
Nordic Skiing						
Men						
15 km Cross-Country Skiing	Haakon Brusveen (NOR)	51:55.5	Sixten Jernberg (SWE)	51:58.6	Veikko Hakulinen (FIN)	52:03.0
30 km Cross-Country Skiing	Sixten Jernberg (SWE)	1:51:03.9	Rolf Rämgard (SWE)	1:51:16.9	Nikolai Anikin (URS)	1:52:28.2
50 km Cross-Country Skiing	Kalevi Hämäläinen (FIN)	2:59:06.3	Veikko Hakulinen (FIN)	2:59:26.7	Rolf Rämgard (SWE)	3:02:46.7
4 x 10 km	Finland	2:18:45.6	Norway	2:18:46.4	USSR	2:21:21.6
Ski Jumping	Helmut Recknagel (GER)★	227.2	Niilo Halonen (FIN)	222.6	Otto Leodolter (AUT)	219.4
Nordic Combined	Georg Thoma (GER)★	457.952	Tormod Knutsen (NOR)	453.000	Nikolai Gusakov (URS)	452.000
Women						
10 km Cross-Country Skiing	Maria Gusakova (URS)	39:46.6	Lyubov Baranova-Kozyryeva (URS)	40:04.2	Radya Jeroschina (URS)	40:06.0
3 x 5 km	Sweden	1:04:21.4	USSR	1:05:02.6	Finland	1:06:27.5
Biathlon	Klas Lestander (SWE)	1:33:21.6	Antti Tyrväinen (FIN)	1:33:57.7	Alexander Privalov (URS)	1:34:54.2
Figure Skating						
Women	Carol Heiss (USA)		Sjoukje Dijkstra (HOL)	1424.8	Barbara Roles (USA)	1414.9
Men	David Jenkins (USA)		Karol Divin (TCH)	1414.3	Donald Jackson (CAN)	1401.0
Pairs	Barbara Wagner/ Robert Paul (CAN)		Marika Kilius/ Hans-Jürgen Bäumler (GER)★	76.8	Nancy Ludington/ Ronald Ludington (USA)	76.2
Speed Skating						
Men						
500 m	Yevgeni Grischin (URS)	40.2	William Disney (USA)	40.3	Rafael Gratsch (URS)	40.4
1500 m	Roald Aas (NOR)	2:10.4			Boris Stenin (URS)	2:11.5
	Yevgeni Grischin (URS)	2:10.4				
5000 m	Viktor Kositschkin (URS)	7:51.3	Knut Johannesen (NOR)	8:00.8	Jan Pesman (HOL)	8:05.1
10,000 m	Knut Johannesen (NOR)	15:46.6	Viktor Kositschkin (URS)	15:49.2	Kjell Bäckman (SWE)	16:14.2
Women						
500 m	Helga Haase (GER)★	45.9	Natalya Dontschenko (URS)	46.0	Jeanne Ashworth (USA)	46.1
1000 m	Klara Guseva (URS)	1:34.1	Helga Haase (GER)★	1:34.3	Tamara Rylova (URS)	1:34.8
1500 m	Lidia Skoblikova (URS)	2:25.2	Elvira Seroczynska (POL)	2:25.7	Helena Pilejczyk (POL)	2:27.1
3000 m	Lidia Skoblikova (URS)	5:14.3	Valentina Stenina (URS)	5:16.9	Eevi Huttunen (FIN)	5:21.0
Ice Hockey	USA		Canada		USSR	

★ representing a combined German team

Rome 1960

August 25 – September 11

Participants: 5346 / Men: 4736, Women: 610, Countries: 83,
Sports: 17, Events: 150
Final Torchbearer: Giancarlo Peris

Medals Table

PLACE	COUNTRY	GOLD	SILVER	BRONZE
1	USSR	43	28	29
2	USA	34	21	16
3	Italy	13	10	13
4	Germany*	12	19	11
5	Australia	8	8	6

Outstanding Athletes

PLACE	NAME (NATIONALITY)	DISCIPLINE	G	S	B
1	Boris Shakhlin (URS)	Gymnastics	4	2	1
2	Larissa Latynina (URS)	Gymnastics	3	2	1
3	Takashi Ono (JPN)	Gymnastics	3	1	2
4	Chris von Saltza (USA)	Swimming	3	1	–
5	Wilma Rudolph (USA)	Athletics	3	–	–

EVENT	GOLD		SILVER		BRONZE	
Athletics						
Men						
100 m	Armin Hary (GER)*	10.2	David Sime (USA)	10.2	Peter Radford (GBR)	10.3
200 m	Livio Berutti (ITA)	20.5	Lester Carney (USA)	20.6	Abdoulaye Seye (FRA)	20.7
400 m	Otis Davis (USA)	44.9	Carl Kaufmann (GER)*	44.9	Malcolm Spence (SAF)	45.5
800 m	Peter Snell (NZL)	1:46.3	Roger Moens (BEL)	1:46.5	George Kerr (ANT)	1:47.1
1500 m	Herbert Elliott (AUS)	3:35.6	Michel Jazy (FRA)	3:38.4	Istvan Rozsavölgyi (HUN)	3:39.2
5000 m	Murray Halberg (NZL)	13:43.4	Hans Grodotzki (GER)*	13:44.6	Kasimierz Zimny (POL)	13:44.8
10,000 m	Pyotr Bolotnikov (URS)	28:32.2	Hans Grodotzki (GER)*	28:37.0	David Power (AUS)	28:38.2
Marathon	Abebe Bikila (ETH)	2:15:16.2	Rhadi Ben Abdesselam (MAR)	2:15:41.6	Barry Magee (NZL)	2:17:18.2
110 m Hurdles	Lee Calhoun (USA)	13.8	Willie May (USA)	13.8	Hayes Jones (USA)	14.0
400 m Hurdles	Glenn Davis (USA)	49.3	Clifton Cushman (USA)	49.6	Richard Howard (USA)	49.7
3000 m Steeplechase	Zdislaw Krzyszkowiak (POL)	8:34.2	Nikolai Sokolov (URS)	8:36.4	Semyon Rischtschin (URS)	8:42.2
4 x 100 m	Germany*	39.5	USSR	40.1	Great Britain	40.2
4 x 400 m	USA	3:02.2	Germany*	3:02.7	Antilles	3:04.0
20 km Walk	Vladimir Golubnitschky (URS)	1:34:07.2	Noel Freeman (AUS)	1:34:16.4	Stanley Vickers (GBR)	1:34:56.4
50 km Walk	Don Thompson (GBR)	4:25:30.0	John Ljunggren (SWE)	4:25:47.0	Abdon Panich (ITA)	4:27:55.4
High Jump	Robert Shavlakadze (URS)	7'1"	Valeri Brumel (URS)	7'1"	John Thomas (USA)	7'0¼"
Pole Vault	Donald Bragg (USA)	15'5"	Ron Morris (USA)	15'1"	Eeles Landström (FIN)	14'11"
Long Jump	Ralph Boston (USA)	26'7½"	Irvin Roberson (USA)	26'7¼"	Igor Ter-Ovanesian (URS)	26'4½"
Triple Jump	Jozef Schmidt (POL)	55'1¾"	Vladimir Goryayev (URS)	54'6¼"	Vitold Kreyer (URS)	53'10¾"
Shot	Bill Nieder (USA)	64'6¾"	Parry O'Brien (USA)	62'8¼"	Dallas Long (USA)	62'4¼"
Discus	Al Oerter (USA)	194'1½"	Richard Babka (USA)	190'4"	Dick Cochran (USA)	187'6"
Hammer	Vasili Rudenkov (URS)	220'1½"	Gyula Zsivotzky (HUN)	215'10"	Tadeusz Rut (POL)	215'4"
Javelin	Viktor Tsibulenko (URS)	277'8"	Walter Krüger (GER)*	260'4"	Gergely Kulcsar (HUN)	257'9"
Decathlon	Rafer Johnson (USA)	8392	Yang Chuan-Kwang (TPE)	8334	Vasili Kusnetsov (URS)	7809
Women						
100 m	Wilma Rudolph (USA)	11.0	Dorothy Hyman (GBR)	11.3	Giuseppina Leone (ITA)	11.3
200 m	Wilma Rudolph (USA)	24.0	Jutta Heine (GER)*	24.4	Dorothy Hyman (GBR)	24.7
800 m	Ludmilla Schevtsova (URS)	2:04.3	Brenda Jones (AUS)	2:04.4	Ursula Donath (GER)*	2:05.6
80 m Hurdles	Irina Press (URS)	10.8	Carol Quinton (GBR)	10.9	Gisela Birkemeyer-Köhler (GER)*	11.0
4 x 100 m	USA	44.5	Germany*	44.8	Poland	45.0
High Jump	Iolanda Balas (ROM)	6'0¾"	Jaroslawa Jozwiakowska (POL)	5'7¼"		
			Dorothy Shirley (GBR)	5'7¼"		
Long Jump	Vera Krepkina (URS)	20'10¾"	Elzbieta Krzesinska (POL)	20'6¾"	Hildrun Claus (GER)*	20'4¼"
Shot	Tamara Press (URS)	56'9¾"	Johanna Lüttge (GER)*	54'5¾"	Earlene Brown (USA)	53'10¾"
Discus	Nina Ponomaryeva (URS)	180'9"	Tamara Press (URS)	172'6"	Lia Manoliu (ROM)	171'9"
Javelin	Elvira Ozolina (URS)	183'7½"	Dana Zátopková (TCH)	176'5"	Birute Kalediena (URS)	175'4"
Swimming						
Men						
100 m Freestyle	John Devitt (AUS)	55.2	Lance Larson (USA)	55.2	Manuel Dos Santos (BRA)	55.4
400 m Freestyle	Murray Rose (AUS)	4:18.3	Tsuyoshi Yamanaka (JPN)	4:21.4	John Konrads (AUS)	4:21.8
1500 m Freestyle	John Konrads (AUS)	17:19.6	Murray Rose (AUS)	17:21.7	George Breen (USA)	17:30.6
100 m Backstroke	David Theile (AUS)	1:01.9	Frank McKinney (USA)	1:02.1	Robert Bennett (USA)	1:02.3
200 m Breaststroke	Bill Mulliken (USA)	2:37.4	Yoshihiko Osaki (JPN)	2:38.0	Wilger Mensonides (HOL)	2:39.7
200 m Butterfly	Michael Troy (USA)	2:12.8	Neville Hayes (AUS)	2:14.6	David Gillanders (USA)	2:15.3
4 x 200 m Freestyle Relay	USA	8:10.2	Japan	8:13.2	Australia	8:13.8
4 x 100 m Medley Relay	USA	4:05.4	Australia	4:12.0	Japan	4:12.2

Rome 1960

EVENT	GOLD		SILVER		BRONZE	
Springboard Diving	Gary Tobian (USA)	170.00	Samuel Hall (USA)	167.08	Juan Batello (MEX)	162.30
Highboard Diving	Robert Webster (USA)	165.56	Gary Tobian (USA)	165.25	Brian Phelps (GBR)	157.13
Water Polo	Italy		USSR		Hungary	
Women						
100 m Freestyle	Dawn Fraser (AUS)	1:01.2	Chris von Saltza (USA)	1:02.8	Natalie Steward (GBR)	1:03.1
400 m Freestyle	Chris von Saltza (USA)	4:50.6	Jane Cederquist (SWE)	4:53.9	Catarina Lagerberg (HOL)	4:56.9
100 m Backstroke	Lynn Burke (USA)	1:09.3	Natalie Steward (GBR)	1:10.8	Satoko Tanaka (JPN)	1:11.4
200 m Breaststroke	Anita Lonsbrough (GBR)	2:49.5	Wiltrud Urselmann (GER)★	2:50.0	Barbara Göbel (GER)★	2:53.6
100 m Butterfly	Carolyn Schuler (USA)	1:09.5	Marianne Heemskerk (HOL)	1:10.4	Janice Andrew (AUS)	1:12.2
4 x 100 m Freestyle	USA	4:08.9	Australia	4:11.3	Germany	4:19.7
4 x 100 m Medley Relay	USA	4:41.1	Australia	4:45.9	Germany	4:47.6
Springboard Diving	Ingrid Krämer (GER)★	155.81	Paula J. Myers-Pope (USA)	141.24	Elizabeth Ferris (GBR)	139.09
Highboard Diving	Ingrid Krämer (GER)★	91.28	Paula J. Myers-Pope (USA)	88.94	Ninelia Krutova (URS)	86.99

Boxing

EVENT	GOLD	SILVER	BRONZE
Flyweight(-112½ lb)	Gyula Török (HUN)	Sergei Sivko (URS)	Kiyoshi Tanabe (JPN)
			Abdel Elgiundi (VAR)
Bantamweight (-119 lb)	Oleg Grigoryev (URS)	Primo Zamparini (ITA)	Oliver Taylor (AUS)
			Brunon Bendig (POL)
Featherweight (-126 lb)	Francesco Musso (ITA)	Jerzy Adamski (POL)	Jorma Limmonen (FIN)
			William Meyers (SAF)
Lightweight (-132 lb)	Kasimierz Pazdzior (POL)	Sandro Lopopoli (ITA)	Richard McTaggart (GBR)
			Abel Laudonio (ARG)
Light-Welterweight (-140 lb)	Bohumil Nemecek (TCH)	Clement Quartey (GHA)	Quincey Daniels (USA)
			Marian Kasprzyk (POL)
Welterweight (-148 lb)	Giovanni Benvenuti (ITA)	Yuri Radonyak (URS)	Leszek Drogosz (POL)
			James Lloyd (GBR)
Light-Middleweight (-157 lb)	Wilbert McClure (USA)	Carmelo Bossi (ITA)	Boris Lagutin (URS)
			Bill Fisher (USA)
Middleweight (-165 lb)	Edward Crook (USA)	Tadeusz Walasek (POL)	Ion Monea (ROM)
			Yevgeni Feofanov (URS)
Light-Heavyweight (-178½ lb)	Cassius Clay (USA)	Zbigniew Pietrzykowski (POL)	Giulio Sarandi (ITA)
			Antony Madigan (AUS)
Heavyweight (+178½ lb)	Franco De Piccoli (ITA)	Daniel Bekker (SAF)	Günter Siegmund (GER)★
			Josef Nemec (TCH)

Weightlifting

EVENT	GOLD		SILVER		BRONZE	
Bantamweight (-123½ lb)	Charles Vinci (USA)	345.0	Yoshinobu Miyake (JPN)	337.5	Esmail Khan(IRN)	330.0
Featherweight (-132¼ lb)	Yevgeni Minayev (URS)	372.5	Isaac Berger (USA)	362.5	Sebastino Mannironi (ITA)	352.5
Lightweight (-148¾ lb)	Viktor Bushuyev (URS)	397.5	Howe-Liang Tan (SIN)	380.0	Abdul Wahid Aziz (IRQ)	380.0
Middleweight (-165½ lb)	Alexander Kurynov (URS)	473.5	Thomas Kono (USA)	427.5	Gyözö Veres (HUN)	405.0
Light-Heavyweight(-182 lb)	Ireneusz Palinski (POL)	442.5	James George (USA)	430.0	Jan Bochenek (POL)	420.0
Middle-Heavyweight (-192½ lb)	Arkadi Vorobyev (URS)	472.5	Trofim Lomakin (URS)	457.5	Louis Martin (GBR)	445.0
Heavyweight (+192½ lb)	Yuri Vlassov (URS)	537.5	James Bradford (USA)	512.5	Norbert Schemansky (USA)	500.0

Greco-Roman Wrestling

EVENT	GOLD	SILVER	BRONZE
Flyweight (-114½ lb)	Dumitru Pirvulescu (ROM)	Osman Sayed (UAE)	Mohamed Paziraye (IRN)
Bantamweight (-125¾ lb)	Oleg Karavayev (URS)	Ion Cernea (ROM)	Petrov Dinko (BUL)
Featherweight (-136½ lb)	Müzahir Sille (TUR)	Imre Polyák (HUN)	Konstantin Vyrupayev (URS)
Lightweight (-147½lb)	Avtandil Koridze (URS)	Bronislav Martinovic (YUG)	Gustaf Freij (SWE)
Welterweight (-160¾ lb)	Mithat Bayrak (TUR)	Günther Maritschnigg (GER)★	René Schiermeyer (FRA)
Middleweight (-174 lb)	Dimiter Dobrev (BUL)	Lothar Metz (GER)★	Ion Taranu (ROM)
Light-Heavyweight (-191¾ lb)	Tevfik Kis (TUR)	Krali Bimbalov (BUL)	Givi Kartoziya (URS)
Heavyweight (+191¾ lb)	Ivan Bogdan (URS)	Wilfried Dietrich (GER)★	Bohumil Kubát (TCH)

Freestyle Wrestling

EVENT	GOLD	SILVER	BRONZE
Flyweight (-114½ lb)	Ahmet Bilek (TUR)	Masayuki Matsubara (JPN)	Mohamed Saifpour Saidabadi (IRN)
Bantamweight (-125¾ lb)	Terrence McCann (USA)	Nejdet Zalev (BUL)	Tadeusz Trojanowski (POL)
Featherweight (-136½ lb)	Mustafa Dagistanli (TUR)	Stantcho Ivanov (BUL)	Vladimir Rubashvili (URS)
Lightweight (-147½ lb)	Shelby Wilson (USA)	Vladimir Sinyavski (URS)	Enyu Dimov (BUL)
Welterweight (-160¾ lb)	Douglas Blubaugh (USA)	Ismail Ogan (TUR)	Muhammed Bashir (PAK)
Middleweight (-174 lb)	Hasan Güngör (TUR)	Georgi Skhirtladze (URS)	Hans Y. Antonsson (SWE)
Light-Heavyweight (-191¾ lb)	Ismet Atli (TUR)	Cholam-R. Takhti (IRN)	Anatoli Albul (URS)
Heavyweight (+191¾ lb)	Wilfried Dietrich (GER)★	Hamit Kaplan (TUR)	Savkus Dzarasov (URS)

Fencing

EVENT	GOLD		SILVER		BRONZE	
Individual Foil - Men	Viktor Zhdanovich (URS)	7	Yuri Sissikin (URS)	4	Albert Axelrod (USA)	3

EVENT	GOLD		SILVER		BRONZE	
Team Foil – Men	USSR		Italy		Germany★	
Individual Épée	Giuseppe Delfino (ITA)	5	Allan Jay (GBR)	5	Bruno Khabarov (URS)	4
Team Épée	Italy		Great Britain		USSR	
Individual Saber	Rudolf Kárpáti (HUN)	5	Zoltán Horváth (HUN)	4	Wladimiro Calarese (ITA)	4
Team Saber	Hungary		Poland		Italy	
Individual Foil – Women	Heidi Schmid (GER)★	6	Valentina Rastvorova (URS)	5	Maria Vicol (ROM)	4
Team Foil – Women	USSR		Hungary		Italy	
Modern Pentathlon						
Individual	Ferenc Németh (HUN)	5024	Imre Nagy (HUN)	4988	Robert L. Beck (USA)	4981
Team	Hungary	14863	USSR	14309	USA	14192
Canoeing						
Men						
1000 m Kayak Singles K1	Erik Hansen (DEN)	3:53.00	Imre Szöllösi (HUN)	3:54.02	Gert Fredriksson (SWE)	3:55.89
1000 m Kayak Pairs K2	Sweden	3:34.73	Hungary	3:34.91	Poland	3:37.34
4 x 500 m Kayak Singles Relay K1	Germany★	7:39.43	Hungary	7:44.02	Denmark	7:46.09
1000 m Canadian Singles C1	János Parti (HUN)	4:33.93	Alexander Silayev (URS)	4:34.41	Leon Rotman (ROM)	4:35.87
1000 m Canadian Pairs C2	USSR	4:17.94	Italy	4:20.77	Hungary	4:20.89
Women						
500 m Kayak Singles K1	Antonina Seredina (URS)	2:08.08	Therese Zenz (GER)★	2:08.22	Daniela Walkowiak (POL)	2:10.46
500 m Kayak Pairs K2	USSR	1:54.76	Germany★	1:56.66	Hungary	1:58.22
Rowing						
Single Sculls	Vyacheslav Ivanov (URS)	7:13.96	Achim Hill (GER)★	7:20.21	Teodor Kocerka (POL)	7:21.26
Double Sculls	Czechoslovakia	6:47.50	USSR	6:50.49	Switzerland	6:50.59
Coxless Pairs	USSR	7:02.01	Austria	7:03.17	Finland	7:03.80
Coxed Pairs	Germany★	7:29.14	USSR	7:30.17	USA	7:34.58
Coxless Fours	USA	6:26.26	Italy	6:28.78	USSR	6:29.62
Coxed Fours	Germany★	6:39.12	France	6:41.62	Italy	6:43.72
Coxed Eights	Germany★	5:57.18	Canada	6:01.52	Czechoslovakia	6:04.84
Yachting						
Finn Class	Paul Elvström (DEN)	8171	Alexander Chuchelov (URS)	6250	André Neli (BEL)	5934
International Star	USSR	7619	Portugal	6695	USA	6269
Flying Dutchman	Norway	6774	Denmark	5991	Germany★	5882
Dragon	Greece	6733	Argentina	5715	Italy	5704
5.5 m	USA	6900	Denmark	5678	Switzerland	5122
Cycling						
Individual Road Race (108¾ miles)	Viktor Kapitonov (URS)	4:20:37.0	Livio Trape (ITA)	4:20:37.0	Willy van den Berghen (BEL)	4:20:57.0
100 km Road Team Time Trial	Italy	2:14:33.53	Germany★	2:16:56.31	USSR	2:18:41.67
1000 m Time Trial	Sante Gaiardoni (ITA)	1:07.27	Dieter Gieseler (GER)★	1:08.75	Rostislav Vargashkin (URS)	1:08.86
1000 m Sprint	Sante Gaiardoni (ITA)		Leo Sterckx (BEL)		Valentino Gasparella (ITA)	
2000 m Tandem	Italy		Germany★		USSR	
4000 m Team Pursuit	Italy	4:30.90	Germany★	4:35.78	USSR	
Equestrianism						
Three-Day Event	Lawrence Morgan (AUS)	+ 7.15	Neale Lavis (AUS)	– 16.50	Anton Bühler (SUI)	– 51.21
Three-Day Event (Team)	Australia	-128.18	Switzerland	-386.02	France	-515.71
Grand Prix (Dressage)	Sergei Filatov (URS)	2144.0	Gustav Fischer (SUI)	2087.0	Josef Neckermann (GER)★	2082.0
Grand Prix (Jumping)	Raimondo D' Inzeo (ITA)	–12	Piero D' Inzeo (ITA)	–16	David Broome (GBR)	–23
Grand Prix (Jumping) Team	Germany★	-46.50	USA	-66.00	Italy	-80.50
Shooting						
Free Rifle (3 Positions)	Hubert Hammerer (AUT)	1129	Hans Spillmann (SUI)	1127	Vasili Borissov (URS)	1127
Small-Bore Rifle (Prone)	Peter Kohnke (GER)★	590	James Hill (USA)	589	Forcella. Pelliccioni (VEN)	587
Small-Bore Rifle (3 Positions)	Viktor Shamburkin (URS)	1149	Marat Niyasov (URS)	1145	Klaus Zähringer (GER)★	1139
Rapid-Fire Pistol	William McMillan (USA)	587/147	Pentti Linnosvuo (FIN)	587/139	Alexander Zabelin (URS)	587/135
Free Pistol (50 m)	Alexei Gushchin (URS)	560	Makhmud Umarov (URS)	552/26	Yoshihisa Yoshikawa (JPN)	552/20
Olympic Trap Shooting	Ion Dumitrescu (ROM)	192	Galliano Rossini (ITA)	191	Sergei Kalinin (URS)	190
Gymnastics						
Men						
Individual Combined Exercises	Boris Shakhlin (URS)	115.95	Takashi Ono (JPN)	115.90	Yuri Titov (URS)	115.60
Team	Japan	575.20	USSR	572.70	Italy	559.05
Parallel Bars	Boris Shakhlin (URS)	19.400	Giovanni Carminucci (ITA)	19.375	Takashi Ono (JPN)	19.350

EVENT	GOLD		SILVER		BRONZE	
Floor	Nobuyuki Aihara (JPN)	19.450	Yuri Titov (URS)	19.325	Franco Menichelli (ITA)	19.275
Horse Vault	Boris Shakhlin (URS)	19.350			Vladimir Portnoi (URS)	19.225
	Takashi Ono (JPN)	19.350				
Horizontal Bar	Takashi Ono (JPN)	19.600	Masao Takemoto (JPN)	19.525	Boris Shakhlin (URS)	19.475
					Velik Kapaszov (BUL)	19.425
Rings	Albert Azaryan (URS)	19.725	Boris Shakhlin (URS)	19.500	Takashi Ono (JPN)	19.425
Pommel Horse	Boris Shakhlin (URS)	19.375	Shuji Tsurumi (JPN)	19.150		
	Eugen Ekman (FIN)	19.375				
Women						
Individual Combined Exercises	Larissa Latyniná (URS)	77.031	Sofia Muratova (URS)	76.696	Polina Astakova (URS)	76.164
Team	USSR	382.320	Czechoslovakia	373.323	Romania	372.053
Floor	Larissa Latynina (URS)	19.583	Polina Astakova (URS)	19.532	Tamara Lyukina (URS)	19.449
Horse Vault	Margarita Nikolayeva (URS)	19.316	Sofia Muratova (URS)	19.049	Larissa Latynina (URS)	19.016
Beam	Eva Bosaková (TCH)	19.283	Larissa Latynina (URS)	19.233	Sofia Muratova (URS)	19.232
Asymmetrical Bars	Polina Astakova (URS)	19.616	Larissa Latynina (URS)	19.416	Tamara Lyukina (URS)	19.399
Basketball						
	USA		USSR		Brazil	
Soccer						
	Yugoslavia		Denmark		Hungary	
Hockey						
	Pakistan		India		Spain	

* Representing a combined German team

Innsbruck 1964

January 29 – February 9

Participants: 1091 / Men: 891, Women: 200, Countries: 36,
Sports: 8, Events: 34
Final Torchbearer: Joseph Rieder

Medals Table

PLACE	COUNTRY	GOLD	SILVER	BRONZE
1	USSR	11	8	6
2	Austria	4	5	3
3	Norway	3	6	6
4	Finland	3	4	3
5	France	3	4	–

Outstanding Athletes

PLACE	NAME (NATIONALITY)	DISCIPLINE	G	S	B
1	Lidia Skoblikova (URS)	Speed Skating	4	–	–
2	Klaudia Boyarskikh (URS)	Nordic Skiing	3	–	–
3	Eero Mäntyranta (FIN)	Nordic Skiing	2	1	–
4	Sixten Jernberg (SWE)	Nordic Skiing	2	–	1
5	Toralf Engan (NOR)	Nordic Skiing	1	1	–
	Christine Goitschel (FRA)	Alpine Skiing	1	1	–
	Marielle Goitschel (FRA)	Alpine Skiing	1	1	–
	Veikko Kankkonen (FIN)	Nordic Skiing	1	1	–
	Yevdokia Mekshilo (URS)	Nordic Skiing	1	1	–
	Assar Rönnlund (SWE)	Nordic Skiing	1	1	–

EVENT	GOLD		SILVER		BRONZE	
Alpine Skiing						
Men						
Downhill	Egon Zimmermann (AUT)	2:18.16	Leo Lacroix (FRA)	2:18.90	Wolfgang Bartels (GER)*	2:19.48
Slalom	Josef Stiegler (AUT)	1:46.71	William Kidd (USA)	1:47.09	James Heuga (USA)	1:48.05
Giant Slalom	François Bonlieu (FRA)	2:11.13	Karl Schranz (AUT)	2:11.27	Josef Stiegler (AUT)	2:11.52
Women						
Downhill	Christl Haas (AUT)	1:55.39	Edith Zimmermann (AUT)	1:56.42	Traudl Hecher (AUT)	1:56.66
Slalom	Christine Goitschel (FRA)	1:29.86	Marielle Goitschel (FRA)	1:30.77	Jean Saubert (USA)	1:31.36
Giant Slalom	Marielle Goitschel (FRA)	1:52.24	Christine Goitschel (FRA)	1:53.11		
			Jean Saubert (USA)	1:53.11		
Nordic Skiing						
Men						
15 km Cross-Country Skiing	Eero Mäntyranta (FIN)	50:54.1	Harald Grönningen (NOR)	51:34.8	Sixten Jernberg (SWE)	51:42.2
30 km Cross-Country Skiing	Eero Mäntyranta (FIN)	1:30:50.7	Harald Grönningen (NOR)	1:32.02.3	Igor Voronchikin(URS)	1:32.15.8

EVENT	GOLD		SILVER		BRONZE	
50 km	Sixten Jernberg (SWE)	2:43:52.6	Assar Rönnlund (SWE)	2:44:58.2	Arto Tiainen (FIN)	2:45:30.4
4 x 10 km	Sweden	2:18:34.6	Finland	2:18:42.4	USSR	2:18:46.9
Ski Jumping (70 m)	Veikko Kankkonen (FIN)	229.9	Toralf Engan (NOR)	226.3	Torgeir Brandtzæg (NOR)	222.9
Ski Jumping (90 m)	Toralf Engan (NOR)	230.7	Veikko Kankkonen (FIN)	228.9	Torgeir Brandtzæg (NOR)	227.2
Nordic Combined	Tormod Knutsen (NOR)	469.28	Nikolai Kiselyev (URS)	453.04	Georg Thoma (GER)★	452.88
Women						
5 km	Klaudia Boyarskikh (URS)	17:50.5	Mirja Lehtonen (FIN)	17:52.9	Alevtina Koltshina (URS)	18:08.4
10 km	Klaudia Boyarskikh (URS)	40:24.3	Yevdokia Mekshilo (URS)	40:26.6	Maria Gusakova (URS)	40:46.6
3 x 5 km	USSR	59:20.2	Sweden	1:01:27.0	Finland	1:02:45.1
Biathlon						
20 km	Vladimir Melanin (URS)	1:20:26.8	Alexander Privalov (URS)	1:23:42.5	Olav Jordet (NOR)	1:24:38.8
Figure Skating						
Women	Sjoukje Dijkstra (HOL)		Regine Heitzer (AUT)		Petra Burka (CAN)	
Men	Manfred Schnelldorfer (GER)★		Alain Calmat (FRA)		Scott Allen (USA)	
Pairs	Ludmilla Belousova/		Marika Kilius/		Debbi Wilkes/	
	Oleg Protopopov (URS)		Hans-Jürgen Bäumler (GER)★		Guy Revell (CAN)	
Speed Skating						
Men						
500 m	Richard McDermott (USA)	40.1	Yevgeni Grischin (URS)	40.6		
			Vladimir Orlov (URS)	40.6		
			Alv Gjestvang (NOR)	40.6		
1500 m	Ants Antson (URS)	2:10.3	Cornelis Verkerk (HOL)	2:10.6	Villy Haugen (NOR)	2:11.2
5000 m	Knut Johannesen (NOR)	7:38.4	Per Ivar Moe (NOR)	7:38.6	Fred Anton Maier (NOR)	7:42.0
10,000 m	Jonny Nilsson (SWE)	15:50.1	Fred Anton Maier (NOR)	16:06.0	Knut Johannesen (NOR)	16:06.3
Women						
500 m	Lidia Skoblikova (URS)	45.0	Irina Yegorova (URS)	45.4	Tatyana Sidorova (URS)	45.5
1000 m	Lidia Skoblikova (URS)	1:33.2	Irina Yegorova (URS)	1:34.3	Kaija Mustonen (FIN)	1:34.8
1500 m	Lidia Skoblikova (URS)	2:22.6	Kaija Mustonen (FIN)	2:25.5	Berta Kolokoltseva (URS)	2:27.1
3000 m	Lidia Skoblikova (URS)	5:14.9	Valentina Stenina (URS)	5:18.5		
			Pil Hwa Han (PRK)	5:18.5		
Bobsledding						
2-Man Bob	Great Britain I	4:21.90	Italy II	4:22.02	Italy I	4:22.63
4-Man Bob	Canada I	4:14.46	Austria I	4:15.48	Italy II	4:15.60
Lugeing						
Singles (Men)	Thomas Köhler (GER)★	3:26.77	Klaus-Michael Bonsack (GER)★	3:27.04	Hans Plenk (GER)★	3:30.15
Singles (Women)	Ortrun Enderlein (GER)★	3:24.67	Ilse Geisler (GER)★	3:27.42	Helene Thurrier (AUT)	3:29.06
2-Man Luge	Josef Feistmantl/		Reinhold Senn/		Walter Aussendorfer/	
	Manfred Stengl (AUT)	1:41.62	Helmut Thaler (AUT)	1:41.91	Sigisfred Mair (ITA)	1:42.87
Ice Hockey						
	USSR		Sweden		Czechoslovakia	

★ representing a combined German team

Tokyo 1964

October 10 – October 24

Participants: 5140 / Men: 4457, Women: 683, Countries: 93,
Sports: 19, Events: 163
Final Torchbearer: Yoshinori Sakai

TOKYO 1964

Medals Table

PLACE	COUNTRY	GOLD	SILVER	BRONZE
1	USA	36	28	28
2	USSR	30	31	35
3	Japan	16	5	8
4	Germany★	10	21	19
5	Italy	10	10	7

Outstanding Athletes

PLACE	NAME (NATIONALITY)	DISCIPLINE	G	S	B
1	Don Schollander (USA)	Swimming	4	–	–
2	Vera Cáslavská (TCH)	Gymnastics	3	1	–
	Yukio Endo (JPN)	Gymnastics	3	1	–
	Sharon Stouder (USA)	Swimming	3	1	–
5	Stephen Clark (USA)	Swimming	3	–	–

Tokyo 1964

EVENT	GOLD		SILVER		BRONZE	
Athletics						
Men						
100 m	Robert Hayes (USA)	10.0	Enrique Figuerola (CUB)	10.2	Harry Jerome (CAN)	10.2
200 m	Henry Carr (USA)	20.3	Otis Paul Drayton (USA)	20.5	Edwin Roberts (TRI)	20.6
400 m	Michael Larrabee (USA)	45.1	Wendell Mottley (TRI)	45.2	Andrzej Badenski (POL)	45.6
800 m	Peter Snell (NZL)	1:45.1	William Crothers (CAN)	1:45.6	Wilson Kiprugut (KEN)	1:45.9
1500 m	Peter Snell (NZL)	3:38.1	Josef Odlozil (TCH)	3:39.6	John Davies (NZL)	3:39.6
5000 m	Robert Schul (USA)	13:48.8	Harald Norpoth (GER)★	13:49.6	William Dellinger (USA)	13:49.8
10,000 m	William Mills (USA)	28:24.4	Mohamed Gammoudi (TUN)	28:24.8	Ronald Clarke (AUS)	28:25.8
Marathon	Abebe Bikila (ETH)	2:12:11.2	Basil Heatley (GBR)	2:16:19.2	Kokichi Tsuburaya (JPN)	2:16:22.8
110 m Hurdles	Hayes Jones (USA)	13.6	Blaine Lindgren (USA)	13.7	Anatoli Mikhailov (URS)	13.7
400 m Hurdles	"Rex" Cawley (USA)	49.6	John Cooper (GBR)	50.1	Salvatore Morale (ITA)	50.1
3000 m Steeplechase	Gaston Roelants (BEL)	8:30.8	Maurice Herriott (GBR)	8:32.4	Ivan Belyayev (URS)	8:33.8
4 x 100 m	USA	39.0	Poland	39.3	France	39.3
4 x 400 m	USA	3:00.7	Great Britain	3:01.6	Trinidad	3:01.7
20 km Walk	Kenneth Matthews (GBR)	1:29:34.0	Dieter Lindner (GER)★	1:31:13.2	Vladimir Golubnichy (URS)	1:31:59.4
50 km Walk	Abdon Pamich (ITA)	4:11:12.4	Paul V. Nihill (GBR)	4:11:31.2	Ingvar Pettersson (SWE)	4:14:17.4
High Jump	Valeri Brumel (URS)	7'1¾"	John Thomas (USA)	7' 1¾"	John Rambo (USA)	7'1¾"
Pole Vault	Fred Hansen (USA)	16'8¾"	Wolfgang Reinhardt (GER)★	16'6¾"	Klaus Lehnertz (GER)★	16'4¾"
Long Jump	Lynn Davies (GBR)	26'5½"	Ralph Boston (USA)	26'4"	Igor Ter-Ovanesyan (URS)	26'2½"
Triple Jump	Jozef Schmidt (POL)	55'3¾"	Oleg Fedoseyev (URS)	54'4¾"	Viktor Kravchenko (URS)	54'4¼"
Shot	Dallas Long (USA)	66'8¼"	Randy Matson (USA)	66'3¼"	Vilmos Varju (HUN)	63'7¼"
Discus	Al Oerter (USA)	200'1½"	Ludvik Danek (TCH)	198'6¾"	David Weill (USA)	195'2"
Hammer	Romuald Klim (URS)	228'9½"	Gyula Zsivótzky (HUN)	226'8"	Uwe Beyer (GER)★	223'4½"
Javelin	Pauli Nevala (FIN)	271'2"	Gergely Kulcsar (HUN)	270'1"	Janis Lusis (URS)	264'2"
Decathlon	Willi Holdorf (GER)★	7887	Rein Aun (URS)	7842	Hans-Joachim Walde (GER)★	7809
Women						
100 m	Wyomia Tyus (USA)	11.4	Edith McGuire (USA)	11.6	Ewa Klobukowska † (POL)	11.6
200 m	Edith McGuire (USA)	23.0	Irena Kirszenstein (POL)	23.1	Marilyn Black (AUS)	23.1
400 m	Betty Cuthbert (AUS)	52.0	Ann Packer (GBR)	52.2	Judith Amoore (AUS)	53.4
800 m	Ann Packer (GBR)	2:01.1	Maryvonne Dupureur (FRA)	2:01.9	Ann Chamberlain (NZL)	2:02.8
80 m Hurdles	Karin Balzer (GER)★	10.5	Tereza Ciepla (POL)	10.5	Pamela Kilborn (AUS)	10.5
4 x 100 m	Poland	43.6	USA	43.9	Great Britain	44.0
High Jump	Iolanda Balas (ROM)	6'2¾"	Michele Brown-Mason (AUS)	5'10¾"	Taisia Chenchik (URS)	5'10"
Long Jump	Mary Rand (GBR)	22'2¼"	Irena Kirszenstein (POL)	21'7¾"	Tatyana Schelkanova (URS)	21'0¾"
Shot	Tamara Press (URS)	59'6"	Renate Garisch (GER)★	57'9¼"	Galina Zybina (URS)	57'3"
Discus	Tamara Press (URS)	187'10½"	Ingrid Lotz (GER)★	187'8"	Lia Manoliu (ROM)	186'10½"
Javelin	Mihaela Penes (ROM)	198'7½"	Marta Rudas (HUN)	191'2"	Yelena Gorchakova (URS)	187'2"
Pentathlon	Irina Press (URS)	5246	Mary Rand (GBR)	5035	Galina Bystrova (URS)	4956

† 1967 Barred from competing as a result of a negative sex test

EVENT	GOLD		SILVER		BRONZE	
Swimming						
Men						
100 m Freestyle	Don Schollander (USA)	53.4	Robert McGregor (GBR)	53.5	Hans-Joachim Klein (GER)★	54.0
400 m Freestyle	Don Schollander (USA)	4:12.2	Frank Wiegand (GER)★	4:14.9	Allan Wood (AUS)	4:15.1
1500 m Freestyle	Robert Windle (AUS)	17:01.7	John Nelson (USA)	17:03.0	Allan Wood (AUS)	17:07.7
200 m Backstroke	Jed Graef (USA)	2:10.3	Gary Dilley (USA)	2:10.5	Robert Bennett (USA)	2:13.1
200 m Breaststroke	Ian O'Brien (AUS)	2:27.8	Georgi Prokopenko (URS)	2:28.2	Chester Jastremski (USA)	2:29.6
200 m Butterfly	Kevin Berry (AUS)	2:06.6	Carl Robie (USA)	2:07.5	Fred Schmidt (USA)	2:09.3
400 m Medley	Richard Roth (USA)	4:45.4	Roy Saari (USA)	4:47.1	Gerhard Hetz (GER)★	4:51.0
4 x 100 m Freestyle	USA	3:33.2	Germany★	3:37.2	Australia	3:39.1
4 x 200 m Freestyle	USA	7:52.1	Germany★	7:59.3	Japan	8:03.8
4 x 100 m Medley	USA	3:58.4	Germany★	4:01.6	Australia	4:02.3
Springboard Diving	Ken Sitzberger (USA)	159.90	Francis Gorman (USA)	157.63	Larry Andreasen (USA)	143.77
Highboard Diving	Robert Webster (USA)	148.58	Klaus Dibiasi (ITA)	147.54	Thomas Gompf (USA)	146.57
Water Polo	Hungary		Yugoslavia		USSR	
Women						
100 m Freestyle	Dawn Fraser (AUS)	59.5	Sharon Stouder (USA)	59.9	Kathleen Ellis (USA)	1:00.8
400 m Freestyle	Virginia Duenkel (USA)	4:43.3	Marilyn Ramenofsky (USA)	4:44.6	Terri L. Stickles (USA)	4:47.2
100 m Backstroke	Cathy Ferguson (USA)	1:07.7	Christine Caron (FRA)	1:07.9	Virginia Duenkel (USA)	1:08.0
200 m Breaststroke	Galina Prozumenschikova (URS)	2:46.4	Claudia Kolb (USA)	2:47.6	Svetlana Babanina (URS)	2:48.6
100 m Butterfly	Sharon Stouder (USA)	1:04.7	Ada Kok (HOL)	1:05.6	Kathleen Ellis (USA)	1:06.0
400 m Medley	Donna De Varona (USA)	5:18.7	Sharon Finneran (USA)	5:24.1	Martha Randall (USA)	5:24.2
4 x 100 m Freestyle	USA	4:03.8	Australia	4:06.9	Netherlands	4:12.0
4 x 100 m Medley	USA	4:33.9	Netherlands	4:37.0	USSR	4:39.2
Springboard Diving	Ingrid Engel-Krämer (GER)★	145.00	Jeanne Collier (USA)	138.36	Mary Willard (USA)	138.18
Highboard Diving	Lesley Bush (USA)	99.80	Ingrid Engel-Krämer (GER)★	98.45	Galina Alexeyeva (URS)	97.60

EVENT	GOLD		SILVER		BRONZE	
Boxing						
Flyweight (-112½ lb)	Fernando Atzori (ITA)		Artur Olech (POL)		Stanislav Sorokin (URS)	
					Robert Carmody (USA)	
Bantamweight (-119 lb)	Takao Sakurai (JPN)		Chung Shin-Cho(KOR)		Juan Fabila Mendoza (MEX)	
					Washington Rodriguez (URU)	
Featherweight (-126 lb)	Stanislav Stepashkin (URS)		Anthony Villanueva (PHI)		Heinz Schulz (GER)★	
					Charles Brown (USA)	
Lightweight (-132 lb)	Józef Grudzien (POL)		Vellikton Barannikov (URS)		James McCourt (IRL)	
					Ronald Harris (USA)	
Light-Welterweight (-140 lb)	Jerzy Kulej (POL)		Yevgeni Frolov (URS)		Eddie Blay (GHA)	
					Habib Galhia (TUN)	
Welterweight (-148 lb)	Marian Kasprzyk (POL)		Ritschardas Tamulis (URS)		Pertti Purhonen (FIN)	
					Silvano Bertini (ITA)	
Light-Middleweight (-157 lb)	Boris Lagutin (URS)		Joseph Gonzales (FRA)		Nojim Maiyegun (NGA)	
					Jozef Grzesiak (POL)	
Middleweight (-165 lb)	Valeri Popentschenko (URS)		Emil Schulz (GER)★		Francesco Valle (ITA)	
					Tadeusz Walasek (POL)	
Light-Heavyweight (-178½ lb)	Cosimo Pinto (ITA)		Alexei Kisselyov (URS)		Alexandar Nikolov (BUL)	
					Zbiegniew Pietrzykowski (POL)	
Heavyweight (+178½ lb)	Joe Frazier (USA)		Hans Huber (GER)★		Guiseppe Ros (ITA)	
					Vadim Yemelyanov (URS)	
Weightlifting						
Bantamweight (-123½ lb)	Alexei Vakhonin (URS)	357.5	Imre Földi (HUN)	355.0	Shiro Ichinoseki (JPN)	347.5
Featherweight (-132¼ lb)	Yoshinobu Miyake (JPN)	397.5	Isaac Berger (USA)	382.5	Mieczyslaw Nowak (POL)	377.5
Lightweight (- 148¾ lb)	Waldemar Baszanowski (POL)	432.5	Vladimir Kaplunov (URS)	432.5	Marian Zielinski (POL)	420.0
Middleweight (- 165½ lb)	Hans Zdrazila (TCH)	445.0	Viktor Kurentsov (URS)	440.0	Masashi Ouchi (JPN)	437.5
Light-Heavyweight (-182 lb)	Rudolf Plukfelder (URS)	475.0	Geza Toth (HUN)	467.5	Gyözö Veres (HUN)	467.5
Middle-Heavyweight (-198½ lb)	Vladimir Golovanov (URS)	487.5	Louis Martin (GBR)	475.0	Ireneusz Palinski (POL)	467.5
Heavyweight (+198½ lb)	Leonid Zhabotinsky (URS)	572.5	Yuri Vlassov (URS)	570.0	Norbert Schemansky (USA)	537.5
Greco-Roman Wrestling						
Flyweight (-114½ lb)	Tsutomu Hanahara (JPN)		Angel Kerezov (BUL)		Dumitru Pirvulescu (ROM)	
Bantamweight (-125¾ lb)	Masamitsu Ichiguchi (JPN)		Vladien Trostiansky (URS)		Ion Cernea (ROM)	
Featherweight (-138¾ lb)	Imre Polyák (HUN)		Roman Rurua (URS)		Branislav Martinovic (YUG)	
Lightweight (-156¼ lb)	Kazim Ayvaz (TUR)		Valeriu Bularca (ROM)		David Gvantseladze (URS)	
Welterweight (-172 lb)	Anatoli Kolesov (URS)		Cyril Todorov (BUL)		Bertil Nyström (SWE)	
Middleweight (-191¾ lb)	Branislav Simic (YUG)		Jiri Kormanik (TCH)		Lothar Metz (GER)★	
Light-Heavyweight (-213¾ lb)	Boyan Radev (BUL)		Per Svensson (SWE)		Heinz Kiehl (GER)★	
Heavyweight (+213¾ lb)	Istvan Kozma (HUN)		Anatoli Roschin (URS)		Wilfried Dietrich (GER)★	
Freestyle Wrestling						
Flyweight (-114½ lb)	Yoshikatsu Yoshida (JPN)		Chang Chang-Sun(KOR)		Said Aliaakbar Haydari (IRN)	
Bantamweight (- 125¾ lb)	Yojiro Uetake (JPN)		Hüseyn Akbas (TUR)		Aidyn Ibragimov (URS)	
Featherweight (-138¾ lb)	Osamu Watanabe (JPN)		Stantcho Ivanov (BUL)		Nodar Kokaschvili (URS)	
Lightweight (-154¼ lb)	Enyu Valtschev (BUL)		Klaus Jürgen Rost (GER)★		Iwao Horiuchi (JPN)	
Welterweight (-172 lb)	Ismail Ogan (TUR)		Guliko Sagaradze (URS)		Mohamad-Ali Sanatkaran (IRN)	
Middleweight (-191¾ lb)	Prodan Gardschev (BUL)		Hasan Güngör (TUR)		Daniel Brand (USA)	
Light-Heavyweight (- 213¾ lb)	Alexander Medved (URS)		Ahmet Ayik (TUR)		Said Mustafov (BUL)	
Heavyweight (+213¾ lb)	Alexander Ivanitsky (URS)		Liutvi Djiber (BUL)		Hamit Kaplan (TUR)	
Judo						
Lightweight (-138¾ lb)	Takehide Nakatani (JPN)		Eric Hänni (SUI)		Oleg Stepanov (URS)	
					Aron Bogolubov (URS)	
Middleweight (154¼lb-176¼ lb)	Isao Okano (JPN)		Wolfgang Hofmann (GER)★		James Bergman (USA)	
					Kim Eui-Tae (KOR)	
Heavyweight (+205 lb)	Isao Inokuma (JPN)		Al Harold Rogers (USA)		Anzor Kiknadze (URS)	
					Parnaoz Chikviladze (URS)	
Open Category	Antonius Geesink (HOL)		Akio Kaminaga (JPN)		Klaus Glahn (GER)★	
					Theodore Boronovskis (AUS)	
Fencing						
Individual Foil - Men	Egon Franke (POL)	3	Jean-Claude Magnan (FRA)	2	Daniel Revenu (FRA)	1
Team Foil - Men	USSR		Poland		France	
Individual Épée	Grigori Kriss (URS)	2+1	Henry Hoskyns (GBR)	2	Guram Kostova (URS)	1
Team Épée	Hungary		Italy		France	
Individual Saber	Tibor Pézsa (HUN)	2+1	Claude Arabo (FRA)	2	Umar Mavlikhanov (URS)	1

EVENT	GOLD		SILVER		BRONZE	
Team Saber	USSR		Italy		Poland	
Individual Foil – Women	Ildiko Ujlaki-Rejto (HUN)	2+2	Helga Mees (GER)★	2+1	Antonella Ragno (ITA)	2
Team Foil – Women	Hungary		USSR		Germany★	
Modern Pentathlon						
Individual	Ferenc Török (HUN)	5516	Igor Novikov (URS)	5067	Albert Mokeyev (URS)	5039
Team	USSR	14961	USA	14189	Hungary	14173
Canoeing						
Men						
1000 m Kayak Singles K1	Rolf Peterson (SWE)	3:57.13	Mihaly Hesz (HUN)	3:57.28	Aurel Vernescu (ROM)	4:00.77
1000 m Kayak Pairs K2	Sweden	3:38.54	Netherlands	3:39.30	Germany★	3:40.69
1000 m Kayak Fours K4	USSR	3:14.67	Germany★	3:15.39	Romania	3:15.51
1000 m Canadian Singles C1	Jürgen Eschert (GER)★	4:35.14	Andrei Igorov (ROM)	4:37.89	Yevgeni Penyayev (URS)	4:38.31
1000 m Canadian Pairs C2	USSR	4:04.64	France	4:06.52	Denmark	4:07.48
Women						
500 m Kayak Singles K1	Ludmila Khvedosyak (URS)	2:12.87	Hilde Lauer (ROM)	2:15.35	Marcia Jones (USA)	2:15.68
500 m Kayak Pairs K2	Germany★	1:56.95	USA	1:59.16	Romania	2:00.25
Rowing						
Single Sculls	Vyacheslav Ivanov (URS)	8:22.51	Achim Hill (GER)★	8:26.24	Gottfried Kottmann (SUI)	8:29.68
Double Sculls	USSR	7:10.66	USA	7:13.16	Czechoslovakia	7:14.23
Coxless Pairs	Canada	7:32.94	Netherlands	7:33.40	Germany★	7:38.63
Coxed Pairs	USA	8:21.23	France	8:23.15	Netherlands	8:23.42
Coxless Fours	Denmark	6:59.30	Great Britain	7:00.47	USA	7:01.37
Coxed Fours	Germany★	7:00.44	Italy	7:02.84	Netherlands	7:06.46
Coxed Eights	USA	6:18.23	Germany★	6:23.29	Czechoslovakia	6:25.11
Yachting						
Finn Class	Willi Kuhweide (GER)★	7638	Peter Barrett (USA)	6373	Henning Wind (DEN)	6190
International Star	Bahamas	5664	USA	5585	Sweden	5527
Flying Dutchman	New Zealand	6255	Great Britain	5556	USA	5158
Dragon	Denmark	5854	Germany★	5826	USA	5523
5.5-m	Australia	5981	Sweden	5254	USA	5106
Cycling						
Individual Road Race (121 miles)	Mario Zanin (ITA)	4:39:51.63	Kjell A. Rodian (DEN)	4:39:51.65	Walter Godefroot (BEL)	4:39:51.74
Team Road Race	Netherlands	2:26:31.19	Italy	2:26:55.39	Sweden	2:27:11.52
1000-m-Time-Trial	Patrick Sercu (BEL)	1:09.59	Giovanni Pettenella (ITA)	1:10.09	Pierre Trentin (FRA)	1:10.42
1000-m-Sprint	Giovanni Pettenella (ITA)		Sergio Bianchetto (ITA)		Daniel Morelon (FRA)	
2000-m-Tandem	Italy		USSR		Germany★	
4000-m-Individual Pursuit	Jiri Daler (TCH)	5:04.75	Giorgio Ursi (ITA)	5:05.96	Preben Isaksson (DEN)	5:01.90
4000-m-Team Pursuit	Germany★	4:35.67	Italy	4:35.74	Netherlands	4:38.99
Equestrianism						
Three-Day Event	Mauro Checcoli (ITA)	64.40	Carlos Alberto Moratorio (ARG)	56.40	Fritz Ligges (GER)★	49.20
Three-Day Event (Team)	Italy	85.80	USA	65.86	Germany	56.73
Grand Prix (Dressage)	Henri Chammartin (SUI)	1504	Harry Boldt (GER)★	1503	Sergei Filatov (URS)	1486
Grand Prix (Dressage) Team	Germany★	2558.0	Switzerland	2526.0	USSR	2311.0
Grand Prix (Jumping)	Pierre Jonquères d'Oriola (FRA)	-9	Hermann Schridde (GER)★	-13.75	Peter Robeson (GBR)	-16.00
Grand Prix (Jumping) Team	Germany★	-68.50	France	-77.75	Italy	-88.50
Shooting						
Free Rifle (3 Positions)	Gary Anderson (USA)	1153	Shota Kveliashvili (URS)	1144	Martin Gunnarsson (USA)	1136
Small-Bore Rifle (Prone)	Laszló Hammerl (HUN)	597	Lones Wigger (USA)	597	Tommy Pool (USA)	596
Small-Bore Rifle (3 Positions)	Lones Wigger (USA)	1164	Velitchko Khristov (BUL)	1152	Laszló Hammerl (HUN)	1151
Rapid-Fire Pistol	Pentti Linnosvuo (FIN)	592	Ion Tripsa (ROM)	591	Lubomir Nacovsky (TCH)	590
Free Pistol (50 m)	Väino Markkanen (FIN)	560	Franklin Green (USA)	557	Yoshihisa Yoshikawa (JPN)	554
Olympic Trap Shooting	Ennio Mattarelli (ITA)	198	Pavel Senichev (URS)	194/25	William Morris (USA)	194/24
Gymnastics						
Men						
Individual Combined Exercises	Yukio Endo (JPN)	115.95	Shuji Tsurumi (JPN)	115.40		
			Viktor Lisitsky (URS)	115.40		
			Boris Shakhlin (URS)	115.40		
Team	Japan	577.95	USSR	575.45	Germany★	565.10
Parallel Bars	Yukio Endo (JPN)	19.675	Shuji Tsurumi (JPN)	19.450	Franco Menichelli (ITA)	19.35

EVENT	GOLD		SILVER		BRONZE	
Floor	Franco Menichelli (ITA)	19.450	Viktor Lisitsky (URS)	19.350		
			Yukio Endo (JPN)	19.350		
Horse Vault	Haruhiro Yamashita (JPN)	19.600	Viktor Lisitsky (URS)	19.325	Hannu Rantakari (FIN)	19.300
Horizontal Bar	Boris Shakhin (URS)	19.625	Yuri Titov (URS)	19.550	Miroslav Cerar (YUG)	19.500
Rings	Takuji Hayata (JPN)	19.475	Franco Menichelli (ITA)	19.425	Boris Shaklin (URS)	19.400
Pommel Horse	Miroslav Cerar (YUG)	19.525	Shuji Tsurumi (JPN)	19.325	Yuri Tsapenko (URS)	19.200
Women						
Individual Combined Exercises	Vera Cáslavská (TCH)	77.564	Larissa Latynina (URS)	76.998	Polina Astakhova (URS)	76.965
Team	USSR	380.890	Czechoslovakia	379.989	Japan	377.889
Floor	Larissa Latynina (URS)	19.599	Polina Astakhova (URS)	19.500	Anikó Ducza (HUN)	19.300
Horse Vault	Vera Cáslavská (TCH)	19.483	Larissa Latynina (URS)	19.283		
			Birgit Radochla (GER)★	19.283		
Beam	Vera Cáslavská (TCH)	19.449	Tamara Manina (URS)	19.399	Larissa Latynina (URS)	19.382
Asymmetrical Bars	Polina Astakova (URS)	19.332	Katalin Makray (HUN)	19.216	Larissa Latynina (URS)	19.199
Basketball	USA		USSR		Brazil	
Soccer	Hungary		Czechoslovakia		Germany★	
Hockey	India		Pakistan		Australia	
Volleyball						
Men	USSR		Czechoslovakia		Japan	
Women	Japan		USSR		Poland	

★ representing a combined German team

Grenoble 1968

Participants: 1158 / Men: 947, Women: 211, Countries: 37,
Sports: 8, Events: 35
Final Torchbearer: Alain Calmat

February 4 – February 18
(Official Opening Ceremony February 6)

Medals Table

PLACE	COUNTRY	GOLD	SILVER	BRONZE
1	**Norway**	6	6	2
2	**USSR**	5	5	3
3	**France**	4	3	2
4	**Italy**	4	–	–
5	**Austria**	3	4	4

Outstanding Athletes

PLACE	NAME (NATIONALITY)	DISCIPLINE	G	S	B
1	**Jean-Claude Killy (FRA)**	Alpine Skiing	3	–	–
2	**Toini Gustafsson (SWE)**	Nordic Skiing	2	1	–
3	**Ole Ellefsæter (NOR)**	Nordic Skiing	2	–	–
	Harald Grönningen (NOR)	Nordic Skiing	2	–	–
	Eugenio Monti (ITA)	Bobsledding	2	–	–
	Luciano de Paolis (ITA)	Bobsledding	2	–	–

EVENT	GOLD		SILVER		BRONZE	
Alpine Skiing						
Men						
Downhill	Jean-Claude Killy (FRA)	1:59.85	Guy Périllat (FRA)	1:59.93	Jean-Daniel Dätwyler (SUI)	2:00.32
Slalom	Jean-Claude Killy (FRA)	1:39.73	Herbert Huber (AUT)	1:39.82	Alfred Matt (AUT)	1:40.09
Giant Slalom	Jean-Claude Killy (FRA)	3:29.28	Willy Favre (SUI)	3:31.50	Heinrich Messner (AUT)	3:31.83
Women						
Downhill	Olga Pall (AUT)	1:40.87	Isabelle Mir (FRA)	1:41.33	Christl Haas (AUT)	1:41.41
Slalom	Marielle Goitschel (FRA)	1:25.86	Nancy Greene (CAN)	1:26.15	Annie Famose (FRA)	1:27.89
Giant Slalom	Nancy Greene (CAN)	1:51.97	Annie Famose (FRA)	1:54.61	Fernande Bochatay (SUI)	1:54.74
Nordic Skiing						
Men						
15 km Cross-Country Skiing	Harald Grönningen (NOR)	47:54.2	Eero Mäntyranta (FIN)	47:56.1	Gunnar Larsson (SWE)	48:33.7
30 km Cross-Country Skiing	Franco Nones (ITA)	1:35:39.2	Odd Martinsen (NOR)	1:36:28.9	Eero Mäntyranta (FIN)	1:36:55.3

EVENT	GOLD		SILVER		BRONZE	
50 km Cross-Country Skiing	Ole Ellefsæter(NOR)	2:28:45.8	Vyacheslav Vedenine (URS)	2:29:02.5	Josef Haas (SUI)	2:29.14.8
4 x 10 km	Norway	2:08:33.5	Sweden	2:10:13.2	Finland	2:10:56.7
Ski Jumping (70 m Hill)	Jiri Raska (TCH)	216.5	Reinhold Bachler (AUT)	214.2	Baldur Preiml (AUT)	212.6
Ski Jumping (90 m Hill)	Vladimir Belusov (URS)	231.3	Jiri Raska (TCH)	229.4	Lars Grini (NOR)	214.3
Nordic Combined	Franz Keller (FRG)	449.04	Alois Kälin (SUI)	447.99	Andreas Kunz (GDR)	444.10
Women						
5 km Cross-Country Skiing	Toini Gustafsson (SWE)	16:45.2	Galina Kulakova (URS)	16:48.4	Alevtina Koltchina (URS)	16:51.6
10 km Cross-Country Skiing	Toini Gustafsson (SWE)	36:46.5	Berit Mørdre (NOR)	37:54.6	Inger Aufles (NOR)	37:59.9
3 x 5 km	Norway	57:30.0	Sweden	57:51.0	USSR	58:13.6
Biathlon						
20 km	Magnar Solberg (NOR)	1:13:45.9	Alexander Tikhonov (URS)	1:14:40.4	Vladimir Gundartsev (URS)	1:18:27.4
4 x 7.5 km	USSR	2:13:02.4	Norway	2:14:50.2	Sweden	2:17:26.3
Figure Skating						
Women	Peggy Fleming (USA)		Gaby Seyfert (GDR)		Hana Masková (TCH)	
Men	Wolfgang Schwarz (AUT)		Timothy Wood (USA)		Patrick Péra (FRA)	
Pairs	Ludmilla Belousova/		Tatyana Schuk/		Margot Glockshuber/	
	Oleg Protopopov (URS)		Alexander Gorelik (URS)		Wolfgang Danne (FRG)	
Speed Skating						
Men						
500 m	Erhard Keller (FRG)	40.3	Magne Thomassen (NOR)	40.5		
			Richard McDermott (USA)	40.5		
1500 m	Cornelis Verkerk (HOL)	2:03.4	Ard Schenk (HOL)	2:05.0		
			Ivar Eriksen (NOR)	2:05.0		
5000 m	Fred Anton Maier (NOR)	7:22.4	Cornelis Verkerk (HOL)	7:23.2	Petrus Nottet (HOL)	7:25.5
10,000 m	Johnny Höglin (SWE)	15:23.6	Fred Anton Maier (NOR)	15:23.9	Örjan Sandler (SWE)	15:31.8
Women						
500 m	Ludmila Titova (URS)	46.1	Mary Meyers (USA)	46.3		
			Dianne Holum (USA)	46.3		
			Jennifer Fish (USA)	46.3		
1000 m	Carolina Geijssen (HOL)	1:32.6	Ludmila Titova (URS)	1:32.9	Dianne Holum (USA)	1:33.4
1500 m	Kaija Mustonen (FIN)	2:22.4	Carolina Geijssen (HOL)	2:22.7	Christina Kaiser (HOL)	2:24.5
3000 m	Johanna Schut (HOL)	4:56.2	Kaija Mustonen (FIN)	5:01.0	Christina Kaiser (HOL)	5:01.3
Bobsledding						
2-Man Bob	Italy I	4:41.54	West Germany I	4:41.54	Romania I	4:44.46
4-Man Bob	Italy I	2:17.39	Austria I	2:17.48	Switzerland I	2:18.04
Lugeing						
Singles (Men)	Manfred Schmid (AUT)	2:52.48	Thomas Köhler (GDR)	2:52.66	Klaus-Michael Bonsack (GDR)	2:53.33
Singles (Women)	Erica Lechner (ITA)	2:28.66	Christa Schmuck (FRG)	2:29.37	Angelika Dünhaupt (FRG)	2:29.56
2-Man Luge	Klaus-Michael Bonsack/		Manfred Schmid/		Wolfgang Winkler/	
	Thomas Köhler (GDR)	1:35.85	Ewald Walch (AUT)	1:36.34	Fritz Nachmann (FRG)	1:37.29
Ice Hockey						
	USSR		Czechoslovakia		Canada	

Mexico City 1968

October 12 – October 27

Participants: 5530/ Men: 4749, Women: 781, Countries: 112,
Sports: 18, Events: 172
Final Torchbearer: Norma Enriqueta Basilio de Sotelo

Medals Table

PLACE	COUNTRY	GOLD	SILVER	BRONZE
1	USA	45	28	34
2	USSR	29	32	30
3	Japan	11	7	7
4	Hungary	10	10	12
5	GDR	9	9	7

Outstanding Athletes

PLACE	NAME (NATIONALITY)	DISCIPLINE	G	S	B
1	Vera Cáslavská (TCH)	Gymnastics	4	2	–
2	Akinori Nakayama (JPN)	Gymnastics	4	1	1
3	Charles Hickcox (USA)	Swimming	3	1	–
4	Sawao Kato (JPN)	Gymnastics	3	–	1
5	Debbie Meyer (USA)	Swimming	3	–	–

EVENT	GOLD		SILVER		BRONZE	
Athletics						
Men						
100 m	Jim Hines (USA)	9.9	Lennox Miller (JAM)	10.0	Charlie Greene (USA)	10.0
200 m	Tommie Smith (USA)	19.8	Peter Norman (AUS)	20.0	John Carlos (USA)	20.0
400 m	Lee Evans (USA)	43.8	Larry James (USA)	43.9	Ronald Freeman (USA)	44.4
800 m	Ralph Doubell (AUS)	1:44.3	Wilson Kiprugut (KEN)	1:44.5	Thomas Farrell (USA)	1:45.4
1500 m	Kipchoge Keino (KEN)	3:34.9	Jim Ryun (USA)	3:37.8	Bodo Tümmler (FRG)	3:39.0
5000 m	Mohamed Gammoudi (TUN)	14:05.0	Kipchoge Keino (KEN)	14:05.2	Naftali Temu (KEN)	14:06.4
10,000m	Naftali Temu (KEN)	29:27.4	Mamo Wolde (ETH)	29:28.0	Mohamed Gammoudi (TUN)	29:34.2
Marathon	Mamo Wolde (ETH)	2:20:26.4	Kenji Kimihara (JPN)	2:23:31.0	Michael Ryan (NZL)	2:23:45.0
110 m Hurdles	Willie Davenport (USA)	13.3	Ervin Hall (USA)	13.4	Eddy Ottoz (ITA)	13.4
400 m Hurdles	David Hemery (GBR)	48.12	Gerhard Hennige (FRG)	49.02	John Sherwood (GBR)	49.03
3000 m Steeplechase	Amos Biwott (KEN)	8:51.0	Benjamin Kogo (KEN)	8:51.6	George Young (USA)	8:51.8
4 x 100 m	USA	38.2	Cuba	38.3	France	38.4
4 x 400 m	USA	2:56.1	Kenya	2:59.6	FRG	3:00.5
20 km Walk	Vladimir Golubnichi (URS)	1:33:58.4	José Pedraza (MEX)	1:34:00.0	Nikolai Smaga (URS)	1:34:03.0
50 km Walk	Christoph Höhne (GDR)	4:20:13.6	Antal Kiss (HUN)	4:30:17.0	Larry Young (USA)	4:31:55.4
High Jump	Dick Fosbury (USA)	7'4¼"	Edward Caruthers (USA)	7'3½"	Valentin Gavrilov (URS)	7'2½"
Pole Vault	Robert Seagren (USA)	17'8½"	Claus Schiprowski (FRG)	17'8½"	Wolfgang Nordwig (GDR)	17'8½"
Long Jump	Bob Beamon (USA)	29'2½"	Klaus Beer (GDR)	26'10½"	Ralph Boston (USA)	26'9¼"
Triple Jump	Viktor Saneyev (URS)	57'0¾"	Nelson Prudencio (BRA)	56'7¾"	Giuseppe Gentile (ITA)	56'5¾"
Shot	Randy Matson (USA)	67'4½"	George Woods (USA)	66'0"	Eduard Grischin (URS)	65'10¾"
Discus	Al Oerter (USA)	212'6"	Lothar Milde (GDR)	206'11"	Ludvik Danek (TCH)	206'5"
Hammer	Gyula Zsivótzky (HUN)	240'8"	Romuald Klim (URS)	240'5"	Lázár Lovász (HUN)	228'11"
Javelin	Janis Lusis (URS)	295'7"	Jorma Kinnunen (FIN)	290'7"	Gergely Kulcsar (HUN)	285'7½"
Decathlon	William Toomey (USA)	8193	Hans- Joachim Walde (FRG)	8111	Kurt Bendlin (FRG)	8064
Women						
100 m	Wyomia Tyus (USA)	11.0	Barbara Ferrell (USA)	11.1	Irena Szewinska-Kirszenstein (POL)	11.1
200 m	Irena Szewinska-Kirszenstein (POL)	22.5	Raelene Boyle (AUS)	22.7	Jennifer Lamy (AUS)	22.8
400 m	Colette Besson (FRA)	52.0	Lillian Board (GBR)	52.1	Natalya Pechenkina (URS)	52.2
800 m	Madeline Manning (USA)	2:00.9	Ilona Silai (ROM)	2:02.5	Maria Gommers (HOL)	2:02.6
80 m Hurdles	Maureen Caird (AUS)	10.3	Pam Kilborn (AUS)	10.4	Chi Cheng (TPE)	10.4
4 x 100 m	USA	42.8	Cuba	43.3	USSR	43.4
High Jump	Miloslava Rezková (TCH)	5'11½"	Antonina Okorokova (URS)	5'10¾"	Valentina Kozyr (URS)	5'10¾"
Long Jump	Viorica Viscopoleanu (ROM)	22'4½"	Sheila Sherwood (GBR)	21'10¾"	Tatyana Talysheva (URS)	21'10"
Shot	Margitta Helmboldt (GDR)	64'4"	Marita Lange (GDR)	61'7¼"	Nadyezhda Chizhova (URS)	63'6"
Discus	Lia Manoliu (ROM)	191'2"	Liesel Westermann (FRG)	189'6"	Jolán Kleiber (HUN)	180'1"
Javelin	Angéla Németh (HUN)	198'0"	Mihaela Penes (ROM)	196'7"	Eva Janko (HUN)	190'5"
Pentathlon	Ingrid Becker (FRG)	5098	Liese Prokop (AUT)	4966	Annamária Tóth (HUN)	4959
Swimming						
Men						
100 m Freestyle	Michael Wenden (AUS)	52.2	Ken Walsh (USA)	52.8	Mark Spitz (USA)	53.0
200 m Freestyle	Michael Wenden (AUS)	1:55.2	Don Schollander (USA)	1:55.8	John Nelson (USA)	1:58.1
400 m Freestyle	Michael Burton (USA)	4:09.0	Ralph Hutton (CAN)	4:11.7	Alain Mosconi (FRA)	4:13.3
1500 m Freestyle	Michael Burton (USA)	16:38.9	John Kinsella (USA)	16:57.3	Gregory Brough (AUS)	17:04.7
100 m Backstroke	Roland Matthes (GDR)	58.7	Charles Hickcox (USA)	1:00.2	Ron Mills (AUS)	1:00.5
200 m Backstroke	Roland Matthes (GDR)	2:09.6	Mitchel Ivey (USA)	2:10.6	Jack Horsley (USA)	2:10.9
100 m Breaststroke	Don McKenzie (USA)	1:07.7	Vladimir Kosinsky (URS)	1:08.0	Nikolai Pankin (URS)	1:08.0
200 m Breaststroke	Felipe Muñoz (MEX)	2:28.7	Vladimir Kosinsky (URS)	2:29.2	Brian Job (USA)	2:29.9

EVENT	GOLD		SILVER		BRONZE	
100 m Butterfly	Douglas Russell (USA)	55.9	Mark Spitz (USA)	56.4	Ross Wales (USA)	57.2
200 m Butterfly	Carl Robie (USA)	2:08.7	Martin Woodroffe (GBR)	2:09.0	John Ferris (USA)	2:09.3
200 m Medley	Charles Hickcox (USA)	2:12.0	Gregory Buckingham (USA)	2:13.0	John Ferris (USA)	2:13.3
400 m Medley	Charles Hickcox (USA)	4:48.4	Gary Hall (USA)	4:48.7	Michael Holthaus (FRG)	4:51.4
4 x 100 m Freestyle Relay	USA	3:31.7	USSR	3:34.2	Australia	3:34.7
4 x 200 m Freestyle Relay	USA	7:52.3	Australia	7:53.7	USSR	8:01.6
4 x 100 m Medley Relay	USA	3:54.9	GDR	3:57.5	USSR	4:00.7
Springboard Diving	Bernard Wrightson (USA)	170.15	Klaus Dibiasi (ITA)	159.74	James Henry (USA)	158.09
Highboard Diving	Klaus Dibiasi (ITA)	164.18	Alvaro Gaxiola (MEX)	154.49	Edwin Young (USA)	153.93
Water Polo	Yugoslavia	USSR	USSR		Hungary	
Women						
100 m Freestyle	Jan Henne (USA)	1:00.0	Susan Pedersen (USA)	1:00.3	Linda Gustavson (USA)	1:00.3
200 m Freestyle	Debbie Meyer (USA)	2:10.5	Jan Henne (USA)	2:11.0	Jane Barkman (USA)	2:11.2
400 m Freestyle	Debbie Meyer (USA)	4:31.8	Linda Gustavson (USA)	4:35.5	Karen Moras (AUS)	4:37.0
800 m Freestyle	Debbie Meyer (USA)	9:24.0	Pamela Kruse (USA)	9:35.7	Maria-Teresa Ramirez (MEX)	9:38.5
100 m Backstroke	Kaye Hall (USA)	1:06.2	Elaine Tanner (CAN)	1:06.7	Jane Swagerty (USA)	1:08.1
200 m Backstroke	Lilian Watson (USA)	2:24.8	Elaine Tanner (CAN)	2:27.4	Kaye Hall (USA)	2:28.9
100 m Breaststroke	Djurdjica Bjedov (YUG)	1:15.8	Galina Prozumenschikova (URS)	1:15.9	Sharon Wichman (USA)	1:16.1
200 m Breaststroke	Sharon Wichman (USA)	2:44.4	Djurdjica Bjedov (YUG)	2:46.4	Galina Prozumenschikova (URS)	2:47.0
100 m Butterfly	Lynette McClements (AUS)	1:05.5	Ellie Daniel (USA)	1:05.8	Susan Shields (USA)	1:06.2
200 m Butterfly	Ada Kok (HOL)	2:24.7	Helga Lindner (GDR)	2:24.8	Ellie Daniel (USA)	2:25.9
200 m Medley	Claudia Kolb (USA)	2:24.7	Susan Pedersen (USA)	2:28.8	Jan Henne (USA)	2:31.4
400 m Medley	Claudia Kolb (USA)	5:08.5	Lynn Vidali (USA)	5:22.2	Sabine Steinbach (GDR)	5:25.3
4 x 100 m Freestyle Relay	USA	4:02.5	FDR	4:05.7	Canada	4:07.2
4 x 100 m Medley Relay	USA	4:28.3	Australia	4:30.0	FRG	4:36.4
Springboard Diving	Sue Gossick (USA)	150.77	Tamara Pogozheva (URS)	145.30	Keala O'Sullivan (USA)	145.23
Highboard Diving	Milena Duchková (TCH)	109.59	Natalya Lobanova (URS)	105.14	Ann Peterson (USA)	101.11
Boxing						
Light-Flyweight (- 105¾ lbs)	Francisco Rodriguez (VEN)		Jee Yong-Ju (KOR)		Harlan Marbley (USA)	
					Hubert Skrzypczak (POL)	
Flyweight (- 112½ lbs)	Ricardo Delgado (MEX)		Artur Olech (POL)		Servillo Oliveira (BRA)	
					Leo Rwabwogo (UGA)	
Bantamweight (- 119 lbs)	Valeri Sokolov (URS)		Eridadi Mukwanga (UGA)		Eiji Morioka (JPN)	
					Chang Kyou-Chull (KOR)	
Featherweight (- 126 lbs)	Antonio Roldan (MEX)		Albert Robinson (USA)		Philipp Waruinge (KEN)	
					Ivan Michailov (BUL)	
Lightweight (- 132 lbs)	Ronald Harris (USA)		Józef Grudzien (POL)		Calistrat Cutov (ROM)	
					Zvonimir Vujin (YUG)	
Light-Welterweight (- 140 lbs)	Jerzy Kulej (POL)		Enrique Regueiferos (CUB)		Arto Nilsson (FIN)	
					James Wallington (USA)	
Welterweight (- 148 lbs)	Manfred Wolke (GDR)		Joseph Bessala (CMR)		Vladimir Musalinov (URS)	
					Mario Guilloti (ARG)	
Light-Middleweight (- 157 lbs)	Boris Lagutin (URS)		Rolando Garbey (CUB)		John Baldwin (USA)	
					Günther Meier (FRG)	
Middleweight (- 165 lbs)	Christopher Finnegan (GBR)		Alexei Kisselyov (URS)		Agustin Zaragoza (MEX)	
					Alfred Jones (USA)	
Light-Heavyweight (- 178½ lbs)	Dan Poznyak (URS)		Ion Monea (ROM)		Georgy Stankov (BUL)	
					Stanislav Gragan (POL)	
Heavyweight (+ 178½ lbs)	George Foreman (USA)		Jonas Chepulis (URS)		Giorgio Bambini (ITA)	
					Joaquin Rocha (MEX)	
Weightlifting						
Bantamweight (- 123½ lbs)	Mohammad Nassiri (IRN)	367.5	Imre Földi (HUN)	367.5	Henryk Trebicki (POL)	357.5
Featherweight (- 132¼ lbs)	Yoshinobu Miyake (JPN)	392.5	Dito Shanidze (URS)	387.5	Yoshiyuki Miyake (JPN)	385.0
Lightweight (- 148¾ lbs)	Waldemar Baszanowski (POL)	437.5	Parviz Jalayer (IRN)	422.5	Marian Zielinski (POL)	420.0
Middleweight (- 165½ lbs)	Viktor Kurentsov (URS)	475.0	Masashi Ouchi (JPN)	455.0	Károly Bakos (HUN)	440.0
Light-Heavyweight (- 182 lbs)	Boris Selitsky (URS)	485.0	Viktor Belyayev (URS)	485.0	Norbert Ozimek (POL)	472.5
Middle-Heavyweight (- 198½ lbs)	Kaarlo Kangasniemi (FIN)	517.5	Jan Talts (URS)	507.5	Marek Golab (POL)	495.0
Heavyweight (+ 198½ lbs)	Leonid Zhabotinski (URS)	572.5	Serge Reding (BEL)	555.0	Joe Dube (USA)	555.0
Greco-Roman Wrestling						
Flyweight (- 114½ lbs)	Petar Kirov (BUL)		Vladimir Bakulin (URS)		Miroslav Zeman (TCH)	
Bantamweight (- 125¾ lbs)	János Varga (HUN)		Ion Baciu (ROM)		Ivan Kochergin (URS)	
Featherweight (- 138¾ lbs)	Roman Rurua (URS)		Hideo Fujimoto (JPN)		Simeon Popescu (ROM)	
Lightweight (- 154¼ lbs)	Munji Mumemura (JPN)		Stefan Horvat (YUG)		Petros Galaktopoulos (GRE)	
Welterweight (- 172 lbs)	Rudolf Vesper (GDR)		Daniel Robin (FRA)		Károly Bajkó (HUN)	

EVENT	GOLD		SILVER		BRONZE	
Middleweight (- 191¾ lbs)	Lothar Metz (GDR)		Valentin Olenik (URS)		Branislav Simic (YUG)	
Light-Heavyweight (- 213¾ lbs)	Boyan Radev (BUL)		Nikolai Yakovenko (URS)		Nicolae Martinescu (ROM)	
Heavyweight (+ 213¾ lbs)	István Kozma (HUN)		Anatoli Roschin (URS)		Petr Kment (TCH)	
Freestyle Wrestling						
Flyweight (- 114½ lbs)	Shigeo Nakata (JPN)		Richard Sanders (USA)		Surenjav Sukhbaatar (MGL)	
Bantamweight (- 125¾ lbs)	Yojiro Uetake (JPN)		Donald Behm (USA)		Abutaleb Gorgori (IRN)	
Featherweight (- 138¾ lbs)	Masaaki Kaneko (JPN)		Enyu Todorov (BUL)		Shamseddin Seyed-Abbassi (IRN)	
Lightweight (- 154¼ lbs)	Abdollah M. Ardabili (IRN)		Enyu Valtschev (BUL)		Sereeter Danzandarjaa (MGL)	
Welterweight (- 172 lbs)	Mahmut Atalay (TUR)		Daniel Robin (FRA)		Dagvasuren Purev (MGL)	
Middleweight (- 191¾ lbs)	Boris Gurevitch (URS)		Munkbat Jigjid (MGL)		Prodan Gardschev (BUL)	
Light-Heavyweight (- 213¾ lbs)	Ahmet Ayik (TUR)		Shota Lomidze (URS)		József Csatári (HUN)	
Heavyweight (+ 213¾ lbs)	Alexander Medved (URS)		Osman Duraliev (BUL)		Wilfried Dietrich (FRG)	
Fencing						
Individual Foil - Men	Ion Drimba (ROM)	4	Jenö Kamuti (HUN)	3	Daniel Revenu (FRA)	3
Team Foil - Men	France		USSR		Poland	
Individual Épée	Gyözö Kulcsár (HUN)	4+2	Grigori Kriss (URS)	4/10/8	Gianluigi Saccaro (ITA)	4/10/7
Team Épée	Hungary		USSR		Poland	
Individual Saber	Jerzy Pawlowski (POL)	4+1	Mark Rakita (URS)	4	Tibor Pézsa (HUN)	3
Team Saber	USSR		Italy		Hungary	
Individual Foil - Women	Elena Novikova (URS)	4	Pilar Roldan (MEX)	3/14	Ildiko Ujlaki-Rejtö (HUN)	3/16
Team Foil - Women	USSR		Hungary		Romania	
Modern Pentathlon						
Individual	Björn Ferm (SWE)	4964	András Balczó (HUN)	4953	Pavel Lednev (URS)	4795
Team	Hungary	14325	USSR	14248	France	13289
Canoeing						
Men						
1000 m Kayak Singles K1	Mihály Hesz (HUN)	4:02.63	Alexander Shaparenko (URS)	4:03.58	Erik Hansen (DEN)	4:04.39
1000 m Kayak Pairs K2	USSR	3:37.54	Hungary	3:38.44	Austria	3:40.71
1000 m Kayak Fours K4	Norway	3:14.38	Romania	3:14.81	Hungary	3:15.10
1000 m Canadian Singles C1	Tibor Tatai (HUN)	4:36.14	Detlef Lewe (FRG)	4:38.31	Vitali Galkov (URS)	4:40.42
1000 m Canadian Pairs C2	Romania	4:07.18	Hungary	4:08.77	USSR	4:11.30
Women						
500 m Kayak Singles K1	Ludmila Pinayeva (URS)	2:11.09	Renate Breuer (FRG)	2:12.71	Viorica Dumitru (ROM)	2:13.22
500 m Kayak Pairs K2	FRG	1:56.44	Hungary	1:58.60	USSR	1:58.61
Rowing						
Single Sculls	Henri Jan Wienese (HOL)	7:47.80	Jochen Meissner (FRG)	7:52.00	Alberto Demiddi (ARG)	7:57.19
Double Sculls	USSR	6:51.82	Netherlands	6:52.80	USA	6:54.21
Coxless Pairs	GDR	7:26.56	USA	7:26.71	Denmark	7:31.84
Coxed Pairs	Italy	8:04.81	Netherlands	8:06.80	Denmark	8:08.07
Coxless Fours	GDR	6:39.18	Hungary	6:41.64	Italy	6:44.01
Coxed Fours	New Zealand	6:45.62	GDR	6:48.20	Switzerland	6:49.04
Coxed Eights	FRG	6:07.00	Australia	6:07.98	USSR	6:09.11
Yachting						
Finn Class	Valentin Mankin (URS)	11.7	Hubert Raudaschl (AUT)	53.4	Fabio Albarelli (ITA)	55.1
International Star	USA	14.4	Norway	43.7	Italy	44.7
Flying Dutchman	Great Britain	3.0	FRG	43.7	Brazil	48.4
Dragon	USA	6.0	Denmark	26.4	GDR	32.7
5.5 m	Sweden	8.0	Switzerland	32.0	Great Britain	39.8
Cycling						
Individual Road Race (122 mi)	Pierfranco Vianelli (ITA)	4:41:25.24	Leif Mortenson (DEN)	4:42:49.71	Gösta Pettersson (SWE)	4:43:15.24
100 km Road Team Time Trial	Netherlands	2:07:49.06	Sweden	2:09:26.60	Italy	2:10:18.74
1000 m time Trial	Pierre Trentin (FRA)	1:03.91	Niels-Christian Fredborg (DEN)	1:04.61	Janusz Kierzkowski (POL)	1:04.63
1000 m Sprint	Daniel Morelon (FRA)		Giordano Turrini (ITA)		Pierre Trentin (FRA)	
2000 m Tandem	France		Netherlands		Belgium	
4000 m Individual Pursuit	Daniel Rebillard (FRA)	4:41.71	Mogens Frey Jensen (DEN)	4:42.43	Xaver Kurmann (SUI)	4:39.42
4000 m Team Pursuit	Denmark	4:22.44	FRG★	4:18.94	Italy	4:18.35

★The winning W. German team were demoted to 2nd place owing to an illegal push-start.

EVENT	GOLD		SILVER		BRONZE	
Equestrianism						
Three-Day Event	Jean-Jacques Guyon (FRA)	-38.86	Derek Allhusen (GBR)	-41.61	Michael Page (USA)	-53.31
Three-Day Event (Team)	Great Britain	-175.93	USA	-245.87	Australia	-331.26
Grand Prix (Dressage)	Ivan Kizimov (URS)	1572	Josef Neckermann (FRG)	1546	Reiner Klimke (FRG)	1537
Grand Prix (Dressage) Team	FRG	2699	USSR	2657	Switzerland	2547
Grand Prix (Jumping)	William Steinkraus (USA)	-4	Marion Coakes (GBR)	-8	David Broome (GBR)	-12
Grand Prix (Jumping) Team	Canada	-102.75	France	-110.50	FRG	-117.25
Shooting						
Free Rifle (3 Positions)	Gary Anderson (USA)	1157	Vladimir Kornev (URS)	1151	Kurt Müller (SUI)	1148
Small-Bore Rifle (Prone)	Jan Kurka (TCH)	598	László Hammerl (HUN)	598	Ian Ballinger (NZL)	597
Small-Bore Rifle (3 Positions)	Bernd Klingner (FRG)	1157	John Writer (USA)	1156	Vitali Parkimovich (URS)	1154
Rapid-Fire Pistol	Josef Zapedzki (POL)	593	Marcel Rosca (ROM)	591/147	Renart Suleimanov (URS)	591/146
Free Pistol (50 m)	Grigori Kossykh (URS)	562/30	Heinz Mertel (FRG)	562/26	Harald Vollmar (GDR)	560
Skeet Shooting	Yevgeni Petrov (URS)	198/25	Romano Garagnani (ITA)	198/24/25	Konrad Wirnhier (FRG)	198/24/23
Trap Shooting	John Braithwaite (GBR)	198	Thomas Garrigus (USA)	196/25/25	Kurt Czekalla (GDR)	198/25/23
Gymnastics						
Men						
Individual Combined Exercises	Sawao Kato (JPN)	115.90	Mikhail Voronin (URS)	115.85	Akinori Nakayama (JPN)	115.65
Team	Japan	575.90	USSR	571.10	GDR	557.15
Parallel Bars	Akinori Nakayama (JPN)	19.475	Mikhail Voronin (URS)	19.425	Viktor Klimenko (URS)	19.225
Floor	Sawao Kato (JPN)	19.475	Akinori Nakayama (JPN)	19.400	Takashi Kato (JPN)	19.275
Horse Vault	Mikhail Voronin (URS)	19.000	Yukio Endo (JPN)	18.950	Sergei Diomidov (URS)	18.925
Horizontal Bar	Mikhail Voronin (URS)	19.550	Eizo Kenmotsu (JPN)	19.375		
	Akinori Nakayama (JPN)	19.550				
Rings	Akinori Nakayama (JPN)	19.450	Mikhail Voronin (URS)	19.325	Sawao Kato (JPN)	19.225
Pommel Horse	Miroslav Cerar (YUG)	19.325	Olli Eino Laiho (FIN)	19.225	Mikhail Voronin (URS)	19.200
Women						
Individual Combined Exercises	Vera Cáslavská (TCH)	78.25	Zinaida Voronina (URS)	76.85	Natalya Kuchinskaya (URS)	76.75
Team	USSR	382.85	Czechoslovakia	382.20	GDR	379.10
Floor	Larissa Petrik (URS)	19.675	Natalya Kuchinskaya (URS)	19650		
	Vera Cáslavská (TCH)	19.675				
Horse Vault	Vera Cáslavská (TCH)	19.775	Erika Zuchold (GDR)	19.625	Zinaida Voronina (URS)	19.500
Beam	Natalya Kuchinskaya (URS)	19.650	Vera Cáslavská (TCH)	19.575	Larissa Petrik (URS)	19.250
Asymmetrical Bars	Vera Cáslavská (TCH)	19.650	Karin Janz (GDR)	19.500	Zinaida Voronina (URS)	19.425
Basketball						
	USA		Yugoslavia		USSR	
Soccer						
	Hungary		Bulgaria		Japan	
Hockey						
	Pakistan		Australia		India	
Volleyball						
Men	USSR		Japan		Czechoslovakia	
Women	USSR		Japan		Poland	

Sapporo 1972

February 3 – February 13

Participants: 1006 / Men: 800, Women: 206, Countries: 35,

Sports: 8, Events: 35

Final Torchbearer: Hideki Takada

Medals Table

PLACE	COUNTRY	GOLD	SILVER	BRONZE
1	USSR	8	5	3
2	GDR	4	3	7
3	Switzerland	4	3	3
4	Netherlands	4	3	2
5	USA	3	2	3

Outstanding Athletes

PLACE	NAME (NATIONALITY)	DISCIPLINE	G	S	B
1	Galina Kulakova (URS)	Nordic Skiing	3	–	–
	Ard Schenk (HOL)	Speed Skating	3	–	–
3	Vyacheslav Vedenine (URS)	Nordic Skiing	2	0	1
4	Marie-Thérèse Nadig (SUI)	Alpine Skiing	2	–	–
5	Pål Tyldum (NOR)	Nordic Skiing	1	2	–

EVENT	GOLD		SILVER		BRONZE	
Alpine Skiing						
Men						
Downhill	Bernhard Russi (SUI)	1:51.43	Roland Collombin (SUI)	1:52.07	Heinrich Messner (AUT)	1:52.40
Slalom	Francisco Ochoa (ESP)	1:49.27	Gustavo Thöni (ITA)	1:50.28	Rolando Thöni (ITA)	1:50.30
Giant Slalom	Gustavo Thöni (ITA)	3:09.62	Edmund Bruggmann (SUI)	3:10.75	Werner Mattle (SUI)	3:10.99
Women						
Downhill	Marie-Thérèse Nadig (SUI)	1:36.68	Annemarie Pröll (AUT)	1:37.00	Susan Corrock (USA)	1:37.68
Slalom	Barbara Cochran (USA)	1:31.24	Daniele Debernard (FRA)	1:31.26	Florence Steurer (FRA)	1:32.69
Giant Slalom	Marie-Thérèse Nadig (SUI)	1:29.90	Annemarie Pröll (AUT)	1:30.75	Wiltrud Drexel (AUT)	1:32.35
Nordic Skiing						
Men						
15 km Cross-Country Skiing	Sven-Ake Lundbäck (SWE)	45:28.24	Fedor Simaschov (URS)	46:.00.84	Ivar Formo (NOR)	46:02.86
30 km Cross-Country Skiing	Vyacheslav Vedenine (URS)	1:36:31.15	Pål Tyldum (NOR)	1:37:25.30	Johannes Harviken (NOR)	1:37:32.44
50 km Cross-Country Skiing	Pål Tyldum (NOR)	2:43:14.75	Magne Myrmo (NOR)	2:43:29.45	Vyacheslav Vedenine (URS)	2:44:00.19
4 x 10 km	USSR	2:04:47.94	Norway	2:04:57.06	Switzerland	2:07:00.06
Ski Jumping (70 m Hill)	Yukio Kasaya (JPN)	244.2	Akitsugu Konno (JPN)	234.8	Seiji Aochi (JPN)	229.5
Ski Jumping (90 m Hill)	Wojciech Fortuna (POL)	219.9	Walter Steiner (SUI)	219.8	Rainer Schmidt (GDR)	219.3
Nordic Combined	Ulrich Wehling (GDR)	413.340	Rauno Miettinen (FIN)	405.505	Karl-Heinz Luck (GDR)	398.800
Women						
5 km Cross-Country Skiing	Galina Kulakova (URS)	17:00.50	Marjatta Kajosmaa (FIN)	17:05.50	Helena Sikolová (TCH)	17:07.32
10 km Cross-Country Skiing	Galina Kulakova (URS)	34:17.82	Alevtina Olunina (URS)	34:54.11	Marjatta Kajosmaa (FIN)	34:56.45
3 x 5 km	USSR	48:46.15	Finland	49:19.37	Norway	49:51.49
Biathlon						
20 km	Magnar Solberg (NOR)	1:15:55.50	Hansjörg Knauthe (GDR)	1:16:07.60	Lars Arvidsson (SWE)	1:16:27.03
4 x 7.5 km	USSR	1:51:44.92	Finland	1:54:37.25	GDR	1:54:57.67
Figure Skating						
Women	Beatrix Schuba (AUT)		Karen Magnussen (CAN)		Janet Lynn (USA)	
Men	Ondrej Nepela (TCH)		Sergei Chetverukhin (URS)		Patrick Péra (FRA)	
Pair	Irina Rodnina/ Alexei Ulanov (URS)		Ludmilla Smirnova/ Andrei Suraikin (URS)		Manuela Gross/ Uwe Kagelmann (GDR)	
Speed Skating						
Men						
500 m	Erhard Keller (FRG)	39.44	Hasse Borjes (SWE)	39.69	Valeri Muratov (URS)	39.80
1500 m	Ard Schenk (HOL)	2:02.96	Roar Grönvold (NOR)	2:04.26	Göran Claeson (SWE)	2:05.8
5000 m	Ard Schenk (HOL)	7:23.61	Roar Grönvold (NOR)	7:28.18	Sten Stensen (NOR)	7:33.39
10,000 m	Ard Schenk (HOL)	15:01.35	Cornelis Verkerk (HOL)	15:04.70	Sten Stensen (NOR)	15:07.08
Women						
500 m	Anne Henning (USA)	43.33	Vera Krasnova (URS)	44.01	Ludmila Titova (URS)	44.45
1000 m	Monika Pflug (FRG)	1:31.40	Atje Keulen-Deelstra (HOL)	1:31.61	Anne Henning (USA)	1:31.62
1500 m	Dianne Holum (USA)	2:20.85	Christina Baas-Kaiser (HOL)	2:21.05	Atje Keulen-Deelstra (HOL)	2:22.05
3000 m	Christina Baas-Kaiser (HOL)	4:52.14	Dianne Holum (USA)	4:58.67	Atje Keulen-Deelstra (HOL)	4:59.91

EVENT	GOLD		SILVER		BRONZE	
Bobsledding						
2-Man Bob	FRG II	4:57.07	FRG I	4:58.84	Switzerland I	4:59.33
4-Man Bob	Switzerland I	4:43.07	Italy I	4:43.83	FRG I	4:43.92
Lugeing						
Men's Singles	Wolfgang Scheidel (GDR)	3:27.58	Harald Ehrig (GDR)	3:28.39	Wolfram Fiedler (GDR)	3:28.73
Women's Singles	Anna-Maria Müller (GDR)	2:59.18	Ute Rührold (GDR)	2:59.49	Margit Schumann (GDR)	2:59.54
2-Man Luge	Paul Hildgartner/ Walter Plaikner (ITA)	1:28.35			Klaus Bonsack/ Wolfram Fiedler (GDR)	1:29.16
	Horst Hörnlein/ Reinhard Bredow (GDR)	1:28.35				
Ice hockey						
	USSR		USA		Czechoslovakia	

Munich 1972

August 26 – September 11

Participants: 7123 / Men: 6065, Women: 1058, Countries: 121,
Sports: 21, Events: 195
Final Torchbearer: Günter Zahn

Medals Table

PLACE	COUNTRY	GOLD	SILVER	BRONZE
1	USSR	50	27	22
2	USA	33	31	30
3	East Germany	20	23	23
4	West Germany	13	11	16
5	Japan	13	8	8

Outstanding Athletes

PLACE	NAME (NATIONALITY)	DISCIPLINE	G	S	B
1	Mark Spitz (USA)	Swimming	7	–	–
2	Sawao Kato (JPN)	Gymnastics	3	2	–
3	Shane Gould (AUS)	Swimming	3	1	1
4	Olga Korbut (URS)	Gymnastics	3	1	–
5	Melissa Belote (USA)	Swimming	3	–	–
	Sandra Neilson (USA)	Swimming	3	–	–

EVENT	GOLD		SILVER		BRONZE	
Athletics						
Men						
100 m	Valeri Borzov (URS)	10.14	Robert Taylor (USA)	10.24	Lennox Miller (JAM)	10.33
200 m	Valeri Borzov (URS)	20.00	Larry Black (USA)	20.19	Pietro Mennea (ITA)	20.30
400 m	Vincent Matthews (USA)	44.66	Wayne Collett (USA)	44.80	Julius Sang (KEN)	44.92
800 m	Dave Wottle (USA)	1:45.9	Yevgeni Arzhanov (URS)	1:45.9	Mike Boit (KEN)	1:46.0
1500 m	Pekka Vasala (FIN)	3:36.3	Kipchoge Keino (KEN)	3:36.8	Rodney Dixon (NZL)	3:37.5
5000 m	Lasse Viren (FIN)	13:26.4	Mohamed Gammoudi (TUN)	13:27.4	Ian Stewart (GBR)	13:27.6
10,000 m	Lasse Viren (FIN)	27:38.4	Emiel Puttemans (BEL)	27:39.6	Miruts Yifter (ETH)	27:41.0
Marathon	Frank Shorter (USA)	2:12:19.8	Karel Lismont (BEL)	2:14:31.8	Mamo Wolde (ETH)	2:15:08.4
110 m Hurdles	Rodney Milburn (USA)	13.24	Guy Drut (FRA)	13.34	Thomas Hill (USA)	13.48
400 m Hurdles	John Akii-Bua (UGA)	47.82	Ralph Mann (USA)	48.51	David Hemery (GBR)	48.52
3000 m Steeplechase	Kipchoge Keino (KEN)	8:23.6	Benjamin Jipcho (KEN)	8:24.6	Tapio Kantanen (FIN)	8:24.8
4 x 100 m	USA	38.19	USSR	38.50	FRG	38.79
4 x 400 m	Kenya	2:59.8	Great Britain	3:00.5	France	3:00.7
20 km Walk	Peter Frenkel (GDR)	1:26:42.4	Vladimir Golubnichi (URS)	1:26:55.2	Hans Reimann (GDR)	1:27:16.6
50 km Walk	Bernd Kannenberg (FRG)	3:56:11.6	Veniamin Soldatenko (URS)	3:58:24.0	Larry Young (USA)	4:00:46.0
High Jump	Yuri Tarmak (URS)	7'3¾"	Stefan Junge (GDR)	7'3"	Dwight Stones (USA)	7'3"
Pole Vault	Wolfgang Nordwig (GDR)	18'0½"	Robert Seagren (USA)	17'8½"	Jan Johnson (USA)	17'6½"
Long Jump	Randy Williams (USA)	27'0¼"	Hans Baumgartner (FRG)	26'10"	Arnie Robinson (USA)	26'4"
Triple Jump	Viktor Saneyev (URS)	56'11"	Jörg Drehmel (GDR)	56'9¼"	Nelson Prudencio (BRA)	55'11¼"
Shot	Wladyslaw Komar (POL)	69'6"	George Woods (USA)	69'5¼"	Hartmut Briesenick (GDR)	69'4¼"
Discus	Ludvik Danek (TCH)	211'3"	Jay Silvester (USA)	208'4"	Rickard Bruch (SWE)	208'0"
Hammer	Anatoli Bondarchuk (URS)	247'8"	Jochen Sachse (GDR)	245'11"	Vasili Khmelevski (URS)	242'10½"
Javelin	Klaus Wolfermann (FRG)	296'10"	Janis Lusis (URS)	296'9"	William Schmidt (USA)	276'11½"
Decathlon	Nikolai Avilov (URS)	8454	Leonid Litvinenko (URS)	8035	Ryszard Katus (POL)	7984

EVENT	GOLD		SILVER		BRONZE	
Women						
100 m	Renate Stecher (GDR)	11.07	Raelene Boyle (AUS)	11.23	Silvia Chivas (CUB)	11.24
200 m	Renate Stecher (GDR)	22.40	Raelene Boyle (AUS)	22.45	Irena Szewinska-Kirszenstein (POL)	22.74
400 m	Monika Zehrt (GDR)	51.08	Rita Wilden (FRG)	51.21	Kathy Hammond (USA)	51.64
800 m	Hildegard Falck (FRG)	1:58.6	Niole Sabaite (URS)	1:58.7	Gunhild Hoffmeister (GDR)	1:59.2
1500 m	Ludmila Bragina (URS)	4:01.4	Gunhild Hoffmeister (GDR)	4:02.8	Paola Cacchi (ITA)	4:02.9
100 m Hurdles	Annelie Ehrhardt (GDR)	12.59	Valeria Bufanu (ROM)	12.84	Karin Balzer (GDR)	12.90
4 x 100 m	FRG	42.81	GDR	42.95	Cuba	43.36
4 x 400 m	GDR	3:23.0	USA	3:25.2	FRG	3:26.5
High Jump	Ulrike Meyfarth (FRG)	6'3½"	Yordanka Blagoyeva (BUL)	6'2"	Ilona Gusenbauer (AUT)	6'2"
Long Jump	Heide Rosendahl (FRG)	22'3"	Diana Yorgova (BUL)	27'2½"	Eva Suranova (TCH)	21'10¼"
Shot	Nadyezhda Chizhova (URS)	69'0"	Margitta Gummel (GDR)	66'4½"	Ivanka Khristova (BUL)	63'6"
Discus	Faina Melnik (URS)	218'7"	Argentina Menis (ROM)	213'5"	Vassilka Stoyeva (BUL)	211'1"
Javelin	Ruth Fuchs (GDR)	209'7"	Jaqueline Todten (GDR)	205'2"	Kathy Schmidt (USA)	196'8"
Pentathlon	Mary Peters (GBR)	4801	Heide Rosendahl (FRG)	4791	Burglinde Pollak (GDR)	4768
Swimming						
Men						
100 m Freestyle	Mark Spitz (USA)	51.22	Jerry Heidenreich (USA)	51.65	Vladimir Bure (URS)	51.77
200 m Freestyle	Mark Spitz (USA)	1:52.78	Steven Genter (USA)	1:53.73	Werner Lampe (FRG)	1:53.99
400 m Freestyle	Bradford Cooper (AUS)	4:00.27	Steven Genter (USA)	4:01.94	Tom McBreen (USA)	4:02.64
1500 m Freestyle	Michael Burton (USA)	15:52.58	Graham Windeatt (AUS)	15:58.48	Douglas Northway (USA)	16:09.25
100 m Backstroke	Roland Matthes (GDR)	56.58	Mike Stamm (USA)	57.70	John Murphy (USA)	58.35
200 m Backstroke	Roland Matthes (USA)	2:02.82	Mike Stamm (USA)	2:04.09	Mitchell Ivey (USA)	2:04.33
100 m Breaststroke	Nobutaka Taguchi (JPN)	1:04.94	Tom Bruce (USA)	1:05.43	John Hencken (USA)	1:05.61
200 m Breaststroke	Jonn Hencken (USA)	2:21.55	David Wilkie (GBR)	2:23.67	Nobutaka Taguchi (JPN)	2:23.88
100 m Butterfly	Mark Spitz (USA)	54.27	Bruce Robertson (CAN)	55.56	Jerry Heidenreich (USA)	55.74
200 m Butterfly	Mark Spitz (USA)	2:00.70	Gary Hall (USA)	2:02.86	Robin Backhaus (USA)	2:03.23
200 m Medley	Gunnar Larsson (SWE)	2:07.17	Alexander McKee (USA)	2:08.37	Steven Furniss (USA)	2:08.45
400 m Medley	Gunnar Larsson (SWE)	4:31.981	Alexander McKee (USA)	4:31.983	Andras Hargitay (HUN)	4:32.700
4 x 100 m Freestyle Relay	USA	3:26.42	USSR	3:29.72	GDR	3:32.42
4 x 200 m Freestyle Relay	USA	7:35.78	FRG	7:41.69	USSR	7:45.76
4 x 100 m Medley Relay	USA	3:48.16	GDR	3:52.12	Canada	3:52.26
Springboard Diving	Vladimir Vasin (URS)	594.06	Franco Cagnotto (ITA)	591.63	Craig Lincoln (USA)	577.29
Highboard Diving	Klaus Dibiasi (ITA)	504.12	Richard Rydze (USA)	480.75	Franco Cagnotto (ITA)	475.83
Water Polo	USSR		Hungary		USA	
Women						
100 m Freestyle	Sandra Neilson (USA)	58.59	Shirley Babashoff (USA)	59.02	Shane Gould (AUS)	59.06
200 m Freestyle	Shane Gould (AUS)	2:03.56	Shirley Babashoff (USA)	2:04.33	Keena Rothhammer (USA)	2:04.92
400 m Freestyle	Shane Gould (AUS)	4:19.04	Novella Calligaris (ITA)	4:22.44	Gudrun Wegner (GDR)	4:23.11
800 m Freestyle	Keena Rothhammer (USA)	8:53.68	Shane Gould (AUS)	8:56.39	Novella Calligaris (ITA)	8:57.46
100 m Backstroke	Melissa Belote (USA)	1:05.78	Andrea Gyarmati (HUN)	1:06.26	Susan Atwood (USA)	1:06.34
200 m Backstroke	Melissa Belote (USA)	2:19.19	Susan Atwood (USA)	2:20.38	Donna Marie Gurr (CAN)	2:23.22
100 m Breaststroke	Catherine Carr (USA)	1:13.58	Galina Stepanova (URS)	1:14.99	Beverley Whitfield (AUS)	1:15.73
200 m Breaststroke	Beverley Whitfield (AUS)	2:41.71	Dana Schoenfield (USA)	2:42.05	Galina Stepanova (URS)	2:42.36
100 m Butterfly	Mayumi Aoki (JPN)	1:03.34	Roswitha Beier (GDR)	1:30.61	Andrea Gyarmati (HUN)	1:03.73
200 m Butterfly	Karen Moe (USA)	2:15.57	Lynn Colella (USA)	2:16.34	Ellie Daniel (USA)	2:16.74
200 m Medley	Shane Gould (AUS)	2:23.07	Kornelia Ender (GDR)	2:23.59	Lynn Vidali (USA)	2:24.06
400 m Medley	Gail Neall (AUS)	5:02.97	Leslie Cliff (CAN)	5:03.57	Novella Calligaris (ITA)	5:03.99
4 x 100 m Freestyle Relay	USA	3:55.19	GDR	3:55.55	FRG	3:57.93
4 x 100 m Medley Relay	USA	4:20.75	GDR	4:24.91	FRG	4:26.46
Springboard Diving	Maxine King (USA)	450.03	Ulrika Knape (SWE)	434.19	Marina Janicke (GDR)	430.92
Highboard Diving	Ulrika Knape (SWE)	390.00	Milena Duchková (TCH)	370.92	Marina Janicke (GDR)	360.54
Boxing						
Light-Flyweight (- 105¾ lbs)	György Gedo (HUN)		U Gil Kim (PRK)		Enrique Rodriguez (ESP) / Ralph Evans (GBR)	
Flyweight (- 112½ lbs)	Gheorghi Kostadinov (BUL)		Leo Rwabwogo (UGA)		Douglas Rodriguez (CUB) / Leszek Blazynski (POL)	
Bantamweight (- 119 lbs)	Orlando Martinez (CUB)		Alfonso Zamora (MEX)		George Turpin (GBR) / Ricardo Carreras (USA)	
Featherweight (- 126 lbs)	Boris Kusnetzov (URS)		Philip Waruinge (KEN)		Clemente Rojas (COL) / Andras Botos (HUN)	
Lightweight (- 132 lbs)	Jan Szczepanski (POL)		Laszlo Orban (HUN)		Alfonso Perez (COL) / Samuel Mbugua (KEN)	

EVENT	GOLD		SILVER		BRONZE	
Light-Welterweight (- 140 lbs)	Ray Seales (USA)		Anghel Angelov (BUL)		Zvonimir Vujin (YUG) Issak Daborg (NIG)	
Welterweight (- 148 lbs)	Emilio Correa (CUB)		János Kajdi (HUN)		Dick Tiger Murunga (KEN) Jesse Valdez (USA)	
Light-Middleweight (- 157 lbs)	Dieter Kottysch (FRG)		Wieslaw Rudkowski (POL)		Alan Minter (GBR) Peter Tiepold (GDR)	
Middleweight (- 165 lbs)	Vyacheslav Lemeschev (URS)		Reima Virtanen (FIN)		Marvin Johnson (USA) Prince Amartey (GHA)	
Light-Heavyweight (- 178½ lbs)	Mate Parlov (YUG)		Gilberto Carillo (CUB)		Janusz Gortat (POL) Isaak Ikhouria (NGR)	
Heavyweight (+ 178½ lbs)	Teofilo Stevenson (CUB)		Ion Alexe (ROM)		Peter Hussing (FRG) Hasse Thomsen (SWE)	
Weightlifting						
Flyweight (- 114½ lbs)	Zymunt Smalcerz (POL)	337.5	Lajos Szuecs (HUN)	330.0	Sandor Holczreiter (HUN)	327.5
Bantamweight (- 123½ lbs)	Imre Földi (HUN)	377.5	Mohammed Nassiri (IRN)	370.0	Gennadi Chetin (URS)	367.5
Featherweight (- 132¼ lbs)	Norair Nurikyan (BUL)	402.5	Dito Shanidze (URS)	400.0	Janos Benedek (HUN)	390.0
Lightweight (- 148¾ lbs)	Mukharbi Kirzhinov (URS)	460.0	Mladen Koutchev (BUL)	450.0	Zbigniev Kaczmarek (POL)	437.5
Middleweight (- 165½ lbs)	Yordan Bikov (BUL)	485.0	Mohammed Trabulsi (LIB)	472.5	Anselmo Silvino (ITA)	470.0
Light-Heavyweight (- 182 lbs)	Leif Jensen (NOR)	507.5	Norbert Ozimek (POL)	497.5	György Horvath (HUN)	495.0
Middle-Heavyweight (- 198½ lbs)	Andon Nikolov (BUL)	525.0	Atanas Chopov (BUL)	517.5	Hans Bettembourg (SWE)	512.5
Heavyweight (- 242½ lbs)	Jan Talts (URS)	580.0	Alexander Kraitchev (BUL)	562.5	Stefan Grützner (GDR)	555.0
Super-Heavyweight (+ 242½ lbs)	Vasili Alexeyev (URS)	640.0	Rudolf Mang (FRG)	610.0	Gerd Bonk (GDR)	572.5
Greco-Roman Wrestling						
Light-Flyweight (- 105¾ lbs)	Gheorg Berceanu (ROM)		Rahim Aliabadi (IRN)		Stefan Anghelov (BUL)	
Flyweight (- 114½ lbs)	Petar Kirov (BUL)		Koichiro Hirayama (JPN)		Giuseppe Bognanni (ITA)	
Bantamweight (- 125¾ lbs)	Rustem Kasakov (URS)		Hans-Jürgen Veil (FRG)		Risto Björlin (FIN)	
Featherweight (- 136½ lbs)	Georgi Markov (BUL)		Heinz-Helmut Wehling (GDR)		Kazimierz Lipien (POL)	
Lightweight (- 149¾ lbs)	Shamil Khisamutdinov (URS)		Stoyan Apostolov (BUL)		Gian Matteo Ranzi (ITA)	
Welterweight (- 163 lbs)	Vitezslav Macha (TCH)		Petros Galaktopoulos (GRE)		Jan Karlsson (SWE)	
Middleweight (- 180¾ lbs)	Csaba Hegedus (HUN)		Anatoli Nazarenko (URS)		Milan Nenadic (YUG)	
Light-Heavyweight (- 198¼ lbs)	Valeri Rezanzev (URS)		Josip Corak (YUG)		Czeslaw Kwiecinski (POL)	
Heavyweight (- 220¼ lbs)	Nicolae Martinescu (ROM)		Nikolai Yakovenko (URS)		Ferenc Kiss (HUN)	
Super-Heavyweight (+ 220¼ lbs)	Anatoli Roschin (URS)		Alexander Tomov (BUL)		Victor Dolipschi (ROM)	
Freestyle Wrestling						
Light-Flyweight (- 105¾ lbs)	Roman Dimitriev (URS)		Ognian Nikolov (BUL)		Ebrahim Javadpour (IRN)	
Flyweight (- 114½ lbs)	Kiyomi Kato (JPN)		Arsen Alakhverdiev (URS)		Hyong Kim Gwong (PRK)	
Bantamweight (- 125¾ lbs)	Hideaki Yanagida (JPN)		Richard Sanders (USA)		László Klinga (HUN)	
Featherweight (- 136½ lbs)	Zagalav Abdulbekov (URS)		Vehbi Akdag (TUR)		Ivan Krastev (BUL)	
Lightweight (- 149¾ lbs)	Dan Gable (USA)		Kikuo Wada (JPN)		Ruslan Ashuralyev (URS)	
Welterweight (- 163 lbs)	Wayne Wells (USA)		Jan Karlsson (SWE)		Adolf Seger (FRG)	
Middleweight (- 180¾ lbs)	Levan Tediashvili (URS)		John Peterson (USA)		Vasile Jorga (ROM)	
Light-Heavyweight (- 198¼ lbs)	Ben Peterson (USA)		Gennadi Strakhov (URS)		Karoly Bajko (HUN)	
Heavyweight (- 220¼ lbs)	Ivan Yarygin (URS)		Khorloo Baianmunkh (MGL)		Jószef Csatári (HUN)	
Super-Heavyweight (+ 220¼ lbs)	Alexander Medved (URS)		Osman Duraliev (BUL)		Chris Taylor (USA)	
Judo						
Lightweight (- 138¾ lbs)	Takao Kawaguchi (JPN)		Bakhaavaa Buidaa (MGL) (disqualified after positive drug test)		Yong Ik Kim (PRK) Jean-Jacques Monuier (FRA)	
Welterweight (- 154¼ lbs)	Toyokazu Nomura (JPN)		Anton Zajkowski (POL)		Anatoli Novikov (URS) Dietmar Höttger (GDR)	
Middleweight (- 176¼ lbs)	Shinobu Sekine (JPN)		Oh Seung-Lip (KOR)		Brian Jacks (GBR) Jean-Paul Coché (FRA)	
Light-Heavyweight (- 205 lbs)	Shota Chochoshvili (URS)		David Starbrook (GBR)		Paul Barth (FRG) Chiaki Ishii (BRA)	
Heavyweight (+ 205 lbs)	Wilhelm Ruska (HOL)		Klaus Glahn (FRG)		Givi Onashvili (URS) Motoki Nishimura (JPN)	
Open Class	Wilhelm Ruska (HOL)		Vitali Kuznetsov (URS)		Jean-Claude Brondani (FRA) Angelo Parisi (GBR)	
Fencing						
Individual Foil - Men	Witold Woyda (POL)	5	Jenö Kamuti (HUN)	4	Christian Noël (FRA)	2
Team Foil - Men	Poland		USSR		France	
Individual Épée	Csaba Fenyresi (HUN)	4	Jacques La Dagaillerie (FRA)	3	Gyözö Kulcsár (HUN)	3
Team Épée	Hungary		Switzerland		USSR	
Individual Saber	Viktor Sidyak (URS)	4	Peter Maroth (HUN)	3	Vladimir Nazlimov (URS)	3

EVENT	GOLD		SILVER		BRONZE	
Team Saber	Italy		USSR		Hungary	
Individual Foil - Women	Antonella Ragno-Lonzi (ITA)	4	Ildiko Bobis (HUN)	3	Galina Gorokhova (URS)	3
Team Foil - Women	USSR		Hungary		Romania	
Modern Pentathlon						
Individual	András Balczó (HUN)	5412	Boris Onischenko (URS)	5335	Pavel Lednev (URS)	5328
Team	USSR	15968	Hungary	15348	Finland	14812
Canoeing						
Men						
1000 m Kayak Singles K 1	Alexander Shaparenko (URS)	3:48.06	Rolf Peterson (SWE)	3:48.35	Geza Csapó (HUN)	3:49.38
1000 m Kayak Pairs K 2	USSR	3:31.23	Hungary	3:32.00	Poland	3:33.83
1000 m Kayak Fours K 4	USSR	3:14.02	Romania	3:15.07	Norway	3:15.27
1000 m Canadian Singles C 1	Ivan Patzaichin (ROM)	4:08.94	Tamas Wichmann (HUN)	4:12.42	Detlef Lewe (FRG)	4:13.63
1000 m Canadian Pairs C2	USSR	3:52.60	Romania	3:52.63	Bulgaria	3:58.10
Women						
500 m Kayak Singles K 1	Yulia Ryabchinskaya (URS)	2:03.17	Mieke Jaapies (HOL)	2:04.03	Anna Pfeffer (HUN)	2:05.50
500 m Kayak Pairs K 2	USSR	1:53.50	GDR	1:54.30	Romania	1:55.01
Slalom Racing						
Kayak Singles	Siegbert Horn (GDR)	268.56	Norbert Sattler (AUT)	270.76	Harald Gimpel (GDR)	277.95
Canadian Singles	Reinhard Eiben (GDR)	315.84	Reinhold Kauder (FRG)	327.89	Jamie McEwan (USA)	335.95
Canadian Pairs	GDR	310.68	FRG	311.90	France	315.10
Kayak Singles (Women)	Angelika Bahmann (GDR)	364.50	Gisela Grothaus (FRG)	398.15	Magdalena Wunderlich (FRG)	400.50
Rowing						
Single Sculls	Yuri Malishev (URS)	7:10.12	Alberto Demiddi (ARG)	7:11.53	Wolfgang Güldenpfennig (GDR)	7:14.45
Double Sculls	USSR	7:01.77	Norway	7:02.58	GDR	7:05.55
Coxless Pairs	GDR	6:53.16	Switzerland	6:57.06	Netherlands	6:58.70
Coxed Pairs	GDR	7:17.25	Czechoslovakia	7:19.57	Romania	7:21.36
Coxless Fours	GDR	6:24.27	New Zealand	6:25.64	FRG	6:28.41
Coxed Fours	FRG	6:31.85	GDR	6:33.30	Czechoslovakia	6:35.64
Coxed Eights	New Zealand	6:08.94	USA	6:11.61	GDR	6:11.67
Yachting						
Finn Class	Serge Maury (FRA)	58.0	Ilias Hatzipavlis (GRE)	71.0	Viktor Potapov (URS)	74.7
International Star	Australia	28.1	Sweden	44.0	FRG	44.4
Flying Dutchman	Great Britain	22.7	France	40.7	FRG	51.1
International Tempest	USSR	28.1	Great Britain	34.4	USA	47.7
Dragon	Australia	13.7	GDR	41.7	USA	47.7
International Soling	USA	8.7	Sweden	31.7	Canada	47.1
Cycling						
Individual Road Race (113¼ mi)	Hennie Kuiper (HOL)	4:14:37.0	Kevin Sefton (AUS)	4:15:04.0	Jaime Huelamo (ESP) (Medal withdrawn - disqualified)	
100 km Road Team Time Trial	USSR	2:11:17.8	Poland	2:11:47.5	Medal withdrawn (HOL disqualified)	
1000 m Time Trial	Niels Fredborg (DEN)	1:06.44	Danny Clark (AUS)	1:06.87	Jürgen Schütze (GDR)	1:07.02
1000 m Sprint	Daniel Morelon (FRA)		John Michael Nicholson (AUS)		Omar Phakadze (URS)	
2000 m Tandem	USSR		GDR		Poland	
4000 m Individual Pursuit	Knut Knudsen (NOR)	4:45.74	Xaver Kurmann (SUI)	4:51.96	Hans Lutz (FRG)	4:50.80
4000 m Team Pursuit	FRG	4:22.14	GDR	4:25.25	Great Britain	4:23.78
Equestrianism						
Three-Day Event	Richard Meade (GBR)	57.73	Alessandro Argenton (ITA)	43.33	Jan Jönsson (SWE)	39.67
Three-Day Event - Teams	Great Britain	95.53	USA	10.81	FRG	18.00
Grand Prix (Dressage)	Liselott Linsenhoff (FRG)	1229	Elena Petruchkova (URS)	1185	Josef Neckermann (FRG)	1177
Grand Prix (Dressage) Team	USSR	5095	FRG	5083	Sweden	4849
Grand Prix (Jumping)	Graziano Mancinelli (ITA)	8/0	Ann Moore (GBR)	8/3	Neal Shapiro (USA)	8/8
Grand Prix (Jumping) Team	FRG	32.00	USA	32.25	Italy	48.00
Shooting						
Free Rifle (3 Positions)	Lones Wigger (USA)	1155	Boris Melnik (URS)	1155	Lajos Papp (HUN)	1149
Small-Bore Rifle (Prone)	Ho Jun Li (PRK)	599	Viktor Auer (USA)	598	Nicolae Rotaru (ROM)	598
Small-Bore Rifle (3 Positions)	John Writer (USA)	1166	Lanny Bassham (USA)	1157	Werner Lippoldt (GDR)	1153
Rapid-Fire Pistol	Jósef Zapedszki (POL)	595	Ladislav Faita (TCH)	594	Viktor Torshin (URS)	593
Free Pistol (50 m)	Ragnar Shanakar (SWE)	567	Dan Iuga (ROM)	562	Rudolf Dollinger (AUT)	560
Running Game Target	Lakov Zhelezniak (URS)	569	Helmut Bellingrodt (COL)	565	John Kynoch (GBR)	562

EVENT	GOLD		SILVER		BRONZE	
Skeet Shooting	Konrad Wirnhier (FRG)	195/25	Yevgeni Petrov (URS)	195/24	Michael Buchheim (GDR)	195/23
Trap Shooting	Angelo Scalzone (ITA)	199	Michel Carrega (FRA)	198	Silvano Basagni (ITA)	195
Archery						
Men	John William (USA)	2528	Gunnar Jarvil (SWE)	2481	Kyösti Laasonen (FIN)	2467
Women	Doreen Wilber (USA)	2424	Irena Szydlowska (POL)	2407	Emma Gapchenko (URS)	2403
Gymnastics						
Men						
Individual Combined Exercises	Sawao Kato (JPN)	114.650	Eizo Kenmotsu (JPN)	114.575	Akinori Nakayama (JPN)	114.325
Team	Japan	571.25	USSR	564.05	GDR	559.70
Parallel Bars	Sawao Kato (JPN)	19.475	Shigeru Kasamatsu (JPN)	19.375	Eizo Kenmotsu (JPN)	19.250
Floor	Nikolai Andrianov (URS)	19.175	Akinori Nakayama (JPN)	19.125	Shigeru Kasamatsu (JPN)	19.025
Horse Vault	Klaus Köste (GDR)	18.850	Viktor Klimenko (URS)	18.825	Nikolai Andrianov (URS)	18.800
Horizontal Bar	Mitsuo Tsukahara (JPN)	19.725	Sawao Kato (JPN)	19.525	Shigeru Kasamatsu (JPN)	19.450
Rings	Akinori Nakayama (JPN)	19.350	Mikhail Voronin (URS)	19.275	Mitsuo Tsukahara (JPN)	19.225
Pommel Horse	Viktor Klimenko (URS)	19.125	Sawao Kato (JPN)	19.000	Eizo Kenmotsu (JPN)	18.950
Women						
Individual Combined Exercises	Ludmila Tourischeva (URS)	77.025	Karin Janz (GDR)	76.875	Tamara Lazakovitch (URS)	76.850
Team	USSR	380.50	GDR	376.55	Hungary	368.25
Floor	Olga Korbut (URS)	19.575	Ludmila Tourischeva (URS)	19.550	Tamara Lazakovitch (URS)	19.450
Horse Vault	Karin Janz (GDR)	19.525	Erika Zuchold (GDR)	19.275	Ludmila Tourischeva (URS)	19.250
Beam	Olga Korbut (URS)	19.400	Tamara Lazakovitch (URS)	19.375	Karin Janz (GDR)	18.975
Asymmetrical Bars	Karin Janz (GDR)	19.675	Olga Korbut (URS)	19.450		
			Erika Zuchold (GDR)	19.450		
Basketball						
	USSR		USA		Cuba	
Soccer						
	Poland		Hungary		GDR★	
					USSR★	
Handball						
	Yugoslavia		Czechoslovakia		Romania	
Hockey						
	West Germany		Pakistan		India	
Volleyball						
Men	Japan		GDR		USSR	
Women	USSR		Japan		North Korea	

★ GDR and USSR declared joint bronze medalists as result was still a draw at end of extra time.

Innsbruck 1976

February 4 – February 15

Participants: 1123 / Men: 892, Women: 231, Countries: 37,
Sports: 8, Events: 37
Final Torchbearers: Christl Haas and Josef Feistmantl

Medals Table

PLACE	COUNTRY	GOLD	SILVER	BRONZE
1	USSR	13	6	8
2	GDR	7	5	7
3	USA	3	3	4
4	Norway	3	3	1
5	FRG	2	5	3

Outstanding Athletes

PLACE	NAME (NATIONALITY)	DISCIPLINE	G	S	B
1	Rosi Mittermaier (FRG)	Alpine Skiing	2	1	–
	Raisa Smetanina (URS)	Nordic Skiing	2	1	–
3	Tatyana Averina (URS)	Speed Skating	2	–	2
4	Nikolai Kruglov (URS)	Biathlon	2	–	–
	Meinhard Nehmer (GDR)	Bobsledding	2	–	–
	Bernhard Germedshausen (GDR)	Bobsledding	2	–	–

EVENT	GOLD		SILVER		BRONZE	
Alpine Skiing						
Men						
Downhill	Franz Klammer (AUT)	1:45.73	Bernhard Russi (SUI)	1:46.06	Herbert Plank (ITA)	1:46.59
Slalom	Piero Gros (ITA)	2:03.29	Gustav Thöni (ITA)	2:03.73	Willy Frommelt (LIE)	2:04.28
Giant Slalom	Heini Hemmi (SUI)	3:26.97	Ernst Good (SUI)	3:27.17	Ingemar Stenmark (SWE)	3:27.41
Women						
Downhill	Rosi Mittermaier (FRG)	1:46.16	Brigitte Toschnig (AUT)	1:46.68	Cynthia Nelson (USA)	1:47.50
Slalom	Rosi Mittermaier (FRG)	1:30.54	Claudia Giordani (ITA)	1:30.87	Hanni Wenzel (LIE)	1:32.20
Giant Slalom	Kathy Kreiner (CAN)	1:29.13	Rosi Mittermaier (FRG)	1:29.25	Danielle Debernard (FRA)	1:29.95
Nordic Skiing						
Men						
15 km Cross-Country Skiing	Nikolai Bayukov (URS)	43:58.47	Yevgeni Beliayev (URS)	44:01.10	Arto Koivisto (FIN)	44:19.25
30 km Cross-Country Skiing	Sergei Savelyev (URS)	1:30:29.38	Bill Koch (USA)	1:30:57.84	Ivan Garanin (URS)	1:31:09.29
50 km	Ivar Formo (NOR)	2:37:30.05	Gert-Dietmar Klause (GDR)	2:38:13.21	Benny Södergren (SWE)	2:39:39.21
4 x 10 km	Finland	2:07:59.72	Norway	2:09:58.36	USSR	2:10:51.46
Ski Jumping (70 m Hill)	Hans-Georg Aschenbach (GDR)	252.0	Jochen Danneberg (GDR)	246.2	Karl Schnabl (AUT)	242.0
Ski Jumping (90 m Hill)	Karl Schnabl (AUT)	234.8	Toni Innauer (AUT)	232.9	Henry Glass (GDR)	221.7
Nordic Combined	Ulrich Wehling (GDR)	423.39	Urban Hettich (FRG)	418.90	Konrad Winkler (GDR)	417.47
Women						
5 km Cross-Country Skiing	Helena Takalo (FIN)	15:48.69	Raisa Smetanina (URS)	15:49.73	Nina Baldycheva (URS)	16:12.82
10 km Cross-Country Skiing	Raisa Smetanina (URS)	30:13.41	Helena Takalo (FIN)	30:14.28	Galina Kulakova (URS)	30:38.61
4 x 5 km	USSR	1:07:49.76	Finland	1:08:36.57	DDR	1:09:57.95
Biathlon						
20 km	Nikolai Kruglov (URS)	1:14:12.26	Heikki Ikola (FIN)	1:15:54.10	Alexander Elizarov (URS)	1:16:05.57
4 x 7.5 km	USSR	1:57:55.64	Finland	2:01:45.58	GDR	2:04:08.61
Figure Skating						
Women	Dorothy Hamill (USA)		Dianna de Leeuw (HOL)		Christine Errath (GDR)	
Men	John Curry (GBR)		Vladimir Kovalev (URS)		Toller Cranston (CAN)	
Pairs	Irina Rodnina/Alexander Zaitsev (URS)		Romy Kerner/Rolf Österreich (GDR)		Manuela Gross/Uwe Kagelmann (GDR)	
Ice Dance	Ludmilla Pakhomova/ Alexander Gorshkov (URS)		Irina Moiseyeva/ Andrei Minenko (URS)		Collen O'Connor/James Millns (USA)	
Speed Skating						
Men						
500 m	Yevgeni Kulikov (URS)	39.17	Valeri Muratov (URS)	39.25	Daniel Immerfall (USA)	39.54
1000 m	Peter Mueller (USA)	1:19.32	Jörn Didriksen (NOR)	1:20.45	Valeri Muratov (URS)	1:20.57
1500 m	Jan Egil Storholt (NOR)	1:59.38	Yuri Kondakov (URS)	1:59.97	Hans van Helden (HOL)	2:00.87
5000 m	Sten Stensen (NOR)	7:24.28	Piet Kleine (HOL)	7:26.47	Hans van Helden (HOL)	7:26.54
10,000 m	Piet Kleine (HOL)	14:50.59	Sten Stensen (NOR)	14:53.30	Hans van Helden (HOL)	15:02.02
Women						
500 m	Sheila Young (USA)	42.76	Cathy Priestner (CAN)	43.12	Tatyana Averina (URS)	43.17
1000 m	Tatyana Averina (URS)	1:28.43	Leah Poulos (USA)	1:28.57	Sheila Young (USA)	1:29.14
1500 m	Galina Stepanskaya (URS)	2:16.58	Sheila Young (USA)	2:17.06	Tatyana Averina (URS)	2:17.96
3000 m	Tatyana Averina (URS)	4:45.19	Andrea Mitscherlich (GDR)	4:45.23	Lisbeth Korsmo (NOR)	4:45.24
Bobsledding						
2-Man Bob	GDR I	3:44.42	FRG I	3:44.99	Switzerland I	3:45.70
4-Man Bob	GDR I	3:40.43	Switzerland II	3:40.89	FRG I	3:41.37
Lugeing						
Men's Singles	Detlef Günther (GDR)	3:27.688	Josef Fendt (FRG)	3:28.196	Hans Rinn (GDR)	3:28.574
Women's Singles	Margit Schumann (GDR)	2:50.621	Ute Rührold (GDR)	2:50.846	Elisabeth Demleitner (FRG)	2:51.056
2-Man Luge	Hans Rinn/ Norbert Hahn (GDR)	1:25.604	Hans Brandner/ Balthasar Schwarm (FRG)	1:25.889	Rudolf Schmid/ Franz Schachner (AUT)	1:25.919
Ice Hockey						
	USSR		Czechoslovakia		FRG	

Montreal 1976

July 17 – August 1

Participants: 6028 / Men: 4781, Women: 1247, Countries: 92,
Sports: 21, Events: 198
Final Torchbearers: Sandra Henderson and Stéphane Prefontaine

Medals Table

PLACE	COUNTRY	GOLD	SILVER	BRONZE
1	USSR	49	41	35
2	GDR	40	25	25
3	USA	34	35	25
4	FRG	10	12	17
5	Japan	9	6	10

Outstanding Athletes

PLACE	NAME (NATIONALITY)	DISCIPLINE	G	S	B
1	Nikolai Andrianov (URS)	Gymnastics	4	2	1
2	Kornelia Ender (GDR)	Swimming	4	1	–
	John Naber (USA)	Swimming	4	1	–
4	Nadia Comaneci (ROM)	Gymnastics	3	1	1
5	Nelli Kim (URS)	Gymnastics	3	1	–

EVENT	GOLD		SILVER		BRONZE	
Athletics						
Men						
100 m	Hasely Crawford (TRI)	10.06	Donald Quarrie (JAM)	10.08	Valeri Borsov (URS)	10.14
200 m	Donald Quarrie (JAM)	20.23	Millard Hampton (USA)	20.29	Dwayne Evans (USA)	20.43
400 m	Alberto Juantorena (CUB)	44.26	Fred Newhouse (USA)	44.40	Herman Frazier (USA)	44.95
800 m	Alberto Juantorena (CUB)	1:43.5	Ivo van Damme (BEL)	1:43.9	Richard Wohlhuter (USA)	1:44.1
1500 m	John Walker (NZL)	3:39.2	Ivo van Damme (BEL)	3:39.3	Paul-Heinz Wellmann (FRG)	3:39.3
5000 m	Lasse Viren (FIN)	13:24.8	Dick Quax (NZL)	13:25.2	Klaus-P. Hildenbrand (FRG)	13:25.4
10,000 m	Lasse Viren (FIN)	27:44.4	Carlos Lopez (POR)	27:45.2	Brendan Foster (GBR)	27:54.9
Marathon	Waldemar Cierpinski (GDR)	2:09:55.0	Frank Shorter (USA)	2:10:45.8	Karel Lismont (BEL)	2:11:12.6
110 m Hurdles	Guy Drut (FRA)	13.30	Alejandro Casanas (CUB)	13.33	Willie Davenport (USA)	13.38
400 m Hurdles	Edwin Moses (USA)	47.64	Michael Shine (USA)	48.69	Yevgeni Gavrilenko (URS)	49.45
3000 m Steeplechase	Anders Gärderud (SWE)	8:08.0	Bronislaw Malinowski (POL)	8:09.1	Frank Baumgartl (GDR)	8:10.4
4 x 100 m	USA	38.33	GDR	38.66	USSR	38.78
4 x 400 m	USA	2:58.65	Poland	3:01.43	FRG	3:01.98
20 km Walk	Daniel Bautista (MEX)	1:24:40.6	Hans-Peter Reimann (GDR)	1:25:13.8	Peter Frenkel (GDR)	1:25:29.4
High Jump	Jacek Wszola (POL)	7'4½"	Gregory Joy (CAN)	7'3¾"	Dwight Stones (USA)	7'3"
Pole Vault	Tadeusz Slusarski (POL)	18'0½"	Antti Kalliomäki (FIN)	18'0½"	David Roberts (USA)	18'0½"
Long Jump	Arnie Robinson (USA)	27'4¾"	Randy Williams (USA)	26'7¼"	Frank Wartenberg (GDR)	26'3¾"
Triple Jump	Viktor Saneyev (URS)	56'8¾"	James Butts (USA)	56'8½"	Joao de Oliveira (BRA)	55'5½"
Shot	Udo Beyer (GDR)	69'0¾"	Yevgeni Mironov (URS)	69'0"	Alexander Baryshnikov (URS)	68'10¾"
Discus	Mac Wilkins (USA)	221'5"	Wolfgang Schmidt (GDR)	217'3"	John Powell (USA)	215'7"
Hammer	Yuri Sedykh (URS)	254'4"	Alexei Spiridonov (URS)	249'7"	Anatoli Bondarchuk (URS)	247'8"
Javelin	Miklos Nemeth (HUN)	310'4"	Hannu Siitonen (FIN)	288'5"	Gheorghe Megelea (ROM)	285'11"
Decathlon	Bruce Jenner (USA)	8617	Guido Kratschmer (FRG)	8411	Nikolai Avilov (URS)	8369
Women						
100 m	Annegret Richter (FRG)	11.08	Renate Stecher (GDR)	11.13	Inge Helten (FRG)	11.17
200 m	Bärbel Eckert (GDR)	22.37	Annegret Richter (FRG)	22.39	Renate Stecher (GDR)	22.47
400 m	Irena Szewinska (POL)	49.29	Christina Brehmer (GDR)	50.51	Ellen Streidt (GDR)	50.55
800 m	Tatyana Kazankina (URS)	1:54.9	Nikolina Shtereva (BUL)	1:55.4	Elfie Zinn (GDR)	1:55.6
1500 m	Tatyana Kazankina (URS)	4:05.5	Gunhild Hoffmeister (GDR)	4:06.0	Ulrike Klapezynski (GDR)	4:06.1
100 m Hurdles	Johanna Schaller (GDR)	12.77	Tatyana Anisimova (URS)	12.78	Natalya Lebedeva (URS)	12.80
4 x 100 m	GDR	42.55	FRG	42.59	USSR	43.09
4 x 400 m	GDR	3:19.2	USA	3:22.8	USSR	3:24.2
High Jump	Rosemarie Ackermann (GDR)	6'4"	Sara Simeoni (ITA)	6'3¼"	Yordanka Blagoyeva (BUL)	6'3¼"
Long Jump	Angela Voigt (GDR)	22'0¾"	Kathy McMillan (USA)	21'10¼"	Lidia Alfeyeva (URS)	21'8"
Shot	Ivanka Khristova (BUL)	69'5¼"	Nadyezhda Chizhova (URS)	68'9¼"	Helena Fibingerová (TCH)	67'9¼"
Discus	Evelin Schlaak (GDR)	226'4"	Maria Vergova (BUL)	220'9"	Gabriele Hinzmann (GDR)	219'3"
Javelin	Ruth Fuchs (GDR)	209'7"	Marion Becker (FRG)	212'3"	Kathy Schmidt (USA)	209'10"
Pentathlon	Siegrun Siegl (GDR)	4745	Christine Laser (GDR)	4745	Burglinde Pollak (GDR)	4740
Swimming						
Men						
100 m Freestyle	Jim Montgomery (USA)	49.99	Jack Babashoff (USA)	50.81	Peter Nocke (FRG)	51.31
200 m Freestyle	Bruce Furniss (USA)	1:50.29	John Naber (USA)	1:50.50	Jim Montgomery (USA)	1:50.58
400 m Freestyle	Brian Goodell (USA)	3:51.93	Tim Shaw (USA)	3:52.54	Vladimir Raskatov (URS)	3:55.76
1500 m Freestyle	Brian Goodell (USA)	15:02.40	Bobby Hackett (USA)	15:03.91	Stephen Holland (AUS)	15:04.66
100 m Backstroke	John Naber (USA)	55.49	Peter Rocca (USA)	56.34	Roland Matthes (GDR)	57.22
200 m Backstroke	John Naber (USA)	1:59.19	Peter Rocca (USA)	2:00.55	Dan Harrigan (USA)	2:01.35
100 m Breaststroke	John Hencken (USA)	1:03.11	David Wilkie (GBR)	1:03.43	Arvidas Iuozaytis (URS)	1:04.23

EVENT	GOLD		SILVER		BRONZE	
200 m Breaststroke	David Wilkie (GBR)	2:15.11	John Hencken (USA)	2:17.26	Richard Colella (USA)	2:19.20
100 m Butterfly	Matt Vogel (USA)	54.35	Joe Bottom (USA)	54.50	Gary Hall (USA)	54.65
200 m Butterfly	Mike Bruner (USA)	1:59.23	Steven Gregg (USA)	1:59.54	Bill Forrester (USA)	1:59.96
400 m Medley	Rod Strachan (USA)	4:23.68	Alexander McKee (USA)	4:24.62	Andrei Smirnov (URS)	4:26.90
4 x 200 m Freestyle	USA	7:23.22	USSR	7:27.97	Great Britain	7:32.11
4 x 100 m Medley	USA	3:42.22	Canada	3:45.94	FRG	3:47.29
Springboard Diving	Phil Boggs (USA)	619.05	Franco Cagnotto (ITA)	570.48	Alexander Kosenkov (URS)	567.24
Highboard Diving	Klaus Dibiasi (ITA)	600.51	Greg Louganis (USA)	576.99	Vladimir Aleynik (URS)	548.61
Water Polo	Hungary		Italy		Netherlands	
Women						
100 m Freestyle	Kornelia Ender (GDR)	55.65	Petra Priemer (GDR)	56.49	Enith Brigitha (HOL)	56.65
200 m Freestyle	Kornelia Ender (GDR)	1:59.26	Shirley Babashoff (USA)	2:01.22	Enith Brigitha (HOL)	2:01.40
400 m Freestyle	Petra Thümer (GDR)	4:09.89	Shirley Babashoff (USA)	4:10.46	Shannon Smith (CAN)	4:14.60
800 m Freestyle	Petra Thümer (GDR)	8:37.14	Shirley Babashoff (USA)	8:37.59	Wendy Weinberg (USA)	8:42.60
100 m Backstroke	Ulrike Richter (GDR)	1:01.83	Birgit Treiber (GDR)	1:03.41	Nancy Garapick (CAN)	1:03.71
200 m Backstroke	Ulrike Richter (GDR)	2:13.43	Birgit Treiber (GDR)	2:14.97	Nancy Garapick (CAN)	2:15.60
100 m Breaststroke	Hannelore Anke (GDR)	1:11.16	Lubov Rusanova (URS)	1:13.04	Marina Kosheveya (URS)	1:13.30
200 m Breaststroke	Marina Kosheveya (URS)	2:33.35	Marina Yurchenia (URS)	2:36.08	Lubov Rusanova (URS)	2:36.22
100 m Butterfly	Kornelia Ender (GDR)	1:00.13	Andrea Pollack (GDR)	1:00.98	Wendy Boglioli (USA)	1:01.17
200 m Butterfly	Andrea Pollack (GDR)	2:11.41	Ulrike Tauber (GDR)	2:12.50	Rosemarie Gabriel (GDR)	2:12.86
400 m Medley	Ulrike Tauber (GDR)	4:42.77	Cheryl Gibson (CAN)	4:48.10	Becky Smith (CAN)	4:50.48
4 x 100 m Freestyle	USA	3:44.82	GDR	3:45.50	Canada	3:48.81
4 x 100 m Medley	GDR	4:07.95	USA	4:14.55	Canada	4:15.22
Springboard Diving	Jennifer Chandler (USA)	506.19	Christa Köhler (GDR)	469.41	Cynthia McIngvale (USA)	466.83
Highboard Diving	Elena Vaytsekhovskaya (URS)	406.59	Ulrika Knape (SWE)	402.60	Deborah Wilson (USA)	401.07
Boxing						
Light-Flyweight (- 105¾ lbs)	Jorge Hernandez (CUB)		Byong Uk Li (PRK)		Payao Pooltarat (THA)	
					Orlando Maldonado (PUR)	
Flyweight (- 112½ lbs)	Leo Randolph (USA)		Ramon Duvalon (CUB)		David Torosyan (URS)	
					Leszek Blazynski (POL)	
Bantamweight (- 119 lbs)	Yong Jo Gu (PRK)		Charles Mooney (USA)		Patrick Cowdell (GBR)	
					Hwang Chulsoon (KOR)	
Featherweight (- 126 lbs)	Angel Herrera (CUB)		Richard Nowakowski (GDR)		Leszek Kosedowski (POL)	
					Juan Paredes (MEX)	
Lightweight (- 132 lbs)	Howard Davis (USA)		Simion Cutov (ROM)		Vasili Solomin (URS)	
					Ace Rusevski (YUG)	
Light-Welterweight (- 140 lbs)	Sugar Ray Leonard (USA)		Andres Aldama (CUB)		Vladimir Kolev (BUL)	
					Kacimierz Szcerba (POL)	
Welterweight (- 148 lbs)	Jochen Bachfeld (GDR)		Pedro Gamarro (VEN)		Reinhard Skricek (FRG)	
					Victor Zilberman (ROM)	
Light-Middleweight (- 157 lbs)	Jerzy Rybicki (POL)		Tadija Kacar (YUG)		Viktor Savchenko (URS)	
					Rolando Garbey (CUB)	
Middleweight (- 165 lbs)	Michael Spinks (USA)		Rufat Riskiev (URS)		Alec Nastac (ROM)	
					Luis Martinez (CUB)	
Light-Heavyweight (- 178½ lbs)	Leon Spinks (USA)		Sixto Soria (CUB)		Costica Danifoiu (ROM)	
					Janusz Gortat (POL)	
Heavyweight (+ 178½ lbs)	Teofilo Stevenson (CUB)		Mircea Simon (ROM)		Johnny Tate (USA)	
					Clarence Hill (BER)	
Weightlifting						
Flyweight (- 114¾ lbs)	Alexander Voronin (URS)	242.5	György Koszegi (HUN)	237.5	Mohammed Nassiri (IRN)	235.0
Bantamweight (- 123½ lbs)	Norair Nurikyan (BUL)	262.5	Grzegorz Cziura (POL)	252.5	Kenkichi Ando (JPN)	250.0
Featherweight (- 132¼ lbs)	Nikolai Kolesnikov (URS)	285.0	Georgi Todorov (BUL)	280.0	Kazumasa Hirai (JPN)	275.0
Lightweight (- 148¾ lbs)	Pyotr Korol (URS)	305.0	Daniel Senet (FRA)	300.0	Kazimierz Czarnicki (POL)	295.0
Middleweight (- 165½ lbs)	Yordan Mitkov (BUL)	335.0	Vartan Militosyan (URS)	330.0	Peter Wenzel (GDR)	327.5
Light-Heavyweight (- 182 lbs)	Valeri Shari (URS)	365.0	Trendachil Stoichev (BUL)	360.0	Peter Baczako (HUN)	345.0
Middle-Heavyweight (- 198½ lbs)	David Rigert (URS)	382.5	Lee James (USA)	362.5	Atanas Chopov (BUL)	360.0
Heavyweight (+ 198½ lbs)	Yuri Zaitsev (URS)	385.0	Krastio Semerdiev (BUL)	385.0	Tadeusz Rutkowski (POL)	377.5
Super-Heavyweight (+ 247⅓ lbs)	Vasili Alexeyev (URS)	440.0	Gerd Bonk (GDR)	405.0	Helmut Losch (GDR)	387.5
Greco-Roman Wrestling						
Light-Flyweight (- 105¾ lbs)	Alexei Shumakov (URS)		Gheorge Berceanu (ROM)		Stefan Anghelov (BUL)	
Flyweight (- 114½ lbs)	Vitali Konstantinov (URS)		Nicu Ginga (ROM)		Koichiro Hirayama (JPN)	
Bantamweight (- 125¾ lbs)	Pertti Ukkola (FIN)		Ivan Frgic (YUG)		Farhat Mustafin (URS)	
Featherweight (- 136½ lbs)	Kazimierz Lipien (POL)		Nelson Davidian (URS)		Laszlo Reczi (HUN)	
Lightweight (- 149¾ lbs)	Suren Nalbandyan (URS)		Stefan Rusu (ROM)		Heinz-Helmut Wehling (GDR)	

EVENT	GOLD		SILVER		BRONZE	
Welterweight (- 163 lbs)	Anatoli Bykov (URS)		Vitezslav Macha (TCH)		Karl-Heinz Helbing (FRG)	
Middleweight (- 180¹/₄ lbs)	Momir Petkovic (YUG)		Vladimir Cheboksarov (URS)		Ivan Kolev (BUL)	
Light-Heavyweight (- 198¹/₄ lbs)	Valeri Rezanzev (URS)		Stoyan Nikolov (BUL)		Czeslaw Kwiecinski (POL)	
Heavyweight (- 220¹/₄ lbs)	Nikolai Bolboshin (URS)		Kamen Goranov (BUL)		Andrzej Skrzylewski (POL)	
Super-Heavyweight (+ 220¹/₄ lbs)	Alexander Kolchinski (URS)		Alexander Tomov (BUL)		Roman Codreanu (ROM)	
Freestyle Wrestling						
Light-Flyweight (- 105¹/₄ lbs)	Khassan Issayev (BUL)		Roman Dmitriev (URS)		Akira Kudo (JPN)	
Flyweight (- 114¹/₂ lbs)	Yuji Takada (JPN)		Alexander Ivanov (URS)		Hae Sup Jeon (KOR)	
Bantamweight (- 125¹/₄ lbs)	Vladimir Umin (URS)		Hans-Dieter Bruchert (GDR)		Masao Arai (JPN)	
Featherweight (- 136¹/₂ lbs)	Jung Mo Yang (KOR)		Zeveg Oidov (MGL)		Gene Davis (USA)	
Lightweight (- 149¹/₄ lbs)	Pavel Pinigin (URS)		Lloyd Keaser (USA)		Yasaburo Sugawara (JPN)	
Welterweight (- 163 lbs)	Jiichiro Date (JPN)		Mansour Barzegar (IRN)		Stanley Dziedzic (USA)	
Middleweight (- 180¹/₄ lbs)	John Peterson (USA)		Viktor Novoshilev (URS)		Adolf Seger (FRG)	
Light-Heavyweight (- 198¹/₄ lbs)	Levan Tediashvili (URS)		Benjamin Peterson (USA)		Stelica Morcov (ROM)	
Heavyweight (- 220¹/₄ lbs)	Ivan Yarygin (URS)		Russell Hellickson (USA)		Dimo Kostov (BUL)	
Super-Heavyweight (+ 220¹/₄ lbs)	Soslan Andyev (URS)		Jószef Balla (HUN)		Ladislav Simon (ROM)	
Judo						
Lightweight (- 138³/₄ lbs)	Hector Rodriguez (CUB)		Chang Eun-Kyung (KOR)		Jozsef Tuncsik (HUN)	
					Felice Mariani (ITA)	
Welterweight (- 154¹/₄ lbs)	Vladimir Nevzorov (URS)		Koji Kuramoto (JPN)		Patrick Vial (FRA)	
					Marian Talaj (POL)	
Middleweight (- 176¹/₄ lbs)	Isamu Sonoda (JPN)		Valeri Dvoinikov (URS)		Slavko Obadov (YUG)	
					Park Yung-Chul (KOR)	
Light-Heavyweight (- 205 lbs)	Kazuhiro Ninomiya (JPN)		Ramaz Harshiladze (URS)		David Starbrook (GBR)	
					Jörg Röthlisberger (SUI)	
Heavyweight (+ 205 lbs)	Sergei Novikov (URS)		Günther Neureuther (FRG)		Allen Coage (USA)	
					Sumio Endo (JPN)	
Open Class	Haruki Uemura (JPN)		Keith Remfry (GBR)		Jeaki Cho (KOR)	
					Shota Chochoshvili (URS)	
Fencing						
Individual Foil – Men	Fabio dal Zotto (ITA)	4	Alexander Romankov (URS)	4	Bernard Talvard (FRA)	3
Team Foil – Men	FRG		Italy		France	
Individual Épée	Alexander Pusch (FRG)	3/2	Jürgen Hehn (FRG)	3/1	Gyözö Kulcsár (HUN)	3/0
Team Épée	Sweden		FRG		Switzerland	
Individual Saber	Viktor Krovopouskov (URS)	5	Vladimir Nazlimov (URS)	4	Viktor Sidjak (URS)	3
Team Saber	USSR		Italy		Romania	
Individual Foil – Women	Ildiko Schwarczenberger (HUN)	4/1	Maria Consolata Collino (ITA)	4/0	Elena Belova (URS)	3
Team Foil – Women	USSR		France		Hungary	
Modern Pentathlon						
Individual	Janusz Pyciak-Peciak (POL)	5520	Pavel Lednev (URS)	5485	Jan Bartu (TCH)	5466
Team	Great Britain	15559	Czechoslovakia	15451	Hungary	15395
Canoeing						
Men						
500 m Kayak Singles K1	Vasile Diba (ROM)	1:46.11	Zoltan Sztanity (HUN)	1:46.95	Rüdiger Helm (GDR)	1:48.30
1000 m Kayak Singles K1	Rüdiger Helm (GDR)	3:48.20	Geza Csapó (HUN)	3:48.34	Vasile Diba (ROM)	3:49.65
500 m Kayak Pairs K2	GDR	1:35.87	USSR	1:36.81	Romania	1:37.43
1000 m Kayak Pairs K2	USSR	3:29.01	GDR	3:29.33	Hungary	3:30.36
1000 m Kayak Fours K4	USSR	3:08.69	Spain	3:08.95	GDR	3:10.76
500 m Canadian Singles C1	Alexander Rogov (URS)	1:59.23	John Wood (CAN)	1:59.58	Matja Ljubek (YUG)	1:59.60
1000 m Canadian Singles C1	Matja Ljubek (YUG)	4:09.51	Vasili Urchenko (URS)	4:12.57	Tamás Wichmann (HUN)	4:14.11
500 m Canadian Pairs C2	USSR	1:45.81	Poland	1:47.77	Hungary	1:48.35
1000 m Canadian Pairs C 2	USSR	3:52.76	Romania	3:54.28	Hungary	3:55.66
Women						
500 m Kayak Singles K1	Carola Zirzow (GDR)	2:01.05	Tatyana Korshunova (URS)	2:03.07	Klara Rajnai (HUN)	2:05.01
500m Kayak Pairs K2	USSR	1:51.15	Hungary	1:51.69	GDR	1:51.81
Rowing						
Men						
Single Sculls	Pertti Karppinen (FIN)	7:29.03	Peter-Michael Kolbe (FRG)	7:31.67	Joachim Dreifke (GDR)	7:38.03
Doubles Sculls	Norway	7:13.20	Great Britain	7:15.25	GDR	7:17.45
Coxless Pairs	GDR	7:23.31	USA	7:26.73	FRG	7:30.03

EVENT	GOLD		SILVER		BRONZE	
Coxed Pairs	GDR	7:58.99	USSR	8:01.82	Czechoslovakia	8:03.28
Coxless Quadruple Sculls	GDR	6:18.65	USSR	6:19.89	Czechoslovakia	6:21.77
Coxless Fours	GDR	6:37.42	Norway	6:41.22	USSR	6:42.52
Coxed Fours	USSR	6:40.22	GDR	6:42.70	FRG	6:46.96
Coxed Eights	GDR	5:58.29	Great Britain	6:00.82	New Zealand	6:03.51
Women						
Single Sculls	Christina Scheiblich (GDR)	4:05.56	Joan Lind (USA)	4:06.21	Elena Antonova (URS)	4:10.24
Double Sculls	Bulgaria	3:44.36	GDR	3:47.86	USSR	3:49.93
Coxless Pairs	Bulgaria	4:01.22	GDR	4:01.61	FRG	4:02.35
Coxed Quadruple Sculls	GDR	3:29.99	USSR	3:32.49	Romania	3:32.76
Coxed Fours	GDR	3:45.08	Bulgaria	3:48.24	USSR	3:49.38
Coxed Eights	GDR	3:33.32	USSR	3:36.17	USA	3:38.68
Yachting						
Finn Class	Jochen Schümann (GDR)	35.4	Andrei Balashov (URS)	39.7	John Bertrand (AUS)	46.4
International Tempest	Sweden	14.0	USSR	30.4	USA	32.7
Flying Dutchman	FRG	34.7	Great Britain	51.7	Brazil	52.1
International Tornado	Great Britain	18.0	USA	36.0	FRG	37.7
International 470	FRG	42.4	Spain	49.7	Australia	57.0
International Soling	Denmark	46.7	USA	47.4	GDR	47.4
Cycling						
Individual Road Race (108¼ mi)	Bernt Johansson (SWE)	4:46:52	Giuseppe Martinelli (ITA)	4:47:23	Mieczyl Nowicki (POL)	4:47:23
100 km Road Team Time Trial	USSR	2:08:53	Poland	2:09:13	Denmark	2:12:20
1000 m Time Trial	Klaus-Jürgen Grünke (GDR)	1:05.927	Michel Vaarten (BEL)	1:07.516	Niels Fredborg (DEN)	1:07.617
1000 m Sprint	Anton Tkac (TCH)		Daniel Morelon (FRA)		Hans-Jürgen Geschke (GDR)	
4000 m Individual Pursuit	Gregor Braun (FRG)	4:47.61	Herman Ponsteen (HOL)	4:49.72	Thomas Huschke (GDR)	4:52.71
4000 m Team Pursuit	FRG	4:21.06	USSR	4:27.15	Great Britain	4:22.41
Equestrianism						
Three-Day Event	Edmund Coffin (USA)	114.99	John Plumb (USA)	125.85	Karl Schultz (FRG)	129.45
Three-Day Event, Team	USA	441.00	FRG	584.60	Australia	599.54
Grand Prix (Dressage)	Christine Stückelberger (SUI)	1486	Harry Boldt (FRG)	1435	Reiner Klimke (FRG)	1395
Grand Prix (Dressage) Team	FRG	5155	Switzerland	4684	USA	4670
Grand Prix (Jumping)	Alwin Schockemöhle (FRG)	0	Michel Vaillancourt (CAN)	12/4	François Mathy (BEL)	12/8
Grand Prix (Jumping) Team	France	40	FRG	44	Belgium	63
Shooting						
Small-Bore Rifle (Prone)	Karlheinz Smieszek (FRG)	599	Ulrich Lind (FRG)	597	Gennadi Lushchikov (URS)	595
Small-Bore Rifle (3 Positions)	Lanny Bassham (USA)	1162	Margaret Murdock (USA)	1162	Werner Seibold (FRG)	1160
Rapid-Fire Pistol	Norbert Klaar (GDR)	597	Jürgen Wiefel (GDR)	596	Roberto Ferraris (ITA)	595
Free Pistol (50 m)	Uwe Potteck (GDR)	573	Harald Vollmar (GDR)	567	Rudolf Dollinger (AUT)	562
Running Game Target	Alexander Gasov (URS)	579	Alexander Kedyarov (URS)	576	Jerzy Greszkiewicz (POL)	571
Skeet Shooting	Josef Panacek (TCH)	198	Eric Swinkels (HOL)	198	Wieslaw Gawlikowski (POL)	196
Trap Shooting	Donald Haldeman (USA)	190	Armando Silva Marques (POR)	189	Ubaldesco Baldi (ITA)	189
Archery						
Women	Luann Ryan (USA)	2499	Valentina Kovpan (URS)	2460	Zebiniso Rustamova (URS)	2407
Men	Darrell Pace (USA)	2571	Hiroshi Michinaga (JPN)	2502	Giancarlo Ferrari (ITA)	2495
Gymnastics						
Men						
Individual Combined Exercises	Nikolai Andrianov (URS)	116.650	Sawao Kato (JPN)	115.650	Mitsuo Tsukahara (JPN)	115.575
Team	Japan	576.85	USSR	576.45	GDR	564.65
Parallel Bars	Sawao Kato (JPN)	19.675	Nikolai Andrianov (URS)	19.500	Mitsuo Tsukahara (JPN)	19.475
Floor	Nikolai Andrianov (URS)	19.450	Vladimir Marchenko (URS)	19.425	Peter Korman (USA)	19.300
Horse Vault	Nikolai Andrianov (URS)	19.450	Mitsuo Tsukahara (JPN)	19.375	Hiroshi Kajiyama (JPN)	19.275
Horizontal Bar	Mitsuo Tsukahara (JPN)	19.675	Eizo Kenmotsu (JPN)	19.500	Henri Boerio (FRA)	19.475
					Eberhard Gienger (FRG)	19.475
Rings	Nikolai Andrianov (URS)	19.650	Alexander Ditiatin (URS)	19.550	Dan Grecu (ROM)	19.500
Pommel Horse	Zoltan Magyar (HUN)	19.700	Eizo Kenmotsu (JPN)	19.575	Nikolai Andrianov (URS)	19.525
Women						
Individual Combined Exercises	Nadia Comaneci (ROM)	79.275	Nelli Kim (URS)	78.675	Ludmila Tourischeva (URS)	78.625
Team	USSR	390.35	Romania	387.15	GDR	385.10
Floor	Nelli Kim (URS)	19.850	Ludmila Tourischeva (URS)	19.825	Nadia Comaneci (ROM)	19.750
Horse Vault	Nelli Kim (URS)	19.800	Carola Dombeck (GDR)	19.650		
			Ludmila Tourischeva (URS)	19.650		
Beam	Nadia Comaneci (ROM)	19.950	Olga Korbut (URS)	19.725	Teodora Ungureanu (ROM)	19.700

EVENT	GOLD		SILVER		BRONZE	
Asymmetrical Bars	Nadia Comaneci (ROM)	20.000	Teodora Ungureanu (ROM)	19.800	Marta Egervari (HUN)	19.775
Team Gymnastics	Sweden	74.20	USSR	73.00	Poland	74.00
Basketball						
Men	USA		Yugoslavia		USSR	
Women	USSR		USA		Bulgaria	
Soccer						
	GDR		Poland		USSR	
Handball						
Men	USSR		Romania		Poland	
Women	USSR		GDR		Hungary	
Hockey						
	New Zealand		Australia		Pakistan	
Volleyball						
Men	Poland		USSR		Cuba	
Women	Japan		USSR		South Korea	

Lake Placid 1980

Participants: 1072 / Men: 839, Women: 233, Countries: 37,
Sports: 8, Events: 38
Final Torchbearer: Charles Morgan Kerr

February 12 – February 24
(Official Opening Ceremony
February 13)

Medals Table

PLACE	COUNTRY	GOLD	SILVER	BRONZE
1	USSR	10	6	6
2	GDR	9	7	7
3	USA	6	4	2
4	Austria	3	2	2
5	Sweden	3	–	1

Outstanding Athletes

PLACE	NAME (NATIONALITY)	DISCIPLINE	G	S	B
1	Eric Heiden (USA)	Speed Skating	5	–	–
2	Nikolai Simyatov (URS)	Nordic Skiing	3	–	–
3	Hanni Wenzel (LIE)	Alpine Skiing	2	1	–
4	Anatoli Alyiabiev (URS)	Biathlon	2	–	1
5	Barbara Petzold (GDR)	Nordic Skiing	2	–	–
	Ingemar Stenmark (SWE)	Alpine Skiing	2	–	–

EVENT	GOLD		SILVER		BRONZE	
Alpine Skiing						
Men						
Downhill	Leonhard Stock (AUT)	1:45.50	Peter Wirnsberger (AUT)	1:46.12	Steve Podborski (CAN)	1:46.62
Slalom	Ingemar Stenmark (SWE)	1:44.26	Phil Mahre (USA)	1:44.76	Jacques Luthy (SUI)	1:45.06
Giant Slalom	Ingemar Stenmark (SWE)	2:40.74	Andreas Wenzel (LIE)	2:41.49	Hans Enn (AUT)	2:42.51
Women						
Downhill	Annemarie Moser-Pröll (AUT)	1:37.52	Hanni Wenzel (LIE)	1:38.22	Marie-Theres Nadig (SUI)	1:38.36
Slalom	Hanni Wenzel (LIE)	1:25.09	Christa Kinshofer (FRG)	1:26.50	Erika Hess (SUI)	1:27.89
Giant Slalom	Hanni Wenzel (LIE)	2:41.66	Irene Epple (FRG)	2:42.12	Perrine Pelen (FRA)	2:42.41
Nordic Skiing						
Men						
15 km Cross-Country Skiing	Thomas Wassberg (NOR)	41:57.63	Juha Mieto (FIN)	41:57.64	Ove Aunli (NOR)	42:28.62
30 km Cross-Country Skiing	Nikolai Simyatov (URS)	1:27:02.80	Vasili Rochev (URS)	1:27:34.22	Ivan Lebanov (BUL)	1:28:03.87
50 km Cross-Country Skiing	Nikolai Simyatov (URS)	2:27:24.60	Juha Mieto (FIN)	2:30:20.52	Alexander Savyalov (URS)	2:30:51.52
4 x 10 km	USSR	1:57:03.46	Norway	1:58:45.77	Finland	2:00:00.18
Ski Jumping (70 m Hill)	Toni Innauer (AUT)	266.3	Manfred Deckert (GDR)	249.2		
			Hirokazu Yagi (JPN)	249.2		
Ski Jumping (90 m Hill)	Jouko Törmänen (FIN)	271.0	Hubert Neuper (AUT)	262.4	Jari Puikkonen (FIN)	248.5
Nordic Combined	Ulrich Wehling (GDR)	432.20	Juuko Karjalainen (FIN)	429.50	Konrad Winkler (GDR)	425.32

EVENT	GOLD		SILVER		BRONZE	
Women						
5 km Cross-Country Skiing	Raisa Smetanina (URS)	15:06.92	Hikka Riihivuori (FIN)	15:11.96	Kvéta Jeriová (TCH)	15:23.44
10 km Cross-Country Skiing	Barbara Petzold (GDR)	30:31.54	Hikka Riihivuori (FIN)	30:35.05	Helena Takalo (FIN)	30:45.25
4 x 5 km	GDR	1:02:11.10	USSR	1:03:18.30	Norway	1:04:13.50
Biathlon						
10 km	Frank Ullrich (GDR)	32:10.69	Vladimir Alikin (URS)	32:53.10	Anatoli Alyabiev (URS)	33:09.16
20 km	Anatoli Alyabiev (URS)	1:08:16.31	Frank Ullrich (GDR)	1:08:27.79	Eberhard Rösch (GDR)	1:11:11.73
4 x 7.5 km	USSR	1:34:03.27	GDR	1:34:56.99	FRG	1:37:30.26
Figure Skating						
Women	Anett Pötzsch (GDR)		Linda Fratianne (USA)		Dagmar Lurz (FRG)	
Men	Robin Cousins (GBR)		Jan Hoffmann (GDR)		Charles Tickner (USA)	
Pairs	Irina Rodnina/		Marina Cherkassova/		Manuela Mager/	
	Alexander Zaitsev (URS)		Sergei Shakhray (URS)		Uwe Bewersdorff (GDR)	
Ice Dance	Natalya Linichuk/		Krisztina Regoczy/		Irina Moisseyeva/	
	Gennadi Karponosov (URS)		András Sallay (HUN)		Andrei Minenkov (URS)	
Speed Skating						
Men						
500 m	Eric Heiden (USA)	38.03	Yevgeni Kulikov (URS)	38.37	Lieuwe de Boer (HOL)	38.48
1000 m	Eric Heiden (USA)	1:15.18	Gaetan Boucher (CAN)	1:16.68	Frode Ronning (NOR)	1:16.91
					Vladimir Lobanov (URS)	1:16.91
1500 m	Eric Heiden (USA)	1:55.44	Kai Arne Stenshjemmet (NOR)	1:56.81	Jerje Andersen (NOR)	1:56.92
5000 m	Eric Heiden (USA)	7:02.29	Kai Arne Stenshjemmet (NOR)	7:03.28	Tom Erik Oxholm (NOR)	7:05.59
10,000 m	Eric Heiden (USA)	14:28.13	Piet Kleine (HOL)	14:36.03	Tom Erik Oxholm (NOR)	14:36.60
Women						
500 m	Karin Enke (GDR)	41.78	Leah Poulos-Mueller (USA)	42.26	Natalya Petruseva (URS)	42.42
1000 m	Natalya Petruseva (URS)	1:24.10	Leah Poulos-Mueller (USA)	1:25.41	Silvia Albrecht (GDR)	1:26.46
1500 m	Annie Borckink (HOL)	2:10.95	Ria Visser (HOL)	2:12.35	Sabine Becker (GDR)	2:12.38
3000 m	Björg Eva Jensen (NOR)	4:32.13	Sabine Becker (GDR)	4:32.79	Elisabeth Heiden (USA)	4:33.77
Bobsledding						
2-Man Bob	Switzerland II	4:09.36	GDR II	4:10.89	GDR I	4:11.08
4-Man Bob	GDR I	3:59.92	Switzerland I	4:00.87	GDR II	4:00.97
Lugeing						
Men's Singles	Bernhard Glass (GDR)	2:54.796	Paul Hildgartner (ITA)	2:55.372	Anton Winkler (FRG)	2:56.545
Women's Singles	Vera Sosulya (URS)	2:36.537	Melitta Sollmann (GDR)	2:37.657	Ingrida Amantova (URS)	2:37.817
2-Man Luge	Hans Rinn/		Peter Gschnitzer/		Georg Fluckinger/	
	Norbert Hahn (GDR)	1:19.331	Karl Brunner (ITA)	1:19.606	Karl Schrott (AUT)	1:19.795
Ice Hockey						
	USA		USSR		Sweden	

Moscow 1980

July 19 – August 3

Participants: 5217 / Men: 4043, Women: 1124, Countries: 80,
Sports: 21, Events: 204
Final Torchbearer: Sergey Belov

Medals Table

PLACE	COUNTRY	GOLD	SILVER	BRONZE
1	USSR	80	69	46
2	GDR	47	37	42
3	Bulgaria	8	16	17
4	Cuba	8	7	5
5	Italy	8	3	4

Outstanding Athletes

PLACE	NAME (NATIONALITY)	DISCIPLINE	G	S	B
1	Alexander Ditiatin (URS)	Gymnastics	3	4	1
2	Caren Metschuk (GDR)	Swimming	3	1	–
3	Barbara Krause (GDR)	Swimming	3	–	–
	Rica Reinisch (GDR)	Swimming	3	–	–
	Vladimir Salnikov (URS)	Swimming	3	–	–
	Vladimir Parfenovich (URS)	Canoeing	3	–	–

EVENT	GOLD		SILVER		BRONZE	
Athletics						
Men						
100 m	Allan Wells (GBR)	10.25	Silvio Leonard (CUB)	10.25	Petr Petrov (BUL)	10.39
200 m	Pietro Mennea (ITA)	20.19	Allan Wells (GBR)	20.21	Donald Quarrie (JAM)	20.29
400 m	Viktor Markin (URS)	44.60	Richard Mitchell (AUS)	44.84	Frank Schaffer (GDR)	44.87
800 m	Steve Ovett (GBR)	1:45.4	Sebastian Coe (GBR)	1:45.9	Nikolai Kirov (URS)	1:46.0
1500 m	Sebastian Coe (GBR)	3:38.4	Jürgen Straub (GDR)	3:38.8	Steve Ovett (GBR)	3:39.0
5000 m	Miruts Yifter (ETH)	13:21.0	Suleiman Nyambui (TAN)	13:21.6	Kaarlo Maaninka (FIN)	13:22.0
10,000 m	Miruts Yifter (ETH)	27:42.7	Kaarlo Maaninka (FIN)	27:44.3	Mohammed Kedir (ETH)	27:44.7
Marathon	Waldemar Cierpinski (GDR)	2:11:03	Gerard Nijboer (HOL)	2:11:20	Sat. Dzhumanazarov (URS)	2:11:35
110 m Hurdles	Thomas Munkelt (GDR)	13.39	Alejandro Casanas (CUB)	13.40	Alexander Puchkov (URS)	13.44
400 m Hurdles	Volker Beck (GDR)	48.70	Vasili Arkhipenko (URS)	48.86	Gary Oakes (GBR)	49.11
3000 m Steeplechase	Bronislaw Malinowski (POL)	8:09.7	Filbert Bayi (TAN)	8:12.5	Eshetu Tura (ETH)	8:13.6
4 x 100 m	USSR	38.26	Poland	38.33	France	38.53
4 x 400 m	USSR	3:01.1	GDR	3:01.3	Italy	3:04.3
20 km Walk	Maurizio Damilano (ITA)	1:23:35.5	Pyotr Pochenchuk (URS)	1:24:45.4	Roland Wieser (GDR)	1:25:58.2
50 km Walk	Hartwig Gander (GDR)	3:49:24	Jorge Llopart (ESP)	3:51:25	Yevgeni Ivchenko (URS)	3:56:32
High Jump	Gerd Wessig (GDR)	7'8¾"	Jacek Wszola (POL)	7'7"	Jörg Freimuth (GDR)	7'7"
Pole Vault	Wladislaw Kozakiewicz (POL)	18'11½"	Konstantin Volkov (URS)	18'6½"		
			Tadeusz Slusarski (POL)	18'6½"		
Long Jump	Lutz Dombrowski (GDR)	28'0¼"	Frank Paschek (GDR)	26'11¼"	Valeri Podluzhni (URS)	26'10"
Triple Jump	Jaak Uudmae (URS)	56'11"	Viktor Saneyev (URS)	56'6¾"	Joao de Oliveira (BRA)	56'6"
Shot	Vladimir Kiselyev (URS)	70'0½"	Alexander Baryshnikov (URS)	69'2"	Udo Beyer (GDR)	69'1¼"
Discus	Viktor Rashchupkin (URS)	218'7"	Imrich Bugar (TCH)	217'9"	Luis Delis (CUB)	217'7"
Hammer	Yuri Sedykh (URS)	268'4"	Sergei Litvinov (URS)	264'6"	Yuri Tamm (URS)	259'0"
Javelin	Dainis Kula (URS)	299'2"	Alexander Makarov (URS)	294'1"	Wolfgang Hanisch (GDR)	284'6"
Decathlon	Daley Thompson (GBR)	8495	Yuri Kutsenko (URS)	8331	Sergei Zhelanov (URS)	8135
Women						
100 m	Ludmila Kondratyeva (URS)	11.06	Marlies Göhr (GDR)	11.07	Ingrid Auerswald (GDR)	11.14
200 m	Bärbel Wöckel (GDR)	22.03	Natalya Bochina (URS)	22.19	Merlene Ottey (JAM)	22.20
400 m	Marita Koch (GDR)	48.88	Jarmila Kratochvilova (TCH)	49.46	Christina Lathan (GDR)	49.66
800 m	Nadyezhda Olizarenko (URS)	1:53.2	Olga Mineyeva (URS)	1:54.9	Tatyana Providokhina (URS)	1:55.5
1500 m	Tatyana Kazankina (URS)	3:56.6	Christiane Wartenberg (GDR)	3:57.8	Nadyezhda Olizarenko (URS)	3:59.6
100 m Hurdles	Vera Komisova (URS)	12.56	Johanna Klier (GDR)	12.63	Lucyna Langer (POL)	12.65
4 x 100 m	GDR	41.60	USSR	42.10	Great Britain	42.43
4 x 400 m	USSR	3:20.2	GDR	3:20.4	Great Britain	3:27.5
High Jump	Sara Simeoni (ITA)	6'5½"	Urszula Kielan (POL)	6'4½"	Jutta Kirst (GDR)	6'4½"
Long Jump	Tatyana Kolpakova (URS)	23'2"	Brigitte Wujak (GDR)	23'1¼"	Tatyana Skachko (URS)	23'0"
Shot	Ilona Slupianek (GDR)	73'6¼"	Svetlana Krachevskaya (URS)	70'3¼"	Margitta Pufe (GDR)	69'6¾"
Discus	Evelin Jahl (GDR)	229'6"	Maria Petkova-Vergova (BUL)	222'9"	Tatyana Lesovaya (URS)	221'1"
Javelin	Maria Caridad-Colon (CUB)	224'5"	Saida Gunba (URS)	222'2"	Ute Hommola (GDR)	218'4"
Pentathlon	Nadia Tkachenko (URS)	5083	Olga Rukavishnikova (URS)	4937	Olga Kuragina (URS)	4875
Swimming						
Men						
100 m Freestyle	Jörg Woithe (GDR)	50.40	Per Alvar Holmertz (SWE)	50.91	Per Johansson (SWE)	51.29
200 m Freestyle	Sergei Kopliakov (URS)	1:49.81	Andrei Krylov (URS)	1:50.76	Graeme Brewer (AUS)	1:51.60
400 m Freestyle	Vladimir Salnikov (URS)	3:51.31	Andrei Krylov (URS)	3:53.24	Ivar Stukolkin (URS)	3:53.95
1500 m Freestyle	Vladimir Salnikov (URS)	14:58.27	Alexander Chaev (URS)	15:14.30	Max Metzker (AUS)	15:14.49
100 m Backstroke	Bengt Baron (SWE)	56.63	Viktor Kusnetsov (URS)	56.99	Vladimir Dolgov (URS)	57.63

EVENT	GOLD		SILVER		BRONZE	
200 m Backstroke	Sandor Wladar (HUN)	2:01.93	Zoltan Verraszto (HUN)	2:02.40	Mark Kerry (AUS)	2:03.14
100 m Breaststroke	Duncan Goodhew (GBR)	1:03.34	Arsen Miskarov (URS)	1:03.82	Peter Evans (AUS)	1:03.96
200 m Breaststroke	Robertas Zhulpa (URS)	2:15.85	Alban Vermes (HUN)	2:16.93	Arsen Miskarov (URS)	2:17.28
100 m Butterfly	Paer Arvidsson (SWE)	54.92	Roger Pyttel (GDR)	54.94	David Lopez (ESP)	55.13
200 m Butterfly	Sergei Fesenko (URS)	1:59.76	Philip Hubble (GBR)	2:01.20	Roger Pyttel (GDR)	2:01.39
400 m Medley	Alexander Sidorenko (URS)	4:22.89	Sergei Fesenko (URS)	4:23.43	Zoltan Verraszto (HUN)	4:24.24
4 x 200 m Freestyle	USSR	7:23.50	GDR	7:28.60	Brazil	7:29.30
4 x 100 m Medley	Australia	3:45.70	USSR	3:45.92	Great Britain	3:47.71
Springboard Diving	Alexander Portnov (URS)	905.025	Carlos Giron (MEX)	892.140	Franco Cagnotto (ITA)	871.500
Highboard Diving	Falk Hoffmann (GDR)	835.650	Vladimir Heynik (URS)	819.705	David Ambartsumyan (URS)	817.440
Water Polo	USSR		Yugoslavia		Hungary	
Women						
100 m Freestyle	Barbara Krause (GDR)	54.79	Caren Metschuk (GDR)	55.16	Ines Diers (GDR)	55.65
200 m Freestyle	Barbara Krause (GDR)	1:58.33	Ines Diers (GDR)	1:59.64	Carmela Schmitt (GDR)	2:01.44
400 m Freestyle	Ines Diers (GDR)	4:08.76	Petra Schneider (GDR)	4:09.16	Carmela Schmitt (GDR)	4:10.86
800 m Freestyle	Michelle Ford (AUS)	8:28.90	Ines Diers (GDR)	8:32.55	Heike Dähne (GDR)	8:33.48
100 m Backstroke	Rica Reinisch (GDR)	1:00.86	Ina Kleber (GDR)	1:02.07	Petra Riedel (GDR)	1:02.64
200 m Backstroke	Rica Reinisch (GDR)	2:11.77	Cornelia Polit (GDR)	2:13.75	Birgit Treiber (GDR)	2:14.14
100 m Breaststroke	Ute Geweniger (GDR)	1:10.22	Elvira Vasilkova (URS)	1:10.41	Susanne Schultz-Nielsson (DEN)	1:11.16
200 m Breaststroke	Lina Kachushite (URS)	2:29.54	Svetlana Varganova (URS)	2:29.61	Yulia Bogdanova (URS)	2:32.39
100 m Butterfly	Caren Metschuk (GDR)	1:00.42	Andrea Pollack (GDR)	1:00.90	Christiane Knacke (GDR)	1:01.44
200 m Butterfly	Ines Geissler (GDR)	2:10.44	Sybille Schönrock (GDR)	2:10.45	Michelle Ford (AUS)	2:11.66
400 m Medley	Petra Schneider (GDR)	4:36.29	Sharon Davies (GBR)	4:46.83	Agnieszka Czopek (POL)	4:48.17
4 x 100 m Freestyle	GDR	3:42.71	Sweden	3:48.93	Netherlands	3:49.51
4 x 100 m Medley	GDR	4:06.67	Great Britain	4:12.24	USSR	4:13.61
Springboard Diving	Irina Kalinina (URS)	725.910	Martina Proeber (GDR)	698.895	Karin Guthke (GDR)	685.245
Highboard Diving	Martina Jäschke (GDR)	595.250	Servard Emirzyan (URS)	576.466	Liana Tsotadze (URS)	575.925
Boxing						
Light-Flyweight (- 105¾ lbs)	Shamil Sabirov (URS)		Hipolito Ramos (CUB)		Ismail Mustafov (BUL)	
					Byong Uk Li (PRK)	
Flyweight (- 112½ lbs)	Petar Lessov (BUL)		Viktor Miroshnichenko (URS)		Janos Varadi (HUN)	
					Hugh Russell (IRL)	
Bantamweight (- 119 lbs)	Juan Bautista Hernandez (CUB)		Bernardo José Pinango (VEN)		Michael Anthony (GUY)	
					Dimitru Cipere (ROM)	
Featherweight (- 126 lbs)	Rudi Fink (GDR)		Adolfo Horta (CUB)		Krzysztof Kosedowski (POL)	
					Viktor Rybakov (URS)	
Lightweight (- 132 lbs)	Angel Herrera (CUB)		Viktor Demianenko (URS)		Richard Nowakowski (GDR)	
					Kazimierz Adach (POL)	
Light-Welterweight (- 140 lbs)	Patrizio Oliva (ITA)		Serik Konakbayev (URS)		Anthony Willis (GBR)	
					José Aguilar (CUB)	
Welterweight (- 148 lbs)	Andres Aldama (CUB)		John Mugabi (UGA)		Karl-Heinz Krüger (GDR)	
					Kazimierz Szczerba (POL)	
Light-Middleweight (- 157 lbs)	Armando Martinez (CUB)		Alexander Koshkin (URS)		Detlef Kästner (GDR)	
					Jan Franck (TCH)	
Middleweight (- 165 lbs)	José Gomez (CUB)		Viktor Savchenko (URS)		Valentin Silaghi (ROM)	
					Jerzy Rybicki (POL)	
Light-Heavyweight (- 178½ lbs)	Slobodan Kacar (YUG)		Pawel Skrzecz (POL)		Herbert Bauch (GDR)	
					Ricardo Rojas (CUB)	
Heavyweight (+ 178½ lbs)	Teofilo Stevenson (CUB)		Pyotr Zayev (URS)		Istvan Levai (HUN)	
					Jürgen Fanghänel (GDR)	
Weightlifting						
Flyweight (- 114½ lbs)	Kanybek Osmonaliev (URS)	540 lbs	Ho Bong Chol (PRK)	540 lbs	Han Gyong Si (PRK)	540 lbs
Bantamweight (- 123¼ lbs)	Daniel Nunez (CUB)	606¼lbs	Yurik Sarkisian (URS)	595 lbs	Tadeusz Dembonczyk (POL)	584 lbs
Featherweight (- 132¼ lbs)	Viktor Mazin (URS)	639¼ lbs	Stefan Dimitrov (BUL)	633¾ lbs	Marek Seweryn (POL)	622¾ lbs
Lightweight (- 148¾ lbs)	Yanko Rusev (BUL)	755 lbs	Joachim Kunz (GDR)	738½ lbs	Mintcho Pachov (BUL)	716 lbs
Middleweight (- 165½ lbs)	Asen Zlatev (BUL)	793½ lbs	Alexander Pervy (URS)	788 lbs	Nedeltcho Kolev (BUL)	760 lbs
Light-Heavyweight (- 182 lbs)	Yurik Vardanyan (URS)	881¾ lbs	Blagoi Blagoyev (BUL)	821 lbs	Dusan Poliacik (TCH)	810 lbs
Middle-Heavyweight (- 198½ lbs)	Peter Baczako (HUN)	832 lbs	Rumen Alexandrov (BUL)	826½ lbs	Frank Mantek (GDR)	815½ lbs
First Heavyweight (- 220½ lbs)	Ota Zaremba (CSR)	870¾ lbs	Igor Nikitin (URS)	865½ lbs	Alberto Blanco (CUB)	848¾ lbs
Second Heavyweight (- 242½ lbs)	Leonid Taranenko (URS)	931¼ lbs	Valentin Christov (BUL)	892¾ lbs	György Szalai (HUN)	859¾ lbs
Super-Heavyweight (+ 242½ lbs)	Sultan Rakhmanov (URS)	970 lbs	Jürgen Heuser (GDR)	903¾ lbs	Tadeusz Rutkowski (POL)	898¼ lbs
Greco-Roman Wrestling						
Light-Flyweight (- 105¾ lbs)	Zaksylik Ushkempirov (URS)		Constantin Alexandru (ROM)		Ferenc Seres (HUN)	
Flyweight (- 114½ lbs)	Vakhtang Blagidze (URS)		Lajos Racz (HUN)		Mladen Mladenov (BUL)	
Bantamweight (- 125¾ lbs)	Shamil Serikov (URS)		Jozef Lipien (POL)		Benni Ljungbeck (SWE)	

EVENT	GOLD		SILVER		BRONZE	
Featherweight (– 136½ lbs)	Stilianos Migiakis (GRE)		István Tóth (HUN)		Boris Kramorenko (URS)	
Lightweight (– 149¼ lbs)	Stefan Rusu (ROM)		Andrzej Supron (POL)		Lars-Erik Skjöld (SWE)	
Welterweight (– 163 lbs)	Ferenc Kocsis (HUN)		Anatoli Bykov (URS)		Mikko Huhtala (FIN)	
Middleweight (– 180¾ lbs)	Gennadi Korban (URS)		Jan Polgowicz (POL)		Pavel Pavlov (BUL)	
Light-Heavyweight (– 198¼ lbs)	Norbert Nottny (HUN)		Igor Kanygin (URS)		Petre Disu (ROM)	
Heavyweight (– 220½ lbs)	Gheorghi Raikov (BUL)		Roman Bierla (POL)		Vasile Andrei (ROM)	
Super-Heavyweight (+ 220½ lbs)	Alexander Kolchinski (URS)		Alexander Tomov (BUL)		Hassan Bchara (LIB)	
Freestyle Wrestling						
Light-Flyweight (– 105¼ lbs)	Claudio Pollio (ITA)		Se Hong Jang (PRK)		Sergei Kornilayev (URS)	
Flyweight (– 114½ lbs)	Anatoli Beloglazov (URS)		Wladyslaw Stecyk (POL)		Nermedin Selimov (BUL)	
Bantamweight (– 119 lbs)	Sergei Beloglazov (URS)		Ho Pyong Li (PRK)		Dugarsuren Quinbold (MGL)	
Featherweight (– 136½ lbs)	Magomedgasan Abushev (URS)		Mikho Dukov (BUL)		Georges Hadjionnides (GRE)	
Lightweight (– 149¼ lbs)	Saipulla Absaidov (URS)		Ivan Yankov (BUL)		Saban Sejdi (YUG)	
Welterweight (– 163 lbs)	Valentin Raitschev (BUL)		Jamtsying Davaajav (MGL)		Dan Karabin (TCH)	
Middleweight (– 180¾ lbs)	Ismail Abilov (BUL)		Mahomet Aratsilov (URS)		István Kovács (HUN)	
Light-Heavyweight (– 198¼ lbs)	Sanasar Oganesyan (URS)		Uwe Neupert (GDR)		Alexander Cichon (POL)	
Heavyweight (– 220½ lbs)	Ilya Mate (URS)		Slavtcho Tchervenkov (BUL)		Julius Strnisko (TCH)	
Super-Heavyweight (+ 220½ lbs)	Soslan Andiev (URS)		Jószef Balla (HUN)		Adam Sandurski (POL)	
Judo						
Super-Lightweight (– 132½ lbs)	Thierry Rey (FRA)		José Rodrigez (CUB)		Tibor Kincses (HUN) Aramby Emizh (URS)	
Welterweight (– 143¼ lbs)	Nikolai Solodukhin (URS)		Tsendying Damdin (MGL)		Ilian Nedkov (BUL) Janusz Pawlowski (POL)	
Lightweight (– 156½ lbs)	Enzio Gamba (ITA)		Neil Adams (GBR)		Karl Heinz Lehmann (GDR) Ravdan Davaadalai (MGL)	
Light-Middleweight (– 171¾ lbs)	Shota Khabaleri (URS)		Juan Ferrer (CUB)		Bernard Tchoullouyan (FRA) Harald Heinke (GDR)	
Middleweight (– 189½ lbs)	Jörg Röthlisberger (SUI)		Isaac Azcuy Oliva (CUB)		Detlev Ultsch (GDR) Alexander Yatskevich (URS)	
Light-Heavyweight (– 209¼ lbs)	Robert van de Walle (BEL)		Tengiz Khubuluri (URS)		Dietmar Lorenz (GDR) Henk Numann (HOL)	
Heavyweight (+ 209¼ lbs)	Angelo Parisi (FRA)		Dimitar Zaprianov (BUL)		Vladimir Kocman (TCH) Radomir Kovacevic (YUG)	
Open Class	Dietmar Lorenz (GDR)		Angelo Parisi (FRA)		Andras Ozsvar (HUN) Arthur Mapp (GBR)	
Fencing						
Individual Foil – Men	Vladimir Smirnov (URS)	4	Pascal Jolyot (FRA)	4	Alexander Romankov (URS)	5
Team Foil – Men	France		USSR		Poland	
Individual Épée	Johan Harmenberg (SWE)	4	Ernõ Kolczonay (HUN)	3	Philippe Riboud (FRA)	3
Team Épée	France		Poland		USSR	
Individual Saber	Viktor Krovopouskov (URS)	4	Mikhail Burtsev (URS)	4	Imre Gedovari (HUN)	3
Team Saber	USSR		Italy		Hungary	
Individual Foil – Women	Pascale Trinquet (FRA)	4	Magda Maros (HUN)	3	Barbara Wysoczanska (POL)	
Team Foil – Women	France		USSR		Hungary	
Modern Pentathlon						
Individual	Anatoli Starostin (URS)	5568	Tamás Szombathelyi (HUN)	5502	Pavel Lednev (URS)	5282
Team	USSR	16126	Hungary	15912	Sweden	15845
Canoeing						
Men						
500 m Kayak Singles K1	Vladimir Parfenovich (URS)	1:43.43	John Sumegi (AUS)	1:44.12	Vasile Diba (ROM)	1:44.90
1000 m Kayak Singles K1	Rüdiger Helm (GDR)	3:48.77	Alain Lebas (FRA)	3:50.20	Ion Birladeanu (ROM)	3:50.49
500 m Kayak Pairs K2	USSR	1:32.38	Spain	1:33.65	GDR	1:34.00
1000 m Kayak Pairs K2	USSR	3:26.72	Hungary	3:28.49	Spain	3:28.66
1000 m Kayak Fours K4	GDR	3:13.76	Romania	3:15.35	Bulgaria	3:15.46
500 m Canadian Singles C1	Sergei Postrekhin (URS)	1:53.37	Lubomir Lubenov (BUL)	1:53.49	Olaf Heukrodt (GDR)	1:54.38
1000 m Canadian Singles C1	Lubomir Lubenov (BUL)	4:12.38	Sergei Postrekhin (URS)	4:13.53	Eckhard Leue (GDR)	4:15.02
500 m Canadian Pairs C2	Hungary	1:43.39	Romania	1:44.12	Bulgaria	1:44.83
1000 m Canadian Pairs C2	Romania	3:47.65	GDR	3:49.93	USSR	3:51.28
Women						
500 m Kayak Singles K1	Birgit Fischer (GDR)	1:57.96	Vanya Ghecheva (BUL)	1:59.48	Antonina Melnikova (URS)	1:59.66
500 m Kayak Pairs K2	GDR	1:43.88	USSR	1:46.91	Hungary	1:47.95

EVENT	GOLD		SILVER		BRONZE	
Rowing						
Men						
Single Sculls	Pertti Karppinen (FIN)	7:09:61	Vasili Yakusha (URS)	7:11.66	Peter Kersten (GDR)	7:14.88
Doubles Sculls	GDR	6:24.33	Yugoslavia	6:26.34	Czechoslovakia	6:29.07
Coxless Pairs	GDR	6:48.01	USSR	6:50.50	Great Britain	6:51.47
Coxed Pairs	GDR	7:02.54	USSR	7:03.35	Yugoslavia	7:04.92
Coxless Quadruple Sculls	GDR	5:49.81	USSR	5:51.47	Bulgaria	5:52.38
Coxless Fours	GDR	6:08.17	USSR	6:11.81	Great Britain	6:16.58
Coxed Fours	GDR	6:14.51	USSR	6:19.05	Poland	6:22.52
Coxed Eights	GDR	5:49.05	Great Britain	5:51.92	USSR	5:52.66
Women						
Single Sculls	Sanda Toma (ROM)	3:40:69	Antonina Makhina (URS)	3:41.65	Martina Schröter (GDR)	3:43.54
Double Sculls	USSR	3:16.27	GDR	3:17.63	Romania	3:18.91
Coxless Pairs	GDR	3:30.49	Poland	3:30.95	Bulgaria	3:32.39
Coxless Quadruple Sculls	GDR	3:15.32	USSR	3:15.73	Bulgaria	3:16.10
Coxed Fours	GDR	3:19.27	Bulgaria	3:20.75	USSR	3:20.92
Coxed Eights	GDR	3:03.32	USSR	3:04.29	Romania	3:05.63
Yachting						
Finn-Class	Esko Rechardt (FIN)	36.7	Wolfgang Mayrhofer (AUT)	46.7	Andrei Balaschov (URS)	47.4
International Star	USSR	24.7	Austria	31.7	Italy	36.1
Flying Dutchman	Spain	19.0	Ireland	30.0	Hungary	45.7
International Tornado	Brazil	21.4	Denmark	30.4	Sweden	33.7
International 470	Brazil	36.4	GDR	38.7	Finland	39.7
International Soling	Denmark	23.0	USSR	30.4	Greece	31.1
Cycling						
Individual Road Race (117½ mi)	Sergei Sukhoruchenkov (URS)	4:48:28	Czeslaw Lang (POL)	4:51:26	Yuri Barinov (URS)	4:51:26
100 km Road Team Time Trial	USSR	2:01:21.7	GDR	2:02:53.2	Czechoslovakia	2:02:53.9
1000 m Time Trial	Lothar Thoms (GDR)	1:02.955	Alexander Pantilov (URS)	1:04.845	David Weller (JAM)	1:05.241
1000 m Sprint	Lutz Hesslich (GDR)		Yave Cahard (FRA)		Sergei Kopylov (URS)	
4000 m Individual Pursuit	Robert Dill-Bundi (SUI)	4:35.66	Alain Bondue (FRA)	4:42.96	Hans-Henrik Oersted (DEN)	4:36.54★
4000 m Team Pursuit	USSR	4:15.70	GDR	4:19.67	Czechoslovakia	

★The bronze medal time was decided in a separate race, which is why it is faster than for silver.

Equestrianism						
Three-Day Event	Federico Roman (ITA)	-108.60	Alexander Blinov (URS)	-120.80	Yuri Salnikov (URS)	-151.60
Three-Day Event. Team	USSR	-457.00	Italy	-656.20	Mexico	-1172.85
Grand Prix (Dressage)	Elisabeth Theurer (AUT)	1370	Yuri Kovshov (URS)	1300	Viktor Ugryumov (URS)	1234
Grand Prix (Dressage) Team	USSR	4383.0	Bulgaria	3580.0	Romania	3346.0
Grand Prix (Jumping)	Jan Kowalczyk (POL)	-8	Nikolai Korolkov (URS)	-9.50	Joaquín Perez de las Heras (MEX)	-12
Grand Prix (Jumping) Team	USSR	-16.00	Poland	-32.00	Mexico	-39.25
Shooting						
Small-Bore Rifle (Prone)	Karoly Varga (HUN)	599	Hellfried Heilfort (GDR)	599	Petr Zaprianov (BUL)	598
Small-Bore Rifle (3 Positions)	Viktor Vlassov (URS)	1173	Bernd Hartstein (GDR)	1166	Sven Johansson (SWE)	1165
Rapid-Fire Pistol	Corneliu Ion (ROM)	596	Jürgen Wiefel (GDR)	596	Gerhard Petrisch (AUT)	596
Free Pistol (50 m)	Alexander Melentyev (URS)	581	Harald Vollmar (GDR)	568	Lubcho Diakov (BUL)	565
Running Game Target	Igor Sokolov (URS)	589	Thomas Pfeffer (GDR)	589	Alexander Gasov (URS)	587
Skeet Shooting	Hans Kjeld Rasmussen (DEN)	196	Lars-Göran Carlsson (SWE)	196	Roberto Castrillo (CUB)	196
Trap Shooting	Luciano Giovanetti (ITA)	198	Rustam Yambulatov (URS)	196	Jörg Damme (GDR)	196
Archery						
Men	Tomi Poikalainen (FIN)	2455	Boris Isachenko (URS)	2452	Giancarlo Ferrari (ITA)	2449
Women	Keto Losaberidse (URS)	2491	Natalya Butuzova (URS)	2477	Paivi Merilouto (FIN)	2449
Gymnastics						
Men						
Individual Combined Exercises	Alexander Ditiatin (URS)	118.650	Nikolai Andrianov (URS)	118.225	Stoyan Deltschev (BUL)	118.000
Team	USSR	589.60	GDR	581.15	Hungary	575.00
Parallel Bars	Alexander Tkachov (URS)	19.775	Alexander Ditiatin (URS)	19.750	Roland Brückner (GDR)	19.650
Floor	Roland Brückner (GDR)	19.750	Nikolai Andrianov (URS)	19.725	Alexander Ditiatin (URS)	19.700
Horse Vault	Nikolai Andrianov (URS)	19.825	Alexander Ditiatin (URS)	19.800	Roland Brückner (GDR)	19.775
Horizontal Bar	Stojan Deltschev (BUL)	19.825	Alexander Ditiatin (URS)	19.750	Nikolai Andrianov (URS)	19.675
Rings	Alexander Ditiatin (URS)	19.875	Alexander Tkachov (URS)	19.725	Jiri Tabák (TCH)	19.600
Pommel Horse	Zoltan Magyar (HUN)	19.925	Alexander Ditiatin (URS)	19.800	Michael Nikolay (GDR)	19.775

EVENT	GOLD		SILVER		BRONZE	
Women						
Individual Combined Exercises	Yelena Davydova (URS)	79.150	Nadia Comaneci (ROM)	79.075		
			Maxi Gnauck (GDR)	79.075		
Team	USSR	394.90	Romania	393.50	GDR	392.55
Floor	Nadia Comaneci (ROM)	19.875			Maxi Gnauck (GDR)	19.825
	Nelli Kim (URS)	19.875			Natalya Shaposhnikova (URS)	19.825
Horse Vault	Natalya Shaposhnikova (URS)	19.725	Steffi Kräker (GDR)	19.675	Melita Ruhn (ROM)	19.650
Beam	Nadia Comaneci (ROM)	19.800	Yelena Davydova (URS)	19.750	Natalya Shaposhnikova (URS)	19.725
Asymmetrical Bars	Maxi Gnauck (GDR)	19.875	Emilia Eberle (ROM)	19.850	Maria Filatova (URS)	19.775
					Steffi Kräker (GDR)	19.775
					Mehta Ruhn (ROM)	19.775
Basketball						
Men	Yugoslavia		Italy		USSR	
Women	USSR		Bulgaria		Yugoslavia	
Soccer						
	Czechoslovakia		GDR		USSR	
Handball						
Men	GDR		USSR		Romania	
Women	USSR		Yugoslavia		GDR	
Hockey						
Men	India		Spain		USSR	
Women	Zimbabwe		Czechoslovakia		USSR	
Volleyball						
Men	USSR		Bulgaria		Romania	
Women	USSR		GDR		Bulgaria	

Sarajevo 1984

Participants: 1274 / Men: 1000, Women: 274, Countries: 49,
Sports: 8, Events: 39
Final Torchbearer: Sandra Dubravčič

February 7 – February 19
(Official Opening Ceremony on February 8)

Medals Table

PLACE	COUNTRY	GOLD	SILVER	BRONZE
1	GDR	9	9	6
2	USSR	6	10	9
3	USA	4	4	–
4	Finland	4	3	6
5	Sweden	4	2	2

Outstanding Athletes

PLACE	NAME (NATIONALITY)	DISCIPLINE	G	S	B
1	Marja-Liisa Hämäläinen (FIN)	Nordic Skiing	3	–	1
2	Karin Enke (GDR)	Speed Skating	2	2	–
3	Gunde Svan (SWE)	Nordic Skiing	2	1	1
4	Gaetan Boucher (CAN)	Speed Skating	2	–	1
5	Wolfgang Hoppe (GDR)	Bobsledding	2	–	–
	Dietmar Schauerhammer (GDR)	Bobsledding	2	–	–
	Tomas Wassberg (SWE)	Nordic Skiing	2	–	–

EVENT	GOLD		SILVER		BRONZE	
Alpine Skiing						
Men						
Downhill	Bill Johnson (USA)	1:45.59	Peter Müller (SUI)	1:45.86	Anton Steiner (AUT)	1:45.95
Slalom	Phil Mahre (USA)	1:39.21	Steven Mahre (USA)	1:39.62	Didier Bouvet (FRA)	1:40.20
Giant Slalom	Max Julen (SUI)	2:41.18	Juriy Franko (YUG)	2:41.41	Andreas Wenzel (LIE)	2:41.75
Women						
Downhill	Michaela Figini (SUI)	1:13.36	Maria Walliser (SUI)	1:13.41	Olga Chartová (TCH)	1:13.53
Slalom	Paoletta Magoni (ITA)	1:36.47	Perrine Pelen (FRA)	1:37.38	Ursula Konzett (LIE)	1:37.50
Giant Slalom	Debbie Armstrong (USA)	2:20.98	Christin Cooper (USA)	2:21.38	Perrine Pelen (FRA)	2:21.40

EVENT	GOLD		SILVER		BRONZE	
Nordic Skiing						
Men						
15 km Cross-Country Skiing	Gunde Svan (SWE)	41:25.6	Aki Karvonen (FIN)	41:34.9	Harri Kirvesniemi (FIN)	41:45.6
30 km Cross-Country Skiing	Nikolai Simyatov (URS)	1:28:56.3	Alexander Zavialov (URS)	1:29:23.3	Gunde Svan (SWE)	1:29:35.7
50 km Cross-Country Skiing	Thomas Wassberg (SWE)	2:15:55.8	Gunde Svan (SWE)	2:16:00.7	Aki Karvonen (FIN)	2:17:04.7
4 x 10 km	Sweden	1:55:06.3	USSR	1:55:16.5	Finland	1:56:31.4
Ski Jumping (70 m Hill)	Jens Weissflog (GDR)	215.2	Matti Nykänen (FIN)	214.0	Jari Puikkonen (FIN)	212.8
Ski Jumping (90 m Hill)	Matti Nykänen (FIN)	231.2	Jens Weissflog (GDR)	213.7	Pavel Ploc (TCH)	202.9
Nordic Combined	Tom Sandberg (NOR)	422.595	Jouko Karjalainen (FIN)	416.900	Rauno Ylipulli (FIN)	410.825
Women						
5 km Cross-Country Skiing	Marja-Liisa Hämäläinen (FIN)	17:04.0	Berit Aunli (NOR)	17:14.1	Kvetoslava Jeriová (TCH)	17:18.3
10 km Cross-Country Skiing	Marja-Liisa Hämäläinen (FIN)	31:44.2	Raisa Smetanina (URS)	32:02.9	Brit Pettersen (NOR)	32:12.7
20-km-Cross-Country Skiing	Marja-Liisa Hämäläinen (FIN)	1:01:45.0	Raisa Smetanina (URS)	1:02:26.7	Anne Jahren (NOR)	1:03:13.6
4 x 5 km	Norway	1:06:49.7	Czechoslovakia	1:07:34.7	Finland	1:07:36.7
Biathlon						
10 km	Eirik Kvalfoss (NOR)	30:53.8	Peter Angerer (FRG)	31:02.4	Matthias Jakob (GDR)	31:10.5
20 km	Peter Angerer (FRG)	1:11:52.7	Frank-Peter Rötsch (GDR)	1:13:21.4	Eirik Kvalfoss (NOR)	1:14:02.4
4 x 7.5 km	USSR	1:38:51.70	Norway	1:39:03.10	FRG	1:39:05.10
Figure Skating						
Women	Katarina Witt (GDR)		Rosalyn Summers (USA)		Kira Ivanova (URS)	
Men	Scott Hamilton (USA)		Brian Oser (CAN)		Jozef Sabovcik (TCH)	
Pairs	Elena Valova/		Kitty Carruthers/		Larissa Selesnewa/	
	Oleg Vasiliyev (URS)		Peter Carruthers (USA)		Oleg Makarow (URS)	
Ice Dance	Jayne Torvill/		Natalya Bestemianova/		Marina Klimova/	
	Christopher Dean (GBR)		Andrei Bukin (URS)		Sergei Ponomarenko (URS)	
Speed Skating						
Men						
500 m	Sergei Fokitchev (URS)	38.19	Yoshihiro Kitazawa (JPN)	38.30	Gaetan Boucher (CAN)	38.39
1000 m	Gaetan Boucher (CAN)	1:15.80	Sergei Khlebnikov (URS)	1:16.63	Kai Arne Engelstad (NOR)	1:16.75
1500 m	Gaetan Boucher (CAN)	1:58.36	Sergei Khlebnikov (URS)	1:58.83	Oleg Bogiev (URS)	1:58.89
5000 m	Tomas Gustafson (SWE)	7:12.28	Igor Malkov (URS)	7:12.30	Rene Schöfisch (GDR)	7:17.49
10,000 m	Igor Malkov (URS)	14:39.90	Tomas Gustafson (SWE)	14:39.95	Rene Schöfisch (GDR)	14:46.91
Women						
500 m	Christa Rothenburger (GDR)	41.02	Karin Enke (GDR)	41.28	Natalya Chive (URS)	41.50
1000 m	Karin Enke (GDR)	1:21.61	Andrea Schöne (GDR)	1:22.83	Natalya Petruseva (URS)	1:23.21
1500 m	Karin Enke (GDR)	2:03.42	Andrea Schöne (GDR)	2:05.29	Natalya Petruseva (URS)	2:05.78
3000 m	Andrea Schöne (GDR)	4:24.79	Karin Enke (GDR)	4:26.33	Gabi Schönbrunn (GDR)	4:33.13
Bobsledding						
2-Man Bob	GDR II	3:25.56	GDR I	3:26.04	USSR II	3:26.16
4-Man Bob	GDR I	3:20.22	GDR II	3:20.78	Switzerland I	3:21.39
Lugeing						
Men's Singles	Paul Hildgartner (ITA)	3:04.258	Sergei Danilin (URS)	3:04.962	Valeri Dudin (URS)	3:05.012
Women's Singles	Steffi Martin (GDR)	2:46.570	Bettina Schmidt (GDR)	2:46.873	Ute Weiss (GDR)	2:47.248
2-Man Luge	Hans Stanggassinger/		Yevgeni Belusov/		Jörg Hoffmann/	
	Franz Wembacher (FRG)	1:23.620	Alexander Beliakov (URS)	1:23.660	Jochen Pietzsch (GDR)	1:23.887
Ice Hockey						
	USSR		Czechoslovakia		Sweden	

Los Angeles 1984

July 28 – August 12

Participants: 6797 / Men: 5230, Women: 1567, Countries: 140,
Sports: 21, Events: 221
Final Torchbearer: Rafer Johnson

Medals Table

PLACE	COUNTRY	GOLD	SILVER	BRONZE
1	USA	83	61	30
2	Romania	20	16	17
3	FRG	17	19	23
4	China	15	8	9
5	Italy	14	6	12

Outstanding Athletes

PLACE	NAME (NATIONALITY)	DISCIPLINE	G	S	B
1	Jecaterina Szabó (ROM)	Gymnastics	4	1	–
2	Carl Lewis (USA)	Athletics	4	–	–
3	Li Ning (CHN)	Gymnastics	3	2	1
4	Valerie Brisco-Hooks (USA)	Athletics	3	–	–
	Richard Carey (USA)	Swimming	3	–	–
	Ian Ferguson (NZL)	Canoeing	3	–	–

EVENT	GOLD		SILVER		BRONZE	
Athletics						
Men						
100 m	Carl Lewis (USA)	9.99	Sam Graddy (USA)	10.19	Ben Johnson (CAN)	10.22
200 m	Carl Lewis (USA)	19.80	Kirk Baptiste (USA)	19.96	Thomas Jefferson (USA)	20.26
400 m	Alonzo Babers (USA)	44.27	Gabriel Tiacoh (CIV)	44.54	Antonio McKay (USA)	44.71
800 m	Joaquim Cruz (BRA)	1:43.00	Sebastian Coe (GBR)	1:43.64	Earl Jones (USA)	1:43.83
1500 m	Sebastian Coe (GBR)	3:32.53	Steve Cram (GBR)	3:33.40	José Abascal (ESP)	3:34.30
5000 m	Said Aouita (MAR)	13:05.59	Markus Ryffel (SUI)	13:07.54	Antoaio Leitao (POR)	13:09.20
10,000 m	Alberto Cova (ITA)	27:47.54	Michael McLeod (GBR)*	28:06.22	Mike Musyoki (KEN)	28:06.46
Marathon	Carlos Lopes (POR)	2:09:21	John Treacy (IRL)	2:09:56	Charles Spedding (GBR)	2:09:58
110 m Hurdles	Roger Kingdom (USA)	13.20	Greg Foster (USA)	13.23	Arto Bryggare (FIN)	13.40
400 m Hurdles	Edwin Moses (USA)	47.75	Danny Harris (USA)	48.13	Harald Schmid (FRG)	48.19
3000 m Steeplechase	Julius Korir (KEN)	8:11.80	Joseph Mahmoud (FRA)	8:13.31	Brian Diemer (USA)	8:14.06
4 x 100 m	USA	37.83	Jamaica	38.62	Canada	38.70
4 x 400 m	USA	2:57.91	Great Britain	2:59.13	Nigeria	2:59.32
20 km Walk	Ernesto Canto (MEX)	1:23:13	Raul Gonzalez (MEX)	1:23:20	Maurizio Damilano (ITA)	1:23:26
50 km Walk	Raul Gonzalez (MEX)	3:37:26	Bo Gustafsson (SWE)	3:53:19	Sandro Bellucci (ITA)	3:53:45
Long Jump	Carl Lewis (USA)	28'0¼"	Gary Honey (AUS)	27'0½"	Giovanni Evangelisti (ITA)	27'0½"
High Jump	Dietmar Mögenburg (FRG)	7' 8½"	Patrik Sjöberg (SWE)	7'7¾"	Zhu Jianhua (CHN)	7'7"
Pole Vault	Pierre Quinon (FRA)	18'0¼"	Mike Tully (USA)	18'6½"	Earl Bell (USA)	18'4½"
Triple Jump	Al Joyner (USA)	56'7½"	Mike Conley (USA)	56'4½"	Keith Connor (GBR)	55'4½"
Shot	Alessandro Andrei (ITA)	69'9"	Michael Carter (USA)	69'2½"	Dave Laut (USA)	68'9¾"
Discus	Rolf Danneberg (FRG)	218'6"	Mac Wilkins (USA)	217'6"	John Powell (USA)	214'9"
Hammer	Juha Tiainen (FIN)	256'2"	Karl-Hans Riehm (FRG)	255'10"	Klaus Ploghaus (FRG)	251'7"
Javelin	Aro Härkönen (FIN)	284'8"	David Ottley (GBR)	281'3"	Kenth Eldebrink (SWE)	274'8"
Decathlon	Daley Thompson (GBR)	8798	Jürgen Hingsen (FRG)	8673	Siegfried Wentz (FRG)	8412
			*Martti Väiniö (FIN) disqualified from 2nd position after failing a drugs test.			
Women						
100 m	Evelyn Ashford (USA)	10.97	Alice Brown (USA)	11.13	Merlene Ottey (JAM)	11.16
200 m	Valerie Brisco-Hooks (USA)	21.81	Florence Griffith (USA)	22.04	Merlene Ottey (JAM)	22.09
400 m	Valerie Brisco-Hooks (USA)	48.83	Chandra Cheeseborough (USA)	49.05	Kathryn Cook (GBR)	49.42
800 m	Doina Melinte (ROM)	1:57.60	Kim Gallagher (USA)	1:58.63	Fita Lovin (ROM)	1:58.83
1500 m	Gabriella Dorio (ITA)	4:03.25	Doina Melinte (ROM)	4:03.76	Maricica Puica (ROM)	4:04.15
3000 m	Maricica Puica (ROM)	8:35.96	Wendy Sly (GBR)	8:39.47	Lynn Williams (CAN)	8:42.14
Marathon	Joan Benoit (USA)	2:24:52	Grete Waitz (NOR)	2:26:18	Rosa Mota (POR)	2:26:57
100 m Hurdles	Benita Fitzgerald-Brown (USA)	12.84	Shirley Strong (GBR)	12.88	Kim Turner (USA)	13.06
					Michele Chardonnet (FRA)	13.06
400 m Hurdles	Nawal El Moutawakel (MAR)	54.61	Judi Brown (USA)	55.20	Cristina Cojocaru (ROM)	55.41
4 x 100 m	USA	41.65	Canada	42.77	Great Britain	43.11
4 x 400 m	USA	3:18.29	Canada	3:21.21	FRG	3:22.98
High Jump	Ulrike Meyfarth (FRG)	6'7½"	Sara Simeoni (ITA)	6'6¾"	Joni Huntley (USA)	6'5½"
Long Jump	Anis Stanciu-Cusmir (ROM)	22'10"	Vali Ionescu (ROM)	22'4¼"	Susan Hearnshaw (GBR)	22'3¾"
Shot	Claudia Losch (FRG)	67'2¼"	Mihaela Loghin (ROM)	67'2"	Gael Martin (AUS)	62'11½"
Discus	Ria Stalman (HOL)	214'5"	Leslie Deniz (USA)	212'9"	Florenta Craciunescu (ROM)	208'9"
Javelin	Tessa Sanderson (GBR)	228'2"	Tiina Lillak (FIN)	226'4"	Fatima Whitbread (GBR)	220'5"
Heptathlon	Glynis Nunn (AUS)	6390	Jackie Joyner (USA)	6385	Sabine Everts (FRG)	6363
Swimming						
Men						
100 m Freestyle	Ambrose Gaines (USA)	49.80	Mark Stockwell (AUS)	50.24	Per Johansson (SWE)	50.31

EVENT	GOLD		SILVER		BRONZE	
200 m Freestyle	Michael Gross (FRG)	1:47.44	Michael Heath (USA)	1:49.10	Thomas Fahrner (FRG)	1:49.69
400 m Freestyle	George Dicarlo (USA)	3:51.23	John Mykkanen (USA)	3:51.49	Justin Lemberg (AUS)	3:51.79
1500 m Freestyle	Michael O'Brien (USA)	15:05.20	George Dicarlo (USA)	15:10.59	Stefan Pfeiffer (FRG)	15:12.11
100 m Backstroke	Richard Carey (USA)	55.79	David Wilson (USA)	56.35	Mike West (CAN)	56.49
200 m Backstroke	Richard Carey (USA)	2:00.23	Frederic Delcourt (FRA)	2:01.75	Cameron Henning (CAN)	2:02.37
100 m Breaststroke	Steve Lundquist (USA)	1:01.65	Victor Davis (CAN)	1:01.99	Peter Evans (AUS)	1:02.97
200 m Breaststroke	Victor Davis (CAN)	2:13.34	Glenn Beringen (AUS)	2:15.79	Etienne Dagon (SUI)	2:17.41
100 m Butterfly	Michael Gross (FRG)	53.08	Pablo Morales (USA)	53.23	Glenn Buchanan (AUS)	53.85
200 m Butterfly	Jon Sieben (AUS)	1:57.04	Michael Gross (FRG)	1:57.40	Rafael Vidal Castro (VEN)	1:57.51
200 m Medley	Alex Baumann (CAN)	2:01.42	Pedro Morales (USA)	2:03.05	Neil Cochran (GBR)	2:04.38
400 m Medley	Alex Baumann (CAN)	4:17.41	Ricardo Prado (BRA)	4:18.45	Robert Woodhouse (AUS)	4:20.50
4 x 100 m Freestyle Relay	USA	3:19.03	Australia	3:19.68	Sweden	3:22.69
4 x 200 m Freestyle Relay	USA	7:16.59	FRG	7:16.73	Great Britain	7:24.78
4 x 100 m Medley Relay	USA	3:39.30	Canada	3:43.23	Australia	3:43.25
Springboard Diving	Greg Louganis (USA)	754.41	Tan Liangde (CHN)	662.31	Ronald Merriott (USA)	661.32
Highboard Diving	Greg Louganis (USA)	710.91	Bruce Kimball (USA)	643.50	Li Kongzheng (CHN)	638.28
Water Polo	Yugoslavia		USA		FRG	
Women						
100 m Freestyle	Carrie Steinseifer (USA)	55.92			Annemarie Verstappen (HOL)	56.08
	Nancy Hogshead (USA)	55.92				
200 m Freestyle	Mary Wayte (USA)	1:59.23	Cynthia Woodhead (USA)	1:59.50	Annemarie Verstappen (HOL)	1:59.69
400 m Freestyle	Tiffany Cohen (USA)	4:07.10	Sarah Hardcastle (GBR)	4:10.27	June Croft (GBR)	4:11.49
800 m Freestyle	Tiffany Cohen (USA)	8:24.95	Michelle Richardson (USA)	8:30.73	Sarah Hardcastle (GBR)	8:32.60
100 m Backstroke	Theresa Andrews (USA)	1:02.55	Betsy Mitchell (USA)	1:02.63	Jolanda de Rover (HOL)	1:02.91
200 m Backstroke	Jolanda de Rover (HOL)	2:12.38	Amy White (USA)	2:13.04	Aneta Patrascoiu (ROM)	2:13.29
100 m Breaststroke	Petra van Staveren (HOL)	1:09.88	Anne Ottenbrite (CAN)	1:10.69	Catherine Poirot (FRA)	1:10.70
200 m Breaststroke	Anne Ottenbrite (CAN)	2:30.38	Susan Rapp (USA)	2:31.15	Ingrid Lempereur (BEL)	2:31.40
100 m Butterfly	Mary T. Meagher (USA)	59.26	Jenna Johnson (USA)	1:00.19	Karin Seick (FRG)	1:00.36
200 m Butterfly	Mary T. Meagher (USA)	2:06.90	Karen Philipps (AUS)	2:10.56	Ina Beyermann (FRG)	2:11.91
200 m Medley	Tracy Caulkins (USA)	2:12.64	Nancy Hogshead (USA)	2:15.17	Michele Pearson (AUS)	2:15.92
400 m Medley	Tracy Caulkins (USA)	4:39.24	Suzanne Landells (AUS)	4:48.30	Petra Zindler (FRG)	4:48.57
4 x 400 m Freestyle Relay	USA	3:43.43	Netherlands	3:44.40	FRG	3:45.56
4 x 100 m Medley Relay	USA	4:08.34	FRG	4:11.97	Canada	4:12.98
Springboard Diving	Silvie Bernier (CAN)	530.70	Kelly McCormick (USA)	527.46	Christina Seufert (USA)	517.62
Highboard Diving	Zhou Jihong (CHN)	378.81	Michele Mitchell (USA)	367.35	Wendy Wyland (USA)	365.52
Synchronized Swimming						
Solo	Tracie Ruiz (USA)	198.467	Carolyn Waldo (CAN)	195.300	Miwako Motoyoshi (JPN)	187.050
Duet	USA	99.00	Canada	98.20	Japan	97.00
Boxing						
Light-Flyweight (– 105¹/₄ lbs)	Paul Gonzales (USA)		Salvatore Todisco (ITA)		Keith Mwila (ZAM)	
					José Marcelino Bolivar (VEN)	
Flyweight (– 112¹/₂ lbs)	Steven McCrory (USA)		Redzep Redzepovski (YUG)		Eyup Can (TUR)	
					Ibrahim Bilali (KEN)	
Bantamweight (– 119 lbs)	Maurizio Stecca (ITA)		Hector Lopez (MEX)		Dale Walters (CAN)	
					Pedro Nolasco (DOM)	
Featherweight (– 126 lbs)	Meldrick Taylor (USA)		Peter Konyegwachie (NGR)		Omar Catari Peraza (VEN)	
					Turgut Aykac (TUR)	
Lightweight (– 132 lbs)	Pernell Whitaker (USA)		Luis Ortiz (PUR)		Martin Ndongo Ebanga (CMR)	
					Cun Chil-Sung (KOR)	
Light-Welterweight (– 140 lbs)	Jerry Page (USA)		Dhawee Umponmaha (THA)		Mirko Puzovic (YUG)	
					Mircea Fulger (ROM)	
Welterweight (– 148 lbs)	Mark Breland (USA)		An Young-Su (KOR)		Joni Nyman (FIN)	
					Luciano Bruno (ITA)	
Light-Middleweight (– 157 lbs)	Frank Tate (USA)		Shawn O'Sullivan (CAN)		Manfred Zielonka (FRG)	
					Christophe Tiozzo (FRA)	
Middleweight (– 165 lbs)	Shin Joon-Sup (KOR)		Virgil Hill (USA)		Mohammed Zaoui (ALG)	
					Aristides Gonzales (PUR)	
Light-Heavyweight (– 178¹/₂ lbs)	Anton Josipovic (YUG)		Kevin Barry (NZL)		Mustapha Moussa (ALG)	
					Evander Holyfield (USA)	
Heavyweight (– 200¹/₂ lbs)	Henry Tillman (USA)		Willie Dewit (CAN)		Angelo Musone (ITA)	
					Arnold Vanderlijde (HOL)	
Super-Heavyweight (+ 200¹/₂ lbs)	Tyrell Biggs (USA)		Francesco Damiani (ITA)		Robert Wells (GBR)	
					Azis Salihu (YUG)	

EVENT	GOLD		SILVER		BRONZE	
Weightlifting						
Flyweight (- 114½ lbs)	Zeng Guoqiang (CHN)	518 lbs	Zhou Peishun (CHN)	518 lbs	Kazushito Manabe (JPN)	512½ lbs
Bantamweight (- 123½ lbs)	Wu Shude (CHN)	589½ lbs	Lai Runming (CHN)	584 lbs	Masahiro Kotaka (JPN)	556½ lbs
Featherweight (- 132¼ lbs)	Chen Weiqiang (CHN)	622¾ lbs	Gelu Radu (ROM)	617¼ lbs	Tsai Wen-Yee (KOR)	600¾ lbs
Lightweight (- 148¾ lbs)	Yao Jingyuan (CHN)	705¼ lbs	Andrei Socaci (ROM)	688¾ lbs	Jouni Gronman (FIN)	688¾ lbs
Middleweight (- 165½ lbs)	Karl-Heinz Radschinsky (FRG)	749½ lbs	Jacques Demers (FRA)	738½ lbs	Dragomir Cioroslan (ROM)	733 lbs
Light-Heavyweight (- 182 lbs)	Petre Becheru (ROM)	782½ lbs	Robert Kabbas (AUS)	755 lbs	Ryoji Isaoka (JPN)	749½ lbs
Middle-Heavyweight (- 198½ lbs)	Nicu Vlad (ROM)	865¼ lbs	Petre Dumitru (ROM)	793½ lbs	David Mercer (GBR)	771 lbs
First Heavyweight 100 kg (- 220½ lbs)	Rolf Milser (FRG)	848¾ lbs	Vasile Gropa (ROM)	843¼ lbs	Pekka Niemi (FIN)	810 lbs
Second Heavyweight (- 242½ lbs)	Norberto Oberburger (ITA)	859¾ lbs	Stefan Tasnadi (ROM)	837¾ lbs	Guy Carlton (USA)	832 lbs
Super-Heavyweight (+ 242½ lbs)	Dean Lukin (AUS)	909¼ lbs	Mario Martinez (USA)	903¾ lbs	Manfred Nerlinger (FRG)	876¼ lbs
Greco-Roman Wrestling						
Light-Flyweight (- 105¾ lbs)	Vincenzo Maenza (ITA)		Markus Scherer (FRG)		Ikuzo Saito (JPN)	
Flyweight (- 114½ lbs)	Atsuji Miyahara (JPN)		Daniel Aceves (MEX)		Bang Dae-Du (KOR)	
Bantamweight (- 125¾ lbs)	Pasquale Passarelli (FRG)		Masaki Eto (JPN)		Haralambos Holidis (GRE)	
Featherweight (- 136½ lbs)	Kim Weon-Kee (KOR)		Kentolle Johansson (SWE)		Hugo Dietsche (SUI)	
Lightweight (- 149¾ lbs)	Vlado Lisjak (YUG)		Tapio Sipila (FIN)		James Martinez (USA)	
Welterweight (- 163 lbs)	Jonko Salomäki (FIN)		Roger Tallroth (SWE)		Stefan Rusu (ROM)	
Middleweight (- 180¾ lbs)	Ion Draica (ROM)		Dimitrios Thanopoulos (GRE)		Sören Claeson (SWE)	
Light-Heavyweight (- 198¼ lbs)	Steven Fraser (USA)		Ilie Matei (ROM)		Frank Andersson (SWE)	
Heavyweight (- 220½ lbs)	Vasile Andrei (ROM)		Greg Gibson (USA)		Jozef Tertelje (YUG)	
Super-Heavyweight (+ 220½ lbs)	Jeffrey Blatnick (USA)		Refik Memisevic (YUG)		Victor Dolipschi (ROM)	
Freestyle Wrestling						
Light-Flyweight (- 105¾ lbs)	Robert Weaver (USA)		Takashi Irie (JPN)		Do Son-Gab (KOR)	
Flyweight (- 114½ lbs)	Saban Trstena (YUG)		Kim Jong-Kiu (KOR)		Yuji Takada (JPN)	
Bantamweight (- 125¾ lbs)	Hideaki Tomiyama (JPN)		Barry Davis (USA)		Kim Eui-Kon (KOR)	
Featherweight (- 136½ lbs)	Randy Lewis (USA)		Kosei Akaishi (JPN)		Lee Jung-Keun (KOR)	
Lightweight (- 149¾ lbs)	You In-Tak (KOR)		Andrew Rein (USA)		Jukka Rauhala (FIN)	
Welterweight (- 163 lbs)	David Shultz (USA)		Martin Knosp (FRG)		Saban Sejdi (YUG)	
Middleweight (- 180¾ lbs)	Mark Shultz (USA)		Hideyuki Nagashima (JPN)		Chris Rinke (CAN)	
Light-Heavyweight (- 198¼ lbs)	Ed Banach (USA)		Akira Ota (JPN)		Noel Loban (GBR)	
Heavyweight (- 220½ lbs)	Lou Banach (USA)		Joseph Atiyeh (SYR)		Vasile Pascasu (ROM)	
Super-Heavyweight (+ 220½ lbs)	Bruce Baumgartner (USA)		Bob Molle (CAN)		Ayhan Taskin (TUR)	
Judo						
Super-Lightweight (- 132½ lbs)	Shinji Hosokawa (JPN)		Kim Jae-Jup (KOR)		Edward Liddle (USA) Neil Eckersley (GBR)	
Welterweight (- 143¼ lbs)	Yoshiyuki Matsuoka (JPN)		Hwang Jung-Oh (KOR)		Josef Reiter (AUT) Marc Alexandre (FRA)	
Lightweight (- 156½ lbs)	Keun Ahn-Beyong (KOR)		Ezio Gamba (ITA)		Luis Onmura (BRA) Kenneth Brown (GBR)	
Light-Middleweight (- 171¾ lbs)	Frank Wieneke (FRG)		Neil Adams (GBR)		Mircea Fratica (ROM) Michel Nowak (FRA)	
Middleweight (- 189½ lbs)	Peter Seisenbacher (AUT)		Robert Berland (USA)		Walter Carmona (BRA) Seiki Nose (JPN)	
Light-Heavyweight (- 209¼ lbs)	Ha Hyoung-Zoo (KOR)		Douglas Vieira (BRA)		Günther Neureuther (FRG) Bjarni Fridriksson (ISL)	
Heavyweight (+ 209¼ lbs)	Hitoshi Saito (JPN)		Angelo Parisi (FRA)		Mark Berger (CAN) Cho Yong-Chul (KOR)	
Open Class	Yasuhiro Yamashita (JPN)		Mohamed Rashwan (EGY)		Arthur Schnabel (FRG) Mihai Cioc (ROM)	
Fencing						
Individual Foil, Men	Mauro Numa (ITA)		Matthias Behr (FRG)		Stefano Cerioni (ITA)	
Team Foil, Men	Italy		FRG		France	
Individual Épée	Philippe Boisse (FRA)		Björne Vaggo (SWE)		Philippe Riboud (FRA)	
Team Épée	FRG		France		Italy	
Individual Saber	Jean-François Lamour (FRA)		Marco Marin (ITA)		Peter Westbrook (USA)	
Team Saber	Italy		France		Romania	
Individual Foil, Women	Ju Jie Luan (CHN)		Cornelia Hanisch (FRG)		Dorina Vaccaroni (ITA)	
Team Foil, Women	FRG		Romania		France	
Modern Pentathlon						
Individual	Daniele Masala (ITA)	5 469	Svante Rasmusson (SWE)	5 456	Carlo Massullo (ITA)	5 406
Team	Italy	16 060	USA	15 568	France	15 565

EVENT	GOLD		SILVER		BRONZE	
Canoeing						
Men						
500 m Kayak Singles K1	Ian Ferguson (NZL)	1:47.84	Lars-Erik Moberg (SWE)	1:48.18	Bernard Bregeon (FRA)	1:48.41
1000 m Kayak Singles K1	Alan Thompson (NZL)	3:45.73	Milan Janic (YUG)	3:46.88	Greg Barton (USA)	3:47.38
500 m Kayak Pairs K2	New Zealand	1:34.21	Sweden	1:35.26	Canada	1:35.41
1000 m Kayak Pairs K2	Canada	3:24.22	France	3:25.97	Australia	3:26.80
1000 m Kayak Fours K4	New Zealand	3:02.28	Sweden	3:02.81	France	3:03.94
500 m Canadian Singles C1	Larry Cain (CAN)	1:57.01	Henning Jakobsen (DEN)	1:58.45	Costica Olaru (ROM)	1:59.86
1000 m Canadian Singles C1	Ulrich Eicke (FRG)	4:06.32	Larry Cain (CAN)	4:08.67	Henning Jakobsen (DEN)	4:09.50
500 m Canadian Pairs C2	Yugoslavia	1:43.67	Romania	1:45.68	Spain	1:47.71
1000 m Canadian Pairs C2	Romania	3:40.60	Yugoslavia	3:41.56	France	3:48.01
Women						
500 m Kayak Singles K1	Agneta Andersson (SWE)	1:58.72	Barbara Schüttpelz (FRG)	1:59.93	Annemiek Derckx (HOL)	2:00.11
500 m Kayak Pairs K2	Sweden	1:45.25	Canada	1:47.13	FRG	1:47.32
500 m Kayak Fours K4	Romania	1:38.34	Sweden	1:38.87	Canada	1:39.40
Rowing						
Men						
Single Sculls	Pertti Karppinen (FIN)	7:00.24	Peter Michael Kolbe (FRG)	7:02.19	Robert Mills (CAN)	7:10.38
Doubles Sculls	USA	6:36.87	Belgium	6:38.19	Yugoslavia	6:39.59
Coxless Pairs	Romania	6:45.39	Spain	6:48.47	Norway	6:51.81
Coxed Pairs	Italy	7:05.99	Romania	7:11.21	USA	7:12.81
Coxless Quadruple Sculls	FRG	5:57.55	Australia	5:57.98	Canada	5:59.07
Coxless Fours	New Zealand	6:03.48	USA	6:06.10	Denmark	6:07.72
Coxed Fours	Great Britain	6:18.64	USA	6:20.28	New Zealand	6:23.68
Coxed Eights	Canada	5:41.32	USA	5:41.74	Australia	5:42.40
Women						
Single Sculls	Valeria Racila (ROM)	3:40.68	Charlotte Geer (USA)	3:43.89	Ann Haesebrouck (BEL)	3:45.72
Double Sculls	Romania	3:26.77	Netherlands	3:29.13	Canada	3:29.82
Coxless Pairs	Romania	3:32.60	Canada	3:36.06	FRG	3:40.50
Coxed Quadruple Sculls	Romania	3:14.11	USA	3:15.57	Denmark	3:16.02
Coxed Fours	Romania	3:19.38	Canada	3:21.55	Australia	3:23.29
Coxed Eights	USA	2:59.80	Romania	3:00.87	Netherlands	3:02.92
Yachting						
Finn Class	Russel Coutts (NZL)	34.7	John Bertrand (USA)	37.0	Terry Neilson (CAN)	37.7
International Star	USA	29.7	FRG	41.4	Italy	43.5
Flying Dutchman	USA	19.7	Canada	22.7	Great Britain	48.7
International Tornado	New Zealand	14.7	USA	37.0	Australia	50.4
International 470	Spain	33.7	USA	43.0	France	49.9
International Soling	USA	33.7	Brazil	43.4	Canada	49.7
Windglider Class	Stephan van den Berg (HOL)	27.7	Randall Steele (USA)	46.0	Bruce Kendall (NZL)	46.4
Cycling						
Men						
Road Race (118¼ mi)	Alexi Grewal (USA)	4:59.57	Steve Bauer (CAN)	4:59.7	Dag Otto Lauritzen (NOR)	5:00.18
100 km Road Team Time Trial	Italy	1:58.28	Switzerland	2:02.38	USA	2:02.46
1000 m Time Trial	Fredy Schmidtke (FRG)	1:06.10	Curtis Harnett (CAN)	1:06.44	Fabrice Colas (FRA)	1:06.65
1000 m Sprint	Mark Gorski (USA)		Nelson Vails (USA)		Tsutomu Sakamoto (JPN)	
4000 m Individual Pursuit	Steve Hegg (USA)	4:39.35	Rolf Gölz (FRG)	4:43.82	Leonard Nitz (USA)	4:44.03
4000 m Team Pursuit	Australia	4:25.99	USA	4:29.85	FRG	4:25.60
Individual Points Race	Roger Ilegems (BEL)		Uwe Messerschmidt (FRG)		José Manuel Youshimatz (MEX)	
Women						
Road Race (49¼ mi)	Connie Carpenter-Phinney (USA)	2:11.14	Rebecca Twigg (USA)		Sandra Schumacher (FRG)	
Shooting						
Men						
Small-Bore Rifle (Prone)	Edward Etzel (USA)	599	Michel Bury (FRA)	596	Michael Sullivan (GBR)	596
Small-Bore Rifle (3 Positions)	Malcolm Cooper (GBR)	1173	Daniel Nipkow (SUI)	1163	Alister Allan (GBR)	1162
Rapid Fire Pistol	Takeo Kamachi (JPN)	595	Corneliu Ion (ROM)	593	Rauno Bies (FIN)	591
Free Pistol (50 m)	Xu Haifeng (CHN)	566	Ragnar Skanaker (SWE)	565	Wang Yifu (CHN)	564
Running Game Target	Li Yuwei (CHN)	587	Helmut Bellingrodt (COL)	584	Huang Shiping (CHN)	581
Skeet Shooting	Matthew Dryke (USA)	198	Ole Riber Rasmussen (DEN)	196/25	Luca Scribani-Rossi (ITA)	196/24
Trap Shooting	Luciano Giovanetti (ITA)	192	Francisco Boza (PER)	192	Daniel Carlisle (USA)	192
Air Rifle	Philippe Heberle (FRA)	589	Andreas Kronthaler (AUT)	581	Barry Dagger (GBR)	587

EVENT	GOLD		SILVER		BRONZE	
Women						
Sport Pistol	Linda Thom (CAN)	585	Ruby Fox (USA)	585	Patricia Dench (AUS)	583
Standard Rifle	Wu Xiaoxuan (CHN)	581	Ulrike Holmer (FRG)	578	Wanda Jewell (USA)	578
Air Rifle	Pat Spurgin (USA)	393	Edith Gufler (ITA)	391	Wu Xiaoxuan (CHN)	389
Archery						
Men	Darrell Pace (USA)	2616	Richard McKinney (USA)	2564	Hiroshi Yamamoto (JPN)	2563
Women	Seo Hyang-Soon (KOR)	2568	Li Lingjuan (CHN)	2559	Kim Jin-Ho (KOR)	2555
Equestrianism						
Three-Day Event	Mark Todd (NZL)	51.60	Karen Stives (USA)	54.20	Virginia Holgate (GBR)	56.80
Three-Day Event, Team	USA	186.00	Great Britain	189.20	FRG	234
Grand Prix (Dressage)	Reiner Klimke (FRG)	1504	Anne Grethe Jensen (DEN)	1442	Otto Hofer (SUI)	1364
Grand Prix (Dressage) Team	FRG	4955	Switzerland	4673	Sweden	4630
Grand Prix (Jumping)	Joe Fargis (USA)		Conrad Homfeld (USA)	-4	Heidi Robbiani (SUI)	-8
Grand Prix (Jumping) Team	USA	12.00	Great Britain	36.75	FRG	39.25
Gymnastics						
Men						
Individual Combined Exercises	Koji Gushiken (JPN)	118.700	Peter Vidmar (USA)	118.675	Li Ning (CHN)	118.575
Team	USA	591.40	China	590.80	Japan	586.70
Parallel Bars	Bart Conner (USA)	19.950	Nobuyuki Kajitani (JPN)	19.925	Mitchell Gaylord (USA)	19.850
Floor	Li Ning (CHN)	19.925	Lou Yun (CHN)	19.775	Koji Sotomura (JPN)	19.700
					Philippe Vatuone (FRA)	19.700
Horse Vault	Lou Yun (CHN)	19.950	Li Ning (CHN)	19.825		
			Mitchell Gaylord (USA)	19.825		
			Koji Gushiken (JPN)	19.825		
			Shinji Morisue (JPN)	19.825		
Horizontal Bar	Shinji Morisue (JPN)	20.000	Tong Fei (CHN)	19.955	Koji Gushiken (JPN)	19.950
Rings	Koji Gushiken (JPN)	19.850			Mitchell Gaylord (USA)	19.825
	Li Ning (CHN)	19.850				
Pommel Horse	Li Ning (CHN)	19.950			Timothy Daggett (USA)	19.825
	Peter Vidmar (USA)	19.950				
Women						
Individual Combined Exercises	Mary Lou Retton (USA)	79.175	Ecaterina Szabó (ROM)	79.125	Simona Pauca (ROM)	78.675
Team	Romania	392.20	USA	391.20	China	388.60
Floor	Ecaterina Szabó (ROM)	19.975	Julianne McNamara (USA)	19.950	Mary Lou Retton (USA)	19.775
Horse Vault	Ecaterina Szabó (ROM)	19.875	Mary Lou Retton (USA)	19.850	Lavinia Agache (ROM)	19.750
Beam	Simona Pauca (ROM)	19.800			Kathy Johnson (USA)	19.650
	Ecaterina Szabó (ROM)	19.800				
Asymmetrical Bars	Ma Yanhong (CHN)	19.950			Mary Lou Retton (USA)	19.800
	Julianne McNamara (USA)	19.950				
Modern Rhythmic	Lori Fung (CAN)	57.950	Doina Staiculescu (ROM)	57.900	Regina Weber (FRG)	57.700
Basketball						
Men	USA		Spain		Yugoslavia	
Women	USA		South Korea		China	
Soccer	France		Brazil		Yugoslavia	
Handball						
Men	Yugoslavia		FRG		Romania	
Women	Yugoslavia		South Korea		China	
Hockey						
Men	Pakistan		FRG		Great Britain	
Women	Netherlands		FRG		USA	
Volleyball						
Men	USA		Brazil		Italy	
Women	China		USA		Japan	

Calgary 1988

February 13 – February 28

Participants: 1423 / Men: 1110, Women: 313, Countries: 57,
Sports: 8, Events: 46
Final Torchbearer: Robyn Perry

Medals Table

PLACE	COUNTRY	GOLD	SILVER	BRONZE
1	USSR	11	9	9
2	GDR	9	10	6
3	Switzerland	5	5	5
4	Finland	4	1	2
5	Sweden	4	–	2

Outstanding Athletes

PLACE	NAME (NATIONALITY)	DISCIPLINE	G	S	B
1	Yvonne van Gennip (HOL)	Speed Skating	3	–	–
	Matti Nykänen (FIN)	Nordic Skiing	3	–	–
3	Tamara Tichonova (URS)	Nordic Skiing	2	1	–
4	Tomas Gustafson (SWE)	Speed Skating	2	–	–
	Frank-Peter Roetsch (GDR)	Biathlon	2	–	–
	Vreni Schneider (SUI)	Alpine Skiing	2	–	–
	Gunde Svan (SWE)	Nordic Skiing	2	–	–
	Alberto Tomba (ITA)	Alpine Skiing	2	–	–

EVENT	GOLD		SILVER		BRONZE	
Alpine Skiing						
Men						
Downhill	Pirmin Zurbriggen (SUI)	1:59.63	Peter Müller (SUI)	2:00.14	Franck Piccard (FRA)	2:01.24
Slalom	Alberto Tomba (ITA)	1:39.47	Frank Wörndl (FRG)	1:39.53	Paul Frommelt (LIE)	1:39.84
Giant Slalom	Alberto Tomba (ITA)	2:06.37	Hubert Strolz (AUT)	2:07.41	Pirmin Zurbriggen (SUI)	2:08.39
Super G	Franck Piccard (FRA)	1:39.66	Helmut Mayer (AUT)	1:40.96	Lars-Börje Eriksson (SWE)	1:41.08
Combined	Hubert Strolz (AUT)	36.55	Bernhard Gstrein (AUT)	43.45	Paul Accola (SUI)	48.24
Women						
Downhill	Marina Kiehl (FRG)	1:25.86	Brigitte Oertli (SUI)	1:26.61	Karen Percy (CAN)	1:26.62
Slalom	Vreni Schneider (SUI)	1:36.69	Mateja Svet (YUG)	1:38.37	Christa Kinshofer-Güthlein (FRG)	1:38.40
Giant Slalom	Vreni Schneider (SUI)	2:06.49	Christa Kinshofer-Güthlein (FRG)	2:07.42	Maria Walliser (SUI)	2:07.72
Super G	Sigrid Wolf (AUT)	1:19.03	Michela Figini (SUI)	1:20.03	Karen Percy (CAN)	1:20.29
Combined	Anita Wachter (AUT)	29.25	Brigitte Oertli (SUI)	29.48	Maria Walliser (SUI)	51.28
Nordic Skiing						
Men						
15 km Cross-Country Skiing (Classical)	Mikhail Devyatarov (URS)	41:18.9	Pal-Gunnar Mikkelsplass (NOR)	41:33.4	Vladimir Smirnov (URS)	41:48.5
30 km Cross-Country Skiing (Classical)	Alexei Prokurorov (URS)	1:24:26.3	Vladimir Smirnov (URS)	1:24:35.1	Vegard Ulvang (NOR)	1:25:11.6
50 km Cross-Country Skiing (Freestyle)	Gunde Svan (SWE)	2:04:30.9	Maurillo de Zolt (ITA)	2:05:36.4	Andi Grünenfelder (SUI)	2:06:01.9
4 x 10 km	Sweden	1:43:58.6	USSR	1:44:11.3	Czechoslovakia	1:45:22.7
Women						
5 km Cross-Country Skiing (Classical)	Marjo Matikainen (FIN)	15:04.0	Tamara Tichonova (URS)	15:05.3	Vida Venciene (URS)	15:11.1
10 km Cross-Country Skiing (Classical)	Vida Venciene (URS)	30:08.3	Raisa Smetanina (URS)	30:17.0	Marjo Matikainen (FIN)	30:20.5
20 km Cross-Country Skiing	Tamara Tichonova (URS)	55:53.6	Anfissa Rezova (URS)	56:12.8	Raisa Smetanina (URS)	57:22.1
4 x 5 km	USSR	59:51.1	Norway	1:01:33.0	Finland	1:01:53.8
Ski Jumping						
Ski Jumping (70 m Hill)	Matti Nykänen (FIN)	229.1	Pavel Ploc (TCH)	212.1	Jiri Malec (TCH)	211.8
Ski Jumping (90 m Hill)	Matti Nykänen (FIN)	224.0	Erik Johnson (NOR)	207.9	Matjaz Debelak (YUG)	207.7
Ski Jumping, Team	Finland	634.4	Yugoslavia	625.5	Norway	596.1
Nordic Combined – Individual	Hippolyt Kempf (SUI)	432.230	Klaus Sulzenbacher (AUT)	429.375	Allar Levandi (URS)	422.590
Nordic Combined – Team	FRG	792.08	Switzerland	791.40	Austria	785.90
Biathlon						
10 km	Frank-Peter Roetsch (GDR)	25:08.1	Valeri Medvetsev (URS)	25:23.7	Sergei Chepikov (URS)	25:29.4
20 km	Frank-Peter Roetsch (GDR)	56:33.3	Valeri Medvetsev (URS)	56:54.6	Johann Passler (ITA)	57:10.1
4 x 7.5 km	USSR	1:22:30.0	FRG	1:23:37.4	Italy	1:23:51.5
Figure Skating						
Women	Katarina Witt (GDR)		Elizabeth Manley (CAN)		Debra Thomas (USA)	
Men	Brian Boitano (USA)		Brian Orser (CAN)		Viktor Petrenko (URS)	
Pairs	Yekaterina Gordeyeva/ Sergei Grinkov (URS)		Yelena Valova/ Oleg Vasiliyev (URS)		Jill Watson/ Peter Oppegard (USA)	

EVENT	GOLD		SILVER		BRONZE	
Ice Dance	Natalya Bestemianova/ Andrei Bukin (URS)		Marina Klimova/ Sergei Ponomarenko (URS)		Tracy Wilson/ Robert McCall (CAN)	
Speed Skating						
Men						
500 m	Uwe-Jens Mey (GDR)	36.45	Jan Ykema (HOL)	36.76	Akira Kuroiwa (JPN)	36.77
1000 m	Nikolai Gulyatev (URS)	1:13.03	Uwe-Jens Mey (GDR)	1:13.11	Igor Szelesovzki (URS)	1:13.19
1500 m	André Hoffman (GDR)	1:52.06	Eric Flaim (USA)	1:52.12	Michael Hadschieff (AUT)	1:52.31
5000 m	Tomas Gustafson (SWE)	6:44.63	Leo Visser (HOL)	6:44.98	Gerard Kemkers (HOL)	6:45.92
10,000 m	Tomas Gustafson (SWE)	13:48.20	Michael Hadschieff (AUT)	13:56.11	Leo Visser (HOL)	14:00.55
Women						
500 m	Bonnie Blair (USA)	39.10	Christa Rothenburger (GDR)	39.12	Karin Kania (GDR)	39.24
1000 m	Christa Rothenburger (GDR)	1:17.65	Karin Kania (GDR)	1:17.70	Bonnie Blair (USA)	1:18.31
1500 m	Yvonne van Gennip (HOL)	2:00.68	Karin Kania (GDR)	2:00.82	Andrea Ehrig (GDR)	2:01.49
3000 m	Yvonne van Gennip (HOL)	4:11.94	Andrea Ehrig (GDR)	4:12.09	Gabi Zange (GDR)	4:16.92
5000 m	Yvonne van Gennip (HOL)	7:14.13	Andrea Ehrig (GDR)	7:17.12	Gabi Zange (GDR)	7:21.61
Lugeing						
Men's Singles	Jens Müller (GDR)	3:05.548	Georg Hackl (FRG)	3:05.916	Yuri Kcharchenko (URS)	3:06.274
Women's Singles	Steffi Walter (GDR)	3:03.973	Ute Oberhoffner (GDR)	3:04.105	Cerstin Schmidt (GDR)	3:04.181
2-Man Luge	Jörg Hoffman/Jochen Pietzch (GDR)	1:31.940	Stefan Krausse/ Jan Behrendt (GDR)	1:32.039	Thomas Schwab/ Wolfgang Staudinger (FRG)	1:32.274
Bobsledding						
2-Man Bob	USSR I	3:53.48	GDR I	3:54.19	GDR II	3:54.64
4-Man Bob	Switzerland I	3:47.51	GDR I	3:47.58	USSR II	3:48.26
Ice Hockey	USSR		Finland		Sweden	

Seoul 1988

September 17 – October 2

Participants: 8465 / Men: 6279, Women: 2186, Countries: 159,
Sports: 23, Events: 237
Final Torchbearers: Son Kee-Chung, Lim Chun-Ae, Chung Sun-Man, Kim
Won-Tak, Sohn Mi-Chung

Medals Table

PLACE	COUNTRY	GOLD	SILVER	BRONZE
1	USSR	55	31	46
2	GDR	37	35	30
3	USA	36	31	27
4	South Korea	12	11	10
5	FRG	11	14	15

Outstanding Athletes

PLACE	NAME (NATIONALITY)	DISCIPLINE	G	S	B
1	Kristin Otto (GDR)	Swimming	6	–	–
2	Matt Biondi (USA)	Swimming	5	1	1
3	Vladimir Artemov (URS)	Gymnastics	4	1	–
4	Daniela Silivas (ROM)	Gymnastics	3	2	1
5	Florence Griffith-Joyner (USA)	Athletics	3	1	–

EVENT	GOLD		SILVER		BRONZE	
Athletics						
Men						
100 m★	Carl Lewis (USA)	9.92★	Linford Christie (GBR)	9.97	Calvin Smith (USA)	9.99
200 m	Joe DeLoach (USA)	19.75	Carl Lewis (USA)	19.79	Robson da Silva (BRA)	20.04
400 m	Steven Lewis (USA)	43.87	Butch Reynolds (USA)	43.93	Danny Everett (USA)	44.09
800 m	Paul Ereng (KEN)	1:43.45	Joaquim Cruz (BRA)	1:43.90	Said Aouita (MAR)	1:44.06
1500 m	Peter Rono (KEN)	3:35.96	Peter Elliott (GBR)	3:36.15	Jens-Peter Herold (GDR)	3:36.21
5000 m	John Ngugi (KEN)	13:11.70	Dieter Baumann (FRG)	13:15.52	Hansjörg Kunze (GDR)	13:15.73
10,000 m	Brahim Boutaib (MAR)	27:21.44	Salvatore Antibo (ITA)	27:23.55	Kipkemboy Kimeli (KEN)	27:25.16
Marathon	Gelindo Bordin (ITA)	2:10:32	Douglas Wakihuriu (KEN)	2:10:47	Ahmed Saleh (DJI)	2:10:59
110 m Hurdles	Roger Kingdom (USA)	12.98	Colin Jackson (GBR)	13.28	Anthony Campbell (USA)	13.38
400 m Hurdles	Andre Philipps (USA)	47.19	Amadou Dia Ba (SEN)	47.23	Edwin Moses (USA)	47.56

EVENT	GOLD		SILVER		BRONZE	
3000 m Steeplechase	Julius Kariuki (KEN)	8:05.51	Peter Koech (KEN)	8:06.79	Mark Rowland (GBR)	8:07.96
4 x 100 m	USSR	38.19	Great Britain	38.28	France	38.40
4 x 400 m	USA	2:56.16	Jamaica	3:00.30	FRG	3:00.56
20 km Walk	Jozef Pribilinec (TCH)	1:19.57	Ronald Weigel (GDR)	1:20.00	Maurizio Damilano (ITA)	1:20:14
50 km Walk	Vyacheslav Ivanenko (URS)	3:38:29	Ronald Weigel (GDR)	3:38:56	Hartwig Gauder (GDR)	3:39:45
High Jump	Gennadi Avdeyenko (URS)	7'9¼"	Hollis Conway (USA)	7'8¼"	Rudolf Povarnitsin (URS)	7'8¼"
					Patrick Sjöberg (SWE)	7'8¼"
Pole Vault	Sergei Bubka (URS)	19'4¼"	Rodion Gataullin (URS)	19'2¼"	Grigori Yegorov (URS)	19'0¼"
Long Jump	Carl Lewis (USA)	28'7¼"	Mike Powell (USA)	27'10¼"	Larry Myricks (USA)	27'1¼"
Triple Jump	Khristo Markov (BUL)	57'9¼"	Igor Lapshin (URS)	57'5¼"	Alexander Kovalenko (URS)	57'2"
Shot	Ulf Timmermann (GDR)	73'8¼"	Randy Barnes (USA)	73'5¼"	Werner Günthör (SUI)	72'1¼"
Discus	Jürgen Schult (GDR)	225'9"	Romas Ubartas (URS)	221'5"	Rolf Danneberg (FRG)	221'1"
Hammer	Sergei Litvinov (URS)	278'2"	Yuri Sedych (URS)	274'10"	Yuri Tamm (URS)	266'3"
Javelin	Tapio Korjus (FIN)	276'6"	Jan Zelezny (TCH)	276'0"	Seppo Räty (FIN)	273'2"
Decathlon	Christian Schenk (GDR)	8488	Torsten Voss (GDR)	8399	Dave Steen (CAN)	8328

★Race Winner Ben Johnson (Can; 9.79) was disqualified for failing a drugs test

Women

100 m	Florence Griffith-Joyner (USA)	10.54	Evelyn Ashford (USA)	10.83	Heike Drechsler (GDR)	10.85
200 m	Florence Griffith-Joyner (USA)	21.34	Grace Jackson (JAM)	21.72	Heike Drechsler (GDR)	21.95
400 m	Olga Brizgina (URS)	48.65	Petra Müller (GDR)	49.45	Olga Nasarova (URS)	49.90
800 m	Sigrun Wodars (GDR)	1:56.10	Christine Wachtel (GDR)	1:56.64	Kim Gallagher (USA)	1:56.91
1500 m	Paula Ivan (ROM)	3:53.96	Lelute Baikauskaite (URS)	4:00.24	Tatyana Samolenko (URS)	4:00.30
3000 m	Tatyana Samolenko (URS)	8:26.53	Paula Ivan (ROM)	8:27.15	Yvonne Murray (GBR)	8:29.02
10 000 m	Olga Bondarenko (URS)	31:05.21	Elizabeth McColgan (GBR)	31:08.44	Yelena Yupiyeva (URS)	31:19.82
Marathon	Rosa Mota (POR)	2:25:40	Lisa Martin (AUS)	2:25:53	Katrin Dörre (GDR)	2:26:21
100 m Hurdles	Yordanka Donkova (BUL)	12.38	Gloria Siebert (GDR)	12.61	Claudia Zaczkiewicz (FRG)	12.75
400 m Hurdles	Debra Flintoff-King (AUS)	53.17	Tatyana Ledovskaya (URS)	53.18	Ellen Fiedler (GDR)	53.63
4 x 100 m	USA	41.98	GDR	42.09	USSR	42.75
4 x 400 m	USSR	3:15.18	USA	3:15.51	GDR	3:18.29
High Jump	Louise Ritter (USA)	6'8"	Stefka Kostadinova (BUL)	6'7"	Tamara Bykova (URS)	6'6¼"
Long Jump	Jackie Joyner-Kersee (USA)	24'3¼"	Heike Drechsler (GDR)	23'8¼"	Galina Chistyakova (URS)	23'4"
Shot	Natalya Lisovskaya (URS)	72'11¼"	Kathrin Neimke (GDR)	69'1¼"	Li Meisu (CHN)	69'1¼"
Discus	Martina Hellmann (GDR)	237'2"	Diana Gansky (GDR)	235'10"	Szvetanka Christova (BUL)	228'10"
Javelin	Petra Felke (GDR)	245'0"	Fatima Whitbread (GBR)	230'8"	Beate Koch (GDR)	220'9"
Heptathlon	Jackie Joyner-Kersee (USA)	7291	Sabine John (GDR)	6897	Anke Behmer (GDR)	6858

Swimming

Men

50 m Freestyle	Matt Biondi (USA)	22.14	Thomas Jager (USA)	22.36	Gennadi Prigoda (URS)	22.71
100 m Freestyle	Matt Biondi (USA)	48.63	Christopher Jacobs (USA)	49.08	Stephan Caron (FRA)	49.62
200 m Freestyle	Duncan Armstrong (AUS)	1:47.25	Anders Holmertz (SWE)	1:47.89	Matt Biondi (USA)	1:47.99
400 m Freestyle	Uwe Dassler (GDR)	3:46.95	Duncan Armstrong (AUS)	3:47.15	Artur Wojdat (POL)	3:47.34
1500 m Freestyle	Vladimir Salnikov (URS)	15:00.40	Stefan Pfeiffer (FRG)	15:02.69	Uwe Dassler (GDR)	15:06.15
100 m Backstroke	Daichi Suzuki (JPN)	55.05	David Berkhoff (USA)	55.18	Igor Polianski (URS)	55.20
200 m Backstroke	Igor Polianski (URS)	1:59.37	Frank Baltrusch (GDR)	1:59.60	Paul Kingsman (NZL)	2:00.48
100 m Breaststroke	Adrian Moorhouse (GBR)	1:02.04	Károly Guttler (HUN)	1:02.05	Dmitri Volkov (URS)	1:02.20
200 m Breaststroke	Jozef Szábó (HUN)	2:13.52	Nick Gillingham (GBR)	2:14.12	Sergio Lopez (ESP)	2:15.21
100 m Butterfly	Anthony Nesty (SUR)	53.00	Matt Biondi (USA)	53.01	Andy Jameson (GBR)	53.30
200 m Butterfly	Michael Gross (FRG)	1:56.94	Benny Nielsen (DEN)	1:58.24	Anthony Mosse (NZL)	1:58.28
200 m Medley	Tamas Darnyi (HUN)	2:00.17	Patrick Kühl (GDR)	2:01.61	Vadim Yaroshchuk (URS)	2:02.40
400 m Medley	Tamas Darnyi (HUN)	4:14.75	David Wharton (USA)	4:17.36	Stefano Battistelli (ITA)	4:18.01
4 x 100 m Freestyle	USA	3:16.53	USSR	3:18.33	GDR	3:19.82
4 x 200 m Freestyle	USA	7:12.51	GDR	7:13.68	FRG	7:14.35
4 x 100 m Medley	USA	3:36.93	Canada	3:39.28	USSR	3:39.96
Springboard Diving	Greg Louganis (USA)	730.80	Tan Liangde (CHN)	704.88	Li Deliang (CHN)	665.28
Highboard Diving	Greg Louganis (USA)	638.61	Xiong Ni (CHN)	637.47	Jesus Mena (MEX)	594.93
Water Polo	Yugoslavia		USA		USSR	

Women

50 m Freestyle	Kristin Otto (GDR)	25.49	Yang Wenyi (CHN)	25.64	Katrin Meissner (GDR)	25.71
					Jill Sterkel (USA)	25.71
100 m Freestyle	Kristin Otto (GDR)	54.93	Zhuang Yong (CHN)	55.47	Cathérine Plewinski (FRA)	55.49
200 m Freestyle	Heike Friedrich (GDR)	1:57.65	Sivia Poll (CRC)	1:58.67	Manuela Stellmach (GDR)	1:59.01
400 m Freestyle	Janet Evans (USA)	4:03.85	Heike Friedrich (GDR)	4:05.94	Anke Möhring (GDR)	4:06.62
800 m Freestyle	Janet Evans (USA)	8:20.20	Astrid Strauss (GDR)	8:22.09	Julie McDonald (AUS)	8:22.93
100 m Backstroke	Kristin Otto (GDR)	1:00.89	Krisztina Egerszegi (HUN)	1:01.56	Cornelia Sirch (GDR)	1:01.57

EVENT	GOLD		SILVER		BRONZE	
200 m Backstroke	Krisztina Egerszegi (HUN)	2:09.29	Kathrin Zimmermann (GDR)	2:10.61	Cornelia Sirch (GDR)	2:11.45
100 m Breaststroke	Tania Dangalakova (BUL)	1:07.95	Antoaneta Frenkeva (BUL)	1:08.74	Silke Hörner (GDR)	1:08.83
200 m Breaststroke	Silke Hörner (GDR)	2:26.71	Huang Xiaomin (CHN)	2:27.49	Antoaneta Frenkeva (BUL)	2:28.34
100 m Butterfly	Kristin Otto (GDR)	59.00	Birte Weigang (GDR)	59.45	Quian Hong (CHN)	59.52
200 m Butterfly	Kathleen Nord (GDR)	2:09.51	Birte Weigang (GDR)	2:09.91	Mary T. Meagher (USA)	2:10.80
200 m Medley	Daniela Hunger (GDR)	2:12.59	Elena Dendeberova (URS)	2:13.31	Noemi Ildiko Lung (ROM)	2:14.85
400 m Medley	Janet Evans (USA)	4:37.76	Noemi Lung (ROM)	4:39.46	Daniela Hunger (GDR)	4:39.76
4 x 100 m Freestyle	GDR	3:40.63	Netherlands	3:43.39	USA	3:44.25
4 x 100 m Medley	GDR	4:03.74	USA	4:07.90	Canada	4:10.49
Springboard Diving	Gao Min (CHN)	580.23	Qing Li (CHN)	534.33	Kelly McCormick (USA)	533.19
Highboard Diving	Xu Yanmei(CHN)	445.20	Michele Mitchell (USA)	436.95	Wendy Lian Williams (USA)	400.44
Synchronized Swimming						
Solo	Carolyn Waldo (CAN)	200.150	Tracie Ruiz-Conforto (USA)	197.633	Mikako Kotani (JPN)	191.850
Duet	Canada	197.717	USA	197.284	Japan	190.959
Boxing						
Light-Flyweight (- 105¾ lbs)	Ivailo Christov (BUL)		Michael Carbajal (USA)		Robert Isaszegi (HUN)	
					Leopoldo Serantes (PHI)	
Flyweight (- 112½ lbs)	Kim Kwang Sun (KOR)		Andreas Tews (GDR)		Mario Gonzalez (MEX)	
					Timofei Skriabin (URS)	
Bantamweight (- 119 lbs)	Kennedy McKinney (USA)		Alexander Christov (BUL)		Phajol Moolsan (THA)	
					Jorge Julio Rocha (COL)	
Featherweight (- 126 lbs)	Giovanni Parisi (ITA)		Daniel Dumitrescu (ROM)		Abdelhak Achik (MAR)	
					Lee Jae Hiuk (KOR)	
Lightweight (- 132 lbs)	Andreas Zülow (GDR)		George Cramne (SWE)		Nerguy Enchbat (MGL)	
					Romallis Ellis (USA)	
Light-Welterweight (- 140 lbs)	Vyacheslav Yanovski (URS)		Graham Cheney (AUS)		Reiner Gies (FRG)Lars Myberg (SWE)	
					Lars Myberg (SWE)	
Welterweight (- 148 lbs)	Robert Wangila (KEN)		Laurent Boudouani (FRA)		Jan Dydak (POL)	
					Kenneth Gould (USA)	
Light-Middleweight (- 157 lbs)	Park Si Hun (KOR)		Roy Jones (USA)		Richard Woodhall (GBR)	
					Raymond Downey (CAN)	
Middleweight (- 165 lbs)	Henry Maske (GDR)		Egerton Marcus (CAN)		Chris Sande (KEN)	
					Hussain Syed (PAK)	
Light-Heavyweight (- 178½ lbs)	Andrew Maynard (USA)		Nuramgomed Shanavasov (URS)		Henryk Petrich (POL)	
					Damir Skaro (YUG)	
Heavyweight (- 200½ lbs)	Ray Mercer (USA)		Baik Hyun Man (KOR)		Andrzej Golota (POL)	
					Arnold Vanderlijde (HOL)	
Super-Heavyweight (+ 200½ lbs)	Lennox Lewis (CAN)		Riddick Bowe (USA)		Alexander Miroshnichenko (URS)	
					Janusz Zarenkiewicz (POL)	
Weightlifting						
Flyweight (- 114½ lbs)	Sevdalin Marinov (BUL)	595 lbs	Chun Byung-Kwan (KOR)	573 lbs	He Zhuoquiang (CHN)	567½ lbs
Bantamweight (- 123½ lbs)	Oken Mirzoian (URS)	644¾ lbs	He Yiangqiang (CHN)	633¾ lbs	Liu Shoubin (CHN)	589¼ lbs
Featherweight (- 132¼ lbs)	Nahim Süleymanoglu (TUR)	755 lbs	Stefan Topourov (BUL)	688¾ lbs	Ye Huanming (CHN)	633¾ lbs
Lightweight (- 148¾ lbs)	Joachim Kunz (GDR)	749½ lbs	Israil Militosian (URS)	744 lbs	Li Jinhe (CHN)	716½ lbs
Middleweight (- 165½ lbs)	Borislav Gidikov (BUL)	826½ lbs	Ingo Steinhöfel (GDR)	793½ lbs	Alexander Varbanov (BUL)	788 lbs
Light-Heavyweight (- 182 lbs)	Israil Arsamakov (URS)	832 lbs	Istvan Messzi (HUN)	815½ lbs	Lee Hyung Kun (KOR)	810 lbs
Middle-Heavyweight (- 198½ lbs)	Anatoli Khrapaty (URS)	909½ lbs	Nail Muchamediarov (URS)	881¾ lbs	Slawomir Zawada (POL)	881¾ lbs
First Heavyweight 100 kg (- 220½ lbs)	Pavel Kuznetzov (URS)	936¾ lbs	Nicu Vlad (ROM)	887¼ lbs	Peter Immesberger (FRG)	870¾ lbs
Second Heavyweight (- 242½ lbs)	Juri Zacharevich (URS)	1,003 lbs	Jozsef Jacso (HUN)	942½ lbs	Ronny Weller (GDR)	936¾ lbs
Super-Heavyweight (+ 242½ lbs)	Alexander Kurlovich (URS)	1,019 lbs	Manfred Nerlinger (FRG)	947¾ lbs	Martin Zawieja (FRG)	914¾ lbs
Greco-Roman Wrestling						
Light-Flyweight (- 105¾ lbs)	Vincenzo Maenza (ITA)		Andrzej Chlab (POL)		Bratan Tzenov (BUL)	
Flyweight (- 114½ lbs)	Jon Rönningen (NOR)		Atsuji Miyahara (JPN)		Lee Jae Suk (KOR)	
Bantamweight (- 125¾ lbs)	Andras Sike (HUN)		Stoyan Balov (BUL)		Haralambos Holidis (GRE)	
Featherweight (- 136½ lbs)	Kamandar Madzhidov (URS)		Yivko Vangyelov (BUL)		An Dae Hyun (KOR)	
Lightweight (- 149¾ lbs)	Levon Zhulfalakian (URS)		Kim Sung Moon (KOR)		Tapio Sipilä (FIN)	
Welterweight (- 163 lbs)	Kim Young Nam (KOR)		Daulet Turlykanow (URS)		Jozef Tracz (POL)	
Middleweight (- 180¾ lbs)	Mikhail Mamiashvili (URS)		Tibor Komaronyi (HUN)		Kim Sang Kyu (KOR)	
Light-Heavyweight (- 198¼ lbs)	Atanas Komchev (BUL)		Harri Koskela (FIN)		Vladimir Popov (URS)	
Heavyweight (- 220½ lbs)	Andrzej Wronski (POL)		Gerhard Himmel (FRG)		Dennis Koslowski (USA)	
Super-Heavyweight (+ 220½ lbs)	Alexander Karelin (URS)		Rangel Guerovski (BUL)		Tomas Johansson (SWE)	
Freestyle Wrestling						
Light-Flyweight (- 105¾ lbs)	Takashi Kobayashi (JPN)		Ivan Tzonov (BUL)		Sergei Karamchakov (URS)	
Flyweight (- 114½ lbs)	Mitsuru Sato (JPN)		Saban Trstena (YUG)		Vladimir Togusov (URS)	

EVENT	GOLD		SILVER		BRONZE	
Bantamweight (- 125¾ lbs)	Sergei Beloglassov (URS)		Askari Mohammadian (IRN)		Noh Kyung Sun (KOR)	
Featherweight (- 114½ lbs)	John Smith (USA)		Stephan Sarkissian (URS)		Simeon Schterev (BUL)	
Lightweight (- 149¾ lbs)	Arsen Fadzayev (URS)		Park Jang Soon (KOR)		Nate Carr (USA)	
Welterweight (- 163 lbs)	Kenneth Monday (USA)		Adlan Varayev (URS)		Rakhmad Sofiadi (BUL)	
Middleweight (- 180¾ lbs)	Han Myung Woo (KOR)		Necmi Gencalp (TUR)		Josef Lohyna (TCH)	
Light-Heavyweight (- 198¼ lbs)	Macharbek Hadarchev (URS)		Akira Ota (JPN)		Kim Tae Woo (KOR)	
Heavyweight (- 220½ lbs)	Vasile Puscasu (ROM)		Leri Kabelov (URS)		William Scherer (USA)	
Super-Heavyweight (+ 220½ lbs)	David Gobedishvili (URS)		Bruce Baumgartner (USA)		Andreas Schröder (GDR)	
Judo						
Super-Lightweight (- 132½ lbs)	Kim Jae Yup (KOR)		Kevin Asano (USA)		Shinji Hosokawa (JPN) Amiran Totikashvili (URS)	
Half-Lightweight (- 143¼ lbs)	Lee Kyung Keun (KOR)		Janusz Pawlowski (POL)		Bruno Carabetta (FRA) Yosuke Yamamoto (JPN)	
Lightweight (- 156½ lbs)	Marc Alexandre (FRA)		Sven Loll (GDR)		Michael Swain (USA) Georgi Tenadze (URS)	
Light-Middleweight (- 171¾ lbs)	Waldemar Legien (POL)		Frank Wieneke (FRG)		Torsten Bréchôt (GDR) Bashir Varayev (URS)	
Middleweight (- 189½ lbs)	Peter Seisenbacher (AUT)		Vladimir Chestakov (URS)		Ben Spijkers (HOL) Akinobu Osako (JPN)	
Light-Heavyweight (- 209¼ lbs)	Aurelio Miguel (BRA)		Marc Meiling (FRG)		Robert van de Walle (BEL) Dennis Stewart (GBR)	
Heavyweight (+ 209½ lbs)	Hitoshi Saito (JPN)		Henry Stöhr (GDR)		Cho Young Chul (KOR) Grigori Verichev (URS)	
Fencing						
Individual Foil - Men	Stefano Cerioni (ITA)		Udo Wagner (GDR)		Alexander Romankov (URS)	
Team Foil - Men	USSR		FRG		Hungary	
Individual Saber	Jean-François Lamour (FRA)		Janusz Olech (POL)		Giovanni Scalzo (ITA)	
Team Saber	Hungary		USSR		Italy	
Individual Épee	Arnd Schmitt (FRG)		Philippe Riboud (FRA)		Andrei Shuvalov (URS)	
Team Épee	France		FRG		USSR	
Individual Foil - Women	Anja Fichtel (FRG)		Sabine Bau (FRG)		Zita Funkenhauser (FRG)	
Team Foil - Women	FRG		Italy		Hungary	
Modern Pentathlon						
Individual	Janós Martinek (HUN)	5404	Carlo Massullo (ITA)	5379	Vachtang Yagorashvili (URS)	5367
Team	Hungary	15886	Italy	15571	Great Britain	15276
Canoeing						
Men						
500 m Kayak Singles K1	Zsolt Gyulay (HUN)	1:44.82	Andreas Stähle (GDR)	1:46.38	Paul MacDonald (NZL)	1:46.46
1000 m Kayak Singles K1	Greg Barton (USA)	3:55.27	Grant Davies (AUS)	3:55.28	André Wohllebe (GDR)	3:55.55
500 m Kayak Pairs K2	New Zealand	1:33.98	USSR	1:34.15	Hungary	1:34.32
1000 m Kayak Pairs K2	USA	3:32.42	New Zealand	3:32.71	Australia	3:33.76
1000 m Kayak Fours K4	Hungary	3:00.20	USSR	3:01.40	GDR	3:02.37
500 m Canadian Singles C1	Olaf Heukrodt (GDR)	1:56.42	Mikhail Slivinski (URS)	1:57.26	Martin Marinov (BUL)	1:57.27
1000 m Canadian Singles C1	Ivan Klementiev (URS)	4:12.78	Jörg Schmidt (GDR)	4:15.83	Nikolai Bukalov (URS)	4:18.94
500 m Canadian Pairs C2	USSR	1:41.77	Poland	1:43.61	France	1:43.81
1000 m Canadian Pairs C2	USSR	3:48.36	GDR	3:51.44	Poland	3:54.33
Women						
500 m Kayak Singles K1	Vania Guechava (BUL)	1:55.19	Birgit Schmidt (GDR)	1:55.31	Izabela Dylewska (POL)	1:57.38
500 m Kayak Pairs K2	GDR	1:43.46	Bulgaria	1:44.06	Netherlands	1:46.00
500 m Kayak Fours K4	GDR	1:40.78	Hungary	1:41.88	Bulgaria	1:42.63
Rowing						
Men						
Single Sculls	Thomas Lange (GDR)	6:49.86	Peter-Michael Kolbe (FRG)	6:54.77	Eric Verdonk (NZL)	6:58.66
Double Sculls	Netherlands	6:21.13	Switzerland	6:22.59	USSR	6:22.87
Coxless Pairs	Great Britain	6:36.84	Romania	6:38.06	Yugoslavia	6:41.01
Coxed Pairs	Italy	6:58.79	GDR	7:00.63	Great Britain	7:01.95
Coxless Quadruple Sculls	Italy	5:53.37	Norway	5:55.08	GDR	5:56.13
Coxless Fours	GDR	6:03.11	USA	6:05.33	FRG	6:06.22
Coxed Fours	GDR	6:10.74	Romania	6:13.58	New Zealand	6:15.78
Coxed Eights	FRG	5:46.05	USSR	5:48.01	USA	5:48.26

EVENT	GOLD		SILVER		BRONZE	
Women						
Single Sculls	Jutta Behrendt (GDR)	7:47.19	Anne Marden (USA)	7:50.28	Magdalena Georgieva (BUL)	7:53.65
Double Sculls	GDR	7:00.48	Romania	7:04.36	Bulgaria	7:06.03
Coxless Pairs	Romania	7:28.13	Bulgaria	7:31.95	New Zealand	7:35.68
Coxed Quadruple Sculls	GDR	6:21.06	USSR	6:23.47	Romania	6:23.81
Coxed Fours	GDR	6:56.00	China	6:58.78	Romania	7:01.13
Coxed Eights	GDR	6:15.17	Romania	6:17.44	China	6:21.83
Yachting						
Finn Class	José Luis Doreste (ESP)	38.1	Peter Holmberg (ISV)	40.4	John Cutler (NZL)	45.0
International Star	Great Britain	45.7	USA	48.0	Brazil	50.0
Flying Dutchman	Denmark	31.4	Norway	37.4	Canada	48.4
International Tornado	France	16.0	New Zealand	35.4	Brazil	40.1
470 Women	USA	26.7	Sweden	40.0	USSR	45.4
470 Men	France	34.7	USSR	46.0	USA	51.0
International Soling	GDR	11.7	USA	14.0	Denmark	52.7
Surfing	Bruce Kendall (NZL)	35.4	Jan Boersma (AHO)	42.7	Michael Gebhardt (USA)	48.0
Cycling						
Men						
Road Race (122¼ mi)	Olaf Ludwig (GDR)	4:32:22	Bernd Gröne (FRG)	4:32:25	Christian Henn (FRG)	4:32:46
100 km Road Team Time Trial	GDR	1:57:47.7	Poland	1:57:54.2	Sweden	1:59:47.3
Sprint	Lutz Hesslich (GDR)		Nikolai Kovche (URS)		Gary Neiwand (AUS)	
1000 m Time Trial	Alexander Kirichenko (URS)	1:04.499	Martin Vinnicombe (AUS)	1:04.784	Robert Lechner (FRG)	1:05.114
4000 m Individual Pursuit	Gintautas Umaras (URS)	4:32.00	Dean Woods (AUS)	4:35.00	Bernd Dittert (GDR)	4:34.17
4000 m Team Pursuit	USSR	4:13.31	GDR	4:14.09	Australia	4:16.02
Individual Points Race	Dan Frost (DEN)	38	Leo Peelen (HOL)	26	Marat Ganeyev (URS)	46/1
Women						
Road Race (51 mi)	Monique Knol (HOL)	2:00:52	Jutta Niehaus (FRG)		Laima Zilporite (URS)	
Sprint	Erika Salumäe (URS)		Christa Luding-Rothenburger (GDR)		Connie Paraskevin-Young (USA)	
Equestrianism						
Three-Day Event	Mark Todd (NZL)	42.60	Ian Stark (GBR)	52.80	Virginia Leng (GBR)	62.00
Three-Day Event, Team	FRG	225.95	Great Britain	256.80	New Zealand	271.20
Grand Prix (Dressage)	Nicole Uphoff (FRG)	1521	Margitt Otto-Crepin (FRA)	1462	Christine Stückelberger (SUI)	1417
Grand Prix (Dressage) Team	FRG	4302	Switzerland	4164	Canada	3969
Grand Prix (Jumping)	Pierre Durand (FRA)	1.25	Greg Best (USA)	4.00	Karsten Huck (FRG)	4.00
Grand Prix (Jumping) Team	FRG	17.25	USA	20.50	France	27.50
Shooting						
Men						
Small-Bore Rifle (Prone)	Miroslav Varga (TCH)	703.9	Cha Yuong Chul (KOR)	702.8	Attila Zahonyi (HUN)	701.9
Small-Bore Rifle (3 Positions)	Malcolm Cooper (GBR)	1279.3	Alister Allan (GBR)	1275.6	Kirill Ivanov (URS)	1275.0
Rapid-Fire Pistol	Afanasi Kuzmin (URS)	698	Ralf Schumann (GDR)	696	Zoltan Kovacs (HUN)	693
Free Pistol (50 m)	Sorin Babii (ROM)	660	Ragnar Skanaker (SWE)	657	Igor Bassinski (URS)	657
Running Game Target	Tor Heiestad (NOR)	689	Huang Shiping (CHN)	687	Gennadi Avramenko (URS)	686
Air Pistol	Taniou Kiriakov (BUL)	687.9	Erich Buljung (USA)	687.9	Xu Haifeng (CHN)	684.5
Skeet Shooting	Axel Wegner (GDR)	222	Alfonso de Iruarrizaga (CHI)	221	Jorge Guardiola (ESP)	220
Trap Shooting	Dmitri Monakov (URS)	222.8	Miloslav Bednarik (TCH)	222/7	Frans Peeters (BEL)	219/16
Air Rifle	Goran Maksimovic (YUG)	695.6	Nicolas Berthelot (FRA)	694.2	Johann Riederer (FRG)	694.0
Women						
Sports Pistol	Nino Salukvadze (URS)	690	Tomoko Hasegawa (JPN)	686	Jasna Sekaric (YUG)	686
Small-Bore Rifle (3 Positions)	Silvia Sperber (FRG)	685.6	Vessela Lecheva (BUL)	683.2	Valentina Cherkassova (URS)	681.4
Air Rifle	Irina Chilova (URS)	498.5	Silvia Sperber (FRG)	497.5	Anna Malukina (URS)	495.8
Air Pistol	Jasna Sekaric (YUG)	489.5	Nino Salukvadze (URS)	487.9	Marina Dobrancheva (URS)	485.2
Archery						
Men						
Individual	Jay Barrs (USA)	338	Park Sung Soo (KOR)	336	Vladimir Echeyev (URS)	335
Team	South Korea	986	USA	972	Great Britain	968
Women						
Individual	Kim Soo Nyung (KOR)	344	Wang Hee Kyung (KOR)	332	Yun Young Sook (KOR)	327
Team	South Korea	982	Indonesia	952	USA	952

EVENT	GOLD		SILVER		BRONZE	
Gymnastics						
Men						
Individual Combined Exercises	Vladimir Artemov (URS)	119.125	Valeri Lyukin (URS)	119.025	Dmitri Biloserchev (URS)	118.975
Team	USSR	593.35	GDR	588.45	Japan	585.60
Parallel Bars	Vladimir Artemov (URS)	19.925	Valeri Lyukin (URS)	19.900	Sven Tippelt (GDR)	19.750
Floor	Sergei Kharkov (URS)	19.925	Vladimir Artemov (URS)	19.900	Lou Yun (CHN)	19.850
Horse Vault	Lou Yun (CHN)	19.875	Sylvio Kroll (GDR)	19.862	Park Jong Hoon (KOR)	19.775
Horizontal Bar	Vladimir Artemov (URS)	19.900			Holger Behrendt (GDR)	19.800
	Valeri Lukin (URS)	19.900			Marius Gherman (ROM)	19.800
Rings	Holger Behrendt (GDR)	19.925			Sven Tippelt (GDR)	19.875
	Dmitri Biloserchev (URS)	19.925				
Pommel Horse	Lubomir Gueraskolv (BUL)	19.950				
	Zsolt Borkai (HUN)	19.950				
	Dmitri Biloserchev (URS)	19.950				
Women						
Individual Combined Exercises	Elena Shushunova (URS)	79.662	Daniela Silivas (ROM)	79.637	Svetlana Boginskaya (URS)	79.400
Team	USSR	395.475	Romania	394.125	GDR	390.875
Floor	Daniela Silivas (ROM)	19.937	Svetlana Boginskaya (URS)	19.887	Diana Doudeva (BUL)	19.850
Horse Vault	Svetlana Boginskaya (URS)	19.905	Gabriela Potorac (ROM)	19.830	Daniela Silivas (ROM)	19.818
Beam	Daniela Silivas (ROM)	19.924	Elena Shushunova (URS)	19.875	Gabriela Potorac (ROM)	19.837
					Phoebe Mills (USA)	19.837
Asymmetrical Bars	Daniela Silivas (ROM)	20.000	Dagmar Kersten (GDR)	19.987	Elena Shushunova (URS)	19.962
Modern Rhythmic	Marina Lobach (URS)	60.000	Adriana Dunavska (BUL)	59.950	Alexandra Timoshenko (URS)	59.875
Tennis						
Men						
Individual	Miloslav Mecir (TCH)		Tim Mayotte (USA)		Stefan Edberg (SWE)	
					Brad Gilbert (USA)	
Doubles	Ken Flach/Robert Seguso (USA)		Emilio Sanchez/Sergio Casal (ESP)		Stefan Edberg/Anders Jarryd (SWE)	
					Miroslav Mecir/Milan Srejber (TCH)	
Women						
Individual	Steffi Graf (FRG)		Gabriela Sabatini (ARG)		Zina Garrison (USA)	
					Manuela Maleeva (BUL)	
Doubles	Pam Shriver/Zina Garrison (USA)		Jana Novotna/Helena Sukova (TCH)		Steffi Graf/Claudia Kohde-Kilsch (FRG)	
					Elizabeth Smylie/Wendy Turnbull (AUS)	
Table Tennis						
Men						
Individual	Yoo Nam Kyu (KOR)		Kim Ki Taik (KOR)		Erik Lindh (SWE)	
Doubles	China		Yugoslavia		South Korea	
Women						
Individual	Chen Jing (CHN)		Li Huifeng (CHN)		Jiao Zhimin (CHN)	
Doubles	South Korea		China		Yugoslavia	
Basketball						
Men	USSR		Yugoslavia		USA	
Women	USA		Yugoslavia		USSR	
Soccer						
	USSR		Brazil		FRG	
Handball						
Men	USSR		South Korea		Yugoslavia	
Women	South Korea		Norway		USSR	
Hockey						
Men	Great Britain		FRG		Netherlands	
Women	Australia		South Korea		Netherlands	
Volleyball						
Men	USA		USSR		Argentina	
Women	USSR		Peru		China	

Albertville 1992

February 8 – February 23

Participants: 1801 / Men: 1313, Women: 488, Countries: 64,
Sports: 10, Events: 57
Final Torchbearers: Michel Platini and François-Cyrille Grange

Medals Table

PLACE	COUNTRY	GOLD	SILVER	BRONZE
1	Germany	10	10	6
2	Unified Team	9	6	8
3	Norway	9	6	5
4	Austria	6	7	8
5	USA	5	4	2

Outstanding Athletes

PLACE	NAME (NATIONALITY)	DISCIPLINE	G	S	B
1	Lyubov Yegorova (EUN)	Nordic Skiing	3	2	–
2	Vegard Ulvang (NOR)	Nordic Skiing	3	1	–
	Bjørn Dæhlie (NOR)	Nordic Skiing	3	1	–
4	Mark Kirchner (GER)	Biathlon	2	1	–
	Gunda Niemann (GER)	Speed Skating	2	1	–

EVENT	GOLD		SILVER		BRONZE	
Alpine Skiing						
Men						
Downhill	Patrick Ortlieb (AUT)	1:50.37	Franck Piccard (FRA)	1:50.42	Günther Mader (AUT)	1:50.47
Slalom	Finn Christian Jagge (NOR)	1:44.39	Alberto Tomba (ITA)	1:44.67	Michael Tritscher (AUT)	1:44.85
Giant Slalom	Alberto Tomba (ITA)	2:06.98	Marc Girardelli (LUX)	2:07.30	Kjetil Andre Aamodt (NOR)	2:07.82
Super-G	Kjetil Andre Aamodt (NOR)	1:13.04	Marc Girardelli (LUX)	1:13.77	Jan Einar Thorsen (NOR)	1:13.83
Combined	Josef Polig (ITA)	14.58	Gianfranco Martin (ITA)	14.90	Steve Locher (SUI)	18.16
Women						
Downhill	Kerrin Lee-Gartner (CAN)	1:52.55	Hilary Lindh (USA)	1:52.61	Veronika Wallinger (AUT)	1:52.64
Slalom	Petra Kronberger (AUT)	1:32.68	Anneliese Coberger (NZL)	1:33.10	Bianca Fernandez-Ochoa (ESP)	1:33.35
Giant Slalom	Pernilla Wilberg (SWE)	2:12.74	Diann Roffe (USA)	2:13.71		
			Anita Wachter (AUT)	2:13.71		
Super-G	Deborah Compagnoni (ITA)	1:21.22	Carole Merle (FRA)	1:22.63	Katja Seizinger (GER)	1:23.19
Combined	Petra Kronberger (AUT)	2.55	Anita Wachter (AUT)	19.39	Florence Masnada (FRA)	21.38
Freestyle/Moguls, Men	Edgar Grospiron (FRA)	25.81	Olivier Allamand (FRA)	24.87	Nelson Carmichael (USA)	24.82
Freestyle/Moguls, Women	Donna Weinbrecht (USA)	23.69	Elisabeta Koyevnikova (EUN)	23.50	Stine Lise Hattestad (NOR)	23.04
Nordic Skiing						
Men						
10 km Cross-Country Skiing (Classical)	Vegard Ulvang (NOR)	27:36.0	Marco Albarello (ITA)	27:55.2	Christer Majbäck (SWE)	27:56.4
15 km Combined	Bjørn Daehlie (NOR)	1:05:37.9	Vegard Ulvang (NOR)	1:06:31.3	Giorgio Vanzetta (ITA)	1:06:32.3
30 km Cross-Country Skiing (Classical)	Vegard Ulvang (NOR)	1:22:27.8	Bjørn Daehlie (NOR)	1:23:14.0	Terje Langli (NOR)	1:23:42.5
50 km Cross-Country Skiing (Freestyle)	Bjørn Daehlie (NOR)	2:03:41.5	Maurilio de Zolt (ITA)	2:04:39.1	Georgio Vanzetta (ITA)	2:06:42.1
4 x 10 km Relay	Norway	1:39:26.0	Italy	1:40:52.7	Finland	1:41:22.9
Ski Jumping (90 m Hill)	Ernst Vettori (AUT)	222.8	Martin Höllwarth (AUT)	218.1	Toni Nieminen (FIN)	217.0
Ski Jumping (120 m Hill)	Toni Nieminen (FIN)	239.5	Martin Höllwarth (AUT)	227.3	Heinz Kullin (AUT)	214.8
Ski Jumping, Team	Finland	644.4	Austria	642.9	Czech Republic	620.1
Nordic Combined, Individual	Fabrice Guy (FRA)		Sylvain Guillaume (FRA)		Klaus Sulzenbacher (AUT)	
Nordic Combined, Team	Japan		Norway		Austria	
Women						
5 km Cross-Country Skiing (Classical)	Marjut Lukkarinen (FIN)	14:13.80	Lyubov Yegorova (EUN)	14:14.70	Yelena Wälbe (EUN)	14:22.7
10 km Combined	Lyubov Yegorova (EUN)	40:08.40	Stefania Belmondo (ITA)	40:31.80	Yelena Wälbe (EUN)	40:51.7
15 km Cross-Country Skiing (Classical)	Lyubov Yegorova (EUN)	42:20.80	Marjut Lukkarinen (FIN)	43:29.90	Yelena Wälbe (EUN)	43:42.3
30 km Cross-Country Skiing (Freestyle)	Stefania Belmondo (ITA)	1:22:30.10	Lyubov Yegorova (EUN)	1:22:52.0	Yelena Wälbe (EUN)	1:24:13.9
4 x 5 km	Unified Team	59:34.80	Norway		Italy	
Biathlon						
Men						
10 km	Mark Kirchner (GER)	26:02.3	Ricco Gross (GER)	26:18.0	Harri Eloranta (FIN)	26:26.6
20 km	Yevgeni Redkin (EUN)	57:34.4	Mark Kirchner (GER)	57:40.8	Mikael Löfgren (SWE)	57:59.4
4 x 7.5 km	Germany	1:24:43.5	Unified Team	1:25:06.3	Sweden	1:25:38.2
Women						
7.5 km	Anfissa Retzova (EUN)	24:29.2	Antje Misersky (GER)	24:45.1	Yelena Byelova (EUN)	24:50.8
15 km	Antje Misersky (GER)	51:47.2	Svetlana Pecherskaya (EUN)	51:58.5	Myriam Bedard (CAN)	52:15.0
3 x 7.5 km	France	1:15:55.6	Germany	1:16:18.4	Unified Team	1:16:54.6

EVENT	GOLD		SILVER		BRONZE	
Figure Skating						
Women	Kristi Yamaguchi (USA)		Midori Ito (JPN)		Nancy Kerrigan (USA)	
Men	Viktor Petrenko (EUN)		Paul Wylie (USA)		Petr Barna (TCH)	
Pairs	Natalya Mishkutionok/		Yelena Beschke/		Isabelle Brasseur/	
	Artur Dimitriyev (EUN)		Denios Petrov (EUN)		Lloyd Eisler (CAN)	
Ice Dance	Marina Klimova/		Isabelle Duchesnay/		Maya Usova/	
	Sergei Ponomarenko (EUN)		Paul Duchesnay (FRA)		Alexander Schulin (EUN)	
Speed Skating						
Men						
500 m	Uwe-Jens Mey (GER)	37.14	Toshiyuki Kuroiwa (JPN)	37.18	Junichi Inoue (JPN)	37.26
1000 m	Olaf Zinke (GER)	1:14.85	Kim Yoon-Man (KOR)	1:14.86	Yukinori Miyabe (JPN)	1:14.92
1500 m	Johann Olav Koss (NOR)	1:54.81	Adne Soendral (NOR)	1:54.85	Leo Visser (HOL)	1:54.90
5000 m	Geir Karlstad (NOR)	6:59.97	Falko Zandstra (HOL)	7:02.28	Leo Visser (HOL)	7:04.96
10,000 m	Bart Veldkamp (HOL)	14:12.12	Johann Olav Koss (NOR)	14:14.58	Geir Karlstad (NOR)	14:18.13
Women						
500 m	Bonnie Blair (USA)	40.33	Ye Qiabo (CHN)	40.51	Christa Luding (GER)	40.57
1000 m	Bonnie Blair (USA)	1:21.9	Ye Qiabo (CHN)	1:21.92	Monique Garbrecht (GER)	1:22.10
1500 m	Jacqueline Börner (GER)	2:05.87	Gunda Niemann (GER)	2:05.92	Seiko Hashimoto (JPN)	2:06.88
3000 m	Gunda Niemann (GER)	4:19.90	Heike Warnicke (GER)	4:22.88	Emese Hunyady (AUT)	4:24.64
5000 m	Gunda Niemann (GER)	7:31.57	Heike Warnicke (GER)	7:37.59	Claudia Pechstein (GER)	7:39.80
Short Track						
1000 m Men Individual	Kim Ki-Hoon (KOR)	1:30.76	Frederic Blackburn (CAN)	1:31.11	Lee Joon-Ho (KOR)	1:31.16
5000 m Men Relay	South Korea	7:14.02	Canada	7:14.06	Japan	7:18.18
500 m Women Individual	Cathy Turner (USA)	47.04	Yan Li (CHN)	47.08	Hwang Ok-Sil (PRK)	47.23
3000 m Women Relay	Canada	4:36.62	USA	4:37.85	Unified Team	4:42.69
Lugeing						
Men's Singles	Georg Hackl (GER)	3:02.363	Markus Prock (AUT)	3:02.669	Markus Schmidt (AUT)	3:02.942
Women's Singles	Doris Neuner (AUT)	3:06.696	Angelika Neuner (AUT)	3:06.769	Susi Erdmann (GER)	3:07.115
2-Man Luge	Stefan Krausse/		Yves Mankel/		Hansjörg Raffl/	
	Jan Behrendt (GER)	1:32.053	Thomas Rudolph (GER)	1:32.239	Norbert Hubert (ITA)	1:32.649
Bobsledding						
2-Man Bob	Switzerland I	1:00.84	Germany I	1:00.90	Germany II	1:01.14
4-Man Bob	Austria I	3:53.90	Germany I	3:53.92	Switzerland I	3:54.13
Ice Hockey	Unified Team		Canada		Czech Republic	

Barcelona 1992

July 25 – August 8

Participants: 9364 / Men: 6657. Women: 2707. Countries: 169.
Sports: 24. Evemts: 257
Final Torchbearer: Antonio Rebollo

Medals Table

PLACE	COUNTRY	GOLD	SILVER	BRONZE
1	Unified Team	45	38	28
2	USA	37	34	37
3	Germany	33	21	28
4	China	16	22	16
5	Cuba	14	6	11

Outstanding Athletes

PLACE	NAME (NATIONALITY)	DISCIPLINE	G	S	B
1	Vitali Sherbo (EUN)	Gymnastics	6	–	–
2	Yevgeni Sadovi (EUN)	Swimming	3	–	–
3	Krisztina Egerszegi (HUN)	Swimming	3	–	–
4	Alexander Popov (EUN)	Swimming	2	2	–
5	Tatyana Goutsou (EUN)	Gymnastics	2	1	1

EVENT	GOLD		SILVER		BRONZE	
Athletics						
Men						
100 m	Linford Christie (GBR)	9.96	Frank Fredericks (NAM)	10.02	Dennis Mitchell (USA)	10.04
200 m	Mike Marsh (USA)	20.01	Frank Fredericks (NAM)	20.13	Michael Bates (USA)	20.38

EVENT	GOLD		SILVER		BRONZE	
400 m	Quincy Watts (USA)	43.50	Steve Lewis (USA)	44.21	Samson Kitur (KEN)	44.24
800 m	William Tanui (KEN)	1:43.66	Nixon Kiprotich (KEN)	1:43.70	Johnny Gray (USA)	1:43.97
1500 m	Fermin Ruiz (ESP)	3:40.12	Rachid El Basir (ESP)	3:40.62	Mohamed Sulaiman (QAT)	3:40.69
5000 m	Dieter Baumann (GER)	13:12.52	Paul Bitok (KEN)	13:12.71	Fita Bayisa (ETH)	13:13.03
10,000 m	Khalid Skah (MAR)	27:46.70	Richard Chelimo (KEN)	27:47.72	Addis Abebe (ETH)	28:00.07
Marathon	Hwang Young-Cho (KOR)	2:13:23	Koichi Morishita (JPN)	2:13:45	Stephan Freigang (GER)	2:14:00
110 m Hurdles	Mark McKoy (CAN)	13.12	Tony Dees (USA)	13.24	Jack Pierce (USA)	13.26
400 m Hurdles	Kevin Young (USA)	46.78	Winthrop Graham (JAM)	47.66	Kriss Akabusi (GBR)	47.82
3000 m Steeplechase	Mathew Birir (KEN)	8:08.84	Patrick Sang (KEN)	8:09.55	William Mutwol (KEN)	8:10.74
4 x 100 m	USA	37.40	Nigeria	37.98	Cuba	38.00
4 x 400 m	USA	2:55.74	Cuba	2:59.51	Great Britain	2:59.73
20 km Walk	Daniel Montero Plaza (ESP)	1:21:45	Guillaume Leblanc (CAN)	1:22:25	Giovanni De Benedictis (ITA)	1:23:11
50 km Walk	Andrei Perlov (EUN)	3:50:13	Carlos Carbajal (MEX)	3:52:09	Ronald Weigel (GER)	3:53:45
High Jump	Javier Sotomayor (CUB)	7'8"	Patrick Sjöberg (SWE)	7'8"	Artur Partyka (POL)	7'8"
					Timothy Forsyth (AUS)	7'8"
					Hollis Conway (GBR)	7'8"
Pole Vault	Maxim Tarassov (EUN)	19'0¼"	Igor Trandenkov (EUN)	19'0¼"	Javier Garcia (ESP)	18'10"
Long Jump	Carl Lewis (USA)	28'5¼"	Mike Powell (USA)	28'4"	Joe Greene (USA)	27'4¼"
Triple Jump	Michael Conley (USA)	59'7¼"	Charles Simpkins (USA)	57'8¾"	Frank Rutherford (BAH)	56'11¼"
Shot	Michael Stulce (USA)	71'2"	James Doehring (USA)	68'9"	Vyacheslav Lycho (EUN)	68'8¼"
Discus	Romas Ubartas (LIT)	213'7½"	Jürgen Schult (GER)	213'0½"	Roberto Moya (CUB)	210'4¼"
Javelin	Jan Zelezny (TCH)	294'2"	Seppo Räty (FIN)	284'1½"	Steve Backley (GBR)	273'6½"
Hammer	Andrei Abduvalyev (EUN)	270'9½"	Igor Astapkovich (EUN)	268'10½"	Igor Nikulin (EUN)	266'11¾"
Decathlon	Robert Zmelik (TCH)	8611	Antonio Peñalver (ESP)	8412	David Johnson (USA)	8309
Women						
100 m	Gail Devers (USA)	10.82	Juliet Cuthbert (JAM)	10.83	Irina Privalova (EUN)	10.84
200 m	Gwen Torrence (USA)	21.81	Juliet Cuthbert (JAM)	22.02	Merlene Ottey (JAM)	22.09
400 m	Marie-José Perec (FRA)	48.83	Olga Brysgina (EUN)	49.05	Ximena Gaviria (COL)	49.64
800 m	Ellen van Langen (HOL)	1:55.54	Lilia Nurutdinova (EUN)	1:55.99	Ana Quirot (CUB)	1:56.80
1500 m	Hassiba Boulmerka (ALG)	3:55.30	Ludmila Rogacheva (EUN)	3:56.91	Qu Yunxia (CHN)	3:57.08
3000 m	Yelena Romanova (EUN)	8:46.04	Tatyana Dorovskich (EUN)	8:46.85	Angela Chalmers (CAN)	8:47.22
10,000 m	Derartu Tulu (ETH)	31:06.02	Elena Meyer (RSA)	31:11.75	Lynn Jennings (USA)	31:19.89
Marathon	Valentina Yegorova (EUN)	2:32:41	Yuko Arimori (JPN)	2:32:49	Lorraine Moller (NZL)	2:33:59
100 m Hurdles	Paraskevi Patoulidou (GRE)	12.64	Lavonna Martin (USA)	12.69	Jordanka Donkova (BUL)	12.70
400 m Hurdles	Sally Gunnell (GBR)	53.23	Sandra Farmer-Patrick (USA)	53.69	Janeene Vickers (USA)	54.31
4 x 100 m	USA	42.11	Unified Team	42.16	Nigeria	42.81
4 x 400 m	Unified Team	3:20.20	USA	3:20.92	Great Britain	3:24.23
10 km Walk	Chen Yueling (CHN)	44:32	Yelena Nikolayeva (EUN)	44:33	Li Chunxiu (CHN)	44:41
High Jump	Heike Henkel (GER)	6'7¼"	Galina Astafei (ROM)	6'6½"	Joanet Quintero (CUB)	6'5½"
Long Jump	Heike Drechsler (GER)	23'5"	Inessa Kravets (EUN)	23'4¼"	Jackie Joyner-Kersee (USA)	23'2¼"
Shot	Svetlana Kriveleova (EUN)	69'1"	Huang Zhihong (CHN)	67'1¾"	Kathrin Neimke (GER)	64'10½"
Discus	Maritza Marten (CUB)	229'10"	Zvetanka Christova (BUL)	222'4½"	Daniela Costian (AUS)	217'3¾"
Javelin	Silke Renke (GER)	224'2½"	Natalya Shikolenko (EUN)	223'11¼"	Karen Forkel (GER)	219'4"
Heptathlon	Jackie Joyner-Kersee (USA)	7044	Irina Belova (EUN)	6845	Sabine Braun (GER)	6649
Swimming						
Men						
50 m Freestyle	Alexander Popov (EUN)	21.91	Matt Biondi (USA)	22.09	Tom Jager (USA)	22.30
100 m Freestyle	Alexander Popov (EUN)	49.02	Gustavo Borges (BRA)	49.43	Stephan Caron (FRA)	49.50
200 m Freestyle	Yevgeni Sadovi (EUN)	1:46.70	Anders Holmertz (SWE)	1:46.86	Antti Kasvio (FIN)	1:47.63
400 m Freestyle	Yevgeni Sadovi (EUN)	3:45.00	Kieren Perkins (AUS)	3:45.16	Anders Holmertz (SWE)	3:46.77
1500 m Freestyle	Kieren Perkins (AUS)	14:43.48	Glen Housman (AUS)	14:55.29	Jörg Hoffmann (GER)	15:02.29
100 m Backstroke	Mark Tewksbury (CAN)	53.98	Jeff Rouse (USA)	54.04	David Berkhoff (USA)	54.78
200 m Backstroke	Martin Lopez-Zubero (ESP)	1:58.47	Vladimir Selkov (EUN)	1:58.87	Stefano Battistelli (ITA)	1:59.40
100 m Breaststroke	Nelson Diebel (USA)	1:01.50	Norbert Rosza (HUN)	1:01.68	Philip Rogers (AUS)	1:01.76
200 m Breaststroke	Mike Barrowman (USA)	2:10.16	Norbert Rozsa (HUN)	2:11.23	Nick Gillingham (GBR)	2:11.29
100 m Butterfly	Pablo Morales (USA)	53.32	Rafal Szukala (POL)	53.35	Anthony Nesty (SUR)	53.41
200 m Butterfly	Melvin Stewart (USA)	1:56.26	Danyon Loader (NZL)	1:57.93	Franck Esposito (FRA)	1:58.51
200 m Medley	Tamas Darnyi (HUN)	2:00.76	Gregory Burgess (USA)	2:00.97	Attila Czene (HUN)	2:01.00
400 m Medley	Tamas Darnyi (HUN)	4:14.23	Eric Namesnik (USA)	4:15.57	Luca Sacchi (ITA)	4:16.34
4 x 100 m Freestyle	USA	3:16.74	Unified Team	3:17.56	Germany	3:17.90
4 x 200 m Freestyle	Unified Team	7:11.95	Sweden	7:15.51	USA	7:16.23
4 x 100 m Medley	USA	3:36.93	Unified Team	3:38.56	Canada	3:39.66
Springboard Diving	Mark Lenzi (USA)	676.53	Tan Liangde (CHN)	645.57	Dmitri Sautin (EUN)	627.78
Highboard Diving	Sun Shuwei (CHN)	677.31	Scott Donie (USA)	633.63	Xiong Ni (CHN)	600.15
Water Polo	Italy		Spain		Unified Team	

EVENT	GOLD		SILVER		BRONZE	
Women						
50 m Freestyle	Yang Wenyi (CHN)	24.79	Zhuang Yong (CHN)	25.08	Angel Martino (USA)	25.23
100 m Freestyle	Zhuang Yong (CHN)	54.64	Jenny Thompson (USA)	54.84	Franziska von Almsick (GER)	54.94
200 m Freestyle	Nicole Haislett (USA)	1:57.90	Franziska van Almsick (GER)	1:58.00	Kerstin Kielgass (GER)	1:59.67
400 m Freestyle	Dagmar Hase (GER)	4:07.18	Janet Evans (USA)	4:07.37	Hayley Lewis (AUS)	4:11.22
800 m Freestyle	Janet Evans (USA)	8:25.52	Hayley Lewis (AUS)	8:30.34	Jana Hanke (GER)	8:30.99
100 m Backstroke	Krisztina Egerszegi (HUN)	1:00.68	Tunde Szabo (HUN)	1:01.14	Lea Loveless (USA)	1:01.43
200 m Backstroke	Krisztina Egerszegi (HUN)	2:07.06	Dagmar Hase (GER)	2:09.46	Nicole Stevenson (AUS)	2:10.20
100 m Breaststroke	Yelena Rudkovskaya (EUN)	1:08.00	Anita Nall (USA)	1:08.17	Samantha Riley (AUS)	1:09.25
200 m Breaststroke	Kyoko Iwasaki (JPN)	2:26.65	Li Lin (CHN)	2:26.85	Anita Nall (USA)	2:26.88
100 m Butterfly	Qian Hong (CHN)	58.62	Christine Ahmann-Leighton (USA)	58.74	Cathérine Plewinski (FRA)	59.01
200 m Butterfly	Summer Sanders (USA)	2:08.67	Wang Xiaohong (CHN)	2:09.01	Susan O'Neill (AUS)	2:09.03
200 m Medley	Li Lin (CHN)	2:11.65	Summer Sanders (USA)	2:11.91	Daniela Hunger (GER)	2:13.92
400 m Medley	Krisztina Egerszegi (HUN)	4:36.54	Li Lin (CHN)	4:36.73	Summer Sanders (USA)	4:37.58
4 x 100 m Freestyle	USA	3:39.46	China	3:40.12	Germany	3:41.60
4 x 100 m Medley	USA	4:02.54	Germany	4:05.19	Unified Team	4:06.44
Springboard Diving	Gao Min (CHN)	572.40	Irina Laschko (EUN)	514.14	Brita Baldus (GER)	503.07
Highboard Diving	Fu Mingxia (CHN)	461.43	Yelena Miroschina (EUN)	411.63	Mary Ellen Clark (USA)	401.91
Synchronized Swimming						
Solo	Kristen Babb-Sprague (USA)	191.848	Sylvie Frechette (CAN)	191.717	Fumiko Okuno (JPN)	187.056
Duet	USA	192.175	Canada	189.394	Japan	186.868
Boxing						
Light-Flyweight (- 105¾ lbs)	Rogelio Marcelo Garcia (CUB)		Daniel Bojinov (BUL)		Jan Quast (GER) Roel Velasco (PHI)	
Flyweight (- 112½ lbs)	Chol Su Choi (PRK)		Raul Gonzales (CUB)		Istvan Kovacs (HUN) Timothy Austin (USA)	
Bantamweight (- 119 lbs)	Joel Casamayor (CUB)		Wayne McCullough (IRL)		Mohamed Achik (MAR) Gwang Sik Li (PRK)	
Featherweight (- 126 lbs)	Andreas Tews (GER)		Faustino Reyes (ESP)		Hocine Soltani (ALG) Ramazi Paliani (EUN)	
Lightweight (- 132 lbs)	Oscar de la Hoya (USA)		Marco Rudolph (GER)		Sung Sik Hong (KOR) Namjil Bayarsaikhan (MGL)	
Light-Welterweight (- 140 lbs)	Hector Vinent (CUB)		Mark Leduc (CAN)		Jyri Kjäll (FIN) Leonard Doroftei (ROM)	
Welterweight (- 148 lbs)	Michael Carruth (IRL)		Juan Hernandez (CUB)		Anibal Acevedo Santiago (PUR) Arkom Chenglai (THA)	
Light-Middleweight (- 157 lbs)	Juan Lemus Garcia (CUB)		Orhan Delibas (HOL)		Robin Reid (GBR) Gyorgy Mizsei (HUN)	
Middleweight (- 165 lbs)	Ariel Hernandez (CUB)		Chris Byrd (USA)		Chris Johnson (CAN) Seung Bae Lee (KOR)	
Light-Heavyweight (- 178½ lbs)	Torsten May (GER)		Rostislav Saulischni (EUN)		Zoltan Beres (HUN) Wojciech Bartnik (POL)	
Heavyweight (- 200½ lbs)	Felix Savon (CUB)		David Izonritei (NGR)		Arnold Vanderlijde (HOL) David Tua (NZL)	
Super-Heavyweight (+ 200½ lbs)	Roberto Balado Mendez (CUB)		Richard Igbineghu (NGR)		Brian Nielsen (DEN) Svilen Aldinov Rusinov (BUL)	
Weightlifting						
Flyweight (- 114¼ lbs)	Ivan Ivanov (BUL)		Lin Qisheng (CHN)		Traian Joachim Ciharean (ROM)	
Bantamweight (- 123½ lbs)	Chun Byung-Kwan (KOR)		Liu Shoubin (CHN)		Luo Jianming (CHN)	
Featherweight (- 132¼ lbs)	Naim Süleymanoglu (TUR)		Nikolai Peshalov (BUL)		He Yinggiang (CHN)	
Lightweight (- 148¾ lbs)	Israel Militosiyan (EUN)		Yoto Yotov (BUL)		Andreas Behm (GER)	
Middleweight (- 165½ lbs)	Fedor Kassapu (EUN)		Pablo Rodriguez (CUB)		Myong Nam Kim (PRK)	
Light-Heavyweight (- 182 lbs)	Pyrros Dimas (GRE)		Krzysztof Siemion (POL)		Ibragim Samadov (EUN)	
Middle-Heavyweight (- 198½ lbs)	Kakhi Kakhiashvili (EUN)		Sergei Syrtsov (EUN)		Sergiusz Wolczaniecki (POL)	
First Heavyweight (- 220½ lbs)	Viktor Tregubov (EUN)		Timur Taimassov (EUN)		Waldemar Malak (POL)	
Second Heavyweight (- 242½ lbs)	Ronny Weller (GER)		Artur Akoev (EUN)		Stefan Botev (BUL)	
Super-Heavyweight (+ 242½ lbs)	Alexander Kurlovich (EUN)		Leonid Taranenko (EUN)		Manfred Nerlinger (GER)	
Greco-Roman Wrestling						
Light-Flyweight (- 105¾ lbs)	Oleg Kucherenko (EUN)		Vincenzo Maenza (ITA)		Wilber Sanchez (CUB)	
Flyweight (- 114½ lbs)	Jon Rönningen (NOR)		Alfred Ter-Mkrychan (EUN)		Min Kyung-Kap(KOR)	
Bantamweight (- 125¾ lbs)	Han Bong An (KOR)		Rifat Yildiz (GER)		Shang Zetian (CHN)	
Featherweight (- 136½ lbs)	Akif Pirim (TUR)		Sergei Martynov (EUN)		Juan Maren (CUB)	
Lightweight (- 149¾ lbs)	Attila Repka (HUN)		Islan Duguchiyev (EUN)		Rodney Smith (USA)	
Welterweight (- 163 lbs)	Minazakan Iskandarian (EUN)		Jozef Tracz (POL)		Torbjörn Kornbakk (SWE)	

EVENT	GOLD		SILVER		BRONZE	
Middleweight (- 180¾ lbs)	Peter Farkas (HUN)		Pjotr Stepien (POL)		Daulet Turhlyhanov (EUN)	
Light-Heavyweight (- 198¼ lbs)	Maik Bullmann (GER)		Hakki Basar (TUR)		Gogui Koguashvili (EUN)	
Heavyweight (- 220½ lbs)	Hector Milian (CUB)		Dennis Koslowski (USA)		Sergei Demiashkievich (EUN)	
Super-Heavyweight (+ 220½lbs)	Alexander Karelin (EUN)		Tomas Johansson (SWE)		Ion Grigoras (ROM)	
Freestyle Wrestling						
Light-Flyweight (- 105¾ lbs)	Kim Il (PRK)		Kim Jong-Shin (KOR)		Vugar Orudyev (EUN)	
Flyweight (- 114½lbs)	Li Hak-Son (PRK)		Harry Lee Jones (USA)		Valentin Jordanov (BUL)	
Bantamweight (- 125¾ lbs)	Alejandro Puerto (CUB)		Sergei Smal (EUN)		Kim Yong-Sik (PRK)	
Featherweight (- 136½ lbs)	John Smith (USA)		Asgari Mohammedian (IRN)		Lazaro Reinoso (CUB)	
Lightweight (- 149¾ lbs)	Arsen Fadzayev (EUN)		Valentin Getsov (BUL)		Kosei Akaishi (JPN)	
Welterweight (- 163 lbs)	Park Jang-Soon (KOR)		Kenneth Monday (USA)		Amir Khadem (IRN)	
Middleweight (- 180¾ lbs)	Kevin Jackson (USA)		Elemadi Jabrailov (EUN)		Rasul Khadem (IRN)	
Light-Heavyweight (- 198¼ lbs)	Maharbeg Chadartsev (EUN)		Kenan Simsek (TUR)		Christopher Campbell (USA)	
Heavyweight (- 220½ lbs)	Leri Chabelov (EUN)		Heiko Balz (GER)		Ali Kayali (TUR)	
Super-Heavyweight (+ 220½ lbs)	Bruce Baumgartner (USA)		Jeffrey Thue (CAN)		David Gobedyishvili (EUN)	
Judo						
Men						
Super-Lightweight (- 132¼ lbs)	Nazim Gusseinov (EUN)		Hyun Yoon (KOR)		Tadanor Koshino (JPN)	
					Richard Trautmann (GER)	
Half-Lightweight (- 143¼ lbs)	Rogerio Sampaio Cardoso (BRA)		Jozsef Csak (HUN)		Udo Quellmalz (GER)	
					Israel Hernandez Planas (CUB)	
Lightweight (- 156½ lbs)	Toshihiko Koga (JPN)		Bertalan Haitos (HUN)		Hoon Chung (KOR)	
					Shay Oren Smadga (ISR)	
Light-Middleweight (- 171¾ lbs)	Hidehiko Yoshida (JPN)		Jason Morris (USA)		Bertrand Damaisin (FRA)	
					Kim Byung-Joo (KOR)	
Middleweight (- 189½ lbs)	Waldemar Legien (POL)		Pascal Tayot (FRA)		Hirotaka Okada (JPN)	
					Nicolas Gill (CAN)	
Light-Heavyweight (- 209¼ lbs)	Antal Kovacs (HUN)		Raymond Stevens (GBR)		Theo Meijer (HOL)	
					Dmitri Sergeyev (EUN)	
Heavyweight (+ 209¼ lbs)	David Shashaleshvili (EUN)		Naoya Ogawa (JPN)		David Douillet (FRA)	
					Imre Csosz (HUN)	
Women						
Super-Lightweight (- 105¾ lbs)	Cecile Nowak (FRA)		Ryoko Tamura (JPN)		Hulya Senyurt (TUR)	
					Amarilis Savon Carmenaty (CUB)	
Half-Lightweight (- 114½ lbs)	Almudena Munoz (ESP)		Noriko Mizogushi (JPN)		Li Zhongyun (CHN)	
					Susan Rendle (GBR)	
Lightweight (- 123½ lbs)	Miriam Blasco (ESP)		Nicola Fairbrother (GBR)		Chiyori Tateno (JPN)	
					Driulis Gonzales Morales (CUB)	
Light-Middleweight (- 134½ lbs)	Cathérine Fleury (FRA)		Yael Arad (ISR)		Di Zhang (CHN)	
					Yelena Petrova (EUN)	
Middleweight (- 145½ lbs)	Odalis Reve Jimenez (CUB)		Emanuela Pierantozzi (ITA)		Heidi Rakels (BEL)	
					Kate Howey (GBR)	
Light-Heavyweight (- 158¾ lbs)	Kim Mi-Jung (KOR)		Yoko Tanabe (JPN)		Laetitia Meignan (FRA)	
					Irene de Kok (HOL)	
Heavyweight (+ 158¾ lbs)	Zhuang Xiaoyan (CHN)		Estela Rodriquez Villanueva (CUB)		Natalia Lupino (FRA)	
					Yoko Sakaue (JPN)	
Fencing						
Individual Foil - Men	Philippe Omnes (FRA)		Sergei Golubitski (EUN)		Elvis Gregory (CUB)	
Team Foil - Men	Germany		Cuba		Poland	
Individual Saber	Benco Szabo (HUN)		Marco Marin (ITA)		Jean-François Lamour (FRA)	
Team Saber	Unified Team		Hungary		France	
Individual Épée	Eric Srecki (FRA)		Pavel Kolobkov (EUN)		Jean-Michel Henry (FRA)	
Team Épée	Germany		Hungary		Unified Team	
Individual Foil - Women	Giovanna Trillini (ITA)		Wang Huifeng (CHN)		Tatyana Sadovskaya (EUN)	
Team Foil - Women	Italy		Germany		Romania	
Modern Pentathlon						
Individual	Arkadlusz Skrzypaszek (POL)	5559	Attila Mizser (HUN)	5446	Eduard Zanovka (EUN)	5361
Team	Poland	16018	Unified Team	15924	Italy	15760

EVENT	GOLD		SILVER		BRONZE	
Canoeing						
Men						
500 m Kayak Singles K 1	Mikko Kolehmainen (FIN)	1:40.34	Zsolt Gyulay (HUN)	1:40.64	Knut Holman (NOR)	1:40.71
1,000 m Canadian Singles C 1	Clint Robinson (AUS)	3:37.26	Knut Holman (NOR)	3:37.50	Greg Barton (USA)	3:37.93
500 m Kayak Pairs K 2	Germany	1:28.27	Poland	1:29.84	Italy	1:30.00
1000 m Kayak Pairs K 2	Germany	3:16.10	Sweden	3:17.70	Poland	3:18.86
1000 m Kayak Fours K4	Germany	2:54.18	Hungary	2:54.82	Australia	2:56.97
500 m Canadian Singles C 1	Nikolai Buchalov (BUL)	1:51.15	Mikhail Slivinski (EUN)	1:51.40	Olaf Heukrodt (GER)	1:53.00
1000 m Canadian Singles C 1	Nikolai Buchalov (BUL)	4:05.92	Ivan Klementyev (LIT)	4:06.60	Gyorgy Zala (HUN)	4:07.35
500 m Canadian Pairs C 2	Unified Team	1:41.54	Germany	1:41.68	Bulgaria	1:41.94
1,000 m Canadian Pairs C 2	Germany	3:37.42	Denmark	3:39.26	France	3:59.51
Women						
500 m Kayak Singles K 1	Birgit Schmidt (GER)	1:51.60	Rita Koban (HUN)	1:51.96	Izabella Dylewska (POL)	1:52.36
500 m Kayak Pairs K 2	Germany	1:40.29	Sweden	1:40.41	Hungary	1:40.81
500 m Kayak Fours K4	Hungary	1:38.22	Germany	1:38.47	Sweden	1:39.79
Canoe Slalom						
Men						
Kayak 1	Pierpaolo Ferrazzi (ITA)	106.89	Sylvain Curinier (FRA)	107.06	Jochen Lettmann (GER)	108.52
Canadian 1	Lukas Pollert (TCH)	113.69	Gareth Marriott (GBR)	116.48	Jacky Avril (FRA)	117.18
Canadian 2	USA	122.41	Czech Republic	124.25	France	124.38
Women						
Kayak 1	Elisabeth Micheler (GER)	126.41	Danielle Woodward (AUS)	128.27	Dana Chladek (USA)	131.75
Rowing						
Men						
Single Sculls	Thomas Lange (GER)	6:51.40	Vaclav Chalupa (TCH)	6:52.93	Kajetan Broniewski (POL)	6:56.82
Doubles Sculls	Australia	6:17.32	Austria	6:18.42	Netherlands	6:22.82
Coxless Pairs	Great Britain	6:27.72	Germany	6:32.68	Slovenia	6:33.43
Coxed Pairs	Great Britain	6:49.83	Italy	6:50.98	Romania	6:51.58
Coxless Quadruple Sculls	Germany	5:45.17	Norway	5:47.09	Italy	5:47.33
Coxless Fours	Australia	5:55.04	USA	5:56.68	Slovenia	5:58.24
Coxed Fours	Romania	5:59.37	Germany	6:00.34	Poland	6:03.27
Coxed Eights	Canada	5:29.53	Romania	5:29.67	Germany	5:31.00
Women						
Single Sculls	Elisabeta Lipa (ROM)	7:25.54	Annelies Bredael (BEL)	7:26.64	Silken Laumann (CAN)	7:28.85
Double Sculls	Germany	6:49.00	Romania	6:51.47	China	6:55.16
Coxless Pairs	Canada	7:06.22	Germany	7:07.96	USA	7:08.11
Coxless Quadruple Sculls	Germany	6:20.18	Romania	6:24.34	Unified Team	6:25.07
Coxless Fours	Canada	6:30.85	USA	6:31.86	Germany	6:32.34
Coxed Eights	Canada	6:02.62	Romania	6:06.26	Germany	6:07.80
Yachting						
Finn Class	José van der Ploeg (ESP)	33.4	Brian Ledbetter (USA)	54.7	Craig Monk (NZL)	64.7
International Star	USA	31.4	New Zealand	58.4	Canada	62.7
Flying Dutchman	Spain	29.7	USA	32.7	Denmark	37.7
International Tornado	France	40.4	USA	42.0	Australia	44.4
470 Men	Spain	50.0	USA	66.7	Estonia	68.7
470 Women	Spain	30.7	New Zealand	39.7	USA	42.4
International Soling	Denmark	34.0	USA	24.4	Great Britain	48.0
Lechner A-390. Men	Franck David (FRA)	70.7	Mike Gebhardt (USA)	71.1	Lars Kleppich (AUS)	98.7
Lechner A-390. Women	Barbara Kendall (NZL)	47.8	Zhang Xiadong (CHN)	65.8	Dorien de Vries (HOL)	68.7
Europa Class	Linda Andersen (NOR)	48.7	Natalia Perena (ESP)	57.4	Julia Trotman (USA)	62.7
Cycling						
Men						
Road Race	Fabio Casartelli (ITA)	4:35:21	Hendrick Dekker (HOL)	4:35:22	Dainis Ozols (LIT)	4:35:24
100 km Road Team Time Trial	Germany	2:01:39	Italy	2:02:39	France	2:05:25
Sprint	Jens Fiedler (GER)		Gary Neiwand (AUS)		Curtis Harnett (CAN)	
1000 m Time Trial	Jose Moreno Perinan (ESP)	1:03.342	Shane Kelly (AUS)	1:04.288	Erin Hartwell (USA)	1:04.753
4000 m Individual Pursuit	Christopher Boardman (GBR)		Jens Lehmann (GER)		Gary Anderson (NZL)	
4000 m Team Pursuit	Germany	4:08.791	Australia	4:10.218	Denmark	4:15.860
Individual Points Race	Giovanni Lombardi (ITA)		Leon van Bon (HOL)		Cedric Mathy (BEL)	

EVENT	GOLD		SILVER		BRONZE	
Women						
Road Race	Kathryn Watt (AUS)	2:04:42	Jeannie Longo–Ciprelli (FRA)	2:05:02	Monique Knol (HOL)	2:05:03
Sprint	Erika Salumäe (EST)		Annett Neumann (GER)		Ingrid Haringa (HOL)	
3000 m Individual Pursuit	Petra Rossner (GER)	3:41.753	Kathryn Watt (AUS)	3:43.438	Rebecca Twigg (USA)	3:52.429
Equestrianism						
Three-Day Event	Matthew Ryan (AUS)	70.0	Herbert Blöcker (GER)	81.3	Blyth Tait (NZL)	87.6
Three-Day Event, Team	Australia	288.6	New Zealand	290.8	Germany	300.3
Grand Prix (Dressage)	Nicole Uphoff (GER)	1768	Isabelle Werth (GER)	1762	Klaus Balkenhol (GER)	1694
Grand Prix (Dressage) Team	Germany	5224	Netherlands	4742	USA	4643
Grand Prix (Jumping)	Ludger Beerbaum (GER)	0.00	Piet Raymakers (HOL)	0.25	Norman Joio (USA)	.75
Grand Prix (Jumping)	Netherlands	12	Austria	16.75	France	24.75
Shooting						
Men						
Small-Bore Rifle (Prone)	Lee Eun-Chul (KOR)	702.5	Harald Stenvaag (NOR)	701.4	Stevan Pletikosic (IOP)	701.1
Small-Bore Rifle (3 Positions)	Grachia Petikian (EUN)	1267.4	Robert Foth (USA)	1266.6	Ryohei Koba (JPN)	1265.9
Rapid-Fire Pistol	Ralf Schumann (GER)	885	Afanassis Kusmin (LET)	882	Vladimir Vochmianin (EUN)	882
Free Pistol (50 m)	Konstantin Lukashik (EUN)	658.0	Wang Yifu (CHN)	657.0	Ragnar Skanaker (SWE)	657.0
Running Game Target	Michael Jakosits (GER)	673	Anatoli Asrabayev (EUN)	672	Lubos Racansky (TCH)	670
Air Pistol	Wang Yifu (CHN)	684.8	Sergei Piyanov (EUN)	684.1	Sorin Babii (ROM)	684.1
Trap Shooting	Petr Hrdlicka (TCH)	219	Kazumi Watanabe (JPN)	219	Marco Venturini (ITA)	218
Air Rifle	Yuri Fedkin (EUN)	695.3	Franck Badiou (FRA)	691.9	Johann Riederer (GER)	691.7
Women						
Sports Pistol (3 positions)	Marina Logvinenko (EUN)	684	Li Duihong (CHN)	680	Dorzhsuren Munkbajar (MGL)	679
Small Bore Rifle	Launi Meili (USA)	684.3	Nonka Matova (BUL)	682.7	Malgorzata Ksiazkiewicz (POL)	681.5
Air Rifle	Yeo Kab-Soon (KOR)	498.2	Vesela Lecheva (BUL)	495.3	Aranka Binder (IOP)	495.1
Air Pistol	Marina Logvinenko (EUN)	486.4	Jasna Sekaric (IOP)	486.4	Maria Grusdeva (BUL)	481.6
Mixed						
Skeet Shooting	Shan Zhang (CHN)	223	Juan Jorge Giha Yarur (PER)	222	Bruno Rossetti (ITA)	222
Archery						
Men						
Individual	Sebastien Flute (FRA)	542	Chung Jae-Hun (KOR)	542	Simon Terry (GBR)	528
Team	Spain		Finland		Great Britain	
Women						
Individual	Cho Youn-Jeong (KOR)	552	Kim Nyung Soo (KOR)	543	Natalya Valeyeva (EUN)	526
Team	South Korea	966	China	917	Unified Team	948
Gymnastics						
Men						
Individual Combined Exercises	Vitali Sherbo (EUN)	59.025	Grigori Misyutin (EUN)	58.925	Valeri Belenki (EUN)	58.625
Individual Team	Unified Team	585.450	China	580.375	Japan	578.250
Parallel Bars	Vitali Sherbo (EUN)	9.900	Guo Linyao (CHN)	9.800	Igor Korobchinski (EUN)	9.800
	Li Jing (CHN)	9.812			Masayuki Matsunaga (JPN)	9.800
Floor	Li Xiaoahuang (CHN)	9.925	Grigori Misyutin (EUN)	9.787	Yukio Ikatani (JPN)	9.787
Horse Vault	Vitali Sherbo (EUN)	9.856	Grigori Misyutin (EUN)	9.781	Ok Ryul Yoo (KOR)	9.762
Horizontal Bar	Trent Dimas (USA)	9.875	Grigori Misyutin (EUN)	9.837	Andreas Wecker (GER)	9.837
Rings	Vitali Sherbo (EUN)	9.937	Li Jing (CHN)	9.875	Andreas Wecker (GER)	9.862
					Li Xiaoshuang (CHN)	9.862
Pommel Horse	Vitali Sherbo (EUN)	9.925	Pae Gil-Su (PRK)	9.925	Andreas Wecker (GER)	9.887
Women						
Individual Combined Exercises	Tatyana Gutsu (EUN)	39.737	Shannon Miller (USA)	39.725	Lavinia Milosovici (ROM)	39.687
Team	Unified Team	395.666	Romania	395.079	USA	394.704
Floor	Lavinia Milosovici (ROM)	10.000	Henrietta Onodi (HUN)	9.950	Cristina Bontas (ROM)	9.912
					Tatyana Gutsu (EUN)	9.912
					Shannon Miller (USA)	9.912
Horse Vault	Henrietta Onodi (HUN)	9.925	Lavinia Milosovici (ROM)	9.925	Tatyana Lyssenko (EUN)	9.912
Beam	Tatyana Lyssenko (EUN)	9.975	Li Lu (CHN)	9.912	Shannon Miller (USA)	9.9612
Asymmetrical Bars	Li Lu (CHN)	10.00	Tatyana Gutsu (EUN)	9.975	Shannon Miller (USA)	9.9612
Modern Rhythmic	Alexandra Timoshenko (EUN)	59.037	Carolina Pascual (ESP)	58.100	Oksana Skaldina (EUN)	57.912

EVENT	GOLD	SILVER	BRONZE
Tennis			
Men			
Singles	Marc Rosset (SUI)	Jordi Arrese (ESP)	Goran Ivanisevic (CRO)
			Andrei Cherkassov (EUN)
Doubles	Boris Becker/Michael Stich (GER)	Wayne Ferreira/Piet Norval (RSA)	Goran Ivanisevic/Goran Prpic (CRO)
			Javier Frana/Christian Miniussi (ARG)
Women			
Singles	Jennifer Capriati (USA)	Steffi Graf (GER)	Mary Jo Fernandez (USA)
			Arantxa Sanchez-Vicario (ESP)
Doubles	Gigi Fernandez/ Mary Jo Fernandez (USA)	Conchita Martinez/ Arantxa Sanchez-Vicario (ESP)	Leila Meshki/Natalya Zvereva (EUN)
			Rachel McQuillan/Nicole Proris (AUS)
Table Tennis			
Men			
Singles	Jan-Ove Waldner (SWE)	Jean-Philippe Gatien (FRA)	Ma Wenge (CHN)
			Kim Taek-Soo (KOR)
Doubles	China	Germany	Korea
Women			
Singles	Deng Yaping (CHN)	Hong Qiao (CHN)	Jung Hwa Hyun (KOR)
			Ben Hui Li (PRK)
Doubles	China	China	South Korea
Basketball			
Men	USA	Croatia	Lithuania
Women	Unified Team	China	USA
Soccer	Spain	Poland	Ghana
Handball			
Men	Unified Team	Sweden	France
Women	South Korea	Norway	Unified Team
Hockey			
Men	Germany	Australia	Pakistan
Women	Spain	Germany	Great Britain
Volleyball			
Men	Brazil	Netherlands	USA
Women	Cuba	Unified Team	USA
Badminton			
Men			
Singles	Alan Budi Kusuma (INA)	Ardy Wiranata (INA)	Thomas Stuer-Lauridsen (DEN)
			Hermawan Susanto (INA)
Doubles	South Korea	Indonesia	China
			Malaysia
Women			
Singles	Susi Susanti (INA)	Soo Hyun Bang (KOR)	Hua Huang (CHN)
			Tang Jiuhong (CHN)
Doubles	South Korea	China	China
			South Korea
Baseball	Cuba	Chinese Taipei	Japan

Lillehammer 1994

February 12 - February 27

Participants: 1737 / Men: 1217, Women: 520, Countries: 67,
Sports: 10, Events: 61
Final Torchbearer: Prince Haakon of Norway

Medals Table

PLACE	COUNTRY	GOLD	SILVER	BRONZE
1	Russia	11	8	4
2	Norway	10	11	5
3	Germany	9	7	8
4	Italy	7	5	8
5	USA	6	5	2

Outstanding Athletes

PLACE	NAME (NATIONALITY)	DISCIPLINE	G	S	B
1	Lyubov Yegorova (RUS)	Nordic Skiing	3	1	–
2	Johann Olav Koss (NOR)	Speed Skating	3	–	–
3	Manuela di Centa (ITA)	Nordic Skiing	2	2	1
4	Björn Dæhlie (NOR)	Nordic Skiing	2	2	–
5	Myriam Bedard (CAN)	Biathlon	2	–	–
	Bonnie Blair (USA)	Speed Skating	2	–	–
	Chun Lee-Kyung (KOR)	Short Track	2	–	–
	Markus Wasmeier (GER)	Alpine Skiing	2	–	–
	Jens Weissflog (GER)	Nordic Skiing	2	–	–

EVENT	GOLD		SILVER		BRONZE	
Alpine Skiing						
Men						
Downhill	Tommy Moe (USA)	1:45.75	Kjetil-Andre Aamodt (NOR)	1:45.79	Edward Podivinsky (CAN)	1:45.87
Slalom	Thomas Stangassinger (AUT)	2:02.02	Alberto Tomba (ITA)	2:02.17	Jure Kosir (SLO)	2:02.53
Giant Slalom	Markus Wasmeier (GER)	2:52.46	Urs Kälin (SUI)	2:52.48	Christian Mayer (AUT)	2:52.58
Super-G	Markus Wasmeier (GER)	1:32.53	Tommy Moe (USA)	1:32.61	Kjetil Andre Aamodt (NOR)	1:32.93
Combined	Lasse Kjus (NOR)	3:17.53	Kjetil Andre Aamodt (NOR)	3:18.55	Harald Nielsen (NOR)	3:19.14
Women						
Downhill	Katja Seizinger (GER)	1:35.93	Picabo Street (USA)	1:36.59	Isolde Kostner (ITA)	1:36.85
Slalom	Vreni Schneider (SUI)	1:56.01	Elfi Eder (AUT)	1:56.35	Katja Koren (SLO)	1:56.61
Giant Slalom	Deborah Compagnoni (ITA)	2:30.97	Martina Ertl (GER)	2:32.19	Vreni Schneider (SUI)	2:32.97
Super-G	Diann Roffe (USA)	1:22.15	Svetlana Gladisheva (RUS)	1:22.44	Isolde Kostner (ITA)	1:22.45
Combined	Pernilla Wiberg (SWE)	3:05.16	Vreni Schneider (SUI)	3:05.29	Alenka Dovzan (SLO)	3:06.64
Trick Skiing						
Men						
Moguls	Jean-Luc Brassard (CAN)	27.24	Sergei Shupletsov (RUS)	26.90	Edgar Grospiron (FRA)	26.64
Jumps	Andreas Schönbächler (SUI)	234.67	Philippe Laroche (CAN)	228.63	Lloyd Langlois (CAN)	222.44
Women						
Moguls	Stine Lise Hattestad (NOR)	25.97	Elizabeth McIntyre (USA)	25.89	Elisabeta Koyevnikova (RUS)	25.81
Jumps	Lina Cheryasova (UZB)	166.84	Marie Lindgren (SWE)	165.88	Hilde Synnöve Lid (NOR)	164.13
Nordic Skiing						
Men						
10 km Cross-Country Skiing (Classical)	Björn Daehlie (NOR)	24:20.1	Vladimir Smirnov (KAZ)	24:38.3	Marco Albarello (ITA)	24:42.3
15 km Combined	Björn Daehlie (NOR)	1:00:08.8	Vladimir Smirnov (KAZ)	1:00:38.0	Silvio Fauner (ITA)	1:01:48.6
30 km (Freestylel)	Thomas Alsgaard (NOR)	1:12:26.4	Björn Daehlie (NOR)	1:13:13.6	Mika Myllylä (FIN)	1:14:14.5
50 km (Classical)	Vladimir Smirnov (KAZ)	2:07:20.3	Mika Myllylä (FIN)	2:08:41.9	Sture Sivertsen (NOR)	2:08:49.0
4 x 10 km	Italy	1:41:15.0	Norway	1:41:15.4	Finland	1:42:15.6
Ski Jumping (70 m Hill)	Espen Bredesen (NOR)	282.0	Lasse Ottesen (NOR)	268.0	Dieter Thoma (GER)	260.5
Ski Jumping (90 m Hill)	Jens Weissflog (GER)	274.5	Espen Bredesen (NOR)	266.5	Andreas Goldberger (AUT)	255.0
Ski Jumping Team	Germany	970.1	Japan	956.9	Austria	918.9
Nordic Combined - Individual	Fred Börre Lundberg (NOR)		Takanori Kono (JPN)		Bjarte Engen Vik (NOR)	
Nordic Combined - Team	Japan		Norway		Switzerland	
Women						
5 km (Classical)	Lyubov Yegorova (RUS)	14:08.8	Manuela di Centa (ITA)	14:28.3	Marja-Liisa Kirvesniemi (FIN)	14:36.0
10 km Combined	Lyubov Yegorova (RUS)	41:38.1	Manuela di Centa (ITA)	41:46.4	Stefania Belmondo (ITA)	42:21.1
15 km Freestyle	Manuela di Centa (ITA)	39:44.5	Lyubov Yegorova (RUS)	41:03.0	Nina Gavriluk (RUS)	41:10.4
30 km Classical	Manuela di Centa (ITA)	1:25:41.6	Marit Wold (NOR)	1:25:57.8	Marja-Liisa Kirvesniemi (FIN)	1:26:13.6
4 x 5 km Relay	Russia	57:12.5	Norway	57:42.6	Italy	58:42.6
Biathlon						
Men						
10 km	Sergei Chepikov (RUS)	28:07.0	Ricco Gross (GER)	28:13.0	Sergei Tarassov (RUS)	28:27.4

EVENT	GOLD		SILVER		BRONZE	
20 km	Sergei Tarassov (RUS)	57:25.3	Frank Luck (GER)	57:28.7	Sven Fischer (GER)	57:41.9
4 x 7.5 km	Germany	1:30.22.1	Russia	1:31:23.6	France	1:32:31.3
Women						
7.5 km	Myriam Bédard (CAN)	26:08.8	Svetlana Paramygina (BLR)	26:09.9	Valentina Tserbe (UKR)	26:10.0
15 km	Myriam Bédard (CAN)	52:06.2	Anne Briand (FRA)	52:53.3	Uschi Disl (GER)	53:15.3
4 x 7.5 km	Russia	1:47:19.5	Germany	1:51:16.5	France	1:52:28.3
Figure Skating						
Women	Oksana Bayul (UKR)		Nancy Kerrigan (USA)		Lu Chen (CHN)	
Men	Alexei Urmanov (RUS)		Elvis Stojko (CAN)		Philippe Candeloro (FRA)	
Pairs	Ekaterina Gordeyeva/		Natalia Mishkutionok/		Isabelle Brasseur/	
	Sergei Grinkov (RUS)		Artur Dimitriyev (RUS)		Lloyd Eisler (CAN)	
Ice Dance	Oksana Grichuk/		Maya Usova/		Jayne Torvill/	
	Yevgeni Platov (RUS)		Alexander Shulin (RUS)		Christopher Dean (GBR)	
Speed Skating						
Men						
500 m	Alexander Golubyov (RUS)	36.33	Sergei Klevshenya (RUS)	36.39	Manabu Horii (JPN)	36.53
1000 m	Dan Jansen (USA)	1:12.43	Igor Shelesovski (BLR)	1:12.72	Sergei Klevshenya (RUS)	1:12.85
1500 m	Johann Olav Koss (NOR)	1:51.29	Rintje Ritsma (HOL)	1:51.99	Falko Zandstra (HOL)	1:52.38
5000 m	Johann Olav Koss (NOR)	6:34.96	Kjell Storelid (NOR)	6:42.68	Rintje Ritsma (HOL)	6:43.94
10,000 m	Johann Olav Koss (NOR)	13:30.55	Kjell Storelid (NOR)	13:49.25	Bart Veldkamp (HOL)	13:56.73
Women						
500 m	Bonnie Blair (USA)	39.25	Susan Auch (CAN)	39.61	Franziska Schenk (GER)	39.70
1000 m	Bonnie Blair (USA)	1:18.74	Anke Baier (GER)	1:20.12	Ye Qiaobo (CHN)	1:20.22
1500 m	Emese Hunyady (AUT)	2:02.19	Svetlana Fedotkina (RUS)	2:02.69	Gunda Niemann (GER)	2:03.41
3000 m	Svetlana Bashanova (RUS)	4:17.43	Emese Hunyady (AUT)	4:18.14	Claudia Pechstein (GER)	4:18.34
5000 m	Claudia Pechstein (GER)	7:14.37	Gunda Niemann (GER)	7:14.88	Hiromi Yamamoto (JPN)	7:19.68
Short Track						
500 m Individual - Men	Chae Ji-Hoon (KOR)	43.45	Mirko Vuillermin (ITA)	43.47	Nicholas Gooch (GBR)	43.68
1000 m - Men	Kim Ki-Hoon (KOR)	1:34.57	Chae Ji-Hoon (KOR)	1:34.92	Marc Gagnon (CAN)	1:33.03
5000 m Men	Italy	7:11.74	USA	7:13.37	Australia	7:13.68
500 m Individual - Women	Cathy Turner (USA)	45.98	Zhang Yanmei (CHN)	46.44	Amy Peterson (USA)	46.76
1000 m - Women	Chun Lee-Kyung (KOR)	1:36.87	Nathalie Lambert (CAN)	1:36.97	Kim So-Hee (KOR)	1:37.09
3000 m. - Women	South Korea	4:26.64	Canada	4:32.04	USA	4:39.34
Lugeing						
Men's Singles	Georg Hackl (GER)	3:21.571	Markus Prock (AUT)	3:21.584	Armin Zoeggeler (ITA)	3:21.833
Women's Singles	Gerda Weissensteiner (ITA)	3:15.517	Susi Erdmann (GER)	3:16.276	Andrea Tagwerker (AUT)	3:16.652
2-Man Luge	Kurt Brugger/		Hansjörg Raffl/		Stefan Krausse/	
	Wilfried Huber (ITA)	1:36.720	Norbert Huber (ITA)	1:36.769	Jan Behrendt (GER)	1:36.945
Bobsledding						
2-Man Bob	Gustav Weder/		Reto Götsch/		Gunther Huber/	
	Donat Acklin (SUI I)	3:30.81	Guido Acklin (SUI II)	3:30.86	Stefano Ticci (ITA I)	3:31.01
4-Man Bob	Germany II	3:27.78	Switzerland I	3:27.84	Germany I	3:28.01
Ice Hockey						
	Sweden		Canada		Finland	

Atlanta 1996

July 19 – August 4

Participants: 10,310 / Men: 6797, Women: 3513, Countries: 197
Sports: 26, Events: 271
Final Torchbearer: Muhammad Ali

Medals Table

PLACE	COUNTRY	GOLD	SILVER	BRONZE
1	USA	44	32	25
2	Russia	26	21	16
3	Germany	20	18	27
4	China	16	22	12
5	France	15	7	15

Outstanding Athletes

PLACE	NAME (NATIONALITY)	DISCIPLINE	G	S	B
1	Amy van Dyken (USA)	Swimming	4	–	–
2	Michelle Smith (IRL)	Swimming	3	–	1
3	Alexander Popov (RUS)	Swimming	2	2	–
4	Gary Hall jun. (USA)	Swimming	2	2	–
5	Alexei Nemov (RUS)	Gymnastics	2	1	3

EVENT	GOLD		SILVER		BRONZE	
Athletics						
Men						
100 m	Donovan Bailey (CAN)	9.84	Frankie Fredericks (NAM)	9.89	Ato Boldon (TRI)	9.90
200 m	Michael Johnson (USA)	19.32	Frankie Fredericks (NAM)	19.68	Ato Boldon (TRI)	19.80
400 m	Michael Johnson (USA)	43.49	Roger Black (GBR)	44.41	Davis Kamoga (UGA)	44.53
800 m	Vebjorn Rodal (NOR)	1:42.58	Hezekiel Sepeng (RSA)	1:42.74	Fred Onyancha (KEN)	1:42.79
1500 m	Noureddine Morceli (ALG)	3:35.78	Fermin Cacho (ESP)	3:36.40	Stephen Kipkorir (KEN)	3:36.72
5000 m	Venuste Nyongabo (BUR)	13:07.96	Paul Bitok (KEN)	13:08.16	Khalid Boulami (MAR)	13:08.37
10,000 m	Haile Gebrselassie (ETH)	27:07.34	Paul Tergat (KEN)	27:08.17	Salah Hissou (MAR)	27:24.67
Marathon	Josiah Thugwane (RSA)	2:12:36	Lee Bong-Ju (KOR)	2:12:39	Eric Wainaina (KEN)	2:12:44
110 m Hurdles	Allen Johnson (USA)	12.95	Mark Crear (USA)	13.09	Florian Schwarthoff (GER)	13.17
400 m Hurdles	Derrick Adkins (USA)	47.55	Samuel Matete (ZAM)	47.78	Calvin Davis (USA)	47.96
3000 m Steeplechase	Joseph Keter (KEN)	8:07.12	Moses Kiptanui (KEN)	8:08.33	Alessandro Lambruschini (ITA)	8:11.28
4 x 100 m	Canada	37.69	USA	38.05	Brazil	38.41
4 x 400 m	USA	2:55.99	Great Britain	2:56.60	Jamaica	2:59.42
20 km Walk	Jefferson Perez (ECU)	1:20:07	Ilya Markov (RUS)	1:20:16	Bernardo Segura (MEX)	1:20:23
50 km Walk	Robert Korzeniowski (POL)	3:43:30	Mikhail Shchennikov (RUS)	3:43:46	Valentin Massana (ESP)	3:44:19
High Jump	Charles Austin (USA)	7'10¾"	Artur Partyka (POL)	7'9½"	Steve Smith (GBR)	7'8½"
Pole Vault	Jean Galfione (FRA)	19'5¼"	Igor Trandenkow (UKR)	19'5¼"	Andrei Tiwonchik (GER)	19'5¼"
Long Jump	Carl Lewis (USA)	27'10¾"	James Beckford (JAM)	27'2½"	Joe Greene (USA)	27'0½"
Triple Jump	Kenny Harrison (USA)	59'4¼"	Jonathan Edwards (GBR)	58'8"	Yoelvis Quesada (CUB)	57'2¾"
Shot	Randy Barnes (USA)	70'11¼"	John Godina (USA)	68'2½"	Oleksandr Bagach (UKR)	68'1"
Discus	Lars Riedel (GER)	227'8"	Vladimir Dubrovchik (BLR)	218'6"	Vassili Kaptyukh (BLR)	215'10"
Javelin	Jan Zelezny (CZE)	289'3"	Steve Backley (GBR)	286'10"	Seppo Raty (FIN)	285'4"
Hammer	Balazs Kiss (HUN)	266'6"	Lance Deal (USA)	266'2"	Oleksiy Krykun (UKR)	262'6"
Decathlon	Dan O'Brien (USA)	8824	Frank Busemann (GER)	8706	Tomas Dvorak (CZE)	8664
Women						
100 m	Gail Devers (USA)	10.94	Merlene Ottey (JAM)	10.94	Gwen Torrence (USA)	10.96
200 m	Marie-José Perec (FRA)	22.12	Merlene Ottey (JAM)	22.24	Mary Onyali (NGR)	22.38
400 m	Marie-José Perec (FRA)	48.25	Cathy Freeman (AUS)	48.63	Falilat Ogunkoya (NGR)	49.10
800 m	Svetlana Masterkova (RUS)	1:57.73	Ana Quirot (CUB)	1:58.11	Maria Mutola (MOZ)	1:58.71
1500 m	Svetlana Masterkova (RUS)	4:00.83	Gabriela Szabo (ROM)	4:01.54	Theresia Kiesel (AUT)	4:03.02
5000 m	Wang Junxia (CHN)	14:59.88	Pauline Konga (KEN)	15:03.49	Roberta Brunet (ITA)	15:07.52
10,000 m	Fernanda Ribeiro (POR)	31:01.63	Wang Junxia (CHN)	31:02.58	Gete Wami (ETH)	31:06.65
Marathon	Fatuma Roba (ETH)	2:26:05	Valentina Yegorova (RUS)	2:28:05	Yuko Arimori (JPN)	2:28:39
100 m Hurdles	Lyudmila Engquist (SWE)	12.58	Brigita Bukovec (SLO)	12.59	Patricia Girard (FRA)	12.65
400 m Hurdles	Deon Hemmings (JAM)	52.82	Kim Batten (USA)	53.08	Tonja Buford-Bailey (USA)	53.22
4 x 100 m	USA	41.95	Bahamas	42.14	Jamaica	42.24
4 x 400 m	USA	3:20.91	Nigeria	3:21.04	Germany	3:21.14
10 km Walk	Yelena Nikolayeva (RUS)	41:49	Elisabeta Perrone (ITA)	42:12	Gao Hongmiao (CHN)	42:19
High Jump	Stefka Kostadinova (BUL)	6'8¾"	Niki Bakogianni (GRE)	6'8"	Inga Babakova (UKR)	6'7"
Long Jump	Chioma Ajunwa (NGR)	23'4½"	Fiona May (ITA)	23'0½"	Jackie Joyner-Kersee (USA)	22'11¾"
Triple Jump	Inessa Kravets (UKR)	50'3½"	Inna Lisovskaya (RUS)	49'1¾"	Sarka Kasparkova (CZE)	49'1¾"
Shot	Astrid Kumbernuss (GER)	67'5½"	Sun Xinmei (CHN)	65'2¾"	Irina Khudorozhkina (RUS)	63'6"
Discus	Ilke Wyludda (GER)	228'6"	Natalya Sadova (RUS)	218'1"	Ellina Zvereva (BLR)	215'4"
Javelin	Heli Rantanen (NOR)	222'11"	Louise McPaul (AUS)	215'0"	Trine Hattestad (NOR)	213'2"
Heptathlon	Ghada Shouaa (SYR)	6780	Natasha Sazonovich (BLR)	6563	Denise Lewis (GBR)	6489

EVENT	GOLD		SILVER		BRONZE	
Swimming						
Men						
50 m Freestyle	Alexander Popov (RUS)	22.13	Gary Hall jun. (USA)	22.26	Fernando Scherer (BRA)	22.29
100 m Freestyle	Alexander Popov (RUS)	48.74	Gary Hall jun. (USA)	48.81	Gustavo Borges (BRA)	49.02
200 m Freestyle	Danyon Loader (NZL)	1:47.63	Gustavo Borges (BRA)	1:48.08	Daniel Kowalski (AUS)	1:48.25
400 m Freestyle	Danyon Loader (NZL)	3:47.97	Paul Palmer (GBR)	3:49.00	Daniel Kowalski (AUS)	3:52.15
1500 m Freestyle	Kieren Perkins (AUS)	14:56.40	Daniel Kowalski (AUS)	15:02.43	Graeme Smith (GBR)	15:02.48
100 m Backstroke	Jeff Rouse (USA)	54.10	Rodolfo Cabrera (CUB)	54.98	Neisser Bent (CUB)	55.02
200 m Backstroke	Brad Bridgewater (USA)	1:58.54	Tripp Schwenk (USA)	1:58.99	Emanuele Merisi (ITA)	1:59.18
100 m Breaststroke	Frederick Deburghgraeve (BEL)	1:00.65	Jeremy Linn (USA)	1:00.77	Mark Warnecke (GER)	1:01.33
200 m Breaststroke	Norbert Rozsa (HUN)	2:12.57	Karoly Guttler (HUN)	2:13.03	Alexei Korneyev (RUS)	2:13.17
100 m Butterfly	Denis Pankratov (RUS)	52.27	Scott Miller (AUS)	52.53	Vladislav Kulikov (RUS)	53.13
200 m Butterfly	Denis Pankratov (RUS)	1:56.51	Matt Malchow (USA)	1:57.44	Scott Miller (AUS)	1:57.48
200 m Medley	Attila Czene (HUN)	1:59.91	Jani Sievenen (FIN)	2:00.13	Curtis Myden (CAN)	2:01.13
400 m Medley	Tom Dolan (USA)	4:14.90	Eric Namesnik (USA)	4:15.25	Curtis Myden (CAN)	4:16.28
4 x 100 m Freestyle	USA	3:15.41	Russia	3:17.06	Germany	3:17.20
4 x 200 m Freestyle	USA	7:14.84	Sweden	7:17.56	Germany	7:17.71
4 x 100 m Medley	USA	3:34.84	Russia	3:37.55	Australia	3:39.56
Springboard Diving	Ni Xiong (CHN)	701.46	Yu Zhuocheng (CHN)	690.93	Mark Lenzi (USA)	686.49
Highboard Diving	Dmitri Sautin (RUS)	692.34	Jan Hempel (GER)	663.27	Xiao Hailiang (CHN)	658.20
Water Polo	Spain		Croatia		Italy	
Women						
50 m Freestyle	Amy van Dyken (USA)	24.87	Le Jingyi (CHN)	24.90	Sandra Volker (GER)	25.14
100 m Freestyle	Le Jingyi (CHN)	54.50	Sandra Volker (GER)	54.88	Angel Martino (USA)	54.93
200 m Freestyle	Claudia Poll (CRC)	1:58.16	Franziska van Almsick (GER)	1:58.57	Dagmar Hase (GER)	1:59.56
400 m Freestyle	Michelle Smith (IRL)	4:07.25	Dagmar Hase (GER)	4:08.30	Kirsten Vlieghuis (NED)	4:08.70
800 m Freestyle	Brooke Bennett (USA)	8:27.89	Dagmar Hase (GER)	8:29.91	Kirsten Vlieghuis (NED)	8:30.84
100 m Backstroke	Beth Botsford (USA)	1:01.19	Whitney Hedgepeth (USA)	1:01.47	Marianne Kriel (RSA)	1:02.12
200 m Backstroke	Krisztina Egerszegi (HUN)	2:07.83	Whitney Hedgepeth (USA)	2:11.98	Cathleen Rund (GER)	2:12.06
100 m Breaststroke	Penelope Heyns (RSA)	1:07.73	Amanda Beard (USA)	1:08.09	Samantha Riley (AUS)	1:09.18
200 m Breaststroke	Penelope Heyns (RSA)	2:25.41	Amanda Beard (USA)	2:25.75	Agnes Kovacs (HUN)	2:26.57
100 m Butterfly	Amy van Dyken (USA)	59.13	Liu Limin (CHN)	59.14	Angel Martino (USA)	59.23
200 m Butterfly	Susan O'Neill (AUS)	2:07.76	Petria Thomas (AUS)	2:09.82	Michelle Smith (IRL)	2:09.91
200 m Medley	Michelle Smith (IRL)	2:13.93	Marianne Limpert (CAN)	2:14.35	Lin Li (CHN)	2:14.74
400 m Medley	Michelle Smith (IRL)	4:39.18	Allison Wagner (USA)	4:42.03	Krisztina Egerszegi (HUN)	4:42.53
4 x 100 m Freestyle	USA	3:39.29	China	3:40.48	Germany	3:41.48
4 x 200 m Freestyle	USA	7:59.87	Germany	8:01.55	Australia	8:05.47
4 x 100 m Medley	USA	4:02.88	Australia	4:05.08	China	4:07.34
Springboard Diving	Fu Mingxia (CHN)	547.68	Irina Laschko (RUS)	512.19	Annie Pelletier (CAN)	509.64
Highboard Diving	Fu Mingxia (CHN)	521.58	Annika Walter (GER)	479.22	Mary Ellen Clark (USA)	472.95
Synchronized Swimming	USA	99.720	Canada	98.367	Japan	97.753
Boxing						
Light-Flyweight (- 106 lbs)	Daniel Petrov (BUL)		Mansueto Valesco (PHI)		Oleg Kuryukhin (UKR)	
					Rafael Lozano (ESP)	
Flyweight (- 112 lbs)	Maikro Romero (CUB)		Bulat Dzumadikov (KAZ)		Albert Pakeyev (RUS)	
					Zoltan Lunka (GER)	
Bantamweight (- 119 lbs)	Istvan Kovacs (HUN)		Arnoldo Mesa (CUB)		Raimkul Malakhbekov (RUS)	
					Khadpo Vichairachanun (THA)	
Featherweight (- 125 lbs)	Somluck Kamsing (THA)		Serafim Todorov (BUL)		Pablo Chacon (ARG)	
					Floyd Mayweather (USA)	
Lightweight (- 132 lbs)	Hocine Soltani (ALG)		Tontcho Tontchev (BUL)		Terrance Cauthen (USA)	
					Leonard Doroftei (ROM)	
Light-Welterweight (- 140 lbs)	Hector Vinent (CUB)		Oktay Urkal (GER)		Bolat Niyazymbetov (KAZ)	
					Fathi Missaoui (TUN)	
Welterweight (- 147 lbs)	Oleg Saitov (RUS)		Juan Hernandez (CUB)		Marian Simion (ROM)	
					Daniel Santos (PUR)	
Light-Middleweight (- 156 lbs)	David Reid (USA)		Alfredo Duvergel (CUB)		Karim Tulaganov (UZB)	
					Esmouhan Ibraimov (KAZ)	
Middleweight (- 165 lbs)	Ariel Hernandez (CUB)		Malik Beyleroglu (TUR)		Mohamed Bahari (ALG)	
					Roshii Wells (USA)	
Light-Heavyweight (- 178 lbs)	Vasili Jirov (KAZ)		Lee Seung-Bae (KOR)		Antonio Tarver (USA)	
					Thomas Ulrich (GER)	
Heavyweight (- 201 lbs)	Felix Savon (CUB)		David Defiagbon (CAN)		Nates Jones (USA)	
					Luan Krasniqui (GER)	
Super-Heavyweight (+ 201 lbs)	Vladimir Klichko (UKR)		Paea Wolfgram (TGA)		Alexei Lezin (RUS)	
					Duncan Dokwari (NGR)	

EVENT	GOLD	SILVER	BRONZE
Weightlifting			
Flyweight (- 119 lbs)	Halil Mutlu (TUR)	Zhang Xiangsen (CHN)	Sevdalin Minchev (BUL)
Bantamweight (- 130 lbs)	Tang Ningsheng (CHN)	Leonidas Sabanis (GRE)	Nikolay Pechalov (BUL)
Featherweight (- 141 lbs)	Naim Süleymanoglu (TUR)	Valerios Leonidis (GRE)	Xiao Jiangang (CHN)
Lightweight (- 154 lbs)	Zhang Xugang (CHN)	Kim Myong-Nam (PRK)	Attila Feri (HUN)
Middleweight (- 167½ lbs)	Pablo Lara (CUB)	Yoto Yotov (BUL)	Jon Chol-Ho (PRK)
Light-Heavyweight (- 183 lbs)	Pyrros Dimas (GRE)	Marc Huster (GER)	Andrzej Cofalik (POL)
Middle-Heavyweight (- 200½ lbs)	Alexei Petrov (RUS)	Leonidas Kokas (GRE)	Oliver Caruso (GER)
First Heavyweight (- 218 lbs)	Akakidei Khakiashvilis (GEO)	Anatoli Khrapaty (KAZ)	Denis Gotfrid (UKR)
Second Heavyweight (- 238 lbs)	Timur Taimassov (UKR)	Sergei Syrtsov (RUS)	Nicu Vlad (ROM)
Super-Heavyweight (+ 238 lbs)	Andrei Chemerkin (RUS)	Ronny Weller (GER)	Stefan Botev (AUS)
Greco-Roman Wrestling			
Light-Flyweight (- 105½ lbs)	Sim Kwon-Ho (KOR)	Alexander Pavlov (BLR)	Zafar Gulyov (RUS)
Flyweight (- 114½ lbs)	Arman Nazaryan (ARM)	Brandon Paulson (USA)	Andrei Kalashnikov (UKR)
Bantamweight (- 125½ lbs)	Yovei Melnichenko (KAZ)	Denis Hall (USA)	Cheng Zetian (CHN)
Featherweight (- 136½ lbs)	Wlodzimierz Zawadzki (POL)	Juan Delis (CUB)	Akif Pirim (TUR)
Lightweight (- 149½ lbs)	Ryzsard Wolny (POL)	Ghani Yalouz (FRA)	Alexander Tretyakov (RUS)
Welterweight (- 163 lbs)	Feliberto Aguilera (CUB)	Marko Asell (FIN)	Jozef Tracz (POL)
Middleweight (- 180½ lbs)	Hamza Yerlikaya (TUR)	Thomas Zander (GER)	Valeri Tsilent (BLR)
Light-Heavyweight (- 198 lbs)	Vyachetslav Oleynyk (UKR)	Jacek Fafinski (POL)	Maik Bullman (GER)
Heavyweight (- 220½ lbs)	Andreas Wronski (POL)	Sergei Lishtvan (BLR)	Mikael Ljungberg (SWE)
Super-Heavyweight (- 286 lbs)	Alexander Karelin (RUS)	Matt Ghaffari (USA)	Sergei Moureiko (MDA)
Freestyle Wrestling			
Light-Flyweight (- 105½ lbs)	Kim Il (PRK)	Armen Mkrchyan (ARM)	Alexis Vila (CUB)
Flyweight (- 114½ lbs)	Valentin Jordanov (BUL)	Namig Abdullaeyev (AZE)	Maulen Mamirov (KAZ)
Bantamweight (- 125½ lbs)	Kendall Cross (USA)	Giga Sissaouri (CAN)	Ri Yong-Sam (PRK)
Featherweight (- 136½ lbs)	Thomas Brands (USA)	Jang Jae-Sung (KOR)	Elbrus Tedeyev (UKR)
Lightweight (- 149½ lbs)	Vadim Bogiyev (RUS)	Townsend Saunders (USA)	Zaza Zazirov (UKR)
Welterweight (- 163 lbs)	Buvaisa Saityev (RUS)	Park Jang-Soon (KOR)	Taykuo Ota (JPN)
Middleweight (- 180½ lbs)	Khadshimurad Magomedov (RUS)	Yang Hyun-Mo (KOR)	Amir Khadem Azghadi (IRN)
Light-Heavyweight (- 198 lbs)	Rasul Khadem Azghadi (IRN)	Maharbeg Chadartsev (RUS)	Eldari Kurtanidze (GEO)
Heavyweight (- 220 lbs)	Kurt Angle (USA)	Abbas Jadidi (IRN)	Arwat Sabejew (GER)
Super-Heavyweight (- 286 lbs)	Mahmut Demir (TUR)	Alexei Medvedev (BUL)	Bruce Baumgartner (USA)
Judo			
Men			
Super-Lightweight (- 132 lbs)	Tadahiro Nomura (JPN)	Girolamo Giovanazzo (ITA)	Doripalam Narmandakh (MGL)
			Richard Trautmann (GER)
Half-Lightweight (- 143 lbs)	Udo Quellmalz (GER)	Yukimasa Nakamura (JPN)	Israel Hernandez Plana (CUB)
			Henrique Guimares (BRA)
Lightweight (- 156½ lbs)	Kenzo Nakamura (JPN)	Kwak Dae-Sung (KOR)	James Pedro (USA)
			Christophe Gagliano (FRA)
Light-Middleweight (- 172 lbs)	Djamel Bouras (FRA)	Toshihiko Koga (JPN)	Soso Liparteliani (GEO)
			Cho In-Chul (KOR)
Middleweight (- 189½ lbs)	Jeon Ki-Young (KOR)	Armen Bagdasarov (UZB)	Marko Spittka (GER)
			Mark Huizinga (NED)
Light-Heavyweight (- 209 lbs)	Pawel Nastula (POL)	Kim Min-Soo (KOR)	Stephane Traineau (FRA)
			Miguel Fernandez (BRA)
Heavyweight (+ 209 lbs)	David Douillet (FRA)	Ernesto Perez (ESP)	Harry van Barneveld (BEL)
			Frank Moeller (GER)
Women			
Super-Lightweight (- 106 lbs)	Kye Sun (PRK)	Ryoko Tamura (JPN)	Amarilis Savon Carmenaty (CUB)
			Yolanda Soler (ESP)
Half-Lightweight (- 114 lbs)	Marie-Claire Restoux (FRA)	Hyun Sook-Hee (KOR)	Legna Verdecia (CUB)
			Noriko Sugawara (JPN)
Lightweight (- 123 lbs)	Driulis Gonzalez Morales (CUB)	Jung Sun-Yong (KOR)	Isabel Fernandez (ESP)
			Liu Chuang (CHN)
Light-Middleweight (- 134½ lbs)	Yuko Emoto (JPN)	Gella Van De Caveye (BEL)	Jenny Gal (NED)
			Jung Sung-Sook (KOR)
Middleweight (- 145½ lbs)	Cho Min-Sun (KOR)	Aneta Szczepanska (POL)	Claudia Zwiers (NED)
			Wang Xianbo (CHN)
Light-heavyweight (- 158½ lbs)	Ulla Werbrouck (HUN)	Yoko Tanabe (JPN)	Yelena Scapin (ITA)
			Diadenis Luna (CUB)
Heavyweight (+ 158½ lbs)	Sun Fu-Ming (CHN)	Estela Rodriguez Villanueva (CUB)	Johanna Hagn (GER)
			Christine Cicot (FRA)

EVENT	GOLD		SILVER		BRONZE	
Fencing						
Men						
Individual Foil	Alessandro Puccini (ITA)		Lionel Plumenail (FRA)		Franck Boidin (FRA)	
Team Foil	Russia		Poland		Cuba	
Individual Épée	Alexander Beketov (RUS)		Ivan Trevejo Perez (CUB)		Geza Imre (HUN)	
Team Épée	Italy		Russia		France	
Individual Saber	Sergei Podnyakov (RUS)		Stanislav Sharikov (RUS)		Damien Touya (FRA)	
Team Saber	Russia		Hungary		Italy	
Women						
Individual Foil	Laura Badea (ROM)		Valentin Vezzali (ITA)		Giovanna Trillini (ITA)	
Team Foil	Italy		Romania		Germany	
Individual Épée	Laura Flessel (FRA)		Valerie Barlois (FRA)		Gyorgyi Horvathne-Szalay (HUN)	
Team Épée	France		Italy		Russia	
Modern Pentathlon	Alexander Parygin (KAZ)	5551	Eduard Zanovka (RUS)	5530	Jano Martinek (HUN)	5501
Canoeing						
Men						
500 m Kayak Singles K1	Antonio Rossi (ITA)	1:37.42	Knut Holmann (NOR)	1:38.33	Piotr Markiewicz (POL)	1:38.61
1000 m Kayak Singles K1	Knut Holmann (NOR)	3:25.78	Beniamino Bonomi (ITA)	3:27.07	Clint Robinson (AUS)	3:29.71
500 m Kayak Pairs K2	Germany	1:28.69	Italy	1:28.72	Australia	1:29.40
1000 m Kayak Pairs K2	Italy	3:09.19	Germany	3:10.51	Bulgaria	3:11.20
1000 m Kayak Fours K4	Germany	2:51.52	Hungary	2:53.18	Russia	2:55.99
500 m Canadian Singles C1	Martin Doktor (CZE)	1:49.93	Slavomir Knazovicky (SLO)	1:50.51	Imre Pulai (ITA)	1:50.75
1000 m Canadian Singles C1	Martin Doktor (CZE)	3:54.41	Ivan Klementyev (LAT)	3:54.95	Gyorgy Zala (HUN)	3:56.36
500 m Canadian Pairs C2	Hungary	1:40.42	Moldova	1:40.45	Romania	1:41.33
1000 m Canadian Pairs C2	Germany	3:31.87	Romania	3:32.29	Hungary	3:32.51
Women						
500 m Kayak Singles K1	Rita Koban (HUN)	1:47.65	Caroline Brunet (CAN)	1:47.89	Josefa Idem (ITA)	1:48.73
500 m Kayak Pairs K2	Sweden	1:39.32	Germany	1:39.68	Australia	1:40.64
500 m Kayak Fours K4	Germany	1:31.07	Switzerland	1:32.70	Sweden	1:32.91
Canoe Slalom						
Men						
Kayak 1	Oliver Fix (GER)	141.22	Andraz Vehovar (SLO)	141.65	Thomas Becker (GER)	142.79
Canadian 1	Michal Martikan (SVK)	151.03	Lukas Pollert (CZE)	151.17	Patrice Estanguet (FRA)	152.84
Canadian 2	France	158.82	Czech Republic	160.16	Germany	163.72
Women						
Kayak 1	Stepanka Hilgertova (CZE)	169.49	Dana Chladek (USA)	169.49	Myriam Fox-Jerusalmi (FRA)	171.00
Rowing						
Men						
Single Sculls	Xeno Mueller (SUI)	6:44.85	Derek Porter (CAN)	6:47.45	Thomas Lange (GER)	6:47.72
Double Sculls	Italy	6:16.98	Norway	6:18.42	France	6:19.85
Coxless Pairs	Great Britain	6:20.09	Australia	6:21.02	France	6:22.15
Quadruple Sculls	Germany	5:56.93	USA	5:59.10	Australia	6:01.65
Coxless Fours	Australia	6:06.37	France	6:07.03	Great Britain	6:07.28
Eights	Netherlands	5:42.74	Germany	5:44.58	Russia	5:45.77
Lightweight Double Sculls	Switzerland	6:23.27	Netherlands	6:26.48	Australia	6:26.69
Lightweight Coxless Fours	Denmark	6:09.58	Canada	6:10.13	USA	6:12.29
Women						
Single Sculls	Yekaterina Khodotovich (BLR)	7:32.21	Silken Laumann (CAN)	7:35.15	Trine Hansen (DEN)	7:37.20
Double Sculls	Canada	6:56.84	China	6:58.35	Netherlands	6:58.72
Coxless Pairs	Australia	7:01.39	USA	7:01.78	France	7:03.82
Quadruple Sculls	Germany	6:27.44	Ukraine	6:30.36	Canada	6:30.38
Eights	Romania	6:19.73	Canada	6:24.05	Belorussia	6:24.44
Lightweight Double Sculls	Romania	7:12.78	USA	7:14.65	Australia	7:16.56
Yachting						
Men						
Finn	Mateusz Kusnierewicz (POL)	32	Sebastian Godefroid (BEL)	45	Roy Heiner (NED)	50
470	Ukraine	40	Great Britain	61	Portugal	62
Mistral Sailboard	Nikolas Kaklamanakis (GRE)	17	Carlos Espinola (ARG)	19	Gal Fridman (ISR)	21

EVENT	GOLD		SILVER		BRONZE	
Women						
Europe	Kristine Roug (DEN)	24	Margit Matthijsse (NED)	30	Courtney Becker-Dey (USA)	39
470	Spain	25	Japan	36	Ukraine	38
Mistral Sailboard	Lee Lai-Shan (HKG)	16	Barbara Kendall (NZL)	24	Alessandra Sensini (ITA)	28
Open						
Star	Brazil	25	Sweden	29	Australia	32
Tornado	Spain	30	Australia	42	Brazil	43
Soling	Germany		Russia		USA	
Laser	Robert Scheidt (BRA)	26	Ben Ainslie (GBR)	37	Per Moberg (NOR)	46
Cycling						
Men						
Road Race	Pascal Richard (SUI)	4:53:56	Ralf Sorensen (DEN)	4:53:56	Max Sciandri (GBR)	4:53:58
Road Time Trial	Miguel Indurain (ESP)	1:04.05	Abraham Olano (ESP)	1:04.17	Chris Boardman (GBR)	1:04.36
Sprint	Jens Fiedler (GER)		Marthy Nothstein (USA)		Curtis Harnett (CAN)	
1000 m Time Trial	Florian Rousseau (FRA)	1:02.712	Erin Hartwell (USA)	1:02.940	Takandu Jumonji (JPN)	1:03.261
4000 m Individual Pursuit	Andrea Collinelli (ITA)	4:20.893	Philippe Ermenault (FRA)	4:22.714	Bradley McGee (AUS)	4:26.121
4000 m Team Pursuit	France	4:05.930	Russia	4:07.730	Australia	
Individual Points Race	Silvio Martinello (ITA)	37	Brian Walton (CAN)	29	Stuart O'Grady (AUS)	25
Cross-Country	Bart Brentjens (NED)	2:17:38	Thomas Frischknecht (SUI)	2:20:14	Miguel Martinez (FRA)	2:20:26
Women						
Road Race	Jeannie Longo-Ciprelli (FRA)	2:36:13	Imelda Chiappa (USA)	2:36:38	Clara Hughes (CAN)	2:36:44
Time Trial	Zulfia Zabirova (RUS)	36:40	Jeannie Longo-Ciprelli (FRA)	37:00	Clara Hughes (CAN)	37:13
Sprint	Felicia Ballanger (FRA)		Michelle Ferris (AUS)		Ingrid Haringa (NED)	
3000 m Individual Pursuit	Antonella Bellutti (ITA)	3:33.595	Marion Clignet (FRA)	3:38.571	Judith Arnt (GER)	3:38.744
Individual Points Race	Nathalie Lancien (FRA)	24	Ingrid Haringa (NED)	23	Lucy Tyler-Sharman (AUS)	17
Cross-Country	Paola Pezzo (ITA)	1:50:51	Alison Sydor (CAN)	1:51:58	Susan DiMattei (USA)	1:52:36
Equestrianism						
Three-Day Event	Blyth Tait (NZL)	56.8	Sally Clark (NZL)	60.4	Kerry Millikin (USA)	73.7
Three-Day Event, Team	Australia	203.85	USA	261.10	New Zealand	268.55
Grand Prix (Dressage)	Isabell Werth (GER)	235.09	Anky van Grunsven (NED)	233.02	Sven Rothenberger (NED)	224.94
Grand Prix (Dressage), Team	Germany	5553	Netherlands	5437	USA	5309
Grand Prix (Jumping)	Ulrich Kirchhoff (GER)	1.00	Willi Melliger (SUI)	4.00	Alexandra Ledermann (FRA)	4.00
Grand Prix (Jumping), Team	Germany	1.75	USA	12.00	Brazil	17.25
Shooting						
Men						
Small-Bore Rifle (Prone)	Christian Klees (GER)	704.8	Sergei Belyayev (KAZ)	703.3	Jozef Gonci (SLO)	701.9
Small-Bore Rifle (3 Positions)	Jean-Pierre Amat (FRA)	1273.9	Sergei Belyayev (KAZ)	1272.3	Wolfram Waibel (AUT)	1269.6
Rapid-Fire Pistol	Ralf Schumann (GER)	698.0	Emil Milev (BUL)	692.1	Vladimir Vochmianin (KAZ)	691.5
Free Pistol (50 m)	Boris Kokorev (RUS)	666.4	Igor Basinki (BLR)	662.0	Roberto Di Donna (ITA)	661.8
Running Game Target	Ling Yang (CHN)	685.8	Xiao Jun (CHN)	679.8	Miroslav Janus (CZE)	678.4
Air Pistol	Roberto Di Donna (ITA)	684.2	Wang Yifu (CHN)	684.1	Taniu Kiryakov (BUL)	683.8
Skeet Shooting	Ennio Falco (ITA)	149	Miroslav Rzepkowski (POL)	148	Andrea Benelli (ITA)	147
Trap Shooting	Michael Diamond (AUS)	149	Josh Lakatos (USA)	147	Lance Bade (USA)	147
Double Trap Shooting	Russell Mark (AUS)	189	Albano Pera (ITA)	183	Zhang Bing (CHN)	183
Air Rifle	Artem Khadzhibekov (RUS)	695.7	Wolfram Waibel (AUT)	695.2	Jean-Pierre Amat (FRA)	693.1
Women						
Sports Pistol	Li Duihong (CHN)	687.9	Diana Yorgova (BUL)	684.8	Marina Logvinenko (RUS)	684.2
Small-Bore Rifle (3 Positions)	Alexandra Ivosev (YUG)	686.1	Irina Gerasimenok (POL)	680.1	Renata Mauer (POL)	679.8
Air Rifle	Renata Mauer (POL)	497.6	Petra Horneber (GER)	497.4	Alexandra Ivosev (YUG)	497.2
Air Pistol	Olga Klochneva (RUS)	490.1	Marina Logvinenko (RUS)	488.5	Maria Grusdeva (BUL)	488.5
Double Trap Shooting	Kim Rhode (USA)	141	Susanne Keirmayer (GER)	139	Deserie Huddleston (AUS)	139
Archery						
Men						
Individual	Justin Huish (USA)		Magnus Petersson (SWE)		Oh Kyun-Moon (KOR)	
Team	USA		South Korea		Italy	
Women						
Individual	Kim Kyung-Wook (KOR)		He Ying (CHN)		Olena Sadovnycha (UKR)	
Team	South Korea		Germany		Poland	

EVENT	GOLD		SILVER		BRONZE	
Gymnastics						
Men						
Individual Combined Exercises	Li Xiaoshuang (CHN)	58.423	Alexei Nemov (RUS)	58.374	Vitali Sherbo (BLR)	58.197
Team	Russia	576.778	China	575.539	Ukraine	571.541
Parallel Bars	Rustam Sharipov (UKR)	9.837	Jair Lynch (USA)	9.825	Vitali Sherbo (BLR)	9.800
Floor	Ioannis Melissanidis (GRE)	9.950	Li Xiaoshuang (CHN)	9.837	Alexei Nemov (RUS)	9.800
Horse Vault	Alexei Nemov (RUS)	9.787	Yeo Hong-Chul (KOR)	9.756	Vitali Sherbo (BLR)	9.724
Horizontal Bar	Andreas Wecker (GER)	9.850	Krasimir Dounev (BUL)	9.825	Vitali Sherbo (BLR)	9.800
					Fan Bin (CHN)	9.800
					Alexei Nemov (RUS)	9.800
Rings	Yuri Chechi (ITA)	9.887	Szilveszter Csollany (HUN)	9.812	Dan Burnica (ROM)	9.812
Pommel Horse	Li Donghua (SUI)	9.875	Marius Urzica (ROM)	9.825	Alexei Nemov (RUS)	9.787
Women						
Individual Combined Exercises	Lilia Podkopayeva (UKR)	39.255	Gina Gogean (ROM)	39.075	Lavinia Milosivici (ROM)	39.067
					Simona Amanar (ROM)	39.067
Team	USA	389.225	Russia	388.404	Romania	388.246
Floor	Lilia Podkopayeva (UKR)	9.887	Simona Amanar (ROM)	9.850	Dominique Dawes (USA)	9.837
Horse Vault	Simona Amanar (ROM)	9.825	Mo Huilan (CHN)	9.768	Gina Gogean (ROM)	9.750
Beam	Shannon Miller (USA)	9.862	Lilia Podkopayeva (UKR)	9.825	Gina Gogean (ROM)	9.787
Asymmetrical Bars	Svetlana Chorkina (RUS)	9.850	Bi Wengji (CHN)	9.837		
			Amy Chow (USA)	9.837		
Rhythmic, Individual	Yekaterina Serebryanskaya (UKR)	39.683	Yanina Batyrchina (RUS)	39.382	Yelena Vitrichenko (UKR)	39.331
Rhythmic, Team	Spain	38.933	Bulgaria	38.866	Russia	38.365
Tennis						
Men						
Singles	Andre Agassi (USA)		Sergi Bruguera (ESP)		Leander Paes (IND)	
Doubles	Mark Woodforde/Todd Woodbridge (AUS)		Tim Henman/Neil Broad (GBR)		Marc-Kevin Goellner/David Prinosil (GER)	
Women						
Singles	Lindsay Davenport (USA)		Arantxa Sanchez-Vicario (ESP)		Jana Novotna (CZE)	
Doubles	Gigi Fernandez/ Mary Jo Fernandez (USA)		Jana Novotna/ Helena Sukova (CZE)		Conchita Martinez / Arantxa Sanchez Vicario (ESP)	
Table Tennis						
Men						
Singles	Liu Guoliang (CHN)		Wang Tao (CHN)		Joerg Rosskoff (GER)	
Doubles	China		China		South Korea	
Women						
Singles	Deng Yaping (CHN)		Chen Jung (TPE)		Qiao Hong (CHN)	
Doubles	China		China		South Korea	
Basketball						
Men	USA		Yugoslavia		Lithuania	
Women	USA		Brazil		Australia	
Soccer						
Men	Nigeria		Argentina		Brazil	
Women	USA		China		Norway	
Handball						
Men	Croatia		Sweden		Spain	
Women	Denmark		South Korea		Hungary	
Hockey						
Men	Netherlands		Spain		Australia	
Women	Australia		South Korea		Netherlands	
Volleyball						
Men	Netherlands		Italy		Yugoslavia	
Women	Cuba		China		Brazil	
Beach Volleyball						
Men's Pairs	USA		USA		Canada	
Women's Pairs	Brazil		Brazil		Australia	

EVENT	GOLD	SILVER	BRONZE
Badminton			
Men			
Singles	Poul-Erik Hoyer-Larsen (DEN)	Jiong Dong (CHN)	Rashid Sidek (MAS)
Doubles	Indonesia	Malaysia	Indonesia
Women			
Singles	Bang Soo-Hyun (KOR)	Mia Audina (INA)	Susi Susanti (INA)
Doubles	China	South Korea	China
Mixed Doubles	South Korea	South Korea	China
Baseball	Cuba	Japan	USA
Softball	USA	China	Australia

Nagano 1998

February 7 – February 22

Participants: 2176 / Men: 1389, Women: 787, Countries: 72
Sports: 14, Events: 68
Final Torchbearers: Chris Moon, Tadanori Kono, Masashi Abe, Reiichi
Mikata, Hiromi Suzuki, Masako Chiba, Midori Ito

Medals Table

PLACE	COUNTRY	GOLD	SILVER	BRONZE
1	Germany	12	9	8
2	Norway	10	10	5
3	Russia	9	6	3
4	Canada	6	5	4
5	USA	6	3	4

Outstanding Athletes

PLACE	NAME (NATIONALITY)	DISCIPLINE	G	S	B
1	Larissa Latsutina (RUS)	Cross-country	3	1	1
2	Bjoern Dæhlie (NOR)	Cross-country	3	1	–
3	Katja Seizinger (GER)	Alpine Skiing	2	–	1
	Chun Lee-Kyung (KOR)	Short Track	2	–	1

EVENT	GOLD		SILVER		BRONZE	
Alpine Skiing						
Men						
Downhill	Jean-Luc Cretier (FRA)	1:50.11	Lasse Kjus (NOR)	1:50.51	Hannes Trinkl (AUT)	1:50.63
Slalom	Hans-Petter Buraas (NOR)	1:49.31	Ole Christian Furuseth (NOR)	1:50.64	Thomas Sykora (AUT)	1:50.68
Giant Slalom	Hermann Maier (AUT)	2:38.51	Stefan Eberharter (AUT)	2:39.36	Michael von Grüningen (SUI)	2:39.69
Super-G	Hermann Maier (AUT)	1:34.82	Hans Knauss (AUT)	1:35.43		
			Didier Cuche (SUI)	1:35.43		
Combined	Mario Reiter (AUT)	3:08.06	Lasse Kjus (NOR)	3:08.65	Christian Mayer (AUT)	3:10.11
Women						
Downhill	Katja Seizinger (GER)	1:28.89	Pernilla Wiberg (SWE)	1:29.18	Florence Masnade (FRA)	1:29.37
Slalom	Hilde Gerg (GER)	1:32.40	Deborah Compagnoni (ITA)	1:32.46	Zali Steggall (AUS)	1:32.67
Giant Slalom	Deborah Compagnoni (ITA)	2:50.59	Alexandra Meissnitzer (AUT)	2:51.79	Katja Seizinger (GER)	2:52.61
Super-G	Picabo Street (USA)	1:18.02	Michaela Dorfmeister (AUT)	1:18.03	Alexandra Meissnitzer (AUT)	1:18.09
Combined	Katja Seizinger (GER)	2:40.74	Martina Ertl (GER)	2:40.92	Hilde Gerg (GER)	2:41.50
Biathlon						
Men						
10 km	Ole Einar Björnadalen (NOR)	27:16.2/0	Frode Andresen (NOR)	28:17.8/2	Ville Raikkonen (FIN)	28:21.7/1
20 km	Halvard Hanevold (NOR)	56:16.4/1	Pier Alberto Carrara (ITA)	56:21.9/0	Alexei Aidarov (BLR)	56:46.5/1
Relay 4 x 7.5 km	Germany	1:21:36.2/0	Norway	1:22:19.3/0	Russia	1:22:19.3/0
Women						
7.5 km	Galina Kukleva (RUS)	23:08.0/1	Ursula Disl (GER)	23:08.7/1	Katrin Apel (GER)	23:32.4/1
15 km	Ekaterina Dafovska (BUL)	54:52.0/0	Elena Petrova (RUS)	55:09.8/1	Ursula Disl (GER)	55:17.9/1
Relay 4 x 7.5 km	Germany	1:40:13.6/0	Russia	1:40:25.2/0	Norway	1:40:37.3/2

EVENT	GOLD		SILVER		BRONZE	
Ski Jumping						
Men						
90 m	Jani Soinonen (FIN)	234.5 Pts.	Kazuyoshi Funaki (JPN)	233.5 Pts.	Andreas Wildhölzl (AUT)	232.5 Pts.
120 m	Kazuyoshi Funaki (JPN)	272.3 Pts.	Jani Soinonen (FIN)	260.8 Pts.	Masahiko Harada (JPN)	258.3 Pts.
120 m (Team)	Japan	933.0 Pts.	Germany	897.4 Pts.	Austria	881.5 Pts.
Curling						
Men	Switzerland		Canada		Norway	
Women	Canada		Denmark		Sweden	
Freestyle Skiing						
Men						
Mogul Field	Jonny Moseley (USA)	26.93 Pts.	Janne Lahtela (FIN)	26.00 Pts.	Sami Mustonen (FIN)	25.76 Pts.
Jump	Eric Bergoust (USA)	255.64 Pts.	Sebastien Foucras (FRA)	248.79 Pts.	Dmitri Dashshinski (BLR)	240.79 Pts.
Women						
Mogul Field	Tae Satoya (JPN)	25.06 Pts.	Tatjana Mittermayer (GER)	24.62 Pts.	Kari Traa (NOR)	24.09 Pts.
Jump	Nikki Stone (USA)	193.00 Pts.	Xu Nannan (CHN)	186.97 Pts.	Colette Brand (SUI)	171.83 Pts.
Snowboarding						
Men						
Giant slalom	Ross Rebagliati (CAN)	2:03.96	Thomas Prugger (ITA)	2:03.98	Ueli Kestenholz (SUI)	2:04.08
Halfpipe	Gian Simmen (SUI)	85.2	Daniel Franck (NOR)	82.4	Ross Powers (USA)	82.1
Women						
Giant slalom	Karine Ruby (FRA)	2:17.34	Heidi Renoth (GER)	2:19.17	Brigitte Koeck (AUT)	2:19.42
Halfpipe	Nicola Thost (GER)	74.6	Stine Brun Kjeldaas (NOR)	74.2	Shannon Dunn (USA)	72.8
Figure Skating						
Men	I Kulik (RUS)		Elvis Stojko (CAN)		Philippe Candelore (FRA)	
Women	Tara Lipinski (USA)		Michelle Kwan (USA)		Lu Chen (CHN)	
Pairs	Oksana Kasakova/Artur Dmitriev (RUS)		Elena Bereshnaya /Anton Sikharulidse (RUS)		Mandy Wotzel/Ingo Steuer (GER)	
Ice Dance	Pasha Grishuk/Yevgeni Platov (RUS)		Anjelika Krylova /Oleg Ovsyannikov (RUS)		Marina Anissina/Gwendal Peizerat (FRA)	
Bob-sledding						
Men						
2-man bob	Huber/Tartaglia (ITA)	3:37.24	Pierre Lüders/David Maceachern (CAN)	3:37.24	Christoph Langen/ Markus Zimmermann (GER)	3:37.89
4-man bob	Germany II	2:39.41	Switzerland	2:40.01	UK	2:40.01
	Christoph Langen/Markus Zimmermann/ Marco Jacobs/Olaf Hampel		Marcel Rohner/Markus Nüssli/ Markus Wasser/Beat Seitz		Sean Olsson/Dean Ward /Courtney Rumbolt/Paul Attwood	
					France I	2:40.01
					Bruno Mingeon/Emmanuel Hostache/Eric Le Chanony/Max Robert	
Lugeing						
Men's Singles	Georg Hackl (GER)	2:23.21	Armin Zöggeler (ITA)	2:23.26	Jens Müller (GER)	2:23.342
2-man Luge	Stefan Krausse/Jan Behrendt (GER)	1:41:105	Christopher Thorpe/Gordy Sheer (USA)	1:41.127	Mark Grimette/Brian Martin (USA)	1:41.217
Women's singles	Silke Kraushaar (GER)	3:23.779	Barbara Niedernhuber (GER)	3:23.781	Angelika Neuner (AUT)	3:24.253
Speedskating						
Men						
10,000 m	Gianni Romme (NED)	13:15.33	Bob de Jong (NED)	13:25.76	Rintje Ritsma (NED)	13:28.19
5000 m	Gianni. Romme (NED)	6:22.20	Rintje Ritsma (NED)	6:28.24	Bart Veldkamp (BEL)	6:28.31
1500 m	Aadne Söndral (NOR)	1:47.87	Ids Postma (NED)	1:48.13	Rintje Ritsma (NED)	1:48.52
1000 m	Ids Postma (NED)	1:10.64	Jan Bos (NED)	1:10.71	Hiroyasu Shimizu (JPN)	1:11.0
500 m	Hiroyasu Shimizu (JPN)	1:11.35	Jeremy Wotherspoon (CAN)	1:11.84	Kevin Overland (CAN)	1:11.86
Women						
5000 m	Claudia Pechstein (GER)	6:59.61	G. Niemann-Stirnemann (GER)	6:59.65	Lyudmilla Prokasheva (KAZ)	7:11.14
3000 m	Gunda Niemann-Stirnemann (GER)	4:07.29	Claudia Pechstein (GER)	4:08.47	Anna Friesinger (GER)	4:09.44
1500 m	Marianne Timmer (NED)	1:57.58	Gunda Niemann-Stirnemann (GER)	1:58.66	Christine Witty (USA)	1:58.9
1000 m	Marianne Timmer (NED)	1:16.51	Christine Witty (USA)	1:16.79	Catriona LeMay-Doan (CAN)	1:17.37
500 m	Catriona LeMay-Doan (CAN)	1:16.60	Susan Auch (CAN)	1:16.93	Tomomi Okazaki (JPN)	1:17.10

EVENT	GOLD		SILVER		BRONZE	
Short Track						
Men						
1000 m	Kim Dong-Sung (KOR)	1:32.375	Li Jiajun (CHN)	1:32.428	Eric Bedard (CAN)	1:32.66
500 m	Takafumi Tishitani (JPN)	42.862	An Yulong. (CHN)	43.022	Hitoshi Uematsu (JPN)	43.713
Relay 5000 m	Canada	7:06.075	South Korea	7:06.776	China	7:11.556
Women						
500 m	A. Perreault (CAN)	46.568	Yang Yang (CHN)	46.627	Chun Lee-Kyung (KOR)	46.335
1000 m	Chun Lee-Kyung (KOR)	1:42.776	Yang Yang (CHN)	1:43.343	Won Hye-Kyung (KOR)	1:43.361
Relay 3000 m	South Korea	4:16.260	China	4:16.383	Canada	4:21.205
Ice Hockey						
Men	Czech Republic		Russia		Canada	
Women	USA		Canada		Finland	
Nordic Skiing						
Men						
10 km Cross-country skiing (Classical)	Björn Dæhlie (NOR)	27:24.5	Markus Gandler (AUT)	27:32.5	Mika Myllylä (FIN)	27:40.1
30 km Cross-country skiing (Classical)	Mika Myllylä (FIN)	1:33.55.8	Erling Jevne (NOR)	1:35.27.1	Silvio Fauner (ITA)	1:36.08.5
50 km Cross-country skiing (Freestyle)	Björn Dæhlie (NOR)	2:05.08.2	Niklas Jonsson (SWE)	2:05.16.3	Christian Hoffmann (AUT)	2:06.01.8
15 km Combination	Thomas Alsgaard (NOR)	1:07.01	Björn Dæhlie (NOR)	1:07.02	Vladimir Smirnov (KZE)	1:07.31
Nordic Combination, Individual	Bjarte Engen Vik (NOR)	41:21.1	Samppa Lajunen (FIN)	41:48.6	Valeri Stolyarov (RUS)	41:49.3
Nordic Combination, Team	Norway	54:11.5	Finland	55:30.4	France	55:53.4
Relay 4 x 10 km	Norway	1:10.64	Italy	1:10.71	Finland	1:11.0
Women						
5 km Cross-country skiing (Classical)	Larissa Latsutina (RUS)	17:37.9	Katerina Neumannova (CZE)	17:42.7	Bente Martinsen (NOR)	17:48.4
15 km Cross-country skiing (Classical)	Olga Danilova (RUS)	46:55.4	Larissa Latsutina (RUS)	47:01.0	Anita Moen-Guidon (NOR)	47:52.6
30 km Cross-country skiing (Freestyle)	Juliya Tchepalova (RUS)	1:22.01.5	Stefania Belmondo (ITA)	1:22.11.7	Larissa Latsutina (RUS)	1:23.15.7
10 km Combined	Larissa Latsutina (RUS)	46:06.9	Olga Danilova (RUS)	46:13.4	Katerina Neumannova (CZE)	46:14.2
Relay 4 x 4 10 km	Russia	55:13.5	Norway	55:38.0	Italy	56:53.3

Sydney 2000

15 September – 1 October

Participants: 10,651 / Men: 6582, Women: 4069, Countries: 200
Sports: 28, Events: 300
Final Torchbearer: Cathy Freeman

Medals Table

PLACE	COUNTRY	GOLD	SILVER	BRONZE
1	USA	40	24	33
2	Russia	32	28	28
3	China	28	16	15
4	Australia	16	25	17
5	Germany	13	17	26

Outstanding Athletes

PLACE	NAME (NATIONALITY)	DISCIPLINE	G	S	B
1	Alexei Nemov (RUS)	Gymnastics	2	1	3
2	Ian Thorpe (AUS)	Swimming	3	2	0
3	Marion Jones (USA)	Athletics	3	0	2
4	Dara Torres (USA)	Swimming	2	0	3
5	Inge de Bruijn (NED)	Swimming	3	1	0

EVENT	GOLD		SILVER		BRONZE	
Athletics						
Men						
100 m	Maurice Greene (USA)	9.87	Ato Bolden (TRI)	9.99	Obadele Thompson (BAR)	10.04
200 m	Konstantinos Kenteris (GRE)	20.09	Darren Campbell (GBR)	20.14	Ato Bolden (TRI)	20.20
400 m	Michael Johnson (USA)	43.84	Alvin Harrison (USA)	44.40	Gregory Haughton (JAM)	44.70
800 m	Nils Schumann (GER)	1:45.08	Wilson Kipketer (DEN)	1:45.14	Aissa Said Guerni (ALG)	1:45.16
1500 m	Noah Kiprono Ngenya (KEN)	3:32.07	Hicham El Guerrouj (MAR)	3:32.32	Bernard Kipchirchir Lagat (KEN)	3:32.44
5000 m	Million Wolde (ETH)	13:35.49	Ali Saidi-Sief (ALG)	13:36.20	Brahim Lahlafi (MAR)	13:36.47
10,000 m	Haile Gebrselassie (ETH)	27:18.20	Paul Tergat (KEN)	27:18.29	Assefa Mezegebu (ETH)	27:19.75
Marathon	Kezahegne Abera (ETH)	2:10:11	Eric Wainaina (KEN)	2:10:31	Tesfaye Tola (ETH)	2:11:10
110 m Hurdles	Anier Garcia (CUB)	13.00	Terrence Trammell (USA)	13.16	Mark Crear (USA)	13.22
400 m Hurdles	Angelo Taylor (USA)	47.50	Hadi Al-Somayli (KSA)	47.53	Llewellyn Herbert (RSA)	47.81
3000 m Steeplechase	Reuben Kosgei (KEN)	8:21.43	Wilson Boit Kipketer (KEN)	8:21.77	Ali Ezzine (MAR)	8:22.15
4 x 100 m	USA	37.61	Brazil	37.90	Cuba	38.04
4 x 400 m	USA	2:56.35	Nigeria	2:58.68	Jamaica	2:58.78

EVENT	GOLD		SILVER		BRONZE	
20 km Walk	Robert Korzeniowski (POL)	1:18:59	Noe Hernandez (MEX)	1:19:03	Vladimir Andreyev (RUS)	1:19:27
50 km Walk	Robert Korzeniowski (POL)	3:42:22	Aigars Fadejevs (LAT)	3:43:40	Joel Sanchez (MEX)	3:44:36
High Jump	Sergey Klyugin (RUS)	2.35	Javier Sotomayor (CUB)	2.32	Abderahmane Hammad (ALG)	2.32
Pole Vault	Nick Hysong (USA)	5.90	Lawrence Johnson (USA)	5.90	Maksim Tarasov (RUS)	5.90
Long Jump	Ivan Pedroso (CUB)	8.55	Jai Taurima (AUS)	8.49	Roman Shchurenko (UKR)	8.31
Triple Jump	Jonathan Edwards (GBR)	17.71	Yoel Garcia (CUB)	17.47	Denis Kapustin (RUS)	17.46
Shot	Arsi Harju (FIN)	21.29	Adam Nelson (USA)	21.21	John Godina (USA)	21.20
Discus	Virgilijus Alekna (LTU)	69.30	Lars Riedel (GER)	68.50	Frantz Kruger (RSA)	68.19
Javelin	Jan Zelezny (CZE)	90.17	Steve Backley (GBR)	89.85	Sergey Makarov (RUS)	88.67
Hammer	Szymon Ziolkowski (POL)	80.02	Nicola Vizzoni (ITA)	79.64	Igor Astapkovich (BLR)	79.17
Decathlon	Erki Nool (EST)	8641	Roman Sebrle (CZE)	8606	Chris Huffins (USA)	8595
Women						
100 m	Marion Jones (USA)	10.75	Ekaterini Thanou (GRE)	11.12	Tanya Lawrence (JAM)	11.18
200 m	Marion Jones (USA)	21.84	Pauline Davis-Thompson (BAH)	22.27	Susanthika Jayasinghe (Sri)	22.28
400 m	Cathy Freeman (AUS)	49.11	Lorraine Graham (JAM)	49.58	Katharine Merry (GBR)	49.72
800 m	Maria Mutola (MOZ)	1:56.15	Stephanie Graf (AUT)	1:56.64	Kelly Holmes (GBR)	1:56.80
1500 m	Nouria Merah-Benida (ALG)	4:05.10	Violeta Szekely (ROM)	4:05.15	Gabriela Szabo (ROM)	4:05.27
5000 m	Gabriela Szabo (ROM)	14:40.79	Sonia O'Sullivan (IRL)	14:41.02	Gete Wami (ETH)	14:42.23
10,000 m	Derartu Tulu (ETH)	30:17.49	Gete Wami (ETH)	30:22.48	Fernanda Ribeiro (POR)	30:22.88
Marathon	Naoko Takahashi (JPN)	2:23:14	Lidia Simon (ROM)	2:23:22	Joyce Chepchumba (KEN)	2:24:45
100 m Hurdles	Olga Shishigina (KAZ)	12.65	Gloria Alozie (NGR)	12.68	Melissa Morrison (USA)	12.76
400 m Hurdles	Irina Privalova (RUS)	53.02	Deon Hemmings (JAM)	53.45	Nezha Bideouane (MAR)	53.57
4 x 100 m	Bahamas	41.95	Jamaica	42.13	USA	42.20
4 x 400 m	USA	3:22.62	Jamaica	3:23.25	Russia	3:23.46
20 km Walk	Wang Liping (CHN)	1:29:05	Kjersti Plaetzer (NOR)	1:29:33	Maria Vasco (ESP)	1:30:23
High Jump	Yelena Yelesina (RUS)	2.01	Hestrie Cloete (RSA)	2.01	Oana Manuela Pantelimon (ROM) 1.99 and Kajsa Bergquist (SWE)	
Pole Vault	Stacy Oragila (USA)	4.60	Tatiana Grigorieva (AUS)	4.55	Vala Flosadottir (ISL)	4.50
Long Jump	Heike Drechsler (GER)	6.99	Fiona May (ITA)	6.92	Marion Jones (USA)	6.92
Triple Jump	Tereza Marinova (BUL)	15.20	Tatyana Lebedeva (RUS)	15.00	Olena Hovorova (UKR)	14.96
Shot	Yanina Koarolchik (BLR)	20.56	Larisa Peleshenko (RUS)	19.92	Astrid Kumbernuss (GER)	19.62
Discus	Ellina Zvereva (BLR)	68.40	Anastasia Kelesidou (GRE)	65.71	Irina Yatchenko (BLR)	65.20
Hammer	Kamila Skolimowska (POL)	71.16	Olga Kuzenkova (RUS)	69.77	Kirsten Munchow (GER)	69.28
Javelin	Trine Hattestad (NOR)	68.91m	Mirela Tzelili (GRE)	67.51	Osleidys Menendez (CUB)	66.18
Heptathlon	Denise Lewis (GBR)	6584	Yelena Prokhorova (RUS)	6531	Natalya Sazanovich (BLR)	6527
Swimming						
Men						
50 m Freestyle	Anthony Ervin (USA) and Gary Hall Jr (USA)	21.98			Pieter van den Hoogenband (NED) 22.03	
100 m Freestyle	Pieter van den Hoogenband (NED) 48.30		Alexander Popov (RUS)	48.69	Gary Hall Jr (USA)	48.73
200 m Freestyle	Pieter van den Hoogenband (NED) 1:45.35		Ian Thorpe (AUS)	1:45.83	Massimiliano Rosolino (ITA)	1:46.65
400 m Freestyle	Ian Thorpe (AUS)	3:40.59	Massimiliano Rosolino (ITA)	3:43.40	Klete Keller (USA)	3:47.00
1500 m Freestyle	Grant Hackett (AUS)	14:48.33	Kieren Perkins (AUS)	14:53.59	Chris Thompson (USA)	14:56.81
100 m Backstroke	Lenny Krayzelburg (USA)	53.72	Matthew Welsh (AUS)	54.07	Stev Theloke (GER)	54.82
200 m Backstroke	Lenny Krayzelburg (USA)	1:56.76	Aaron Peirsol (USA)	1:57.35	Matthew Welsh (AUS)	1:57.59
100 m Breaststroke	Domenico Fioravanti (ITA)	1:00.46	Ed Moses (USA)	1:00.73	Roman Sloudnov (RUS)	1:00.91
200 m Breaststroke	Domenico Fioravanti (ITA)	2:10.87	Terence Parkin (RSA)	2:12.50	Davide Rummolo (ITA)	2:12.73
100 m Butterfly	Lars Froelander (SWE)	52.00	Michael Klim (AUS)	52.18	Geoff Huegill (AUS)	52.22
200 m Butterfly	Tom Malchow (USA)	1:55.35	Denys Sylantyev (UKR)	1:55.76	Justin Norris (AUS)	1:56.17
200 m Medley	Massamiliano Rosolino (ITA)	1:58.98	Tom Dolan (USA)	1:59.77	Tom Wilkens (USA)	2:00.87
400 m Medley	Tom Dolan (USA)	4:11.76	Eric Vendt (USA)	4:14.23	Curtis Myden (CAN)	4:15.33
4 x 100 m Freestyle	Australia	3:13.67	USA	3:13.86	Brazil	3:17.40
4 x 200 m Freestyle	Australia	7:07.05	USA	7:12.64	Netherlands	7:12.70
4 x 100 m Medley	USA	3:33.73	Australia	3:35.27	Germany	3:35.88
Springboard Diving	Ni Xiong (CHN)	708.72	Fernando Platas (MEX)	708.42	Dmitri Sautin (RUS)	703.20
10 m Platform Diving	Liang Tian (CHN)	724.53	Jia Hua (CHN)	713.55	Dmitri Sautin (RUS)	679.26
Diving 3 m Synchronized Springboard	N Xiong and H Xiao (CHN)	365.58	D Sautin and A Dobroskok (RUS)	329.97	R Newberry and D Pullar (AUS)	322.86
Diving 10 m Synchronized Platform	D Sautin and I Loukachine (RUS)	365.04	L Tian and J Hu (CHN)	358.74	J Hempel and H Meyer (GER)	338.88
Water Polo	Hungary		Russia		Yugoslavia	
Women						
50 m Freestyle	Inge de Bruijn (NED)	24.32	Therese Alshammar (SWE)	24.51	Dara Torres (USA)	24.63
100 m Freestyle	Inge de Bruijn (NED)	53.83	Therese Alshammar (SWE)	54.33	Jenny Thompson (USA) and Dara Torres (USA)	54.43

Sydney 2000

EVENT	GOLD		SILVER		BRONZE	
Swimming						
Women						
200 m Freestyle	Susie O'Neill (AUS)	1:58.24	Martina Moravcova (SVK)	1:58.32	Claudia Poll (CRC)	1:58.81
400 m Freestyle	Brooke Bennett (USA)	4:05.80	Diana Munz (USA)	4:07.07	Claudia Poll (CRC)	4:07.83
800 m Freestyle	Brooke Bennett (USA)	8:19.67	Yana Klochkova (UKR)	8:22.66	Kaitlin Sandeno (USA)	8:24.29
100 m Backstroke	Diana Mocanu (ROM)	1:00.21	Mai Nakamura (JPN)	1:00.55	Nina Zhivanevskaya (ESP)	1:00.89
200 m Backstroke	Diana Mocanu (ROM)	2:08.16	Roxana Maracineanu (FRA)	2:10.25	Miki Nakao (JPN)	2:11.05
100 m Breaststroke	Megan Quann (USA)	1:07.05	Leisel Jones (AUS)	1:07.49	Penny Heyns (RSA)	1:07.55
200 m Breaststroke	Agnes Kovacs (HUN)	2:24.35	Kristy Kowal (USA)	2:24.56	Amanda Beard (USA)	2:25.35
100 m Butterfly	Inge de Bruijn (NED)	56.61	Martina Moravcova (SVK)	57.97	Dara Torres (USA)	58.20
200 m Butterfly	Misty Hyman (USA)	2:05.88	Susie O'Neill (AUS)	2:06.58	Petria Thomas (AUS)	2:07.12
200 m Medley	Yana Klochkova (UKR)	2:10.68	Beatrice Caslaru (ROM)	2:12.57	Cristina Teuscher (USA)	2:13.32
400 m Medley	Yana Klochkova (UKR)	4:33.59	Yasuko Tajima (JPN)	4:35.96	Beatrice Caslaru (ROM)	4:37.18
4 x 100 m Freestyle	Australia	3:13.67	USA	3:13.86	Brazil	3:17.40
4 x 200 m Freestyle	USA	7:57.80	Australia	7:58.52	Germany	7:58.64
Springboard Diving	Mingxia Fu (CHN)	609.42	Jungjing Guo (CHN)	597.81	Doerte Lindner (GER)	574.35
10 m Platform Diving	Laura Wilkinson (USA)	543.75	Na Li (CHN)	542.01	Anne Montminy (CAN)	540.15
Synchronized Diving 3 m Platform	V Ilyina and I Pakhalina (RUS)	332.64	M Fu and J Guo (CHN)	321.60	G Sorokina and O Zhupyna (UKR)	290.34
Synchronized Diving 10 m Platform	N Li and X Sang (CHN)	345.12	E Heymans and A Montminy (CAN)	312.03	R Gilmore and L Tourky (AUS)	301.50
Synchronized Swimming Duet	Olga Brusnikina and Maria Kiseleva (RUS)	99.580	Miya Tachibana and Miho Takeda (JPN)	98.650	Virginie Dedieu and Myriam Lignot (FRA)	97.437
Synchronised Swimming Team	Russia	99.146	Japan	98.860	Canada	97.357
Water Polo	Australia		USA		Russia	
Boxing						
Light-Flyweight (–48kg)	Brahim Asloum (FRA)		Rafael Munoz (ESP)		Maikro Romero (CUB) Un Chol Kim (PRK)	
Flyweight (–51kg)	Wijan Ponlid (THA)		Bulat Jumadilov (KAZ)		Jerome Thomas (FRA) Volodymyr Sydorenko (UKR)	
Bantamweight (–54kg)	Guillermo Rigondeaux (CUB)		Raimkoul Malakhbekov (RUS)		Sergiy Danylchenko (UKR) Clarence Vinson (USA)	
Featherweight (–57kg)	Bekzat Sattarkhanov (KAZ)		Ricardo Juarez (USA)		Tahar Tamsamani (MAR) Kamil Djamaloudinov (RUS)	
Lightweight (–60kg)	Mario Kindelan (CUB)		Andriy Kotelnyk (UKR)		Cristian Benitez (MEX) Alexandre Maletine (RUS)	
Light-Welterweight (–63.5kg)	Mahammadkodir Abdullayev (UZB)		Ricardo Williams Jnr (USA)		Mohamed Allalou (ALG) Diogenes Luna (CUB)	
Welterweight (–67kg)	Oleg Saitov (RUS)		Sergiy Dotsenko (UKR)		Vitalie Grusac (MDA) Dorel Simion (ROM)	
Light-Middleweight (–71kg)	Yermakhan Ibraimov (KAZ)		Marian Simion (ROM)		Pornchai Thongburan (THA) Jermain Taylor (USA)	
Middleweight (–75kg)	Jorge Gutierrez (CUB)		Gaidarbek Gaidarbekov (RUS)		Vugar Alekperov (AZE) Zsolt Erdei (HUN)	
Light-Heavyweight (–81kg)	Alexandre Lebziak (RUS)		Rudolf Kraj (CZE)		Andriy Fedchuk (UKR) Sergey Mihaylov (UZB)	
Heavyweight (–91kg)	Felix Savon (CUB)		Soultanakhmed Ibraguimov (RUS)		Vladimir Tchanturia (GEO) Sebastian Koeber (GER)	
Super-Heavyweight (+91kg)	Audley Harrison (GBR)		Mukhtarkhan Dildabekov (KAZ)		Paolo Vidoz (ITA) Rustam Saidov (UZB)	
Weightlifting						
Men						
–56 kg	Halil Mutlu (TUR)		Wenxiong Wu (CHN)		Xiangxiang Zhang (CHN)	
56–62 kg	Nikolay Pechalov (CRO)		Leonidas Sampanis (GRE)		Gennady Oleshchuk (BUL)	
62–69 kg	Galabin Boevski (BUL)		Georgi Markov (BUL)		Sergei Lavrenov (BLR)	
69–77 kg	Xugang Zuan (CHN)		Viktor Mitrou (GRE)		Arsen Melikyan (ARM)	
77–85 kg	Pyrros Dimas (GRE)		Marc Huster (GER)		George Asanidze (GEO)	
85–94 kg	Akakios Kakiasvilis (GRE)		Szymon Kolecki (POL)		Alexei Petrov (RUS)	
94–105 kg	Hossein Tavakoli (IRI)		Alan Tsagaev (BUL)		Asaad Said Saif (QAT)	
105+ kg	Hossein Rezazadeh (IRI)		Ronny Weller (USA)		Andrei Chemerkin (RUS)	
Women						
–48 kg	Tara Nott (USA)		Raema Lisa Rumbewas (INA)		Sri Indriyani (INA)	
48–53 kg	Xia Yang (CHN)		Li Feng-Ying (TPE)		Winarni Binti Slamet (INA)	
53–58 kg	Soraya Jimenez Mendivil (MEX)		Song Hui Ri (KOR)		Khassaraporn Suta (THA)	
58–63 kg	Xiaomin Chen (CHN)		Valentine Popova (RUS)		Ioanna Chatziioannou (GRE)	
63–69 kg	Weining Lin (CHN)		Erzsebet Markus (HUN)		Karnam Malleswari (IND)	

EVENT	GOLD	SILVER	BRONZE
69–75 kg	Maria Isabel Urrutia (COL)	Ruth Ogbeifo (NGR)	Yi-Hang Kuo (TPE)
75+ kg	Meiyuan Ding (CHN)	Agata Wrobel (POL)	Cheryl Haworth (USA)
Greco-Roman Wrestling			
48–54 kg	Kwon-Ho Sim (KOR)	Lazaro Rivas (CUB)	Yong Gyun Kang (PRK)
54–58 kg	Armen Nazarian (BUL)	In-Sub Kim (KOR)	Zetian Sheng (CHN)
58–63 kg	Vartares Samourgachev (RUS)	Juan Luis Maren (CUB)	Akaki Chachua (GEO)
63–69 kg	Feliberto Azcuy (CUB)	Katsuhiko Nagata (JPN)	Alexei Glouchkov (RUS)
69–76 kg	Mourat Kardanov (RUS)	Matt James Lindland (USA)	Marco Yli-Hannuksela (FIN)
76–85 kg	Hamza Yerlikaya (TUR)	Sandor Istvan Bardosi (HUN)	Mukran Vakhtangadze (GEO)
85–97 kg	Mikael Ljungberg (SWE)	Davyd Saldadze (UKR)	Garrett Lowney (USA)
97–130 kg	Rulon Gardner (USA)	Aleksands Karelin (RUS)	Dmitri Debelka (BLR)
Freestyle Wrestling			
48–54 kg	Namik Abdullayev (AZE`0	Samuel Henson (USA)	Amiran Karntanov (GRE)
54–58 kg	Alireza Dabir (IRI)	Yevgen Buslovych (UKR)	Terry Brands (USA)
58–63 kg	Mourad Oumakhanov (RUS)	Serafim Barzakov (BUL)	Jae-Sung Jang (KOR)
63–69 kg	Daniel Igali (CAN)	Arsen Gitinov (RUS)	Lincoln McIlravy (USA)
69–76 kg	Brandon Slay (USA)	Eui Jae Moon (KOR)	Adem Bereket (TUR)
76–85 kg	Adam Saitiev (RUS)	Yoel Romero (CUB)	Mogamed Ibragimov (MKD)
85–97 kg	Saghid Mourtasaliyev (RUS)	Islam Bairamukov (KAZ)	Eldari Kurtanidze (GEO)
97–130 kg	David Moussoulbes (RUS)	Artur Taymazov (UZB)	Alexis Rodriguez (CUB)
Judo			
Men			
Super-Lightweight (-60 kg)	Tadahiro Nomura (JPN)	Bu-Kyung Jung (KOR)	Manolo Poulot (CUB) Aidyn Smagulov (KGZ)
Half-Lightweight (60–66 kg)	Huseyin Ozkan (TUR)	Larbi Benboudaoud (FRA)	Girolamo Giovinazzo (ITA) Georgi Vazagashvili (GEO)
Lightweight (66–73 kg)	Giuseppe Maddaloni (ITA)	Tiago Camilo (BRA)	Anatoly Laryukov (BLR) Vsevolods Zelonijs (LAT)
Half-Middleweight (73–81 kg)	Makoto Takimoto (JPN)	In-Chul Cho (KOR)	Alexsei Budolin (EST) Nuno Delgado (POR)
Middleweight (81–90 kg)	Mark Huizinga (NED)	Carlos Honorato (BRA)	Ruslan Mashurenko (UKR) Frederic Demontfaucon (FRA)
Half-Heavyweight (90–100 kg)	Kosei Inoue (JPN)	Nicolas Gill (CAN)	Iouri Stepkine (RUS) Stephane Traineau (FRA)
Heavyweight (over 100 kg)	David Douillet (FRA)	Shinichi Shinohara (JPN)	Tamerlan Tmenov (RUS) Indrek Pertelson (EST)
Women			
Super-Lightweight (-48 kg)	Ryoko Tamura (JPN)	Lioubov Brouletova (RUS)	Anne-Maria Gradante (GER) Ann Simons (BEL)
Half-Lightweight (48–52 kg)	Legna Verdecia (CUB)	Noriko Narazaki (JPN)	Sun Hui Kye (PRK) Yuxiang Liu (CHN)
Lightweight (52–57 kg)	Isabel Fernandez (ESP)	Driulys Gonzalez (CUB)	Kie Kusakabe (JPN) Maria Pekli (AUS)
Half-Middleweight (57–63 kg)	Severine Vandenhende (FRA)	Shufang Li (CHN)	Gella Vandecaveye (BEL) Sun-Sook Jung (KOR)
Middleweight (63–70 kg)	Sibelis Veranes (CUB)	Kate Howey (GBR)	Min-Sun Cho (KOR) Ylenia Scapin (ITA)
Half-Heavyweight (70–78 kg)	Lin Tang (CHN)	Celine Lebrun (FRA)	Simona Marcela Richter (ROM) Emanuela Pierantozzi (ITA)
Heavyweight (+78 kg)	Hua Yuan (CHN)	Daima Mayelis Beltran (CUB)	Seon-Young Kim (KOR) Mayumi Yamashita (JPN)
Taekwondo			
Men			
58 kg	Michail Mouroutsis (GRE)	Gabriel Esparza (ESP)	Chih-Hsiung Huang (TPE)
68 kg	Steven Lopez (USA)	Joon-Sik Sin (KOR)	Hadi Saeibonehkohal (IRI)
80 kg	Angel Matos Fuentes (CUB)	Faissal Ebnoutalib (GER)	Victor Estrada-Garibay (MEX)
80+ kg	Kyong-HUN Kim (KOR)	Daniel Trenton (AUS)	Pascal Gentil (FRA)
Women			
49 kg	Lauren Burns (AUS)	Urbia Rodriguez (CUB)	Shu-Ji Chi (TPE)
57 kg	Jae-Eun Jung (KOR)	Hieu Ngan Tran (VIE)	Hamide Bikcin (TUR)
67 kg	Sun-Hee Lee (KOR)	Trude Gundersen (NOR)	Yoriko Okamoto (JPN)
67+ kg	Zhong Chen (CHN)	Natalia Ivanova (RUS)	Dominique Bosshart (CAN)

EVENT	GOLD		SILVER		BRONZE	
Fencing						
Men						
Individual Épée	Pavel Kolobkov (RUS)		Hugues Obry (FRA)		Sang-Ki Lee (KOR)	
Team Épée	Italy		France		Cuba	
Individual Foil	Young-Ho Kim (KOR)		Ralf Bissdorf (GER)		Dmitri Chevtchenko (RUS)	
Team Foil	France		China		Italy	
Individual Sabre	Mihai Claudiu Covaliu (ROM)		Mathieu Gourdain (FRA)		Wiradech Kothny (GER)	
Team Sabre	Russia		France		Germany	
Women						
Individual Épée	Timea Nagy (HUN)		Gianna Habluetzel-Buerki (SUI)		Laura Flessel-Colovic (FRA)	
Team Épée	Russia		Switzerland		China	
Individual Foil	Valentina Vezzali (ITA)		Rita Koenig (GER)		Giovanna Trillini (ITA)	
Team Foil	Italy		Poland		Germany	
Modern Pentathlon						
Men	Dmitry Svatkovsky (RUS)	5376	Gabor Balogh (HUN)	5353	Pavel Dovgal (BLR)	5338
Women	Stephanie Cook (GBR)	5318	Emily de Riel (USA)	5310	Kate Allenby (GBR)	5273
Canoeing						
Men						
500 m Kayak Singles K1	Knut Holmann (NOR)	1:57.847	Petar Merkov (BUL)	1:58.393	Michael Kolganov (ISR)	1:59.563
1000 m Kayak Singles K1	Knut Holmann (NOR)	3:33.269	Petar Merkov (BUL)	3:34.649	Tim Brabants (GBR)	3:35.057
500 m Kayak Pairs K2	Hungary	1:47.055	Australia	1:47.895	Germany	1:48.771
1000 m Kayak Pairs K2	Italy	3:14.461	Sweden	3:16.075	Hungary	3:16.357
1000 m Kayak Fours K4	Hungary	2:55.188	Germany	2:55.704	Poland	2:57.192
500 m Canadian Singles C1	Gyorgy Kolonics (HUN)	2:24.813	Maksim Opalev (RUS)	2:25.809	Andreas Dittmer (GER)	2:27.591
1000 m Canadian Singles C1	Andreas Dittmer (GER)	3:54.379	Ledys Frank Balceiro (CUB)	3:56.071	Steve Giles (CAN)	3:56.437
500 m Canadian Pairs C2	Hungary	1:51.284	Poland	1:51.536	Romania	1:54.260
1000 m Canadian Pairs C2	Romania	3:37.355	Cuba	3:38.753	Germany	3:41.129
Women						
500 m Kayak Singles K1	Josefa Idem Guerrini (ITA)	2:13.848	Caroline Brunet (CAN)	2:14.646	Katrin Borchert (AUS)	2:15.138
500 m Kayak Pairs K2	Germany	1:56.996	Hungary	1:58.580	Poland	1:58.787
500 m Kayak Fours K2	Germany	1:34.53	Hungary	1:34.94	Romania	1:37.01
Canoe Slalom						
Men						
Slalom C1	Tony Estanguet (FRA)	231.87	Michal Martikan (SVK)	233.76	Juraj Mincik (SVK)	234.22
Slalom C2	Slovakia	237.74	Poland	243.81	Czechoslovakia	249.45
Slalom K1	Thomas Schmidt (GER)	217.25	Paul Ratcliffe (GBR)	223.71	Pierpaolo Ferrazzi (ITA)	225.03
Women						
Slalom K1	Stepanka Hilgertova (CZE)	247.04	Brigitte Guibal (FRA)	251.88	Anne-Lise Bardet (FRA)	254.77
Rowing						
Men						
Single Sculls	Rob Waddell, (NZL)	6:48.90	Xeno Mueller (SUI)	6:50.55	Marcel Hacker (GER)	6:50.83
Double Sculls	Slovenia	6:16.63	Norway	6:17.98	Italy	6:20.49
Coxless Pairs	France	6:32.97	USA	6:33.80	Australia	6:34.26
Quadruple Sculls	Italy	5:45.56	Netherlands	5:47.91	Germany	5:48.64
Coxless Fours	Great Britain	5:56.24	Italy	5:56.62	Australia	5:57.61
Eights	Great Britain	5:33.08	Australia	5:33.88	Croatia	5:34.85
Lightweight Double Sculls	Poland	6:21.75	Italy	6:23.47	France	6:24.85
Lightweight Coxless Fours	France	6:01.68	Australia	6:02.09	Denmark	6:03.51
Women						
Single Sculls	Ekaterina Karsten (BLR)	7:28.14	Rumyana Neykova (BUL)	7:28.15	Katrin Rutschow-Stomporowski (GER)	7:28.99
Double Sculls	Germany	6:55.44	Netherlands	7:00.36	Lithuania	7:01.71
Coxless Pairs	Romania	7:11.00	Australia	7:12.56	USA	7:13.00
Quadruple Sculls	Germany	6:19.58	Great Britain	6:21.64	Russia	6:21.65
Eights	Romania	6:06.44	Netherlands	6:09.39	Canada	6:11.58
Lightweight Double Sculls	Romania	7:02.64	Germany	7:02.95	USA	7:06.37

EVENT	GOLD		SILVER		BRONZE	
Yachting						
Men						
Finn	Iain Percy (GBR)	35	Luca Devoti (ITA)	46	Fredrik Loof (SWE)	47
470	Australia	38	USA	42	Argentina	57
Mistral Sailboard	Christoph Sieber (AUT)	38	Carlos Espinola (ARG)	43	Aaron McIntosh (NZL)	48
Women						
Europe	Shirley Robertson (GBR)	37	Margriet Matthysse (NED)	39	Serena Amato (ARG)	51
470	Australia	33	USA	47	Ukraine	48
Mistral Sailboard	Alessandra Sensini (ITA)	15	Amelie Lux (GER)	15	Barbara Kendall (NZL)	19
Open						
Star	USA	34	Great Britain	35	Brazil	39
Tornado	Austria	16	Australia	25	Germany	38
Soling	Denmark		Germany		Norway	
Laser	Ben Ainslie (GBR)	42	Robert Scheidt (BRA)	44	Michael Blackburn (AUS)	60
49er	Finland	55	Great Britain	60	USA	64
Cycling						
Men						
Road Race	Jan Ullrich (GER)	5:29:08	Alexandre Vinokourov (KAZ)	5:29:17	Andreas Kloeden (GER)	5:29:20
Road Time Trial	Vyatcheslav Ekimov (RUS)	57:40	Jan Ullrich (GER)	57:48	Lance Armstrong (USA)	57:74
1000 m Sprint	Marty Nothstein (USA)		Florian Rousseau (FRA)		Jens Fiedler (GER)	
Olympic Sprint	France		Great Britain		Australia	
1000 m Time Trial	Jason Queally (GBR)	1:01.609	Stefan Nimke (GER)	1:02.487	Shane Kelly (AUS)	1:02.818
4000 m Individual Pursuit	Robert Bartko(GER)	4:18.515	Jens Lehmann (GER)	4:23.824	Brad McGee (AUS)	4:19.250
4000 m Team Pursuit	Germany	3:59.710	Ukraine	4:04.520	Great Britain	4:01.979
Individual Points Race	Juan Llaneras (SPA)	14	Milton Wynants (URU)	18	Alexey Markov (RUS)	16
Keirin	Florian Rousseau (FRA)		Gary Neiwand (AUS)		Jens Fiedler (GER)	
Madison	Australia	26	Belgium	22	Italy	15
Mountain Bike	Miguel Martinez (FRA)	2:09:02.50	Filip Meirhaeghe (BEL)	2:10:05.51	Christoph Sauser (SUI)	2:11:21.00
Women						
Road Race	Leontien Zijlaard (NED)	3:06:31	Hanka Kupfernagel (GER)	3:06:31	Diana Ziliute (LIT)	3:06:31
Time Trial	Leontien Zijlaard (NED)	42:00	Mari Holden (USA)	42:37	Jeannie Longo-Ciprelli (FRA)	42:52
500 m Time Trial	Felicia Ballanger (FRA)	34.140	Michelle Ferris (AUS) 3	4.696	Cuihua Jiang (CHN)	34.768
Sprint	Felicia Ballanger (FRA)		Oksana Grichina (RUS)		Iryna Yanovych (UKR)	
3000 m Individual Pursuit	Leontien Zijlaard (NED)		Marion Clignet (FRA)		Yvonne McGregor (GBR)	
Individual Points Race	Antonella Bellutti (ITA)	19	Leontien Zijlaard (NED)	16	Olga Slioussareva (RUS)	15
Mountain Bike	Paola Pezzo (ITA)	1:49:24.38	Barbara Blatter (SUI)	1:49:51.42	Margarita Fullana (SPA)	1:49:57.39
Equestrian						
Three-Day Event	David O'Connor (USA)	34.00	Andrew Hoy (AUS)	39.80	Mark Todd (NZL)	42.00
Three-Day Event, Team	Australia	146.80	Great Britain	161.00	USA	175.80
Grand Prix (Dressage)	Anky van Grunsven (NED)	239.18	Isabell Werth (GER) Gigolo	234.19	Ulla Salzgeber (GER) Rusty	230.57
Grand Prix (Dressage), Team	Germany	5632	Netherlands	5579	USA	5166
Grand Prix (Jumping)	Jeroen Dubbeldam (NED)	4.00	Albert Voorn (NED)	4.00	Khaled Al Eid (KSA)	4.00
Grand Prix (Jumping), Team	Germany	15.00	Switzerland	16.00	Brazil	24.00
Individual Dressage Freestyle to Music	Anky van Grunsven (NED)	1721	Isabelle Werth (GER)	1644	Ulla Salzgeber (GER)	1613
Shooting						
Men						
Small-Bore Rifle (Prone)	Jonas Edman (SWE)	701.3	Torben Grimmel (DEN)	700.4	Serguei Martynov (BLR)	700.3
Small-Bore Rifle (3 Positions)	Rajmond Debevec (SLO)	1275.1	Juha Hirvi (FIN)	1270.5	Harald Stenvaag (NOR)	1268.6
Rapid Fire Pistol	Serguei Alifirenko (RUS)	687.6	Michel Ansermet (SUI)	686.1	Iulian Raicea (ROM)	684.6
Free Pistol	Tanyu Kiriakov (BUL)	666.0	Igor Basinsky (BLR)	663.3	Martin Tenk (CZE)	662.5
Running Game Target	Ling Yang (CHN)	681.1	Oleg Moldovan (MDA)	681.0	Zhiyuan Niu (CHN)	677.4
Air Pistol	Franck Dumoulin (FRA)	688.9	Yifu Wang (CHN)	686.9	Igor Basinsky (BLR)	682.7
Air Rifle	Yalin Cai (CHN)	696.4	Artem Khadjibekov (RUS)	695.1	Evgeni Aleinikov (RUS)	693.8
Skeet Shooting	Mykola Milchev (UKR)	150	Petr Malek (CZE)	148	James Graves (USA)	147
Trap Shooting	Michael Diamond (AUS)	147	Ian Peel (GBR)	142	Giovanni Pellielo (ITA)	140
Double Trap Shooting	Richard Faulds (GBR)	187	Russell Mark (AUS)	187	Fehaid Al Deehani (KUW)	186
Women						
Sport Pistol	Maria Grozdeva (BUL)	690.3	Luna Tao (CHN)	689.8	Lolita Evglevskaya (BLR)	686.0
Small-Bore Rifle (3 Positions)	Renata Mauer-Rozanska (POL)	684.6	Tatiana Goldobina(RUS)	680.9	Maria Feklistova (RUS)	679.9
Air Rifle	Nancy Johnson (USA)	497.7	Cho-Hyun Kang (KOR)	497.5	Jing Gao (CHN)	497.2
Air Pistol	Luna Tao (CHN)	488.2	Jasna Sekaric (YUG)	486.5	Anne-Marie Forder (AUS)	484

EVENT	GOLD		SILVER		BRONZE	
Shooting						
Women						
Skeet	Zemfira Meftakhetdinova (AZE)	98	Svetlana Demina (RUS)	95	Diana Igaly (HUN)	93
Trap	Daina Gudzineviciute (LTU)	93	Delphine Racinet (FRA)	92	E Gao (CHN)	90
Archery						
Men						
Individual	Simon Fairweather (AUS)		Victor Wunderle (USA)		Wietse van Alten (NED)	
Team	Korea		Italy		USA	
Women						
Individual	Mi-Jin Yun (KOR)		Nam-Soon Kim (KOR)		Soo-Nyung Kim (KOR)	
Team	South Korea		Ukraine		Germany	
Gymnastics						
Men						
Individual Combined Exercises	Alexei Nemov (RUS)	58.474	Wei Yang (CHN)	58.361	Oleksandr Beresh (UKR)	58.212
Team	China	231.919	Ukraine	230.306	Russia	230.019
Parallel Bars	Li Xiaopeng (CHN)	9.825	Joo-Hung Lee (KOR)	9.812	Alexei Nemov (RUS)	9.800
Floor	Igor Vihrovs (LTU)	9.812	Alexei Nemov (RUS)	9.800	Iordan Iovtchev (BUL)	9.787
Horse Vault	Gervasio Deferr (SPA)	9.712	Alexey Bondarenko (RUS)	9.587	Leszek Blanik (POL)	9.475
Horizontal Bar	Alexei Nemov (RUS)	9.787	Benjamin Varonian (FRA)	9.787	Joo-Hung Lee (KOR)	9.775
Rings	Szilveszter Csollany (HUN)	9.850	Dimosthenis Tampakos (GRE)	9.762	Iordan Iovtchev (BUL)	9.737
Pommel Horse	Marius Daniel Urzica (ROM)	9.862	Eric Poujade (FRA)	9.825	Alexei Nemov (RUS)	9.800
Trampoline	Alexandre Moskalenko (RUS)	41.7	Ji Wallace (AUS)	39.3	Mathieu Turgeon (CAN)	39.1
Women						
Individual Combined	Simona Amanar (ROM)	38.642	Maria Olaru (ROM)	38.581	Liu Xuan (CHN)	38.418
Team	Romania	154.608	Russia	154.403	China	154.008
Floor	Elena Zamolodtchikova (RUS)	9.850	Svetlana Khorkina (RUS)	9.812	Simona Amanar (ROM)	9.712
Horse Vault	Elena Zamolodtchikova (RUS)	9.731	Andreea Raducan (ROM)	9.693	Ekaterina Lobazniouk (RUS)	9.674
Beam	Liu Xuan (CHN)	9.825	Ekaterina Lobazniouk (RUS)	9.787	Elena Prodounova (RUS)	9.775
Asymmetrical Bars	Svetlana Khorkina (RUS)	9.862	Ling Jie (CHN)	9.837	Yang Yun (CHN)	9.787
Rhythmic, Individual	Yulia Barsukova (RUS)	39.632	Yulia Raskina (BLR)	39.548	Alina Kabaeva (RUS)	39.466
Rhythmic, Team	Russia	39.500	Belarus	39.500	Greece	39.283
Trampoline	Irina Karavaeva (RUS)	38.90	Oxana Tsyhuleva (UKR)	37.70	Karen Cockburn (CAN)	37.40
Tennis						
Men's Singles	Yevgeny Kafelnikov (RUS)		Tommy Haas (GER)		Arnaud di Pasquale (FRA)	
Men's Doubles	Canada		Australia		Spain	
Women's Singles	Venus Williams (USA)		Elena Dementieva (RUS)		Monica Seles (USA)	
Women's Doubles	USA		Netherlands		Belgium	
Table Tennis						
Men's Singles	Kong Linghui (CHN)		Jan-Ove Waldner (SWE)		Liu Guoliang (CHN)	
Men's Doubles	China		China		France	
Women's Singles	Wang Nan (CHN)		Li Ju (CHN)		Jing Chen (TPE)	
Women's Doubles	China		China		Korea	
Basketball						
Men	USA		France		Lithuania	
Women	USA		Australia		Brazil	
Soccer						
Men	Cameroon		Spain		Chile	
Women	Norway		USA		Germany	
Handball						
Men	Russia		Sweden		Spain	
Women	Denmark		Hungary		Norway	
Hockey						
Men	Netherlands		Korea		Australia	
Women	Australia		Argentina		Netherlands	
Volleyball						
Men	Yugoslavia		Russia		Italy	
Women	Cuba		Russia		Brazil	

EVENT	GOLD		SILVER		BRONZE	
Beach Volleyball						
Men's Pairs	USA		Brazil		Germany	
Women's Pairs	Australia		Brazil		Brazil	
Badminton						
Men's Singles	Ji Xinpeng (CHN)		Hendrawan (INA)		Xia Xuanze (CHN)	
Men's Doubles	Indonesia		Korea		Korea	
Women's Singles	Gong Zhichao (CHN)		Camilla Martin (DEN)		Ye Zhaoying (CHN)	
Women's Doubles	China		China		China	
Mixed Doubles	China		Indonesia		Great Britain	
Baseball	USA		Cuba		Korea	
Softball	USA		Japan		Australia	
Triathlon						
Men	Simon Whitfield (CAN)	1:48:24.02	Stephan Vuckovic (GER)	1:48:37.58	Jan Rehula (CZE)	1:48:46.64
Women	Brigitte McMahon (SUI)	2:00:40.52	Michellie Jones (AUS)	2:00:42.55	Magli Messmer (SUI)	2:01:08.83

Salt Lake City 2002

8 February – 24 February

Participants: 2399 / Men: 1513, Women: 886, Countries: 77

Sports: 7, Events: 78

Final Torchbearers: The American ice hockey team, gold medal winners in Lake Placid, 1980

Medals Table

PLACE	COUNTRY	GOLD	SILVER	BRONZE
1	Germany	12	16	7
2	Norway	11	7	6
3	USA	10	13	11
4	Canada	6	4	7
5	Russia	6	4	5

Outstanding Athletes

PLACE	NAME (NATIONALITY)	DISCIPLINE	G	S	B
1	Ole Einar Bjoerndalen (NOR)	Biathlon	4	0	0
2	Janica Kostelic (CRO)	Skiing	3	1	0
3	Jochem Uytdehaage (NED)	Skating	2	1	0
4	Stephan Eberharter (AUT)	Skiing	1	1	1
5	Sabine Voelker (GER)	Skating	0	2	1

EVENT	GOLD		SILVER		BRONZE	
Alpine Skiing						
Men						
Downhill	Fritz Strobl (AUT)	1:39.13	Lasse Kjus (NOR)	1:39.35	Stephan Eberharter (AUT)	1:39.41
Slalom	Jean-Pierre Vidal (FRA)	1:41.06	Sebastien Amiez (FRA)	1:41.82	Benjamin Raich (AUT)	1:42.41
Giant Slalom	Stephan Eberharter (AUT)	2:23.28	Bode Miller (USA)	2:24.16	Lasse Kjus (NOR)	2:24.32
Super-G	Kjetil Andre Aamodt (NOR)	1:21.58	Stephan Eberharter (AUT)	1:21.68	Andreas Schifferer (AUT)	1:21.83
Combined	Kjetil Andre Aamodt (NOR)	3:17.56	Bode Miller (USA)	3:17.84	Benjamin Raich (AUT)	3:18.26
Women						
Downhill	Carole Montillet (FRA)	1:39.56	Isolde Kostner (ITA)	1:40.01	Renate Goetschl (AUT)	1:40.39
Slalom	Janica Kostelic (CRO)	1:46.10	Laure Pequegnot (FRA)	1:46.17	Anja Paerson (SWE)	1:47.09
Giant Slalom	Janica Kostelic (CRO)	2:30.01	Anja Paerson (SWE)	2:31.33	Sonja Nef (SUI)	2:31.67
Super-G	Daniela Ceccarelli (ITA)	1:13.59	Janica Kostelic (CRO)	1:13.64	Karen Putzer (ITA)	1:13.86
Combined	Janica Kostelic (CRO)	2:43.28	Renate Goetschl (AUT)	2:44.77	Martina Ertl (GER)	2:45.16
Biathlon						
Men						
10 km	Ole Einar Bjoerndalen (NOR)	24:51.3	Sven Fischer (GER)	25:20.2	Wolfgang Perner (AUT)	25:44.4
Pursuit	Ole Einar Bjoerndalen (NOR)	57:25.9	Raphael Poiree (FRA)	+43.0	Ricco Gross (GER)	+56.0
20 km	Ole Einar Bjoerndalen (NOR)	51:03.3	Frank Luck (GER)	51:39.4	Victor Maigourov (RUS)	51:40.6
Relay 4 x 7.5 km	Norway	1:23:42.3	Germany	1:24:27.6	France	1:24:36.6

EVENT	GOLD		SILVER		BRONZE	
Biathlon						
Women						
7.5 km	Kati Wilhelm (GER)	20:41.4	Uschi Disl (GER)	20:57.0	Magdalena Forsberg (SWE)	21:20.4
Pursuit	Olga Pyleva (RUS)	52:51.9	Kati Wilhelm (GER)	+5.3	Irina Nikoultchina (BUL)	+8.1
15 km	Andrea Henkel (GER)	47:29.1	Liv Grete Poiree (NOR)	47:37.0	Magdalena Forsberg (SWE)	48:08.3
Relay 4 x 7.5 km	Germany	1:27:55.0	Norway	1:28:25.6	Russia	1:29:19.7
Ski Jumping						
Men						
90 m	Simon Ammann (SUI)	269.0	Sven Hannawald (GER)	267.5	Adam Malysz (POL)	263.0
120 m	Simon Ammann (SUI)	281.4	Adam Malysz (POL)	269.7	Matti Hautamaeki (FIN)	256.0
120 m (Team)	Germany	974.1	Finland	974.0	Slovenia	946.3
Curling						
Men	Norway		Canada		Switzerland	
Women	Great Britain		Switzerland		Canada	
Freestyle Skiing						
Men						
Mogul Field	Janne Lahtela (FIN)	27.97	Travis Mayer (USA)	27.59	Richard Gay (FRA)	26.91
Aerials	Ales Valenta (CZE)	257.02	Joe Pack (USA)	251.64	Alexei Grichin (BLR)	251.19
Women						
Mogul Field	Kari Traa (NOR)	25.94	Shannon Bahrke (USA)	25.06	Tae Satoya (JPN)	24.85
Aerials	Alisa Camplin (AUS)	193.47	Veronica Brenner (CAN)	190.02	Deidra Dionne (CAN)	189.26
Snowboarding						
Men						
Giant Slalom	Philipp Schoch (SUI)		Richard Richardsson (SWE)		Chris Klug (USA)	
Halfpipe	Ross Powers (USA)	46.1	Danny Kass (USA)	42.5	Jarret Thomas(USA)	42.1
Women						
Giant Slalom	Isabelle Blanc (FRA)		Karine Ruby (FRA)		Lidia Trettel (ITA)	
Halfpipe	Kelly Clark (USA)	47.9	Doriane Vidal (FRA)	43.0	Fabienne Reuteler (SUI)	39.7
Figure Skating						
Men	Alexei Yagudin (RUS)		Evgeni Plushenko (RUS)		Timothy Goebel (USA)	
Women	Sarah Hughes (USA)		Irina Slutskaya (RUS)		Michelle Kwan (USA)	
Pairs	Elena Berezhnaya and Anton Sikharulidze (RUS)		Xue Shen and Hongbo Zhao (CHN)		Jamie Sale and David Pelletier (CAN)	
Ice Dance	Marina Anissina and Gwendal Peizerat (FRA)		Irina Lobacheva and Ilia Averbukh (RUS)		Barbara Fusar Poli and Maurizio Margaglio (ITA)	
Bob-sledding						
Men						
2-man bob	Germany I	3:10.11	Switzerland I	3:10.20	Switzerland II	3:10.62
4-man bob	Germany II	3:07.51	United States I	3:07.81	USA II	3:07.86
Women						
2-woman bob	USA II	1:37.76	Germany I	1:38.06	Germany II	1:38.29
Lugeing						
Men's Singles	Armin Zoeggeler (ITA)	2:57.941	Georg Hackl (GER)	2:58.270	Markus Prock (AUT)	2:58.283
2-man Luge	Patric-Fritz Leitner and Alexander Resch (GER)	1:26.082	Mark Grimmette and Brian Martin (USA)	1:26.216	Chris Thorpe and Clay Ives (USA)	1:26.220
Women's Singles	Sylke Otto (GER)	2:52.464	Barbara Niedernhuber (GER)	2:52.785	Silke Kraushaar (GER)	2:52.865
Speedskating						
Men						
10,000 m	Jochem Uytdehaage (NED)	12:58.92	Gianni Romme (NED)	13:10.03	Lasse Saetre (NOR)	13:16.92
5000 m	Jochem Uytdehaage (NED)	6:14.66	Derek Parra (USA)	6:17.98	Jens Boden (GER)	6:21.73
1500 m	Derek Parra (USA)	1:43.95	Jochem Uytdehaage (NED)	1:44.57	Adne Sondral (NOR)	1:45.26
1000 m	Gerard van Velde (NED)	1:7.18	Jan Bos (NED)	1:07.53	Joey Cheek (USA)	1:07.61
500 m	Casey FitzRandolph (USA)	1:09.23	Hiroyasu Shimizu (JPN)	1:09.26	Kip Carpenter(USA)	1:09.47

EVENT	GOLD		SILVER		BRONZE	
Women						
5000 m	Claudia Pechstein (GER)	6:46.91	Gretha Smit (NED)	6:49.22	Clara Hughes (CAN)	6:53.53
3000 m	Claudia Pechstein (GER)	3:57.70	Renate Groenewold (NED)	3:58.94	Cindy Klassen (CAN)	3:58.97
1500 m	Anni Friesinger (GER)	1:54.02	Sabine Voelker (GER)	1:54.97	Jennifer Rodriguez (USA)	1:55.32
1000 m	Chris Witty (USA)	1:13.83	Sabine Voelker(GER)	1:13.96	Jennifer Rodriguez (USA)	1:14.24
500 m	Catriona LeMay Doan (CAN)	1:14.75	Monique Garbrecht-Enfeldt (GER)	1:14.94	Sabine Voelker (GER)	1:15.19
Short Track						
Men						
1500 m	Apolo Anton Ohno (USA)	2:18.541	Jiajun Li (CHN)	2:18.731	Marc Gagnon (CAN)	2:18.806
1000 m	Steven Bradbury (AUS)	1:29.109	Apolo Anton Ohno (USA)	1:30.160	Mathieu Turcotte (CAN)	1:30.563
500 m	Marc Gagnon (CAN)	41.802	Jonathan Guilmette (CAN)	41.994	Rusty Smith (USA)	42.027
Relay 5000 m	Canada	6:51.579	Italy	6:56.327	China	6:59.633
Women						
500 m	Yang A Yang (CHN)	44.187	Evgenia Radanova (BUL)	44.252	Chunlu Wang (CHN)	44.272
1000 m	Yang A Yang (CHN)	1:36.391	Gi-Hyun Ko (KOR)	1:36.427	Yang S Yang (CHN)	1:37.008
1500 m	Gi-Hyun Ko (KOR)	2:31.581	Sun-Kyung Choi (KOR)	2:31.610	Gugenia Radanova (BUL)	2:31.723
Relay 3000 m	Korea	4:12.793	China	4:13.236	Canada	4:15.738
Ice Hockey						
Men	Canada		USA		Russia	
Women	Canada		USA		Sweden	
Nordic Skiing						
Men						
Nordic Combined, Sprint	Samppa Lajunen (FIN)		Ronny Ackermann (GER)		Felix Gottwald (AUT)	
Nordic Combined, Individual	Samppa Lajunen (FIN)		Jaakko Tallus (FIN)		Felix Gottwald (AUT)	
Nordic Combined, Team	Finland		Germany		Austria	
1.5 km Sprint	Tor Arne Hetland (NOR)	2:56.9	Peter Schlickenrieder (GER)	2:57.0	Cristian Zorzi (ITA)	2:57.2
15 km	Andrus Veerpalu (EST)	37:07.4	Frode Estil (NOR)	37:43.4	Jaak Mae (EST)	37:50.8
30 km	Johann Muehlegg (ESP)	1:09:28.9	Christian Hoffman (AUT)	1:11:31.0	Mikhail Botvinov (AUT)	1:11:32.3
50 km	Mikhail Ivanov (RUS)	2:06:20.8	Andrus Veerpalu (EST)	2:06:44.5	Odd-Bjoern Hjelmeset (NOR)	2:08:41.5
Combined Pursuit	Johann Muehlegg (ESP)	49:20.4	Thomas Alsgaard (NOR) and Frode Estil (NOR)	49:48.9		
Relay 4 x 10 km	Norway	1:32:45.5	Italy	1:32:45.8	Germany	1:33:54.5
Women						
1.5 km Sprint	Julija Tchepalova (RUS)	3:10.6	Evi Sachenbacher (GER)	3:12.2	Anita Moen (NOR)	3:12.7
10 km	Bente Skari (NOR)	28:05.6	Olga Danilova (RUS)	28:08.1	Julija Tchepalova (RUS)	28:09.9
15 km	Stefania Belmondo (ITA)	39:54.4	Larissa Lazutina (RUS)	39:56.2	Katerina Neumannova (CZE)	40:01.3
30 km	Gabriella Paruzzi (ITA)	1:30:57.1	Stefania Belmondo (ITA)	1:31:01.6	Bente Skari (NOR)	1:31:36.3
Combined Pursuit	Olga Danilova (RUS)	24:52.1	Larissa Lazutina (RUS)	24:59.0	Beckie Scott (CAN)	25:09.9
Relay 4 x 5 km	Germany	49:30.6	Norway	49:31.9	Switzerland	50:03.6

Index

The index contains the names of competitors and personalities mentioned in the text. A page number in italics indicates that the person is featured in an illustration.

Aamodt, Kjetil Andre *187*, 203
Aas, Roald 98
Abbagnale, Carmine *179*
Abbagnale, Giuseppe *179*
Abbott, Margaret 21, 22
Abera, Gezagne *224*
Aberg, Georg 34
Abrahams, Harold *45*, *46*, 154
Ackermann, Ronny 235
Ackermann, Rosemarie *144*
Acklin, Donat *189*, *205*
Acklin, Guido 205
Adisson, Franck 195
Adler, Margarete 34
Agassi, Andre 215
Ahlgren, Anders 34
Akabusi, Kriss 192
Albert, Prince, of Monaco *236*
Albright, Tenley 82, *89*, *90*
Alekna, Virgilijus 245
Alexeyev, Vasili 147
Ali, Muhammad 207, *209*
   see also Clay, Cassius
Aliabadi, Rahim *135*
Allan, Alister 175
Allen, Scott 108
Alt, Robert *91*
Altwegg, Jeanette *73*, 74, *82*
Ambrosini, Ernesto 38
amateurism 12
   see also professionalism
   challenged 61
   redefined 163
Amokachi, Daniel 215
Amoore, Judith 112
Ampthill, Arthur O. 11
Amunike, Emmanuel 215
ancient Olympics 8, *9*, *9, 10*, 239
Andersen, Carl-Albert 23
Andersen, Greta *79*
Andersen, Hjalmar "Hjallis" *80*
Andersen, Reidar 67
Andersen-Schiess, Gaby 165
Anderson, Gary 196
Anderson, Miller 87
Andersson, Volger 51
Andiev, Soslan *157*
André, Georges 30, *46*
Andriakopoulos, Nikolaos 19
Andrieux, Michel *227*
Angelopoulos-Daskalaki, Gianna 239, *239*
Angerer, Peter *160*
Angst, Heinrich *91*
Anikin, Nikolai 98
Annan, Alyson 233
Antibo, Salvatore 177
Aochi, Seiji 127
Aouita, Said *176*
Apel, Katrin *218*
Applegarth, William *34*
Arai, Shigeo *71*
Argenton, Alessandro *136*
Armano, Mario 118
Armstrong, Debbie *160*
Armstrong, Duncan 178
Armstrong, Eileen 38
Arnheiter, Albert *35*
Arnold, Thomas 9
Artemov, Vladimir *180*
arts competitions, last 77
Aryault, Arthur *104*
Ashford, Evelyn *164*
Ashworth, Jeanne 99
Asikainen, Alfred 34
Asrabayev, Anatoli *197*
Astafei, Galina *193*
Astakhova, Polina *115*
Aste, Paul 107
Auch, Susan 205
Audley, Gordon 82
Aun, Rein 111
Avilov, Nikolai 144
awards

Merit for Alpinism 41
   special Olympic *173*
Ayat, Albert 21
Azaryan, Albert 94, 104

Babashoff, Shirley 134
Babayaro, Celestine 215
Babcock, Harry 34
Babka, Richard 102
Bachler, Reinhold 118
Backhaus, Robin 134
Bacon, Charles *31*
Bader, Pepi 129
Bahmann, Angelika 134
Baier, Anke 205
Baier, Ernst *65*, 67
Bailey, Donovan *209*
Bailey, Emmanuel McDonald 87
Baillet-Latour, Henri de *11*, 37, 53, 73
Bakken, Jill 233, *236*
Bakogianni, Niki 240, *241*
Balas, Iolanda *104*
Balck, Viktor *10*, 11
Balkenhol, Klaus *199*
Ball, Rudi 69
Balla, József 156
Ballangrud, Ivar 49, 51, *59*, *64*, 65
Baptiste, Kirk 165
Barinov, Yuri 156
Baron, Mietje 55
Bartholomew, Kenneth *74*
Basar, Hakki *198*
Bau, Sabine *181*
Bauer, Rudolf 21
Baugniet, Pierre 74
Baumann, Alex *166*
Baumann, Dieter 177
Bäumler, Hans-Jürgen *99*, 107
Baxter, Alain 233, *233*
Baxter, Irving 22, 23
Bayul, Oksana 201, *204*
Bea, Sebastien 227
Beamon, Bob 120, 121, 193
Beaurepaire, Frank 237
Beck, Hans 58
Becker, Boris *199*
Becker, Elizabeth 47
Becker, Ingrid 122
Becker, Thomas 211
Becker-Dey, Courtney 211
Bédard, Myriam *203*
Beerli, Joseph 67
Behmer, Anke 176
Behr, Matthias 167
Behrendt, Jan *189*, 205
Beiser, Trude 75
Bell, Florence 55
Belmondo, Stefania *186*, *203*
Belousova, Ludmilla 106, 107, *119*
Belova, Irina 193
Belusov, Vladimir *118*
Benoit, Joan 165
Berceanu, Gheorghe *135*
Beresford, Jack 71
Berg, Stephan van den 163
Berge, Guttorm 82
Berglund, Hans *79*
Bergmann, Gretel 69
Bergström, Hjalmar *66*
Berthod, Madeleine *91*
Bertini, Romeo 47
Besson, Colette *122*
Bestemianova, Natalya *173*
Bibbia, Nino 73
Biebl, Heidi *97*, *99*
Bief, Jacqueline du 82
Biellmann, Denise *151*
Bikila, Abebe *101*, *116*
Biller, John 27, 30
Bion, Victor 37
Biondi, Matt 175, *178*
Bjoerndalen, Ole Einer *236*
Black, Larry 133

Blagoyeva, Yordanka 133, 144
Blair, Bonnie *204*
Blankers-Koen, Fanny 76, 77, *79*, 85
Blasco, Miriam *198*
Bleibtrey, Ethelda *39*
Blitz, Gérard 39
Blixen-Finecke, Hans von 35
Board, Lillian *122*
Boardman, Chris 196
Bobrov, Vsevolod 89
Bochatay, Fernande 118
Böck, Hermann 82
Böckl, Willy 42
Bode, Harro 147
Bogdan, Ivan 104
Boginskaya, Svetlana *181*
Böhling, Ivar 34
Boit, Philip 219
Boitano, Brian *171*
Boiteux, Jean 87
Boland, John Pius 17
Bolden, Jeanette 164
Boldt, Harry *114*, 147
Boltenstern, Gustaf-Adolf 35
Bonaly, Surya 188
Bondarchuk, Anatoli 144
Bonde, Carl 35
Bonderenko, Aleksei 228
Bonk, Gerd 147
Bonlieu, François 109
Bonna, Narve 43
Booth, Mitch 195
Borckink, Annie 149
Bordin, Gelindo 175
Borg, Arne 47
Börjes, Hasse 128
Börner, Jacqueline 188
Boronovskis, Theodore 114
Borzov, Valeri *133*
Boston, Ralph *102*, 111
Boutaib, Brahim 177
Boutaib, Hammou *192*
Bouvier, Charles 67
Bowden, Norris 90
Boyarskikh, Klaudia 109
boycotts
   calls for 69
   political 12, 143, 149, 153, 163
   religious 21, 23
Boyle, Raelene 133
Bozon, Charles 99
Bradbury, Steven 233, *236*
Bradley, Tom 163, *169*
Braglia, Alberto *34*
Brand, Esther *86*
Brandtzæg, Torgeir 108
Brasher, Chris 94
Brassard, Jean-Luc *205*
Braun, Gregor *146*
Braun, Sabine 193
Bredesen, Espen *203*
Brehmer, Christina 144
Breitkreutz, Emil 27
Briand, Ann 203
Bricker, Calvin 34
Briesenick, Hartmut 134
Brightwell, Robbie *113*
Brigitha, Enith 145
Broome, David 104
Brown, Alice 164
Brown, Ivan 67
Brown, Judi 164
Brown, Leroy 47
Brown, Ron 165
Browning, David 87
Bruce, Charles G. 41
Brugger, Kurt *204*
Bruggmann, Edmund 129
Bruguera, Sergi 215
Brundage, Avery
   IOC President 11, 12, 111
   Munich terrorist attack 131, 137
   politics and sport 69,
      "Schranz" case 127
   US ice hockey teams 73
Brunet, Pierre *51*
Brunette, Eugène 41
Brunner, Karl 150
Brunner, Melitta 51
Brusveen, Haakon 98
Bubka, Sergei 175, 177
Buchanan, Glenn 166

Buchner, Annemarie "Mirl" *83*
Budd, Frank *103*
Bukin, Andrei *173*
Bullmann, Maik *198*
Buraas, Hans-Petter *218*
Bure, Vladimir 134
Burger, Fritzi 50, 58
Burghley, Lord David *53*, 54
Burka, Petra 108
Burke, Lynn *103*
Burke, Thomas 18, *19*
Busch, Christian *27*
Busch, Christian 27
Buslyovych, Yevgeni *231*
Butler, Everard 35
Butovsky, Alexei *10*
Button, Richard "Dick" *74*, *81*, *82*
Byberg, Thomas *74*
Byrd, Chris *58*, *198*
Bystrova, Galina 112

Calligaris, Novella 134
Callot, Ernest 11
Callot, Henri 19
Callus, Ashley 223
Calmat, Alain 108
Calnan, George C. *62*
Campbell, Darren *241*
Candeloro, Philippe 205
Capadrutt, Reto 58
Cariou, Jean 35
Carlos, John 121, *122*
Carminucci, Giovanni 104
Caroli, Guido *90*
Caron, Stephan 178
Carpenter, Connie *169*
Carreras, José 192
Carroll, Daniel 225
Caruthers, Edward 123
Casey, Levi 54
Čáslavská, Vera 111, *115*, 121, 125
Cass, Danny 237
Ceccarelli, Daniela *234*, 249
Cha Yuong Chul 182
Chammartin, Henri 114
Chandler, Richard 9
Charpentier, Robert 69
Chataway, Christopher 86
Checcoli, Mauro 114
Cheeseborough, Chandra 164
Chelimo, Richard *192*
Chemerkin, Andrei 207, *213*
Chen Jing 180
Chepulis, Jonas 124
Cherkassova, Marina 150
Cherkassova, Valentina 182
Chetverukhin, Sergei 128
Chilova, Irina 182
Chistyakova, Galina 176
Chivas, Silvia 133
Cho Youn-Jeong 196
Christensen, Hans, 78
Christie, Linford *190*, *192*, 209
Christopoulos, Stephanos 19
Chudina, Alexandra 86
Chukarin, Viktor *85*, *87*, 95,
Chukhrai, Sergei 156
Chun Lee-Kyung 205
Chung Jae-Hun 196
Ciorosian, Dragomir 169
Clark, Ellery *17*, 18
Clark, Robert 70
Clarke, Ronald 122
Clausen, Stefani 39
Clay, Cassius *105*, 114 see also Ali, Muhammad
Cloete, Hestie 225
Clotworthy, Robert 87
Cloughen, Robert *31*
Cochran, Barbara Ann 129
Cochran, Richard 102
Coe, Sebastian 153, 154, *155*, 163
Cojocaru, Cristina 164
Colket, Meredith B. 23
Colledge, Cecilia *65*, 67
Colliard, Renée *89*, *91*
Collombin, Roland 129
Colò, Zeno *83*
Colombo, Jürgen *136*
Comaneci, Nadia *142*
Compagnoni, Deborah *187*
Connolly, James *17*, 18

Conrad, Reinaldo 147
Consolini, Adolfo *79*, 102
Conte, Antonio 21
Cook, Myrtle 55
Coomber, Alex 233
Cooper, Charlotte 21
Cooper, Christin *161*
Cooper, Malcolm *175*
Copeland, Lillian *63*
Coray, Albert 27
Corradini, Deedee *11*
Costie, Candy 166
Coubertin, Pierre de
   biography 9
   German ban 45
   Merit for Alpinism award 41
   new events 33
   Olympic flag design 13
   Olympic principles 25, 37
   Olympic revival 9–10
   Paris 1900 22
   women participants 53
Cousins, Robin *151*
Couttet, James 74
Crammond, John *73*
Cranz, Christl *65*
Crothers, Bill *113*
Cruz, Joaquim 163, *176*
Csik, Ferenc 71
Csollany, Szilveszter *229*
Cuff, Leonard A. 11
Cuhel, Frank 54
Cullmann, Bernd 102
Curry, John 139, 141
Curtis, Charles 62
Curtis, Thomas 18, *19*
Curtius, Ernst 9
Cuthbert, Betty 93, *94*, 113
Cuthbert, Juliet *192*

Dabir, Alireza *231*
Dæhlie, Björn 107, *184*, 201, 203, 217, 218
Dafoe, Frances 90
Dalinsh, Janis 63
Daly, John 27
Damme, Ivo van 143, *144*
Daniels, Charles 25, 27
Danne, Wolfgang 119
Danneberg, Rolf *165*
Dänzer, Frieda 91
D'Arcy, Victor 35
Darnyi, Tamas 194
Da Silva, Adhemar Ferreira 86
Dätwyler, Jean-Daniel 119
Daume, Willi, 153
Davenport, Lindsay 215
David, Franck 195
Davies, Lynn *111*
Davis, Otis *103*
D'Ayen, Elisabeth 38
Dean, Christopher *158*, 159, *204*
Décugis, Max 38
Deferr, Gervasio 229
Degener, Richard 71
DeMar, Clarence 47
Dementieva, Elena 231
Demers, Jacques 169
Desjardins, Ulise Joseph 55, *166*
Devers, Gail 191, *192*, 209
Devonish, Arnoldo 86
De Witt, Lincoln *232*
Dibiasi, Klaus 123
Di Capua, Giuseppe *179*
Di Centa, Manuela *203*
Didrikson, Mildred "Babe" *61*, 63
Diem, Carl 69, 81
Diener, Gottfried *91*
Diesch, Eckart *146*
Diesch, Jörg *146*
Dietrich, Wilfried *104*, 124
Dijkstra, Sjoukje 99, 107, 108
Dildabekov, Mukhtarkhan 223
Dillard, Harrison 79
Dimas, Pyrros 240, *241*
Dimas, Trent 196
DiMattei, Susan 213
D'Inzeo, Piero 104
D'Inzeo, Raimondo 104
disabled athletes, integration 171, 224
discontinued events (Summer Games)

cricket 22
golf 22
Greek-style discus 30
motorboating 29
outdoor handball 77
polo 77
rope climbing *19*
rugby 22
swimming obstacle races *23*
tug-of-war *23*
underwater swimming 23
weight throwing 37 .
Disl, Uschi 203
Disney, William 98
Ditiatin, Alexander *153, 157*
Dixon, Craig 98
Dixon, Robin *109* .
Domian, Thomas *179*
Donchenko, Natalia 99
D'Oriola, Pierre Jonquères *114*
Douglas, Johnny *29*
Douillet, David *231*
Doyle, Arthur Conan *31*
Draeger, Richard 105
Draves, Victoria *79*
Dream Team 191, *199, 214*
Drechsler, Heike 176, *191*
Dreifke, Joachim *145*
Dressel, Vally 34
Drosin, Deena *244*
Drost, Johannes 23
drugs
 compulsory testing 117, 191
 positive tests 13, 175, 176, 223,
  228, 233
 strychnine 27
Dubravčič, Sandra *160*
Duchesnay, Isabelle 188
Duchesnay, Paul 188
Ducza, Anikó 115
Dunavska, Adriana 180
Durack, Fanny 34
Duraliev, Osman 124
Dvorak, Charles 27
Dyken, Amy van 207, *210*
Dzarasov, Savkus 104

Eagan, Edward *59*
Eberhard, Paul 75
Eberharter, Stephen *233*
Eckert, Bärbel 145
Edenhauser, Georg 67
Edström, Johannes Sigfrid *11*, 12, 73,
 74, 77
Edward, Harry *39*
Edwards, Jonathan 223, *224*
Edwards, Phil 61
Egerszegi, Krisztina 178, *191, 194*
Eichholz, Armin *179*
Eicker, Peter 147
Eidenbenz, Hans *50*
Eiffel Tower *20*
Ekimov, Viacheslev *228*
Ekman, Eugen 104
electronic timing, introduced 33
Elek, Ilona *70*, 77
Elliott, Launceston *19*
Elliott, Peter 176
Ellis, Kathleen *112*
Enck, Schuyler 47
Ender, Kornelia 134, *145*
Enderlein, Ortrun 109, 117
Endo, Yukio *115*
Endrich, Felix *75*
Engan, Toralf 108
Englund, Nils-Joel *66*
Enke, Karin *161*
Erdmann, Susi 188, 205
Ereng, Paul *176*
Eriksen, Stein *81, 82, 83*
Eriksson, Henry *78*
Eriksson, Lars-Börje 172
Eriksson, Sven 67
'ethnic minorities', events for 25
Eto, Masaki *169*
Eugster, Hans 87
Evangelisti, Giovanni 165
Evans, Janet 195, *209*
Evans, Peter 155
Evensen, Bernt 51, 58
Evenson, Thomas 61
Everts, Sabine *165*
Ewell, Norwood *79*

Ewing, Pat *168*
Ewry, Ray 21, 22, *27*, 29, *30*

Fahrner, Thomas, 166
Fairweather, Simon *230*
Falk, Paul *82*
Falk, Ria *82*
Famose, Annie 118
Farrell, John O'Neil 51
Farstad Sverre 74
Fasser, Ekkehard *173*
Fassi, Carlo 141
Fässler, Marcel *173*
Favor-Hamilton, Suzy *225*
Favre, Willy 119
Feierabend, Fritz 75
Felke, Petra *177*
Fernandez, Gigi *199*, 215
Fernandez, Mary Jo *199*, 215
Ferreira, Wayne 199
Ferris, Elizabeth 102
Fiasconato, Marcello 144
Fichtel, Anja *181*
Fickeisen, Otto *35*
Fickeisen, Rudolf *35*
Figini, Mechela *172*
Filatov, Sergei 114
Findlay, Conn 105
Finnegan, Chris *124*
Fischer, Birgit *226*
Fischer, Sven *203*
Fiske, William *59*
Fitch, Horatio 45
Fitzgerald, Robert *74*
Fix, Oliver *210*
Flameng, Léon 19
Flanagan, John 23, *25*
Fleming, Peggy 119
Flessel, Laura *181*
Fletcher, Caroline 47
Fletcher, Jenny *34*
Florijn, Roland *179*
Floth, Horst 129
Flowers, Vonetta 233, *236*
Fluckinger, Georg 150
Flute, Sebastien *197*
Flynn, Patrick *38*
Fonst, Ramón 21
Forbes, John 195
Foreman, George 114, *124*
Forgues, Wilfrid 195
Formo, Ivar 141
Forshaw, Joseph 31
Fortuna, Wojciech 127
Fosbury, Richard "Dick" 121, 122
Foulon, Emmanuel 22
Frandl, Josefine 91
Franko, Jure 161
Fraser, Dawn *92, 93, 111, 112*
Fraser, Gretchen *73, 75*
Frazier, Herman 144
Frazier, Joe *114*
Fredericks, Frankie 192
Freeman, Cathy *222*
Freiermuth, Rico 161
Frey, Konrad *71*
Frigerio, Ugo 63
Friman, Jaakko 45
Fullana, Margarite 228
Fu Mingxia 195, 210
Funkenhauser, Zita *181*
Furniss, Bruce 145
Fydler, Chris 223

Gabl, Franz 74
Gagnon, Marc 201
Gaisreiter, Stefan 129
Gammoudi, Mohamed 122
Gao Min 178, 195
Garatti-Saville, Eleanor *62*
Garbrecht, Monique 188
Gardas, Hubert *156*
Gärdin, Gösta *79*
Gardner, Maureen 77
Garrett, Robert *17, 18*, 22, 23
Gartmann, Arnold *67*
Gataullin, Rodion 177
Gautschi, Georges 42
Gavrilov, Valentin 123
Gaxiola, Alvaro 123
Gaynor, William J. *35*
Gebhardt, Mike 195
Gebhardt, Willibald *10*

Gebrselassie, Haile *244*
Geesink, Antonius *111, 114*
Geier, Oscar 58
Geijssen, Carolina 117
Geisler, Ilse 109
Gennip, Yvonne van *171*
Genter, Steven 134
Georgantas, Nicolaos 27
Georgiadis, Ioannis 19
Gerevich, Aladár 77, *79, 101*
Gerhard, Friedrich 70
Gerschwiler, Hans 74
Gimpel, Harald 134
Giobellina, Silvio 161
Gladisheva, Svetlana 203
Glahn, Klaus 114
Glockshuber, Margot 119
Göbel, Barbara *103*
Goedrich, August 19
Goetschl, Renate 235
Goitschel, Christine 108, 117
Goitschel, Marielle 108, 109, *117,*
 118
Gönczy, Lajos 22
Gonzalez, Driulis *213*
Gooch, Nicholas 205
Goodhew, Duncan *155*
Gorchakova, Yelena 87
Gordien, Fortune 78
Gordon-Watson, Mary 136
Gorelik, Alexander 119
Gorshkov, Alexander 139, 140
Götschi, Reto 205
Gould, Shane *131, 134*
Gouskos, Miltiades 18
Graddy, Sam 165
Graf, Stephanie 245
Graf, Steffi 175, *181*
Grafström, Gillis 38, 42, 57, *40, 49*
Gratsch, Rafael 98
Gravelotte, Eugène-Henri 19
Gray, Clifford *59*
Green, Thomas *63*
Greene, Albert 71
Greene, Maurice 223, *225*
Greene, Nancy *118*
Gretzky, Wayne 217
Grichuk, Oksana *204*
Griffin, Merritt 30
Griffith-Joyner, Florence *174, 177*
Grini, Lars 118
Grischin, Yevgeni 89, *98, 99*
Grishuk, Pasha 220
Grogan, James 82
Grönningen, Harald 109
Gropa, Vasile 169
Grospiron, Edgar 205
Gross, Manuela 128
Gross, Michael *163, 166*
Gross, Ricco *203*
Grothaus, Gisela 134
Gröttumsbraaten, Johan
 1924 Chamonix 42
 1928 St Moritz 49, 50
 1932 Lake Placid *56*, 57, 58
Grumlaux, Emile 22
Grunsven, Anky van *229*
Grut, Torben 34
Grut, William *79*
Gschnitzer, Peter 150
Guerovski, Rangel 182
Guillaume, Sylvain *186*
Guillemot, Joseph 38
Gunnell, Sally *192*
Günther, Detlef 141
Gusakova, Maria 109
Gusenbauer, Ilona 132
Guseva, Klara 97, 99
Gustafson, Tomas *173*
Gustafsson, Toini *117*
Guth, Jiři *10*, 11
Gutterson, Albert 34
Guttler, Károly 178
Guy, Fabrice *186*
Gyarmati, Olga 77
Gyenge, Valéria *85*

Haas, Christl 118
Haase, Helga 97, *99*
Hackett, Grant 236
Hackl, Georg *189*
Hadschieff, Michael 173

Hagen, Oddbjörn *67*
Hahn, Archie *26*
Hahn, Norbert 141, *150*
Hakulinen, Veikko *89, 91, 98*
Hall, Gary 134
Hall, Gary Jr. *210*
Halmay, Zoltán 23
Halswelle, Wyndham *31*
Hämäläinen, Kalevi 98
Hämäläinen, Marja-Liisa *159*
Hambrook, Sharon 166
Hamill, Dorothy 140
Hamilton, Scott *161*
Hammerer, Resi 75
Hampson, Thomas *61*
Hanevold, Halvard *219*
Hanisch, Cornelia *167*
Hansen, Fred *113*
Happe, Ursula *95*
Harding, Tonya, 201
Hare, Truxton 23
Haringa, Ingrid 196
Haritz, Günter *136*
Harrigan, Dan 145
Harris, Danny 164
Harrison, Audley 223
Hartel, Lis 85
Hartwell, Erin 196
Hary, Armin *101, 102*
Hase, Dagmar *194*
Hasse, Kurt 70
Hasu, Heikki *75*
Hatch, Annia *247*
Hattestad, Trine *225*
Haug, Thorleif *41, 42*
Haugen, Anders 43
Hawkins, George *31*
Hayes, John Joseph 31
Hearn, Lacey 27
Heath, Michael 166
Heaton, Jennison 49
Heaton, John 49, 58
Hecher, Traudl 99
Hedlund, Per Erik *49, 50*
Hefferon, Charles 31
Hegge, Ole 50
Hehn, Jürgen *146*
Heiden, Eric *148, 149*
Heidenreich, Jerry 134
Heilfort, Hellfried 156
Heine, Jutta 102
Heinrich, Prinz 50
Heiss, Carol 90, 97, *99*
Helden, Hans van 139
Helgesen, Finn *74, 82*
Helten, Inge *144*
Heltzer, Regine 108
Hemery, David 122
Hempel, Udo *136*
Henard, Nicolas 195
Henkel, Heike *193*
Henning, Anne 128
Henrichs, Karlheinz *114*
Henry, Kenneth *82, 98*
Henie, Sonja
 1924 Chamonix 42
 1928 St Moritz *48*, 49, 50, *51*
 1932 Lake Placid 57, *57*, 58, *58*
 1936 Garmisch-Partenkirchen
  65, *66*, 67
 title defence *171, 172*
Herber, Maxi 65
Herbert, Charles 11
Herbert, Garry *194*
Hernandez, Ariel *198*
Herold, Jens-Peter 176
Herouin, Henri 22
Hess, Hans *51*
Heuga, James 109
Heuser, Jürgen 156
Hickcox, Charles 123
Hicks, Thomas *24, 26, 27, 28*
Hill, James 105
Hilman, Harry *31*
Hines, Jim 121
Hingsen, Jürgen 165
Hinterseer, Ernst 99
Hochleitner, Dorothea 91
Hodge, Percy *38*
Hofmann, Fritz 18, 27
Hogenson, William 26
Holdorf, Willi 110
Holidis, Haralambos 169, 240

Holloway, J.J. *25*
Höllwarth, Martin 186
Holman, Dorothy 38
Holmertz, Anders 178
Honey, Gary 165
Hoogenband, Pieter van den *226*
Höppe, Wolfgang *159, 161*
Hoppenberg, Ernst 23
Horgan, Dennis 23
Horine, George 34
Horn, Siegbert *134*
Hornfischer, Kurt *71*
Horr, Marquis 30
Houghton, Julian Brooke *146*
Hoyt, William 18
Hradetzky, Gregor *71*
Hubacher, Edy 129
Hubbard, William Dehart 47
Huber, Günther 205
Huber, Hans 114
Huber, Herbert 119
Huber, Norbert 188, 205
Huber, Sebastian *51*
Huber, Wilfried *205*
Hübner, Frank 147
Hughes, Sarah 233, *237*
Huhtala, Martti 75
Huhtanen, Veikko 77
Huish, Justin *213*
Hultén, Vivi-Anne 67
Hurd, Alexander 58
Huschke, Thomas 147
Hussein, King 237
Huttunen, Eevi 99
Hyman, Dorothy 102
Hymen, Misty *226*
Hysong, Nick *225*

Ihbe, Ernst *71*
Ilmanen, Sakari *38*
Imbach, Joseph 45
Indurain, Miguel *207, 213*
Innis, Hubert van 22
'intermediate' Olympics 10-11, 18,
 25
Ismayr, Rudolf 70
Iso-Hollo, Volmari 61, *69*
Israelsson, Sven 75
Ito, Midori 188
Ivanov, Vyacheslav 111

Jackson, Marjorie 85
Jacobi, Joe *194*
Jacobs, Christopher 178
Jaffee, Irving *57, 58, 59*
Jager, Thomas 178
Jagge, Finn Christian *187*
Jakobsson, Ludovika 38
Jakobsson, Walter 38
Jakosits, Michael *197*
Jamison, Herbert, *18*
Janz, Karin 124, 134, *135*
Jarvis, John 23
Jefferson, Thomas 165
Jenkins, David 90, 97,
Jenkins, Hayes Alan *90*, 97
Jenner, Bruce *144*
Jensen, Björg Eva 149
Jensen, Viggo 19
Jernberg, Sixten 91, 98, 107, 109
Jewtraw, Charles *42*
Jiao Zhimin 180
Jinnear, William 35
Jipcho, Benjamin 133
Job, Brian 124
Jochum-Beiser, Trude *83*
Johannesen, Knut 98, 108
Johansen, Arne 82
Johansson, Claes 34
Johansson, Greta 34
Johansson, Tomas 182
John, Sabine 176
Johnson, Ben 165, 175, *176*
Johnson, Dave 193
Johnson, Earl 47
Johnson, Earvin "Magic" *191*
Johnson, Michael 207, *207*, 209,
 224
Joly, Andrée *51*
Jonath, Arthur 62
Jones, Marion 223, *223*
Jonsson, Gustaf 51
Jönsson, Jan *136*

Joseph, John 29
Josephson, Karen *194*
Josephson, Sarah *194*
Joyner, Jackie (later Joyner-Kersee, Jackie) *165*, *176 193*
Jozwiakowska, Jaroslawa 102
Juantorena, Alberto *144*
judges
  impartial 29
  pressurized 233, 236
judging
  electronic timing 33
  photo-finishing 33, *35*
Julen, Max *160*
Julin, Magda 38
Jun Sun-Jong *213*

Kabaeva, Alina *229*
Kagelmann, Uwe 128
Kahanamoku, "Duke" Paoa *33*
Kaiser, Otto 51
Kaklamanakis, Nikolas *211*
Kakousis, Perikles 240, *240*
Kälin, Alois *119*
Kälin, Urs 203
Kaminaga, Akio 114
Kankonnen, Veikko 108
Kannenberg, Bernd *132*
Kantanen, Tapio 133
Kaplan, Hamit 104
Kapus, Franz *91*
Karakalos, Telemachos 19
Karelin, Alexander *182*
Karlsson, Nils *72*
Karlstad, Geir 173
Karntanov, Admiran *241*
Karppinen, Klaes *66*
Karppinen, Pertti *145*, *169*
Kaspar, Felix 67
Kassaya, Yukio 127
Kato, Sawao 124, *135*
Kaufmann, Carl 102
Kazankina, Tatyana *154*
Kealoha, Warren *39*
Kedir, Mohammed 154
Kegeris, Raymond 39
Keino, Kipchoge 122, *132*, 176
Keleti, Agnes *95*
Keller, Erhard *118*, 127, *128*
Keller, Franz *117*, *119*
Kelly, Shane 196
Kemeny, Ferenc *10*, 11
Kemkers, Gerard 173
Kempf, Hippolyt *173*
Kemser, Franz *83*
Kennedy, Edward 82
Kennedy, Karol 82
Kenteris, Konstantinos 240, *241*
Kerr, Charles Morgan *150*
Kerr, Robert *31*
Kerrigan, Nancy 188, 201, 205
Keulen-Deelstra, Atje 128
Khorkina, Svetlana *228*
Khudorozhkina, Irina *209*
Kidd, William 109
Kiehl, Marina *172*
Kielan, Urszula 154
Kiely, Thomas *25*
Kilian, Hanns 51
Kilius, Marika *99*, 107
Killanin, Michael Morris *11*, 131, 153
Killy, Jean-Claude *116*, 117, *119*, 185
Kim Hyong Hun *231*
Kim Ki-Hoon 201, 205
Kim Ki Taik 180
Kim, Nelli *145*
Kimball, Bruce 166
King, Charles 27
Kinshofer-Güthlein, Christa 172
Kiprugut, Wilson *113*
Kirchhoff, Ulrich *213*
Kirchner, Andreas 161
Kirchner, Mark *185*, *187*, *203*
Kirksey, Morris M. *39*
Kirov, Nikolai 154
Kirst, Jutta 154
Kirszenstein, Irena 112
Kiviat, Abel 33
Kjus, Lasse 233
Klammer, Franz 139, 141
Klein, Hans-Joachim 112

Klein, Manfred *179*
Klein, Martin *34*
Kleine, Piet 139, 185
Kleppich, Lars 195
Klim, Michael 223
Klimenko, Viktor 134
Klimke, Reiner *114*, 124, 147, *169*
Klimova, Marina 173, *185*, *188*
Klingström, Lennart *79*
Knol, Monique *181*
Knösel, Angela 117
Knox, Debbie *236*
Koch, Beate 177
Kohnke, Peter *104*
Kolbe, Peter-Michael *145*, 169, 178
Kolehmainen, Hannes *33*, 85
Kolokoltseva, Berta 108
Kolshin, Pavel 91
Koltschina, Alevtina 109
Komar, Wladyslaw *134*
Kong Linghui *247*
Konno, Akitsugu 127
Konno, Ford 87
Konstantinidis, Aristidis 19
Kontoev, German 241
Korbut, Olga *131*, 134, *135*
Kosakiewicz, Wladyslaw *155*
Kosheveya, Marina 143
Kosinsky, Vladimir 124
Kositschkin, Viktor 98
Koss, Johann Olav *201*
Kostadinova, Stefka *193*, 240
Kostelic, Janica 233, *235*
Kostner, Isolde 203, *235*
Kovacs, Antal *198*
Kovacs, József *94*
Kraenzlein, Alvin 21, 22
Krämer, Ingrid *103*
Kratschmer, Guido *144*, 165
Krausse, Stefan *189*, 205
Krayzelburg, Lenny *227*
Kreiner, Kathy 141
Kröcher, Rabod Wilhelm 35
Kronberger, Petra *185*, *187*
Krutova, Ninelia 102
Kryczka, Kelly 166
Kubat, Bohumil 104
Kuchinskaya, Natalya 124
Kuck, John *55*
Kuhn, Friedrich *83*
Kulakova, Galina *127*, *129*
Kulcsar, Gyözö 147
Kumbernuss, Astrid *209*
Kungler, Frank 240
Kunz, Andreas 119
Kunze, Hansjörg 177
Kurlovich, Alexander *198*
Kusik, Mikhail 35
Kusuma, Allen *199*
Kuts, Vladimir *93*, *94*
Kuttin, Heinz 186
Kwan, Michelle 237

LaBeach, Lloyd *79*
Lajunen, Samppa *234*
Lammers, Georg *54*
Lamour, Jean-François *180*
Lampe, Werner 134
Landvoigt, Bernd *156*
Landvoigt, Jörg *156*
Lane, Francis 18
Lane, Frederick 21, 23
Lang, Czeslaw 156
Lange, Thomas 178
Langen, Christopher *221*
Langen, Ellen van 191
Lanig, Hans Peter 99
Lannoy, Micheline 74
Larsen, Roald 51
Larsson, Erik August *65*
Latynina, Larissa *93*, *101*, 111, 115
Lauer, Martin, 102
Lazakovitch, Tamara 134
Leahy, Con 30
Leahy, Patrick 22
Lecheva, Vessela 182
Lee Joo-Hyung 223
Lee Lai-Shan 211
Lee, Samuel *79*

LeGendre, Robert *47*
Lehmann, Bernhard 159, 161
Lehmann, Jen 196
Lehnertz, Klaus 112
Lehtonen, Eero 47
Lehtonen, Mirja 109
Leitner, Matthias 99
Lemke, Wilhelm 27
Leng, Virginia 180
Lenglen, Suzanne *37*, *38*
Leonard, Silvio 154
Leonard, Sugar Ray 114
Leone, Giuseppina 102
Lerwill, Sheila 86
Lestander, Klas 97
Leutenegger, Hans 129
Lewden, Pierre 47
Lewis, Carl
  1984 Los Angeles *162*, 163, *165*, 165
  1988 Seoul 176, *176*
  1992 Barcelona 193, *193*
  1996 Atlanta 207, 209, *209*
Lewis, Denise 223
Lewis, Lennox 114, *182*
Li Huifeng 180
Li Jiajun 236
Li Ju 230
Li Kongzheng 166
Li Lu *196*
Li Ning 167
Li Xiaopeng *223*
Li Xiaoshuang *213*
Liddell, Eric *45*
Liesche, Hans 34
Ligges, Fritz 114
Lightbody, James 26
Lillak, Tiina 165
Lindh, Erik 180
Linkovesi, Leo 128
Linsenhoff, Liselotte 124
Lippert, Rudolf 70
Lis, Andrzej 156
Lismont, Karel 133
Lissitski, Viktor 115
Liu Guoliang 236
Liu Guoliang *236*
Ljunggren, John 102
Lobatsch, Marina *180*
Loday, Yves *195*
Logan, William 58, *59*
Lohse, Rene 220
Lomberg, Charles 35
London, Jack 54
Lonsbrough, Anita *103*
Lopes, Carlos *164*
Lorenz, Karl 71
Lorz, Fred 25
Losch, Helmut 147
Louganis, Greg *163*, *166*, 179
Loughran, Beatrix 42, *51*
Lou Yun 167
Louis, Spyridon 16, 17, 240, *240*
Lowe, Douglas 46
Lu Chen 205
Lucchesi-Palli, Ferdinando 11
Luck, Frank 203
Luding-Rothenburger, Christa *181* 188
Ludington, Nancy 99
Ludington, Ronald 99
Lukin, Dean 169
Luna Tao *246*
Lundkvist, Erik *53*
Lusis, Janis 133
Lüthy, Jacques 150
Lutz, Hans 146
Lykkeberg, Peder 23
Lynn, Janet 128
Lyssenko, Tatyana 196

Maaninka, Kaarlo 154
McCall, Robert 173
Maccario, Augusto *38*
McCluskey, Joseph 61
McCormick, Pat *95*
McCracken, Josiah 23
McDermott, Donald *82*
McDermott, Richard 118
MacDonald, Fiona *236*
McGrath, Matthew *47*
McGregor, Robert 112

McKane, Kathleen, *38*, 39
McKenley, Herb 87
McKenzie, Donald 123
MacMillan, Shannon 215
McTaggart, Dick *93*
Madison, Helen 62
Maennig, Wolfgang *179*
Maenza, Vincenzo 169
Magnussen, Karen 128
Mahlendorf, Walter 102
Mahre, Phil 150, *159*
Mahre, Steve *159*
Mahringer, Erika 75
Maier, Fred Anton 108
Maier, Hermann *218*
Maier, Otto *35*
Makarov, Sergei *245*
Makino, Shozo 71
Malek, Petr 231
Mangiarotti, Edoardo 101
Maniami-Tzehlili, Mirella 225
Manina, Tamara 115
Mankel, Yves 188
Manley, Dorothy 78
Mäntyranta, Eero 109, 119
Marcus, Egerton *182*
Martin, Lisa 177
Martin, Louis 23
Martin, Paul 47
Martin, Rhona *236*
Martinez, Conchita 198
Martinez, Mario 169
Martinsen, Odd 119
Martinsson, Barbro 117
Maske, Henry *182*
Masková, Hana 119
Masson, Paul 18
Mastenbroek, Hendrika "Ria" 69
Masterkova, Svetlana *209*
Mathias, Bob, *85*
Mathisen-Lunding, Hans 70
Mathy, François 147
Matt, Alfred 119
Matthes, Roland 123, 145
Matthijsse, Margit 211
Mattle, Werner 129
Mayer, Christian 203
Mayer, Helene *55*, 69, 70
Mayer, Helmut 172
Mayotte, Tim 181
Mazzarocchi, Tserafino 34
Mead Lawrence, Andrea *81*
Meade, Richard *136*
Meagher, Mary T. 166
Mecir, Miloslav 175, *181*
medals
  1896 Athens 17
  modern awards 25
  redesigned *239*
  three-level podium 61, *62*
Medica, Jack 71
Medved, Alexander 124
Meier, Kurt 173
Meissner, Jochen 125
Mekshilo, Yevdokia 109
Mellinghaus, Matthias *179*
Mena, Jesus 178
Menendez, Osleidys 225
Menichelli, Franco 115
Mennea, Pietro 133, *154*
Merah-Benida, Nouria 225
Merle, Carole 187
Merriott, Ronald 166
Messner, Heinrich 119, 129
Metcalfe, Ralph 60, *62*
Meyer, Antoinette 75
Meyer, Debbie 123
Meyfarth, Ulrike *132*, 163
Mezin, Andrei 217
Mickler, Ingrid *131*
Milchev, Mykola *231*
Miller, Bode *235*
Miller, Cheryl *169*
Miller, Lennox 133
Miller, Shannon *213*
Miller, William 61
Mills, Robert 169
Mills, Ronald 123
Milosovici, Lavinia *196*
Milser, Rolf *169*

Mimoun, Alain *86*, *94*
Minton, Robert 58
Minuzzo, Giuliana (later Chenal-Minuzzo, Giuliana) *83*, 89
Mir, Isabelle 118
Miskarov, Arsen 155
Misyutin, Grigori 196
Mitchell, Dennis 192
Mitchell, H. Kent 105
Mittermaier, Rosi 138, 139
Miyahara, Atsuji 182
Miyazaki, Yasuji *61*
Mjoen, Haakon 117
Moe, Per Ivar 108
Moe, Tommy *203*
Moen-Guidon, Anita *219*
Moers, Karl von 35
Mohr, Ernst 27
Molitor, Karl 74
Möllenkamp, Thomas *179*
Monti, Eugenio *118*
Montillet, Carole *235*
Montgomery, Tim *244*
Moon Kyung-Ya 169
Moore, Bella *19*
Moorehouse, Adrian *178*
Morales, Pablo 166
Moratorio, Carlos Alberto 114
Morell, Curdin 188
Moreno, José Manuel *196*
Morris, Glenn *70*
Morrow, Bobby Joe *94*
Morton, Margaret *236*
Moseley, Jonny *218*
Moser-Pröll, Annemarie *149*
Moses, Edwin 143, 153, *164*, 192
Mota, Rosa 165, *177*
Motoyoshi, Miwako 166
Mougin, Eugène 22
Mouroutsis, Michalis 246
Moutawakel, Natal El 163, *164*
Muckelt, Ethel 42
Muelegg, Johann 233, *235*
Mühe, Lotte *55*
Mukhatshova, Lyubov 129
Müller, Anna-Maria 117
Müller, Peter 161, 172
Muñoz, Felipe 125
Muratov, Valentin 94
Muratov, Valeri 128
Murphy, Edward *59*
Murphy, Ted 227
Musiol, Bogdan 161
Mustonen, Kaija 99, 108
Musy, Pierre 67
Myers, Kenneth 225

Naber, John *145*
Nadig, Marie-Theres *127*
Nägle, Hans *51*
Nagy, László 82, 90
Nagy, Marianne 82, 90
Nakayama, Akinori 125
Nansen, Egil 81
Nansen, Fridtjof 81
Nash, Ted *104*
Nash, Tony 109
Neckermann, Josef *114*, 124, 136
Neilson, Sandra 134
Nemov, Alexei 223
Nepela, Ondrej 128
Nerlinger, Manfred 169, 198
Nervi, Pier Luigi 101
Nesty, Anthony 175
Neumann, Anett 196
Neuner, Angelika 188, *221*
Neuner, Doris 188
new events (Summer Games)
  50 km road walk *63*
  200 m (women) 77
  400 m hurdles (women) 163, *164*
  athletics relays 29
  baseball *199*
  basketball 69
  basketball (women) 143, *146*
  beach volleyball *214*
  boxing 25
  canoe slalom *134*
  canoeing 69, *71*
  cross-country cycling (women) *213*
  cycling road time trial *213*

hammer 23
handball (women) 143
heptathlon (women) 163, *165*
individual épée (women) 213
judo 111, *111*, *114*
long jump (women) 77, *77*
modern pentathlon 33
rowing (women) 143
sailing 21
shot put (women) 77
soccer (women) *214*
swimming (women) *34*
synchronized swimming
    (women) 163, *166*
table tennis 175, *180*
taekwondo 246
volley ball 111
windsurfing 163
new events (Winter Games)
30 km cross-country *91*
5000 m speed skating (women)
    171
Alpine combined 65
biathlon 97
curling 217, *221*
downhill 73, 74, *74*
freestyle skiing 185, *189,* 201
ice dancing 139, *140*
luge 107, *109*
Nordic relay 65, *66*
Nordic team combined 171
short-track speed skating 185,
    201
skeleton sledding 49
ski jumping team 171
slalom 73, 75, *75*
snowboarding 217
speed skating indoors 171
speed skating (women) 97, *99*
super giant slalom 171, *172*
two-man bob *59*
Newhouse, Fred 144
Newton, Arthur 27
Ngugi, John 175, *177*
Nieberl, Lorenz *83*
Niedernhuber, Barbara 221
Nielsen, Laila Schou 67
Niemann, Gunda *188*
Niemi, Pekka 169
Nieminen, Toni 185, *186*
Nikolopoulos, Alexandros 19
Nikolopoulos, Stamatios 18
Nilsson, Johnny 108
Nones, Francesco *119*
Nordlander, Axel 35
Norheim, Sondre 81
Norman, Peter *122*
Norton, Ray *103*
Norval, Piet 199
Notary, Keith 195
Novotna, Jana 215
Numa, Mauro 167
Nunn, Glynis 163, *165*
Nurmela, Sulo *66*
Nurmi, Paavo
    1920 Antwerp 37, *37*, 38, *38*
    1924 Paris *44*, 45, *46*, 47
    1928 Amsterdam 53, 54, 55
    1952 Helsinki 85, 86, *86*
Nyambui, Suleyman *155*
Nykänen, Matti *160*, 171

O'Brian, Jay *59*
O'Brien, Dan *209*
Ochoa, Francisco Fernández 127,
    129
O'Connor, David *229*
Oda, Mikio *54*
Ödegaard, Reidar 50
Oerter, Al *102*, 121
Oertli, Brigitte 172
Ogiwara, Kenji *187*
Olech, Janusz *180*
Oliva, Isaac Azcuy 156
Olivas, Daniela *175*, *181*
Olizarenko, Nadyezhda *154*
Olliwier, Eva 38
Olympic flag *12*, 13, 37
Olympic flame *12*, 13, 53
Olympic oath, first taken 37
Olympic posters *14-15*
Olympic stadia, Athens 242-3,
    242-3
Olympic villages 45, 61

Olyunina, Alevtina 129
Omnes, Philippe *197*
Ono, Takashi 104
Opel, Georg von *104*
Oppelt, Kurt *90*
Oreiller, Henri *73*, *74*
Orser, Brian 171
Ortlieb, Patrick *187*
Osborn, Harold 45, *46*
Osborn, Ruth 62
Osler, Andreas 81, *83*
Östrand, Olof 87
Ostermeyer, Micheline *79*
Osthoff, Oscar 240
Ottey, Merlene 164, *192*, 209
Otto, Kristin 175, *178*
Otto, Ellen 70
Otto, Louise 34
Otto-Crepin, Margitt 180
Ouden, Willemijntje den *62*
Overland, Kevin 220
Ovett, Steve 153, *155*
Owens, Jesse *68*, 69, 163

Packer, Ann *113*
Paddock, Charles W. *36*, *39*
Paes, Leander 215
Pakhomova, Ludmilla 139, 140
Pall, Olga 118
Palusalu, Kristjan 71
Pamich, Abdon 102
Pankratov, Denis *210*
Papasideris, Georgios 18
Papp, László *95*
Paramygina, Svetlana 203
Paraskevopoulo, Panagiotis 18
Parfenovich, Vladimir *156*
Parker, Bridget 136
Parker, Jack 70
Paruzzi, Gabriella 249
Passarelli, Pasquale 169
Patoulidou, Paraskevi 191, *241*
Patterson, Floyd 114
Pattisson, Rodney *146*
Paul, Robert 99
Pawlik, Eva 73, 74
Payne, Thelma 38
Pechstein, Claudia 188, *220*
Pedroso, Ivan *225*
Peirsol, Aaron 227
Peitsch, Hugo 27
Pelen, Perrine *161*
Pelle, István *63*
Pelletier, David *237*
Pelliccioni, Forcella 105
Peñalver, Antonio 193
Péra, Patrick *119*, 128
Percy, Karen *172*
Perec, José-Marie *209*
Périllat, Guy, 99, 119
Pesmann, Jan 98
Peters, Mary 133, *134*
Petersson, William *37*
Petrik, Larissa 124
Petrov, Petr 154
Petzold, Barbara *151*
Pezzo, Paola *213*, *228*
Pflug, Monika *128*
photo-finishing, introduced 33, *35*
photographic monopoly
    attempted 53
Piccard, Franck *172*
Pierce, Henry *61*
Pietri, Dorando *28*, *31*
Pietrzykowski, Zbigniew 105
Pilejczyk, Helena 99
Pinsent, Matthew *194*, *211*
Pirie, Gordon *94*
Pitou, Penny 99
Planck-Szabo, Herma 42
Platov, Yevgeni *204*, *220*
Plewinski, Catherine 178
Poalis, Luciano de *118*
Podivinsky, Edward 203
politics
    boycotts due to 12, 143, 149,
        153, 163
    international 85, 93
    national 33, 85, 121
    racial 65, 69, 121, *122*
post-war excluded countries 37,
    45, 77
Pollak, Burglinde 134
Pollay, Heinz 70

Ponomarenko, Sergei 173,185, *188*
Ponsteen, Herman 147
Pope-Myers, Paula 102
Popov, Alexander *210*
Porter, Harry *30*
Porter, William *78*
Pospičil, František, 139
Pötzsch, Anett *151*
Poujadeic 228
Powell, John 165
Powell, Mike 121, *193*
Powers, Ross *237*
Pratt, Daria 22
Pravda, Christian 82, 83
Preiml, Baldur 118
Preis, Ellen 70
Press, Irina *113*
Press, Tamara *111*
Priemer, Petra 145
Prigoda, Gennadi 178
Prinstein, Myer 21, 22
Privalova, Irina *192*
Prock, Markus 188
professionalism 13, 33, 65
    see also amateurism
    permitted 163
    Schrantz case 127
Prokop, Liese 123
Protopopov, Oleg 106, 107, *119*
Puccini, Alessandro 246
Pusch, Alexander *146*
Pyrgos, Leon 19

Qian Hong 178
Quarrie, Donald *154*
Quintero, Anna *193*

Rabe, Bahne *179*
Racansky, Lubos 196
Rada, Edi 74
Radke-Batschauer, Lina 53
Radschinsky, Karl-Heinz 169
Raducan, Andreea 229
Raffl, Hansjörg 188, 205
Rakhmanov, Sultan 157
Rämgard, Rolf 98
Rand, Mary 112, *113*
Rankin, Janice 229
Raška, Jiří 117, *118*
Rau, Richard 35
Rausch, Emil 25
Rautavaara, Tapio 77
Razazedeh, Hossein 230
Rebagliati, Ross 217, *218*
Recknagel, Helmut 97
Redgrave, Steven *194*, *207*, *211,*
    226
Redkin, Yevgeni 185
O'Brien... Redinhard,Wolfgang 112
Regnell, Lisa 34
Reichert, Ossi *91*
Reiff, Gaston 78
Reinalter, Edy 74
Reinhard, Wolfgang 112
Reinisch, Rica 153
Reiter, Mario *219*
Remigino, Lindy 87
Retton, Mary Lou *167*
Reyes, Faustino *198*
Richards, Alma 34
Richards, Vincent 45, 175
Richter, Annegret *144*
Rieder, Josef 108
Riefenstahl, Leni 69
Rienks, Nicolas *179*
Riggin, Aileen 37, *38*, *39*, 47
Rinn, Hans 141, *150*
Risma, Rintje *220*
Ritola, Ville *46*, 55
Robertson, Bruce 134
Robertson, Dave 22
Robertson, Irvin 102
Robertson, Lawson 27
Robertson, Ronald 99
Robeson, Peter 114
Rocca, Peter 145
Rochow, Friedrich von 35
Rodnina, Irina *128,* 149, *151*
Rodochla, Birgit 115
Roetsch, Frank-Peter *173*
Roffe, Diann *202*
Rohan, Jiří 195
Roles, Barbara 99

Rolland, Jean Christophe *227*
Römay, Fernando *168*
Ronningen, Jon 182
Rono, Peter 176
Root, Elbert 71
Rose, Murray 93
Rose, Ralph 27, *30*, *33*
Rosenberg, Margarete 34
Rosendahl, Heide *131*, *133*, 134
Rosenfeld, Fanny 55
Rossetti, Bruno *197*
Rothenburger, Christa *161*, 181,
    188
Rothhammer, Keena 134
Röthlisberger, Jürg *157*
Roubanis, Georgios 240
Roug, Kristine *211*
Ruberl, Karl 23
Rudolph, Thomas 188
Rudolph, Wilma *100*, 101, *103*
Ruiz, Tracie 163, *166*
Ruska, Wilhelm *131*, 135
Russl, Bernhard *129*
Rutherford, Walter 22
Rutkowski, Tadeusz 156
Ruud, Birger *57*, 58, *67*, 75
Rylova, Tamara 99
Ryun, Jim 122

Sabatini, Gabriela 181
Sadovi, Yevgeni 191, *194*
Sailer, Anton 'Toni' *88*, 89, 117, 119
Saito, Eishiro 217
Sakai, Yoshinoro *112*
Salminen, Ilmari 69
Salnikov, Vladimir 152, 153, *155*
Salumäe, Erika *181*, *196*
Salzmann, Urs 161
Samaranch, Juan Antonio
    IOC President *10*, 153
    Olympic commercialization 13,
        191
    Olympic award 172
    Sarajevo site 159
Samse, Leroy 27
Sanchez Vicario, Arantxa 198, 215
Sanderson, Tessa *165*
Sands, Charles E. 22
Sandurski, Adam 156
Sattler, Norbert 134
Saubert, Jean 108
Savon, Felix *213*
Savyalov, Alexander 150
Sayre, John 104
Schade, Herbert *86*
Schäfer, Karl *57*, *66*
Schauerhammer, Dietmar 159, 161
Scheiblich, Christine 145
Schenk, Ard *126*, 127
Schenk, Christian *177*
Schenk, Franziska 205
Scherer, Markus 169
Schindelholz, Lorenz 188
Schjelderup, Thorleif 75
Schlunegger, Hedy 75
Schmal, Adolf 18
Schmid, Franz 61
Schmid, Harald 164
Schmid, Toni 61
Schmidt, Bill 133
Schmidt, Eugen 18, *19*
Schmidt, Markus 188
Schnabl, Karl 139, 141
Schneider, Othmar 82, *83*
Schneider, Vreni 172, 202
Schnelldorfer, Manfred 107, 108
Schockemöhle, Alwin *146*
Schoenfield, Alvin 22
Schollander, Don *111*, *112*
Scholz, Jackson 46
Scholz, Lilly 51
Schönbrunn, Gabi 161
Schöne, Andrea 161
Schöpf, Regina 90
Schrader, Hilde *53*, 55
Schranz, Karl 12, 109, 117, 127
Schridde, Hermann 114
Schrott, Karl 150
Schuba, Beatrix 127, *128*
Schuhmann, Carl *17*, 19
Schultz, Eckhardt *179*
Schultz, Ernst 23
Schultz, Karl 147

Schumacher, Günther *136*, *146*
Schümann, Jochen 144
Schumann, Margit 140
Schut, Johanna 117
Schwarz, Elisabeth *90*
Schwarz, Wolfgang *119*
Scott, Barbara Ann *73*, *74*
Scott, Clyde 78
Scott, Sheila 172
Searle, Greg *194*
Searle, Jonathan *194*
Sedykh, Yuri *144*
Ségura, Louis 34
Seibt, Helmut 82
Seiwald, Brigitte 118
Seizinger, Katja *187*
Seyfert, Gaby 119
Seyffarth, Ake *74*
Shakhlin, Boris *95*, *104*, 115
Shakhray, Sergei 150
Shan Zhang *197*
Shcherbakov, Leonid 86
Shea, Jack *233*
Shea, John 57, *58*, 149
Sheldon, Lewis P. 22
Sheldon, Richard 23
Sherbo, Vitali *191*, *196*
Sheridan, Martin *26*, *29*, *30*
Sherwood, John 122
Shimuzu, Hiroyasu 217
Shinohara, Shinichi 231
Shirley, Dorothy 102
Shorter, Frank *132*
Shuk, Tatyana 119
Shulin, Alexander *204*
Shupletsov, Sergei 205
Shushunova, Elena 181
Sidorova, Tatyana 108
Sidorova, Yevgeniya 90
Sieben, Jon 166
Sieberl, Helmut 82
Sikharulidze, Anton *237*
Silvas, Daniela *175*, *181*
Sime, David *102*
Simek, Miroslav 195
Simeoni, Sara 144, *153*, *155*
Simura, Saeko 166
Simyatov, Nikolai *151*
Sirch, Cornelia 178
Six, Alexandre 23
Skah, Khalid *192*
Skoblikova, Lidia, 97, 99, 107, 108
Skutnabb, Julius 42, 51
Sloane, William M. 11
Slusarski, Tadeusz 154
Slutskaya, Irina *237*
Smetanina, Raisa 139, 185
Smirnov, Vladimir *202*
Smith, Calvin 165
Smith, Caroline 47
Smith, Ethel 55
Smith, Lewis 165
Smith, Michelle *207*, *210*
Smith, Randy 195
Smith, Tommie 121, *122*
Smithson, Forrest 31
Snell, Peter *113*
Soldatenko, Venyamin 133
Somfay, Elemé 47
Somody, István 30
Southwood, Leslie 71
Soye, Emanuel de Blommaert de 35
Spedding, Charlie 165
Speirs, Annie 34
Spence, Malcolm 103
Sperber, Silvia *182*
Spinks, Leon 114
Spinks, Michael 114
Spinks, Terry *93*
Spinnler, Adolf 27
Spiridonov, Alexei 144
Spiss, Toni 83
Spitz, Mark *130*, 131, *135*, 175
Stack, Frank 58, *59*
Stadler, Joseph 27
Stalman, Rita 163
Stark, Ian 180
Starostin, Anatoli 157
Staub, Roger 99
Stecher, Renate *133*, 144
Steer, Irene *34*
Steinbauer, Walter 129
Stenen, Ole 58
Stenin, Boris 98

Stenina, Valentina 99, 108
Stenmark, Ingemar 149, *150*
Stenroos, Albin *46*
Stettler, Heinz 161
Steuer, Anni *70*
Stevens, Curtis *59*
Stevens, Hubert *59*
Stevens, Raymond *198*
Steward, Natalie 102
Stich, Michael *199*
Sticker, Josefine 34
Stiegler, Josef "Pepi" *99, 107, 109*
Stindt, Hermine 34
Stock, Leonhard *150*
Stocker, Werner *173*
Stojko, Elvis 205
Stork, Hermann 71
Stouder, Sharon *112*
Strassberger, Josef *55*
Straub, Jürgen *155*
Strausbaugh, Scott *194*
Street, Picabo *234*
Streidt, Ellen 144
Strickland, Shirley de la Hunty 78, 85, 93
Strobl, Fritz *233*
Strömstad, Thoralf 42, 43
Strug, Kerri 207, *213*
Stubbendorff, Ludwig *70*
Stückelberger, Christine 147, 180
Sugiura, Shigeo *71*
Sukhoruchenkov, Sergei 156
Süleymanoglu, Naim *182, 213*
Sullivan, James E. 27
Sun Shuwei *195*
Sun Xinmei *209*
Suraikin, Andrei 128
Susanti, Susi 199
Svenson, Sten *104*
Svet, Mateja *172*
Sweeney, Michael 22
Sydor, Alison 213
Szabó, Ecaterina *163, 167*
Szewinska, Irena 133, *143, 144*
Szöke, Katalin *87*
Szokoli, Alajos 18

Taber, Norman 33
Taguchi, Masaharu *71*
Tagwerker, Andrea 205
Taipale, Armas *33,*
Takemoto, Maseo 104
Tampakos, Dimosthenis 229
Tan Liangde 166, 195
Tanaka, Satoko 102
Taranenko, Leonid 198
Taurima, Jai *225*
Taylor, Elizabeth *70*
Taylor, Henry 29
Taylor, Morgan *54*
Taylor, Robert 133
television
    first live broadcasts 89
    rights 12–13, 127, 163, 171, 191
Temes, Judit 87

Tergat, Paul 209
Termeulen, Johanna 87
Ter-Ovanesian, Igor 102
terrorist attacks
    1972 Munich 12, 131, *137*
    1996 Atlanta 207, *215*
Tews, Andreas *198*
Thams, Jacob Tullin *43*
Theodorescu, Monica *199*
Thoma, Dieter 203
Thoma, Georg *96, 97*
Thomassen, Magne 118
Thompson, Daley *153, 163, 165*
Thompson, Don *102*
Thompson, Earl 37
Thomson, Earl 70
Thöni, Gustavo *127, 129*
Thöni, Rolando 129
Thorpe, Ian *223*
Thorpe, Jim *32, 33, 35*
Thunberg, Clas 42, 49, *51, 58*
Thurner, Helene 109
Tian Liang *227*
Ticci, Stefano 205
Tikhonov, Viktor 188
timing
    automatic 61
    electronic 33
Timoshenko, Alexandra 180, *196*
Titov, Yuri 94, 104
Tkachenko, Nadia 153
Tola, Tesfaye 224
Tolan, Eddie *60, 62*
Tomba, Alberto *129, 170, 187, 201*
Tomkins, James 227
Tomlinson, Chris *244*
Tootell, Fred *47*
Töpel, Hjördis 47
Topurov, Stefan 182
Torchebœuf, Emile 22
Torrence, Gwen *192, 209*
Torvill, Jayne *158, 159, 204*
Tosi, Giuseppe 78
Tóth, Annamaria 123
Traun, Fritz 17
Treacy, John 165
Trenton, Daniel *231*
Tretyak, Vladislav *161*
Trillini, Giovanna *197*
Trinquet, Pascale 156
Trudeau, Pierre 143
Tsiklitiras, Konstantinos 30, 240
Tsitas, Georgios 19
Tsurumi, Shuji 115
Tümmler, Bodo 123
Tuulos, Vilho 54
Tweddle, Elizabeth *244*
Twigg, Rebecca *169*
Tyler, Albert *18*

Ubartas, Romas *193*
Ueberroth, Peter 163, *169*
Ulanov, Alexei *128*, 149
Ulvang, Vegard *185, 186*
Uphoff, Nicole 180, *199*

Urmanov, Alexei *204*
Urselmann, Wiltrud *103*
Urzica, Marius 229
Usova, Maya *204*
Utterström, Sven *57*
Utzschneider, Peter *129*

Vaillancourt, Michel 147
Valenta, Ales *234*
Valentine, Howard 27
Valla, Trebisonda *70*
Varga, Béla 34
Varga, Karoly *157*
Varga, Miroslav *182*
Vehovar, Andraz 210
Veldkamp, Bart 185
Vendeville, Charles de 23
Verkerk, Cornelis 117
Vermes, Alban 154
Verner, W. Frank 27
Versis, Sotirios 18
Vettori, Ernst *186*
Vezzali, Valentina *230*
Vikelas, Dimitrios *10, 11, 17*
Vilagos, Penny 195
Vilagos, Vicky 195
Vinjarengen, Hans 58
Vinson, Maribel 58
Viren, Lasse *132, 143*
Visser, Leo 173
Vizzoni, Nicola 225
Voge, Ingo 161
Volkov, Dmitri 178
Volkov, Konstantin 154
Vonhof, Peter *146*
Voronin, Mikhail 124
Voronina, Zinaida 124
Voss, Torsten 177
Vuarnet, Jean *99*
Vuillermin, Mirko 205

Wachter, Anita *185*
Wagner, Barbara *99*
Wagner, Katrin *226*
Wahlberg, Kaare 58
Wailes, Richard *104*
Wainaina, Eric 224
Wainwright, Helen 38
Waitz, Grete 165
Wajsowna, Jadwiga 62
Walasiewicz, Stanislawa 61
Wälbe, Yelena 186
Walde, Hans-Joachim 111
Waldo, Carolyn 166
Walker, Leroy *11*
Waller, Friedrich *75*
Walliser, Maria 172
Wangenheim, Konrad von 70
Wang Nan *230*
Warnicke, Heike 188
Wartenberg, Christiane 154
Washbond, Alan 67
Wasmeier, Markus *201, 202*
Wassberg, Thomas 160
Wayne, Marshall *71*

Weber, Adolf 27
Weber, Wilhelm 27
Wecker, Andreas 196
Weder, Gustav *189, 205*
Wegner, Gudrun 134
Wehling, Ulrich *149, 151*
Weigang, Birte 178
Weise, Eberhard 161
Weissensteiner, Gerda *205*
Weissflog, Jens 161
Weissmuller, Johnny *45, 52, 47, 61, 93*
Weller, Ronny 207, *213*
Wells, Allan *154*
Wendl, Ingrid 90
Wentz, Siegfried 165
Wenzel, Andreas 150, 161
Wenzel, Hanni *150*
Werth, Isabelle *199*
Wessling, Ansgar *179*
Wetzig, Roland 161
Weyer, Willi 153
Whitbread, Fatima 165, 177
White, Albert 166
White, Isabelle 34
Whitier, Paula 22
Wicki, Jean 129
Wide, Edvin *46, 55*
Widemann, Lydia 81
Wiegand, Frank 112
Wiegand, Otto 27
Wienese, Henri Jan 125
Wieslander, Hugo 35
Wightmann, Hazel 45
Wiklund, Elis *66*
Wikström, Axel *66*
Wilker, Hermann *35*
Wilkie, David *143*
Wilkins, Louis 27
Wilkins, Mac 165
Williams, Percy *54*
Williams, Venus *231*
Wills, Helen 45, 175
Wilson, Alexander 61
Wilson, James 38
Wilson, Tracy *173*
Winkler, Hans Günter *95, 136*
Winkler, Kati 220
Winter, John *79*
Winter Olympics
    alternation with Summer Games 201
    inauguration 11, 41
    as International Winter Sports Week 40-3, *40-3*
    winter sports, inclusion with Summer Games 11, 29
Witt, Katarina *159, 171, 173*
Wohlhuter, Richard 144
Wolde, Mamo 133
Wolf, Sigrid *172*
Wolfermann, Klaus *132*
women participants
    distances run 53

first 11–12, 21, 53
    gender testing 117
    track and field events 53
Wolkowisky, Ruben 237
Wood, Allan 112
Wood, Timothy 119
Woods, George 134
Woosnam, Max 39
World Exhibitions
    Olympics as part of 10, *20, 21, 25*
    professional athletes at *22*
Wotherspoon, Jeremy 220
Wrede, Ludwig 51
Wrightson, Bernie 123
Wunderle, Victor 230
Wunderlich, Erhard *168*
Wunderlich, Magdalena 134

Xenakis, Thomas 19
Xiong Ni 178
Xuan Liu *228*
Xu Yanmei 178

Yagudin, Alexei 237
Yamaguchi, Kristi *189*
Yarur, Juan Jorge Giha 197
Ye Huanming 182
Yegorov, Grigori 177
Yegorova, Irina 108
Yegorova, Lyubov 185, 186, *200, 201*
Yelisina, Yelena *225*
Yifter, Miruts 153, *155*
Yoo Nam Kyu *180*
Young, Edwin 123
Young, Kevin *192*
Young, Larry 133
Young, Sheila 140
Yusa, Masanori *71*

Zahonyi, Attila *182*
Zahourek, Berta 34
Zaitsev, Alexander 149, 151
Zamolodtichikova, Elena *228*
Zandoella, Roberto 118
Zaprianov, Petr 156
Zátopek, Emil
    1948 London 77, 78, *78*
    1952 Helsinki 84, 85, 86, *86*
Zátopková, Dana *86*
Zelezny, Jan 209
Zerba, Valentina 203
Zhuang Yong 178
Zhulpa, Robertas 155
Zimmerer, Wolfgang *129*
Ziolkowski, Szymon 225
Zmelik, Robert *193*
Zubiaur, José B. 11
Zuchold, Erika 124, 134
Zurbriggen, Pirmin *171, 172*

Picture credits:

(b = bottom, t = top, c = center, l = left, r = right)

The publishers would like to thank the following agencies for the photographs used inside this book. The figures in brackets indicate the number of photographs each agency supplied. Allsport, London (10); Archiv für Kunst und Geschichte, Berlin (26); Associated Press, Frankfurt (6); Associated Press, London (8); Associated Sports Photography, Leicester (13); Heinrich von der Becke (15); Bertelsmann Lexikon Verlag, Gütersloh (151); Bettmann Archive Inc., New York (66); Bibliothèque Nationale, Paris (1); Bildarchiv Preussischer Kulterbesitz, Berlin (4); Bongarts, Hamburg (201); Colorsport, London (10); DPA, Frankfurt (44); EMPICS, Nottingham (40); Mary Evans Picture Library, London (2); Historisches Farbarchiv Christa Elsler, Norderney (1); Fencing Photo Library, Karina Hoskyns (1); Frank Spooner Pictures, London (1); Horst Müller, Düsseldorf (63); Hulton Deutsch Collection, London (16); Jurgens Ost + Europa-Photo, Cologne (8); Keystone Pressedienst GmbH, Hamburg (1); Kos Picture Source, London (2); Mirror Syndication, London (4); NAOC, Nagano City (1); Olympic Museum, International Olympic Committee, Lausanne (5); Popperfoto, Northampton (35); Pressefoto Baumann, Ludwigsburg (27); Roger Viollet, Paris (5); Sporting Pictures, London (2); Sportbild-Agentur Schirner, Meersbusch (120); Sportimage, Hamburg (2); Sven Simon, Essen (88); Archiv Umminger, Breitenberg (10); USIS, Bonn (5); Werek, Munich (6); Bongarts, Hamburg (26)

In this 2004 edition the following images were included:

© **ATHOC:** 239br, 242tr& br (K.Vergas), 242bl (A.N.A), 243t (G.Prinos), 243bl (C.Cunliffe), 243cr (C.Voulgari); **Corbis:** 3br (Mantey S./Corbis Sygma), 7br (Duomo), 13b (Gyori Antoine/Corbis Sygma), 15r (Kontos Yannis/Corbis Sygma), 223ct (Seguin Franck/Corbis Sygma), 232 (Chris Trotman/Duomo), 237(Chris Trotman/Duomo), 238 (Sygma), 241tr (Orban/Corbis Sygma), 241 (LeSegretain P./Corbis Sygma), 248 (Tim De Waele/Isosport), 250(Yue/China Feature/Corbis Sygma), 251 crb (Bruce Connolly), 251br(Liu Liqun); **EMPICS:** 224bc, 228br, 239 crb, 241cr, bl, 244tl, bl, 251tr; **Getty Images:** 224br, 225bl, 225cl, 225crb, 229c, cl, bl, cr, br, 231cbl, bl, 234tr, cr, br, bl, 235bl, 236bl, 237br, 239crt, 244cr, 246tl, tr, cr, 247t, bl, 249tr, 251crt; **La Presse, Turin:** 249 (all except tr); **Popperfoto:** 3tr, 223t, 223cb, 224bl, 226cr, 227tl, 230tr, 233tr, crt, crb, 234tl, 235tl, tr, br, 236tl, tr, cr, br, 237tl, tr, cl, 239tr, 240tr, 245bl, 245tr, br; **Popperfoto/Reuters:** 11, 222, 223b, 224tl, 224tr, 225tr, 225crt, 225bl, 225br, 226 (all except cr), 227bl, br, tr, 228, tl, tr, bl, 229tl, tr, cr, br, bc, 230tl, bl, 231tl, tr, 233br, 240bl, 241tl, 242tl, 244tr, 246b, 247br; **Reuters:** 225c, 231ct, 239l; **International Olympic Committee, Lausanne:** 15cr, 233l.